THE BARBECUE! BIBLE

THE BARBECUE! BIBLE

BY STEVEN RAICHLEN

ILLUSTRATIONS BY MARGARET CHODOS-IRVINE

WORKMAN PUBLISHING • NEW YORK

Photography credits:
Pages xxii, 40, 112, 178, 458 © Steven Raichlen; page 24 © Mark
Greenberg/Envision; pages 70, 370 © J.B. Marshall/Envision; page 102
© 1995 Bruno Barbey/Magnum Photos, Inc.; page 152 © 1998 Costa
Manos/Magnum Photos, Inc.; page 202 © Jean Higgins/Envision;
pages 236, 340 © 1970 Costa Manos/Magnum Photos, Inc.; page 286 ©
Sheilah Scully; page 400 © 1995 Thomas Hoepker/Magnum Photos,
Inc.; page 416 © StockFood America/Bischof; page 434 © 1998 Simon
Russell; page 488 © Dennie Cody/FPG International; page 510 © 1966
Bruno Barbey/Magnum Photos, Inc.

Library of Congress Cataloging-in-Publication Data
Raichlen, Steven.
The barbecue bible by Steven Raichlen; illustrations by Margaret
Chodos-Irvine.
p. cm.
Includes index.
ISBN 0-7611-1317-7 (hb).—ISBN 0-7611-1179-4 (pb)
1. Barbecue cookery. I. Title.
TX840.B3R35 1998
641.5'784—dc21   98-17053
                                                               CIP

Cover design by Paul Hanson
Book design by Lisa Hollander

Cover photographs: author © Anthony Loew; chicken and grilled
vegetable plate © Greg Schneider; red chile pepper © StockFood
America/Conrad; bell peppers © StockFood America/Bumann; all
other jacket photographs © Louis Wallach

Workman books are available at special discounts when purchased
in bulk for premiums and sales promotions as well as for fund-raising
or educational use. Special editions or book excerpts can be created
to specification. For details, contact the Special Sales Director at the
address below.

Workman Publishing Company, Inc.
708 Broadway
New York, NY 10003-9555

First printing June 1998
10 9 8 7 6 5 4 3 2 1

Every family needs
a patriarch.
Ours was my grandfather, Dear.

―――――――

This book is dedicated
in loving memory
to Samuel Israel Raichlen.

ACKNOWLEDGMENTS

The most gratifying part of writing any book is thanking the people who helped make it possible. *The Barbecue Bible* involved a proverbial cast of thousands.

First and foremost, I thank my wife, Barbara, who brought me to an environment where I could grill all year round (Miami), accompanied me on much of the world's barbecue trail, and relived it in a three-year frenzy of recipe testing in our backyard. Barb, you're the best.

Next, I want to thank the whole crew at Workman Publishing.

Peter Workman encouraged me to expand my original and rather modest proposal into a book of biblical proportions. Words simply aren't adequate to thank my editor, Suzanne Rafer, who patiently wrestled a manuscript of more than 2,000 pages into a book that actually fit between two covers, working with unwavering diligence, dedication, and verve to meet an impossible deadline. It's easy to see why authors would kill to work with her.

Margery Tippie had the daunting task of copyediting the book, and her professionalism and extraordinary attention to detail were exceeded only by her patience and hard work. The same is true for Charles Pierce, who helped polish the manuscript line by line, word by word. Paul Hanson, designed the lively cover of the book and Lisa Hollander, assisted by Kristen M. Nobles, Jeanne Hogle, and Lori Malkin, is responsible for the lovely design. Artist Margaret Chodos-Irvine brought my words to life with her charming drawings and lino prints. Assistant editor Carrie Schoen and proofreader Barbara Mateer also toiled tirelessly on the project, and Cathy Dorsey made index sense of it all.

It was a great pleasure to work for the first time with Workman publicists Ellen Morgenstern and Jackie Mills, and again with the irrepressible Susan Schwartzman. As always, I also thank Andrea Glickson, Jenny Mandell, Pat Upton, Janet Harris, David Schiller, and all my other colleagues at Workman.

I was also assisted by an extraordinary staff in Miami—editorial assistants Blanca Silva, Lorraine Massey, and Donna Morton de Souza and recipe testers Elida Proenza and Roger Thrailkill. Boris Djokic kept the computers humming and offered insight into the grilling of his native Yugoslavia, while my cousin David Raichlen helped with the anthropological research. While I was writing the book, my stepson Jake opened a restaurant, at JADA (check it out the next time you're in South Miami). This is a very handy thing to have happen when you're developing recipes for a cookbook the size of this one. I'd like to thank Jake and his partner David Gordon and the whole team at JADA for their enthusiasm and support.

I'd like to thank my colleagues and fellow cookbook authors—both in the United States and abroad—for sharing their enormous expertise (and their favorite barbecue joints): Burton Anderson, Najmieh Batmanglij, Giuliano Bugialli, Darra Goldstein, Jessica Harris, Madhur Jaffrey, Patsy Jamieson, Nancy Harmon Jenkins, John Mariani, Joan Nathan, David Rosengarten, Nicole Routhier, Julie Sahni, Mimi Sheraton, Nina Simonds, Anne Willan, Anya Von Bremsen, and Patricia Wells.

I had a lot of great chefs in my court for this project, too. The short list would include Rick Bayless, Alain Ducasse, George Germon, Vinod Kapor, Johanne Killeen, Emeril Lagasse, Mark Miller, Mark Militello, Stephan Pyles, Charlie Trotter, and, of course, Chris Schlesinger (who brought grilling into the twenty-first century). Don Hysko of Peoples Woods educated me on the fine points of grilling with natural wood and charwood.

I'd also like to thank my colleagues at Weber-Stephen Products, first for sharing their expertise with me (not to mention the opportunity to experience sub-zero grilling at their proving grounds in Palatine, Illinois, in the middle of winter): Mike Kempster Sr., Mark Kempster Jr., Betty Hughes, Kirk Cleveland, Tom Wenke, Jim Forbes, Edna Schlosser, and the exuberant Elizabeth Karmel.

A big thanks to three special friends: Kathleen Cornelia, Katherine Kenny, and Milton Eber.

In researching this book, I had the help of hundreds of tourism officials and barbecue buffs both in the United States and abroad. I could never thank all the people who helped me, but I'd like to acknowledge as many as I can.

Argentina: Eduardo Piva, Enrique Capozzolo, and Gloria Pacheca of the Argentina National Tourist Office.

Australia: Peter Hackworth of the Chili Queens and New York Latin restaurant in Brisbane.

Azerbaijan: Peter Richards of the Hyatt Regency Baku.

Brazil: Sara Widness of Kaufman Widness Communications; Marius Fontena of Churrascaria Marius; Yara Castro Roberts and Belita Castro.

China/Hong Kong: Trina Dingler Ebert of Aman Resorts in Hong Kong; Angela Herndon of Lou Hammond & Associates; Margaret Sheriden, formerly of the *South China Morning Post*.

Curaçao: Traci La Rosa and Mark Walsh of Peter Martin Associates, Inc.; the Curaçao Tourist Development Bureau.

France: Marion Fourestier and Robin Massee of the French Government Tourist Office.

French West Indies: Myron Clement and Joe Petrocik of Clement-Petrocik Co.; the French West Indies Tourist Board; My friend Eric Troncani of the Carl Gustaf Hotel.

India: T. Balakrishnan, Y. K. Jain, Seema Schahi of the Indian Goverment Tourist Office; Chef Manjit S. Gill of the Welcomgroup; Chefs Nakkul Anand, Geeta Kranhke, Shishir Baijal, Gev Desai, and J. P. Singh of the Maurya Sheraton Hotel & Towers in New Delhi; Chefs Mohamed Farooq and Amitabh Devendra at the Mughal Sheraton in Agra; Chefs Manu Mehta and Nisar Waris of the Rajputana Palace Sheraton in Jaipur.

Indonesia: Fauzi Bowo, Madi Chusnun, and Yuni Syafril of the Indonesia Tourist Promotion Office; William W. Wongso of the William F & B Management Co. in Jakarta.

Israel: Don Weitz of the Israeli Government Tourist Office; Ehud Yonay of Greater Galilee Gourmet, Inc.

Italy: Juliet Cruz of the Italian Trade Commission; Maria and Angelo Leocastre of the Villa Roncalli in Foligno.

Jamaica: Patricia Hannan and Jackie Murray of the Jamaica Tourist Board; Winston Stoner of Busha Browne's Company, Ltd.

Japan: Eriko Kawaguchi, M. B. Maslowski, Osamu Akiyama, and Nobuko Misawa of the Japan National Tourist Organization; Lucy Seligman, editor of the *Gochiso-sama*.

Korea: Sang-hoon Rah, Sean Nelan, and Peter Jang of the Korea National Tourism Corporation; Mr. Park of Samwon Garden

Macao: Eric L. Chen of the Government Tourist Office in Macao.

Malaysia: Azizah Aziz of Tourism Malaysia.

Mexico: Lori Jones and Patricia Echenique of the Mexican Tourism Board; Tom Fisher and Alina Gambor of Burson Marsteller; Jesus Arroyo Bergeyre of Arroy Restaurantes.

Monaco: Emmanuelle Perrier of the Monaco Tourism Bureau.

Morocco: Pamela Windo (friend and guide extraordinaire).

Republic of georgia:: My e-mail pal Betsy Haskell of Betsy's Hotel in Tbilisi.

Singapore: Mak Ying Kwan and Faizah Hanim Ahmad of the Singapore Tourist Promotion Board.

South Africa: Heather Kowadla and Laura Morrill of Lou Hammond & Associates; Christina Martin of the Christina Martin School of Food & Wine in KuaZulu Natal; Alicia Wilkinson of the Silwood Kitchen Cookery School in Capetown.

Spain: Alejandro Gomez Marco and Maria Luisa Albacar of the Oficina Española de Turismo; Ana Rodriguez of the Hotel Ritz in Madrid.

Thailand: Kim Vacher-Ta of Tourism Authority of Thailand; Phenkhae Chattanont of the Oriental Bangkok Hotel; Ann Laschever of Lou Hammond and Associates.

Trinidad: Michael De Peaza, Nancy Pierre, and Tony Poyer of the Trinidad Tourism Development Bureau.

Turkey: Murat Barlas and Ayfer Unsal; Mustafa Siyahhan of the Turkish Tourist Office in Washington, D.C.; Mehmet Dogan of the Tourism Office in Gaziantep.

United States: Karen Adler of Pig Out Publications, Inc.; Judith Fertig, Danny Edwards of Little Jake's Eat It and Beat It, and Lindsey Shannon of BB's Lawnside in Kansas City; Mike Alexander and Mike DeMaster of Sonny Bryan's in Dallas; Roy and Jane Barber and Barry Maxwell of the Memphis in May International Festival, Inc.

Uruguay: Alexis Parodi of the Ministerio de Turismo del Uruguay.

Vietnam: Trai Thi Duong of the Truc Orient Express and Binh Van Duong of Le Truc.

Finally, a huge thanks to all the grill jockeys and pit bosses—both named in this book and unnamed—for sharing with me their skills, knowledge, time, food, and unbridled passion for grilling. Barbecue buffs have a reputation for secrecy, but everywhere I went, people welcomed me into their hearts and their kitchens. I thank them for 3 ½ extraordinary years on the barbecue trail.

CONTENTS

A CRASH COURSE ON GRILLING AND BARBECUING 1

Everything you need to know in order to grill and barbecue like a pro—in no time flat. How to master direct and indirect grilling; pit barbecuing; grilling on a rotisserie; and grilling without a grate. What to look for in equipment; how to buy the right fuel, how to light it, and how to keep it lit. Plus the scoop on accessories.

THIRST QUENCHERS 25

Cooking over a hot grill can work up a powerful thirst, and pit masters world-wide know that there are more ways to quench it than with beer. Here, then, is a mix of coolers—with and without alcohol—to accompany any barbecue.

WARM-UPS 41

Set your barbecue off to the happiest start with a selection of appetizing openers: Silver Paper Chicken, Hong Kong Honey-Glazed Wings, Shrimp Mousse on Sugar-

cane. Or how about a smoky Grilled Corn Chowder? They're all so good they taste like the main event themselves.

BLAZING SALADS 71

Salads play two roles in the world of barbecue. Some, like Grilled Vegetable Caponata and Grilled Pork with a Sweet-Tart Dressing, are themselves grilled dishes. Others set off a grilled dish perfectly. You need go no farther than this chapter to enjoy both kinds.

GRILLED BREAD 103

From irresistible Grilled Garlic Bread Fingers to Catalan Tomato Bread to from-scratch Tandoori-Baked Flat Breads—whether ready-made or homemade, the grill gives bread unmatched flavor and crispness.

WHAT'S YOUR BEEF 113

Texas-Style Barbecued Brisket and Brazilian Stuffed Rib Roast; Stet's Steak and Bengali Shish Kebabs; Saigon Market Beef Sticks and Korean Grilled Short Ribs. Beef on the grill—savory, succulent, sensational—a perfect match of food and fire.

HIGH ON HOG 153

Time to go whole hog! Cook up the tenderest North Carolina-Style Pulled Pork or fieriest Jamaican Jerk Pork Tenderloin. Feast on Pork with Moorish Seasonings, Sweet and Garlicky Pork Chops, or finger-licking Memphis-Style Ribs.

A LITTLE LAMB 179

So much of the world's barbecuers love to grill lamb that it's no wonder the selection of dishes is outstanding. Try Capetown Lamb from South Africa, "Onion Water" Lamb Chops from Afghanistan, and The Real Turkish Shish Kebab from Turkey (of course!).

GROUND MEAT, BURGERS, AND SAUSAGES 203

The U.S. might have the best burgers, but wait till you taste the ground meat concoctions the rest of the world has to offer—Indonesian Flying Fox Satés, Oasis Kebabs from the Middle East, The Original Karim's Seekh Kebab from India—proving that the appeal of flavorful ground meat is universal.

BIRD MEETS GRILL 237

The world loves a great grilled chicken, and here are the recipes to help you achieve greatness: Thai Chicken Satés Served in Lettuce Leaves, Sea Captain's Chicken Tikka, and Bahamian Grilled Chicken, to name a few. But don't overlook other birds that cook up deliciously on the grill, as well—check out the recipes for quail, duck, and turkey.

WATER MEETS FIRE: FISH ON THE GRILL

Fresh fish, perfectly grilled, is spectacularly succulent. Don't miss Whole Grilled Snapper with South African Spices, Grilled Sea Bass with Fresh Artichoke Salad, Grilled Salmon Kiev, and Sole with Catalan Fruits and Nuts.

HOT SHELLS: LOBSTERS, SHRIMP, SCALLOPS & CLAMS

Grilled Spiny Lobster with Basil Butter, Scallop Kebabs with Pancetta, Lemon, and Basil, Oysters with Horseradish Cream, and enough shrimp recipes to keep the barbie fired up for weeks. Here is shellfish at its best!

VEGETABLES: GREENS MEET GRILL

There is probably no better way to heighten the natural flavor of a vegetable than by grilling. Proof is no farther away than Georgian Vegetable Kebabs, Tandoori Cauliflower, Argentinian Grilled Eggplant, Chorizo

Grilled Mushrooms, and wonderfully warming Grilled Sweet Potatoes with Sesame Dipping Sauce.

VEGETARIAN GRILL

No longer only just for meat-eaters, now you can serve up a complete range of vegetarian dishes at a barbecue, including The Original Grilled Pizza, exotic Indian Spinach-Cheese Kebabs, a lush Provençal Dagwood, and steak-like Grilled Portobello Mushroom Sandwiches with Basil Aïoli.

RICE, BEANS, AND BEYOND

Most of the world's great grilled dishes are accompanied by flavorfully prepared grains and beans. Dig into Persian-Style Steamed Rice and Quick and Smoky Baked Beans. And for something less expected, how about a Grilled Yorkshire Pudding?

SIDEKICKS: PICKLES, RELISHES, SALSAS & SLAWS

Bring on the condiments, those savory, fiery, sweet, and utterly satisfying gowiths that dress up any barbecue. Central Asian Pickles, Onion Relish with Pomegranate Molasses, Pineapple Chutney, "Dog's Nose" Salsa, and Tomato Peanut Sambal will add pizzazz to even the simplest grilled chicken, steak, or fish.

SAUCES 459

All great pit masters are judged on their barbecue sauces and you'll match the best of them with this far-reaching collection. From a sweet-sour Basic Barbecue Sauce to a contemporary Ginger-Plum Barbecue Sauce to a mouth-scorching Portuguese *piri-piri*, there are plenty to match any grilled dish.

RUB IT IN 489

Memphis Rub and Indian Roasted Spice Powder; Mexican Smoked Chile Marinade and Teriyaki Marinade; Roquefort Butter, Ketjap Butter, and Bourbon Butter Basting Sauce. A full selection of rubs, marinades, butters, and bastes add zip to even the simplest fare.

FIRE AND ICE: DESSERTS 511

No great barbecue is complete without a great dessert. Whether you end with a final flourish on the grill or with a luscious frozen dessert, you won't go wrong. Don't forget to leave room for Grilled Sugar-Dipped Pineapple, Balinese Grilled Bananas in Coconut Milk Caramel, Persian Lemon and Rosewater "Sundae" with Sour Cherry Syrup, and Coconut Ice Cream.

THREE YEARS ON THE BARBECUE TRAIL

Half a million years ago, the world witnessed a revolution. An ape-like creature destined to become man became the first animal to cook its dinner. The mastery of fire by *Homo erectus* around 500,000 B.C. resulted in nothing less than the rise of civilization. Anthropologists have argued that the primitive act of roasting meat over fire ultimately led to language, art, religion, and complex social organization. In other words, you could say that grilling begat civilization.

How our forebears learned to grill remains a matter of speculation. Perhaps the first barbecue was the result of a forest fire, which roasted venison, bison, and other game on the hoof in a natural conflagration. Perhaps a haunch of meat fell into a campfire. Perhaps lightning struck a tree and transformed it into charcoal. In any case, archeological evidence suggests that by 125,000 B.C. man was using live fire to cook his meat and to help him extract from the bones a morsel particularly prized in prehistoric times: marrow.

The following millennia brought countless refinements to the art of cooking, from the invention of pottery and pots and pans to the bread machine and microwave oven. But when it comes to bringing out the primal flavor of food, nothing can rival grilling over a live fire.

This truth has not been lost to cultures as diverse as the Greek, Japanese, Australian, South African, and Argentinian. Grilling remains our most universal and universally beloved method of cooking. And in the past ten years, our own country has experienced a veritable grill mania.

It is this shared experience—and a desire to learn more about the cultures that produced its infinite regional variations—that led me to write this book.

Why I Wrote This Book

The idea for the book came to me shortly after moving from Boston to Miami. South Florida is enough to sharpen anyone's appetite for grilling. First, there's the climate, which makes year-round grilling not only a possibility but almost a duty. (How different Miami is from Boston, where grilling in the winter requires donning arctic apparel!)

Then there's Miami's dizzying cultural diversity. Dade County, which includes Miami, is 50 percent Hispanic, and Miami itself is home to the nation's largest Cuban, Nicaraguan, Colombian, and Haitian communities. But "Hispanic" only begins to describe what's going on in Miami's markets and restaurants: Not only are the countries of the Caribbean and South America represented, but virtually every country in Europe, Africa, and Asia as well. Global cuisine isn't simply a curiosity or luxury here in South Florida. It's a way of life.

So an idea began to take hold of my imagination: to explore how the world's oldest and most universal cooking method varies from country to country, region to region, and culture to culture. To travel the world's barbecue trail—if such a trail existed—and learn how pit masters and grill jockeys solve that age-old problem: how to cook food over live fire without burning it.

I resolved to explore the *asados* of Argentina and the *churrascos* of Brazil; to taste Jamaica's jerk and Mexico's *barbacoa*. I'd visit Greece to discover the secret of *souvlaki* and Italy to learn how to make an authentic *bistecca alla fiorentina*. My research introduced me to eat *mechouie* in Morocco and *koftas* in the Middle East, *donner kebab* in Turkey, and tandoori in India. I would visit the birthplace of

Japanese yakitori, Indonesian *saté,* and Korean *kui* and *bool kogi.*

Of course, there'd be lots of live-fire cooking to investigate in my own country: from the ribs of Kansas City and Memphis to the pulled pork of the Carolinas and the slow-smoked briskets of Texas. I'd check out the wood-burning grills of California and the hearthside cookery of New England. The more I delved into the world of barbecuing and grilling, the more I became convinced that it is more than just another technique in a cook's repertoire. It's even more than a cultural phenomenon. The world over, it's a way of life.

It wouldn't hurt, I reasoned, that grilling and barbecuing fit so nicely into the contemporary North American lifestyle. These ancient methods support the four dominant trends in modern American cooking: our passion for explosive flavors; our fast-paced lifestyle, with its need for quick, easy cooking methods; our mushrooming health consciousness and desire to eat foods that are low in fat but high in flavor; our desire to turn our homes into our entertainment centers, to transform the daily necessity of food preparation into recreation—even fun.

If ever there was a cooking method to take us into the next millennium, it is grilling. We see its growing popularity in the sky-rocketing sales of barbecue grills (currently, more than 70 percent of Americans own grills). We see it in the proliferation of barbecue festivals and restaurants with wood-burning grills.

The truth is that—in terms of ease, speed, and intensity of flavor—nothing can rival grilling. And as more Americans travel the barbecue trail and discover the regional subtleties of grilling, the movement will only grow.

I shared my idea with Peter Workman and Suzanne Rafer of Workman Publishing, who responded with an enthusiasm that matched my own. In fact, they encouraged me to broaden the scope of the original book from the 12 countries on which I had initially planned to focus to the entire world of grilling. (Easy for them to do! They wouldn't have to worry about jet lag, visas, complex travel arrangements, vaccinations that turned my arms into pincushions, and gastrointestinal perils that would challenge the limits of my culinary curiosity.)

A proposal was written. A contract was executed.

And only then did I panic.

How would I visit more than 25 countries in the space of three years? How would I overcome local language barriers and sometimes less than favorable attitudes to American journalists? And even if I could communicate with street cooks and chefs, how would I persuade them to share their grilling secrets? How would I ferret out the best barbecue (and best places to have it) in countries I knew only from guidebooks?

I realized I had taken on the biggest challenge of my life.

How I Wrote This Book

I began, as any journalist does, with research. I read exhaustively both cookbooks and travel books. I queried colleagues with expertise in the various countries I planned to visit. I consulted with tourism bureaus and cultural attachés. I spoke with food and cookware importers, travel agents, anthropologists, foreigners I met here and abroad—anyone who could shed insight into the grilling of a particular country.

My informants included fellow journalists, university professors, business travelers, diplomats, and flight attendants. Some of my best information came from taxi drivers. (Of all professions, cabbies seem to possess the most unerring knowledge of who serves the best barbecue.) I planned as much as I could, then I made sure I was in the right place to capitalize on chance.

I speak French and Spanish and a smattering of Italian, Portuguese, and German (the latter is useful in Turkey), so in countries where these languages are spoken, I was able to work on my own. In countries where I didn't speak the language, I found guides or interpreters. And of course I developed my own sign language:

> "I" (point to me)
>
> "write" (move my fingers to mime writing)
>
> "about food" (raise an imaginary fork or chopsticks to my lips or rub my belly)
>
> "I would like to" (again point to me)
>
> "watch" (point to my eye)
>
> "you cook." (mime the act of grilling, mixing, chopping, or stir-frying)

I took with me one of my previous cookbooks. I would show the recipes and point to the photograph of me on the back cover.

I feared my efforts would be met with suspicion, secrecy, and rejection, but almost everywhere I went I encountered openness, warmth, and welcome. Virtually all of the grill jockeys I interviewed were not only willing but happy to share their knowledge. On many occasions, I was invited into the kitchen. I tried my hand at molding *kofta* meat onto skewers, fanning the coals, or slapping *naan* on the inside walls of a blazing tandoor. My efforts generally evoked peals of good-natured laughter.

I found myself in many places not frequented by most travelers, having experiences that ranged from fascinating to hair-raising. In Mexico I nibbled cactus worms and crickets as a prelude to barbecue. (The latter tasted like potato chips with legs.) In Uruguay I sampled testicles, tripe, intestines, kidneys, and blood sausage. In Bali I paid a 6 A.M. visit to the local *babi guli* (roast pork) man, who rewarded my punctuality by letting me help him slaughter a suckling pig. In Bangkok I was the guest of honor at an Isarn (northeastern Thai) restaurant whose fly-filled kitchen overlooked a stagnant canal. (I forced myself to eat with the enthusiasm appropriate to a guest of honor, and no one was more surprised than I when I *didn't* get sick.

Some of the world's best barbecue was off limits because of political turmoil. I would have liked to have visited Afganistan, Iraq, Iran, and some of the more turbulent former Soviet republics. Instead, I found experts and restaurants specializing in those cuisines in this country.

Barbecue buffs have a reputation for being a secretive bunch (at least in the United States), but virtually everywhere I traveled on the barbecue trail, cooks were happy to share their recipes and expertise. Some scrawled recipes for me, to be translated back at my hotel. Others drew pictures in my notebook to explain where a particular piece of meat came from or

how to execute a particular cut. When possible, I credit the extraordinary grill hockeys I met by name (or at least by the name of their establishment).

Recipes are the heart of any cookbook, of course. In this one you'll find more than 500, covering everything from Brazilian *churrasco* to Balinese shrimp satés to Memphis-style ribs. The essays describing some of my experiences are intended for the traveler (both active and armchair), as well as the cook.

My three years on the barbecue trail passed in what seems like the blink of any eye.

As I sit here writing these words, I picture all the remarkable places I've been, the kind, generous people I've met, and the extraordinary food I've been lucky enough to sample. And yet I can't help but feel there's so much more I would have liked to have accomplished. The world of barbecue is so vast and complex, any survey is bound to have blind spots. I honestly believe I could spend the rest of my life writing about barbecuing and grilling and still find new things to discover.

About the Recipes

When writing the recipes, I've tried to be as authentic as possible. But I've also taken into account the fact that certain foods, seasonings, and cooking equipment simply aren't available in the United States (not to mention the fact that our tastes and aesthetics are different). Whenever I depart from a traditional recipe, I've tried to suggest the way it would be made in its country of origin.

In my three years on the barbecue trail, I sampled many dishes I know most Americans would never dream of preparing at home. (A few that come to mind are Uruguay's *choto* (grilled coiled lamb's intestines) and Indonesia's *saté padang* (kebabs of beef entrails served in a fiery gravy). I've tried to describe these dishes in the essays and boxes in this book. I hope you'll give them a try when you travel.

As I quickly discovered on the barbecue trail, grilling is an art, not a science. Many cooks work in unbelievably primitive conditions. Indeed, one of the reasons I'm drawn to grilling is that it's so forgiving in terms of measurements and proportions. I hope you'll use the recipes in this book as I do, that is, as a broad guideline. If you don't feel like eating beef, make the recipe with chicken or seafood. Most of the marinades and rubs in this book—listed either as freestanding recipes or subrecipes in more elaborate preparations—can be used with any type of grilled fare. You'll also notice that there is often more than one way to cook a particular dish. As I always say in my cooking classes: There's no

such thing as a mistake in the kitchen, just a new recipe waiting to be discovered.

Seasoning, marinating, and grilling are the cornerstones of live-fire cooking, which brings me to what I call the Barbecue Bible Method, and as you will see, it's very simple. First marinate the meat, or rub it with spices. Then let the meat absorb the seasonings for as long as recommended or as long as you have time for. Finally, grill it over whatever sort of fuel on whatever sort of equipment you feel most comfortable using. That's it.

Of course, I hope to expand your horizons—to inspire you to try new techniques and new flavors. But the bottom line is that I want you to make these recipes. Remember, cooking isn't brain surgery. This is especially true for what is surely the world's easiest cooking method, grilling.

Beating a Path to the World's Best Barbecue

Grilling is done, in some form or other, in virtually every country in the world. In some regions, it's a marginal technique—something you do outdoors, for example, when you lack access to a proper kitchen. Or something a low-wage street

vendor does, lacking the knowledge or material resources to practice a more sophisticated style of cooking.

In other countries, grilling lies at the core of the culture's culinary identity. The grills may range from the shoebox–size braziers used in Southeast Asia to the behemoth fire pits found in South America and the American South. The preparations may be as simple as Argentina's *bife de lomo* (grilled tenderloin seasoned only with salt) or as complex as Vietnam's *bo bun* (thinly sliced, lemongrass-marinated beef eaten with noodles, chiles, crisp vegetables, aromatic herbs, and rice paper.)

In researching my world tour of grilling and barbecue, I discovered that there is a barbecue belt that encircles the globe. Or more specifically, that there are six great barbecue zones. The United States and Mexico and the Caribbean comprises the first. Standing alone as the second is South America. On the other side of the Atlantic, the barbecue zone stretches from the Mediterranean Basin to the Middle East (number three) and from Arab North Africa to South Africa via the continent's western coast (number four).

The largest contiguous barbecue zone starts in Turkey and runs east through the Caucasus Mountains, Central Asia, Iraq, Iran, Afghanistan, Pakistan, and India (number five). In the thirteenth century, the Mongols, led by Genghis Khan, spread their love of grilled meats as far west as Turkey. The Arab world refined the idea, then shipped it back via the Mogul rulers to the Indian subcontinent and possibly beyond to Indonesia.

The last great barbecue zone follows the eastern rim of the Pacific, stretching from Australia and Indonesia to Korea. Along the way, some of the world's most interesting grilling can be found in Singapore, Malaysia, Thailand, Vietnam, Macao, and Japan.

Thus, most of the world's grilling take place in the tropics, which you'd expect, given the proclivity of most humans in hot climates to cook outdoors. (Furthermore, most of the world's spices grow in the tropics, which adds interest to the marinades and condiments traditionally associated with grilling.) But a great deal of remarkable live-fire cooking lies squarely outside the tropics: Consider Japan, Argentina, and our own United States.

What's almost as interesting as where people do live-fire cooking is where they don't.

Grilling has never played much of a role in two of the world's gastronomic superpowers: northern Europe and China. And although grilling is found in Africa, more often than not charcoal fires are used to heat stew pots and frying pans, not to cook the meats directly.

My first year on the barbecue trail, I focused my efforts in my own hemisphere. My first stop was the Jamaican town Boston Beach, birthplace of jerk. I island hopped my way across the Caribbean, stopping for French West Indian *boucanée* (chicken smoked over sugarcane), Trinidadian *choka* (spiced, grilled vegetables), *lechon asado* (Hispanic roast pig). The North American concept of barbecue (the intense spicing and slow smoky grilling) originated in the Caribbean, and the tradition remains alive and flourishing.

Next I headed for South America, home to some of the world's most heroic grilling. I dined in stylish *churrascarias* in Rio de Janeiro, at the homey grill stalls of Montevideo's Mercado del Puerto, and at landmark steak houses in Buenos Aires. I watched whole sides of beef being roasted in front of a campfire on an *estancia* (ranch) in the Pampas. South American grilling, I learned, represents one end of the barbecue spectrum, emphasizing simplicity and directness of flavor. Argentinians don't even bother with marinades for most meats: the seasonings are limited to sea salt and the perfume of wood smoke.

The second year, I turned my attention to Asia. I visited Indonesia, birthplace of the saté and home to what is probably the world's single largest repertoire of grilled dishes. I sampled dozens of different types of satés—a small fraction of what's actually eaten in Indonesia. I learned that small is beautiful: Indonesian satés are cooked on grills the size of a shoebox and served on skewers as slender as broom straws.

Indonesia and my next destination, Singapore and Malaysia, possess some of the world's most complex marinades and spice mixtures. On the island of Penang in northern Malaysia, I watched grill jockeys pound ginger, chiles, galangal, lemongrass, kaffir lime leaves, shrimp paste, and coconut milk into fragrant paste for seasoning grilled meats and seafood. I scorched my tongue on the fiery *achars* (pickles) and *sambals* (relishes) that accompany grilled fare in Southeast Asia. This complex seasoning of grilled meats stands at the opposite end of the spectrum from the simple grilled meats of South America.

One common complaint about barbecue in the West is that it's so, well, relentlessly carnivorous. In Thailand and Vietnam I found the perfect model for healthy barbecue: the pairing of small portions of grilled meats with large amounts of vegetables, rice, and noodles. The Thai often eat barbecued food wrapped in lettuce leaves (a practice echoed by Koreans), while in Vietnam the wrapping is done in crêpe-like sheets of rice paper. Fish sauce–based dipping sauces, toasted peanuts, sliced chiles, and fragrant basil and mint sprigs are often combined with grilled meats in a single, explosively flavorful bite.

As I moved north, the fish sauce and coconut milk marinades gave way to soy sauce and five-spice powder mixtures in Hong Kong and Macao and to sweet sesame marinades in Korea. In Japan (land of my birth, by the way), I sat elbow to elbow with Japanese businessmen in crowded Tokyo yakitori parlors, enjoying sweet-salty teriyaki and pungent barbecue sauces made from miso (cultured soybean paste) and *umeboshi* (pickled plums). I feasted on fabled Kobe beef and on ingredients I never knew you could grill, like okra and ginkgo nuts. Here, too, I learned that small is beautiful and that barbecue could be as subtle as haiku.

The third year, I focused my research on the Near East and the Mediterranean Basin. Turkish cooks introduced me to an astonishing array of kebabs and grilled vegetables. In Morocco I discovered *mechouie* (pit-roasted lamb), not to mention French-style brochettes flavored with pungent North African spices. In France I experienced the heady pleasures of grilling over grapevines. (One night, I drove 400 miles to taste grilled escargots in a tiny village near Perpignon.) Italy, Spain, and Portugal impressed me with their wealth of simply grilled seafoods and vegetables.

Along the way, I filled in my travels: Mexico for its *barbacoas* and *carne asado;* India for its extraordinary tandoori and grilled breads; Israel for its *shwarma, kofta,* and grilled foie gras. I crisscrossed the United Stated, savoring pulled pork in the Carolinas, brisket in Texas, and ribs in Kansas City and Memphis.

All told, I traveled more than 150,000 miles to 25 countries on 5 continents.

Don't ask me what my favorite barbecue is. It would be a little like asking the parents of a large family to name their favorite child.

I loved the plate-burying abundance of an Argentinian steak as much as the delicacy of Japanese yakitori. I loved the straightforwardness of Italian *bistecca alla fiorentina* as much as the complex layering of flavor characteristic of Indian tandoori. I loved the eat-with-your-fingers informality of North American barbecue and the chic of a Brazilian *churrascaria.* I loved the Asian-style grilling, with its modest portions of grilled meats in relation to the generous serving of starches and vegetables. But I wouldn't snub my nose at a thick, juicy hamburger made from freshly ground sirloin charred over blazing hickory or mesquite.

Come to think of it, during three long years on the barbecue trail, there wasn't a single meal I didn't enjoy. So, as they say in Spanish, *buen provecho;* in Vietnamese, *chuc qui ban an ngon;* in Hindi, *aap kha lijiya;* in Japanese, *itadakimasu;* in Arabic, *bessahaa;* in Hebrew, *b'teavon;* in Korean, *jharr chop su se yo;* in French, *bon appétit;* in Chinese, *man man chi.* In other words, dig in!

—Steven Raichlen

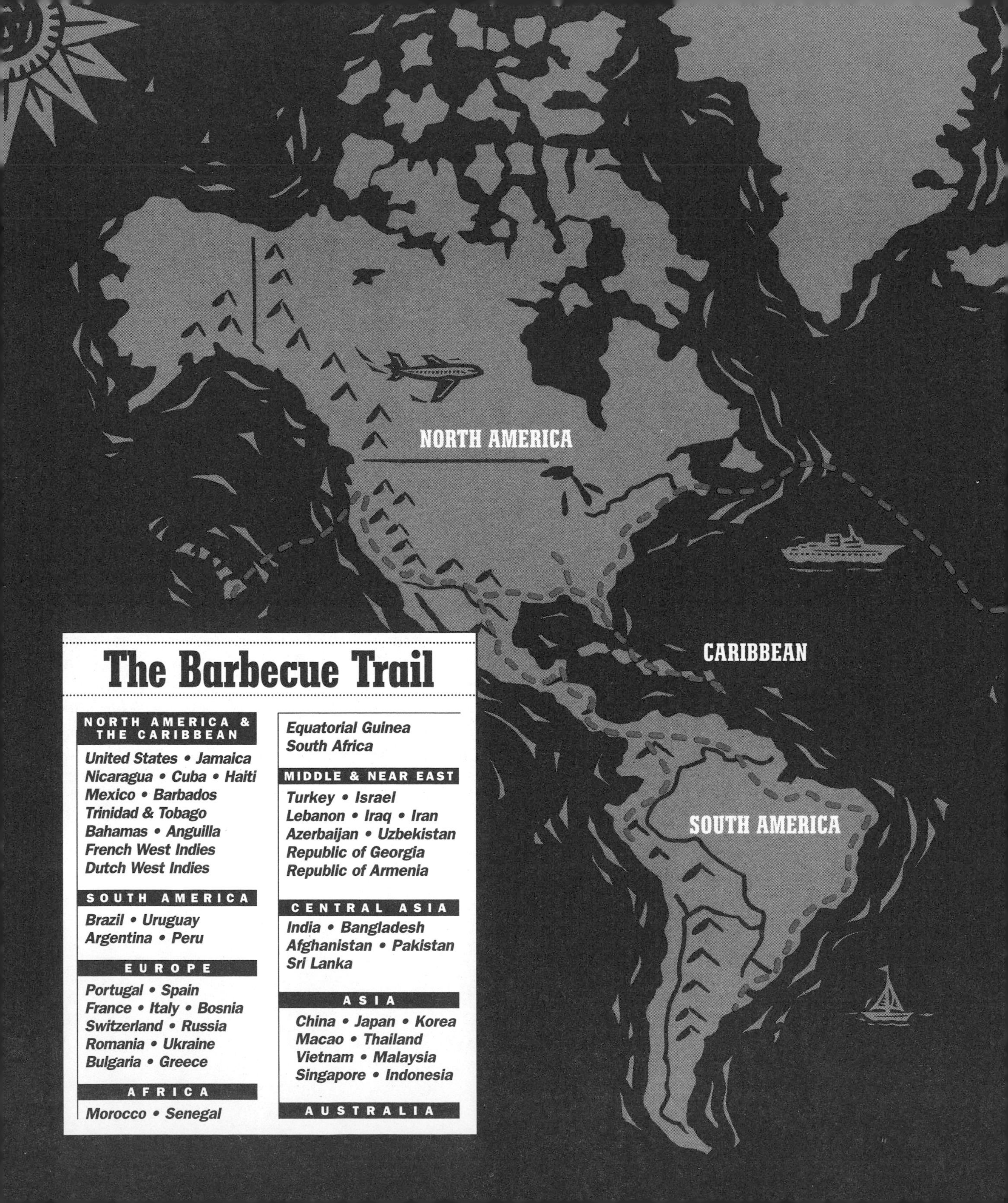

NORTH AMERICA

CARIBBEAN

SOUTH AMERICA

The Barbecue Trail

NORTH AMERICA & THE CARIBBEAN

United States • Jamaica
Nicaragua • Cuba • Haiti
Mexico • Barbados
Trinidad & Tobago
Bahamas • Anguilla
French West Indies
Dutch West Indies

SOUTH AMERICA

Brazil • Uruguay
Argentina • Peru

EUROPE

Portugal • Spain
France • Italy • Bosnia
Switzerland • Russia
Romania • Ukraine
Bulgaria • Greece

AFRICA

Morocco • Senegal
Equatorial Guinea
South Africa

MIDDLE & NEAR EAST

Turkey • Israel
Lebanon • Iraq • Iran
Azerbaijan • Uzbekistan
Republic of Georgia
Republic of Armenia

CENTRAL ASIA

India • Bangladesh
Afghanistan • Pakistan
Sri Lanka

ASIA

China • Japan • Korea
Macao • Thailand
Vietnam • Malaysia
Singapore • Indonesia

AUSTRALIA

A CRASH COURSE ON
Grilling and Barbecuing

> *"Cooks are made, grillers are born."*
> —FRENCH PROVERB

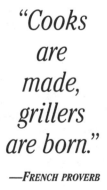

Men don't have an exclusive on grilling beef in Central America

 rilling is the oldest, most widespread and most forgiving method of cooking. Over the centuries, there have been countless refinements to the process of cooking food over fire: from grills and grates to rotisseries and turnspits to gas grills and infrared burners. These refinements have enabled us to cook an ever wider repertory of ingredients on the grill, but the basic principles remain the same, as does the primal pleasure of fire-cooked foods.

THE PROCESS

A lot of confusion surrounds the terms *grilling* and *barbecuing,* compounded by the fact that we use *barbecue* to refer to many different aspects of live-fire cooking: from a piece of cooking equipment (the grill) to one or more cooking methods (using that grill) to specific dishes, such as Texas- or North Carolina–style barbecue. We also use the term more broadly to refer to the act of cooking outdoors, to a meal cooked and served outdoors, and to a social gathering featuring barbecued food.

Much of the confusion lies in the fact that we often use the same piece of equipment (the "barbecue grill") for the high-heat direct method known as grilling, for the low-heat, smoke-cook method that constitutes true barbecue, and for the moderate-heat method known as indirect grilling.

All three methods, although related, are quite different. Understanding these differences will enable you to produce great fire-cooked fare every time.

Grilling

Grilling is a high-heat cooking method done directly over live flames, cooking the food in a matter of minutes. The three operative concepts here are "direct," "high heat," and "minutes." Grilled

Grilling Indoors

The advent of the first stovetop electric grills brought into the kitchen what had been traditionally an outdoor cooking method. These grills feature an electric heating element beneath a metal grate—a sort of inverted broiler. But is this really grilling? A purist would say no. Indeed, conspicuously absent is the first qualification: live fire. But electric grills do offer the dry high-heat searing and charring so prized in outdoor grilling. I'm not sure that a blindfolded eater could tell the difference between outdoor and indoor grilled food that has been marinated well. And it certainly enables Frost Belters to enjoy grill-style food all year long.

This brings me to skillet grills, those frying pans with parallel raised ridges on the bottom that are designed to simulate grill marks. Here again, a purist might be tempted to dismiss these devices. Certainly there's no live fire. But the ridges create the smoky charring and inviting grill marks so typical of grilling. Skillet grilling is no substitute for outdoor grilling, but it can serve the apartment dweller who wants to approximate a grilled flavor.

food is cooked directly over and just a few inches away from the flames or glowing coals at a temperature in excess of 500°F (some restaurant grills achieve temperatures of 800° to 1,000°F). This high heat chars the surface of the food, sealing in juices and creating the smoky, caramelized crust we so prize in grilled fare.

True grilling is best suited to thin or small tender cuts of meat or other foods, including kebabs, burgers, sausages, steaks, and chops; chicken pieces or breasts; fish fillets, steaks, or small whole fish or shellfish; vegetables; even breads—in short, any food that benefits from relatively brief cooking over high heat. Time is of the essence; since true grilling means the food will be cooked quickly, it should be done to order. Indeed, one of the greatest pleasures of grilled food is its immediacy: You literally watch it being cooked.

Grilling is by far the world's most common live-fire cooking method, practiced on six continents in restaurants, street stalls, and backyards, by rich and poor alike. Grilling is essentially the same, whether it's done over a campfire-size pit in Argentina or on a shoebox-size saté grill in Bali.

Barbecuing

Barbecuing lies at the opposite end of the spectrum from true grilling. It is a long, slow, indirect, low-heat method that uses smoldering logs or charcoal and wood chunks to smoke-cook the food, usually some sort of meat. "Indirect" means that the heat source is located away from the food to be cooked. In traditional American pit barbecue, the heat source is a separate firebox, which is attached to but not part of the actual cooking chamber. When barbecuing is done on a charcoal or gas grill, a low fire is maintained on one side or around the periphery of the grill and the food is cooked on the other side or in the center.

When I say slow, I mean *slow*. Kansas City's famous KC Masterpiece restaurants cook their baby back ribs for 10 hours, their pork shoulders for 16 hours. When I say low, I mean *low*. The temperature of the pit at Dallas's legendary Sonny Bryan's never rises above 225°F. Low heat generates smoke (the wood smolders, it doesn't burn), and this smoke gives barbecue its characteristic flavor. Smoke is a natural preservative, and in the days before refrigeration it was probably used first and foremost to keep meats and seafood from spoiling.

The long, slow, low, indirect heat of barbecue is ideally suited to large pieces of meat, like whole pigs and turkeys. It's also perfect for cuts with lots of tough connec-tive tissue, like brisket and spareribs. Barbecue was tradi-tionally associated with the poorer echelons of society. Unable to afford the prestige cuts, they created a cuisine based on inexpensive cuts, meats that are revered as barbecue today.

Barbecuing is primarily a New World phenomenon, originating in the Caribbean and reaching its apotheosis in Texas, Tennessee, Missouri, and the American South in general. The *poulet boucanée* (Buccaneer-Style Chicken) of the French West Indies is a sort of bar-becue. So is Jamaica's jerk, although the meat is cooked directly over live, albeit low-burn-ing, coals.

The Birth of the Kettle Grill

*I*n a cooking method as ancient and universal as grilling, it seems unlikely that a single individual could be responsible for the invention of a new technique. Nonetheless, one person did revolutionize the art of outdoor cookery in North America by combining the techniques of grilling and barbecuing in a single device: the kettle grill. His name was George Stephen, and the method he pioneered is now known as indirect grilling.

The year was 1951. The place was Palatine, Illinois. Like many Americans in those halcyon days of the 1950s, Stephen was an avid barbecue buff. But the flat, brazier-style grills popular in those days didn't work well in rainy or windy weather. He was frustrated.

At the time, Stephen worked at the Weber Brothers Metal Works, a manu-facturer of nautical buoys. In a stroke of genius, he had the idea to fit a metal grate into one of the spun metal bowls used for buoy making. He then fash-ioned a cover with vents out of the same metal. In July 1952, George Stephen began marketing his grill as "George's Kettle" which was promptly nicknamed the "Sputnik" on account of its rotund shape.

The advantage of the deep, cov-ered kettle grill wasn't simply that it deflected wind and rain. Rather, it was the way it enabled the user to transform the grill into a sort of oven where foods could be roasted—or for that matter barbecued—by the heat of glowing charcoal.

Today the Weber Kettle remains the world's best-selling charcoal grill.

Indirect Grilling

Indirect grilling is a hybrid method, invented in this century, that bridges the gap between barbecuing and grilling. As in barbecuing, the food is cooked adjacent to, not directly over, the coals. But the cooking takes place in the same chamber as the fire and the temperature is usually higher—generally 350° to 400°F. Wood chips or chunks are often placed on the coals or other heat source to generate smoke, as with barbecue. But just as often, indirect grilling is done without smoke.

When indirect grilling on a charcoal grill, the coals are placed on the sides or periphery of the firebox; the food is in the center of the grate. With a gas grill, the burners on one side (or the front and back of the grill) are lit and the food is placed over the nonlit burner.

The beauty of indirect grilling is that it turns your barbecue grill into a sort of oven. This enables you to cook large cuts (prime rib, turkey, whole fish) or fatty cuts of meat (duck, chicken, ribs) without burning them.

Indirect grilling gives you the best of both grilling and barbecuing—the charcoal flavor of the former, the tenderness and smokiness of the latter—without the drawbacks. Indirect grilling is a lot more forgiving than direct grilling in terms of timing and temperature control. And it's a lot faster than true barbecue, which can take 6 to 12 hours.

The majority of the recipes in this book, as in the world of barbecue at large, are grilled. A substantial number call for indirect grilling. Several recipes, like the Texas Brisket and the North Carolina–Style Pulled Pork Shoulder, are cooked long enough and at a low enough heat to qualify as true barbecue.

Pit Cooking

Pit cooking is probably the oldest method of live-fire cooking. But today the term can mean very different things depending on where you live.

In Argentina, pit cooking is known as *asado*. Large cuts of meats (even whole lambs or pigs) are roasted on T-shaped spits placed upright in a circle around a blazing campfire. I've observed such campfires in ranch settings and in restaurants in downtown Buenos Aires. The heat is direct, but not directly under the meat, nor is it as hot as grilling over a grate. With a moderate flame, a side of beef or a whole goat cooks in 4 to 6 hours.

Barbecue buffs in the Carolinas, Texas, and the Midwest call their cookers "pits," although most are brick constructions that stand above ground; some are portable trailer-mounted cookers fashioned from fuel tanks. In these areas in the old days, barbecue was no doubt smoke-cooked over shallow pits in the ground.

True pit cooking takes place in a hole in the ground. You've experienced it if you've ever been to a traditional New England clambake or to a Hawaiian luau. Pit cooking is popular in Mexico, where famous pit-cooked dishes include *barbacoa* (pit-cooked goat or lamb wrapped in cactus or avocado leaves) and *pebil* (pit-cooked pork wrapped in banana leaves).

In this type of pit cooking, a large hole is dug in the ground, then lined with stones and firewood. The fire is ignited and allowed to burn down to glowing coals. Then the food—usually a large cut of meat, like a whole pig or goat—is wrapped in a flame-retardant material, such as banana leaves or seaweed, and placed in the pit, which is covered with dirt, sand, more seaweed, or a tarpaulin. The food cooks underground for 12 to 24 hours. When dug out, it is incredibly flavorful and fall-off-the-bone tender.

But is it barbecue?

True, we're talking about an indirect cooking method, and the wood embers impart at least a trace of smoke flavor. But it's also true that the low, wet heat that does the cooking is actually more akin to steaming or roasting.

Like so much in the realm of live-fire cooking, whether pit cooking is or isn't barbecue is a matter of debate.

GEARING UP

Now that I've cleared up the differences between grilling and barbecuing, let's examine the gear—the grills and accessories—you need available for live-fire cooking.

Charcoal or Gas?

The great debate over the merits of charcoal versus gas has raged ever since utility companies introduced the first gas grills (built-in pedestal models) in the 1950s. Charcoal grills can be time-consuming, unpredictable, and messy—all reasons why grill buffs love them. Most professionals favor charcoal over gas.

The vast majority of cooks I met on the global barbecue trail cook over either wood or charcoal. This is certainly in part because of the flavor, but there's an economic explanation as well. Charcoal is readily available in the Third World, and a charcoal grill can be fashioned from materials scavenged from the trash heap. In other words, charcoal grilling requires very little capital investment. When used properly, a charcoal grill produces a clean, high heat you simply can't achieve with propane.

But gas grills have their partisans—among them some very high profile chefs. Michelin three-star chef Alain Ducasse made gas the fuel of the high-tech, multiple-spit grills he designed for his acclaimed restaurants, Louis XV in Monte Carlo and Alain Ducasse in Paris. The chefs at what is arguably the most famous grill in Tokyo, the inimitably theatrical Inakaya, cook their *robatayaki* over tiny high-tech gas grills. And whatever we Americans may profess in public, the most recent reports show that we buy more gas grills than charcoal.

I own several charcoal grills and can wax as grandiloquent about their virtues and idiosyncrasies as the next guy. But I have to admit that for a workday dinner, I'm more likely to fire up one of our gas grills. Sure, I miss poking the coals around and waltzing the food from hot spots to cold spots. But the push-button ignition, even heat, and ease of cleaning make up for the lack of sport.

Why use gas? In a single word, convenience. Gas grills require no messy charcoal, no special ignition devices, no 40 minutes spent lighting and preheating. (A gas grill preheats in less than 15 minutes.) A gas grill is easier to control and provides a steadier, more even heat than charcoal. It also lasts longer without replenishing: A standard propane tank will give you 12 to 18 hours of nonstop grilling. Besides, you can cover most gas grills, turning them into smokers and indirect cookers.

So why doesn't everyone use a gas grill? Well, gas does have a few drawbacks. You can't get gas to burn quite as hot as charcoal (especially when the latter is fanned), although there is a new generation of gas grills that burn hotter than ever before. Gas is inherently flavorless. The "grilled" flavor you get from a gas grill comes from charring the meat; the "smoke" flavor results when the fat and meat juices burn on the "Flavorizer" bars or lava stones. Gas heat is also a slightly wet heat (when propane is burned, it releases carbon dioxide and water), and purists feel that this moisture adulterates the texture of the meat.

Besides, charcoal has a host of advantages, not the least of which is the thrill most males experience when they set something on fire. Charcoal grilling is a more interactive experience than gas grilling, which makes it, in the eyes of many barbecue buffs, more fun. Charcoal burns hotter than gas and can be "turbocharged" by oxygenating it (ventilating it) with a fan. Indeed, in many parts of the world—especially Asia—the fan or blower is an important item in the grill jockey's toolbox. To the extent that charcoal contains wood, it also generates a natural smoke flavor.

Charcoal grills are cheaper to buy than gas and can be improvised when commercially manufactured grills aren't available. The year I traveled through Europe after college, I took one piece of cooking equipment in my backpack: a wok. Whenever I wanted to barbecue, I simply lined it with foil and filled it with charcoal or briquets.

Which grill to buy depends on your personality and lifestyle. If you enjoy building and tending a fire, if you're interested in the actual process of grilling, not just the results, a charcoal grill is definitely for you. If you're more convenience-oriented and time-starved (and who isn't these days?), you'll probably prefer the push-button ease of a gas grill. Better yet, buy one of each.

Types of Grills

As grill fever continues to sweep North America, an ever-increasing selection of grills—from portable kettle grills to jumbo built-ins, from simple hibachis to high-tech gas grills—has become available. Here's a look at the basic styles, starting with the smallest.

HIBACHI: This small, portable charcoal grill, originally from Japan, is one of the world's best designed live-fire cooking devices. Making a virtue of simplicity, the hibachi consists of a rectangular or oval firebox (traditionally made of a heavy metal, like cast iron, for even heat conduction) surmounted by one or two metal grates. The hibachi is designed for the direct high-heat grilling of teriyaki, kebabs, satés, and small cuts of meat. The cooking temper-

ature is controlled by air vents near the bottom and by raising and lowering the grate. The saté grills of Indonesia and the braziers of Turkey and North Africa are variations on the hibachi.

TABLE GRILL also known as the **Australian grill** or **Argentinian grill:** This long, narrow grill (4 to 6 feet long, 1½ to 2 feet wide) looks like a table surmounted by a grate. Legs or a trolley platform hold the grilling surface at waist height for comfortable cooking. Charcoal versions have a shallow firebox for the coals and an adjustable grate. Gas versions feature thermostatic heat control. Table grills are used for the direct high-heat cooking of large numbers of steaks, chops, shrimp, and lobster. You often find them at communal or charity barbecues. When Australians speak of barbecue grills, this is what they mean.

KETTLE GRILL: This uniquely American grill has a deep rounded bowl with a grate in the bottom for holding the charcoal (or wood chunks) and a grate on top for the food. The lid is also bowl-shaped, which allows you to turn the grill into a smoker (when you use wood chips) or an outdoor oven. Kettle

grills can be used for direct high-heat grilling, but what makes them unique is their ability to do indirect grilling and barbecuing. To this end, the best kettle grills have hinged grates for easy access to the coals and slotted side baskets that hold the charcoal for indirect grilling. The cooking temperature is controlled by vents on the bottom and in the lid. Kettle grills come in both round and square designs.

55-GALLON STEEL DRUM GRILL: This variation on the kettle grill is especially popular on the professional barbecue circuit. A couple of hours of welding is all it takes to cut a 55-gallon industrial steel drum in half lengthwise and install legs, a chimney, a grate, and hinges and handles for raising and lowering the lid. The hefty size of these grills enables you to cook large cuts of meats (including whole pigs). It's also easy to build a fire on one side of the drum (or in a separate firebox) for the smoky, low-heat, indirect cooking needed to make fall-off-the-bone-tender barbecue. Variations on the 55-gallon steel drum grill include the smaller 10-gallon versions made from propane

What to Look For

With more choices than ever, buying a grill can be almost as daunting as purchasing a car or a computer. Here's what I look for when buying a grill.

CHARCOAL GRILLS

ESSENTIAL FEATURES (applies to hibachis, table grills, kettle grills, and 55-gallon drums):

- Sturdy, nonwobbly legs

- A heavy-gauge metal bowl or firebox with a tight-fitting lid (except hibachis; they have no lid)

- A grate at the bottom of the bowl for holding the charcoal

- Air vents on both the top and bottom for temperature control (except hibachis; they have no top vents)

- A solid-feeling cooking grate (in the case of a hibachi or table grill, one that's easy to raise and lower)

- Wooden or heatproof handles

DESIRABLE OPTIONAL FEATURES:

- A built-in thermometer

- Slotted metal or wire side baskets to hold the coals for indirect cooking

- A hinged grate that offers easy access to the fire, so you can add coals as needed

- An ash catcher on the bottom for easy cleaning and disposal

- A side table for additional workspace

- Fittings for a rotisserie

GAS GRILLS

ESSENTIAL FEATURES:

- Sturdy construction

- A thick, heavy firebox and tight-fitting lid for even heat conduction

- Electric ignition

- At least two (preferably three) separate heating zones

- Adjustable controls that enable you to set the grill on high, medium, and low. The high setting should give you a consistent grilling temperature of 500°F. This usually (but not always) means a grill with at least 33,000 BTUs.

- A gas gauge

- A built-in thermometer

DESIRABLE OPTIONAL FEATURES:

- Side tables for extra workspace

- A gas burner on one side for heating sauces and accompaniments

- Fittings for a rotisserie and smoker box

- A warming rack

- A spider guard for keeping insects out of the burners

- A glass window in the cover

---

tanks, common in the Caribbean, and the jumbo 200- or 500-gallon versions made from furnace oil tanks, popular at barbecue festivals.

GAS GRILL: Another American invention, the gas grill consists of a metal box lined with tube-shaped liquid-propane burners. Surmounting these burners is a heating surface, sometimes a row of inverted V-shaped metal bars, sometimes lava stones or ceramic briquets. Propane has no flavor of its own as it burns, but a smoke flavor is created when the meat juices and melting fat sizzle on the stones or metal bars. These days, most gas grills have two or three separate cooking zones, so you can set them up for indirect grilling.

BUILT-IN GRILL: These brick or stone behemoths began to appear in the 1950s, the golden age of backyard barbecue. There are two types: the raised hearth style with a built-in chimney and the southern-style barbecue pit. The former—charcoal- or wood-burning—was designed for the direct high-heat grilling of steaks, chicken, and burgers. The latter was built for the long, slow smoke-cooking essential to making barbecue. With the increased mobility of the American family (the average American moves once every four years), built-ins have largely disappeared, and I must say I miss them. They gave me the sense of comfort and community I feel when I sit in front of a fireplace. However, a new generation of built-ins has started to appear—a veritable high-tech outdoor cooking center that's as likely to be fueled by propane or natural gas as by wood or charcoal.

The Scoop on Accessories

Owning the right accessories won't automatically make you a great griller, but it's a lot harder to be one without them. Here are the essentials and the not-so-essential-but-usefuls. One excellent mail-order source for grilling accessories is the Grill Lover's Catalog, published by Char-Broil, P.O. Box 1300, Columbus, GA 31902-1300; (800) 241-8981.

ESSENTIALS:

- Chimney starter (if you have a charcoal grill); see page 12

- Wire brush for cleaning the grate

- Two or more sets of long-handled tongs. (I particularly like the spring-loaded tongs sold at restaurant supply houses and cookware shops)

- One or more long-handled spatulas, preferably with crooked (offset) blades

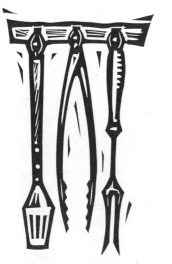

- Two long-handled basting brushes (natural bristles, please; nylon will melt. You may also want to invest in a mop-style baster, which looks like a miniature mop)

- One set of heavy-duty oven mitts

- Three sharp knives: chef's (8 to 12 inches), paring, and carving

- Carving fork

- Instant-read meat thermometer

- Disposable aluminum foil drip pans (these are essential for indirect cooking and barbecuing and are also useful for soaking wood chips and holding marinates. They are available at just about any supermarket)

- Roll of heavy-duty aluminum foil

- Roll of paper towels

- Water pistol (useful for taming flare-ups)

- Plastic or rubber gloves (wear them when you rub spices into pork and ribs)

- An assortment of metal and bamboo skewers

- Stopwatch or timer

- Portable spotlight for grilling at night (there's nothing harder than grilling when you can't see the food)

- Dry spray-type fire extinguisher

LUXURIES:

- A flat vegetable grate or basket grill with small holes that allow the smoke and flames to pass through but keep the vegetable pieces from falling through the grate

- A hinged fish grilling basket that allows you to grill and turn a whole fish

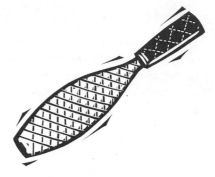

- A motorized rotisserie that mounts on the grill (it's great for whole chickens and legs of lamb)

- A larding iron, a long slender tool with a V-shaped blade that enables you to insert strips of ham, cheese, or vegetables into a roast

- An electric spice mill (looks like a coffee grinder)—great for grinding whole spices to make rubs that taste like they mean it

- A meat grinder like grandma used to use (a grinder works much better than a food processor for grinding meat)

- A kitchen syringe—useful for injecting bastes into turkey breasts, pork roasts, and other dry meats to moisturize them from the inside

- A sprayer or mister for basting grilled meats with vinegar or other flavorings. Use the commonplace garden variety for vinegar. One company makes a mister you can use with olive oil—Liquid Motion, Inc., 109 Kettle Creek, Weston, CT 06883; phone: (203) 226-6981

FUEL FOR THE FIRE

Now that you have the information you need to buy a grill, let's look at the fuel options for firing up your grill.

Black Gold— Charcoal

About 300,000 years ago, give or take a few millennia, our prehistoric forebears made a revolutionary discovery: Charred wood (charcoal) burns cleaner, hotter, and much more efficiently than fresh wood.

Charcoal is made by burning wood without allowing complete combustion (it has nothing to do with coal, which is a carbon-based mineral). It was probably discovered by accident when someone shoveled dirt or sand on a campfire. Deprived of oxygen, the wood continued to smolder, just enough to evaporate the water and resins, but not enough to consume all the combustible components.

Cordwood contains 20 to 30 percent water; charred wood contains 2 to 3 percent. This gives charcoal many advantages: It burns faster and hotter (as much as 200 degrees hotter), and it's easier to transport and store. Charcoal is the preferred cooking fuel for more than half the world's population; it is used throughout Africa, the Caribbean, and Asia.

Particularly delicious is the coconut charcoal (made from coconut shells) used in Southeast Asia.

Most of the world uses lump charcoal, but in North America it's the briquet that reigns supreme. The good news about charcoal briquets is that they're more uniform in shape, size, and consistency than charred wood. The bad news is that, like sausage, you never quite know what's in them (see "Types of Charcoal" this page). Some briquets are made from charred hardwood with natural plant starches as a binder. Other briquets contain wood scraps, tree bark, sawdust, coal dust, borax, limestone, and/or sodium nitrate held together with a petroleum-based binder.

The Flavorful Fuel: Wood

Wood was the first fuel that man used for grilling. In many ways it remains the best. Wood burns hot and long, releasing flavorful smoke that enhances any

Types of Charcoal

Charcoal is the most popular fuel for backyard grilling. Here are the basic types.

CHARWOOD, also known as lump charcoal or chunk charwood charcoal: The fuel preferred by chefs, charwood is made by burning whole logs or large pieces of wood in a kiln without oxygen. It is sold in irregularly shaped pieces and burns clean and hot.

NATURAL BRIQUETS: Made from pulverized charwood, these briquets are held together with natural starches.

COMPOSITION BRIQUETS: Made from burned wood, wood scraps, and/or coal dust, these briquets have paraffin or petroleum binders.

food cooked in its presence. (Whatever the virtues of charwood or charcoal in terms of convenience and temperature control, they are essentially flavorless. The only way to produce a real smoke flavor with charcoal is to toss wood chips on the coals.)

Wood's superiority as a cooking fuel is attested to by its universal popularity in North and South America and Europe. From

Cooking with Wood

For years, I've used wood chips for fuel and wood chunks to add a smoke flavor when cooking on a gas or charcoal grill. But it never occurred to me that I could grill on an all-wood fire at home. I always assumed that wood grilling was meant only for restaurant food—something to be done over an industrial-strength grill and therefore beyond the reach of the home cook.

Then I met Jerry Lawson. Jerry is the president of W W Wood, Inc., of Pleasanton, Texas, and an avid griller. His company sells a line of natural wood products—hefty chunks of hickory or mesquite packaged in flammable paper sacks. All you do is lay the sack flat in your grill and light the corners; in 10 or 15 minutes, you have a dandy blaze for grilling.

I've since learned that many companies sell wood chunks in affordable bulk packaging. (Look for them at the sources listed below.)

Wood chunks turn out to be a cinch to light in a chimney starter. Simply ball up three or four sheets of newspaper in the bottom section (or use a paraffin starter), place the wood chunks in the top (filling it most of the way up), and light the paper. You should have blazing coals in 10 to 15 minutes. Dump them out into the grill and use tongs or a spatula to spread them out evenly over the bottom. Let the wood burn until glowing red, 3 to 5 minutes, and get ready for one of the best taste sensations of your life.

Cooking with wood is pretty much like cooking over charcoal. But keep in mind that wood can burn hotter, so you might not need quite as much. Because of the high heat, it's best to leave the grill uncovered. (Use any recipe that calls for direct grilling.) Use only dried natural hardwood. Softwoods, like pine, produce an unpleasant resiny flavor, and lumber scraps may be treated with carcinogenic chemicals.

WHAT WOOD TO USE

Does it really make a difference what sort of wood you grill on? Charlie Trotter thinks so. Chicago's preeminent chef varies the woods in his grill according to the season. "In the winter, we use heavier woods, like oak and hickory," explains Trotter, "moving to lighter woods, like alder and locust, in the springtime, and fruitwoods, like cherry, in the summer." The fact is that woods are to grilling what spices are to rubs; they add flavor to whatever you cook over them.

ALDER: A good clean wood from the Pacific Northwest. Good for salmon, turkey, and chicken.

APPLE: Tangy and clean-flavored. Good for chicken, pork, and game.

CHERRY: Sweet and fruity, with distinct cherry overtones. Use for duck and other poultry.

GRAPEVINE TRIMMINGS: The preferred fuel in France. Burns at a high heat, imparting a clean, dare I say vinous, smoke flavor. Grape wood is well suited to steaks and other meats, seafood, and escargots.

HICKORY: Rich and smoky. The traditional wood for American barbecue. Good for pork.

MAPLE: Mellow, mild, and sweet. Use with poultry, seafood, and pork.

MESQUITE: Robustly flavored and smoky. The ultimate wood for beef in the style of Texas and northern Mexico.

OAK: A European favorite, and the wood preferred by professional chefs. Its clean, well-rounded flavor is equally well suited to poultry, seafood, and meat.

PECAN: A southern American favorite. Similar to hickory, only milder.

WHERE TO BUY WOOD

W W WOOD, INC.
P.O. Box 398
Pleasanton, TX 78064
(830) 569-2501

CHAR-BROIL
P.O. Box 1240
Columbus, GA 31902
(800) 241-7548

NATURE'S OWN/PEOPLES WOODS
75 Mill Street
Cumberland, RI 02864
(800) 729-5800

Boy Scout campfires to the wood-burning grills at the trendiest restaurants, wood fire–cooked food has an irresistible appeal. This truth is not lost on Tuscan cooks, Argentinian *asadors,* and the new generation of American chefs, many of whom have made the wood-burning grill the focal point of their restaurants.

Wood does have its drawbacks, however. First, it's bulky. Logs are harder to light than charcoal and take longer to reach the ideal cooking temperature. Heat control can be tricky, and it's wasteful to build a log fire to cook for only one or two people.

However, when it comes to smoke flavor, nothing can beat a wood fire. In the box opposite you'll find instructions for building a wood fire. If cooking over wood is impractical for your particular setup, you can achieve a wood-grilled flavor by tossing wood chips or chunks on your grill.

Almost any hardwood is a candidate for

grilling. (Hardwood comes from deciduous trees—trees that lose their leaves in winter.) Oak is probably the most popular wood on a worldwide basis, burning hot and clean and producing a distinctive but not overpowering smoke flavor. Hickory is popular in the South and the Midwest (Kansas City–style barbecue would be sorry stuff without it), burning somewhat slower than oak, producing a rich, sweet smoky taste.

Conventional wisdom holds that the only wood you should never use for grilling is a softwood, like pine or spruce. It's true that evergreen trees are loaded with resins, which cause dangerous flare-ups and impart a sooty, tarry taste to foods cooked over them. But even here I've found exceptions to the rule. One autumn I stumbled upon a village cookout in Bavaria, where bratwurst was being grilled over pinecones. The resulting resin flavor was delicious.

Finally, a word of caution to home handymen and -women who may be tempted to use wood

scraps for their barbecues. Plywood and pressure-treated lumber, which contain toxic chemicals, should be avoided at all costs.

Tanked on Gas

Gas grills run on liquid propane, which is available at grill shops, hardware stores, and RV centers. The standard tank holds about 20 pounds of propane, which will burn for 12 to 18 hours, depending on the usage and the temperature of the grill.

Most of the newer gas grills come with gas gauges. On mine, you set the gauge when the tank is empty, then you fill the tank. *Cook's Magazine* offers a handy tip for assessing the gas level in your propane tank if you don't have a gauge: Tilt the tank slightly, and pour a cup of boiling water over the outside of the tank. Feel the tank with your hand. It is empty where the metal feels warm. There is propane where the tank remains cool.

When filling a new propane tank, the air must be removed first. Advise the service person that you are filling a new tank, so he or she can bleed the tank properly. Transport the filled tank in an upright position. I keep a milk crate in the trunk of my car for this purpose.

Some of the new high-tech built-in grills run on natural gas. Contact your local utility company for hookup.

HOW TO LIGHT UP AND COOK ON A CHARCOAL GRILL

So now you know about the various types of grills and fuels. The next thing to master is cooking over live fire. Let's begin with a charcoal grill.

Starters

When I was 8 years old, my mother gave me a lesson—and a heart-stopping fright—on the wrong way to light a charcoal grill. She threw a match on the briquets, then poured gasoline on top. It was only the quick thinking of our neighbor that averted a tragedy: he knocked the exploding gas can out of Mom's hands and pushed her away from the fire. We all learned a valuable lesson: If you do use a petroleum-based starter, never, *ever* use gasoline. Pour the starter on the coals as directed in the instructions, seal the container, and move it away from the grill *before* you strike the match.

Actually, liquid starters have fallen out of fashion. The theory is that lighter fluids leave a foul-tasting oily residue. And in some states they're considered pollutants and are outlawed. I'm not sure how much residue survives when the coals have been properly preheated, but many people are turned off by the thought of having a petroleum product burning under their food.

The contemporary alternative is the paraffin starter, which looks like a milk-white ice cube. To use paraffin starters, place two or three cubes in the center of your grill and pile a mound of charcoal over them, or put them in the bottom of a chimney starter (see the next paragraph). Touch a match to a corner of a cube to light it.

The ignition aid most favored by grill buffs these days is the chimney starter, a device of elegant simplicity consisting of a 6- to 8-inch-wide cylindrical steel pipe with vent holes at the bottom, grate in the middle, and a heatproof handle. To light charcoal or wood chunks in a chimney

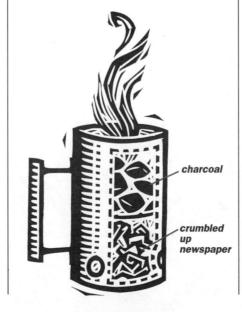

charcoal

crumbled up newspaper

starter, you pile either in the top section and place a few sheets of crumpled newspaper or a couple of paraffin starters in the bottom. Place the chimney on the charcoal grate, touch a lit match to the newspaper or starter, and soon the coals will be blazing. (*Never* light a chimney starter on a wood or otherwise flammable surface.)

When the coals are ready, lift the chimney and dump out the coals in the grill.

An alternative to the chimney starter is the electric starter, a loop-shaped heating element you place under the coals and plug in. Lay the starter on the grate and arrange a tall mound of coals over the heating element. Plug in the starter. The coals will ignite into flame in a matter of minutes. This starter works equally well with wood chunks. The chief drawback to this device is that it requires an electric outlet next to the grill.

Building a Charcoal Fire

Grilling over charcoal has always been as much an art as it is a science because there's no perfectly precise way to control the heat. You need to start with enough coals to cover an area

3 inches larger on all sides than the size of the food you plan to cook. To cook a full meal on a standard 22½-inch kettle grill, this means about 50 briquets.

Light the coals, using one of the methods outlined above. Leave them in the chimney starter (or the pile) until they are all blazing red, about 20 minutes. Then use tongs or a spatula to rake (spread) the coals over the bottom grate in a single layer, and let them burn until they are covered with a thin layer of gray ash, about 5 to 10 minutes. Thus, you need 25 to 30 minutes in all to light and preheat a charcoal grill.

Building a Wood Fire

Wood chunks make a great fuel for charcoal-style grills. (See the box on page 10 for a complete discussion of cooking over wood.)

Direct Grilling on a Charcoal Grill

Direct grilling involves using a high heat to cook relatively thin cuts of meat, like steaks, chops, and kebabs, and vegetables, like peppers and portobello mushrooms. The high heat sears the surface and seals in the juices. When working over high heat, the

Cleaning and Oiling the Grate

Cleanliness may be next to godliness when it comes to personal hygiene, but don't overdo it when it comes to your grill. A firebox seasoned with smoke and spatterings produces better-tasting food than a shiny new grill just out of the box. Don't be gross about it, though. Never leave whole pieces of food encrusted on the grill.

The one exception to the cleanliness rule is the grate, which you should clean thoroughly before and after each use. A clean grate helps prevent foods from sticking and makes the final product taste better. At my house we follow this simple procedure.

Before cooking, when the grill has been preheated to high and the grate is hot, brush the grate vigorously with a long-handled wire brush to loosen any burned-on food or debris. (A metal spatula works well for scraping off large bits.) Brush the grill again when you've finished cooking.

If the grate is to be oiled, wait until it is hot, and oil it just prior to adding the food. There are three techniques for oiling. The first is to remove the grate from the fire and spray it with oil. (Use sturdy spring-loaded tongs and a heavy oven mitt or pot holders to lift the grill.) *Never* spray the grate over the fire: you'll spark a Vesuvian flare-up.

For the second method, the grate remains on the grill. Pour ¼ to ½ cup of vegetable oil into a small bowl. Fold a paper towel to create a pad about ¾ inch thick, 1 inch wide, and 3 inches long. Holding this pad with long-handled tongs, dip it in the oil, then rub it over the bars of the hot grate.

The third method—my favorite—is also with grate in place. Rub the hot grate with a piece of beef, bacon, or chicken fat (hold the fat with tongs or with a carving fork).

total cooking time, depending on the size of the food, will be 4 to 20 minutes (4 minutes for small satés, 20 minutes for a large T-bone steak). In many parts of the world, cooks boost the heat of the coals even further by oxygenating them with a fan or an electric blower.

top grate

bottom grate

coals and fire

The most common error people make when grilling is trying to work over a heat that is too high, or too low. The traditional test is to hold your hand about 6 inches above the coals. If you can count slowly to three before having to pull your hand away, the fire is the right temperature for direct grilling (about 500°F).

Direct grilling is generally done with the grill uncovered—especially when cooking small cuts of meat, like kebabs and satés, or highly flammable foods, like bread. Larger cuts of meat need to be cooked using the indirect method.

Two-Tiered Grilling: When direct-grilling over charcoal, I like to use the two-tier method: Spread one third of the coals in a single layer over one side (one half) of the grill, the other two thirds in a double

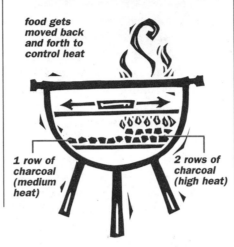

food gets moved back and forth to control heat

1 row of charcoal (medium heat)

2 rows of charcoal (high heat)

layer on the other side. Leave a small side portion of the grill free of coals. This arrangement gives you a super-hot heat source for searing, a moderately hot heat source for cooking, and a warm spot for keeping cooked foods warm. You control the heat by moving the food from one area to the other.

Indirect Grilling on a Charcoal Grill

Try cooking a whole chicken or a 4-pound fish over a super-hot fire, and you'll wind up with a carbonized exterior and a heart of uncooked flesh. Thicker foods should cook over a lower heat for a longer period of time, anywhere from 30 minutes to 2 hours. So how do you achieve this sort of heat on a charcoal grill?

The answer is to use the indirect method. In indirect grilling, the coals are pushed to the sides of the grill and the food cooks in the center—over a drip pan, not over the coals. The grill is always covered, and the vents in the lid and in the bottom of the grill are used to regulate the heat (open to raise the temperature, close to lower it). The temperature in indirect grilling, about 350°F, is usually lower than in direct.

To set up your grill for indirect grilling, light the coals using one of the methods described earlier. When they are blazing red, use

When to Cover the Grill

A lot of ink—and emotion—has been spilled over when or if to cover the grill.

The majority of the world's grill jockeys, from Singapore to São Paolo, work over direct flames without covering the grill. But if you want to make American-style barbecue, covering is absolutely essential. Covering turns your grill into an oven/barbecue pit.

My rule is this: When using the direct grilling method to cook kebabs, satés, breads, small vegetables, thin steaks, boneless chicken breasts, and other thin cuts of meat that require a high or medium-high heat and a short cooking time (2 to 4 minutes per side or less), leave the grill uncovered.

When direct-grilling thicker cuts of meat, such as beef or fish steaks, pork chops, or spatchcocked chickens, cover the grill after searing.

When using the indirect grilling method to cook whole chickens or other birds, roasts, bone-in leg of lamb, shellfish in the shell, and other large pieces of food, cover the grill.

When spit-roasting poultry or roasts, cover the grill if possible.

When to Use a Drip Pan

When grilling food by the indirect method, including barbecuing, it's a good idea to use a drip pan.

The drip pan serves two purposes: First, it collects the drippings from ribs, ducks, and other fatty foods. Second, Some grill jockeys use it to hold water, beer, wine, marinades, and other flavorful liquids to create a steamy environment that keeps the food moist during prolonged cooking.

The disposable aluminum foil roasting pans that you find in supermarkets make great drip pans. When you are indirect grilling, place the pan between the mounds of hot coals under the grate.

Many gas grills have built-in drip pans. If yours does, you don't have to add another.

tongs to transfer them to opposite sides of the grill, arranging them in two piles. Some grills have special half-moon-shaped baskets to hold the coals at the sides; others have wire fences that hook onto the bottom grate. Let the coals burn until they are covered with a thin layer of gray ash. Set the drip pan in the center of the grill, between the mounds of coals. Place the food on the grate over the drip pan, and cover the grill. You'll need to add about 10 to 12 fresh briquets to each side after an hour of cooking (see Refueling

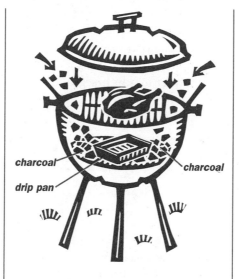

charcoal

charcoal

drip pan

a Charcoal Grill this page).

If you want to add a smoke flavor, add 1 to 2 cups of presoaked wood chips, or 2 to 4 chunks, to the coals just before you start to cook, and again whenever you replenish the coals (about once an hour).

Barbecuing on a Charcoal Grill

Barbecuing on a charcoal grill works just like indirect cooking, except that you work at an even lower temperature (275°F to 300°F) and you always add wood chips to generate the smoke that gives barbecued foods their characteristic flavor.

USING WOOD CHIPS: Wood chunks and chips are widely available at gourmet shops, hardware stores, and supermarkets. Look for hard-

wood chunks, such as hickory, oak, cherry, alder, or mesquite (see the box on page 10). Do not use sawdust, which is designed for smokers, not grills. Soak the wood chunks or chips in a bowl of cold water to cover for 1 hour. This slows the rate of combustion, so the wood will smolder, not burn.

Add 1 to 2 cups of soaked, drained wood chips, or 2 to 4 chunks, to the coals when you start to barbecue, and again whenever you replenish the coals (about once an hour; see the next section).

Refueling a Charcoal Grill

As charcoal burns, it gradually generates less and less heat. After an hour, that initial 500°F flame will have dropped 100 to 200 degrees. When you are using a prolonged cooking method, like indirect grilling or barbecuing, you'll need to replenish the coals every hour, or any time the temperature in the grill drops by more than 50°F. Most newer grills have thermometers built into the lids. If yours doesn't, you can measure the temperature by inserting a grill thermometer through one of the top vent holes. For a 22½-inch grill, you'll need to add about 20 to 24 coals at a time (10 to 12 coals per side) to replenish the fire.

You can add fresh coals either prelighted or not. If you are adding unlighted coals, leave the grill uncovered for 5, so the air speeds combustion. This method is the easiest, but it has one potential drawback: As the new coals light, they sometimes emit a bitter smoke that can make your food taste ashy. (Charwood ignites instantly, so you won't get this burned, ashy taste.)

To avoid this problem, light the replenishment coals in a chimney starter in another grill or on a concrete slab (never on a wood surface) 15 to 20 minutes before you will need them. Then add the lighted coals to the side baskets with tongs.

HOW TO LIGHT UP AND COOK ON A GAS GRILL

You don't need a degree in engineering to light a gas grill, but here, too, there are a few watch points.

Lighting the Grill

First, be sure you have enough gas (that's where the gas gauge comes in). There's nothing worse than starting to cook a whole brisket or ham and running out of gas halfway through.

Uncover the grill, set the starting burner on high, and light it with the ignition switch (or if you have an old model, a match). Make sure the burner is lit. Most gas grills have a peephole located under the burner control knob for viewing the burner.

Should the gas fail to light after you've pushed the ignition switch for a few seconds, shut the grill down, wait a few minutes to let the grill air out, and then try again. Many men (myself included), lack a patience gene (not to mention a common sense gene), so I mention this for anyone falling into that category: Do not keep the gas flowing while you keep pressing a balky ignition switch. The firebox will fill with gas, and when the spark finally comes, the gas will ignite with explosive force.

Once the master burner is lit, light the others, setting all on high. Preheat the grill to the desired temperature. This will take 10 to 15 minutes. Don't skimp on this preheating time—that's one of the most common mistakes people make when using a gas grill. (It is best to preheat the grill to high then lower to the desired temperature.)

Direct Grilling on a Gas Grill

Set the burner dials on high and preheat the grill until the internal temperature is at least 500°F. (The temperature is usually measured at the lid level of the firebox, so it may be somewhat higher than the temperature at the grate.) You'll probably need to light all the burners to achieve this high heat. Once the desired temperature is reached, you can shut off one or more burners if you don't need the whole surface of the grate.

To direct-grill at medium-high heat, set the burner dials on medium-high, so that the internal temperature reaches at least 400°F.

Indirect Grilling on a Gas Grill

Nothing could be easier than setting up a gas grill for indirect grilling. You'll need a grill with at least two heating zones (right side and left side), preferably three (front, middle, and back or left, right, and center). Preheat the grill to high, as described above.

Making Crosshatch Grill Marks

*I*s there anything handsomer than fish steaks or veal chops neatly crosshatched with grill marks? You'll be amazed to know how easy it is to achieve this professional look at home.

Preheat the grill to *high* and thoroughly clean, preheat, and oil the grate. Place the steaks or chops on the grill, all lined up in the same direction. After 2 minutes, use a spatula or tongs to rotate each piece 45 degrees to make a diagonal crosshatch or 90 degrees to make a square crosshatch. Cook until seared to taste, about 2 minutes more.

Invert the steaks and repeat the procedure on the other side. The exact cooking times will depend on what you're cooking, the thickness of the steak or chop, and how you like it cooked.

To indirect-grill on a two-zone grill, reduce the heat on one side to medium-high or medium and turn the other side off. Place the food and drip pan (if using—many gas grills have built-in drip pans) on the *off* side. Adjust the gas flow so that the temperature inside the firebox stays around 350°F.

For a three-zone grill, set the front and rear (or left and right) burners on medium, leaving the center burner off. Place the food and drip pan in the center. Again, adjust the gas flow so that the temperature inside the firebox stays around 350°F.

Barbecuing on a Gas Grill

*T*o barbecue on a two-zone grill, reduce the heat on one side to medium-low and turn the other side off. Place the food to be cooked on the *off* side. Adjust the gas flow so that the temperature inside the firebox stays around 275° to 300°F.

For a three-zone grill, set the front and rear (or left and right) burners on medium-low, leaving the center burner off. Place the food and drip pan in the center. Again, adjust the gas flow so that the temperature inside the firebox stays around 275° to 300°F.

Using Wood Chips on a Gas Grill

*G*as grills present a special challenge for the cook who wants to add the heady flavor of wood smoke. Many gas grills are equipped with smoker boxes (a metal box with holes in it to let the smoke out), but unless the grill is operating at full blast, it doesn't get hot enough to make the wood smolder. (This is not a problem on a charcoal grill, where the wood comes in direct contact with the glowing coals.) But if you run a gas grill on high, the temperature will be too hot for indirect grilling or barbecuing.

There is a way to get around this problem. Put all the presoaked wood chips in the smoker box and position the box directly over one of the burners. Preheat the grill to high until the smoke billows then lower the heat to the desired temperature for indirect grilling or barbecuing (or follow the manufacturer's instructions).

If your grill lacks a smoker box, you can buy one from a grill supply shop (see Mail-Order Sources); or you can improvise one, using a small loaf pan or metal pie tin.

The Ten Commandments of Perfect Grilling

1. *BE ORGANIZED.* Have everything you need for grilling—the food, marinade, basting sauce, seasonings, and equipment—on hand and at grillside before you start grilling.

2. *GAUGE YOUR FUEL.* There's nothing worse than running out of charcoal or gas in the middle of grilling. When using charcoal, light enough to form a bed of glowing coals 3 inches larger on all sides than the surface area of the food you're planning to cook. (A 22½-inch grill needs one chimney's worth of coals.) When cooking on a gas grill, make sure the tank is at least one-third full.

3. *PREHEAT THE GRILL TO THE RIGHT TEMPERATURE.* Remember: Grilling is a high-heat cooking method. In order to achieve the seared crust, charcoal flavor, and handsome grill marks associated with masterpiece grillmanship, you must cook over a high heat. How high? At least 500°F. Although I detail this elsewhere, it is worth repeating: When using charcoal, let it burn until it is covered with a thin coat of gray ash. Hold your hand about 6 inches above the grate. After 3 seconds, the force of the heat should force you to snatch your hand away. When using a gas grill, preheat to high (at least 500°F); this takes 10 to 15 minutes. When indirect grilling, preheat the grill to 350°F.

4. *KEEP IT CLEAN.* There's nothing less appetizing than grilling on dirty old burnt bits of food stuck to the grate. Besides, the food will stick to a dirty grate. Clean the grate twice: once after you've preheated the grill and again when you've finished cooking. The first cleaning will remove any bits of food you may have missed after your last grilling session. Use the edge of a metal spatula to scrape off large bits of food, a stiff wire brush to finish scrubbing the grate.

5. *KEEP IT LUBRICATED.* Oil the grate just before placing the food on top, if necessary (some foods don't require that the grates be oiled). Spray it with oil (away from the flames—see page 13), use a folded paper towel soaked in oil, or rub it with a piece of fatty bacon, beef fat, or chicken skin.

6. *TURN, DON'T STAB.* The proper way to turn meat on a grill is with tongs or a spatula. Never stab the meat with a carving fork—unless you want to drain the flavor-rich juices onto the coals.

7. *KNOW WHEN TO BASTE.* Oil-and-vinegar-, citrus-, and yogurt-based bastes and marinades can be brushed on the meat throughout the cooking time. (If you baste with a marinade that you used for raw meat or seafood, do not apply it during the last 3 minutes of cooking.) When using a sugar-based barbecue sauce, apply it toward the end of the cooking time. The sugar in these sauces burns easily and should not be exposed to prolonged heat.

8. *KEEP IT COVERED.* When cooking larger cuts of meat and poultry, such as a whole chicken, leg of lamb, or prime rib, use the indirect method of grilling or barbecuing (see pages 14 and 16). Keep the grill tightly covered and resist the temptation to peek. Every time you lift the lid, you add 5 to 10 minutes to the cooking time.

9. *GIVE IT A REST.* Beef, steak, chicken—almost anything you grill—will taste better if you let it stand on the cutting board for a few minutes before serving. This allows the meat juices, which have been driven to the center of a roast or steak by the searing heat, to return to the surface. The result is a juicier, tastier piece of meat.

10. *NEVER DESERT YOUR POST.* Grilling is an easy cooking method, but it demands constant attention. Once you put something on the grill (especially when using the direct method), stay with it until it's cooked. This is not the time to answer the phone, make the salad dressing, or mix up a batch of your famous *mojitos.*

Above all, have fun. Remember that grilling isn't brain surgery. And that's the gospel!

PUTTING IT ALL TOGETHER

As you use the recipes in this book, you'll be instructed to preheat the grill, set it up for direct or indirect cooking, and make various adjustments in the temperature. Here are brief explanations of these instructions.

Preheat the grill to high

If you are using a charcoal grill, light the coals by one of the methods described in "Lighting and Cooking on a Charcoal Grill." Rake the hot coals over the bottom of the grill. (If desired, use the two-tiered method described on page 14 for better heat control.) Open the top and bottom vents wide. Use the 3-second test to determine when the coals are the proper temperature for cooking: Hold your hand about 6 inches above the coals. If you can keep it there for 3 seconds (count "one one-thousand, two one-thousand, three one-thousand") and only 3 seconds, the fire is the right temperature. If you have a thermometer, the surface temperature of the grilling area should be about 500°F. Allow about 30 minutes to bring the coals to the right temperature for cooking.

If you are using a gas grill, set all the burner dials on high. Preheat the grill until the internal temperature is at least 500°F. This will take 10 to 15 minutes.

Preheat the grill to medium-high

For a charcoal grill, light the coals as described earlier, but rake them out into a thinner layer or let them burn for another 5 to 10 minutes longer. You should be able to hold your hand over the fire for 5 seconds.

For a gas grill, preheat to high, then turn the burner dials down to medium-high. The firebox temperature should be about 400°F.

Preheat the grill to medium

For a charcoal grill, light the coals as described earlier, but rake them out into a yet thinner layer or let them burn for another 5 to 10 minutes. You should be able to hold your hand over the fire for 7 seconds.

For a gas grill, preheat to high, then turn the burner dials down to medium. The firebox temperature should be about 350°F.

Preheat the grill to medium-low

For a charcoal grill, light the coals as described earlier, but rake them out into a yet thinner layer or let them burn for 5 to 10 minutes longer than you did for medium. You should be able to hold your hand over the fire for 10 seconds.

For a gas grill, preheat to high, then turn the burner dials down to medium-low. The firebox tempera-ture should be about 325°F.

Preheat the grill to low

For a charcoal grill, light the coals as described earlier. Rake out the coals in a very thin layer or let them burn for 15 to 20 minutes longer. You should be able to hold your hand over the coals for 12 seconds.

For a gas grill, preheat to high, then turn the burner dials down to low. The firebox temperature should be about 300°F.

Set the grill up for direct cooking

For a charcoal grill, light the coals as described on page 12. Rake them out directly under the section of the grate where you plan to do the cooking. You may wish to use the two-tiered method outlined on page 14

For a gas grill, it's best to pre-heat the whole grill, then turn off the burners you don't need. Gas grills respond almost instanta-neously; control the heat by adjusting the gas flow.

Set the grill up for indirect cooking—charcoal

Follow the instructions on page 14.

Set the grill up for indirect cooking—gas

Follow the instructions on page 16.

SPECIAL SETUPS

The world of grilling is so varied, it would take volumes to describe all the different configurations. Here are a few special setups you can use to do global grilling in your backyard.

Rotisserie Cooking

Spit roasting, also known as rotisserie grilling, has fallen somewhat out of fashion. When I was a kid, everyone in the neighborhood had a rotisserie attachment for their grill. Most grill manufacturers still make these attachments, and I'm not sure why people don't use them more. Perhaps in this burger-and-chicken-breast era, we're too hurried for the time it takes to spit-roast a chicken or leg of lamb.

This is a shame, because nothing can beat the gentle, even heat and internal basting that comes with spit roasting. Spit roasting combines the charring properties of direct grilling with the gently penetrating heat of indirect cooking. The rotating motion bastes the meat with the melting fat. These virtues are not lost on the French or the Brazilians, who have made the rotisserie the focal point of their grilling.

Rotisserie grilling is particularly well suited to chicken, game hens, and ducks, not to mention cylindrical roasts like pork loins and boneless rib roasts. I know a pit man in Uruguay who cooks garlic rolls on the rotisserie. In Paris, I've seen cooks grill spareribs, lamb shanks, and whole lambs and suckling pigs on the spit.

You can prepare rotisseried foods on either a charcoal or a gas grill. When buying a rotisserie attachment, look for a motor with an on-off switch (adjustable speeds are nice, too) and a long enough cord to reach the available outlet. Be sure the device comes with a mounting bracket that will fit on your grill.

The spit itself should have adjustable prongs for holding the food in place. Another nice feature is a counterweight, which helps reduce the strain on the motor.

To set up a charcoal grill, build a fire, following one of the procedures outlined on page 12. When the coals are hot, rake them into two parallel rows, one about 4 inches in front of where the spit will turn and one about 4 inches behind where the spit will turn. Place a drip pan in the center, between the rows of coals. Skewer the food on the spit and turn on the motor. Add 10 to 12 fresh coals per side every hour.

To rotisserie on a gas grill, you need a grill with multiple burners arranged front to back. To set up a gas grill, preheat the front and rear burners to high. Leave the center burner off. Place a drip pan on the grilling grate in the center. Skewer the food on the spit, and turn on the motor. Note that when setting up a gas grill, you might have to put the drip pan under the grate because the rotisserie attachment sits so low. Fancier gas grills usually have built-in drip pans, eliminating the need for this step.

Approximate Times for Rotisserie Cooking*

1 chicken (3½ lbs)	40 to 60 min
1 game hen (2 lbs)	25 to 30 min
1 duck (4 to 5 lbs)	1¼ to 1½ hrs
1 butterflied leg of lamb (2 to 3 lbs)	1 to 1½ hrs
1 boneless pork loin (2 to 3 lbs)	1 to 1½ hrs
1 boneless rib roast (about 3 lbs)	1 to 1½ hrs

Times given are for a covered grill. Add 15 to 20 minutes for an uncovered grill.

How to Grill Without a Grate

To most Americans, the grate (the metal grilling rack) is the most important part (or at least the defining part) of a barbecue grill. So you may be surprised to learn that in many parts of the world—from Turkey to Japan to India—grills do not have grates and the food is cooked in midair, as it were, directly over the fire.

Ground meat kebabs, like Indonesian satés and Persian *lula,* do particularly well without a grate, because the meat tends to stick to the metal bars. Many Indian tandoori dishes are covered with a chickpea batter that also tends to stick to the grate, as does the miso glaze so popular in Japanese grill joints.

The easiest way to achieve this effect on an American-style grill is to place two, flat 1-inch-thick bricks or paving stones or pieces of metal pipe on the grill grate, far enough apart so that the ends of the skewers can rest comfortably on them. Place the skewer ends on the bricks; the food will be suspended above the grate and should be fully exposed to the heat.

If you've ever wrestled with ground meat kebabs sticking to the grate, you'll find this simple technique a revelation.

Cooking Satés

The saté is probably the most perfect morsel ever devised by a grill buff. This bite-size kebab on a small bamboo skewer is wildly popular all across Southeast Asia. Japan's yakitori and teriyaki are kissing cousins of saté.

There's only one remotely challenging aspect to cooking a saté. Because bamboo is flammable, you must figure out a way that allows you to cook the meat without burning the skewer. There are two ways to accomplish this. You can soak the skewers in a pan of cold water to cover for 1 hour before using them. Or use a grill that is just wide enough to expose the meat, but not the skewer, to the flames. Specially designed for this purpose are saté grills, long, narrow metal boxes that are quite tiny and portable. Variations turn up from Jakarta to Kyoto and Kuala Lumpur. (I bought one in Jakarta that's 12 inches long and 3 inches wide and was fashioned from a large tin can.)

A Japanese-style hibachi is the closest thing to a saté grill available in North America, and it works quite well for cooking satés. You simply rake the coals right to the edge of the hibachi and place the satés on the grill with the exposed ends of the skewers hanging over the edges.

To cook satés on a larger charcoal grill, bank the coals on one side of the grill. Place the satés on the grate with the exposed ends of the skewers extending away from the coals. Or arrange the satés at the edge of the grate so that the exposed handle parts of the skewers hang over the side of the grill.

To cook satés on a gas grill, light only half the grill. Place the satés over the lit section with the skewers extending over the unlit section. Or arrange the satés at the edge of the grate so that the exposed parts of the skewers hang over the side of the grill.

If the skewers start to burn despite these efforts, simply protect them with strips of heavy-duty aluminum foil.

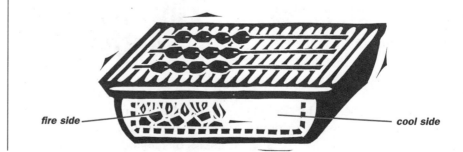

fire side ———   ——— *cool side*

Barbecue Countdown

In grilling, as in life, timing is everything. Here's a basic timetable that will help you get your grill lit, your food marinated and cooked, and your guests fed—without your having a nervous breakdown.

PRELIMINARIES

1. Twelve hours to 1 hour before you plan to serve, immerse the food in its marinade or rub it with its spice mix.

2. Set the table.

3. Prepare the drinks and side dishes.

WITH A CHARCOAL GRILL

1. One hour before you plan to start cooking, soak wood chips or chunks, if you are using them, in cold water to cover.

2. Light the charcoal 30 to 40 minutes before you plan to start cooking.

3. When the coals blaze red (after 15 to 20 minutes), dump them out of the chimney starter and spread them over the bottom of the grill. I like to rake the coals more thickly on one side than the other, so I have a high heat and low heat (see the two-tiered technique on page 14). Let the coals burn until they are covered with a thin layer of gray ash, 5 to 10 minutes more for high heat. Now the fire is ready for grilling. If your recipe calls for a lesser heat, follow the timing instructions outlined on page 19.

4. Clean the grate with a wire brush, and oil it as described on page 13.

5. If you are using wood chips, drain them well and toss them on the coals. Put the food on the grate, and grill. If you will be indirect-grilling for an extended period, light a second batch of coals in the chimney starter after 45 minutes (about 15 minutes before you will need them).

6. After the food is cooked, don't forget to clean the grate again with the wire brush.

WITH A GAS GRILL

Follow the procedure described here, preheating the grill for 15 minutes. If you are using wood chips, place them in the smoker box. Keep the grill on high until the chips begin to smoke, then lower the heat as needed.

IS IT DONE YET?

The only remotely tricky part about barbecuing and grilling is knowing when the food is done. Aficionados use the "poke" method, which is surprisingly accurate when used by a seasoned griller, but for larger cuts of meat, nothing beats the "scientific" method for assessing doneness.

The Artistic Method

The poke method is best for testing the doneness of steaks, chops, chicken breasts, and fish steaks or fillets.

Press the thickest part of the steak or chop with your finger. When it is rare, it will feel soft and yielding—a bit like the flesh between the base of your thumb and forefinger when you bring them loosely together.

When it is medium, the meat will feel slightly resistant—like the flesh between the base of your thumb and forefinger when you make a loose fist.

When well done, the meat will feel resistant and springy—like the flesh between the base of your thumb and forefinger when you make a tight fist.

To test whole chicken for doneness (less artistic, but still not scientific), insert a trussing needle or skewer into the thickest part of one thigh; the juices should come out clear. You can also try wiggling the drumstick; it should feel very loose. Or make a cut between the leg and the body. There should be no redness at the joint (unless you're smoking the chicken—smoke imparts a natural pink glow to meats).

To test fish for doneness, press the thickest part with your finger. The flesh should break into large, firm flakes and should pull away from the bones easily.

The Scientific Method

But what about larger cuts of meat? The only really infallible test is to check the internal temperature with an instant-read meat thermometer. This handy device is available at any cookware shop.

Insert it into the thickest part of the meat, but without touching any bones. (Bones, like metal, conduct heat.) In the meat, poultry, and seafood chapters you'll find tables outlining degrees of doneness and their corresponding temperatures. Internal temperatures are also listed in the recipes when appropriate.Here, then, is a broad guide to doneness.

BEEF AND LAMB	
Rare	140°F
Medium-rare	150°F
Medium	160°F
Well-done	170°F

PORK	
Medium	160°F
Well-done	170°–190°F

CHICKEN, TURKEY, AND QUAIL	
Medium	160°F
Well-done	170°–180°F

DUCK AND SQUAB	
Rare	140°F
Medium	160°F
Well-done	170°F

Thirst Quenchers

"Appetite comes with eating... but thirst departs with drinking."

—FRANÇOIS RABELAIS

Quenching your thirst at Basil's Bar in the West Indies.

"**L**eaded or unleaded?" asked the bartender at a grill shack in Nassau, Bahamas. Leaded or unleaded, indeed! In local parlance, "leaded" refers to a gin-spiked coconut punch called sky juice, while unleaded describes the same drink made without gin. How better to begin a barbecue?

You sure can work up an enormous thirst when grilling. First, because you're outdoors, standing next to a powerful heat source. Second, because the food that comes off the grill demands a full-flavored libation that matches the smoky taste of the fire.

It's hard to imagine a Brazilian barbecue without an icy pitcher of Brazilian Daiquiris (*caipirinhas*) made with cane spirits and lime. Or Turkish kebabs without glasses of Raki (a cocktail made with anise liquor) or a Caribbean cookout without Planter's Punch.

Here you'll find some of the world's best thirst-quenchers, not all of them leaded.

Consider Afghan Yogurt Drink, or *doh,* a Central Asian thirst-quencher made from yogurt, mint, and club soda and enjoyed in one form or another from Baghdad to Kabul. From the *gingere ananas* (Ginger Pineapple Punch) of Senegal to the *bandung* (Rosewater Cooler) of Singapore and Malaysia, you'll find plenty of unleaded treasures to soothe the most stubborn thirst.

Leaded

THE ORIGINAL PINA COLADA

PUERTO RICO

ON THE SIDE

Ramon "Monchito" Marrero Perez knows a thing or two about piña coladas. The bar in San Juan where he works serves more than three hundred of these tropical refreshers a day. Perez claims to have invented the piña colada on a steamy summer day in 1954. Actually, according to Webster's, the term piña colada first appeared in print in 1923. Rum and pineapple juice had been a popular Puerto Rican cocktail for decades (if not centuries). Perez's innovation lay in adding coconut cream for richness and smoothness. Below is Perez's original recipe. For an even more luscious piña colada, substitute 1 cup diced fresh pineapple for the pineapple juice.

¼ cup light rum (Perez uses Bacardi)
¾ cup unsweetened pineapple juice
3 tablespoons coconut cream, such as
   Coco Lopez
2 tablespoons heavy cream
1 cup crushed ice
1 stick or thin wedge fresh pineapple
1 maraschino cherry with stem

Combine the rum, pineapple juice, coconut cream, and heavy cream in a blender with the ice and process until smooth. Pour into a large glass. Garnish with the pineapple stick and cherry and serve immediately.

Serves 2; can be multiplied as desired

BRAZILIAN DAIQUIRI
Caipirinha

BRAZIL

ON THE SIDE

Every rum-drinking nation has a version of the daiquiri, and Brazil's is the *caipirinha* (pronounced "kai-pir-EEN-ya"). Made with only three ingredients—fresh limes, sugar, and cane spirits—the *caipirinha* seems simple enough and it goes down with astonishing ease. But woe betide the person who drinks several in rapid succession, for the *caipir-* *inha* is made with one of the strongest spirits in the western hemisphere: cachaça.

Cachaça (pronounced "ka-SHAH-sa") is a spirit made from sugar cane that's considerably stronger than rum. Cachaça can be found at well-stocked liquor stores, especially in cities with large Brazilian communities. If unavailable, you can use 151 rum or regular white rum. A similar drink, called *caipiroska,* is made with vodka.

What distinguishes the *caipirinha* from the commonplace daiquiri is the conscientious crushing of the limes in the pitcher, an act that extracts the flavorful oils from the rind. It's hard to imagine a *churrasco* (Brazilian barbecue) that would not begin with a pitcher of *caipirinhas*.

8 large, juicy limes
1 cup turbinado sugar (Sugar in the Raw;
    see page 29) or granulated sugar,
    or more to taste
2 cups cachaça, 151 rum, or regular white rum
4 cups ice cubes

1. Roll the limes on a cutting board, pressing with the palms of your hands, to loosen the juices from the pulp. Cut each lime into 8 pieces, then place the pieces in the bottom of a sturdy pitcher. Add 1 cup sugar and pound the pieces with a pestle, potato masher, or wooden spoon to extract as much juice as possible.

2. Stir in the cachaça and ice, then correct the sweetness, adding sugar as necessary for just the right balance of sweet and sour. Serve, if desired, in daiquiri glasses, but regular tumblers will do.

Serves 8

BAHAMIAN SKY JUICE

BAHAMAS

ON THE SIDE

No Bahamian barbecue would be complete without sky juice, a potent brew of coconut water (the clearish liquid inside the coconut), evaporated milk, and gin. When I say potent, I mean potent—it goes down effortlessly and will turn your knees to rubber effortlessly, too.

Sky juice is generally made with gin in the Bahamas—odd for the rum-loving Caribbean yet logical, given the islands' British heritage—but I can report that it's equally delightful made with rum. I like to serve sky juice right in the coconut shell—a presentation that's especially festive at a cookout. Also, I like my sky juice on the sweeter side, but many people don't, so I've made the sugar optional.

4 ripe (hard) coconuts (see Note)
1 cup evaporated milk
1 cup gin or rum
3 tablespoons sugar (optional)
1 teaspoon ground cinnamon
½ teaspoon freshly grated nutmeg

1. Using a screwdriver and hammer, poke through the "eyes" of the coconuts and drain the liquid from each through a strainer into a mixing bowl. You should have about 2 cups coconut water. Reserve the emptied coconuts. Add the evaporated milk, gin, sugar (if using), cinnamon, and nutmeg to the coconut water and stir to dissolve the sugar. Refrigerate the mixture until cold (at least 2 hours) or stir in a few ice cubes.

2. Using a funnel or squirt bottle, pour the sky juice into the reserved coconut shells. Insert straws and serve.

Makes 4 cups, enough to serve 4

Note: When buying coconuts, shake them to hear the water slosh around inside. A dry coconut is sometimes rancid and certainly past its prime.

PLANTER'S PUNCH

CARIBBEAN

ON THE SIDE

ADVANCE PREPARATION: 2 hours to 2 days for steeping the punch

Planter's punch is found throughout the Caribbean. Back in the days of the great plantations, it was the traditional beverage of welcome. The basic recipe calls for orange juice, pineapple juice, guava nectar, and rum, but there are as many variations as there are individual bartenders. Serve it with any of the West Indian–style barbecue dishes in this book.

1 cup dark rum
1 cup fresh orange juice
1 cup unsweetened pineapple juice
1 cup guava nectar
2 tablespoons fresh lime juice
2 tablespoons sugar, or more to taste
½ teaspoon Angostura bitters
½ vanilla bean, split
2 cinnamon sticks (each 3 inches)
2 whole cloves
Ice cubes, for serving

FOR GARNISH:
4 orange slices
4 maraschino cherries with stems
Freshly grated nutmeg

1. Combine the rum, orange juice, pineapple juice, guava nectar, lime juice, sugar, and bitters in a pitcher and stir until the sugar is dissolved. Add the vanilla bean, cinnamon sticks, and cloves. Let the punch steep, covered, in the refrigerator for at least 2 hours or as long as 2 days.

2. Strain the punch into tumblers filled with ice. Garnish each glass with an orange slice and a maraschino cherry. Grate some nutmeg over each serving and serve immediately.

Serves 4

BRAZILIAN COCONUT SHAKE
Batido

BRAZIL

ON THE SIDE

Batido (pronounced "ba-CHEE-do") is the name Brazilians give to a variety of alcoholic milkshakes. The liquor of choice for this recipe would be cachaça (a potent Brazilian cane spirit). If it's unavailable, use regular white rum instead. I serve this exotic creamy milkshake with any barbecue that features Brazilian fare, for example Brazilian Stuffed Rib Roast and Brazilian Pork Rollatini (see Index).

⅓ cup coconut cream, such as Coco Lopez
⅓ cup cachaça or regular white rum
¼ cup sweetened condensed milk
4 cups crushed ice

Combine the coconut cream, cachaça, and condensed milk in a blender with the ice and process until smooth. Pour into tall glasses and serve immediately.

Serves 4

PASSION FRUIT DAIQUIRI

CARIBBEAN

ON THE SIDE

The daiquiri originated at the turn of the century in the nickel-mining town of Daiquiri in southeast Cuba. You don't need a degree in mixology to know that its principle ingredients, then as now, are lime juice, sugar, and rum. Today daiquiris made with a multitude of fruits are enjoyed throughout the Americas. The following passion fruit daiquiri will give you a whole new perspective on, and appreciation for, a Caribbean classic.

¾ cup frozen or bottled passion fruit juice or 15 passion fruits
⅔ cup light rum
6 tablespoons firmly packed light brown sugar
3 cups crushed ice

1. If using frozen or bottled juice, proceed to step 2. If using fresh fruits, cut them in half and scrape out the pulp. Force the pulp through a strainer; you should have about ¾ cup.

2. Combine the pulp, rum, and sugar in a blender with the ice and process until smooth. Pour into martini glasses and serve immediately.

Serves 4

FRENCH WEST INDIAN RUM PUNCH
'Ti Punch

FRENCH WEST INDIES

ON THE SIDE

TURBINADO SUGAR

A *granulated light brown sugar, turbinado sugar is available at natural food stores. In supermarkets, look for the Sugar in the Raw brand.*

'Ti punch (short for "petit punch") is the most elemental of the French West Indian rum drinks—sipped with equal enthusiasm at casual cook shacks and tony restaurants. To partake of the 'ti punch properly, the drinker squeezes the lime in the drink, then stirs to dissolve the sugar. Some people add an ice cube or two, but most Guadeloupeans sip it straight.

Some versions call for the suavity of cane syrup, but most of the 'ti punch I had in Guadeloupe consisted simply of rum, lime, and sugar. Use either white rum or dark, depending on your taste.

3 tablespoons rum
2 teaspoons turbinado sugar (Sugar in the Raw) or granulated sugar
1 lime wedge, for garnish

Place the rum and sugar in a glass (the locals prefer small brandy glasses) and stir lightly with a spoon. Rub around the rim of the glass with the lime wedge, then press it onto the rim. Serve the 'ti punch with a small spoon or stirrer and a lime wedge for squeezing into the drink.

Serves 1; can be multiplied as desired

SMOKY MARTINI

ON THE SIDE

Steak is back. So are cigars and martinis. After a decade of rabid health-consciousness, Americans seem to be relaxing a bit about food and eating wisely, without forsaking a sense of enjoyment. This martini is fortified with a drop of liquid smoke, which makes it perfect for a barbecue.

3 tablespoons gin
½ teaspoon dry Vermouth
1 drop liquid smoke
1 cup ice cubes
Strip of lemon zest

Combine the gin, vermouth, and liquid smoke in a shaker with the ice and stir (do not shake) to mix. Strain the drink into a martini glass. Twist the lemon zest, shiny side down, over the martini, then drop it into the drink. Serve immediately.
Serves 1; can be multiplied as desired

SINGAPORE SLING

ON THE SIDE

It was a typical day on the barbecue trail, hours spent touring cook stalls, sampling satés under the blazing equatorial sun. Actually, tougher than it sounds. So I offered my wife and myself a treat at the end of the day: cocktails at the ultraluxurious Raffles Hotel, where, legend has it, in 1915 the Singapore sling was invented by a Hainanese bartender named Ngiam Tong Boon. Today the drink is served in special monogrammed glasses in the hotel's vertiginously high-ceilinged Bar & Billiard Room. You can serve it with any of the Singapore- or Malaysian-style satés in this book.

½ cup gin
¼ cup cherry brandy
2 tablespoons fresh lime juice
2 tablespoons unsweetened pineapple juice

2 tablespoons fresh orange juice
1 tablespoon Cointreau
1 tablespoon Benedictine
4 dashes Angostura bitters
Ice cubes, for serving
3 cups club soda, or more as needed
4 maraschino cherries, for garnish
4 fresh pineapple slices, for garnish

1. Combine the gin, brandy, fruit juices, Cointreau, Benedictine, and bitters in a pitcher and stir to mix.

2. Place ice cubes in 4 tall glasses, then divide the gin mixture equally among them. Add club soda to fill each glass and garnish with a cherry and a slice of pineapple. Stir with a long-handled spoon and serve immediately.
Serves 4

PISCO SOUR

PERU

ON THE SIDE

The pisco sour isn't what you'd call a hot seller these days, but in the boom time following the California gold rush, this lively cocktail was one of America's most popular drinks. Pisco is the name of a robust brandy made in Peru and Chile from Muscat grapes. Serve pisco sours with any of the *anticuchos* (Peruvian kebabs) in the book or with any other South American barbecue.

½ **cup sugar**
1 **lemon wedge**
¼ **cup fresh lemon juice**
¾ **cup pisco brandy**
½ **teaspoon Angostura bitters**
1 **large egg white (see Note)**
3 **cups crushed ice**

1. Spread ¼ cup of the sugar in a shallow dish. Rub the rims of 4 martini or whisky sour glasses with the cut side of the lemon wedge and dip each glass rim in the sugar, shaking off the excess.

2. Combine the remaining ¼ cup sugar, the lemon juice, brandy, bitters, and egg white in a blender with the ice and process until frothy.

3. Pour the mixture into the prepared glasses and serve immediately.

Serves 4

Note: If you feel nervous about consuming raw egg white, use 1 tablespoon egg substitute.

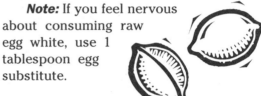

FRONTERA MARGARITA

MEXICO

ON THE SIDE

ADVANCE PREPARATION:
6 to 8 hours for steeping the mixture

The potent tequila and lime thirst-quencher known as margarita is synonymous with good times and Mexican grilling. The best margarita I ever tasted, though, was made, not by a Mexican, but by a gringo, Rick Bayless, owner of two popular Chicago restaurants, Frontera Grill and Topolobampo. Rick lets his tequila steep with lime juice and lime zest for a good part of the day before mixing the drink, which creates a margarita with an uncommon depth of flavor.

1¾ **cups tequila (Rick uses Cuervo Especial Gold)**
¼ **cup orange liqueur (Rick uses the Spanish liqueur Gran Torres)**

1 **cup water**
½ **cup fresh lime juice**
1 **teaspoon finely grated lime zest**
⅓ **cup sugar**
¼ **cup coarse sea salt**
8 **lime wedges, for garnish**
3 to 4 **cups ice cubes, for serving**

1. The morning before you plan to serve the margaritas, combine the tequila, orange liqueur, water, lime juice and zest, and sugar in a pitcher. Stir to dissolve the sugar, then let the mixture steep in the refrigerator, covered, for 6 to 8 hours.

2. Spread the salt in a shallow dish. Rub the rims of 8 martini glasses with the cut side of a lime wedge and dip each glass rim in the salt, shaking off the excess. Add the ice to the margarita mixture and stir (or combine in a shaker and shake), then strain the margari- tas into the prepared glasses. Drop a lime wedge in each glass and serve at once.

Serves 8

MADRID-STYLE SANGRIA

SPAIN

ON THE SIDE

Sangria is one of the most popular beverages for a barbecue, but over the years, there's been a tendency to turn it into a sort of wine-drenched fruit salad. Here's a sangria that's prepared in the style of the tapas bars of Madrid—minimal fruit, not too sweet, and very potent. My wife, Barbara, happens to like a fruity sangria, and when my back is turned, she's apt to add grapes and diced bananas to this recipe. If you like a fruity sangria, do the same.

1 bottle (750 ml) dry red wine,
      preferably Spanish
1 cup gin
1 cup Cognac
1 cup sugar, or more to taste
1 whole lemon
1 whole orange
½ cup fresh lemon juice
½ cup fresh orange juice
3 cinnamon sticks (each 3 inches)
Ice cubes, for serving

1. Combine the wine, gin, Cognac, and 1 cup sugar in a pitcher and stir until the sugar has dissolved. Cut the peel, including the white pith, off the lemon and orange, exposing the flesh. Cut the flesh into ¼-inch dice. Discard any seeds.

2. Stir the diced fruit, fruit juices, and cinnamon sticks into the wine mixture. Taste for sweetness, adding sugar to taste. You can serve the sangria right away, but it will be better if chilled for an hour or so, to "ripen."

3. Serve the sangria in wine glasses over ice.

Serves 6

RAKI

TURKEY

ON THE SIDE

It may be stretching it a bit to call this simple drink a recipe, but so essential is raki (and its Greek counterpart, ouzo) to the enjoyment of barbecue in the eastern Mediterranean and Near East, I'd feel remiss if I didn't include it. Raki is a strong, clear, anise-flavored spirit. By some mysterious chemical reaction, it turns milky white the moment you add water.

1 cup raki or ouzo
1 to 2 cups water
Ice cubes, for serving

Pour two or three fingers (¼ cup) of raki into each of 4 tall glasses. Add water and ice to taste, then stir and serve.

Serves 4

Unleaded

GINGER PINEAPPLE PUNCH
Gingere Ananas

SENEGAL

ON THE SIDE

Spicy, sweet, and refreshing. Such is *gingere ananas,* a popular Senegalese drink that combines the fruitiness of fresh pineapple with the peppery bite of ginger. Serve with Senegalese Grilled Lamb with Onion Mustard Sauce (see Index).

1 piece (4 inches) fresh ginger
3 cups diced fresh pineapple
3 tablespoons sugar, or
    more to taste
3 tablespoons fresh lime juice
4 cups cold water
Ice, for serving

1. Cut the ginger into ¼-inch slices, then combine with the pineapple, 3 tablespoons sugar, the lime juice, and water in a blender and process until smooth.

2. Strain this liquid into a pitcher, pressing the pulp against the strainer with the back of a spoon to extract all the juice. Correct the sweetness, adding more sugar, if desired, then pour into tall glasses over ice and serve immediately.

Serves 4

MANGO NECTAR

CARIBBEAN

ON THE SIDE

Mango and other tropical fruit punches turn up throughout the Caribbean, where they make a refreshing nonalcoholic alternative to the knee-weakening rum drinks associated with the region.

2 cups diced ripe mango (1 large or
    2 medium fruits)
2 cups water, or more as needed
2 tablespoons sugar, or more
    to taste

2 tablespoons fresh lime juice, or
    more to taste
Ice cubes, for serving

Combine the mango, 2 cups water, and 2 tablespoons each sugar and lime juice in a blender and process until smooth. Add water as needed to thin the punch to pourable consistency, and sugar and lime juice to taste. Pour into tall glasses over ice and serve immediately.

Serves 4

PEANUT PUNCH

Peanuts turn up throughout the world of grilling: as a coating for kebabs in West Africa, for example, or as a sauce for satés in Southeast Asia. I discovered this unusual peanut punch at a rough-and-tumble eating pavilion called the Breakfast Shed in Port of Spain, the capital of Trinidad. I guarantee this will forever change the way you think about peanuts.

½ cup creamy peanut butter
½ cup sweetened condensed milk
1 teaspoon vanilla extract
1 teaspoon Angostura bitters
4 cups water
Ice cubes, for serving

Combine the peanut butter, condensed milk, vanilla, bitters, and water in a pitcher and whisk until the peanut butter is dissolved. Pour into tall glasses over ice and serve immediately.

Serves 4

ROSEWATER COOLER
Bandung

Visit the Indian section of any of Singapore's hawkers' centers and you'll find drink vendors purveying a rainbow-colored assortment of exotic drinks. *Bandung* may look like Pepto-Bismol, but its perfumy rosewater flavor is as refreshing as it is unique. Serve with Singapore or Malaysian-style satés.

3 cups cold water
⅓ cup sweetened condensed milk
2 tablespoons rosewater (see Note)
2 tablespoons banana liqueur
2 tablespoons grenadine syrup
Ice cubes, for serving

Combine the water, condensed milk, rosewater, liqueur, and grenadine syrup in a pitcher and stir to mix. Pour into tall glasses over ice and serve immediately.

Serves 4

Note: Rosewater is available at Middle Eastern and Indian markets and many gourmet shops.

MINTED LIMEADE

ON THE SIDE

This summery refresher takes advantage of the perfumed oils in the skin of the lime as well as the sour juice of the pulp. The mint adds a cooling touch that's most welcome next to a hot grill.

8 limes, or enough for 1 cup juice
1 cup sugar, or more to taste
1 bunch fresh mint, rinsed and
   spun dry, 6 to 8 sprigs set
   aside for garnish
5 cups water
Ice cubes, for serving

1. Remove the zest (oil-rich outer peel, green part only) from 4 of the limes, using a vegetable peeler. Combine the zest with 1 cup sugar, the mint, and 1 cup of the water in a small saucepan and bring to a boil over medium-high heat, stirring to dissolve the sugar. Reduce the heat to low and simmer gently for 5 minutes. Remove from the heat and let cool to room temperature, then strain the mixture into a pitcher.

2. Press the juice from all the limes; you should have 1 cup. Add the juice and remaining 4 cups water to the sugar mixture; if a sweeter limeade is desired, whisk in extra sugar. Pour into tall glasses over ice, garnishing each serving with a sprig of mint.

Serves 6 to 8

MINT TEA

ON THE SIDE

Mint tea is more than the national drink of Morocco. It's the very lifeblood of this North African country, an elixir served to guests and family, in restaurants and private homes, at the beginning of a business negotiation or at the end of a meal. It contains only three ingredients, but its preparation has the solemnity of a religious rite. For best results, use a heavy teapot, preferably metal.

Traditionally, Moroccan mint tea is served in small, hand-painted glasses with gold rims. Serve as a prelude or conclusion to Moroccan grilled fare.

1 bunch fresh mint, rinsed and spun dry
1 tablespoon loose black tea, such as
   Ceylon or English Breakfast
3 tablespoons sugar, or to taste
4 cups boiling water

1. Rinse out a 5-cup teapot with boiling water. Twist the bunch of mint a few times between your fingers to bruise the leaves, then combine in the teapot with the black tea and sugar. Fill the teapot with the 4 cups boiling water and let steep for 5 minutes.

2. Serve the tea by straining it into small heatproof glasses or small cups.

Serves 6 to 8

AFGHAN YOGURT DRINK

Doh

AFGHANISTAN

ON THE SIDE

Doh is the national drink of Afghanistan and one of a legion of sour, salted beverages popular throughout central and eastern Asia. I admit that the ingredient combination (yogurt whey, lemon juice, club soda, mint, and salt) may sound strange to a North American, but I promise that you will quickly grow to love it. The salt serves as a valuable rehydrating agent in warm climates.

To be strictly authentic, you'd need one special ingredient to prepare *doh*: yogurt whey, the clear sourish liquid left over from draining yogurt, a procedure basic to many of the Afghan, Iranian, and Indian marinades found in this book. Fortunately, you'll have plenty of yogurt whey left over from making them, but since you shouldn't have to rely on whey to prepare *doh*, I call for an equal amount of undrained yogurt as a substitute.

½ cup yogurt whey or plain whole-milk
    yogurt
½ cup club soda
1 tablespoon fresh lemon juice, or
    more to taste
1 teaspoon dried mint
½ teaspoon salt, or more to taste
Ice cubes, for serving

Combine the yogurt whey, club soda, 1 tablespoon lemon juice, mint, and ½ teaspoon salt in a small pitcher or glass and stir to mix. Correct the seasoning, adding salt or lemon juice to taste. Pour into a tall glass over ice to serve.

Serves 1; can be multiplied as desired

Where to Sample Afghan Grilling

KHYBER PASS
34 St. Marks Place
New York, NY
Phone (212) 473-0989

AFGHAN KEBAB HOUSE
155 W. 46th Street
New York, NY
Phone (212) 768-3874
with other locations in Manhattan

HELMUND
430 Broadway
San Francisco, CA
Phone (915) 362-0641
with other locations in
Cambridge, Massachusetts, and
Baltimore, Maryland

The Afghan Grill

Of all the countries I wanted to visit, but couldn't because of political turmoil, Afghanistan was my biggest disappointment. This landlocked, mountainous nation of 15 million lies at one of the great crossroads of the barbecue trail and at the confluence of four great civilizations: the Middle East, Central Asia, Eastern Asia, and the Indian subcontinent. Afghan grilling weaves culinary influences from all four regions into a cuisine that's uniquely its own.

This truth was brought home to me on my first meal at an Afghanistani restaurant, the Khyber Pass, in New York's East Village. The moment I stepped into the storefront dining room, with its soft lights, kilim carpets, Afghan tapestries, and hand-hammered copperware, I felt I was a million miles away from Manhattan. The house specialties—grilled lamb chops flavored with onion water, fire-charred game hens, and chicken marinated in yogurt and spices and cooked to fall-off-the-bone-tenderness—were exotic, but immediately accessible. I was won over by the way the side dishes of piquant *chatni* (chutneys—tangy table sauces, which in Aftganistan are made from vinegar, herbs—most often cilantro—and ground nuts, not the fruits we are more familiar with) and bracingly tart *torshi* (vegetable pick-

les) counterpointed the richness of the grilled meats.

"Afghanistan lies at the crossroads of Asia," explained the restaurant's manager, Mohamed Noor. Noor reminded me that Alexander the Great conquered the region in the fourth century B.C. on his way from Greece to India. In the thirteenth century A.D., Genghis Khan subdued the area while on his march to Turkey and Eastern Europe. He was followed in the sixteenth century by King Babur, founder of India's Mogul Empire. (Indeed, King Babur is buried outside the capital city of Kabul.) Each of the conquerors and their armies left a mark on Afghan food.

Thus, olive oil, cinnamon, dill, fenugreek, and *kalonji* (nigella seeds, also known as black cumin or black onion seeds) are as popular in Afghanistan as they are in Middle and Near Eastern cooking. From India, Afghans acquired a taste for *garam*

masala (a spice blend whose ingredients include cumin, cinnamon, cloves, and black cardamom seeds) and *chatnis*. As throughout northern India and Central Asia, meats are marinated before grilling in tenderizing pastes of yogurt and spices. The Persian Empire provided the *torshis* and lavash (flat bread) that are indispensable companions to Afghan barbecue.

The focal point of the Afghan kitchen is the grill. Afghanis use simple seasonings to make some of the best grilled food in the world. Marinades run to yogurt (or yogurt cheese) flavored with onion, garlic, chiles, hot red pepper flakes, cumin, and sometimes olive oil. It's not uncommon for meats to be marinated for 48 hours, which makes them extraordinarily juicy and tender.

The accompaniments are simple: thin chewy Afghan bread, nutty rice pilaf, tangy pickles, and coriander sauce.

There are recipes throughout the book for Afghan quail, chicken, and lamb dishes, plus such traditional accompaniments as *doh* (yogurt drink) and *chatni*. All of them are listed in the Index under Afghan recipes. And on the facing page is a short list of Afghan restaurants, where you can sample some of this extraordinary grilling in exotic settings, but without leaving the United States.

PERSIAN YOGURT DRINK
Dugh

IRAN

ON THE SIDE

Dugh is the beverage traditionally served with Iranian (Persian) kebabs. A close cousin of the drink on page 36 from Afghanistan, it's made with whole yogurt instead of whey and flavored with dried rose petals, available in Middle Eastern stores. Salted beverages may seem odd to most North Americans (not to mention ones with pepper), but they're uncannily refreshing.

2 cups plain whole-milk yogurt
1 tablespoon dried mint, plus a pinch or
　　two for garnish
1 tablespoon dried rose petals, plus a

pinch or two for garnish
1 teaspoon salt, or more to taste
1 teaspoon freshly ground black pepper,
　　or more to taste
1 quart club soda
Ice cubes, for serving

Combine the yogurt, 1 tablespoon mint, 1 tablespoon rose petals, salt, and pepper in a pitcher and stir to mix. Add the club soda. Stir gently to mix, adding more salt and pepper, if desired. Pour into tall glasses, over ice, and garnish each glass with a sprinkling of mint and rose petals.
　　　Serves 4 to 6

VIETNAMESE ICED COFFEE

VIETNAM

ON THE SIDE

This isn't like any iced coffee you've probably ever tasted—it combines strongly brewed espresso and sweetened condensed milk. For the Thai version, imagine you're sipping the coffee from an ice-filled plastic bag through a straw—which is how it's served by street vendors in Bangkok.

3 tablespoons sweetened condensed
　　milk
¾ cup brewed espresso, hot
Ice cubes, for serving

Place the condensed milk in the bottom of a tall heatproof glass. Pour in the espresso (in Vietnam it would be drip-brewed right into the glass) and stir with a spoon to blend. Add ice cubes to fill the glass and serve immediately.
　　　Serves 1; can be multiplied as desired

INDIAN YOGURT COOLER
Lassi

INDIA

ON THE SIDE

Lassi is India's answer to the North American milkshake, and a splendid and refreshing answer it is. It's also the perfect beverage to serve with hot and spicy food. (Contrary to popular belief, dairy products are much more effective than beer at extinguishing chile hellfire.) The rosewater and cardamom add a perfumed flavor you'll find exquisitely exotic.

1 cup plain whole-milk yogurt
1½ tablespoons sugar, or more to taste
1 teaspoon rosewater
¼ teaspoon ground cardamom
5 ice cubes, cracked with a mallet
1 teaspoon chopped unsalted pistachio nuts, for garnish

Combine the yogurt, 1½ tablespoons sugar, the rosewater, cardamom, and ice in a blender and blend until smooth. Taste for sweetening, adding sugar to taste. Pour into a tall glass, sprinkle the top with the chopped pistachios, and serve immediately.

Serves 1; can be multiplied as desired

Warm-Ups

"Even an old boot tastes good if it is cooked over charcoal."

—*ITALIAN PROVERB*

A fan enlivens the coals at this saté stand in Bali.

One of the things I like best about grilling is how it leaves you with so much free time. Sure, live-fire cooking can be quick and intense, but there are plenty of idle moments for standing around and chatting with friends.

But just because you're standing around doesn't mean you have to go hungry—indeed, an empty plate is a sad thing at a barbecue. This chapter, a collection of dips, appetizers—even soups—will help yours get off to a rousing start. From familiar dishes, like *baba ganooj* (made the authentic way—by charring the eggplant on the grill) to the more exotic, such as *boka dushi* ("sweet mouth" chicken kebabs from the island of Curaçao), Vietnamese shrimp mousse grilled on sweet, crunchy sugarcane, and even Goat Cheese Grilled in Grape Leaves that would do a Frenchman (or Californian) proud.

You'll find dishes you may never have realized could be grilled, like Indonesian quail egg kebabs or flame-cooked escargots. You'll also taste some of the world's greatest grilled (literally) cheese dishes, from Mexican quesadillas to Argentinian grilled provolone. And then there are those aforementioned grilled soups here (more precisely soups made with grilled vegetables) that will leave your guests raving long after the party is over.

VIETNAMESE GRILLED BEEF AND BASIL ROLLS

VIETNAM

METHOD:
Direct grilling

SPECIAL EQUIPMENT:
10 to 12 short bamboo skewers, soaked for 1 hour in cold water to cover and drained

This recipe was inspired by a classic Vietnamese appetizer, *bo goi la-lot,* beef grilled in *la-lot* leaves. The latter are the crinkly, round, aromatic leaves of a Southeast Asian vine. If you live in a city with a large Vietnamese community, you may be able to find fresh *la-lot* leaves, but if not, don't despair. These delicate rolls are equally delectable made with fresh basil, and that is what I prepare them with here. (For a Japanese touch, you could even use shiso leaves—also known as perilla or beefsteak leaf—which taste like a cross between mint and basil.) Sometimes these rolls are made with thin beef slices, sometimes with ground beef. I've followed the example of the Vietnam House restaurant in Saigon, using the latter. Chopped peanuts add a nice crunchy finish.

8 ounces very lean ground beef
    sirloin
2 cloves garlic, minced
5 teaspoons Asian fish sauce, or more
    to taste
1 tablespoon sugar, or more
    to taste
1 teaspoon freshly ground black pepper
1 or 2 large bunches basil, to yield about
    60 large leaves
3 tablespoons coarsely chopped
    dry-roasted peanuts (optional)

1. Combine the beef, garlic, 5 teaspoons fish sauce, 1 tablespoon sugar, and the pepper in a small bowl. Mix to a smooth paste with your hands, then sauté a small amount of the mixture in a nonstick skillet and taste for seasoning. Add fish sauce or sugar to the remaining mixture as necessary; the mixture should be both salty and sweet.

2. Select 50 to 60 of the largest basil leaves; rinse under cold running water, drain, and blot gently dry with paper towels. Place one leaf, underside up, on your work surface. Depending on the size of the leaf, mound up to 2 teaspoons of the beef mixture in the center of the leaf, then roll up the leaf, from the stem end, into a compact cylinder. Place the roll on a baking sheet, with the leaf tip tucked under, while you repeat the procedure with the remaining beef mixture and basil leaves. Thread the rolls crosswise on the skewers, 5 rolls to a skewer, making sure the place where the leaf ends cross are pierced first (see Note).

3. Preheat the grill to high.

4. When ready to cook, oil the grill grate. Arrange the skewers on the hot grate and grill, turning with tongs, until the rolls are cooked through, 2 to 4 minutes in all. The basil will be lightly browned and the rolls very hot to the touch. Serve the rolls on the skewers with the peanuts sprinkled over them (if using).

Makes 50 to 60 rolls; serves 4 as an appetizer

Note: You can make the rolls to this point up to several hours ahead of time. If not planning to cook immediately, cover loosely with plastic wrap and refrigerate.

The Vietnamese Grill

I have a theory about the best way to eat during the sweltering dog days of summer. I take my cue from sun-belt lands that have scorching climates all year long. Hot climates generally produce cooking styles well suited to warm weather eating. And nowhere is this more true than Vietnam.

I visited Saigon hot on the barbecue trail, and didn't have far to go to strike paydirt. My hotel, the New World, was located across the street from Saigon's Ben Thanh Central Market. And as at markets throughout Southeast Asia, Ben Thanh was teeming with grill jockeys.

A favorite stop was a stall where a woman grilled chicken wings that had been marinating in a fragrant paste of lemongrass, garlic, and fish sauce. Another vendor proffered an egg that had been "hard-boiled" (roasted) over a coconut shell charcoal fire. I wrapped it with a sprig of mint in a lettuce leaf and dipped it in *nuoc cham,* Vietnam's delicate table sauce—a piquant mixture of fish sauce, lime juice, and sugar. The combination was stellar.

Grilling is ubiquitous in Vietnam, first because it produces such flavorful food, and second because it's so cheap to prepare. As in Thailand and Indonesia, coconut is a major crop here and the tree's by-product—coconut husks—makes excellent charcoal.

But grilling isn't only for the poor, a fact brought home to me where I stopped next—a tiny restaurant called Vietnam House. Located on the second floor of a fashionable townhouse on Dong Khoi Street, Vietnam House seems to exist chiefly for the pleasure of deep-pocketed foreigners. This has both advantages and drawbacks: You get to dine among lacquered screens and gilded wood carvings, serenaded by live, twangy Vietnamese classical music and served by waitresses in *ao dai* (slit dresses). On the down side, you feel a little like you're in Epcot.

I wouldn't say Vietnam House specializes in grilled fare, but two items here rank as world-class barbecue. The first is *chao tom,* an ingenious combination of shrimp mousse that is grilled on a piece of sugarcane. You don't really eat the cane, so much as chew it to release the sweet juices.

The other dish is *bo goi la-lot,* beef grilled in *la-lot* leaves and served on tiny skewers. *La-lot* is the piquant leaf of a Southeast Asian vine that reminds me a little of basil. The beef fairly sizzled, its fat counterbalanced by the herbal tang of the leaf.

A counterpointing of grilled meats with vegetables, specifically with lettuce and aromatic herbs, and noodles is one of the hallmarks of Vietnamese cuisine.

A MEAL OUTDOORS

No dish represents the Vietnamese penchant for enriching small portions of grilled meats with a large proportion of noodles and vegetables than *banh hoi thit* (grilled pork with rice noodles) and its sister dish *bo bun* (grilled beef with rice paper). And no one makes them better than the restaurant Thanh Nien.

I enjoyed my grilled pork in the restaurant's airy courtyard. To my left, stood a grove of bamboo; to my right, a thatch-roofed portico. Oscillating fans stirred the torrid air. The tables around me were filled with fledgling capitalists chattering on cellular phones.

As I sipped an icy "33" Export beer, the waitress set before me three plates. The first contained neatly coiled, snowy rice noodles. The second held the actual pork, which had been thinly sliced, marinated in a fragrant mixture of lemongrass, shallots, and vodka, and smokily charred on the grill. The cooked slices were then dusted with an aromatic sprinkling of chopped scallions and toasted peanuts, the former for pungency, the latter for sweetness and crunch.

The final element was a salad platter that turns up on all Vietnamese tables. The refreshing assortment included lettuce and basil leaves, sliced cucumbers, mung bean sprouts, and crisp, pointed slices of star fruit. To eat the dish, you wrap a coil of noodles and a slice of pork in a lettuce leaf, with basil for fragrance and slices of cucumber and star fruit for crispness.

The result is a morsel perfect for summer, being simultaneously hot and cold; crisp, soft, and chewy; sweet, salty, lemony, and aromatic. I can't think of a dish in the West that comes close to achieving such a complex interplay of temperatures, textures, and tastes. And it's fun to eat.

Check the Index under Vietnamese recipes for the many that appear in this book.

VIETNAMESE BEEF JERKY
Thit Bo Kho

VIETNAM

METHOD:
Direct grilling

ADVANCE PREPARATION:
1 to 2 days for marinating and drying the meat

Grilled sugar-cured, dried beef is a popular snack and street food throughout Southeast Asia. Vietnam's version (*thit bo kho*) owes its explosive flavor to a marinade made with lemongrass, chiles, and fish sauce. Traditionally, the cured beef is dried outdoors in the sun—a common sight in Vietnam, but one that may be more difficult to execute in North America. The beef can also be dried on racks in the refrigerator, as I suggest below.

1 pound lean beef sirloin or bottom round in a single piece
2 stalks fresh lemongrass, trimmed, or 2 strips lemon zest (each 2 x ½ inches; removed with a vegetable peeler)
1 clove garlic, chopped
1 to 2 hot red chiles, stemmed and seeded (for spicier jerky, leave the seeds in)
5 tablespoons sugar
½ teaspoon salt
½ teaspoon freshly ground black pepper
2 tablespoons Asian fish sauce
2 tablespoons soy sauce
2 tablespoons vegetable oil, for brushing

1. Cut the beef as thinly as possible into crosswise slices and place in a baking dish. Set aside while you prepare the marinade.

2. Combine the lemongrass, garlic, chiles, sugar, salt, and pepper in a mortar and grind to a smooth paste with the pestle, then work in the fish sauce and soy sauce. If you don't have a mortar and pestle, combine all these ingredients in a blender and process to a smooth purée. Pour the marinade over the meat in the baking dish and toss thoroughly to coat. Cover and let marinate, in the refrigerator, for 2 hours.

3. Remove the beef from the marinade and spread out the slices on a wire rack in a shallow roasting pan. Refrigerate, loosely covered with plastic wrap, until the beef is completely dry, 1 to 2 days.

4. Preheat the grill to high.

5. When ready to cook, oil the grill grate. Arrange the beef slices on the hot grate and grill, turning with tongs, until sizzling, brown, and crisp, 2 to 3 minutes per side, brushing once or twice with oil as the beef cooks. Serve immediately.

Serves 4 as an appetizer, 2 to 3 as an entrée

INDONESIAN BEEF AND COCONUT SATES
Saté Lalat

INDONESIA

METHOD:
Direct grilling

Saté lalat is the smallest of Indonesian satés—not much bigger than a fly, which is what *lalat* literally means.

Typically, the skewers for *saté lalat* are the size of broom straws; the meat portion is about 1 inch long; a serving would include

SPECIAL EQUIPMENT:
30 short bamboo skewers, soaked for 1 hour in cold water to cover and drained

three or four dozen satés. To suit American skewers and appetites, I make my *saté lalats* a little bigger.

A specialty of the island of Madura near Java, *saté lalat* owes its distinctive texture and flavor to the addition of shredded coconut. To be strictly authentic you should use freshly grated coconut, but I like the touch of sweetness (not to mention the convenience) offered by the shredded dried coconut sold at the supermarket. An Indonesian would use fresh turmeric; I approximate its flavor by combining the more readily available ground turmeric and fresh ginger.

These satés are so flavorful you really don't need a sauce.

10 ounces lean ground beef chuck or sirloin
¹⁄₂ teaspoon ground turmeric
2 teaspoons minced or grated fresh ginger
¹⁄₂ cup shredded coconut (dried or fresh, sweetened or unsweetened)
1 tablespoon sweet soy sauce (ketjap manis) or 1¹⁄₂ teaspoons each regular soy sauce and molasses
1 teaspoon fresh lime juice
2 tablespoons peanut or other vegetable oil
¹⁄₄ teaspoon salt, or more to taste
¹⁄₂ teaspoon freshly ground black pepper, or more to taste

1. Combine the beef, turmeric, ginger, coconut, sweet soy sauce, lime juice, oil, ¹⁄₄ teaspoon salt, and ¹⁄₂ teaspoon pepper in a medium-size bowl. Mix to a smooth paste with your hands, then sauté a small amount of the mixture in a nonstick skillet until cooked through and taste for seasoning. Add salt and pepper to the remaining mixture as necessary.

2. Lightly wet your hands with cold water, then take a small amount (about 1 tablespoon) of the meat mixture and mold it around a skewer to form a thin strip about 5 inches long. Continue until all the mixture is used up, placing the satés as they are finished on a platter or baking sheet lined with plastic wrap until ready to cook.

3. Preheat the grill to high.

4. When ready to cook, oil the grill grate. Arrange the satés on the hot grate and grill, turning with tongs, until nicely browned on the outside and cooked through, 2 to 4 minutes in all. Serve immediately.

Serves 4 to 6 as an appetizer, 2 as an entrée

PASTRAMI GRILLED IN GRAPE LEAVES

TURKEY

METHOD:
Direct grilling

ADVANCE PREPARATION:
15 minutes for soaking the grape leaves

Visit the Spice Market (also known as the Egyptian Market) in Istanbul and you'll see long, tongue-shaped strips of orange-brown meat hanging from the shop rafters. This is *basturma,* the cured beef of the Near East and precursor (both historically and linguistically) of North American pastrami. The meat for *basturma* is usually beef, although it is sometimes made with camel, and the spices—salt, pepper, coriander, and paprika—will be familiar to anyone who likes pastrami. However, the flavor of *basturma* is more exotic.

That set me thinking about an appetizer I enjoyed at the Tugra Restaurant at

Istanbul's stately Ciragan Palace Hotel: *basturma* grilled in grape leaves. If you live in an area with a large Middle or Near Eastern community (such as Fresno or Boston), you may be able to find real *basturma*. But a fine version of this dish can be made with pastrami.

In the interest of authenticity, I should note that the cheese is not in the original recipe, but I very much like the way it rounds out the flavors.

16 bottled grape leaves packed in
   brine, drained
6 ounces thinly sliced pastrami or
   basturma
8 crosswise slices string cheese (each about
   ¼ inch thick) or mozzarella (about
   6 ounces; optional)
1 fresh, ripe medium tomato, cut into
   8 thin slices
1 small onion, cut into 8 thin slices
8 paper-thin lemon slices, seeded,
   with rind removed

1. Cover the grape leaves with cold water in a medium-size bowl and let soak for 15 minutes, changing the water two or three times.

2. Drain the grape leaves and blot dry with paper towels. Spread out 8 of the leaves on a work surface. Place a few slices of pastrami in the center of each. Top each portion of pastrami with a slice of cheese, a slice of tomato, a slice of onion, and finally a slice of lemon. Bring the edges of the grape leaf up around the filling. Place a second grape leaf on top and bring the edges down so the filling is entirely covered.

3. Transfer the bundles to a baking sheet or platter, cover loosely with plastic wrap, and refrigerate while you preheat the grill to high.

4. When ready to cook, oil the grill grate. Arrange the bundles on the hot grate and grill, turning with a spatula, until the grape leaves brown and the filling is heated through, 4 to 8 minutes in all.

5. Serve immediately, and eat by unwrapping the grape leaves (they are not eaten) and eating the filling with a fork.

Makes 8 pieces; serves 4 as an appetizer

DUTCH WEST INDIAN CHICKEN KEBABS
Boka Dushi

CURAÇAO

METHOD:
Direct grilling

ADVANCE PREPARATION:
30 minutes for marinating the chicken

This is a dish of three continents. I tasted it at a restaurant in Curaçao, but its roots lie in the East Indies, specifically Java, Indonesia. Its name belies the strong Spanish influence on Curaçaoan culture: in Papiamentu—the local dialect, a musical blend of Spanish, Portuguese, Dutch, and West African languages—*boka* means "mouth" and *dushi* means "sweet." The seasonings and spices for the dish are sold at the Floating Market in Willemstad, a colorful flotilla of Venezuelan produce boats that make the 35-mile journey here to sell comestibles from South America. The assertive flavors of ginger and *sambal ulek* (chile paste) will light up your mouth like a Fourth of July sky. The recipe was inspired by one of

Curaçao's best restaurants, the Indonesia Rijsttafel in Willemstad. As in Asia, dark meat is preferred to white, as it's thought to have a richer flavor. But you could certainly use the same weight in skinless, boneless chicken breasts (you'll need 1½ pounds).

8 chicken thighs (2½ to 3 pounds)
¼ cup sweet soy sauce (ketjap manis) or 2 tablespoons each regular soy sauce and molasses
1 tablespoon fresh lime juice
2 teaspoons grated fresh ginger
1 to 2 teaspoons sambal ulek or other chile paste or sauce
1 teaspoon ground cumin
½ teaspoon ground turmeric
1 cup Dutch West Indian Peanut Sauce (page 473)

1. Skin and bone the chicken thighs, then rinse under cold running water. Drain and blot dry with paper towels. Cut the meat into strips the size of your little finger.

2. Combine the sweet soy sauce, lime juice, ginger, *sambal ulek,* cumin, and turmeric in a large bowl and stir well to blend. Add the chicken and toss thoroughly to coat. Cover and let marinate, in the refrigerator, for 30 minutes.

3. Preheat the grill to high.

4. When ready to cook, drain the chicken strips, then thread them lengthwise on the skewers. Oil the grill grate, and arrange the skewers on the hot grate. Grill until the meat is cooked through, 2 to 4 minutes in all. Serve the *boka dushis* immediately, with ramekins of the Dutch West Indian Peanut Sauce for dipping.

Serves 4 as an appetizer

SILVER PAPER CHICKEN

This recipe was inspired by San Francisco's celebrated dim sum palace, Yank Sing. The original was deep-fried, but grilling produces equally tasty chicken with a fraction of the fat. The foil helps seal in flavor and succulence—and also makes for an offbeat presentation. Five-spice powder is a Chinese seasoning comprised of cinnamon, pepper, cloves, Sichuan peppercorns, and star anise. It imparts an exotically sweet, aromatic flavor to the chicken. Look for five-spice powder in Asian markets, gourmet shops, and in the ethnic foods sections of most supermarkets.

8 chicken thighs (2½ to 3 pounds) or 4 skinless, boneless chicken breast halves (about 1½ pounds)
4 large scallions
½ cup soy sauce
¼ cup sugar
2 tablespoons Chinese rice wine or dry sherry
1 clove garlic, minced
½ teaspoon Chinese five-spice powder

1. If using chicken thighs, remove the skin. Using a sharp cleaver, cut each thigh, through the bone, crosswise in half. If using chicken breasts, cut each into 2-inch pieces for 16 pieces altogether. Rinse the chicken under cold running water, then drain and blot dry with paper towels. Trim the scallions and cut each into four 2-inch sections.

2. Combine the soy sauce, sugar, rice wine, garlic, and five-spice powder in a heavy saucepan and bring to a boil over medium heat. Continue boiling until thick and syrupy, about 5 minutes. Transfer the mixture to a bowl and let cool to room temperature. Add the chicken pieces, toss to coat thoroughly, and let marinate, covered, in the refrigerator, for 2 to 4 hours.

3. Preheat the grill to high.

4. Cut sixteen 6-inch squares of aluminum foil. Place a piece of foil, shiny side down, on your work surface. Drain the chicken, reserving the marinade, and place a piece, along with a piece of scallion, in the center of each piece of foil. Spoon a little marinade on top of each piece of chicken,

then wrap by crinkling the foil together, rather than folding it neatly (see Note).

5. When ready to cook, arrange the bundles on the hot grate and grill, turning with tongs, until the chicken is cooked through, 4 to 8 minutes in all. To test for doneness, unwrap one of the bundles. The chicken should feel firm and hot to the touch. Much of the fun of eating this dish is the surprise that comes with unwrapping the foil, but do warn eaters to open their bundles carefully; the chicken will be very steamy and hot.

Makes 16 pieces; serves 8 as an appetizer

Note: The recipe can be prepared to this point up to 6 hours ahead. Refrigerate until ready to cook.

SAIGON GARLIC-LEMONGRASS WINGS

VIETNAM

METHOD:
Direct grilling

ADVANCE PREPARATION:
4 to 24 hours for marinating the chicken

SPECIAL EQUIPMENT:
12 long bamboo skewers, soaked for 1 hour in cold water to cover and drained

I've always found the best window into a nation's cuisine to be its food markets. The moment I arrived in Saigon, I rushed to the colossal Ben Thanh Market, located across the street from the hotel where I was staying. You can buy just about anything at Ben Thanh: eel, snake, all manner of innards, even grasshoppers. When you tire of shopping, an army of food vendors stands ready to ply you with Vietnamese soups, stews, and barbecue.

Here's how one vendor prepares chicken wings; her recipe is as easy to make as it is flavorful. To increase the surface area of meat exposed to the flames, the wings are spread open as though poised for flight and threaded on a skewer for grilling. Although I spoke no Vietnamese and the vendor spoke no English, the pleasure these delectable wings brought me was obvious.

To be strictly authentic, you'll need lemongrass and fish sauce for the marinade. In a pinch, you could substitute lemon zest and soy sauce.

12 whole chicken wings (2½ to 3 pounds)
4 cloves garlic, peeled
¼ cup chopped shallots
1 piece (1 inch) fresh ginger, peeled and thinly sliced
2 stalks fresh lemongrass, trimmed and sliced, or 2 strips lemon zest (each 2 x ½ inches; removed with a vegetable peeler)
2 tablespoons sugar
⅓ cup Asian fish sauce
3 tablespoons fresh lemon juice
3 tablespoons vegetable oil
¼ cup finely chopped dry-roasted peanuts, for garnish
¼ cup chopped fresh cilantro, for garnish (optional)

1. Rinse the wings under cold running water, then drain and blot dry with paper towels. Make two or three deep slashes, to the bone, in the meaty part of each wing. Set aside while you prepare the marinade.

2. Combine the garlic, shallots, ginger, lemongrass, and sugar in a mortar and grind to a paste with the pestle. Work in the fish sauce, lemon juice, and 1 tablespoon of the oil. Alternatively, process the ingredients in a blender to a smooth purée. Scrape into a large bowl, add the chicken wings, and toss to coat thoroughly. Cover and let marinate, in the refrigerator, for at least 4 hours, but preferably 24, turning the wings occasionally.

3. Preheat the grill to medium-high.

4. When ready to cook, drain the chicken wings, reserving the marinade, then thread each wing on a skewer, running the skewer through all three sections to hold it open as widely as possible. Brush the wings on both sides with the remaining oil. Oil the grill grate and arrange the skewers on the hot grate. Grill, turning several times with tongs, until the thicker wing sections are no longer pink near the bone, 12 to 16 minutes in all. Brush once or twice with the reserved marinade; do not brush during the last 3 minutes of cooking.

5. Transfer the chicken to a serving platter and sprinkle with the peanuts and cilantro (if using). Serve immediately.

Makes 12 whole wings; serves 4 to 6 as an appetizer

STAR ANISE WINGS

MALAYSIA

METHOD:
Direct grilling

ADVANCE PREPARATION:
8 to 24 hours for marinating the chicken

SPECIAL EQUIPMENT:
Rotisserie (optional)

Lee Chun Hock is a jocular grill master who plies his trade in northern Malaysia. I met him on Gurney Road on Penang Island, where he runs a barbecue stall called Ipoh Famous Roasted Chicken Wings. (Ipoh is the name of his boss.) Hock's "pit" is a gleaming stainless rotisserie, where spring chickens are roasted snap-crackle-poppingly crisp over a charcoal fire. He offered me the following recipe on the condition that I give him a winning lottery number. I told him my age, birthday, and street address. I hope he won!

The powerfully flavorful marinade has everything you could wish for; soy sauce for saltiness, sugar and *ketjap manis* for sweetness, star anise and cinnamon sticks for spice. The basting of sesame oil gives the wings a nutty crispness.

12 whole chicken wings (2½ to 3 pounds)
⅓ cup soy sauce
⅓ cup sweet soy sauce (ketjap manis) or
    2½ tablespoons each regular soy sauce
    and molasses
⅓ cup Chinese rice wine or dry sherry
⅓ cup sugar
2 teaspoons freshly ground black pepper
1 teaspoon Accent (MSG; optional)
5 whole star anise
2 cinnamon sticks (each 3 inches)
2 tablespoons dark sesame oil, for basting

1. Rinse the chicken wings under cold running water, then drain and blot dry with paper towels. Make 2 or 3 deep slashes, to the bone, in the meaty part of each wing. Set aside while you prepare the marinade.

2. Combine the soy sauces, rice wine, sugar, pepper, and Accent (if using) in a large nonreactive bowl and whisk until the sugar is dissolved. Add the star anise and cinnamon, then add the wings and turn to coat completely with the marinade. Cover and let marinate, in the refrigerator, for at least 8 and as long as 24 hours.

3. Preheat the grill to high if using the rotisserie, medium-high if grilling directly on the grate. When ready to cook, set the rotisserie in place (if using). Remove the wings from the marinade.

4. *Rotisserie method:* Thread each wing onto the spit, through the excess skin found at the joint. Grill the wings on the spit until the thicker wing sections are no longer pink near the bone, 20 to 30 minutes.

Direct grill method: Oil the grill grate. Arrange the wings on the hot grate and grill, turning with tongs, until cooked as above, 12 to 16 minutes in all.

For both methods: Brush the wings once or twice with sesame oil as they cook.

5. Transfer the wings to a serving platter and serve immediately.

Makes 12 whole wings or about 5 dozen pieces; serves 4 to 6 as an appetizer

AUSTRALIAN BEER-BARBECUED WINGS

AUSTRALIA

METHOD:
Direct grilling

ADVANCE PREPARATION:
4 hours for marinating the chicken

The wing is the choicest morsel of the chicken for grilling, consisting chiefly of skin (rendered crackling crisp by the flames) and bones (which are fun to gnaw, imparting a rich flavor in the process). The little meat there is, is well marbled, so it stays moist throughout the cooking. This truth is not lost on Australians, for whom the art of grilling chicken wings is something of a national pastime. You'll love the tangy, sweet-sour taste of these wings, which owe their uniqueness to a marinade flavored with Australian beer.

FOR THE CHICKEN AND MARINADE:
12 whole chicken wings (2½ to 3 pounds)
¼ cup peanut oil
¼ cup fresh lemon juice
¼ cup Worcestershire sauce
¼ cup Australian beer, such as Foster's
1 teaspoon salt
1 teaspoon freshly ground black pepper

FOR THE BARBECUE SAUCE:
2 tablespoons peanut oil
1 small onion, finely chopped
1 clove garlic, minced
2 teaspoons minced fresh ginger
½ teaspoon hot red pepper flakes
1 cup ketchup
⅓ cup Australian beer, such as Foster's
2 tablespoons fresh lemon juice
2 tablespoons Worcestershire sauce
2 tablespoons red wine vinegar
1 tablespoon firmly packed dark brown sugar
1 tablespoon honey
2 teaspoons soy sauce
1 teaspoon dry mustard
½ teaspoon freshly ground black pepper

1. Rinse the wings under cold running water, then drain and blot dry with paper towels. Make 2 or 3 deep slashes, to the bone, in the meaty part of each wing. Place the chicken in a large nonreactive bowl and stir in the ¼ cup oil, lemon juice, Worcestershire sauce, beer, salt, and pepper. Cover and let marinate, in the refrigerator, for 4 hours, turning the wings occasionally.

2. Meanwhile, prepare the barbecue sauce. Heat the oil in a medium-size heavy saucepan over medium heat. Add the onion, garlic, ginger, and hot pepper flakes and sauté, stirring with a wooden spoon, until the onion and garlic are lightly browned, about 5 minutes. Stir in the ketchup, beer, lemon juice, Worcestershire sauce, vinegar, sugar, honey, soy sauce, mustard, and pepper and bring to a boil. Reduce the heat to low and simmer the sauce gently until thick and richly flavored, 10 to 15 minutes, stirring occasionally. Remove from the heat and measure

out about 1 cup. Set it aside for serving.

3. Preheat the grill to medium-high.

4. When ready to cook, oil the grill grate. Drain the wings and arrange them on the hot grate, pulling them open to expose as much skin as possible to the flames. Grill, turning several times with tongs, until the thicker wing sections are no longer pink near the bone, 12 to 16 minutes in all. Start brushing the wings with the barbecue sauce the last 5 minutes, then transfer to a platter and brush with sauce again.

5. Serve accompanied by the reserved sauce.

Makes 12 whole wings; serves 4 to 6 as an appetizer

SPICY CHILE WINGS

SINGAPORE

METHOD:
Direct grilling

ADVANCE PREPARATION:
6 to 24 hours for marinating the chicken

These spicy wings reflect Singapore's incredible ethnic diversity. Five-spice powder is a Chinese flavoring, while the *ketjap manis* (sweet soy sauce) comes from Indonesia. The frying of the spice paste is characteristic of Malaysian and Nonya ("grandmother") cooking, but the place where I actually sampled the wings was the Arab Market. Frying the spice paste creates a complex flavor that will make these some of the best wings you've ever tasted.

The vendor who shared this recipe with me used parboiled wings, which he slathered with spice paste and finished on the grill. Given the hundreds of wings sold each morning, parboiling was a way for him to shorten the cooking time to a manageable duration. Since you and I are in less of a rush than the average market cook, I suggest you take the time to marinate the raw wings in the spice paste and cook them from start to finish on the grill.

Note that although this recipe may

look a little complicated, the actual preparation time is about 20 minutes.

16 whole chicken wings (about 3½ pounds)
3 large shallots, peeled
6 cloves garlic, peeled
1 piece (1 inch) fresh ginger
2 to 10 Thai, serrano, or small jalapeño chiles, seeded (for hotter wings, leave the seeds in; see Notes)
½ cup vegetable oil
2 tablespoons soy sauce
2 tablespoons sweet soy sauce (ketjap manis) or 1 tablespoon each regular soy sauce and molasses
1 teaspoon Chinese five-spice powder

1. Rinse the wings under cold running water, then drain and blot dry with paper towels. Make 2 or 3 deep slashes, to the bone, in the meaty part of each wing. Place in a large bowl and refrigerate while you prepare the spice paste.

2. Combine the shallots, garlic, ginger, and chiles in a food processor and process to a smooth paste. Add ¼ cup of the oil, the soy sauces, and five-spice powder and process until smooth (see Notes).

3. Heat the remaining ¼ cup oil in a wok or small, heavy skillet over medium heat. Add the spice paste and cook, stirring constantly, until thick, brown, and very flavorful, 8 to 12 minutes. Remove from the heat and let cool completely.

4. Add the cooled spice paste to the chicken and turn the wings to coat thoroughly. Cover and let marinate, in the refrigerator, for at least 6 hours or as long as 24 (the longer the better).

5. Preheat the grill to medium-high.

6. When ready to cook, oil the grill grate. Arrange the wings on the hot grate and grill, turning with tongs, until the thicker wing sections are no longer pink near the bone, 12 to 16 minutes in all.

7. Transfer the wings to a serving platter and serve.

Makes 16 whole wings; serves 4 to 8 as an appetizer

Notes: As elsewhere in this book, I call for a range of chiles. Two seeded chiles will give you piquant wings; 10 unseeded chiles would make even a Malaysian firebrand feel at home.

■ The ingredients for the spice paste can also be puréed in a blender, in which case they can be processed all together.

HONG KONG HONEY-GLAZED WINGS

CHINA

METHOD:
Direct grilling

ADVANCE PREPARATION:
2 to 4 hours for marinating the chicken

SPECIAL EQUIPMENT:
12 long bamboo skewers, soaked for 1 hour in cold water to cover and drained

Here's a simple recipe for Hong Kong–style chicken wings. Brushing honey on during cooking creates an exceptionally crisp, sweet skin.

12 whole chicken wings (2½ to 3 pounds)
4 cloves garlic, minced
1½ teaspoons salt
1½ teaspoons freshly ground black pepper
1 teaspoon Accent (MSG; optional)
½ cup honey, for brushing

1. Rinse the chicken wings under cold running water, then drain and blot dry with paper towels. Make 2 or 3 deep slashes, to the bone, in the meaty part of each wing. Place the wings in a large bowl and sprinkle with the garlic, salt, pepper, and Accent (if using). Turn the wings to coat with the seasonings, then cover and let marinate, in the refrigerator, for 2 to 4 hours.

2. Preheat the grill to medium high.

3. When ready to cook, oil the grill grate. Heat the honey just to warm in a small saucepan on the side burner of the grill, if you have one, or over low heat on the stovetop. Thread each chicken wing on a skewer, running the skewer through all three sections to hold the wing open as wide as possible. Arrange the wings on the hot grate and grill, turning with tongs, until the thicker wing sections are no longer pink near the bone, 12 to 16 minutes in all, brushing the wings during the last 4 minutes of grilling with the warm honey.

4. Transfer the wings to a serving platter and serve at once.

Makes 12 whole wings; serves 4 to 6 as an appetizer

GRILLED CHICKEN WINGS WITH HONG KONG SPICES

Shek O Wings

CHINA

METHOD:
Direct grilling

ADVANCE PREPARATION:
6 to 24 hours for marinating the chicken

SPECIAL EQUIPMENT:
12 long bamboo skewers, soaked for 1 hour in cold water to cover and drained

The seaside community of Shek O lies on the far side of Hong Kong Island, perhaps a half hour drive from the forest of skyscrapers. But the distance might be better measured in centuries than in kilometers. Here, on this island of relentless urban sprawl and frenzied economic development, is a bohemian seaside community with narrow streets, laid-back bars and open-air restaurants, and beaches that are crowded on Sundays with family picnickers.

Grilling normally plays a minor role in Chinese cuisine, but the Sunday crowds transform Shek O beaches into barbecue central. Vendors do a lively business in charcoal and grilling utensils. The grills themselves are ingenious fabrications of chicken wire and rebar (the ribbed metal bars used for reinforcing concrete). The most popular food for grilling is chicken wings, which are marinated in soy sauce and honey. As elsewhere in Asia, the wings are spread open on the skewers like a zigzag to expose the maximum surface area to the fire.

12 whole chicken wings (2½ to 3 pounds)
½ cup soy sauce
⅓ cup honey
1 tablespoon minced fresh ginger
3 cloves garlic, minced
3 scallions, very finely chopped
2 teaspoons Chinese five-spice powder

1. Rinse the chicken wings under cold running water, then drain and blot dry with paper towels. Make 2 or 3 deep slashes, to the bone, in the meaty part of each wing. Set aside while you prepare the marinade.

2. Combine the soy sauce, honey, ginger, garlic, scallions, and five-spice powder in a large bowl and whisk until the honey is dissolved. Set aside about half the marinade in a small covered bowl and refrigerate until ready to grill. Add the wings to the remaining marinade and turn to coat completely. Cover and let marinate, in the refrigerator, for at least 6 hours but preferably 24, turning the wings occasionally.

3. Preheat the grill to medium-high.

4. When ready to cook, drain the chicken wings, then thread each wing on a skewer, running the skewer through all three sections to hold the wing open as wide as possible. Oil the grill grate and arrange the wings on the hot grate. Grill, turning with tongs, until the thicker wing sections are no longer pink near the bone, 12 to 16 minutes in all, brushing the wings as they cook with the reserved marinade. Don't baste during the last 3 minutes of grilling.

5. Transfer the wings to a serving platter and serve at once.

Makes 12 whole wings; serves 4 to 6 as an appetizer

EAT IT AND BEAT IT WINGS

U.S.A.

METHOD:
Indirect grilling

ADVANCE PREPARATION:
24 hours to marinate the chicken

SPECIAL EQUIPMENT:
1½ cups wood chips, preferably hickory, soaked for 1 hour in cold water to cover and drained

A restaurant with a name like Kansas City's Little Jake's Eat It and Beat It takes a pretty rapid-fire approach to customer turnover. When it comes to barbecue, however, proprietor Danny Edwards definitely takes his time. The following wings are marinated in a spice rub overnight, then smoke-grilled until fall-off-the-bone tender. Quantities for the various seasonings are approximate: Add more or less to suit your taste.

12 whole chicken wings (2½ to 3 pounds)
2 teaspoons garlic salt
2 teaspoons black pepper
2 teaspoons cayenne pepper
2 teaspoons crumbled dried oregano

1. Rinse the chicken wings under cold running water, then drain and blot dry with paper towels. Place the wings in a large bowl and sprinkle with the garlic salt, pepper, cayenne, and oregano. Turn the wings to coat with the seasonings, then cover and let marinate, in the refrigerator, for 24 hours.

2. Set up the grill for indirect grilling (see page 14 or 16); with a drip pan in the center.

If using a gas grill: Place all the wood chips in the smoker box and preheat the grill to high; when smoke appears, lower the heat to medium-low.

If using a charcoal grill: Preheat to medium-low. When the coals are ready, toss half the drained wood chips on the coals.

3. *For both methods:* Oil the grill grate and place the wings on the hot grate over the drip pan. Cover the grill and cook the wings until very tender, 1½ to 2 hours; if using charcoal, add 10 to 12 fresh coals and a handful of chips per side after 1 hour.

4. Transfer the wings to a serving platter and serve at once.

Makes 12 whole wings; serves 4 to 6 as an appetizer

GRILLED SHRIMP DIM SUM

CHINA

METHOD:
Direct grilling

SPECIAL EQUIPMENT:
12 short bamboo skewers or wooden toothpicks, soaked for 1 hour in cold water to cover and drained

Grilling is not one of the primary cooking techniques in Chinese cuisine. But many Chinese dishes lend themselves to live-fire cooking. Consider the following shrimp dish, which is traditionally served as dim sum. Grilling the shrimp instead of deep-frying them has the dual advantage of heightening the flavor and reducing the fat.

12 large shrimp
12 scallions
6 lean strips bacon

1. Preheat the grill to medium-high.

2. Peel and devein the shrimp (see page 349). Trim off the greens from the scallions, reserving them for another dish, then trim off the roots; you should be left with 2-inch sections of scallion white. Cut the bacon strips crosswise in half.

3. Nestle each scallion white in the curved hollow of a shrimp, then wrap in a piece of bacon and secure with a bamboo skewer or toothpick by running the skewer or toothpick through the wrapped shrimp.

4. When ready to cook, arrange the dim sum on the hot grate and grill until the shrimp are firm and pink and the bacon is crisp, 2 to 4 minutes per side, turning once with tongs. Serve immediately.

Serves 4

SHRIMP MOUSSE ON SUGARCANE
Chao Tom

VIETNAM

METHOD:
Direct grilling

ADVANCE PREPARATION:
2 hours for chilling the mousse

Chao tom, shrimp mousse grilled on sugarcane, is one of the most distinctive dishes in Vietnam. Talk about a dazzling contrast of flavors and textures, *chao tom* has it all: soft shrimp mousse and crispy, dulcet sugarcane. You don't really eat the cane so much as chew it, which releases sweet juices that balance the saltiness of the shrimp. Fresh sugarcane is available in most major supermarkets.

1 pound large shrimp, peeled and deveined (see page 349)
2 ounces pork fat or salt pork, diced
1 clove garlic, minced
1 scallion, both white and green parts, trimmed and minced
1 tablespoon sugar, or more to taste
1 tablespoon Asian fish sauce
1 tablespoon peanut oil, plus additional for forming the kebabs
1 teaspoon Vietnamese or Thai hot sauce
½ teaspoon salt, or more to taste
½ teaspoon freshly ground black pepper, or more to taste
3 pieces sugarcane (each 6 to 8 inches long)

1. Combine the shrimp, pork fat, garlic, scallion, and 1 tablespoon sugar in a food processor and process to a coarse purée.

Add the fish sauce, 1 tablespoon peanut oil, the hot sauce, salt (if using salt pork, add only ¼ teaspoon salt), and pepper, running the machine in spurts. Sauté a small amount of the mixture in a nonstick skillet and taste for seasoning, adding sugar, salt, or pepper to the remaining mixture as necessary; the mixture should be highly seasoned. Transfer the mixture to a bowl, cover, and refrigerate until well chilled, about 2 hours.

2. Peel the sugarcane with a sharp, heavy knife and cut each piece lengthwise into 4 quarters. Lightly oil the fingers of one hand. Take about 3 tablespoons of the shrimp mixture and mold it around the top half of a piece of sugarcane. This will feel awkward at first, but soon you'll be doing it like a pro. Continue in this fashion until all the sugarcane pieces are prepared. Arrange the kebabs on a lightly oiled plate, cover with plastic wrap, and refrigerate until ready to grill.

3. Preheat the grill to high.

4. When ready to cook, oil the grill grate. Arrange the kebabs on the hot grate and grill, turning once with tongs, until the shrimp mixture is lightly browned, firm, and cooked through, 2 to 3 minutes per side. Serve the kebabs at once, eating by nibbling the shrimp mixture off the cane. Be sure to chew the cane to extract the sweet juice.

Serves 12 as an appetizer

GRILLED SNAILS
Escargots Grillés

FRANCE

METHOD:
Direct grilling

SPECIAL EQUIPMENT:
Vegetable grate or cake rack

No one can accuse me of not going the distance for a recipe. Consider this one, from the restaurant L'Hostal in Castellnou, France (see the facing page).

L'Hostal's chef uses lard for basting the snails. That's right, lard. I know that lard is not the most fashionable ingredient in the United States, but, for starters, it has a unique meaty flavor you just can't duplicate with butter. It's also healthier than butter, believe it or not, containing half the cholesterol and one-third saturated fat of the latter. But you can certainly use butter in the recipe if lard turns you off. By the way, the shallots, garlic, and celery should be chopped so fine they would blow away if you breathed too hard.

Under the best circumstances, you'd build your fire with grapevine trimmings (see Mail-Order Sources). The second best alternative, is charcoal, with a few soaked grapevine trimmings or wine barrel chips (see Mail-Order Sources) tossed on the coals. But rest assured that eminently respectable grilled snails can be cooked on a gas grill.

2 dozen canned escargots with shells
    (if possible, try to buy petits gris)
12 tablespoons lard or unsalted butter, or a
    mixture of both, at room temperature
2 large shallots, very finely minced
3 cloves garlic, very finely minced
1 medium rib celery, very finely minced
3 tablespoons minced fresh Italian (flat-leaf)
    parsley
1 teaspoon fresh thyme leaves or ½ teaspoon
    dried
½ teaspoon curry powder
Salt and freshly ground black pepper, to taste

1. Drain the escargots in a colander and rinse well under cold running water. Drain again and blot dry with paper towels. Melt 3 tablespoons of the lard in a medium-size saucepan over medium heat. Add the shallots, garlic, celery, parsley, thyme, curry powder, and salt and pepper and sauté until the vegetables are soft and translucent but not brown, about 3 minutes. Remove the pan from the heat and let the mixture cool to room temperature.

2. Preheat the grill to high.

3. Whisk the remaining lard into the cooled vegetable mixture, then place a portion of the mixture the size of a hazelnut in each escargot shell, using the tip of a butter knife. Insert the escargot in the shell and fill with some of the remaining vegetable mixture, placing each snail as it is filled on a baking sheet or platter (see Note).

4. When ready to cook, place a vegetable grate or wire cake rack on top of the grill grate. Arrange the snails, open side up, on the rack and grill until the filling is bubbling and fragrant, 3 to 5 minutes. Use tongs to transfer the snails to plates and serve at once.

Makes 2 dozen snails; serves 4 as an appetizer

Note: The recipe can be prepared to this point up to several hours in advance. Refrigerate, loosely covered with plastic wrap, until ready to grill.

Stalking the Elusive Grilled Snail

Barbecue lends itself to obsession. If you're afflicted with an obsessive personality like me and you start to delve into the world of barbecue, you may soon find all your spare time literally going up in smoke. The truth is well known to the legions of barbecue "widows" who have lost their husbands to barbecue contests and smoke fests. This truth became apparent during a 10-day swing through the south of France to study the elusive art of French grilling.

Barbara (my wife) and I had been on the road for about a week, and this being Sunday, it was to be our first night "off" (without any special dining plans). Then I made the fatal mistake of calling French culinary authority Patricia Wells, who told me about grilled snails.

Grilled snails are the specialty of a restaurant called L'Hostal in the hamlet of Castellnou near Perpignan in southwestern France. The problem was that we were in Arles (the Provençal town immortalized by Van Gogh), some 400 miles away.

A call to the restaurant confirmed that yes, they had grilled snails. Yes, I could order them for this evening. No, the restaurant would not be open Monday or Tuesday. Yes, it was too bad we were leaving France on Wednesday. Yes, if we wanted grilled snails, we'd have to eat them that night.

I did some quick calculations. If we left our hotel in 10 minutes and drove a hundred miles an hour, we could be in

Castellnou by sundown. I turned to Barbara and said, "I've just found a place that serves grilled snails."

"Great," she said. "Let's go."

"There's only one problem," I said. "The restaurant is near the Spanish border."

Luckily, when it comes to barbecue, my wife is nearly as obsessive as I am.

True to my calculations, we arrived in Castellnou four hours later, having averaged a hundred miles an hour on the autoroute. The last six miles took us up a steep, winding road to a perfectly restored medieval citadel. We found L'Hostal without much trouble (it being the only restaurant in town). Still vibrating from the drive, we took our seats on a cliffside terrace with a dizzying, dazzling view of the Roussillon Valley.

In the summer, L'Hostal does its grilling in a huge outdoor fireplace. In the winter, the operations are moved to the manorial hearth in the low-ceilinged dining room. The favored fuel here is vine trimmings, branches for delicate

fare, like snails, vine stalks and roots for large cuts of meat. When we arrived sure enough, and sure enough, four dozen tiny snails were sizzling away on a circular wire grill over blazing vine trimmings.

With tolls, gas, and a place to stay for the evening, the trip to Castellnou cost $400. Which makes this one of the most expensive dishes of escargots I've ever eaten. It was worth the drive—and the money—for I've never seen grilled escargot anywhere else.

In one sense, neither you nor I will ever be able to reproduce this recipe at home. We probably can't get the tiny, succulent escargots known locally as *petits gris* ("little grays"). We certainly can't buy them live or feed them on fresh thyme in special cages in our basements. We can't buy snail grills, although a vegetable grate or round cake rack perched on a couple of bricks will work in a pinch.

Ultimately, we will never be able to duplicate the texture and flavor of L'Hostal's grilled snails: the former being soft, moist, even a little "drooly" (*baveuse* in French), the latter being pungent, salty, aromatic, with overtones of thyme and even curry.

But I love a challenge. So, although we may not be able to duplicate the dish, I've come up with a recipe for highly delicious grilled snails inspired by L'Hostal's preparation (see the facing page). As for the grill, well, Barbara is still wondering what happened to our cake rack.

GRILLED EGGPLANT DIP
Choka Dip

TRINIDAD

METHOD:
Direct grilling

There is no shortage of grilled eggplant dishes in the world, but this one—a dip that is a specialty of Trinidad's Indian community—is the only one I know of in which the eggplant is studded with garlic cloves before grilling. What results is an incredible depth of flavor. I often use this Trinidadian technique when I grill eggplant on my own.

Serve as a dip with Grilled Pita Chips.

2 long, slender eggplants (about 2 pounds in all)
8 cloves garlic, cut lengthwise in half
½ cup plain whole-milk yogurt
¼ cup chopped fresh cilantro
3 scallions, both white and green parts, trimmed and finely chopped
2 teaspoons ground coriander
2 teaspoons grated fresh ginger
2 tablespoons fresh lemon juice
2 tablespoons vegetable oil
Salt and freshly ground black pepper, to taste
Grilled Pita Chips (page 104)

1. Preheat the grill to high.

2. Make 8 small slits in each eggplant, using the tip of a paring knife. Insert a half garlic clove in each.

3. When ready to cook, place the eggplants on the hot grate and grill, turning with tongs, until the skin is charred all over and the flesh is very soft, 20 to 30 minutes; the eggplants will have lost their firm shape. Transfer the eggplants to a plate to cool.

4. Using a paring knife, scrape the charred skin off the eggplants. Transfer the eggplant flesh, with its garlic, to a medium-size bowl and mash to a coarse purée with a fork. Stir in the yogurt, cilantro, scallions, coriander, ginger, lemon juice, oil, and salt and pepper. Serve immediately with the pita chips.

Makes about 2½ cups; serves 8 as an appetizer or dip

PERSIAN EGGPLANT DIP WITH WALNUTS

IRAN

METHOD:
Direct grilling

I first sampled this tangy dip at a Persian (Iranian) restaurant in New York called Persepolis. If you think *baba ganooj* is good (see the next recipe), wait until you taste this. What makes it so distinctive is the addition of walnuts and a tangy farmer's cheese called *kashk-bibi*. Before you despair of finding the latter (it's available in Middle Eastern markets), know that its sharp flavor is easily approximated by using feta cheese and a spoonful of feta brine (the liquid in which most fetas come packed).

Serve as a dip with Grilled Pita Chips.

1 large or 2 small eggplants (about
   1 pound in all)
¼ cup walnut pieces, lightly toasted
   (see page 93)
1 ounce feta cheese packed in brine,
   drained but 1 tablespoon
   liquid reserved
1 clove garlic, minced
3 tablespoons plain yogurt, preferably
   whole milk
3 tablespoons extra-virgin olive oil
1 teaspoon fresh lemon juice, or more
   to taste
Salt and freshly ground black pepper,
   to taste
1 tablespoon dried mint
Grilled Pita Chips (page 104)

1. Preheat the grill to high.

2. When ready to cook, place the eggplants on the hot grate and grill, turning with tongs, until the skin is charred all over and the flesh is very soft, 20 to 30 minutes; the eggplants will have lost their firm shape. Transfer the eggplants to a plate to cool.

3. Grind the nuts to a coarse powder in a food processor, running the machine in bursts. Using a paring knife, scrape the charred skin off the eggplants. Transfer the eggplant flesh to the food processor workbowl with the ground nuts. Crumble the feta and add to the processor along with the garlic, then process to a smooth purée. Add the reserved feta liquid, yogurt, 2 tablespoons of the oil, 1 teaspoon lemon juice, and salt and pepper and process until smooth. Taste for seasoning, adding salt or lemon juice as necessary; the mixture should be highly seasoned. Transfer the mixture to a serving bowl. Make a slight hollow in the center of the dip with the back of a spoon and set aside.

4. Heat the remaining 1 tablespoon oil in a small skillet over medium heat. Add the mint and sauté, stirring, until fragrant, about 1 minute. Pour the mint oil into the hollow in the dip and serve immediately with the pita chips.

Makes about 1½ cups; serves 6 to 8 as an appetizer or dip

MIDDLE EASTERN EGGPLANT PUREE WITH TAHINI
Baba Ganooj

MIDDLE EAST

METHOD:
Direct grilling

Baba ganooj is one of those ethnic dishes that has crossed over to the North American mainstream. To prepare it correctly, you must char the eggplant on the grill. The charring imparts an intense characteristic smoke flavor that makes this one of the most popular items on a Middle Eastern *mezze* (appetizer) platter. There's one nontraditional element here—the studding of the eggplant with garlic cloves before grilling—a technique I picked up in Trinidad.

Serve as a dip with Grilled Pita Chips.

2 long, slender eggplants (about
    2 pounds in all)
9 cloves garlic, 8 cut lengthwise in half
    and 1 minced
2 scallions, both white and green parts,
    trimmed and finely chopped
3 tablespoons tahini
3 tablespoons extra-virgin olive oil,
    or more to taste, plus 1 tablespoon
    for serving
3 tablespoons fresh lemon juice, or more
    to taste
Salt and freshly ground black pepper, to taste
Grilled Pita Chips (page 104)

1. Preheat the grill to high.

2. Using the tip of a paring knife, make 8 small slits in each eggplant and insert a half clove garlic in each slit. Set the eggplants aside.

3. When ready to cook, place the eggplants on the hot grate and grill, turning with tongs, until the skin is charred all over and the flesh is very soft, 20 to 30 minutes; the eggplants will have lost their firm shape. Transfer the eggplants to a plate to cool.

4. Using a paring knife, scrape the charred skin off the eggplants. Transfer the eggplant flesh to a food processor. Add the minced garlic, scallions, tahini, 3 tablespoons oil, 3 tablespoons lemon juice, and salt and pepper and process until smooth. Taste for seasoning, adding salt, oil, or lemon juice as necessary; the mixture should be very tangy.

5. Spoon the *baba ganooj* into a serving bowl and drizzle with the remaining 1 tablespoon oil. Scoop up the dip with the pita chips.

Makes about 2¼ cups; serves 8 as an appetizer or dip

YOGURT-CUCUMBER SALAD WITH MINT
Cacik

TURKEY

ON THE SIDE

ADVANCE PREPARATION: *4 hours for draining the yogurt (optional)*

Part dip and part salad, *cacik* (pronounced "ja-jik") turns up on *mezze* (hors d'oeuvre) platters throughout Turkey—not to mention in Greece, where it goes by the name of *tzatziki.* (I see it as eastern Mediterranean guacamole.) I can't think of a more refreshing dish for warm weather than this cooling combination of yogurt, mint, and cucumber—a perfect dip for a summer cookout. For an exceptionally rich *cacik,* drain the yogurt for 4 hours, as described in step 1. But don't worry if you don't have time to drain it—the *cacik* will still be extremely tasty.

Serve as a dip with wedges of fresh pita bread.

2 cups plain whole-milk yogurt (see Note)
1 European (seedless) cucumber or 1 large
    regular cucumber
1 teaspoon salt, or more to taste
1 to 2 cloves garlic, minced
3 tablespoons finely chopped fresh mint or
    dill or 1 tablespoon dried
2 tablespoons extra-virgin olive oil
Freshly ground black pepper, to taste

1. If draining the yogurt, set a yogurt strainer, or regular strainer lined with a double layer of dampened cheesecloth, over a medium-size bowl. Add the 2 cups yogurt and drain, in the refrigerator, for 4 hours. You should wind up with about 1¼ cups.

2. Peel the cucumber and seed it, if necessary (see box, page 90), then coarsely grate or finely chop it. Place the grated cucumber in a colander and toss with ½ teaspoon salt. Let stand, over a bowl or in the sink, for 20 minutes to drain off some of the excess water from the cucumber. Blot the cucumber dry with paper towels.

3. Transfer the drained yogurt to a serving bowl. Stir in the cucumber, garlic, ½ teaspoon salt, 2 tablespoons of the mint, 1 tablespoon of the oil, and pepper. Taste for seasoning, adding salt or pepper as necessary.

4. To serve, make a slight hollow in the center of the *cacik* with the back of a spoon, pouring the remaining oil into the depression (for a less formal presentation, simply drizzle the remaining oil on top). Decorate the top of the *cacik* with the remaining 1 tablespoon mint. (One traditional presentation is to sprinkle the mint in two intersecting lines to make a cross. If you decide to serve the *cacik* this way, don't make a hollow in the yogurt; simply drizzle the top with oil.) Serve immediately.

Makes about 2 cups; serves 4 to 6 as an appetizer

Note: You'll need only 1¼ cups yogurt if you don't plan to drain it.

GRILLED PROVOLONE
Provolone Asado

ARGENTINA

METHOD:
Direct grilling

SPECIAL EQUIPMENT:
Two-pronged barbecue fork

This popular Argentinian appetizer defies the laws of culinary physics. Doesn't cheese melt when heated? Wouldn't it become unmanageably gooey on the grill? The fact is that provolone holds its shape beautifully during grilling, acquiring a silky texture and a charred, smoky flavor that balances the cheese's peppery, pungent bite. One thing is for sure, this dish is certainly popular: Visit any steakhouse in Buenos Aires and you'll see huge platters of provolone slices, stacked up like chips at a casino, ready for grilling.

2 slices (each about 8 ounces and ½ inch thick) aged provolone (the older and firmer the better)
1 to 2 tablespoons olive oil
2 teaspoons dried oregano
Freshly ground black pepper, to taste
Crusty Italian bread, for serving (see Note)

1. Preheat the grill to high.

2. When ready to cook, oil the grill grate. Brush the cheese slices on both sides with oil and sprinkle with half the oregano and some pepper. Place the cheese slices on the hot grate. Cook until the bottom side is browned and beginning to bubble, but not completely melted. This will take 2 to 4 minutes.

3. Pry the cheese slices off the grill with the prongs of a barbecue fork. Invert them, sprinkle with the remaining oregano and additional pepper, and grill the other sides the same way, another 2 to 4 minutes. Transfer the grilled cheese to a plate.

4. To eat, spread the melted cheese on chunks or slices of bread.

Serves 6 to 8 as an appetizer

Note: Although it's not traditional, for an even richer charcoal flavor you could slice the bread and toast it on the grill.

GRILLED QUESADILLAS

MEXICO

METHOD:
Direct grilling

Ten years ago, few of us had ever heard of quesadillas. Now we can't seem to live without them. These Mexican grilled cheese "sandwiches," made from tortillas sandwiched with chiles and cheese, have taken the U.S. by storm. This recipe features a quesadilla that's actually cooked on the grill. Feel free to vary the ingredients for the filling, but don't wander away when cooking them. Tortillas burn like paper.

1¼ cups coarsely grated Jack or
　　sharp white Cheddar cheese
½ cup sour cream
2 scallions, both white and green parts,
　　trimmed and thinly sliced
1 Flame-Roasted Tomato (recipe follows),
　　seeded (see box) and finely diced
¼ cup fresh cilantro leaves
2 to 3 pickled jalapeño chiles, thinly sliced
　　(see Note)
½ teaspoon ground cumin
Salt and freshly ground black pepper, to taste
8 flour tortillas (8 inches each)

1. Preheat the grill to medium-high.

2. Combine the cheese, sour cream, scallions, tomato, cilantro, chiles, and cumin in a small bowl and stir to mix. Add salt and pepper.

3. When ready to cook, lay 4 tortillas out on your work surface and spread them evenly with the cheese mixture. Press the remaining tortillas on top to make a sandwich. Place on the hot grill grate and grill until lightly browned on both sides, 2 to 4 minutes per side, turning carefully with a large spatula. Cut each quesadilla into 8 wedges for serving.

Makes 48 wedges: serves 8 to 12 as an appetizer, 4 as a light entrée

Note: For spicier quesadillas, use thinly sliced fresh jalapeños, with or without the seeds, as desired.

How to Seed a Tomato

Cut the tomato (fresh or roasted) in half crosswise. Holding a half in one hand, cut side down, gently squeeze it to drain out the seeds and liquid. You can help ease them out with your fingers.

Frugal cooks may wish to work over a strainer that's sitting in a bowl. The pulp and seeds that land in the strainer can be pressed with the back of a spoon, extracting the tomato liquid into the bowl. Save the liquid, covered, in the refrigerator for sauces, soups, or drinking.

Flame-Roasted Tomatoes

Some of the recipes in this book call for peeled and seeded tomato. Why bother doing either? Tomato skins (especially when cooked) can form red filaments that get caught in your teeth. Tomato seeds come in a watery pulp that can dilute the flavor of the dish.

Mexicans have devised an ingenious method for peeling tomatoes. They char the tomatoes on the grill (or on a *comal*, or griddle). The charred skins impart a great smoky flavor and slip off easily.

Fresh, ripe tomatoes

1. Preheat the grill to high.

2. When ready to cook, arrange the tomatoes on the hot grill grate and grill, turning with tongs, until the skin blackens and blisters. This will take 8 to 12 minutes, depending on the size of the tomatoes.

Transfer the tomatoes to a plate or platter to cool.

3. Scrape the burnt skin off the tomato with a paring knife. Don't worry if you can't remove every last bit: a little burnt skin adds a nice smoky flavor.

GOAT CHEESE GRILLED IN GRAPE LEAVES

U.S.A

METHOD:
Direct grilling

ADVANCE PREPARATION:
15 minutes to 8 hours for refrigerating the bundles

This dish was inspired by a rustic French cheese called banon (BAN-awh). A specialty of the Alpes Maritime region, this cheese is made from cow's or goat's milk, then wrapped in chestnut leaves and cured with marc (a brandy made from the grape residue after the juice has been extracted), giving it a nutty, slightly winey flavor. I've taken the idea one step further: grilling the cheese in grape leaves. The grilled grape leaves impart a piquant, woodsy flavor to the cheese while keeping it exquisitely moist and creamy. You want to use a soft goat cheese for this recipe; good choices would include Montrachet, bûcheron, or a young crottin de Chavignol.

16 bottled grape leaves packed in brine
8 sun-dried tomatoes, plain or packed
    in oil
8 ounces goat cheese, cut into 8 slices
3 tablespoons pine nuts, toasted (optional;
    see page 93)
1 teaspoon fresh thyme leaves or
    ½ teaspoon dried
Freshly ground black pepper, to taste
1 tablespoon extra-virgin olive oil
16 small, thin slices French bread or
    pumpernickel

1. Soak the grape leaves in cold water to cover in a large bowl for 15 minutes, changing the water 2 or 3 times. If using dry sun-dried tomatoes, soak them in hot water to cover for 15 minutes. If using oil-packed dried tomatoes, there is no need to soak them.

2. Drain the grape leaves and blot dry with paper towels. Place 8 leaves on your work surface. Drain the tomatoes, blot dry, and cut into thin slivers. Place a piece of cheese in the center of each grape leaf. Sprinkle the slivered tomatoes, pine nuts (if using), thyme, and pepper over the cheese and drizzle with oil. Bring the edges of the grape leaf up around the cheese. Place a second grape leaf on top and bring the edges down so the cheese is entirely covered. Refrigerate the bundles for at least 15 minutes or up to 8 hours (loosely cover with plastic wrap for longer refrigeration).

3. Preheat the grill to high.

4. When ready to cook, arrange the cheese bundles on the hot grate and grill until the grape leaves brown and the cheese begins to melt, 2 minutes per side, turning once with a spatula.

5. Place the bread slices on the grate and grill until golden brown, 1 to 2 minutes per side. Serve immediately, unwrapping the grape leaves (they are not eaten) and eating the melted cheese with a fork or spread on the toasted bread.

Makes 8 bundles; serves 4 as an appetizer

BACON GRILLED PRUNES

U.S.A.

METHOD:
Direct grilling

**SPECIAL
EQUIPMENT:**
*16 short thin
bamboo skewers
or wooden tooth-
picks, soaked for
1 hour in cold
water to cover
and drained*

ere's proof that some of the world's
tastiest dishes are also the most simple. This recipe consists of only two
ingredients—bacon and prunes—but the
contrast of sweet and salty, meaty and
fruity, crisp and chewy makes this an irresistible appetizer. I like to use an artisanal
cob-smoked bacon (see Mail-Order
Sources), but a lean supermarket brand
would do perfectly well.

4 lean strips bacon, or more as needed
16 pitted prunes

1. Preheat the grill to high.
2. Cut each strip of bacon crosswise

into 4 pieces; each piece should be just large
enough to wrap up a prune. Wrap each prune
in bacon and secure with a bamboo skewer
or toothpick by running the skewer or toothpick through the center of the prune and out
the other side.

3. When ready to cook, arrange the
prunes on the hot grate and grill, turning
once with tongs, until heated through and
the bacon is crisp, 1 to 3 minutes per side.
Transfer to a platter and serve immediately.
Remove the skewers or toothpicks before
serving, or at least warn everyone of their
presence.

Makes 16 pieces

PANCETTA GRILLED FIGS

ITALY

METHOD:
Direct grilling

**SPECIAL
EQUIPMENT:**
*12 small bamboo
skewers or
wooden
toothpicks,
soaked for 1 hour
in cold water to
cover and
drained*

**ADVANCE
PREPARATION:**
*30 minutes to
marinate the
eggs*

ere's an Italian twist on the preceding
recipe, using fresh figs and pancetta.
The former were once deemed fairly
exotic, but you can now find them in most
supermarkets (and certainly in Italian markets), especially in late spring and summer.
Pancetta is often described as cured Italian
bacon. Unlike our bacon, though, it's never
smoked. Pancetta can be found in Italian
markets, gourmet shops, and an increasing number of supermarkets.

6 thin slices pancetta
12 ripe figs, stemmed (see Note)
12 fresh sage leaves

1. Preheat the grill to high.
2. Cut each strip of pancetta in half; each
piece should be just large enough to wrap up

a fig. Wrap each fig, topped with a sage leaf,
in pancetta, and secure with a small bamboo
skewer or toothpick by running the skewer
or toothpick through the center of the fig and
out the other side.

3. When ready to cook, arrange the figs
on the hot grate and grill, turning once with
tongs, until heated through and the pancetta
is crisp, 2 to 4 minutes per side. Transfer to
a platter and remove the skewers or toothpicks before serving, or at least warn everyone of their presence.

***Makes 12 pieces; serves 4 to 6 as an
appetizer***

Note: You could also use dried figs for
this recipe. Soak them in a bowl of boiled
water (or, better yet, hot Marsala wine or
port) for 30 minutes, or until soft, then drain
and proceed with the recipe.

GRILLED EGGS WITH VIETNAMESE SEASONINGS

VIETNAM

METHOD:
Direct grilling

Here's a Southeast Asian twist on Western hard-cooked eggs. If you're familiar only with the mayonnaise-mustard treatment hard-boiled eggs receive in the West, the vibrant fish sauce–lime juice–chile dipping sauce will come as a revelation! The eggs are roasted over a low flame on the grill, instead of being boiled. This particular recipe was inspired by a street vendor in Saigon, but I've seen similar preparations in Thailand and Singapore.

4 large eggs, at room temperature
3 tablespoons Asian fish sauce
2 tablespoons fresh lime juice
1 tablespoon sugar
1 clove garlic, minced
1 Thai, bird, or serrano chile, thinly sliced
    (for a milder sauce, seed the chile)
1 head Boston lettuce, separated into leaves,
    rinsed, and spun dry
1 small bunch fresh mint, trimmed of large
    stems

1. Preheat the grill to medium.

2. When ready to cook, pierce a tiny hole in the end of each egg with an egg pricker or needle. Place the eggs on the grill and cook until the shell is browned and eggs are completely cooked, 10 to 12 minutes, turning often with tongs to ensure even cooking.

3. Combine the fish sauce, lime juice, sugar, garlic, and chile in a small bowl and stir until the sugar is dissolved. Divide the sauce among 4 tiny bowls. Arrange the lettuce leaves and mint on a platter.

4. Serve the eggs in the shell. To eat, shell the egg and cut it in quarters lengthwise. Each quarter egg should then be wrapped in a lettuce leaf with a sprig of mint, dipped in the sauce, and eaten.

Serves 4 as an appetizer

QUAIL EGG SATES
Saté Telor

INDONESIA

METHOD:
Direct grilling

Saté telor is one of the most unusual satés in Indonesia, tiny kebabs of immature chicken eggs—a specialty of the city of Kudus in central Java. *Saté telor* is the traditional accompaniment to

ayam soto (Javanese chicken soup). I make it with quail eggs, but hard-cooked, quartered chicken eggs are acceptable substitutes. The sweet, peppery glaze and crisply fried shallots make this a must-try

ADVANCE PREPARATION:
1 hour for cooling and marinating the eggs

SPECIAL EQUIPMENT:
8 short bamboo skewers, soaked for 1 hour in cold water to cover and drained

for the adventurous griller. Serve these satés as a pass-around or at-table hors d'oeuvre.

24 quail eggs or 6 chicken eggs
1 cup sweet soy sauce (ketjap manis),
    or ½ cup each regular soy sauce
    and molasses
2 cloves garlic, minced
2 tablespoons firmly packed light brown
    sugar
1 teaspoon freshly ground black pepper
½ teaspoon Accent (MSG; optional)
1 cup vegetable oil, for frying
4 shallots, cut into thin wedges

1. Place the quail or chicken eggs in a large saucepan with cold water to cover and bring gradually to a gentle boil over medium-low heat. Cook the quail eggs for 5 minutes and the chicken eggs for 11 minutes, then remove from the heat. Immediately set the pan with the eggs in the sink and run cold water into it until the shells are cool. Shell the eggs under cold running water. Blot dry with paper towels; if using chicken eggs, cut into quarters lengthwise. Set aside while you prepare the glaze.

2. Combine the sweet soy sauce, garlic, sugar, pepper, and Accent (if using) in a small deep saucepan (see Note) and bring to a boil over medium-high heat, stirring until the sugar is dissolved. Remove the glaze from the heat and set aside to cool to room temperature, about 30 minutes.

3. Add the eggs to the cooled glaze, stirring gently to coat. Set aside to marinate for 30 minutes.

4. Preheat the grill to high.

5. Heat the oil to 350°F in a small skillet (test by adding a piece of shallot; the oil bubbles should dance). Add the shallots and fry until golden brown and crisp, about 2 minutes. Using a slotted spoon, remove the shallots to paper towels to drain.

6. When ready to cook the eggs, remove the eggs from the marinade and thread lengthwise on the skewers, 3 to a skewer. If you are working with egg quarters, gently bring the skewer lengthwise through both the white and the yolk. Oil the grill grate, arrange the satés on the hot grate, and grill, basting with the glaze and turning once with tongs, until the eggs are heated through, 2 to 4 minutes per side. Sprinkle the satés with the fried shallots and serve immediately.

Makes 24 pieces; serves 4 to 8 as an appetizer

Note: The saucepan must be large enough to later hold the eggs but narrow enough so the eggs will be covered by the glaze.

FIRE-CHARRED TOMATO SOUP

U . S . A .

METHOD:
Direct grilling

This smoky tomato soup is a long way from the canned version we're all so familiar with. The charred flavor of the vegetables is reinforced by the fire-toasted ancho chile (the dried version of a poblano chile) and the soup is delectable both hot and cold.

Note that I've made wood chips—not soaked this time—optional. You'll get a richer, smokier flavor if you use them, but the soup will be perfectly delicious even if you don't. Do use the most gorgeous fresh, ripe tomatoes you can find. The results will be well worth the search.

SPECIAL EQUIPMENT:
1 long metal skewer

1 cup dry (unsoaked) wood chips (optional)

4 large fresh, ripe tomatoes (about 3 pounds)
2 medium onions, quartered
2 medium red bell peppers
4 tablespoons extra-virgin olive oil
Salt and freshly ground black pepper, to taste
1 ancho chile (or 2 if you like spicy food) or other large dried chile, such as pasilla
7 cups homemade vegetable or chicken stock canned or low-sodium broth, or more as needed
3 cloves garlic, minced
1 tablespoon balsamic vinegar, or more to taste
1 tablespoon honey, or more to taste
3 tablespoons mixed chopped fresh herbs, such as basil, thyme, chives, and/or Italian (flat-leaf) parsley
½ cup plain yogurt, preferably whole milk, or sour cream

1. *If using a gas grill:* Place the wood chips (if using) in the smoker box. Preheat the grill, gas or charcoal, to high.

2. Cut the tomatoes crosswise into 1-inch-thick slices, cutting out the stem ends. Thread the onion wedges onto a long metal skewer. Brush the tomato slices, onion wedges, and peppers generously with oil, using half of it, and season with salt and pepper.

3. When ready to cook, *if using a charcoal grill,* toss the wood chips (if using) on the coals. *For both methods:* Oil the grill grate. Arrange the tomatoes, onion skewer, and peppers on the hot grate and grill, turning the onion skewer and peppers with tongs and the tomato slices with a spatula, until the vegetables are nicely charred all over. The bell peppers will take the longest, 15 to 20 minutes, the tomatoes the shortest, about 8 minutes in all. As they are done, transfer to a platter to cool.

4. Place the ancho chile on the grate and toast quickly, about 20 seconds per side, just until it becomes smoky and brittle. Take care not to let it burn.

5. Using a paring knife, scrape the charred skin off the onions and peppers (don't worry about removing every last bit). Cut the onions into thin crosswise slices: stem and seed the peppers.

6. Crumble the toasted chile into a small saucepan with 1 cup of the stock. Heat over medium heat until warm, then remove from the heat and let soak until soft, about 5 minutes.

7. Heat the remaining 2 tablespoons oil in a large saucepan over medium heat. Add the garlic and onion and cook until lightly browned, about 5 minutes. Stir in the tomatoes, peppers, remaining 6 cups stock, 1 tablespoon vinegar, 1 tablespoon honey, the chile and its soaking liquid, and salt and pepper. Simmer the soup for 5 minutes. If it seems too thick, add a little more stock.

8. Transfer the soup to a blender and process to a smooth purée, then return it to the saucepan, pressing it through a strainer if necessary to remove any remaining pieces of charred skin. Stir in 2 tablespoons of the herbs and salt and pepper to taste. If a sharper soup is desired, add a little more vinegar; a sweeter soup, a little more honey.

9. To serve, ladle the soup into bowls. Top each serving with a dollop of yogurt and sprinkle with the remaining herbs.

Serves 8 as a first course

GRILLED CORN CHOWDER

U.S.A.

METHOD:
Direct grilling

**SPECIAL
EQUIPMENT:**
*1 cup wood
chips, soaked for
1 hour in cold
water to cover
and drained*

If you like a smoky flavor and you like chowder, you'll love this grilled corn chowder—especially if you grill the corn with wood chips. The open flame seems to intensify the sweetness of all the vegetables.

3 ears of corn, shucked
1 medium onion, peeled and quartered
    (but the root ends left on)
1 medium green bell pepper or poblano chile
1 medium red bell pepper
2 tablespoons olive oil or melted butter, or
    more as needed
Salt and freshly ground black pepper, to taste
2 medium all-purpose potatoes, peeled and
    cut into ¼-inch dice
2 tablespoons all-purpose flour
½ teaspoon fresh thyme leaves or
    ¼ teaspoon dried
4 cups homemade chicken or vegetable
    stock or low-sodium canned broth
1 bay leaf
¾ cup heavy cream or half-and-half
2 tablespoons chopped fresh Italian (flat-leaf)
    parsley, for garnish (optional)

    1. *If using a gas grill:* Place the chips in the smoker box. Preheat the grill, gas or charcoal, to high.

    2. When ready to cook, *if using charcoal,* toss the wood chips on the coals. *For both methods:* Brush the corn, onion, and pep-pers with a little oil and season with salt and pepper. Arrange the vegetables on the hot grate and grill, turning with tongs, until nice-ly charred on all sides, 16 to 20 minutes for the bell peppers, 10 to 12 minutes for the onion quarters, and 8 to 12 minutes for the corn. As they cook, baste the vegetables with additional oil and sprinkle with salt and pepper, removing the vegetables as they are done to a platter to cool.

    3. Cut the corn kernels off the cobs and place in a large saucepan. Using a paring knife, scrape the charred skins off the peppers and onions (don't worry about remov-ing every last bit). Stem and seed the peppers and cut into ¼-inch dice; cut the onion quarters into thin crosswise slices, discarding the roots. Add the peppers and onion to the corn in the saucepan.

    4. Stir the diced potatoes, flour, and thyme into the vegetables and cook the mix-ture over medium-high heat for 2 minutes, stirring frequently to prevent burning. Add the stock and bay leaf and bring to a boil, then reduce the heat to low and cook, uncov-ered, at a gentle simmer until the potatoes are cooked, 8 to 10 minutes. Stir in the cream and cook for 2 minutes longer. Season with salt and pepper and remove from the heat. Remove and discard the bay leaf.

    5. Spoon the chowder into bowls, sprin-kle with the parsley (if using), and serve immediately.

GRILLED GAZPACHO

SPAIN

METHOD:
Direct grilling

Gazpacho is Spain's culinary life blood, a refreshing purée of vegetables that blurs the distinction between soup and salad. Grilling adds a smoky dimen-sion that transforms this warm-weather soup from the realm of refreshing to unforgettable. If using a food processor, purée the vegetables first, then add the liquids.

SPECIAL EQUIPMENT: *2 long bamboo skewers, soaked for 1 hour in cold water to cover and drained*

4 scallions, both white and green parts, trimmed
2 cloves garlic, peeled
1 medium red onion, peeled and quartered (but root ends left on)
1/3 cup extra-virgin olive oil
2 slices (each 3/4 inch) country-style white bread or French bread
5 fresh, ripe medium tomatoes (about 2 1/2 pounds)
1 medium red bell pepper
1 medium green bell pepper
1 medium cucumber, peeled
1/4 cup mixed chopped fresh herbs, such as basil, oregano, tarragon, and/or Italian (flat-leaf) parsley
2 tablespoons red wine vinegar, or more to taste
1/2 to 1 cup cold water, or more as needed
Salt and freshly ground black pepper, to taste

1. Preheat the grill to high.

2. Finely chop the scallion greens and set aside for garnish. Thread the scallion whites crosswise on a skewer and add the garlic cloves. Thread the onion quarters on a second skewer. Lightly brush the scallion whites, garlic, and onion quarters with about a tablespoon of the oil.

3. When ready to cook, oil the grill grate. Place the skewers on the hot grate and grill, turning with tongs, until the vegetables are nicely browned, 4 to 8 minutes in all. Transfer to a plate to cool. Add the bread slices to the grate and grill until darkly toasted, 1 to 2 minutes per side. Set aside. Grill the tomatoes and bell peppers until the skins are nicely charred, about 8 to 12 minutes in all for the tomatoes, 16 to 20 minutes for the peppers. Transfer to a platter to cool. Using a paring knife, scrape the charred skins off the tomatoes, onions, and peppers (don't worry about removing every last bit). Core and seed the peppers.

4. Cut the scallion whites, garlic, onions, toast, tomatoes, bell peppers, and cucumber into 1 inch pieces. Place the pieces in a blender, adding the tomatoes first, along with the herbs, 2 tablespoons vinegar, and the remaining oil. Process to a smooth purée. Thin the gazpacho to pourable consistency with water as needed, and season with salt and pepper.

5. The gazpacho can be served now, but it will taste even better if you chill it for an hour or so to allow the flavors to blend. Just before serving, correct the seasoning, adding salt or vinegar as necessary. To serve, ladle the gazpacho into bowls and sprinkle with the chopped scallion greens.

Serves 8 as a first course

Blazing Salads

Produce arrives by boat at a floating market in Thailand.

As you travel the world's barbecue trail, you come to recognize certain constants. Consider the pairing of grilled meats with salads. Every culture has a selection of salads that are traditionally served with barbecue, from the *kimchis* (pickled salads) that accompany Korean grilled meats to the lavish salad bars (sometimes four dozen different items) found at Brazilian *churrascarias* (barbecue restaurants). Most of these salads are served cold as side dishes (their cool crunch counterpoints the sizzle of the grilled fare), but many are cooked and served hot.

No ingredient is beyond a diehard grill jockey. In this chapter, you'll find recipes for Grilled Eggplant, Tomato, and Pepper Salad, for a Thai grilled pork salad flavored with roasted rice and chiles, and for grilled chicken salads from both India and Iran. And you'll learn how to prepare a classic *salade niçoise* (well, not so classic, as it calls for fresh tuna, not canned) on the grill.

You'll also encounter some of the traditional salad platters that accompany Turkish, Mexican, Indonesian, and Lebanese barbecue. They may not be grilled, but are a must alongside dishes that are flame-cooked. If all this sounds too exotic, there's a potato salad that would do a good old North American barbecue proud.

On the Grill

GRILLED EGGPLANT, TOMATO, AND PEPPER SALAD
Fasouli

METHOD:
Direct grilling

Love of barbecue cuts across race, nationality, and economic class. Some of my best informants have been taxi drivers, most of whom seem to come from other countries. This recipe was inspired by a conversation with an Armenian cabbie in Philadelphia. He called it *fasouli,* which he said means "crazy" or "all mixed up." He preferred to remain anonymous, so wherever he is, thanks for the tip.

The salad can be prepared up to a day ahead of time, but correct the seasoning just before serving.

1 medium eggplant (about 1 pound)
1 large green bell pepper
1 large red bell pepper
1 pound fresh, ripe plum tomatoes
½ cup finely chopped onion
2 cloves garlic, minced
3 tablespoons extra-virgin olive oil
2 tablespoons red wine vinegar, or
    more to taste
½ cup coarsely chopped fresh Italian
    (flat-leaf) parsley
Salt and freshly ground black pepper,
    to taste

1. Preheat the grill to high.

2. When ready to cook, place the eggplant on the hot grate, and grill, turning with tongs as needed, until very soft and charred all over and the flesh is very soft. This will take 20 to 30 minutes. Char the peppers and tomatoes the same way, 16 to 20 minutes for the peppers, about 8 minutes for the tomatoes (see Note). Transfer the charred vegetables to a cutting board to cool.

3. Cut the stem end from the eggplant, then scrape the charred skin off the eggplant, peppers, and tomatoes with a paring knife. Stem and seed the peppers and core the tomatoes. Cut the vegetables into 1-inch cubes or squares and transfer to a serving bowl. Stir in the onion, garlic, oil, 2 tablespoons vinegar, parsley, salt, and pepper. Correct the seasoning, adding salt or vinegar as necessary; the salad should be highly seasoned. Serve immediately or cover and refrigerate for up to 24 hours before serving.

Serves 4 to 6

Note: Cook the tomatoes enough to blister the skins, but not so much that they become soft. The centers should remain firm.

SPANISH GRILLED VEGETABLE SALAD
Escalivada

SPAIN

METHOD:
Direct grilling

GRILLING VEGETABLES
When scraping the blackened skins from the grilled vegetables, don't worry about removing every last bit of charred skin. A little bit left on adds flavor.

Escalivada (sometimes spelled *escalibada*) is a Catalan grilled vegetable salad. (*Escalivar* means, in Catalan, "to cook in hot ashes.") At a minimum, the vegetables would include onions, red bell peppers, and eggplant, with a generous drizzle of fruity Spanish olive oil. A more elaborate version might include leeks, scallions, celery, and tomatoes, topped with a proper vinaigrette. Traditionally, the vegetables are grilled whole and sliced into thin strips for serving, but you get a richer smoke flavor by preslicing the onions and eggplant. It's customary to display the vegetables separately on a plate, but you can also toss them together—making a great topping for grilled bread.

FOR THE VEGETABLES:
1 large onion
1 large or 2 small long, slender eggplants
    (about 1 pound)
1 bunch leeks (the smallest, tenderest
    you can find)
1 bunch scallions
2 medium red bell peppers
4 medium ribs celery
2 tablespoons extra-virgin olive oil,
    preferably Spanish
Salt and freshly ground black pepper, to taste

FOR THE VINAIGRETTE:
2 tablespoons sherry vinegar or red wine
    vinegar, or more to taste
½ teaspoon salt, or more to taste
⅓ cup extra-virgin olive oil, preferably Spanish
3 tablespoons finely chopped fresh Italian
    (flat-leaf) parsley
Freshly ground black pepper, to taste
Lemon wedges, for serving

1. Preheat the grill to high.

2. Peel the onion, leaving the root end intact, then cut through the root into 6 or 8 wedges. Cut the eggplant on the diagonal into ¼-inch slices. Trim the leeks of the dark greens and roots, leaving only the white portion, then cut lengthwise in half and rinse well. Blot the leeks dry with paper towels. Trim the roots off the scallions. Brush the vegetables generously with olive oil and season with salt and pepper.

3. When ready to cook, arrange the vegetables, including the bell peppers and celery, on the hot grate and grill, turning with tongs, until nicely browned, about 12 minutes in all. Transfer the vegetables as they are done to a cutting board to cool.

4. When cool enough to handle, cut the roots off the onion wedges and thinly slice the onions crosswise. Cut the eggplant slices into ¼-inch slivers. Scrape any burnt skin off the peppers, then stem, seed, and thinly slice. Cut the leeks, scallions, and celery into thin crosswise slices. Arrange the vegetable slices in separate piles on plates or a platter.

5. Prepare the vinaigrette. Whisk together the vinegar and salt in a small bowl until the salt is dissolved. Whisk in the olive oil, parsley, and pepper (and additional salt, if needed) to taste. Spoon the vinaigrette over the vegetables and serve with lemon wedges.

Serves 4 to 6

LEBANESE EGGPLANT SALAD
Salafat el Rahab

LEBANON

METHOD:
Direct grilling

Eggplant has a wonderful ability to absorb the smoky flavors of the grill—a truth appreciated by cooks throughout the Middle East. The contrast of charred eggplant and fresh tomato produces an amazingly flavorful salad. I like to use small Italian-style eggplants, which cook through more quickly than the large American eggplants. If the only thing available is the latter, try to find a long, relatively thin eggplant.

3 to 4 small (Italian-style) eggplants or
    1 regular eggplant (about 1 pound in all)
2 fresh, ripe medium tomatoes, seeded
    (see box, page 62) and cut into
    ¼-inch dice
1 bunch fresh Italian (flat-leaf) parsley,
    stemmed and thinly sliced (about ¾ cup)
2 scallions, both white and green parts,
    trimmed and finely chopped
1 clove garlic, minced (optional)
2 tablespoons extra-virgin olive oil, or
    more to taste
2 tablespoons fresh lemon juice, or
    more to taste
Salt and freshly ground black pepper,
    to taste

1. Preheat the grill to high.

2. When ready to cook, place the eggplants on the hot grate and grill until charred all over and the flesh is very soft, turning with tongs as needed. This will take 15 to 20 minutes for small eggplants; up to 30 minutes for large. Transfer the eggplants to a cutting board to cool.

3. Cut the stem ends from the eggplants and scrape off the burnt skin with a paring knife. Cut the flesh into ¼-inch dice and transfer to a serving bowl. Stir in the tomatoes, parsley, scallions, garlic (if using), 2 tablespoons olive oil, 2 tablespoons lemon juice, salt, and pepper. Taste for seasoning, adding more olive oil if the salad seems too dry and salt or lemon juice as necessary; the salad should be highly seasoned.

Serves 4

MOROCCAN EGGPLANT SALAD
Salade d'Aubergines

MOROCCO

METHOD:
Direct grilling

Like many Moroccan salads, this one is traditionally made by frying the eggplant in oil. I've lightened the recipe by charring the eggplant on the grill. In Morocco you'd use small eggplants, but larger, American-style eggplants work well, too. (Increase the cooking time for the latter.) If you're used to Middle Eastern–style eggplant salads, you'll find that the addition of cumin, paprika, and white pepper lends a delectable North African accent to this one.

4 to 6 small (Italian-style) eggplants or
   2 regular eggplants (1½ pounds in all)
3 tablespoons extra-virgin olive oil
3 tablespoons chopped fresh Italian
   (flat-leaf) parsley
2 tablespoons fresh lemon juice, or
   more to taste
1 clove garlic, minced
½ teaspoon ground cumin
½ teaspoon paprika
½ teaspoon freshly ground white pepper
½ teaspoon salt, or more to taste

1. Preheat the grill to medium.

2. When ready to cook, brush the eggplants with about ½ tablespoon of the oil, then place on the hot grate and grill until charred all over and the flesh is very soft, turning with tongs as needed. The whole process will take 15 to 20 minutes for small eggplants; up to 30 minutes for large. Transfer the eggplants to a cutting board to cool.

3. Cut the stem ends from the eggplants and scrape off the charred skin with a paring knife, then finely chop the flesh and transfer to a serving bowl. Stir in the remaining oil, the parsley, 2 tablespoons lemon juice, garlic, cumin, paprika, pepper, and ½ teaspoon salt. Taste for seasoning, adding salt or lemon juice as necessary; the salad should be highly seasoned. Serve at room temperature.

Serves 4

GRILLED ZUCCHINI SALAD

MOROCCO

ON THE SIDE:
Direct grilling

Here's a North American twist on a traditional Moroccan salad. Moroccans would fry the zucchini, but I like the robust flavor imparted by grilling. In Morocco it's customary to serve four to six different salads. Try matching this with the Moroccan Eggplant Salad and the Armenian Grilled Eggplant, Tomato, and Pepper Salad (also in this chapter).

4 small or 3 medium zucchini (about
   1 pound in all), scrubbed and
   trimmed
3 tablespoons extra-virgin olive oil
Salt and freshly ground black pepper,
   to taste
12 large fresh mint leaves, slivered, or
   1 teaspoon dried
2 tablespoons finely chopped fresh
   Italian (flat-leaf) parsley
1 tablespoon fresh lemon juice, or
   more to taste
1 clove garlic, minced
½ teaspoon paprika
¼ teaspoon ground cumin
¼ teaspoon freshly ground white pepper, or
   more to taste

1. Preheat the grill to high.

2. Cut the zucchini into ¼-inch lengthwise slices. Brush each slice with oil (you'll need about 1 tablespoon in all) and season with salt and pepper.

3. When ready to cook, arrange the zucchini slices on the hot grate and grill, turning with tongs, until tender and well browned, 10 minutes in all. Transfer to a cutting board to cool.

4. Cut each zucchini slice crosswise on the diagonal into ¼-inch strips. Transfer the strips to a serving bowl and stir in the remaining 2 tablespoons oil, the mint, parsley, 1 tablespoon lemon juice, garlic, paprika, cumin, and ¼ teaspoon white pepper. Taste for seasoning, adding salt, white pepper, or lemon juice as necessary; the salad should be highly seasoned. Serve at room temperature.

Serves 4

GRILLED VEGETABLE CAPONATA

ITALY

METHOD:
Direct grilling

Caponata is Sicily's answer to Russia's eggplant caviar—a cross between a dip and a salad made with sautéed eggplants, peppers, and other vegetables, invigorated with olives, capers, and pine nuts. It's just the sort of dish that can be electrified by grilling. Caponata can be served by itself as an antipasto, salad, or side dish, and it would be delicious as a topping for *bruschetta*. The one unexpected ingredient in this recipe—cocoa powder—adds a pleasant, bittersweet flavor.

The caponata will keep for a week; just be sure to reseason it before serving.

2 long, slender eggplants (about
　　1½ pounds in all)
8 cloves garlic, peeled and cut
　　lengthwise in half
2 fresh, ripe medium tomatoes
2 medium onions, peeled and cut in
　　quarters (leave on the root ends)
2 medium ribs celery, trimmed
1 medium red bell pepper
1 medium green bell pepper
5 tablespoons extra-virgin olive oil, or as needed
Salt and freshly ground black pepper,
　　to taste
3 tablespoons chopped fresh Italian
　　(flat-leaf) parsley
2 tablespoons pine nuts, toasted
　　(see box, page 93)
2 tablespoons drained capers
2 tablespoons chopped pitted olives
　　(green or black—your choice)
2 tablespoon balsamic vinegar, or
　　more to taste
1½ teaspoons unsweetened cocoa powder

1. Preheat the grill to high.
2. Make 8 slits in each eggplant with the tip of a paring knife and insert a half clove of garlic in each. Lightly brush the eggplants, tomatoes, onions, celery, and bell peppers with oil, using about 2 tablespoons, and season with salt and pepper.

3. When ready to cook, arrange the vegetables on the hot grate. Grill the eggplants until the skin is charred all over and the flesh is very soft, 20 to 30 minutes, turning with tongs as needed. Grill the tomatoes, turning with tongs, until the skin is black and blistered, 8 to 12 minutes. Grill the onions, celery, and peppers the same way; these will take 10 to 20 minutes in all. Transfer the vegetables as they are done to a cutting board to cool.

4. Scrape the charred skin off the vegetables with a paring knife. Remove the stem end from the eggplants and coarsely chop the flesh. Core the tomatoes, then cut crosswise in half, wring out the seeds, and coarsely chop the flesh. Thinly slice the onions, first cutting off the root ends, and celery. Core, seed, and thinly slice the peppers. Transfer the vegetables to a serving bowl.

5. Stir in 3 tablespoons oil, the parsley, pine nuts, capers, olives, 2 tablespoons vinegar, the cocoa powder, and salt and pepper. Toss well to mix. Taste for seasoning, adding salt or vinegar as necessary; the caponata should be highly seasoned. Serve at room temperature.

Serves 6 as an appetizer, 4 as a salad

SPICY THAI GRILLED BEEF SALAD
Yam Nua Yang

THAILAND

METHOD:
Direct grilling

ADVANCE PREPARATION:
2 to 8 hours for marinating the meat

This recipe is modeled on Thailand's famous *yam nua yang,* grilled beef salad. I can't think of a better starter or light main course on a warm summer day. The combination of flavors—fiery chiles, fragrant mint, ginger, and garlic—is explosive . . . and addictive. As in other recipes, I offer a range of chiles: one for the tender of tongue and six (or more) for the pyromaniac. Sometimes the salad is topped with roasted rice powder (see box, page 80) instead of peanuts.

FOR THE BEEF AND MARINADE:
1 flank steak (1¼ to 1½ pounds)
3 tablespoons soy sauce
2 tablespoons Asian fish sauce
2 tablespoons sugar
3 cloves garlic, minced
1 tablespoon minced fresh ginger

FOR THE DRESSING:
3 cloves garlic
1 to 6 Thai, bird, seranno, or
    jalapeño chiles, thinly sliced
    (for a milder dressing, seed the chiles)
1½ tablespoons sugar
3 tablespoons Asian fish sauce
3 tablespoons fresh lemon juice

TO FINISH THE SALAD:
1 head Boston or Bibb lettuce, separated into
    leaves, rinsed, and spun dry
1 cucumber, peeled and thinly sliced
1 small sweet onion, such as Maui or
    Vidalia, very thinly sliced
12 cherry tomatoes, cut in half
12 fresh mint leaves (optional)
¼ cup fresh cilantro leaves
¼ cup coarsely chopped dry-roasted peanuts

1. Lightly score the flank steak in a crosshatch pattern, making the cuts ¼ inch deep. Place the meat in a glass baking dish. Combine the soy sauce, fish sauce, sugar, garlic, and ginger in a mixing bowl and whisk until the sugar dissolves. Pour this mixture over the steak and let marinate, covered, in the refrigerator for at least 2 hours or as long as 8, turning several times.

2. Preheat the grill to high.

3. Prepare the dressing. Grind the garlic, chiles, and sugar to a paste in a mortar with a pestle. Work in the fish sauce and lemon juice. Alternatively, the dressing ingredients can be puréed in a blender.

4. Prepare the salad. Line a platter with the lettuce leaves and arrange the cucumber slices, onion, cherry tomatoes, and mint leaves (if using) on top.

5. When ready to cook, drain the steak. Oil the grill grate, then place the steak on the hot grate and grill until cooked to taste (4 to 6 minutes per side for medium-rare), using tongs to turn. Transfer the steak to a cutting board and let cool slightly or completely. The salad can be served warm or at room temperature. Thinly slice the steak across the grain on the diagonal. Spoon the dressing over the salad and arrange the beef slices on top. Sprinkle with the cilantro and roasted peanuts and serve.

Serves 4

A Tale of Three Barbecues: The Thai Grill

This is a tale of one city—and three barbecues. The first embodies the privileged world of Somerset Maugham, of the jet-setting gentry that frequents one of Asia's grandest hotels. The second and third reflect a more realistic style of Third World dining. All three take place in Thailand's political and cultural capital: Bangkok. And all reflect the Thai love of explosive flavors and their profound reverence for food.

Curiously, I did not think of Thailand as one of the world's great barbecue centers. There isn't a single great barbecued dish in Thailand's pantheon of culinary masterpieces. There's no Thai equivalent to Brazilian *churrasco,* to Italian *bistecca alla fiorentina,* to Persian *chelow kebab,* or American ribs.

Yet everywhere I went in Thailand, I experienced grilling—on the beaches of Samui Island, in the highlands of Chaing Mai, on the crowded streets and back alleys of Bangkok. So strong is the Thai love of *yaang* (live-fire cooking), they reserve it not just for special occasions, but for everyday fare.

Everyday fare? Well that's a mundane way to describe my first experience with Thai grilling: the riverside barbecue at the Oriental Hotel. The Oriental is one of those pleasure palaces built in the last century, on the banks of the Chao Prya River. Joseph Conrad resided there; so did Herman Melville and Somerset Maugham. My room in the Writers Wing was a veritable two-story townhouse, with every architectural amenity and electronic convenience known to modern man.

But what had my jaw dropping was a torchlit barbecue on the riverside terrace. Seated at a pink granite table with teak chairs, I was surrounded by pedestal globe lights entwined with bougainvillaea. Here a whiff of frangipani, there the perfume of jasmine. The longtail boats skimming the Chao Prya River seemed close enough to touch.

As with everything at the Oriental, barbecue is done in a grandiose way, with banks of grills and a buffet line stretching a good fifty feet. There's a seafood station that fairly sparkles with spiny lobsters, slipper lobsters, fresh and salt water prawns, and a fishmonger's assortment of fish, neatly bedded in ice. There are poultry and meat stations, where chicken, duck, squab, beef, and pork emerge sizzling from the grills.

But despite the fancy surroundings, the basic preparations are really quite simple. The marinades are variations on a mixture of fish sauce *(nam*

pla), lime juice, sugar, and garlic. The accompanying table sauces range from a mild, sweet lemon-honey-garlic sauce to an incendiary tincture of chiles, shallots, and fish sauce. I could spend a couple of paragraphs describing the side dishes—the salad spreads, elaborate carved fruit displays, dessert stations where young women in sarongs cook coconut cakes called *kenoms.* But what really impressed me was the straightforwardness of the grilled fare, the elegant simplicity of the fish.

THE HAWKERS' CENTER

A few days later, I experienced a similar barbecue in a considerably different setting: a hawkers' center on a tiny side street off traffic-clogged Silom Road. Hawkers' centers are where ordinary Thais eat—a motley assortment of food stalls and pushcarts selling every imaginable Thai street food, from stir-fries and soups to noodle dishes, like *pad thai.* The air was thick with smoke from charcoal braziers.

I stopped at the cart of a tiny woman for a popular local snack, squid on a stick. She fished the tiny sea creature from a jar where it was marinating in an aromatic mixture of fish sauce, lime juice, palm sugar, garlic, chiles, and lemongrass. The squid went onto a tiny skewer for a two-minute sizzle over the coals. It was sweet, salty, tender, smoky, and absolutely delicious. These, of course are the same flavors I experienced at the Oriental. But this feast cost all of 10 baht (about 45 cents).

It's no accident that fish sauce is a recurring theme in Thai barbecue. This malodorous condiment—made from salted, fermented anchovies—is as essential to Thai cooking as soy sauce is to Japanese and Chinese. Fish sauce has a wonderful way of reinforcing the briny flavor of seafood. I suppose this is the reason it's so popular in Thailand as a marinade and dip for grilled fish.

BARBECUE IN ESARN

Talk to Thais long enough about barbecue and you'll hear the name Esarn. The term refers to both a region and a people: the province in northeastern Thailand adjacent to the Laotian and Cambodian borders, whose inhabitants are of Lao descent.

According to my guide, Nilcharoen Prasertsak, the Esarn became masters of grilling by simple economic necessity. They couldn't afford the oil necessary for stir-frying. So they turned to cooking food over the one commodity even the poor in Thailand have plenty of—coconut shell charcoal. Esarn street vendors are famous throughout Thailand for their *gai yaang* (grilled chicken) and *pla yaang* (grilled fish).

And that is why my next destination was an Esarn neighborhood in the Dusit District of Bangkok. There houses open directly onto the sidewalks, women sit crosslegged, washing dishes, clothes, and children in plastic tubs on the ground. Sun filters through the leaves of scraggly trees, and mangy

dogs lie in the middle of the street. The scene is more reminiscent of a village in the jungle than of an Asian metropolis with seven million inhabitants.

To judge from the smoke in the air, I was certainly in barbecue central. Every square foot of sidewalk seemed to be devoted to some sort of culinary activity. On one street corner a man fanned a charcoal fire that was blazing in a hub cap. Elsewhere, women were pounding garlic and spices in mortars with pestles and shredding green papayas to make a crunchy, fiery Esarn salad called *som tum.*

My destination was Raan Khun Noi (Mr. Noi's Restaurant), located at 52 Sukhantharam Road. It was clearly a class joint—you could tell by the flashing jukebox. There were also a framed picture of the King of Thailand, plastic chairs, and pink-clothed tables, and scrawny kittens foraging for scraps on the floor. There was even air conditioning—a rare luxury in these parts—although there was a 5 baht charge per person for the management to turn it on.

Mr. Noi specializes in the sort of simple but pungent fare for which the Esarn are famous: a *som tum* so laced with chiles, it all but melts your molars; an oxtail soup that soothes your soul while it scorches your gullet; a spatchcocked grilled chicken, all smoky and crisp, redolent with cilantro and garlic. As with most Esarn grilled meats, the chicken was accompanied with a platter of cabbage and celery leaves, basil sprigs, and green beans. The sticky rice came Laotian-style, steamed in a hollow length of bamboo. I devoured it Esarn style—with my fingers.

Despite dubious hygienic conditions, there was such good will and warm hospitality on the part of the staff, I decided to eat whatever was put in front of me. I survived without so much as a hiccough, but I'm not sure I would risk it again.

THAI SATES

Incidentally, there's one grilled dish you don't have to risk your gastrointestinal track to enjoy, a dish you'll find wherever you go in Thailand—high-style restaurant or down home street stall—which is all the more curious, because the dish was invented in a country a thousand miles away: Indonesia. I'm talking, of course, about saté.

Named for the Javanese word meaning to "stick" or "skewer," saté consists of tiny pieces of chicken, pork, or other meats grilled on tiny bamboo skewers. Saté has become quite popular in North America, but nothing here can rival the tiny size and delicate flavor of Thai satés. The sweet soy sauce marinade of Java has given way to a fish sauce–coconut milk mixture. (The oil-rich coconut milk keeps the meat from drying out.) Thai saté is traditionally accompanied by a creamy peanut sauce and a tangy cucumber salad.

Thai barbecue makes the perfect alternative to the meat-laden cookouts of the West. Seafood and vegetables play a major role in Thai grilling. When meats are eaten, it's in small quantities, with a high proportion of vegetables and rice. But even if this is not a concern, you can't beat the dynamic flavors of the Thai grill.

GRILLED PORK WITH A SWEET-TART DRESSING

Pork Laab

METHOD:
Direct grilling

ADVANCE PREPARATION:
1 to 2 hours for marinating the meat

Laab (sometimes written *larb*) refers to a family of Thai salads made with grilled meats, crisp vegetables, and explosively flavored seasonings. This one features pork, which is marinated in a pungent mixture of fish sauce and garlic and grilled just prior to serving.

Roasted rice powder gives the salad a nutty flavor and gritty-crunchy consistency much prized by Southeast Asians. If it seems like too much trouble to make, the salad is still amazingly tasty without it. (Or you could use coarsely chopped peanuts in its place.) As elsewhere in this book, I've called for a range of chiles. A Thai would use the full six—or even more.

FOR THE PORK AND MARINADE/DRESSING:
1 pork tenderloin or 2 pork chops
    (about 8 ounces)
¼ cup Asian fish sauce
¼ cup fresh lime juice
2 tablespoons firmly packed light brown
    sugar or honey
3 cloves garlic, minced
½ teaspoon freshly ground black pepper

FOR THE SALAD:
1 cucumber, peeled, seeded (see box,
    page 90), and thinly sliced
2 cups thinly sliced napa cabbage or
    iceberg lettuce
1 cup mung bean sprouts
2 shallots, sliced paper-thin
1 to 6 Thai, jalapeño, or serrano chiles,
    thinly sliced (for a milder salad,
    seed the chiles)

How to Make Rice Powder

Set a dry skillet over medium heat. Add ¼ cup rice and heat until the grains are lightly toasted and just beginning to brown, shaking the pan to ensure even cooking, 2 to 3 minutes. (Note that the rice will crackle when toasting.) Transfer the rice to a bowl to cool, then grind it to a fine powder in a spice mill or blender. You should end up with ⅓ cup rice powder.

2 scallions, both white and green parts,
    trimmed and thinly sliced
¼ cup fresh mint leaves, plus a few
    whole sprigs for garnish
¼ cup fresh basil leaves
¼ cup fresh cilantro leaves (or more
    mint or basil)
2 tablespoons rice powder, for garnish
    (optional; see box above)

1. Trim any sinew or large pieces of fat off the pork. Combine the ingredients for the marinade/dressing in a medium-size bowl and stir until the sugar is dissolved. Transfer half of this mixture to a second bowl for the dressing. Add the pork to the remainder and let marinate, covered, in the refrigerator for 1 to 2 hours, turning the meat several times.

2. About 45 minutes before serving, preheat the grill to medium-high.

3. When ready to cook, drain the pork and blot dry. Reserve the marinade. Oil the grill grate, then place the pork on the hot grate. Grill the pork until cooked, 6 to 8 minutes per side for a tenderloin, 3 to 6 minutes per side for chops, using tongs to turn and basting only the first side with any excess marinade. When cooked, the internal temperature should be 160°F on an instant-read meat thermometer. Transfer the pork to a cutting board and let rest for 5 minutes.

4. Meanwhile, add the cucumber, napa cabbage, bean sprouts, shallots, chiles, scallions, mint, basil, and cilantro to the dressing in the bowl and toss gently but thoroughly to mix. Mound the salad on plates or a platter. Thinly slice the pork on the diagonal and fan out the slices on top of the salads. Sprinkle the salads with the rice powder (if using), garnish with mint sprigs, and serve immediately.

Serves 4 to 6

PERSIAN CHICKEN SALAD WITH PICKLES AND OLIVES

IRAN

METHOD:
Direct grilling

ADVANCE PREPARATION:
Chicken must be grilled ahead of time

Here's a great way to use up leftover grilled chicken. I first tasted it at a fine Persian restaurant in New York called Persepolis. The combination of chicken and potatoes in a salad is as delectable as it's unexpected.

1 pound large red-skinned potatoes
2 large eggs
Salt, to taste
2 cups finely diced (¼ inch) cold grilled chicken
3 tablespoons finely chopped cornichons or dill pickles
2 medium ribs celery, very finely diced
1 tablespoons chopped pitted green olives
6 tablespoons mayonnaise
2 tablespoons chopped fresh dill, plus a few sprigs for garnish
Freshly ground black pepper, to taste
8 lettuce leaves, rinsed and spun dry, for serving
2 fresh, ripe medium tomatoes, thinly sliced, for garnish
12 black olives, preferably oil-cured, for garnish

1. Place the potatoes and eggs in a pot of cold salted water and bring to a boil over medium heat. Reduce the heat to low and simmer until the potatoes are tender (they will be easy to pierce with a skewer) and the eggs are hard cooked; 11 minutes should do it (see Note). Drain the potatoes and eggs in a colander and rinse under cold water until cool. Drain well.

2. Cut the potatoes into ¼-inch dice, then place in a large bowl. Add the chicken, pickles, celery, olives, mayonnaise, and chopped dill and toss gently but thoroughly to mix. Correct the seasoning, adding salt and pepper to taste. Shell the eggs, cut into ¼-inch dice, and add to the bowl.

3. To serve, line plates or a platter with lettuce leaves. Arrange the tomato slices in a ring around the edge of the plate, overlapping them slightly. Mound the chicken salad in the center and decorate the top with the olives and dill sprigs.

Serves 4

Note: In any case, the eggs will be done after 11 minutes. The potatoes may take longer.

How to Rinse and Dry Cilantro

When it comes to flavoring grilled fare, nothing beats cilantro. The leaves of the coriander plant have an unusually pungent flavor that has endeared it to grill jockeys all over the world.

Once the province of ethnic markets, fresh cilantro is now available in virtually any major supermarket. If you're lucky enough to live in an area with a large Hispanic or Asian community, you may be able to find fresh bunches of cilantro with the roots attached. (The roots are used as a flavoring for marinades and spice pastes throughout Southeast Asia.) Fresh cilantro is often very sandy, so before using it, it's best to give the leaves a good rinsing.

To wash cilantro, hold the bunch by the stems and agitate the leaves in a large bowl of cold water. Change the water once or twice, or until it is free of grit.

To dry cilantro, still holding it by the stems, shake it firmly in a wide arc. (This is best done outdoors, so as not to spatter your walls with water.) Alternatively, shake them (somewhat less enthusiastically) in the sink or blot them dry with paper towels. Or use a salad spinner, once you've plucked off the roots.

To stem cilantro, pluck small sprigs off the large stems. (The small stems are okay to keep and chop.)

To keep leftover cleaned cilantro fresh for later use, loosely wrap it in a moist paper towel and store it in an unsealed plastic bag in the refrigerator. It's important that the bag be unsealed, so that the cilantro leaves can "breathe."

GRILLED CHICKEN SALAD WITH INDIAN SPICES
Murgh Chaat

INDIA

METHOD:
Direct grilling

ADVANCE PREPARATION:
Chicken must be grilled ahead of time

Here's another great way to use up leftover chicken or any grilled chicken. The tangy flavors of cilantro, tomato, and lemon juice make this salad particularly refreshing in the summer.

To be strictly authentic, prepare the salad with a spice mix called *chaat masala*. The mix owes its tartness to the addition of *amchur* (ground green mango) and its sulphury flavor to a mineral called black salt. *Chaat masala* can be bought ready made at an Indian grocery store. Or use the Quick Chaat Mix on the facing page. The flavor won't be quite the same, but the salad will be delectable nonetheless.

1 fresh, ripe medium tomato
½ medium green bell pepper, stemmed and
    seeded
¼ medium red onion
3 cups finely diced (¼ inch) cold grilled
    chicken
¾ cup chopped fresh cilantro
3 tablespoons vegetable oil
3 tablespoons fresh lemon juice, or
    more to taste
½ teaspoon ground cumin
½ teaspoon ground coriander
½ teaspoon freshly ground black pepper
2 teaspoons chaat masala or
    Quick Chaat Mix (recipe follows)
Salt (optional)
Curly leaf lettuce, rinsed and spun dry,
    for serving

1. Cut the tomato, bell pepper, and onion into ¼-inch dice and place in a large bowl with the chicken. Combine the cilantro, oil, 3 tablespoons of the lemon juice, the cumin, coriander, pepper, and half the *chaat masala* in a small bowl and whisk to blend; then pour the mixture over the salad. Toss well to mix and taste the seasoning, adding salt (if using) or lemon juice as necessary; the salad should be highly seasoned.

2. Spoon the salad onto plates lined with lettuce leaves, sprinkle the remaining *chaat masala* over each serving, and serve immediately.

Serves 4

Quick Chaat Mix

Use this as a toasted seasoning mix for grilled chicken or sprinkle it over the *raitas* (yogurt sauces) in this book (see Index).

¼ teaspoon cumin seeds
¼ teaspoon coriander seeds
¼ teaspoon black peppercorns
¼ teaspoon ground ginger
1 teaspoon dried mint leaves
1 teaspoon salt

1. Set a dry skillet over medium heat. Add the cumin seeds, coriander seeds, and peppercorns and heat, shaking the pan occasionally, until the spices are fragrant and toasted, about 2 minutes.

2. Allow the spices to cool, then grind them to a powder in a spice mill. Add the ginger, mint leaves, and salt and continue to grind until finely ground. If not using immediately, store the mixture in a tightly capped small jar in a cool, dry place for up to 2 months.

Makes about 1 tablespoon

GRILLED SALADE NIÇOISE

FRANCE

METHOD:
Direct grilling

This classic salad from Nice is the epitome of Provençal cooking—bright colors and bold flavors in a dish that's refreshing, nourishing, and sustaining. The traditional version is made with boiled vegetables and canned tuna. To make a more interesting salad, I took to grilling fresh tuna instead. It wasn't long before I was grilling the potatoes, onions, and green beans, too.

ADVANCE PREPARATION:
30 minutes for marinating the fish

SPECIAL EQUIPMENT:
Vegetable grate and fish grilling basket (both optional)

Grilling transforms traditional *salade niçoise* into an unforgettable entrée. It's practical, too, as all the ingredients can be grilled ahead. *Haricots verts* are skinny French green beans. Look for them in the produce section of gourmet shops and at specialty greengrocers, or use the skinniest regular green beans you can find.

FOR THE DRESSING:
1 tablespoon fresh lemon juice
2 teaspoons Dijon mustard
1 tablespoon red wine vinegar, or
     more to taste
Salt and freshly ground black pepper, to taste
1 clove garlic, minced
¼ cup extra-virgin olive oil
1 to 2 anchovy fillets, rinsed, blotted dry, and
     finely chopped (optional)
1 tablespoon capers, drained
12 fresh basil leaves, thinly slivered,
     plus 4 to 6 small sprigs for garnish

FOR THE SALAD:
4 fresh tuna steaks (each 6 ounces and
     about 1 inch thick)
4 tablespoons extra-virgin olive oil
2 tablespoons fresh lemon juice
Coarse sea salt and cracked black
     peppercorns, to taste
1 pound small red potatoes, scrubbed
     and cut in half
12 ounces haricots verts or regular green
     beans, ends trimmed
1 large red onion, peeled and cut into
     12 wedges (leave the root ends on)
Salt and freshly ground black pepper, to taste
6 cups mesclun (mixed baby salad greens)
2 large fresh, ripe tomatoes, cut into
     wedges
2 hard-cooked eggs, cut into wedges
⅓ cup niçoise or other black olives, rinsed
     and drained

1. Prepare the dressing. Place the lemon juice, mustard, vinegar, salt, pepper, and garlic in a mixing bowl and whisk until the salt

Mesclun Mix

Mesclun is a mix of baby lettuces and greens, including arugula, oak leaf lettuce, tatsoi, mizuna, mustard greens, and other greens. It is available as a mix at gourmet shops and most supermarkets. But, certainly, you can make your own using the following ingredients (make sure each has been picked young—the leaves should be very small):

Arugula	Mizuna
Bok choy	Mustard greens
Chicory	Spinach
Lettuces	Tatsoi

is dissolved. Whisk in the oil in a thin stream, followed by the anchovies (if using), capers, and basil. Correct the seasoning, adding salt or vinegar as necessary; the dressing should be highly seasoned. Set aside.

2. Place the tuna in a shallow dish with 2 tablespoons olive oil, the lemon juice, salt, and cracked black peppercorns. Turn the fish a couple of times to coat thoroughly with the marinade and let marinate; in the refrigerator, for 30 minutes.

3. Preheat the grill to high.

4. Meanwhile, place the potatoes in a medium-size saucepan with lightly salted water to cover. Bring the potatoes to a boil, reduce the heat, and simmer until just tender, 8 to 10 minutes. Using a slotted spoon, remove the potatoes from the water, refresh under cold running water, and drain again. Return the water in the saucepan to a boil. Add the beans and cook in the rapidly boiling water until crisp-tender, about 1 minute. Drain, refresh under cold running water, and drain again.

5. When ready to cook, if using the vegetable grate, preheat it for 5 minutes. Toss the potatoes, green beans, and onion wedges with the remaining 2 tablespoons oil and season with salt and pepper. Arrange the vegetables on the hot vegetable grate or grill grate and grill until nicely charred on the outside, 3 to 6 minutes per side, using tongs to turn. Transfer to a platter and let cool.

6. Oil the fish grilling basket (if using) or grill grate. Drain the tuna and place it in the basket or on the hot grate; grill until cooked to taste, 4 to 6 minutes per side for medium rare. Transfer the tuna to a cutting board and cut into thin crosswise slices (see Note).

7. Just before serving, mound the mesclun in the center of a large platter and arrange the tomato wedges, beans, potatoes, onion wedges (cut off the bit of root end), hard-cooked eggs, and olives in an attractive pattern around the greens. Fan the tuna slices out over the greens, whisk the dressing, then spoon it over the salad. Garnish with the basil sprigs and serve.

Serves 4 as a light main course

Note: The recipe can be prepared ahead to this point, unless you wish to have the tuna hot. In that case, grill it at the last minute.

On the Side

VIETNAMESE SALAD PLATE

VIETNAM

ON THE SIDE

This fragrant assortment of herbs and vegetables is served alongside Vietnamese grilled fare and noodles. The lettuce leaves are used as wrappers for bite-sized portions of meat and its various accompaniments. The Vietnamese are adept at using chopsticks to do the wrapping—a skill that definitely improves with practice. The basil provides explosive blasts of flavor (often mint and/or cilantro are served as well), while the bean sprouts and cucumber provide a delicious wetness and crunch. If you live in an area with a large Asian community, you may be able to find Thai basil, which has delightful minty overtones.

1 head Boston or Bibb lettuce
1 bunch fresh basil, mint, and/or cilantro
2 cups fresh bean sprouts
2 to 4 serrano or jalapeño chiles, to taste, seeded, if desired
1 medium cucumber, peeled (see box, page 89)
1 starfruit (optional)

Separate the lettuce into leaves, trying to keep the leaves as whole as possible. Rinse and spin dry the lettuce and basil separately, leaving the latter on the stem; rinse and drain the bean sprouts. Thinly slice the chiles, cucumber and starfruit (if using). Arrange the various ingredients in attractive piles on a platter and serve.

Serves 4 to 6

TURKISH RADISH SALAD PLATE

TURKEY

ON THE SIDE

Here's the Turkish version of the fresh vegetable platter that, in one form or another, seems to accompany grilled meats all over the world. If you go to Turkey to experience this, you may be intrigued by a vegetable that looks like a bright red tennis ball. It's actually a jumbo radish. Here, the parsley is for eating, not just to look pretty, so make sure it is very fresh.

Serve the salad with any of the Turkish grilled meat dishes (see Index), squeezing the lemon over all.

1 bunch fresh Italian (flat-leaf)
    parsley
1 bunch radishes, trimmed and halved
2 lemons, cut into wedges and seeded

Rinse the parsley and spin dry, leaving the stems attached. Arrange with the radishes and lemon wedges on plates or a platter and serve.

Serves 4 to 6

Salad Plates

Salad and vegetable plates are one of the constants in the world of grilling—the indispensable accompaniment to grilled meats, be they Indonesian satés, Turkish kebabs, Mexican *carne asado,* or anything in between.

I've included five traditional salad plates I encountered on the barbecue trail. Use them as a starting point to customize your own accompaniments.

LEBANESE CRUDITES PLATE

LEBANON

ON THE SIDE

This vegetable platter (or a variation on it) appears on the table whenever a Lebanese meal is served. The vegetables are eaten by themselves as an hors d'oeuvre or as an accompaniment to grilled meats or seafood (often rolled up in a piece of pita). As you move east, you find a similar vegetable platter accompanying grilled meats in Iran, Iraq, India, and even Indonesia.

Serve this with Grilled Shrimp with Taratoor, the Ground Beef Kebabs, or Armenian Shish Kebab (see Index).

1 bunch scallions, both white and green
     parts, trimmed
1 bunch radishes, trimmed of roots
     and leaves
1 cucumber, cut lengthwise in half,
     then into wedges

2 dill pickles, cut lengthwise in half,
     then into wedges
2 hearts of romaine lettuce,
     separated into leaves, rinsed,
     and spun dry

Arrange the vegetables in an attractive pattern on a platter and serve.
Serves 4 to 6

JAVANESE LONG BEAN SALAD PLATE WITH CABBAGE WEDGES

Lalapan

INDONESIA

ON THE SIDE

This colorful herb and vegetable platter is the traditional Javanese accompaniment to grilled fish. You won't be able to duplicate it exactly, as they use strange aromatic herbs, like *daun mangi* and *daun rispong*, that simply don't exist in the West. (To hint at their flavor, I've called for *epazote*—a Mexican herb—with a clean, woodsy, pleasantly bitter flavor.) Long beans are Asian green beans that can measure up to 18 inches. Look for them at Asian markets or substitute skinny green beans. Serve *lalapan* with any of the Indonesian grilled fish dishes included in this book. Traditionally, the Fiery Chile and Shallot Relish (*sambal chobek;* see Index) would be served as well.

12 ounces long beans or thin green beans,
     ends trimmed off
Salt, to taste
½ medium white cabbage, cored and
     cut into ½-inch wedges

1 medium cucumber, peeled and cut
     into ¼-inch slices
2 fresh, ripe medium tomatoes, cored
     and cut into wedges
1 bunch lemon balm or basil, rinsed
     and patted dry
1 bunch epazote or Italian (flat-leaf)
     parsley, washed and patted dry

1. Cook the long beans in a saucepan of rapidly boiling salted water until crisp-tender, about 3 minutes. Drain well, refresh under cold water, and drain again.

2 Arrange the vegetables and herbs attractively on a platter and serve.
Serves 4 to 6

LONG BEANS WITH FRESH COCONUT
Urap Sayur

BALI

ON THE SIDE

This salad is as complex and delightful as traditional Balinese music, an intricate interplay of flavors and textures—the crunch of long beans, the crispness of coconut, the succulent sweetness of bean sprouts and bell peppers. As noted before, long beans are Asian green beans that grow up to 18 inches in length. Look for them at Asian markets or use regular green beans (the skinniest you can find) or *haricots verts*. Don't be disconcerted by the seemingly large amount of oil. Most of it is discarded. Serve this salad with any of the Balinese satés or grilled dishes in this book (see Index). Note that Indonesian ingredients are described in the Glossary.

FOR THE GARNISH AND DRESSING:
½ cup vegetable oil, preferably canola
9 cloves garlic, thinly sliced
    (about 3 tablespoons), plus
    2 cloves minced
4 to 5 shallots (about 4 ounces),
    thinly sliced (about ⅔ cup), plus
    1 shallot, minced
1 stalk lemongrass, trimmed and minced,
    or 1 strip lemon zest (2 x ½ inches;
    remove with a vegetable peeler)
1 tablespoon minced galangal or
    fresh ginger
¼ cup canned coconut milk
¼ cup fresh lime juice
2 tablespoons palm sugar or firmly packed
    light brown sugar
2 tablespoons Asian fish sauce or
    soy sauce

FOR THE SALAD:
Salt, to taste
8 ounces long beans or thin green beans,
    ends trimmed off
2 cups mung bean sprouts
¼ to ½ cup grated fresh coconut
    (see box, facing page) or unsweetened
    dried coconut
1 medium red bell pepper,
    stemmed, seeded, and cut into
    ¼-inch dice
1 to 4 jalapeño or other hot chiles, and
    minced
Freshly ground black pepper,
    to taste

1. Prepare the garnish. Heat the oil in a small skillet over medium-high heat. Add the sliced garlic and fry until crisp and golden brown, about 1 minute. Using a wire skimmer or slotted spoon, transfer the garlic to paper towels to drain. Fry the sliced shallots the same way, working in several batches if necessary to avoid crowding the pan. Take care not to let the garlic and shallots burn, or they'll become bitter. Blot the garlic and shallots with a paper towel and set aside. Pour off all but 3 tablespoons oil from the skillet and discard.

2. Prepare the dressing. Reheat the oil in the skillet over medium heat. Add the minced garlic and shallot, the lemongrass, and *galangal* and sauté until lightly browned, about 1 minute. Stir in the coconut milk and bring to a boil. Cook until reduced by half, about 3 minutes. Stir in the lime juice, palm sugar, and fish sauce and bring to a boil. Remove the pan from the heat and let the dressing cool.

3. Prepare the salad. Bring a saucepan

with 2 quarts of salted water to a boil.

4. Cut the long beans into $\frac{1}{2}$-inch pieces. Place the mung bean sprouts in a colander in the sink. Cook the long beans in the boiling water until crisp-tender, about 2 minutes. Drain the beans in the colander (the boiling water will blanch the sprouts). Rinse the vegetables under cold running water until the beans are cool, then drain the beans and mung beans well and blot both dry with paper towels.

5. Transfer the long beans and bean sprouts to a large bowl. Stir in the grated coconut, red bell pepper, jalapeño, fried garlic, fried shallots, and dressing (see Note). Toss well to mix. Correct the seasoning, adding salt and pepper to taste. Transfer the salad to an attractive platter and serve.

Serves 4 to 6

Note: The salad can be assembled ahead of time, but add the fried garlic and shallots and dressing at the last minute.

How to Prepare Fresh Coconut

To open a fresh coconut, place it on a rack or in a bowl in the sink. Tap it repeatedly with the back of a cleaver all the way around the middle of the coconut. Rotate the coconut as you tap: soon a crack will appear, then the coconut will break in half. Save the coconut water that falls into the bowl; it's great for drinking or cooking rice. Now, wrap the coconut halves in a kitchen towel and break into pieces with a hammer. Using a paring knife, pry the meat from the shell. (If it's hard to get out, bake the pieces in a 400°F oven for 10 minutes.) Trim the brown skin off the meat. Grate the coconut on a hand grater or in the food processor, using the grating blade.

If you're not going to use all the coconut, place it (either in chunks or grated) in a plastic bag and refrigerate up to 2 days. To keep fresh longer, wrap the prepared coconut in plastic and then in aluminum foil, and freeze for up to 2 months. The average coconut when grated yields about 5 cups.

SPICY JAPANESE BEAN SPROUT SALAD

JAPAN

ON THE SIDE

A meal at a yakitori parlor would include several small dishes of salads as well as grilled fare on a skewer. This one comes from Ton Ton, a bare bones yakitori joint under the elevated railroad near the Ginza district in Tokyo. The dressing contains only six ingredients, but the flavors—sweet, salty, sour, nutty, and fiery—will play pinball with your taste buds.

1 clove garlic
¾ teaspoon salt, or more to taste
1 tablespoon sugar, or more to taste
3 tablespoons rice vinegar, or more
    to taste
2 teaspoons Asian (dark) sesame oil
½ to 1 teaspoon hot red pepper flakes,
    to taste
4 cups mung bean sprouts
    (about 8 ounces)

1. Mash the garlic with ¾ teaspoon salt in a small bowl. Add 1 tablespoon sugar, 3 tablespoons vinegar, the sesame oil, and hot pepper flakes and whisk until the sugar and salt are dissolved. Stir in the bean sprouts and let stand for 5 minutes.

2. Just before serving, taste for seasoning, adding salt, sugar, or vinegar as necessary; the salad should be highly seasoned.

Serves 4 to 6

SHIRAZI CUCUMBER, TOMATO, AND ONION SALAD

IRAN

ON THE SIDE

Tomato, onion, and cucumber salads seem to turn up whenever meats are run through skewers and seared smokily over fire. Here's the Iranian version, named for its birthplace, the city of Shiraz, and robustly flavored with lime juice, parsley, and fresh mint. Serve this salad with any of the Persian kebabs in this book (see Index), accompanied by pieces of lavash or pita bread for dipping.

2 fresh, ripe medium tomatoes, cored
    and cut into ½-inch dice
1 large cucumber, peeled, seeded
    (see box), and cut into ½-inch dice
1 small or medium onion, cut into
    ½-inch dice
½ cup chopped fresh Italian (flat-leaf)
    parsley
½ cup chopped fresh mint
3 scallions, both white and green parts,
    trimmed and finely chopped
1 to 2 cloves garlic, minced
¼ cup fresh lime juice, or more to taste
¼ cup extra-virgin olive oil
Salt and freshly ground black pepper,
    to taste

Combine the tomatoes, cucumber, and onion in a serving bowl with the parsley, mint, scallions, garlic, ¼ cup lime juice, and oil. Toss gently but thoroughly to mix. Add salt and pepper to taste and more lime juice as necessary; the salad should be highly seasoned. Serve immediately.

Serves 4 to 6

To Peel and Seed Cucumbers

Remove cucumber peel in lengthwise strips with a vegetable peeler, leaving about ⅛ inch between each peeled-off strip. That way, when you slice the cucumbers crosswise, you get attractive green stripes on each slice.

To seed a cucumber, cut it in half lengthwise and scrape out the seeds with a melon baller or teaspoon.

BALINESE CUCUMBER SALAD

ON THE SIDE

This curious salad looks a little like green spaghetti. Actually, it's made with long, thin, noodle-like slivers of cucumber. (The easiest way to cut these is on a mandoline or with the julienne disk of a food processor.) There certainly is a universality of serving cucumber salads with barbecue. But what better way to relieve the heat of the fire and the day than with a salad that's as cool as the proverbial cucumber?

3 tablespoons dry-roasted peanuts, coarsely chopped
1 European cucumber (see Note) or 1 large regular cucumber
¼ large sweet onion, such as Vidalia
3 tablespoons rice vinegar
1½ tablespoons sugar, or more to taste
½ teaspoon salt, or more to taste

1. Set a dry skillet over medium heat. Add the peanuts and heat until lightly browned, about 2 minutes, shaking the pan occasionally. Transfer to a plate to cool.

2. Peel and seed the cucumber (see box, facing page). Cut the cucumber crosswise into 3-inch sections, then lengthwise into spaghetti-thin strips. Cut the onion into as thin crosswise slices as possible.

3. Combine the vinegar, sugar, and salt in a serving bowl and whisk until the sugar and salt are dissolved. Taste for seasoning, adding sugar or salt as necessary; the dressing should be both tart and sweet. Stir in the cucumber and onion. Sprinkle the salad with the peanuts and serve.

Serves 4

Note: A European cucumber is the long, thin variety that has few seeds. It is often sold sealed in plastic.

POTATO SALAD WITH CARAMELIZED ONIONS

ON THE SIDE

Potato salad is an immutable fixture for an American barbecue. Here's the Sri Lankan version—spiked with spicy-fried onions—just right for accompanying the Sri Lankan chicken satés or any of the Indian, Pakistani, or Bangladeshi kebabs in this book. I've taken a few liberties with the recipe, such as leaving the potato skins on. As elsewhere, I give a range of heat: Use 2 teaspoons hot paprika if you like a milder potato salad and 6 teaspoons if you like to eat fire.

1½ pounds red-skinned potatoes, preferably very small, scrubbed
Salt, to taste
¼ cup vegetable oil, or more as needed
2 to 6 teaspoons hot paprika (or for a much milder salad, use sweet paprika)
1½ teaspoons ground coriander
½ teaspoon freshly ground black pepper
⅛ teaspoon ground cardamom
1 large onion, very thinly sliced
2 tablespoons fresh lemon juice
3 tablespoons chopped fresh cilantro

1. If using very small new potatoes, cut them in half; cut larger potatoes into ½-inch chunks. Place the potatoes in a medium-size saucepan with lightly salted water to cover and bring to a boil. Reduce the heat to medium and simmer the potatoes until just tender, about 10 minutes.

2. Meanwhile, prepare the onion mixture. Heat ¼ cup oil in a large skillet over high heat. Add the paprika (start with a small amount), coriander, pepper, and cardamom and sauté, stirring, for 15 seconds. Add the onion and sauté for 1 minute. Reduce the heat to medium, then medium-low, and cook the onion until caramelized—that, is very

soft and a deep golden brown—which will take about 20 minutes in all.

3. When the potatoes are done, drain in a colander, rinse under cold running water until cool, and drain again. Set aside while finishing the onion mixture.

4. Stir the cooled potatoes and lemon juice into the onion mixture and cook over medium heat until thoroughly coated, 1 to 2 minutes. Correct the seasoning, adding salt or paprika as necessary; the salad should be highly seasoned. If it looks too dry, add a little more oil. Transfer to a bowl and let cool, then sprinkle with cilantro to serve.

Serves 4

TWO-TONE POTATO SALAD

No barbecue would be complete without potato salad. One day, short on regular potatoes, my wife, Barbara, made this two-tone salad using sweet and baking potatoes. The result was so colorful and tasty we've made it a family standby. You'll be amazed how much flavor the olives and capers add. If you wish to make a conventional potato salad, use all baking potatoes.

FOR THE POTATOES AND DRESSING:
2 large baking potatoes (each 10 ounces)
2 large sweet potatoes (each 10 ounces)
Salt, to taste
⅓ cup mayonnaise
2 tablespoons Dijon mustard
2 tablespoons extra-virgin olive oil
2 tablespoons red wine vinegar, or more to taste
2 tablespoons drained capers
2 tablespoons chopped pitted green olives (with or without pimientos)
Freshly ground black pepper, to taste

FOR THE SALAD:
2 medium ribs celery (with leaves, if possible), finely chopped
2 hard-cooked eggs, coarsely chopped (optional)
3 scallions, both white and green parts, trimmed and finely chopped
½ cup finely chopped red onion
¼ cup chopped fresh Italian (flat-leaf) parsley, plus a few sprigs for garnish
8 pitted black olives, for garnish

1. Peel all the potatoes and cut into ¾-inch cubes. Place the baking potatoes in a large saucepan with 2 quarts lightly salted water. Bring to a boil and cook for 4 minutes. Add the sweet potatoes and simmer until both types of potatoes are just tender, 4 to 6 minutes more.

2. Meanwhile, prepare the dressing. Combine the mayonnaise and mustard in a large serving bowl and whisk until blended and smooth. Whisk in the oil, 2 tablespoons vinegar, capers, green olives, and pepper.

3. Drain the potatoes, then stir into the dressing while still hot. Set aside to cool and absorb the dressing.

4. Prepare the salad. Stir the celery, eggs (if using), scallions, red onion, and chopped parsley gently but thoroughly into the cooled potato mixture. Correct the seasoning, adding salt or vinegar; the salad should be highly seasoned. Garnish the salad with the black olives and parsley sprigs and serve.

Serves 6

SPICY DAIKON

KOREA

ADVANCE PREPARATION: *20 minutes to 8 hours for marinating the salad*

It's hard to imagine a Korean meal without this refreshing salad of crunchy chunks of daikon radish emblazoned with chili powder, vinegar, and garlic. Daikon is a succulent Asian radish that looks like our white (icicle) radish but is much longer and thicker; it has a moist, crisp flesh. Look for it at Asian markets, natural foods stores, and many supermarkets. In a pinch, you could use regular red radishes.

1 daikon radish (12 to 14 ounces)
3 cloves garlic, minced
1 tablespoon minced fresh ginger
2 teaspoons sugar, or more to taste
1 teaspoon salt, or more to taste
1 to 3 teaspoons hot paprika or ½ teaspoon cayenne pepper
2 tablespoons rice vinegar, or more to taste
2 teaspoons soy sauce
1 teaspoon Asian (dark) sesame oil
3 scallions, both white and green parts, trimmed and finely chopped
1½ teaspoons sesame seeds, toasted (see box)

1. Peel the radish with a vegetable peeler and cut off the ends, then cut in quarters lengthwise and crosswise into ½-inch slices.

2. Combine the garlic, ginger, 2 teaspoons sugar, 1 teaspoon salt, and paprika in a serving bowl and mash together with the back of a wooden spoon. Stir in 2 tablespoons vinegar, the soy sauce, sesame oil, scallions, sesame seeds, and daikon. Let stand for 30 minutes, or as long as 8 hours (if 8 hours, cover and refrigerate).

3. Just before serving, correct the seasoning, adding salt, vinegar, or sugar as necessary, the salad should be highly seasoned.

Serves 4 to 6

How to Toast Seeds, Nuts, and Breadcrumbs

Set a dry skillet over medium heat. Add the seeds, nuts, or breadcrumbs and heat until lightly toasted, 3 to 5 minutes, shaking the skillet occasionally. Remove to a plate to cool.

Toasting can also be done in a preheated 350°F oven. Spread out the seeds, nuts, or crumbs on a baking sheet and place in the oven until lightly browned, 5 to 10 minutes. Watch carefully to avoid burning.

SPICY FRUIT IN A TAMARIND DRESSING
Rujak

INDONESIA

ON THE SIDE

This offbeat salad (*rujak*, pronounced "RUE-jack") is one of the national dishes of Indonesia. (Indeed, it turns up throughout Southeast Asia, especially in Singapore and Malaysia.) The pairing of crunchy vegetables and acidic fruits makes an uncommonly refreshing combination for a barbecue. As for the sauce—a sweet, hot, piquant mixture of chiles, peanuts, and tamarind—few salad dressings are more distinctively flavorful or refreshing. There's nothing else quite like it. If tamarind is unavailable, use balsamic vinegar instead.

FOR THE DRESSING:
3 tablespoons dry-roasted peanuts
3 tablespoons tamarind pulp or balsamic vinegar
¾ cup hot water
1 piece (2 inches) ripe banana
2 cloves garlic, minced
1 shallot, minced
1 to 3 jalapeño or other hot chiles, minced (for a milder rujak, seed the chiles)
2 tablespoons Asian fish sauce, sweet soy sauce (ketjap manis), or regular soy sauce
2 tablespoons molasses
1 tablespoon firmly packed brown sugar
1 tablespoon fresh lime juice, or more to taste
Salt, to taste

FOR THE SALAD:
1 starfruit or Asian pear
1 small jicama or large Granny Smith apple (about 8 ounces)
½ fresh pineapple

Grilled Rujak

Rujak vendors in Malaysia sometimes serve this salad on skewers, as ungrilled kebabs. I, too, like to serve it on skewers, but when I do, I lightly grill the kebabs first.

If you want to give it a try, thread the fruit attractively onto short presoaked and drained bamboo skewers and grill for 2 to 4 minutes per side (4 to 8 minutes in all) over high heat. Serve each skewer in a pool of tamarind dressing.

1 cucumber
1 cup mung bean sprouts, rinsed and drained
¼ cup chopped fresh cilantro or scallion greens, for garnish

1. Prepare the dressing. Grind the peanuts to a coarse powder in a food processor, running the machine in spurts. Transfer to a small bowl.

2. Combine the tamarind pulp and hot water in the processor and let stand for 5 minutes to soften. Pulse the machine in short bursts until the flesh comes away from the seeds, about 1 minute. Don't process so much that you crush the seeds. Strain the resulting mixture into the bowl with the peanuts. Discard the seeds and pulp. If using balsamic vinegar, add it and the water to the peanuts.

3. Return the peanut mixture to the processor and add the banana, garlic, shallot, chiles, fish sauce, molasses, sugar, 1 tablespoon lime juice, and salt. Process to a smooth paste. Taste for seasoning, adding salt or lime juice as necessary; the dressing should be highly seasoned. Set aside while you prepare the fruits and vegetables.

4. If using the starfruit, cut it into ¼-inch crosswise slices and set aside; if using the Asian pear, cut it in half lengthwise, core it, and then cut each half into ¼-inch crosswise slices. If using the jicama, peel it, halve it lengthwise, and cut the halves into ¼-inch crosswise slices; if using the apple, prepare as for the Asian pear. Peel and core the pineapple; cut it into 1-inch cubes. Peel the cucumber and cut it into ¼-inch crosswise slices.

5. To serve, pool the dressing on a platter or 4 large salad plates. Arrange the bean sprouts and pineapple in the center and fan the cucumber, jicama, and starfruit slices around them. Garnish with cilantro and serve.

Serves 4

SESAME SPINACH

JAPAN

ON THE SIDE

Simplicity and color are the hallmarks of Japanese salads: the bright greens of spinach, the oranges of carrots, the whites of daikon radish and bean sprouts. Consider this spinach salad, commonly served at yakitori parlors, and which owes its wonderful nutty flavor to sesame oil and toasted sesame seeds. For the best results, use the young, tender, flat-leaf spinach leaves sold in bunches at specialty greengrocers, not those in cellophane bags. Serve with any of the Japanese grilled dishes in this book.

1 pound fresh spinach, stemmed and rinsed
    thoroughly (see box)
Salt, to taste
2 tablespoons sesame seeds, toasted
    (see box, page 93)
1 clove garlic, minced
2 tablespoons mirin (sweet rice wine) or
    cream sherry, or more to taste
1 tablespoon soy sauce, or more to taste
1 tablespoon Asian (dark) sesame oil

1. Cook the spinach in a large saucepan of boiling salted water until just tender,

How to Rinse Salad Greens

Salad greens, such as spinach, are often gritty—especially if you buy them by the bunch at farm stands. To get rid of the grit, separate the leaves from any heavy stems. Place the leaves in a large bowl of cold water and agitate gently with your fingers, allowing the grit to fall to the bottom of the bowl. Lift the leaves out of the water with your hands and place in a colander. Pour out the water and refill the bowl with fresh. Continue washing the greens in this fashion—as many as six times—until grit free. Always transfer the greens to a colander before discarding the water. If you pour the greens with the water into the colander, you'll just wash the grit back on.

about 30 seconds. Drain the spinach in a colander and rinse with ice water. Blot the spinach leaves dry with paper towels.

2. Combine half the sesame seeds, the garlic, 2 tablespoons mirin, 1 tablespoon soy sauce, and the sesame oil in a serving bowl and whisk to mix. Stir in the spinach. Correct the seasoning, adding soy sauce or mirin as necessary; the salad should be a little sweet and a little salty. Sprinkle the spinach with the remaining sesame seeds and serve at room temperature or chilled.

Serves 4 to 6

TOMATO SALAD WITH FETA CHEESE
Shopska Salata

BULGARIA

ON THE SIDE

Late one evening in Washington, D.C., after a grueling day on a book tour, I sat back in my room at the Jefferson Hotel and ordered room service. I was obligingly served by one Kiril Mitov, a young Bulgarian putting himself through school by working the swing shift at the hotel. We got to talking about books and barbecue, and soon he was telling me about cookouts in Sofia. No Bulgarian barbecue would be complete without this salad, he said, which takes its name from a rural region outside Sofia, and it owes its distinctive tang to snow-white Bulgarian feta cheese. *Shopska salata* is the traditional accompaniment to Bulgarian Burgers and Bosnian Three-Meat Patties (see Index).

2 large fresh, ripe tomatoes
1 medium green bell pepper, stemmed and seeded
1 to 2 spring onions, both white and green parts (see Note)
¼ cup coarsely chopped fresh Italian (flat-leaf) parsley
¼ cup extra-virgin olive oil
1 tablespoon red wine vinegar, or more to taste
Salt and freshly ground black pepper, to taste
3 ounces feta cheese, preferably Bulgarian, drained

1. Core the tomatoes and cut into 1-inch cubes. Cut the pepper and onion into ¼-inch dice. Combine the vegetables in a serving bowl with the parsley, olive oil, 1 tablespoon vinegar, and salt and pepper. Toss gently but thoroughly to mix. Correct the seasoning, adding salt, pepper, or vinegar as necessary; the salad should be highly seasoned.

2. Coarsely grate or crumble the cheese on top and serve immediately.

Serves 4

Note: If spring onions are not available, 4 scallions (both white and green parts) or ½ small red onion may be substituted.

TOMATO AND SHALLOT SALAD

SRI LANKA

ON THE SIDE

This tangy dish—part relish and part salad—is one of the innumerable variations on the theme of tomato and onion salad found wherever meat or fish are cooked on a grill. As elsewhere in this book, I offer a range of chiles.

The salad can be served immediately, but it will taste better if you leave it to stand for 15 or 20 minutes, so the flavors have a chance to blend. Be sure to correct the seasoning just before serving. Serve it with the Sri Lankan satés or any of the Indian tandoori in this book (see Index).

3 tablespoons distilled white vinegar, or more to taste
1 teaspoon salt, or to taste
½ teaspoon freshly ground black pepper
3 tablespoons vegetable oil
2 large fresh, ripe tomatoes, cut into ¼-inch dice
½ cup diced (¼-inch) shallots
1 to 4 serrano or jalapeño chiles, thinly sliced crosswise
¼ cup finely chopped fresh cilantro or mint

Combine the vinegar, salt, and pepper in a serving bowl and whisk until the salt is dissolved. Whisk in the oil. Add the tomatoes, shallots, chiles, and cilantro. Correct the seasoning, adding salt or vinegar as necessary; the salad should be highly seasoned. Serve immediately.
Serves 4

SHEPHERD'S SALAD
Coran Salatasi

TURKEY

ON THE SIDE

There are probably as many versions of this colorful salad as there are Turkish cooks to make it. The basic ingredients are onions, tomatoes, and peppers. Here's a more elaborate version that's bursting with Anatolian freshness. Serve as a prelude to any of the Turkish kebabs in this book (see Index).

1 large or 2 small fresh, ripe tomatoes
1 medium cucumber
1 medium green bell pepper
½ small red onion
3 tablespoons chopped fresh Italian (flat-leaf) parsley (optional)
½ cup brine-cured black olives
3 tablespoons extra-virgin olive oil
1 tablespoon red wine vinegar, or more to taste
Salt and freshly ground black pepper, to taste
3 ounces feta cheese, drained and crumbled

1. Core and seed the tomatoes (see box, page 62) and cut into ¼-inch dice. Peel and seed the cucumber (see box, page 89) and cut into ¼-inch dice. Stem and seed the pepper and cut into ¼-inch dice. Cut the onion into ¼-inch dice.

2. Combine the tomatoes, cucumber, bell pepper, onion, parsley (if using), and most of the olives in a serving bowl (see Note). Add the oil, 1 tablespoon vinegar, and salt and pepper and toss gently but thoroughly to mix. Correct the seasoning, adding salt and pepper or vinegar as necessary; the salad should be highly seasoned.

3. Sprinkle the crumbled feta cheese over the salad, decorate with the remaining olives, and serve immediately.

Serves 4

Note: The vegetables can be cut and tossed ahead of time, but for best results don't mix in the dressing more than 20 minutes before serving.

"THREE HOTS" SALAD

KOREA

ON THE SIDE

This spicy salad is one of the half dozen or so condiments that traditionally accompany Korean grilled meat dishes. I first sampled it at Samwon Garden, a mammoth restaurant in Seoul that takes an almost Disneyesque approach to Korean barbecue. The salad acquires its peppery bite from three sources: watercress, mustard greens, and wasabi (Japanese horseradish). The latter is available at Asian markets, natural foods stores, and gourmet shops. If unavailable, use prepared horseradish. Serve it with the Korean Sesame-Grilled Beef or the Korean Grilled Short Ribs (see Index).

2 teaspoons wasabi, or to taste
2 teaspoons water
3 tablespoons rice vinegar
1½ tablespoons sugar
2 teaspoons soy sauce
½ teaspoon salt
½ teaspoon freshly ground black pepper
1 bunch watercress, rinsed, spun dry, and torn into small sprigs
1 bunch mustard greens, stemmed, rinsed, spun dry, and torn into bite-size pieces (2 to 3 cups) or the equivalent in additional watercress

1. Combine the wasabi and water in the bottom of a serving bowl and whisk to make a paste. Let stand 5 minutes.

2. Add the vinegar, sugar, soy sauce, salt, and pepper to the wasabi mixture, and whisk until the sugar and salt are dissolved.

3. Just before serving, add the watercress and mustard greens and toss to mix.

Serves 4 to 6

KOREAN LETTUCE AND ONION SALAD

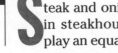

ON THE SIDE

Steak and onions are a marriage made in steakhouse heaven. Koreans display an equal enthusiasm for the combination—witness this tangy onion and lettuce salad, another one that is served with grilled meats at the sprawling Samwon

Garden steakhouse in Seoul. Elsewhere in Korea, I found spring onion and scallion salads prepared in a similar fashion. The sesame seeds and vinegar tend to neutralize the pungency of the onion, especially if you use a sweet onion.

Serve the salad with Korean Sesame-Grilled Beef or Korean Grilled Short Ribs (see Index).

2 tablespoons soy sauce, or more to taste
2 tablespoons rice vinegar, or more to taste
½ teaspoon sugar, or more to taste
½ teaspoon hot paprika or cayenne pepper
2 teaspoons Asian (dark) sesame oil
1½ tablespoons sesame seeds, toasted (see box, page 93)
½ teaspoon freshly ground black pepper
6 to 8 romaine lettuce leaves, rinsed, spun dry, and cut crosswise into ¼-inch strips (about 3 cups)
1 sweet onion, such as Vidalia, Maui, or Walla Walla, thinly sliced (see Note)

1. Combine 2 tablespoons each soy sauce and vinegar and ½ teaspoon each sugar and paprika in a serving bowl and whisk until the sugar is dissolved. Whisk in the sesame oil, sesame seeds, and pepper.

2. Add the lettuce and onion to the dressing and toss gently but thoroughly. Correct the seasoning, adding soy sauce, vinegar, or sugar as necessary; the salad should be highly seasoned. Serve immediately.

Serves 4

Note: If the stronger-tasting yellow onions are the only ones available, you may wish to blanch the slices in boiling water for 10 seconds, then rinse under cold water, to blunt the bite.

LA CABANA'S HOUSE SALAD

ARGENTINA

ON THE SIDE

To visit Buenos Aires without dining at La Cabaña would be a little like going to Agra and skipping the Taj Mahal. Hyperbole, perhaps, but the claim serves to emphasize the preeminence of what is undoubtedly Argentina's most famous steakhouse. Since 1935, La Cabaña has served as a magnet for big-spending beef buffs, and its magnificent high-ceilinged dining room, done in dark woods, wrought iron, and gilded wallpaper, has been a favorite haunt of presidents and kings. (The king of Spain holds court in the rear dining room when visiting Argentina.) Although justly renowned for its beef, La Cabaña serves a wonderful house salad— a welcome respite from the carnivorian onslaught that characterizes a typical Argentinian meal.

FOR THE SALAD:
1 small or ½ large head iceberg lettuce
1 bunch arugula, stemmed, rinsed,
    and dried
2 fresh, ripe medium tomatoes
2 hard-cooked eggs, shelled
1 medium red bell pepper, stemmed and
    seeded
1 cup diced cooked beets
2 medium ribs celery, thinly sliced
1 can (14 ounces) hearts of palm, drained
    and thinly sliced

FOR THE DRESSING:
2 teaspoons Dijon mustard
1 tablespoon red wine vinegar, or
    more to taste
1 tablespoon fresh lemon juice
½ teaspoon salt, or more to taste
½ cup extra-virgin olive oil
½ teaspoon freshly ground black pepper,
    or to taste

1. Core the lettuce and cut it crosswise into ¼-inch slices. Gently toss the lettuce with the arugula in a bowl. Arrange this mixture in the bottom of 6 shallow salad bowls, mounding it toward the center.

2. Cut each tomato into 12 wedges. Cut each hard-cooked egg into 6 wedges. Cut the pepper into 18 thin strips. Arrange the tomato and hard-cooked egg wedges and pepper strips on top of the lettuce in a sunburst pattern (radiating away from the center like the spokes of a wagon wheel), alternating colors.

3. Drain off any liquid that may still remain on the beets and blot dry with paper towels. Mound the beets, celery, and hearts of palm in the center of each portion of salad (see Note).

4. Prepare the dressing. Combine the mustard, vinegar, lemon juice, and salt in a small bowl and whisk until the salt is dissolved. Whisk in the oil and pepper. Correct the seasoning, adding salt or vinegar as necessary; the salad should be highly seasoned. Pour the dressing over the salads and serve immediately.
    Serves 6
    Note: The salads can be prepared ahead to this point. Cover loosely with plastic wrap and refrigerate until ready to serve.

A DIFFERENT GREEK SALAD
Marlo Salata

GREECE

ON THE SIDE

This is a little different from the Greek salads most of us are used to, made as it is with crisp romaine lettuce and aromatic fresh dill. The lemon juice is squeezed directly over the salad; I like to squeeze each half between my fingers to catch the seeds before they fall into the salad.

Serve this salad with the Rotisseried Leg of Lamb with Lemon and Butter, Swordfish Souvlaki (see Index), or any other Greek grilled fare.

1 head romaine lettuce, separated into
   leaves, rinsed, and spun dry
1 clove garlic, cut in half
1 bunch dill, freshly chopped
1 bunch scallions, both white and green
   parts, trimmed and finely chopped
1 to 2 lemons, cut in half
3 to 4 tablespoons extra-virgin olive oil
Salt and freshly ground black pepper,
   to taste
½ cup Kalamata or other Greek olives
4 to 6 ounces feta cheese, drained and
   thinly sliced

1. Cut the romaine leaves crosswise into ½-inch strips. Rub a salad bowl with the cut garlic. Add the romaine, dill, and scallions (see Note).

2. Just before serving, squeeze the lemon juice to taste over the salad and pour the oil on top. Season the salad generously with salt and pepper and toss well to mix. Garnish the salad with the olives and feta and serve.

Serves 4 to 6

Note: The salad can be prepared ahead to this point. Cover loosely with plastic wrap and refrigerate until ready to serve.

Grilled Bread

In Morocco, bread tastes best cooked over blazing wood.

It was bound to happen. After decades of firing up such predictable fare as meat, seafood, and vegetables, grill jockeys are finally discovering bread.

Of course, grilling may have been the original method used to prepare bread. The first ones made by our Neolithic ancestors were likely grain pastes cooked crisp on heated stones next to a campfire. Today, villagers in Lebanon still use this technique for cooking pita bread. And in India, the flat breads called *naan* are baked on the sides of charcoal-fired clay ovens called tandoors, while in Mexico, commercially prepared tortillas are cooked on a metal conveyer belt that passes over open flames.

The easiest way to grill bread is to use the glowing coals as a toaster. But you can also use the flames to cook raw dough. In the following pages you'll find recipes for grilled flat bread and *focaccia* cooked directly over the embers, as well as a direct-grilled version of Indian *naan*. Grilling also makes wonderfully crisp *papadoms* (Indian lentil crisps) that are completely free of the oil normally associated with them.

Whether you start with ready-made bread or homemade dough, you'll find it tastes better cooked on the grill.

GRILLED PITA CHIPS

MIDDLE EAST

METHOD:
Direct grilling

Grilling is a great way to crisp wedges of pita bread for dipping. (It's also a great way to add fresh life to stale pita bread.) For extra color and flavor, sprinkle the chips with white or black sesame seeds before grilling.

3 large or 4 small pita breads
3 tablespoons extra-virgin olive oil
1 tablespoon regular or black sesame
    seeds (optional)

1. Preheat the grill to high.

2. Cut larger pitas into 8 wedges, smaller pitas into 6 wedges (see Note). Generously brush both sides of each wedge with oil.

Sprinkle one side of each wedge with sesame seeds (if using).

3. When ready to cook, arrange the pita wedges on the hot grate, and grill, turning with tongs, until nicely browned, 1 to 2 minutes per side. Place the wedges in a single layer on a tray, platter, or cake rack and allow to cool. The wedges will crisp on cooling.

Makes 24 wedges

Note: For extra-crisp chips, separate each pita into two rounds by cutting it in half horizontally. Cut each round into wedges, brush on both sides with oil (you'll need more oil) and grill. This gives you a thinner and therefore crisper pita chip.

GRILLED BREAD WITH GARLIC CILANTRO BUTTER

U.S.A.

METHOD:
Direct grilling

Grilling produces a garlic bread that is crunchy on the outside and softly chewy on the inside, with a smoky charcoaled flavor. The cilantro lends a Latin touch.

1 loaf bakery-style French bread (about 20
    inches long)
8 tablespoons (1 stick) unsalted butter, at
    room temperature
4 cloves garlic, minced
½ cup minced fresh cilantro
Salt and freshly ground black pepper, to taste

1. Preheat the grill to medium-high.

2. Cut the bread sharply on the diagonal into ¾-inch-thick slices.

3. Cream the butter with a whisk in a mixing bowl. Add the garlic, cilantro, salt, and pepper.

4. When ready to cook, generously brush or spread the bread slices on both sides with the cilantro butter. Arrange the bread slices on the hot grate and grill, turning with tongs as needed, until nicely browned, 2 to 4 minutes per side. Don't take your eyes off the grill for a second; grilled bread burns very easily. Transfer to a bread basket and serve immediately.

Makes 20 to 24 pieces; serves 4 to 6

GRILLED GARLIC BREAD FINGERS

U.S.A.

METHOD:
Direct grilling

Barbecue, by its very nature, requires a lot of standing around the grill waiting for foods to cook. But idle time shouldn't be hungry time. These slender bread strips—nice and garlicky—make a perfect munchie while you're waiting for more substantial fare to cook. Cutting the bread into fingers maximizes the surface area, ensuring even crusting and browning on all sides. The lemon zest adds a dimension you won't find in most garlic breads. And because you maximize the surface area, this recipe works well even on supermarket French bread. In the interest of health, I like to brush the bread with olive oil, but you could certainly use the melted butter.

1 loaf French bread (about 20 to
   24 inches long; see Note)
½ cup extra-virgin olive oil or melted
   unsalted butter
4 cloves garlic, minced
1 teaspoon grated lemon zest
¼ cup minced fresh Italian (flat-leaf) parsley
Salt and freshly ground black pepper, to taste

1. Preheat the grill to medium-high.

2. Cut the loaf crosswise into 4 equal pieces. Then cut each piece lengthwise into 4 equal pieces to make 16 "fingers," each 5 to 6 inches long.

3. Heat the oil in a small saucepan over medium-low heat. Add the garlic, lemon zest, and parsley and simmer until the garlic just begins to brown, 3 to 5 minutes. Remove the garlic oil from the heat and season with salt and pepper.

4. When ready to cook, generously brush the bread fingers all over with the garlic oil. Starting crust side down, arrange the fingers on the hot grate and grill, turning with tongs, until nicely browned, 2 to 4 minutes per side. Don't take your eyes off the grill for a second; grilled bread burns very easily. Transfer to a bread basket and serve immediately.

Makes 16 pieces; serves 6 to 8

Note: My favorite bread for this recipe are the soft, puffy "French" or "Italian" loaves sold in the supermarket bread aisle. You can also use a long, crusty bakery-style baguette, but the result will be *very* crusty.

CATALAN TOMATO BREAD
Pa Amb Tomàquet

SPAIN

METHOD:
Direct grilling

My first meal in Barcelona—at the venerable Los Caracoles restaurant in the medieval quarter—began with this simple bread appetizer, and scarcely a day went by when I wasn't served some variation of it. Catalan Tomato Bread belongs to an ancient family of grilled breads that includes Italian *bruschetta* and Indian *naan*. It offers irrefutable proof that the best dishes are often the easiest.

At its most rudimentary, *pa amb tomà-*

quet consists simply of a slice of grilled bread rubbed with ripe tomatoes and drizzled with olive oil. Like all simple dishes, it requires the best raw materials: crusty country-style bread; squishily ripe tomatoes; fragrant, cold-pressed olive oil. When prepared properly, the bread will be crisp from grilling, but the surface will be just beginning to soften thanks to the juices from the tomatoes. Not everyone in Catalonia uses garlic, so I've made it optional.

There are two ways to serve tomato bread. The first is for the cook to do the rubbing and drizzling. The second is to provide each person with a clove of garlic, half tomato, cruet of oil, and bowl of salt and let him or her do the work. The second way is more fun.

4 fresh, very ripe tomatoes, cut in half
4 cloves garlic, cut in half (optional)
8 slices country-style bread, cut ½ inch thick
Cruet of extra-virgin olive oil
Small bowl of coarse (kosher or sea) salt
Freshly ground black pepper (optional)

1. Preheat the grill to medium-high.

2. Place a half tomato and half garlic clove (if using) on each serving plate.

3. When ready to cook, arrange the bread slices on the hot grate and grill until nicely browned, 2 to 4 minutes per side.

4. Place a piece of grilled bread on each plate. To eat, rub a bread slice with cut garlic (if using), then with cut tomato. Drizzle each slice with oil and sprinkle with salt and pepper, if desired. Serve immediately.
Serves 8

TUSCAN GRILLED GARLIC BREAD
Bruschetta

ITALY

METHOD:
Direct grilling

SPECIAL EQUIPMENT:
1 cup unsoaked wood chips, preferably oak (charcoal grill only; optional)

A slice of grilled bread rubbed with garlic and drizzled with olive oil—*bruschetta* (pronounced "broo-SKEH-tta")—is the ancestor of American garlic bread. Most of us have grown up with baked or toasted versions, but real *bruschetta*—cooked over coals—comes as a revelation. To be strictly authentic, you'd use Tuscan bread, which is remarkable for its dense, slightly crumbly texture and its curious lack of salt. The latter makes the bread taste rather insipid—until you pair it with fruity Tuscan olive oil and sea salt.

Bruschetta offers a remarkable contrast of flavors: the intense, granular saltiness of the topping, the fruitiness of the olive oil, the fragrance of the garlic (which is mellowed by warming), and the scent of smoke. Oh, sure, there are fancier versions of *bruschetta*, but none can rival the elemental flavor of this one. Note that there is no need to soak the wood chips. Unsoaked, the chips will give the *bruschetta* more of a wood flavor than a smoky flavor. Use them with a charcoal grill only.

8 slices of Italian bread (preferably unsalted Tuscan bread), cut ½ inch thick
1 to 2 cloves garlic, cut in half
2 to 3 tablespoons of the best cold-pressed extra-virgin olive oil you can find, preferably Tuscan
Coarse (kosher or sea) salt and freshly ground black pepper

1. Preheat the grill to medium-high.

2. When ready to cook, throw a cupful of unsoaked wood chips on the coals (if using). Arrange the bread slices on the hot grate and grill until nicely browned on both sides, 2 to 4 minutes per side, rotating the slices 60 degrees after 30 seconds or so to create an attractive crosshatch of grill marks. Transfer the bread slices to the cool edge of the grill or warming rack and let cool for 1 minute. This prevents steam from forming on the platter under the bread, which would make the slices soggy.

3. Rub the top of each bread slice generously with cut garlic. Drizzle with oil and sprinkle heavily with salt and pepper. Serve immediately.

Serves 4 to 8

GRILLED FOCACCIA

ITALY

METHOD:
Direct grilling

It's hard to imagine a time when we didn't eat *focaccia*. In the last decade, this puffy Italian flat bread has jumped from the ethnic fringe to the culinary mainstream. *Focaccia* is a very ancient bread whose name comes from the Latin word *focus,* meaning "hearth." There is archeological evidence that the first *focacce* were baked right in or on the embers on hearthstones heated by coals. That set me thinking about cooking the dough directly on the grill. This will make a thinner *focaccia* than the deep-dish pizza thickness you may be accustomed to—it's almost like a cracker.

FOR THE DOUGH:
1 envelope active dry yeast
1 cup warm water
1½ teaspoons sugar
3 tablespoons olive oil
1½ teaspoons salt
3¼ cups unbleached all-purpose flour,
   plus more for dusting
¼ cup fine cornmeal, for dusting

TO FINISH THE BREADS:
3 tablespoons sesame seeds
1 tablespoon coarse (kosher or sea) salt
3 to 4 tablespoons olive oil, for brushing

1. Combine the yeast with the water and sugar in a large bowl and let stand until foamy, about 10 minutes. Stir in 2 tablespoons oil, the salt, and 3 cups flour to form a dough that comes away from the sides of the bowl. Add more flour if necessary.

2. Knead the dough until smooth and elastic either by hand on a floured work surface, in a food processor, or in a mixer fitted with the dough hook; add flour, if necessary. The dough should be soft and pliable, but not sticky. It should take 6 to 8 minutes.

3. Use some of the remaining tablespoon of oil to oil a large bowl. Place the dough in the bowl, brush the top with the remaining oil, cover loosely with plastic wrap, and let rise in a warm, draft-free spot until doubled in bulk, 1 to 2 hours.

4. Punch down the dough and roll it into a cylinder about 2 inches in diameter. Cut the cylinder into 8 equal pieces. Roll each piece of dough into a ball and keep covered with a damp kitchen towel.

5. When you are ready to roll out the breads, preheat the grill to high.

6. Lightly dust the work surface and rolling pin with flour. Roll out the balls one at a time (keeping the others covered) to form circles 6 inches in diameter and ¼ inch thick. Lightly dust the circles with cornmeal and stack them on a plate with a piece of plastic wrap or waxed paper in between. For the best results, finish rolling out the breads not more than 15 minutes before you plan to cook them.

7. To finish the *focacce,* combine the sesame seeds and salt in a small bowl. Lightly brush the top of each *focaccia* with oil and sprinkle with the sesame mixture. When ready to cook, place a few at a time, oiled side down, on the hot grate. Brush the top with more oil and sprinkle with more sesame mixture. Cook the *focacce* until their bottoms are nicely browned and blistered, 2 to 4 minutes. Turn with tongs and cook the second side, 2 to 4 minutes more. Cook all the *focacce* in this fashion and serve.

Makes 8 **focacce;** *serves 4 to 8*

BRUCE FRANKEL'S GRILLED BREAD

U.S.A.

METHOD:
Direct grilling

ADVANCE PREPARATION:
1½ to 2½ hours for the dough to rise

This recipe takes me down memory lane, specifically to a restaurant that helped launch the dining revolution in Boston, a romantic, innovative restaurant run by a visionary chef named Bruce Frankel. Although Panache in Central Square, Cambridge, Massachusetts, closed its doors over a decade ago, and although Frankel has turned his talents to the Internet, my generation of Boston foodies will forever remember Panache with fondness. Bruce used to serve this wonderful grilled bread with goat cheese as an appetizer.

½ envelope active dry yeast
   (1¼ teaspoons)
1 tablespoon molasses
⅔ cup warm water
1½ cups unbleached all-purpose flour,
   plus more for dusting
¾ cup whole-wheat flour
3 tablespoons cornmeal, plus more for
   dusting
½ teaspoon coarse (kosher or sea) salt,
   plus more for sprinkling
3 tablespoons olive oil
Coarsely ground black pepper, to taste
1 tablespoon fresh thyme leaves

1. Combine the yeast with the molasses and 2 tablespoons of the warm water in a large bowl and let stand until foamy, 5 to 10 minutes. Stir in the remaining water, 1½ cups all-purpose flour, the whole-wheat flour, 3 tablespoons cornmeal, and ½ teaspoon salt to form a dough that is soft and pliable, but not sticky. Knead the dough until smooth and elastic either by hand on a floured work surface, in a food processor, or a mixer fitted with a dough hook; add more all-purpose flour, if necessary. It should take 6 to 8 minutes.

2. Use about ½ tablespoon of the oil to lightly oil a large bowl. Place the dough in the bowl, brush the top with another ½ tablespoon oil, cover with a dampened kitchen towel, and let rise in a warm, draft-free spot until doubled in bulk, 1 to 2 hours. Punch the dough down, cover again, and let rise until doubled in bulk again, about 30 minutes.

3. Punch the dough down and divide it into 6 equal pieces. Roll each piece into a ball and keep covered with a damp kitchen towel.

4. Preheat the grill to high.

5. Lightly dust the work surface and rolling pin with flour. Roll out the balls one at a time (keeping the others covered) to form circles 5 inches in diameter and ⅛ inch thick. Lightly dust the circles with cornmeal and stack them on a plate with a piece of plastic wrap or waxed paper in between.

6. When ready to cook, brush the breads with the remaining oil and place, a few at a time, on the hot grate. Grill, turning once with tongs, until puffed and golden brown, 2 to 4 minutes per side. Sprinkle the breads with pepper and the thyme leaves. Serve immediately.

Makes 6 breads; serves 6

TANDOORI-BAKED FLAT BREADS
Naan

INDIA

METHOD:
Direct grilling

ADVANCE PREPARATION:
1 to 2 hours for the dough to rise

Flat breads were the first food cooked in a tandoor (Indian oven) and for me they remain the best. Especially, the light, buttery, yeasted bread known as *naan.* The traditional way to cook *naan* is on the walls of the tandoor. Virtually every residential neighborhood in northern India has a bakery (more like an open-air stall), where barefoot bakers roll and bake *naan* to order.

The procedure is simple enough. When you order *naan,* the baker takes a soft white ball of dough and rolls it into a flat bread. A few slaps from hand to hand stretch the bread into its traditional teardrop shape. Using a pillowlike holder called a *gaddi* (literally "throne"), the baker presses the bread onto the walls of a hot tandoor. The *gaddi* protects his hand— a must when you consider that the temperature of the tandoor can reach 700°F. The bread emerges from the oven puffed and blistered on top and crisp and brown on the bottom. It's sweet and smoky, pliable and moist, and about as delicious as bread gets.

Most of us don't have tandoors, but good results can be obtained with an American-style barbecue grill. Over the years, I've experimented with various techniques, including placing a baking stone in the grill. The best results come with cooking the *naan* directly on the grate over the flames.

1 envelope active dry yeast
5 tablespoons sugar
1 cup warm water
1 egg, beaten
3 tablespoons milk
2 teaspoons salt
4½ to 5 cups unbleached all-purpose
    flour, plus additional for dusting
    and rolling
1 tablespoon vegetable oil
4 tablespoons (½ stick) unsalted butter,
    melted

1. Combine the yeast, 1 tablespoon of the sugar and ¼ cup of the water in a large bowl and let stand until foamy, 5 to 10 minutes. Stir in the remaining sugar, the remaining water, the egg, milk, and salt. Add 4 cups of the flour and stir to form a dough that is soft and pliable, but not sticky. Knead the dough until smooth and elastic either by hand on a floured work surface, in a food processor, or a in mixer fitted with the dough hook; add more flour, if necessary. It should take 6 to 8 minutes.

2. Use ½ tablespoon of the oil to lightly oil a large bowl. Place the dough in the bowl, brush the top with the remaining oil, cover with a clean kitchen towel, and let rise in a warm, draft-free spot until doubled in bulk, 1 to 1½ hours. Punch down the dough and pinch off 2-inch pieces. Roll them between your palms into smooth balls. You should have 14 to 16 balls. Place the balls on a lightly floured baking sheet and cover with a lightly dampened clean kitchen towel. Let rise again until puffy, about 30 minutes.

3. Preheat the grill to high.

4. When ready to cook, place a rolling pin, cutting board, bowl of flour, and the melted butter near the grill. (This is incredibly theatrical; your guests will be amazed.) Roll out a dough ball on a lightly floured cut-

ting board to form a disk about 5 inches in diameter. Gently slap the disk from one hand to the other to stretch it into an elongated 7- to 8-inch circle. (The motion is rather like the "patty cake, patty cake" motion in the nursery rhyme.) Stretch the circle into a traditional teardrop shape and immediately lay it on the hot grate.

5. Cook the bread until the bottom is crusty and browned and the top is puffed and blistered, 2 to 4 minutes. Brush with butter. Invert the *naan* and grill the other side until lightly browned, 2 to 4 minutes. Prepare the remaining *naan* the same way. Brush each *naan* with more butter as it comes off the grill and serve while piping hot. Serve whole, or cut each *naan* into 3 wedges to serve the traditional way.

Makes 14 to 16 **naans;** *serves 7 to 8*

PAPADOMS COOKED OVER THE COALS

INDIA

METHOD:
Direct grilling

*P*apadoms are crisp, spicy, wafer-thin Indian flat breads made from lentil flour and spices. You've probably had them if you've eaten at an Indian restaurant, for *papadoms* are served as both an hors d'oeuvre and with the entrée. They usually come deep-fried at Indian restaurants in North America, an admittedly tasty but greasy preparation, but in India *papadoms* are often cooked on the lid of a tandoor oven or over direct flames to produce audibly crisp wafers without a drop of added fat.

Papadoms are commonly sold boxed, canned, or frozen at Indian markets and gourmet shops. (They're one of the few commercially prepared foods consumed widely in India.) Here's how *papadoms* are served on Bombay's Khau Galli, a kaleido-

scopically colorful street of food stalls near the Zaveri market.

8 papadoms

1. Preheat the grill to high.

2. When ready to cook, place a few papadoms on the hot grill grate. Cook until the bottoms begin to brown and blister, 20 to 40 seconds. Turn the papadoms with tongs and cook the other side the same way. Serve immediately.

Serves 8

JAMAICAN FRY BREAD
Festivals

ON THE SIDE

Festivals—deep-fried breads—are the traditional accompaniment to Jamaican jerk chicken or pork. The following were inspired by a jerk joint in Boston Beach called Sufferer's. (The name is certainly appropriate when you stop to consider how many scotch bonnet chiles go into a single batch of jerk!) For a more fanciful presentation, I like to braid the dough into twists, but you can roll it out and fry it in the traditional cigar shapes.

2 cups unbleached all-purpose flour
¼ cup cornmeal
3 tablespoons sugar
2 tablespoons baking powder
1 teaspoon salt
5 tablespoons unsalted butter,
    chilled
¾ cup evaporated milk, or more
    as needed
2 cups peanut oil for frying, or
    as needed

1. Combine the flour, cornmeal, sugar, baking powder, and salt in a large mixing bowl. Cut in the butter, using two knives. Alternatively, mix the ingredients in a food processor fitted with a chopping blade. The mixture should feel crumbly, like sand. Add enough evaporated milk to obtain a stiff but pliable dough. Stir just to mix.

2. Pinch off walnut-size pieces of dough and roll them between your palms to make long thin ropes. You should have about 24, each one about 10 inches long and ¼ inch thick. Fold the ropes in half and twist them together.

3. Place the oil in a deep-fat fryer or large, deep skillet. Heat over medium-high heat until it reaches 350°F.

4. Gently and carefully lower the festivals into the oil and fry, turning with a slotted spoon, until golden brown, 2 to 40 minutes in all. Transfer the festivals to paper towels to drain and serve while still hot.

Makes about 24 festivals; serves 4 to 6

What's Your Beef?

This woman has spent the last 25 years perfecting her grilling skills at a Central American market.

To judge from the quantity of bison bones found near the fire pits of prehistoric cave dwellers, beef was man's first barbecue. To this day, the popularity of beef remains universal—not to mention at an all-time high. After all, nothing matches the primeval pleasure of sanguine, smokily charred, perfectly cooked beef.

Beef is some of the best food the barbecue trail has to offer, whether you're a Korean enjoying *bool kogi* (sesame-grilled beef), a Russian savoring *shashlik* (kebabs), or a Texan cutting into an oversize steak. What you may not realize is just how widespread and passionate the world's beef eaters are or how astonishingly diverse are the ways to cook beef with live fire.

In this chapter you'll find grilled beef dishes of all sizes, shapes, and cooking methods. Tiny satés from Indonesia, mammoth prime ribs from Great Britain, T-bones from Tuscany, teriyaki from Tokyo, short ribs from Seoul, quickly seared beef from Vietnam, and slow-cooked, smoky briskets from Texas.

You'll also learn how to properly grill a steak and stuff and roll a *matambre* (South American flank steak). In fact, no matter what your beef is, you'll find it in this chapter.

TEXAS-STYLE BARBECUED BRISKET

U.S.A.

METHOD:
Indirect grilling

ADVANCE PREPARATION:
4 to 8 hours for marinating the meat (optional); also, leave yourself 5 to 8 hours for cooking

SPECIAL EQUIPMENT:
6 to 8 cups hickory or mesquite chips or chunks, soaked for 1 hour in cold water to cover and drained

Pork may be the preferred barbecue feast of the Mississippi (think of the pork shoulder of the Carolinas and the ribs of Kansas City and Memphis). But in Texas beef is king. Especially beef brisket, which comes moist and smoky and tender enough to cut with a fork. (Not that any self-respecting Texas barbecue buff would actually eat brisket with a fork.) Barbecued brisket is simultaneously one of the easiest and most challenging recipes in the world of barbecue. It's easy because it requires only one main ingredient—brisket (even the rub is optional). It's challenging because pit masters spend years learning the right combination of smoke (lots), heat (low), and time (measured in half days rather than hours) to transform one of the toughest, most ornery parts of the steer into tender, meaty perfection.

Over the years, I've found that two things help above all: choosing the right cut of brisket—namely, untrimmed, with a thick sheath of fat—and then cooking the brisket in a shallow pan. The latter keeps the juices from dripping onto the fire and the meat from drying out, while allowing for maximum smoke penetration from the top. A whole brisket (the sort cooked by a restaurant) weighs 18 to 20 pounds. Below I call for partially trimmed brisket—a cut weighing 5 to 6 pounds. Do not attempt this recipe with a 2-pound trimmed, fatless brisket; it will turn out much too dry.

1 beef brisket (5 to 6 pounds), with a layer of fat at least ¼ inch thick, preferably ½ inch thick

1 tablespoon coarse (kosher or sea) salt

1 tablespoon chile powder

2 teaspoons sugar

1 teaspoon freshly ground black pepper

1 teaspoon ground cumin

Barbecue Sauce, the Texas Way

The best Texas-style barbecue sauce combines the sweetness of Kansas City–style tomato sauces with the mouth-puckering tartness of a North Carolina vinegar sauce. I've come up with my own version—mix equal parts of Basic Barbecue Sauce with the North Carolina Vinegar Barbecue Sauce (both in the Sauces chapter). Serve it with barbecued brisket, and for a really good sauce, add drippings or a little chopped brisket.

1. Rinse the brisket under cold running water and blot dry with paper towels.

2. Combine the remaining ingredients in a bowl and toss with your fingers to mix. Rub this mixture into the brisket on all sides. If you have time, wrap the brisket in plastic and let marinate, in the refrigerator, for 4 to 8 hours (or even overnight), but don't worry if you don't have time for this—it will be plenty flavorful, even if you cook it right away.

3. Set the grill up for indirect cooking (see page 14 or 16). No drip pan is necessary for this recipe. *If using a charcoal grill,* preheat to low.

If using a gas grill, place as many wood chips as you can in the smoker box and preheat the grill to high. When smoke appears, lower the heat to medium-low.

4. When ready to cook, if using a charcoal grill, toss one-quarter of the wood chips on the coals. Place the brisket, fat side up, in an aluminum foil pan (or make a pan with a double sheet of heavy duty aluminum foil). Place the pan in the center of the hot grate, away from the heat. Cover the grill.

5. Smoke-cook the brisket, using the indirect method, until tender enough to shred with your fingers, 5 to 8 hours. (The cooking time will depend on the size of the brisket and heat of the grill.) Baste the brisket from time to time with the fat and juices that accumulate in the pan. If using charcoal, add 10 to 12 fresh coals per side every hour and toss more wood chips on the fresh coals. (Add about ½ cup chips per side every time you replenish the coals.) With gas, all you need to do is be sure that you start with a full tank of gas.

6. Remove the brisket pan from the grill and let cool for 15 minutes. Transfer the brisket to a cutting board and thinly slice across the grain, using a sharp knife, electric knife, or cleaver. Transfer the sliced meat to a platter, pour the pan juices on top, and serve immediately.

Serves 10 to 12

GRILLED PRIME RIBS OF BEEF WITH GARLIC AND ROSEMARY

U . S . A .

METHOD:
indirect grilling

ADVANCE PREPARATION:
None, but leave yourself about 4 hours for cooking

If you're like most people (including me), you're probably intimidated by the prospect of cooking a standing rib roast. Who wouldn't be? A prime rib represents a formidable piece of meat for even the most seasoned chef: an 18-pound mass of beef and bones that literally takes both hands to lift. It's also expensive—a 7-rib roast can cost upwards of $100. Well, be intimidated no more, because here's an easy, virtually failproof method for cooking perfect, crusty-on-the-outside, meltingly-tender-inside prime ribs every time: Cook it on your barbecue grill using the indirect method.

The only remotely challenging aspect to cooking prime ribs is the timing, and if you figure on 12 to 14 minutes per pound (for a bone-in roast), you'll make a perfect roast every time. Besides, you can let a cooked prime-rib roast stand for up to 30 minutes before carving. Indeed, at least 10 to 15 minutes of standing time is recommended to allow the juices to flow from the center of the roast back to the exterior.

The following recipe calls for a 7-rib roast, which will weigh 16 to 18 pounds and will serve eight Paul Bunyans and twelve normal people. A 2-, 4-, or 6-rib roast would be prepared the same way. For that matter, a boneless rib roast would also be prepared this way (just shorten the cooking time). When buying prime ribs, be sure to choose a roast with a thick jacket of fat. This fat melts during cooking, basting and tenderizing the meat.

And don't fret if you can't find fresh rosemary. The beef will have plenty of flavor with dried rosemary.

Yorkshire Pudding (see Index) makes the perfect accompaniment.

FOR THE BEEF:

1 prime rib beef roast (7 ribs; 16 to 18
    pounds), tied at 2-inch intervals
6 cloves garlic, each clove cut lengthwise
    into 4 pieces
4 to 6 sprigs fresh rosemary or
    1 tablespoon dried

FOR THE RUB:

2 tablespoons black peppercorns
2 tablespoons dried rosemary
2 tablespoons coarse (kosher or sea) salt
2 tablespoons sweet paprika

1. Set the grill up for indirect cooking (see page 14 or 16) and place a large drip pan in the center. Preheat to medium.

2. Using the tip of a slender paring knife, make a series of ½-inch-deep holes in the roast, mostly in the sheath of fat on top, but also on the sides and bottom. The holes should be about 2 inches apart. Insert slivers of garlic in half the holes. Strip the leaves off one or two of the rosemary sprigs and insert them in the remaining holes (or insert the dried rosemary). Slide the remaining sprigs under the string used to tie up the roast.

3. Make the rub. Grind the peppercorns and dried rosemary to a fine powder in a spice mill or blender. Add the salt and paprika and grind to mix. Rub this mixture all over the roast, especially over the sheath of fat on top.

4. When ready to cook, oil the grill grate. Place the roast, fat side up, on the hot grate over the drip pan and cover the grill.

5. Grill the roast until cooked to taste, 3½ to 4 hours for medium-rare for a roast this size, figuring on 12 to 14 minutes per pound. (If using a charcoal grill, you'll need to add 10 to 12 fresh coals per side every hour. If using a gas grill, keep the cover closed at all times.) Use an instant-read thermometer to determine doneness; you'll want to cook the roast to 145°F for medium-rare, 160°F for medium. Transfer the roast to a platter or carving board and cover loosely with aluminum foil. Let the roast rest for 10 to 15 minutes before carving and serving. The easiest way to carve the roast is to cut it into rib sections with a long, slender knife, then into thin slices to serve.

Serves 12 to 16

BRAZILIAN STUFFED RIB ROAST

BRAZIL

METHOD:
*Indirect grilling
or rotisserie*

**SPECIAL
EQUIPMENT:**
*Rotisserie
(optional)*

This grilled stuffed roast is one of the most colorful *churrascuria* offerings ever to grace a plate in Rio. Imagine a boneless beef rib roast generously larded with ham, cheese, carrots, peppers, and other vegetables, then roasted to fork-tenderness on a rotisserie (or using the indirect-grilling method). The stuffing serves a dual purpose, both flavoring the meat and forming a colorful mosaic when the roast is sliced. This recipe was inspired by the restaurant Porcão in Ipanema in Rio de Janeiro.

The easiest way to insert the various ingredients for the stuffing that goes into the meat is to use a larding iron, a sharp implement with a V-shaped metal blade, which you may be able to find at a cookware shop. Alternatively, follow the instructions for larding in the box on the facing page.

1 boneless beef rib roast (3½ to 4 pounds), rolled and tied

2 long slender carrots, peeled and cut lengthwise in half

½ green bell pepper, stemmed, seeded, and cut lengthwise into ½-inch strips

½ red bell pepper, stemmed, seeded, and cut lengthwise into ½-inch strips

1 medium onion, cut into 10 wedges

1 slice (¼ inch thick) smoked ham (about 2 ounces), cut into ¼-inch strips and frozen

1 slice (¼ inch thick) aged provolone or other firm white cheese (about 2 ounces), cut into ¼ inch strips and frozen

2 cloves garlic, cut into matchstick slivers

Salt and freshly ground black pepper, to taste

1. Using a larding iron or sharpening steel, pierce the roast from end to end in 16 to 20 places. The idea is to riddle the meat with slender tunnels that run along the grain.

2. *Insert* the carrot halves, bell pepper strips, thin onion wedges, and ham and cheese strips into these tunnels, gently inching them into the holes. The carrot strips will be long enough to transpierce the meat, but you'll need to double or triple up on the remaining ingredients; insert shorter items from both ends.

3. Make tiny slits, 1 inch apart, in the surface of the roast, using the tip of a paring knife. Insert a sliver of garlic in each. Generously season the roast with salt and pepper (see Note).

4. *Indirect grilling method:* Set up the grill for indirect cooking. (see page 14 to 16) placing a large drip pan in the center. Preheat to medium. When ready to cook, oil the grill grate. Place the roast on the hot grate over the drip pan. Cover the grill and cook the roast to taste: 1 to 1½ hours for medium-rare (145°F on an instant-read thermometer), 1½ to 2 hours for medium (160°F). If using a charcoal grill, add 10 to 12 fresh coals per side every hour.

Rotisserie method: Set up the rotisserie following the instructions on page 20. *If using a gas grill,* preheat the front and rear burners to high. *If using a charcoal grill,* light the coals and rake into rows in front and back, leaving a gap in the center. Skewer the roast on the spit. Rotisserie the roast until cooked to medium-rare (about 145°F on an instant-read thermometer), 1¼ to 1½ hours on a covered rotisserie. For medium (160°F), cook for 1½ to 2 hours. If using a charcoal grill, replenish the coals as needed.

5. Transfer the roast to a cutting board and let rest for 10 minutes. Cut into thin crosswise slices, using an electric knife or sharp carving knife to serve.

Serves 8

Note: The recipe can be prepared up to 8 hours ahead to this point. Store in the refrigerator.

Larding the Beef

Don't despair if you don't have a larding iron. A sharpening steel works just as well. Wash and wipe the steel to remove any metal fillings. Slowly insert the slender end of the steel into one end of the roast and push it through to the other side. Pull it out, leaving a tunnel in the meat. Gently worm the vegetable slivers, cheese, and ham into the tunnel. With shorter vegetables, like pepper strips, you'll have to insert from both ends. Freezing the ham and cheese first makes them easier to insert.

STEAK IN GARLIC-LIME MARINADE
Palomilla

CUBA

METHOD:
Direct grilling

Mention *palomilla* to a Cuban and his eyes will light with pleasure. Like so much grilled fare, *palomilla* (pronounced "pal-o-ME-ya") is a poor man's dish that has been elevated to gastronomic indulgence. The term refers to a thin, flavorful steak cut from the bottom round (*la bola* in Spanish). Because bottom round can be rather tough, the steak is cut thin (about the width of your baby finger) to make it seem more tender.

Where I live in Miami, *palomilla* turns up at Cuban restaurants throughout the city, but no one makes it better than Victor's Cafe. That's because Victor's owner, Sonia Zaldivar, uses prime top butt and she grills the meat over oak, instead of sautéing it in a frying pan. Like most Cuban meats, *palomilla* would traditionally be marinated in *adobo* (a cumin, lime, garlic marinade) before cooking. But Sonia skips the marinating, basting the steak with *adobo* as it cooks.

If you can't find steaks cut from the top butt, you could use shell steaks, or sirloin. The important thing is to cut the steaks thin (no more than ½ inch thick).

Serve with Grilled Polenta or Bahamian Peas and Rice (see Index).

FOR THE ADOBO:
4 cloves garlic
1 teaspoon salt, or more to taste
½ teaspoon ground cumin
½ teaspoon freshly ground black
    pepper, or more to taste
½ cup sour orange juice or
    fresh lime juice
2 tablespoons olive oil

FOR THE STEAKS:
4 beef steaks (each 6 to 8 ounces),
    cut ½ inch thick
2 large onions, cut crosswise into
    ½-inch slices
2 tablespoons olive oil

1. Prepare the *adobo*. Combine the garlic, salt, cumin, and pepper in a mortar and grind to a paste with the pestle. Work in the lime juice and oil to a smooth paste. Alternatively, place all the ingredients in a blender and process to a smooth purée. Correct the seasoning, adding salt and pepper as necessary; the mixture should be highly seasoned.

2. Preheat the grill to high.

3. When ready to cook, oil the grill grate. Brush the onion slices with the oil and arrange on the hot grate. Brush the steaks with the *adobo* mixture and place on the hot grate with the onion (see Note). Grill the steaks to taste, 2 to 3 minutes per side for medium-rare, basting with the *adobo* and rotating 90 degrees after 1 minute to create an attractive crosshatch of grill marks. Always use tongs when moving or turning the steak. Grill the onions until nicely charred, 3 to 4 minutes per side, seasoning with salt and pepper.

4. Transfer the steaks to plates or a platter and brush one final time with the *adobo*. Let stand for 3 minutes, then serve with the grilled onions on the side.

Serves 4

Note: To give the steaks a richer garlic, cumin, and lime flavor, marinate them in the *adobo* in a nonreactive baking dish for 10 minutes before grilling.

How to Grill the Perfect Steak

When Americans are polled about their favorite foods for grilling, steak always heads the list. A slab of beef is the perfect food for the grill: Its broad surface area soaks up charcoal and smoke flavors, and its relative thinness allows for quick cooking.

The most common mistake made in grilling steak is overcooking it; the second most common is undercooking. Here's how to do it just right.

1. **Pick the right kind of steak.** Tender cuts like sirloin, tenderloin, porterhouse, New York strip, and shell steak are the best. Fibrous steaks, like skirt and flank, also taste great grilled—especially when thinly sliced on the diagonal. Save tough cuts like chuck and blade steak for long, slow, moist cooking methods like braising.

2. Some people let the steak come to room temperature before grilling. Most professionals, including myself, don't bother. If you do cook a room temperature steak, reduce the cooking time slightly.

3. **Preheat the grill to high.** If cooking a very thick steak (say a strip steak 2 inches thick), build a two-tiered fire (see page 14). On a gas grill, preheat one side to high, one side to medium-high.

4. **Season the steaks generously with salt and pepper.** Use a coarse-grained salt, like kosher or sea salt. Coarse grain salt crystals dissolve more slowly than fine table salt, so they hold up better during cooking, and steak pros all over the world use this. I always use freshly ground or freshly cracked black pepper and I apply it generously both before and after grilling.

Some people don't add the salt until after cooking. The salt, they argue, draws out the juices. Believe me, you won't get much juice loss in the short time it takes to cook a medium-rare steak. And besides, you can't beat the flavor of salt mixed with caramelized meat juices.

5. **Oil the grill grate.** The easiest way to do this for steak is to use a piece of steak fat held in tongs or at the end of a carving fork. Rub it over the bars of the grate. An oiled rag or folded up paper towels work fine, too.

6. **Place the steaks on the oiled grate,** all lined up in the same direction. After 2 minutes, rotate each steak. Normally I rotate 45 degrees. This cre-

ates an attractive diamond crosshatch of grill marks on the steak. Sometimes I rotate 90 degrees; this produces a square crosshatch. Cook the steak until beads of blood appear on the surface, 1 to 2 minutes for a steak ½ inch thick, 3 to 5 minutes for one 1 inch thick, 6 to 9 minutes for a thickness of 1½ to 2 inches. Turn the steak with tongs or a spatula; never use a fork. The holes made by a fork allow the juices to escape.

7. **Continue cooking the steaks on the other side,** rotating them after 2 minutes. You'll need slightly less time on the second side. The best test for doneness is feel: Press the top with your index finger. A rare steak will be softly yielding; a medium steak will be firmly yielding; a well-done steak will be firm. (See "Is It Done Yet?" on page 22.) Never cut into a steak to test for doneness. This, too, drains the juices.

8. **Transfer the steaks to plates or a platter and season again with salt and pepper.** At this stage, I like to brush my steaks with extra-virgin olive oil (à la Tuscany) or with melted butter (à la Peter Luger, the Brooklyn steak house). This is optional, but it sure rounds out the flavor.

9. **This last step is usually overlooked, but it's the most important.** Let the steaks rest for 2 to 3 minutes before you serve them. This allows the juices to flow back from the center of the meat to the exterior, giving you a moister, juicier steak.

Beef Grilling Chart*

CUT	METHOD	HEAT	DONENESS		
			RARE (140°F)	MEDIUM (160°F)	WELL-DONE (170°F)
STEAKS					
½ INCH THICK	DIRECT	HIGH	1–2 MIN/SIDE	2–3 MIN/SIDE	3–4 MIN/SIDE
1 INCH THICK	DIRECT	HIGH	3–4 MIN/SIDE	4–6 MIN/SIDE	6–7 MIN/SIDE
1½ INCHES THICK	DIRECT	HIGH	4–6 MIN/SIDE	6–8 MIN/SIDE	8–9 MIN/SIDE
FLANK STEAK	DIRECT	HIGH	2–3 MIN/SIDE	4–5 MIN/SIDE	6–7 MIN/SIDE
ROASTS & RIBS					
TENDERLOIN (2–3 LBS)	INDIRECT	HIGH	40–50 MIN	1 HR	DON'T DO IT
TENDERLOIN (4–5 LBS)	INDIRECT	HIGH	1 HR	1¼ HRS	DON'T DO IT
BONELESS RIB (4–6 LBS)	INDIRECT	MEDIUM	1–1½ HRS	1½–2 HRS	DON'T DO IT
STANDING RIB (16–18 LBS, BONE-IN)	INDIRECT	MEDIUM	3 HRS	4 HRS	DON'T DO IT
BRISKET (5–6 LBS)	INDIRECT	MEDIUM-LOW			5–8 HRS
RIBS	INDIRECT	MEDIUM		1½–2 HRS	1½–2 HRS; DONE WHEN TENDER

This chart is offered as a broad guideline to cooking times for the various cuts of meat. Remember, grilling is an art, not a science. When in doubt, refer to times in the individual recipes.

STET'S STEAK

U.S.A.

METHOD:
Direct grilling

My friend Stetson Glimes developed this steak recipe on a camping trip. It's a perfect example of how a few ingredients, when thoughtfully combined, can utterly transform a commonplace dish. Stet is quite emphatic about using freshly ground white pepper, not black.

4 sirloin beefsteaks (10 to 12 ounces each), cut 1 inch thick
¼ cup dry mustard, such as Colman's
¼ cup Worcestershire sauce
Juice of 1 large, juicy lime
Coarse (kosher or sea) salt and freshly ground white pepper, to taste

1. Place the steaks on a platter and sprinkle with half the dry mustard. Pat the steaks with the flat part of a fork to spread the mustard evenly over and into the meat. Sprinkle the steaks with half the Worcestershire sauce, then squeeze half of the lime over

them. Pat with the fork. Season the steaks generously with salt and pepper. Turn the steaks over and spread with the remaining mustard, Worcestershire, and lime juice, and more salt and pepper, patting with the fork. Let the steaks marinate for 15 to 20 minutes while you preheat the grill.

2. Preheat the grill to high.

3. When ready to cook, oil the grill grate. Place the steaks on the hot grate and grill, turning with tongs, until cooked to taste, 4 to 6 minutes per side for medium-rare. Do not rotate steaks here; if you do, you'll jar off the mustard mixture. (Stet serves them Pittsburgh rare—black on the outside, bloody inside.) Transfer the steaks to a platter and let stand for 3 minutes.

4. Thinly slice the steaks on the diagonal, as you would London broil. Let the slices marinate in the meat juices for a minute or two, then serve immediately.

Serves 4

STEAK FROM HELL

MEXICO

METHOD:
Direct grilling

SPECIAL EQUIPMENT:
2 cups mesquite wood chips, soaked for 1 hour in cold water to cover and drained (optional)

EXTRA SALSA

The Steak From Hell recipe includes a salsa to serve with the steaks. If you have any left over, store it in the refrigerator. It's great with chips.

This recipe literally is a "steak from hell." It comes from an unassuming steakhouse in Juarez, Mexico, called Mitla, and *mitla* is the Nahuatl Indian word for "hell." Mitla's steaks owe their extraordinary flavor to the fact that they're cooked over blazing mesquite logs. You can approximate the flavor by tossing mesquite chips on the grill. Note that I call for grilling the tomatoes used in the salsa on a stovetop burner. This is done while the barbecue grill is heating up and allows for the salsa to be prepared in advance.

2 to 4 chiles de arbol or other
    dried hot red chiles (4 give
    you a nice heat)
2 large, fresh, ripe tomatoes
⅓ medium onion, sliced
1 clove garlic, sliced
3 tablespoons coarsely chopped
    fresh cilantro
1 to 2 tablespoons fresh lime juice
Salt and freshly ground black pepper,
    to taste
4 sirloin or T-bone beefsteaks
    (each about ½ inch thick)
4 large or 8 small flour tortillas,
    for serving

1. Preheat the grill to high. *If using a gas grill,* add the wood chips (if using) to the smoker box before preheating.

2. Soak the chiles in a bowl of warm water until pliable, about 20 minutes.

3. Meanwhile, set each tomato directly on a stove burner and roast over high heat until the skins are charred and blistered on all sides, 6 to 8 minutes. Transfer to a plate and let cool. Drain the chiles and remove the seeds if you prefer a milder salsa. Place the chiles in a blender with the tomatoes, onion, garlic, and cilantro. Process to a coarse paste. Add the lime juice and salt and pepper to taste; the salsa should be highly seasoned. Transfer to a serving bowl.

4. When ready to cook, *if using charcoal,* toss the wood chips on the coals. For both gas and charcoal, oil the grill grate. Salt the steaks generously on one side. Place on the hot grate, salt side down, and grill, turning once with tongs, until cooked to taste, 2 to 3 minutes per side for medium-rare. Remove the steaks to a platter and let stand for 3 minutes.

5. Meanwhile, arrange the tortillas on the grate and grill until soft, pliable, but not browned, about 20 seconds per side. Serve the steaks with the tortillas and the salsa on the side.

Serves 4; makes about 1½ cups salsa

In Pursuit of the Best Tuscan Steak

It was one of those days when life on the barbecue trail didn't seem so glamorous. When my destination seemed to recede with each passing kilometer. When the "just another 20 minutes" turned into hour after hour.

My wife, Barbara, and I had come to Tuscany to sample *bistecca alla fiorentina* (Florentine steak). But here we were driving away from Florence, indeed, leaving Tuscany for Umbria. The winding roads and scenic hilltop towns I associate with Tuscany gave way to a roadway clogged with diesel belching trucks and a city crowded with traffic. It seemed an inauspicious start to a quest for a disappearing regional dish.

Yet our destination had come recommended by a highly reliable source. Italian food and wine expert Burton Anderson had mentioned the Villa Roncalli in the sort of conspiratorial whisper that foodies reserve for their personal favorite haunts. "He's one of the last people in Tuscany that serves real Chianina beef," explained Anderson. "I think you'll find his grilling techniques of interest."

We pulled off a crowded road into a long tree-shaded driveway. At the end rose a tall, yellow building with green shutters and brick-colored trim—the Villa Roncalli, formerly a seventeenth century hunting lodge. We stowed our scepticism long enough to check into a simple room with the gorgeous linens and bathroom fixtures we'd come to associate with even the most modest lodgings in Italy.

The dining room opened at 8 P.M., and we were there. The setting certainly looked promising: a large square chamber with a half dozen elegantly set tables. A huge bronze chandelier hung from a dizzyingly high-domed ceiling. An equally monumental mahogany breakfront filled with wine bottles lined the back wall. A waist-high fireplace stood in one corner, but much to my dismay, there was nary a fire in sight.

Because of anti-pollution measures, many restaurants in Florence have given up cooking over the traditional oak fire. But here in the countryside? Well, I couldn't imagine why the Villa Roncalli's fireplace was still cold and bare.

A handsome young woman in a starched, immaculately white, floor-length apron made a majestic entrance. Maria Luisa Leocastre is the owner's daughter, dining room manager, and chef. "If we wouldn't mind,"

she explained, "the kitchen would like to prepare for us a menu *degustazione.*" (They give out menus, but everyone has the *degustazione*.) Of course we wouldn't mind, I said, but, I noted that I would like to try a *bistecca alla fiorentina.*

In gradual succession we were served a delicate salad of *ortie* (wild greens) and shaved Parmesan cheese; a squash blossom filled with velvety ricotta and herbs; and a tiny square of fish cooked in a crust of paper-thin sliced potatoes. There was an exquisite soup made from beans and tiny clams. There was an exquisitely creamy barley risotto. The only thing missing was the beef.

Then at 10:30 P.M., just when I'd completely despaired of ever having my *bistecca,* Maria's father, Angelo Leocastre, made his appearance. Pressed denim shirt. Pleated wool pants. Alligator belt and leather shoes. He looked less like a grill master than an executive on vacation. Angelo dumped a few handfuls of oak on the stone slab floor of the fireplace and with a flourish ignited it with a blowtorch. He switched on a device that looked like a giant hair blower and within minutes the coals blazed red.

A true *bistecca* turns out to be a cross between a T-bone steak and a porterhouse. (It's cut closer to the center of the steer than a North American T-bone, so it includes a full circle of the tenderloin.) The steak Angelo showed me was two fingers thick and as dark red as the local Sagranito wine that filled my glass. He tossed it on a square grill that had legs to hold it over the fire.

"*Veloce, veloce* (fast, fast)," Angelo said, passionately explaining the secret to great *bistecca alla fiorentina.* The key is high heat. Using local oak and a blower to stoke the coals, he claims he can achieve a temperature of 900°F. Within minutes, the outside of the meat had seared to a golden-brown crust. The inside remained moist and sanguine. I noted with interest that Angelo seasoned the meat—a huge sprinkle of salt and white pepper from separate stone bowls—only after he had turned it.

I timed the cooking with a stop watch: exactly 6 minutes per side. Angelo transferred the steak to a platter and basted it generously with olive oil. Generous? I'd say he poured half a cup of green-gold oil over the steak. The aroma generated when the fragrant oil hit the hot meat made my mouth water and my taste buds quake.

There are people who maintain that a steak is a steak is a steak. They haven't tasted Angelo's *bistecca.* To say it cuts like butter wouldn't do justice to its extraordinary tenderness. As for the flavor, I've simply never had beef like it. Somehow, Angelo has achieved the sort of complexity and depth of flavor you would get by aging a Parmesan cheese for three years or a red wine for a couple of decades. It's rich, sonorous, complex, and full-flavored, without being heavy or gamy. It's beef the way it was meant to be

Where to Eat Bistecca alla Fiorentina in Italy

Many restaurants in Tuscany and Umbria (especially in the country) have fireplaces in the dining room or kitchen that double as grills. Here are a few of my favorites:

Villa Roncalli
via Roma 25
Foligno, Perugia
tel. 0742-391091

Cibreo
via dei Macci 118, Florence
tel. 055-2341100

Da Delfina
Artimino near Carmignano
Tuscany
tel. 055-8718074

eaten before the industrialization of cattle raising.

Angelo waved away a plate of vegetables the waitress had brought. "When you eat *fiorentina, fiorentina* is all you eat. The only suitable vegetable is wine," Angelo said with a wink. With it we drank fishbowl-size glasses of a dark red, cedary Santoroso wine. Amazingly enough, considering all the food we'd eaten, with Angelo's help we managed to finish the *bistecca.* The T-bone went to Angelo's waist-high mastif, "Tiny."

Angelo's eyes lit with passion as he described the animal that supplies his *bistecca.* The Chianina is a huge,

snow-white, one-and-a-half-ton steer that owes its extraordinary flavor to a diet of corn, beans, and barley. It's not an animal that lends itself to industrial production, explained Angelo. It takes too long to reach maturity and the "yield" is not efficient.

Angelo knows, perhaps, ten farmers who still raise it. "A labor of love," he said. The future for Chianina does not look particularly promising. "Some day, all our meat will come from Argentina or France," he winced noticeably. "Then there will be no more *fiorentina.*"

After dinner, we followed Angelo into an outbuilding that serves as his studio, where we learned the final secrets of his extraordinary *bistecca.* It's here he ages the beef for 30 days at around 33°F. It will lose about 15 percent of its weight in the process. We admired the prosciutti and sausages hanging from the rafters—all homemade and aged for three years. "We make everything from scratch here," Angelo said with pride.

As the nights turn cool and darkness comes earlier, many of us will forsake our barbecue grills. But this is precisely the sort of weather a Tuscan cherishes for grilling. In Tuscany, grilling is generally done indoors in a fireplace. There's even a special grate with legs at each corner for holding the meat over a pile of coals.

On page 125 you'll find a recipe for *bistecca alla fiorentina* that comes as close as possible to the Italian classic. I can't think of a more compelling reason to keep the fire in your grill burning all autumn or winter long.

RIB STEAKS WITH RED WINE SAUCE AND MARROW

Entrecôte à la Bordelaise

FRANCE

METHOD:
Direct grilling

Here's a recipe from my cooking school days in Paris. An *entrecôte* is a French rib steak, often cooked and served on the bone in plate-burying proportions. In the U.S. I use shell steaks (rib eyes), which are generously marbled and delicious on the grill. As for the term *bordelaise* (Bordeaux style), it refers, logically enough, to a sauce made with reduced red wine and shallots and a garnish of poached marrow. I like to enrich the sauce further by adding sautéed mushrooms. You needn't open a *grand cru* for this recipe, but try to use a wine you wouldn't mind drinking straight. (This is a great way to use up leftover Bordeaux.) Marrow bones can be found at butcher shops and ethnic markets: Ask your butcher to cut the bones on his saw and extract the marrow for you. But even if you can't find marrow, the steaks will still be fabulous without it.

FOR THE STEAKS:
4 beef shell steaks (rib eyes; 8 to 10
    ounces each)
2 tablespoons olive oil
Coarse (kosher or sea) salt and
    cracked black pepper, to taste

FOR THE BORDELAISE SAUCE:
3 tablespoons unsalted butter
½ cup minced shallots
8 ounces fresh white mushrooms, wiped
    clean, and thinly sliced
2 cups dry red wine
1 cup homemade beef stock or low-sodium
    canned beef broth
1 teaspoon cornstarch dissolved in
    1 tablespoon red wine (optional)
Coarse (kosher or sea) salt and freshly
    ground black pepper, to taste

FOR GARNISH:
¼ cup marrow, from 4 marrow bones
2 tablespoons chopped fresh Italian
    (flat-leaf) parsley

1. Rub the steaks on both sides with the oil and season with salt and pepper. Let them come to room temperature while you make the sauce.

2. Melt the butter in a heavy medium-size saucepan. Add the shallots and sauté over medium heat, stirring, until softened and translucent but not brown, about 3 minutes. Add the mushrooms and cook until lightly browned and most of the liquid has evaporated, 3 to 5 minutes. Add the wine and bring to a boil over medium-high heat, then reduce the heat slightly and simmer the wine briskly until reduced by half, about 5 minutes. Add the stock and simmer briskly until the mixture is reduced by half again, 5 minutes more. If you start with very good stock, the mixture may be thick enough to serve as a sauce without the cornstarch. If not, stir the cornstarch-wine mixture into the sauce and bring to a boil; the sauce should thicken slightly. Whisk in salt and pepper as necessary; the sauce should be highly seasoned. Remove from the heat and set aside while you poach the marrow.

3. Pour water to a depth of 1 inch into a shallow pan. Heat to a simmer, add the marrow, and poach until waxy and white, with no remaining red, turning with a skimmer, 15 to 30 seconds. Do not overcook, or the marrow will melt. Transfer the marrow to paper towels to drain; then cut it into thin crosswise slices (see Note).

4. Preheat the grill to high.

5. When ready to cook, oil the grill grate.

Place the steaks on the hot grate and grill until cooked to taste, 4 to 6 minutes per side for medium-rare, rotating the steaks 45 degrees after 2 minutes on each side to create an attractive crosshatch of grill marks; use tongs when moving or turning the steak. While the steak cooks, reheat the sauce, tasting it for seasoning. Transfer the steaks to a platter and let stand for 2 to 3 minutes. Spoon the sauce over the steaks and top with slices of marrow and a sprinkling of parsley. Serve immediately.

Serves 4

Note: The recipe can be prepared several hours ahead to this point.

FLORENTINE-STYLE STEAK
Bistecca alla Fiorentina

ITALY

METHOD:
Direct grilling

SPECIAL EQUIPMENT:
Hand-held hair dryer for charcoal grills

Bistecca alla fiorentina is one of the high holies of Tuscan cuisine. I know that it doesn't sound like much when you describe it: an olive oil–basted, grilled T-bone steak. But here, as in so much of art, perfection lies in the details. The details in this instance include a lengthily aged steak from a rare breed of cattle cooked over an uncommonly high heat and basted with the best olive oil money can buy. *Bistecca* is commonly translated as T-bone steak, although it's actually closer to a porterhouse: Cut closer to the center of the steer, it has a larger piece of tenderloin attached.

On page 122, you can read about a true master in the art of making *bistecca alla fiorentina*. It would be impossible to duplicate his recipe outside of Italy, but his techniques can be adapted to make a highly respectable version with North American beef. The main secret is to find a butcher who will sell you an aged T-bone steak. Oh, you'll also need one unexpected piece of equipment—a hair dryer for fanning the coals!

1 T-bone or porterhouse beefsteak
  (about 2 pounds), cut at least
  1½ inches thick
Coarse (kosher or sea) salt and freshly
  ground white pepper
½ cup of the best cold-pressed extra-virgin
  olive oil you can find (preferably Tuscan)

1. Preheat the grill to high. (Ideally, you'll be using wood or charcoal; the coals should just be beginning to ash over.) If using wood or charcoal, blow the ash off with a hair dryer.

2. When ready to cook, oil the grill grate. Place the steak on the hot grate and point the hair dryer at the coals to fan them to a glowing red. Grill the steak until cooked to taste (about 6 to 8 minutes per side for medium-rare) turning with tongs; generously salt and pepper the steak when you turn it. When done, remove it to a deep serving platter and generously salt and pepper again.

3. Drizzle the oil over the hot steak and let stand for 3 minutes before serving. Cut servings of the beef off the bone for each eater. Mix the oil that collects in the bottom of the platter with the meat juices and spoon these over the steak as a sauce. Uncork an old bottle of Barolo and get ready to enjoy the world's best steak.

Serves 2 to 3; can be multiplied as desired

NICARAGUAN-STYLE STEAK
Churrasco

NICARAGUA

METHOD:
Direct grilling

ADVANCE PREPARATION:
30 minutes for marinating the meat

The word *churrasco* is used throughout Latin America to describe beef cooked on the grill, although the precise meaning varies from country to country. In Brazil, for example, *churrasco* is the generic term for barbecue. In Nicaragua it refers to a broad, thin steak cut from a beef tenderloin. Most steaks are cut across the muscle grain, but Nicaragua's *churrasco* is cut along the grain. What results is a flat, thin piece of meat with a remarkable texture, a steak that's tender enough to cut with a fork. (And the steak's broad surface area readily picks up the smoke flavor from the coals.)

Nicaraguan *churrasco* is always served

with a trio of sauces: *chimichurri* (here used as a marinade as well), *salsa marinara* (Nicaraguan Tomato Sauce), and a spicy pickled onion sauce called *cebollita*. Other accompaniments might include fried plantains (Grilled Plantains, a tasty substitute, appears in this book) and Bahamian Peas and Rice (see Index).

1 piece (1½ pounds) beef tenderloin, preferably center cut
1 large or 2 medium bunches fresh Italian (flat-leaf) parsley, stemmed (about 2 cups leaves)
4 cloves garlic, peeled
1 cup olive oil
¼ cup red wine vinegar, or more to taste
3 tablespoons water
1½ teaspoons salt, or more to taste
1 teaspoon finely ground black pepper, or more to taste

1. Place the piece of tenderloin lengthwise on the cutting board. Holding the knife parallel to the cutting board, cut the meat into 4 flat, even horizontal strips. Place each

strip between two sheets of plastic wrap and pound with the side of a cleaver or with a rolling pin to a thickness of $1/4$ inch. Arrange the steaks in a nonreactive baking dish.

2. Prepare the *chimichurri.* Combine the parsley and garlic in a food processor and process until finely chopped. Add the oil, $1/4$ cup vinegar, water, $1^1/2$ teaspoons salt, and 1 teaspoon pepper and process to make a thick sauce. Correct the seasoning, adding salt, pepper, or vinegar as necessary; the mixture should be highly seasoned. Place half the *chimicurri* in a bowl or crock for serving; pour the remainder over the meat. Cover and let marinate in the refrigerator, 30 minutes, turning several times.

3. Preheat the grill to high.

4. When ready to cook, oil the grill grate. Drain the beef and place it on the hot grate. Grill, turning with tongs, until cooked to taste, 1 to 2 minutes per side for medium-rare. Serve with the remaining *chimichurri* sauce.

Serves 4

Churrasco of Tenderloin Tips
Puntas de Churrasco

Butchers sometimes sell tenderloin "tips" or "tails"—the narrow ends that are too slender to cut into filet mignons. These tips make a wonderful *churrasco* (they're better marbled than the center cuts) and they're a lot less expensive to boot. You may need to butterfly them (see box, page 163) to obtain thin, broad strips.

Substitute $1^3/4$ pounds tenderloin tips for the tenderloin center cut above (you'll need a little more, because the tips are a fattier cut). Trim off any excess fat and proceed as directed.

KOREAN SESAME-GRILLED BEEF
Bool Kogi

KOREA

ADVANCE PREPARATION: *1 to 2 hours for marinating the meat*

Korean food is probably the best-kept secret in Asia. From the moment we landed in Seoul, my wife and I ate extraordinarily well. And despite the time of year (winter) and the weather (frigid), everywhere we went we had barbecue. Most of the meat is grilled to order on a tabletop brazier, which helps warm your frozen fingers as you eat.

Korean barbecue comes in two main varieties: *kalbi kui* (Korean Grilled Short Ribs—see page 146) and *bool kogi,* thin shavings of beef steeped in a sweet-salty sesame marinade and grilled crisply over charcoal. The sugar and sesame oil caramelize during the cooking, giving the meat a candied sweetness. The dish takes its name from the Korean words for "fire" and "meat." The meat is cooked on a grill that looks like a perforated inverted wok.

In Korea *bool kogi* is eaten like moo shu or fajitas, using a lettuce leaf instead of a pancake or tortilla. You roll the meat (and often a grilled garlic clove) in a romaine lettuce leaf, dip it in sauce—here an Asian pear sauce—then pop it into your mouth. The contrast of sweet and salty, of pungent and fruity, of crisp vegetable and chewy but tender meat is unique in the world of barbecue.

FOR THE BEEF AND MARINADE:

2 pounds beef tenderloin tips, or boneless sirloin
½ cup soy sauce
⅓ cup sugar
3 tablespoons sake, rice wine, or sherry
2 tablespoons Asian (dark) sesame oil
8 cloves garlic, thinly sliced
4 scallions, both white and green parts, trimmed and minced
2 tablespoons sesame seeds, toasted (see box, page 93)
½ teaspoon freshly ground black pepper

FOR SERVING:

Garlic Kebabs, prepared through step 2 (optional, page 385)
Asian Pear Dipping Sauce (page 486)
1 head romaine lettuce, separated into leaves, rinsed, and spun dry

1. If using tenderloin tips, butterfly them (see box, page 163) to obtain broad flat pieces of meat; each should be about 4 inch-es long and wide and ¼ inch thick. If using the sirloin, cut it across the grain into ¼-inch slices. Whichever cut you use, pound the slices between two sheets of plastic wrap with the side of a cleaver or with a rolling pin to flatten them to a thickness of ⅛ inch. Place the meat in a large nonreactive baking dish and set aside while you prepare the marinade.

2. Combine all the ingredients for the marinade in a small bowl and whisk until the sugar is dissolved. Pour the mixture over the meat in the baking dish and toss thoroughly to coat. Cover and let marinate, in the refrigerator, for 1 to 2 hours.

3. Preheat the grill to high.

4. When ready to cook, oil the grill grate. Add the garlic kebabs (if using) to the hot grate and grill for 4 to 5 minutes. Then arrange the pieces of meat on the grate and grill, turning with tongs, until nicely browned on both sides, 1 to 2 minutes per side. Turn the garlic kebabs as the meat cooks. Transfer the meat to a platter when it is done and unwrap the garlic.

5. Pour the dipping sauce into 6 small bowls, one for each diner. To eat, take a piece of meat and a grilled garlic clove and wrap them in a lettuce leaf. Dip the leaf in the dipping sauce and eat at once.

Serves 6

GRILLED BEEF OAXACA-STYLE

MEXICO

METHOD:
Direct grilling

Carne asado ("grilled meat") and *carnitas* ("little pieces of grilled meat") describe a snack/street/party food so popular in Mexico, it could qualify as an official state dish. You find these smokily grilled beef bits wherever crowds gather and an enterprising cook has enough space to set up a grill.

The best *carne asado* I've ever tasted was at the Mercado 20 de Noviembre (November 20 Market) in Oaxaca. The contrast of textures and flavors—chewy meat, crisp scallions, juicy salsa, cooling guacamole, and fiery chiles—was as dazzling as the Baroque architecture in the local churches.

Oaxacan *carne asado* makes a wonderful way to entertain, offering your guests a taste experience they're not likely to forget. The following recipe may seem involved, but it's really a series of simple steps. To be strictly authentic, you'd cook the ingredients over wood or charcoal, not gas. But gas will do the trick, too.

2 bunches scallions, both white and green parts, trimmed

8 chiles de agua, cubanelle peppers, bull's horn peppers, jalapeño chiles, or poblano chiles

Coarse (kosher or sea) salt

2 pounds boneless sirloin steak, cut into broad sheets ¼ inch thick (see Note)

16 corn or flour tortillas, or as needed

4 limes, cut into wedges

Oaxacan-Style Guacamole (page 449)

Salsa Mexicana (page 174)

1. Preheat the grill to high.

2. When ready to cook, *if using wood or charcoal,* toss the scallions and chiles right on the charcoals. Cook, turning with tongs, until nicely charred and tender, about 5 minutes per side.

If using gas (or if you don't have easy access to the coals of your grill), cook the scallions and chiles on the grate. After removing, cover the scallions with aluminum foil and set aside while you prepare the chiles.

3. Scrape the skin off the chiles with a sharp knife (don't worry about removing every last bit). Halve them and scrape out the seeds. Cover with foil and set aside.

4. When ready to grill the beef, oil the grill grate. Generously salt the beef and place it on the hot grate. Grill, turning with tongs, about 3 minutes per side for well-done (the way Oaxacans like their beef cooked). While you're at it, throw the tortillas, a few at a time, on the grill for a few seconds to heat them and keep warm in a cloth-lined basket. Transfer the beef to a cutting board and cut into thin strips or ½-inch dice.

5. To serve, set out bowls of limes, guacamole, and salsa. To eat, place a few pieces of beef on a tortilla. Place a grilled scallion and chile half on top. Top with spoonfuls of guacamole and salsa, and a squeeze of lime juice. Roll the whole thing up and eat.

Serves 8

Note: Ask your butcher to cut the beef for you on a meat slicer. The advantage of cutting the steaks so thin is that you maximize the surface area exposed to the heat and smoke.

A SIMPLE MATAMBRE

ARGENTINA

METHOD:
Direct grilling

ADVANCE PREPARATION:
4 to 8 hours for marinating the meat

Matambre (literally, "hunger killer") refers both to a cut of meat and to the series of dishes that are made from it. The cut, which doesn't exist in North America, is a large, ½-inch-thick rectangular muscle from the chest of the cow. Tough but flavorful, *matambre* is always served well done: the prolonged cooking helps break down the tough meat fibers.

The simplest version of *matambre*—the one served as an appetizer at *estancias* (ranches) and steak houses in Argentina—consists of the flat piece of the meat sprinkled with spices, grilled, and cut into 1-inch squares to be served on toothpicks. To re-create it in North America, I like to use skirt steak. Skirt steak is a smaller cut than *matambre,* but the thinness and muscle structure are similar. Skirt steak is more tender, however, so you don't need to cook it as long.

To make a more elaborate *matambre,* the meat is stuffed and rolled into a compact cylinder and grilled over low heat for several hours. Instructions for making a stuffed *matambre* are found below.

FOR THE STEAK AND MARINADE:

1½ pounds beef skirt steaks
1 medium green bell pepper, stemmed, seeded, and finely chopped
2 cloves garlic, minced
¼ cup olive oil
2 tablespoons red wine vinegar
1 teaspoon dried oregano
½ teaspoon hot red pepper flakes
½ teaspoon salt
½ teaspoon finely ground black pepper
2 bay leaves

FOR THE SPICE MIXTURE:

1 teaspoon dried oregano
½ teaspoon hot red pepper flakes
½ teaspoon salt
½ teaspoon finely ground black pepper

1. Arrange the steaks in a nonreactive baking dish and set aside while you prepare the marinade.

2. Combine the bell pepper, garlic, oil, vinegar, oregano, pepper flakes, salt, and pepper in a small bowl and stir to mix well. Pour over the steaks in the baking dish and toss well to coat. Add the bay leaves, cover, and let marinate in the refrigerator, for at least 4 hours, preferably overnight.

3. Preheat the grill to high.

4. Combine the ingredients for the spice mixture in a small bowl.

5. When ready to cook, oil the grill grate. Drain the steaks and place on the hot grate. Sprinkle the steaks with half the spice mixture and grill, turning with tongs, until medium to medium-well done, about 4 minutes per side, sprinkling with the remaining spice mixture after turning.

6. Transfer the steaks to a cutting board and let stand about 3 minutes, then cut into 1-inch squares and serve on toothpicks.

Serves 6 as an appetizer, 4 as a main course

MONTEVIDEAN STUFFED BEEF ROLL
Matambre

URUGUAY

METHOD:
Indirect grilling

This recipe may sound complicated, but it can be assembled in 15 minutes. When people see the results, they'll think you've been working for hours. The cut called for is flank steak, but I've also made it with brisket. If you're not comfortable with your knifesmanship, ask your butcher to butterfly the meat. For more on *matambre,* see page 132.

SPECIAL EQUIPMENT: *Metal skewers or butcher's string for securing the matambre*

½ large red bell pepper, stemmed and seeded
½ large green bell pepper, stemmed and seeded
1 piece (6 ounces) Romano cheese
1 piece (6 ounces) kielbasa sausage
2 large eggs, hard-cooked, peeled, and cooled (optional)
1 long carrot, peeled
6 thin slices bacon
1 beef flank steak (1½ to 1¾ pounds), butterflied (see box, this page)
Salt and freshly ground black pepper, to taste
1 teaspoon dried oregano
½ teaspoon dried sage

1. Set the grill up for indirect cooking (see page 14 or 16), placing a drip pan in the center. Preheat to medium-low.

2. Cut the peppers into ½-inch lengthwise strips. Cut the cheese and sausage lengthwise into strips ½ inch thick. Cut the eggs (if using) lengthwise into quarters. Cut the carrot lengthwise in quarters. Lay the bacon strips on a large (24 × 24 inch) square of heavy-duty aluminum foil, leaving a space of 1 inch between each; the strips should run parallel to the edge of the work surface. Place the butterflied flank steak on top of the bacon so that the grain of the meat (and the seam between the meat halves) runs perpendicular to the bacon.

3. Season the meat generously with salt and pepper and sprinkle with oregano and sage. Arrange strips of sausage in a neat row, end to end, along the edge of the meat closest to you. Place a row of red bell pepper strips next to it, then a row of cheese strips, then carrot strips, then green bell pepper strips, then hard-cooked eggs. Repeat the process until all the ingredients are used up. Leave the last 3 inches of meat uncovered.

4. Starting at the edge closest to you and using the foil to help you, roll up the meat with the filling to make a compact roll. It's a lot like rolling a jelly roll. Pin the top edge shut with metal skewers or tie the *matambre*

closed with a few lengths of butcher's string. Encase the roll in the foil, twisting the ends to make what will look like a large sausage. Poke a few holes in the foil at each end to allow for the release of steam.

5. When ready to cook, place the *matambre* in the center of the grill, away from the fire. Cover the grill. Cook until very tender, 1½ to 2 hours. (If using charcoal, add 10 to 12 fresh coals per side after 1 hour.) To test for doneness, insert a metal skewer right through the foil covering. It should pierce the meat easily and be piping hot to the touch when withdrawn. Transfer the *matambre* to a cutting board and let cool for 15 minutes.

6. Remove the foil and skewers or string, then cut the *matambre* crosswise into 1-inch slices to serve.

Serves 8 as an appetizer, 4 as a main course

Butterflying a Flank Steak

The flank steak you buy should be 10 to 12 inches long and about 6 inches wide. Place the steak at the edge of the cutting board, short side toward you and narrow edge of the long side at your right, if you are righthanded, and at your left, if you are lefthanded. Holding a long, slender sharp knife parallel to the cutting board, cut the steak in half horizontally, starting at the narrow edge of the long side and cutting almost all the way through to the opposite edge. Open out the piece of meat as you would a book and pound it flat with the side of a meat cleaver or with a rolling pin. The object (in the case of a 1½- to 1¾-pound piece of flank steak) is to obtain a 12- to 15-inch square of meat.

Matambre: A Hunger-Killer from South America

El Palenque may not be the fanciest restaurant in Montevideo, Uruguay, but when it comes to eating beef, there's no place I'd rather be. Located in the Mercado del Puerto (Port Market), a nineteenth century covered market that today serves as Montevideo's barbecue headquarters, El Palenque offers a staunchly carnivorous bill of fare that includes *mollejas* (grilled sweetbreads), *choto* (crispy rolled tripe), and an *asado de tira* (long, thin cross section of the rib roast) that literally buries your plate.

But my favorite dish here bears the curious name of *matambre.* Actually, the name says it all. *Hambre* is the Spanish word for "hunger." *Matar* means "to kill." Put them together and you get one of the most distinctive dishes in South America.

Matambres are usually described as rolled, stuffed, baked or grilled flank steaks. But travel around South America and you'll find that they can come flat and plain, as well, and made with a variety of meat cuts, not just flank steak. Traditionally served as an appetizer, *matambres* also come in portions large enough to dwarf the average North American entrée.

For me, the *matambre* reaches its apotheosis at El Palenque. The Montevidean version features a belt-loosening array of sausages, carrots, bell peppers, and cheese rolled in an oregano and sage-scented sheet of flank steak. When sliced widthwise, the *matambre* forms a handsome spiral of beef studded with a colorful mosaic of vegetables, cheese, and sausage. Knowing about the restaurant's mighty portions, I ordered a half serving of Palenque's hunger-killer. The slice was as thick as a phone book. I'd hate to see a full portion.

ARGENTINIAN ROOTS

The first *matambres* appeared in Argentina as steaks seasoned with salt and herbs and cooked flat over glowing coals. Such was the *matambre* I received by way of a welcome at the Estancia La Cinacina, a ranch west of Buenos Aires that stages barbecues and equestrian shows for sightseers. Cut into 1-inch squares and served on toothpicks, this sort of *matambre* makes for a tasty hors d'oeuvre.

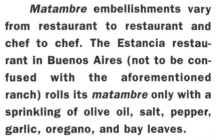

Matambre embellishments vary from restaurant to restaurant and chef to chef. The Estancia restaurant in Buenos Aires (not to be confused with the aforementioned ranch) rolls its *matambre* only with a sprinkling of olive oil, salt, pepper, garlic, oregano, and bay leaves.

In Brazil, I feasted on a splendid *matambre* at the Barra Grill in Rio de Janeiro. True to Brazilian tradition, the meat had been marinated in a spicy garlic-and-lime-based marinade, prior to being rolled with bacon and cheese, and roasted on a spit.

Because of the innate toughness of the cut of meat used in the dish, *matambre* requires lengthy cooking to attain the proper tenderness. You might think that lengthy cooking would be difficult, if not impossible, over a live fire. But South American grill jockeys resort to an ingenious method. They swaddle the *matambre* in aluminum foil and cook it for several hours over a low fire. The foil prevents the outside of the meat from burning, while holding the *matambre* neatly in shape.

On pages 129 and 130 you'll find recipes for two different *matambres* you can prepare on your grill. Whether you serve them as colorful appetizers or main courses, one thing's for sure: They certainly will kill your hunger!

GRILLED BEEF WITH PEANUT FLOUR
Kyinkyinga

WEST AFRICA

METHOD:
Direct grilling

ADVANCE PREPARATION:
2 to 3 hours for marinating the meat

SPECIAL EQUIPMENT:
4 long metal skewers or 8 short bamboo skewers, soaked for 1 hour in cold water to cover and drained

I first learned of *kyinkyinga* (pronounced "chin-CHIN-ga") from an anthropologist who spent several years studying tribes in West Africa. When cooking beef, they hang long strips of it on vertical skewers and cook it upright in front of a campfire. The peanut flour used to coat the meat adds an unexpected crunch and sweet nutty flavor that counterpoints the fiery chile marinade on the beef.

The only remotely difficult aspect to this dish is finding peanut flour. If you live in a city with a West African community, you may be able to find it at a West African grocery store or sometimes at an Asian market. If not, you can order it by mail (see Mail-Order Sources). In a pinch, you can easily grind dry roasted peanuts with a little flour in a food processor.

For the sake of convenience, I cook the meat kebab style. As always, I offer a range of chiles. Four will give you a really hot *kyinkyinga*.

FOR THE BEEF AND MARINADE:
1½ to 2 pounds boneless beef sirloin, cut into 1-inch cubes
1 large onion, cut into chunks
1 green bell pepper, stemmed, seeded, and cut into chunks
6 cloves garlic, peeled
1 to 4 scotch bonnet chiles or 4 to 8 jalapeños, coarsely chopped (for a milder kyinkyinga, seed the chiles)
2 tablespoons chopped fresh ginger
1½ teaspoons salt
1 teaspoon freshly ground black pepper
¼ cup peanut oil

FOR THE KEBABS:
2 large green bell peppers, stemmed, seeded, and cut into 1-inch pieces
1 large onion, cut into 1-inch pieces
1½ cups peanut flour (see Note)

1. Place the beef in a large baking dish and set it aside while you prepare the marinade.

2. Combine the onion, bell pepper, garlic, chiles, ginger, salt, and pepper in a food processor and finely chop. Add the oil and continue processing to a smooth purée. Add the mixture to the beef and toss thoroughly to coat. Cover and let marinate, in the refrigerator, for 2 to 3 hours.

3. Preheat the grill to high.

4. Remove the beef from the marinade and thread it onto the skewers, alternating with pieces of bell pepper and onion. Place the flour on a large plate and roll the kebabs in it so that all sides are generously covered.

5. When ready to cook, oil the grill grate. Arrange the skewers on the hot grate. Grill, turning the kebabs with tongs, until the beef is cooked to taste, 2 to 3 minutes per side (8 to 12 minutes in all), for medium-rare. Serve immediately.

Serves 4

Note: If you don't have peanut flour, grind 1¼ cups dry-roasted peanuts with ¼ cup all-purpose flour as fine as possible in a food processor, running the machine in short bursts. Take care not to overgrind; peanut flour quickly becomes peanut butter.

PERUVIAN BEEF KEBABS

Anticuchos

METHOD:
Direct grilling

**ADVANCE
PREPARATION:**
*2 hours for
marinating the
meat*

**SPECIAL
EQUIPMENT:**
*4 long metal
skewers*

Anticuchos are Peru's national snack, spicy kebabs of beef heart grilled to order by street vendors. As beef hearts aren't part of most of our North American diets, I've redesigned the recipe to be made with sirloin. The traditional recipe calls for two special ingredients: *aji amarillo* and achiote. The first is a fiery yellow chile powder made from the powerful Peruvian chile. The second is the orange seeds of the Caribbean annatto plant. (Annatto seeds—available in Latin American markets, or see Mail-Order Sources—are very hard; grind them in a spice mill.) But if you can't find these ingredients, rest assured that perfectly delectable *anticuchos* can be made using the more readily available substitutions suggested below.

Peruvian Potato Mixed Grill would make a good accompaniment (see Index).

FOR THE BEEF AND MARINADE:
1½ pounds boneless beef sirloin or
  tenderloin, cut into 1-inch cubes
2 cloves garlic, minced
2 to 4 teaspoons aji amarillo (chile powder or
  paste) or hot paprika
1 teaspoon ground annatto seeds or
  ½ teaspoon ground turmeric
1 teaspoon ground cumin
1 teaspoon salt
1 teaspoon freshly ground black pepper
½ cup olive oil
⅓ cup red wine vinegar

FOR THE GLAZE:
3 tablespoons vegetable oil
1 to 3 teaspoons ground aji amarillo
  (chile powder or paste) or hot paprika

1½ teaspoons salt
½ teaspoon freshly ground black pepper
3 tablespoons finely chopped fresh Italian
  (flat-leaf) parsley

FOR THE KEBABS:
1 medium green bell pepper, stemmed,
  seeded, and cut into 1-inch pieces
1 medium red or yellow bell pepper,
  stemmed, seeded, and cut into 1-inch
  pieces

1. Toss the beef with the garlic, chile powder, annatto, cumin, salt, and pepper in a large nonreactive baking dish. Cover and let marinate, in the refrigerator, for 30 minutes.

2. Stir in the oil and vinegar and continue to marinate the beef, in the refrigerator, 1½ hours more.

3. Preheat the grill to high.

4. Prepare the glaze. Heat the oil in a small skillet or saucepan. Add the chile powder, salt, and pepper. Sauté the mixture, stirring, over low heat until orange and fragrant, about 5 minutes. Stir in the parsley and cook for 1 minute. Remove from the heat and set aside to cool.

5. Thread the beef pieces onto the skewers, alternating with squares of bell pepper. Brush the *anticuchos* with half of the glaze.

6. When ready to cook, oil the grill grate. Arrange the skewers on the hot grate. Grill, turning the kebabs with tongs, until the meat is cooked to taste, 2 to 3 minutes per side (8 to 12 minutes in all), for medium-rare. Brush the kebabs as they cook with the remaining glaze. Do not brush within the last 3 minutes of grilling. Serve immediately.
Serves 4

On Trimming Fat from Meat

Throughout this book, I ask you to trim various cuts of meat. What you want to remove is any sinew, gristle, and silverskin. And excess fat—not *all* fat.

By excess fat, I mean large pieces (1 inch or more) of fat or a layer of fat that's more than ½ inch thick. Fat may be bad in nutritional circles. (I should know: I write a series of High-Flavor, Low-Fat cookbooks.) But when it comes to barbecue, fat is good. Well-marbled steaks or briskets covered with a sheath of fat always taste better than absolutely lean cuts of meat.

The reason is simple: Grilling is a dry-cooking method. The blast of dry heat tends to dry meats out. As a well-marbled piece of meat cooks, the fat melts, basting the meat fibers, keeping them moist and succulent.

Besides, there's nothing more delicious than the flame-charred fat at the edge of a steak or rib. Just don't make a steady diet of it!

So the next time you go to trim meat, resist the temptation to remove all the fat. Your barbecue will be much the better for it.

BENGALI SHISH KEBABS

BANGLADESH

METHOD:
Direct grilling

ADVANCE PREPARATION:
2 hours for marinating the meat

SPECIAL EQUIPMENT:
4 long metal skewers or 8 short bamboo skewers, soaked for 1 hour in cold water to cover and drained

Shish kebab is the world's most popular barbecue dish. The meat varies as you move around the world (for that matter, so does the kind of skewer used), but the principle (meat grilled on a stick) remains constant. Here's the Bengali version—a popular after-school snack in Bangladesh, the way burgers are in the U.S. The spicing is more restrained than the tandoori kebabs of India and the mix is rubbed onto the meat before the oil is added for marinating. The dry spices get into the meat better this way.

I call for beef tenderloin here, but you can also use tenderloin tips or sirloin.

FOR THE BEEF AND MARINADE:
1½ pounds beef tenderloin, trimmed and cut into 1-inch cubes
3 cloves garlic, minced

1 tablespoon minced fresh ginger
1½ teaspoons salt
1 tablespoon ground coriander (see Note)
1 teaspoon ground cumin (see Note)
1 teaspoon freshly ground black pepper
½ to 1 teaspoon cayenne pepper, or to taste
3 tablespoons vegetable oil

FOR THE KEBABS:
Tandoori-Baked Flat Breads (page 109) or pita bread
1 cucumber, seeded (see box, page 89) and cut into ½-inch dice
1 tomato, seeded (see box, page 62) and cut into ½-inch dice
1 small onion, cut into ½-inch dice
1 lemon, cut into wedges
Bengali Mango-Tamarind Barbecue Sauce (optional; page 464)

1. Combine the beef, garlic, ginger, salt, and spices in a bowl and toss thoroughly to mix. Add the oil and toss again. Cover and let marinate, in the refrigerator, for 2 hours.

2. Preheat the grill to high.

3. When ready to cook, thread the beef cubes onto the skewers. Oil the grill grate, then arrange the kebabs on the hot grate. Grill, turning the kebabs with tongs, until the beef is cooked to taste, 2 to 3 minutes per side (8 to 12 minutes in all) for medium-rare. Transfer the kebabs to a platter.

4. Arrange the breads of your choice in one layer on the grate and grill until pliable, about 20 seconds per side. Divide the breads among serving plates (if serving as an appe-tizer, cut each bread in half). Unskewer the beef onto the breads (or fold a bread around the meat on each skewer and remove the skewer). Sprinkle the diced cucumber, toma-to, and onion over the meat and squeeze a little lemon juice on top. Spoon the barbecue sauce (if using) on top, or use as a dipping sauce. Serve immediately.

Serves 8 as an appetizer, 4 as an entrée

Note: For extra flavor, start with whole cumin and coriander seeds. Lightly toast them in a dry skillet over medium heat until lightly colored and fragrant, 3 to 5 minutes, shaking the pan frequently, then cool and grind in a food processor.

RUSSIAN BEEF KEBABS
Shashlik

METHOD:
Direct grilling

ADVANCE PREPARATION:
4 to 8 hours overnight for marinating the meat

SPECIAL EQUIPMENT:
4 to 6 long metal skewers

Muscovites love to take to the country on the weekends, and when they do, chances are they'll cook these robust beef kebabs. Grating the onion is a traditional Slavic technique that produces a fuller, richer onion flavor than dicing.

FOR THE BEEF AND MARINADE:
1½ to 2 pounds boneless beef
    sirloin or tenderloin tips
1 large onion, coarsely grated
6 cloves garlic, coarsely grated
½ cup dry red wine
¼ cup red wine vinegar
3 tablespoons olive oil
2 bay leaves
1½ teaspoons salt, or to taste
1½ teaspoons freshly ground pepper

FOR THE KEBABS:
1 large onion, cut into 1-inch pieces
1 large green bell pepper, stemmed,
    seeded, and cut into 1-inch
    pieces

1. Trim any sinew and excess fat off the beef, then cut the meat into 1½-inch cubes. Combine the ingredients for the marinade in a large nonreactive baking dish. Add the meat and toss thoroughly to coat. Cover and let marinate, in the refrigerator, at least 4 hours, but preferably 8, stirring once or twice.

2. Preheat the grill to high.

3. Remove the beef from the marinade and thread onto the skewers, alternating with pieces of onion and bell pepper. When ready to cook, oil the grill grate. Arrange the kebabs on the hot grate and grill, turning with tongs, until the meat is cooked to taste, 2 to 3 minutes per side, (8 to 12 minutes in all), for medium-rare. Baste the beef with any excess marinade as it cooks, but stop basting the last 5 minutes. Serve immediately.

Serves 4 to 6

FIERY STICK MEAT
Suyas

NIGERIA

METHOD:
Direct grilling

ADVANCE PREPARATION:
1 to 2 hours for marinating the meat

SPECIAL EQUIPMENT:
20 short bamboo skewers, soaked for 1 hour in cold water to cover and drained

I first encountered "stick meat" (fiery beef kebabs) at a Nigerian restaurant in Washington, D.C. But it was Dozie Nnamah, a cab driver in Chicago, who set the scene for properly enjoying this popular West African snack.

Imagine you're in your twenties and it's Saturday night in Lagos. You and a bunch of friends crowd into a car for a spin around the city. You crank the radio volume up until it rattles the windshield, listening to Ebenezer Obey, King Sunny Ade, or whoever else is rocking the Nigerian airwaves these days.

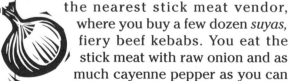

You pick up a couple of six-packs of Gulder or Premier beer. (None for the driver, of course!) The last stop is the nearest stick meat vendor, where you buy a few dozen *suyas,* fiery beef kebabs. You eat the stick meat with raw onion and as much cayenne pepper as you can stand, and that's how it goes—for an evening, at least, it's hard to imagine that life gets better than this.

Note that the meat shouldn't be too lean for stick meat; you need a few pieces of fat to baste and tenderize the beef as it cooks. As usual, I offer a range of heat from the cayenne. At my house, I would use 1 tablespoon cayenne for the marinade.

Serve with plenty of ice-cold beer.

1½ pounds boneless beef sirloin (try to choose a piece with some fat on it, or ask your butcher to give you a piece of beef fat)
3 beef bouillon cubes
1 tablespoon water
1 to 3 teaspoons cayenne pepper, plus 1 tablespoon for serving
1 teaspoon freshly ground black pepper
½ teaspoon salt
2 tablespoons vegetable oil
1 medium onion, cut into ½-inch pieces, for serving

1. Cut the beef into ½-inch cubes. Crumble the bouillon cubes in a large bowl and mix with the water to make a thick paste. Stir in the cayenne, black pepper, and salt. Add in the meat and toss thoroughly to coat. Cover and let marinate, in the refrigerator, for 1 to 2 hours.

2. Preheat the grill to high.

3. Remove the beef from the marinade and thread onto the skewers, 6 to 8 cubes to a skewer, leaving the point (the last ¼ inch of the skewer) exposed. Pour the oil on a plate and roll the skewers around in it to coat the meat.

4. When ready to cook, arrange the skewers on the hot grill grate and grill, turning with tongs, until the meat is cooked to taste, 2 to 3 minutes per side (8 to 12 minutes in all; see Note).

5. Place the onion in a small bowl and the additional 1 tablespoon cayenne pepper in another. To eat, spear a piece of onion on the end of the skewer, then sprinkle the meat with as much additional cayenne as you can bear.

Serves 8 as an appetizer, 4 as an entrée

Note: these times will give you meat that is well-done All the stick meat I've had has been served that way. (It's been made with cheap cuts of meat, so prolonged cooking is required to tenderize it.) To serve medium-rare stick meat, use a more tender cut and cook 1 to 2 minutes per side.

Hawkers' Centers

I am an enthusiastic eater of street food. I love everything about it—its immediacy, its directness, its in-your-face flavors, the fact that you can watch it be made to order and eat it the second it's ready. I love street food for the same reason that I love homey ethnic restaurants: because the owner is putting his energy and money into the food, not the decor.

This is especially true for the satés, kebabs, *anticuchos, tacos al pastor,* and other grilled fare that constitutes some of the world's greatest curbside eating. Many of my happiest moments on the barbecue trail were spent at outdoor markets and street stalls, where you sit so close to the grill, you feel like you're at a barbecue in your own backyard.

The one drawback to street food is hygiene (or its lack). Running water (never mind hot water) is a luxury at many Third World street stalls, as is refrigeration. Food is usually prepared and served with the vendor's bare hands. Eating street food can be like playing culinary roulette. You never know which bite will lead to gastrointestinal distress.

Some years ago, in an effort to make street food more sanitary, the government of Singapore organized the vendors into hawkers' centers, where the cooks—and their customers—could enjoy the health benefits of electricity, refrigera-tion, running water, and a roof over their heads. The hawkers' centers are rigorously regulated by the government, which makes Singapore one of the safest places in the world to enjoy street food. There are dozens of hawkers' centers around Singapore—three of the best are located at Newton Circus, Bugis Square, and the newly restored Clarke Quay.

Hawkers' centers represent democracy and ecumenism at their best. Visit a hawkers' center in Singapore, for example, and you'll find Indonesian saté stands, Muslim bakeries, Chinese noodle stalls, and Indian drink shops. Cell phone–toting Chinese businessmen dine elbow to elbow with turbaned Sikhs.

Following Singapore's example, other nations have begun to organize their street vendors into regulated hawkers' centers. The Sarinah Food Court in the basement of the Sarinah shopping center in Jakarta groups street vendors specializing in dishes from all over Indonesia into a clean, modern Western-style setting. Similar hawkers' centers exist in the basement of department stores throughout Korea, Japan, and Malaysia. One of the world's best hawkers' centers—Gurney Drive in Penang, Malayasia—enjoys a spectacular seaside setting. Where else can you feast on saté and *rujak* with a view of the Andaman Sea?

QUICK PERSIAN BEEF KEBABS

IRAN

METHOD:
Direct grilling

SPECIAL EQUIPMENT:
4 long metal skewers

As a rule, Iranian kebabs are easy to make, but they do require a day or two of marinating. Here, however, is a beef kebab from that country you can make and serve in the time it takes you to preheat the grill. The secret is to use thinly sliced beef tenderloin, which is so tender it needs no advance marinating.

1½ pounds beef tenderloin, all fat and
    sinew trimmed off
1 large onion, cut into 1-inch chunks
3 tablespoons fresh lime juice
3 tablespoons extra-virgin olive oil
1 tablespoon cracked black peppercorns
Salt, to taste
2 tablespoons unsalted butter, in one
    piece, for serving
Lavash (flat bread), for serving

1. Cut the tenderloin crosswise into 1-inch-thick slices. Place the slices flat on the cutting board and cut into 1-inch-wide strips. Cut each strip crosswise into ½-inch-thick pieces. Thread the beef onto the skewers and place them on a large nonreactive platter.

2. Purée the onion in a food processor. Strain the resulting purée over the kebabs, turning to coat all sides. Using a fork, beat the lime juice, oil, pepper, and salt in a small bowl, then pour the mixture over the kebabs, again turning to coat on all sides. Marinate for 15 minutes.

3. Meanwhile, preheat the grill to high.

4. When ready to cook, oil the grill grate. Drain the kebabs, arrange on the hot grate, and grill until cooked to taste, 1 to 2 minutes per side (4 to 8 minutes in all; Iranians like their beef on the medium side of medium-rare). Transfer the kebabs to a platter. With the butter on the end of a fork for easy handling, rub it over each kebab. Serve immediately, with the lavash, using a piece of the bread to protect your hand as you slide the beef off the skewer.

Serves 4

BANI MARINE STREET BEEF KEBABS

MOROCCO

METHOD:
Direct grilling

ADVANCE PREPARATION:
2 to 8 hours for marinating the meat

Bani Marine Street is one of the barbecue lanes in Marrakesh, a crowded street off the Jema al-Fna marketplace lined with simple storefront grill restaurants. You don't really need a menu, since the bill of fare is displayed in the window: lamb chops, liver, *merguez* sausages reddened with paprika and cayenne, and decoratively sculpted mounds of *koefta* (ground spiced lamb). There are also many items Americans don't generally eat, like lamb's testicles and spleen—the latter stuffed with onions and parsley.

A meal at one of these restaurants is a simple but soul-satisfying experience: a dish of olives and a plate of kebabs, served with fiery *harissa,* fire-toasted bread, and shallot relish (a rather ingenious condiment since the parsley neutralizes the pungency of the shallots.) Should you be

SPECIAL
EQUIPMENT:
4 long metal
skewers

in a hurry, the cook will be happy to package these ingredients in a split bread and wrap it in paper for carry-out eating.

As in Indonesia, the meat for the kebabs is diced very small to keep it tender. And it doesn't hurt to put a little fatty beef or beef fat on the kebabs as well as the lean sirloin to keep the meat moist.

1½ pounds boneless beef sirloin
1 medium onion, finely chopped or grated
¼ cup finely chopped fresh Italian (flat-leaf) parsley
1 teaspoon paprika
Salt
½ teaspoon ground cumin, plus 1 tablespoon, for serving
½ teaspoon freshly ground white pepper
2 tablespoons vegetable oil
Moroccan Shallot Relish (page 441)
A Simple Harissa (page 479)
Moroccan bread, French bread, or pita bread

1. Cut the beef into ½-inch cubes. Combine the onion, parsley, paprika, 1 teaspoon salt, ½ teaspoon cumin, the white pepper, and oil in a large baking dish. Add the beef and toss thoroughly to coat. Cover and let marinate, in the refrigerator at least 2 hours but preferably 8.

2. Preheat the grill to high.

3. Thread the beef onto the skewers. When ready to cook, oil the grill grate. Arrange the kebabs on the hot grate and grill, turning once with tongs, until the meat is cooked to taste, 3 to 4 minutes per side for medium (6 to 8 minutes in all; Moroccans tend to eat their beef well-done).

4. To serve, place 1 tablespoon each salt and cumin, in tiny separate bowls and place on the table side by side, along with bowls of the shallot relish and *harissa*. Slide the meat off the skewers onto plates. Let each person season his or her portion to taste with the salt and cumin, then spoon the relish and *harissa* on top. Serve the bread, in chunks, to soak up the juices.

Serves 4

MADEIRA BEEF AND BAY LEAF KEBABS
Espetada

PORTUGAL

METHOD:
Direct grilling

ADVANCE
PREPARATION:
at least 4 hours
for marinating
the meat

SPECIAL
EQUIPMENT:
4 to 6 long metal
skewers

Grilled beef is beloved throughout Portugal, but nowhere as much as on the island of Madeira. Restaurants on this hilly island have a unique accoutrement: an inverted L-shaped metal pole attached to one end of each table. The beef is grilled on special metal skewers with eyelets at the end, which are then brought to the table and hung with great ceremony, from the L-shaped pole, over a bowl piled with Portuguese bread. As the kebabs hang, the meat juices drip onto the bread, which becomes as much a delicacy as the beef.

Unless you have a degree in welding, you probably won't be able to duplicate this arrangement, but you can approximate the effect by serving the kebabs on a platter lined with sliced Portuguese bread. It's interesting to note that in the old days (and still deep in the countryside), the beef was skewered and grilled on branches of the bay leaf tree.

1½ pounds beef tenderloin or boneless sirloin
¼ cup extra-virgin olive oil
¼ cup red wine vinegar
1 onion, finely chopped
½ cup chopped fresh Italian (flat-leaf) parsley
4 cloves garlic, finely chopped
1 teaspoon salt
1 teaspoon freshly ground black pepper
12 bay leaves
Portuguese or other crusty country-style
    bread, for serving

1. Trim any sinews and excess fat off the beef, then cut the meat into 2-inch cubes. Combine the oil, vinegar, onion, parsley, garlic, salt, and pepper in a large nonreactive baking dish. Add the beef and toss thoroughly to coat. Cover and let marinate, in the refrigerator, for 4 to 6 hours.

2. Preheat the grill to high.

3. Remove the beef and bay leaves from the marinade and thread onto the skewers, dividing the bay leaves among the kebabs. When ready to cook, oil the grill grate. Arrange the kebabs on the hot grate and grill, turning with tongs, until the meat is cooked to taste, 2 to 3 minutes per side (8 to 12 minutes in all) for medium-rare. Baste the *espetadas* with any excess marinade, but not during the last 3 minutes.

4. Serve the *espetadas* on or off the skewers on slices or chunks of Portuguese bread for soaking up the juices.

Serves 4 to 6

LEMONGRASS BEEF WITH PEANUTS

THAILAND

METHOD:
Direct grilling

**SPECIAL
EQUIPMENT:**
*28 to 32 short
bamboo skewers,
soaked for 1 hour
in cold water to
cover and
drained*

Variations on these delicate kebabs are to be found throughout South-east Asia. Coriander and sugar may seem like odd flavorings for beef, but the combination works brilliantly. (After all, we North Americans slather sugar-based barbecue sauces on brisket and ribs!)

1½ pounds boneless beef sirloin or top round
2 cloves garlic, peeled
2 stalks lemongrass, trimmed and
    cut into ¼-inch slices, or 2 strips
    lemon zest (each 2 x ½ inches;
    removed with a vegetable peeler)
1 tablespoon coriander seeds
2 tablespoons firmly packed light brown sugar
¼ cup Asian fish sauce
¼ cup coarsely chopped dry-roasted
    peanuts, for garnish

1. Lay the steaks flat on a cutting board and cut crosswise into long, thin strips, each should be about ⅛ inch thick, 1 inch wide, and 4 to 5 inches long. Weave the beef strips lengthwise onto the skewers and set aside in a large baking dish while you prepare the marinade.

2. Combine the garlic, lemongrass, coriander seeds, and brown sugar in a mortar and pound into a coarse paste with the pestle. If you don't have a mortar and pestle, purée the ingredients in a blender. Stir in the fish sauce. Drizzle the marinade over the beef skewers and rub it into the beef to coat as thoroughly as possible. Cover and let marinate, in the refrigerator, for 30 minutes, or until the grill is ready.

3. Preheat the grill to high.

4. When ready to cook, oil the grill grate. Arrange the skewers on the hot grate and grill, turning with tongs, until the meat is cooked to taste, 1 to 2 minutes per side (2 to 4 minutes in all) for medium. Sprinkle the skewers with chopped peanuts and serve at once.

Serves 4

LETTUCE BUNDLES WITH GRILLED BEEF

VIETNAM

METHOD:
Direct grilling

ADVANCE PREPARATION:
30 minutes for marinating the meat and soaking the noodles

SPECIAL EQUIPMENT:
24 short bamboo skewers, soaked for 1 hour in cold water to cover and drained

This dish could be thought of as a Vietnamese taco. Although it doesn't really exist there, I was inspired to create it by a classic Vietnamese dish called *bo bun* (beef with rice paper). It's a fun combination of salad, pasta, and meat courses mixed into a single, satisfying mouthful. It's also a versatile dish that you can prepare with any type of meat (or seafood), a variety of noodles—I've used Thai rice vermicelli, Japanese soba, and Western-style spaghetti. The recipe calls for sirloin, but you could also use shell steak or New York strip.

Rice vermicelli are hair-thin rice noodles. Look for them in Asian markets, natural foods stores, and an increasing number of supermarkets.

1 boneless sirloin beefsteak (about
    1 pound), cut about 1 inch thick
Aromatic Lemongrass Marinade
    (facing page)
4 ounces rice vermicelli, soba noodles,
    angel hair pasta, or spaghetti
1 bunch fresh basil, preferably Thai basil,
    stemmed
1 bunch fresh mint, stemmed (optional)
2 jalapeño chiles, thinly sliced (optional—
    for lettuce bundles with less heat,
    seed the chiles)
1 head Boston or Bibb lettuce, separated
    into leaves, rinsed, and spun dry
Thai Peanut Sauce (page 472)

1. Lay the steak flat on a cutting board. Using a sharp knife, cut it lengthwise into ⅛-inch-wide strips, then transfer to a nonreactive baking dish. Add the marinade and toss the beef to coat thoroughly. Cover and let marinate, in the refrigerator, for 30 minutes.

2. If using rice vermicelli, soak in a bowl in cold water to cover until soft and pliable, about 30 minutes. (If using soba, angel hair, or spaghetti, no soaking is necessary.) Drain the rice noodles and cook in 3 quarts rapidly boiling water until tender, 2 to 4 minutes (6 to 8 minutes if using the other noodles). Drain whichever noodles you used in a colander and rinse with cold water. Drain again and transfer the noodles to a bowl. Arrange the basil, mint (if using), chiles (if using), and lettuce leaves on plates or in bowls. Divide the peanut sauce among 4 small bowls (see Note).

3. Preheat the grill to high.

4. Weave the beef strips lengthwise onto the skewers. When ready to cook, oil the grill grate. Arrange the skewers on the hot grate and grill, turning with tongs, until the meat is cooked to taste, about 1 to 2 minutes per side (2 to 4 minutes in all) for well-done. Transfer to a platter.

5. To eat, wrap a strip of beef, a forkful of noodles, some basil and mint leaves and chile slices (if using) in a lettuce leaf. Slide the skewer out (you can use the lettuce leaves as pot holders for sliding the beef off the skewers). Dip the resulting bundle first into the sauce and then pop it into your mouth—for a contrast of textures, temperatures, and flavors that is dazzling.

Serves 4 as an appetizer, 2 to 3 as an entrée

Note: The recipe can be prepared to this point up to 3 hours in advance. If you do so, cover everything with plastic wrap and refrigerate. Don't heat the grill until you're ready to proceed.

SAIGON MARKET BEEF STICKS

VIETNAM

METHOD:
Direct grilling

ADVANCE PREPARATION:
30 to 60 minutes for marinating the meat

SPECIAL EQUIPMENT:
24 small bamboo skewers, soaked for 1 hour in cold water to cover and drained

These tiny kebabs are the Vietnamese version of satés. You'll find them at the hawkers stands clustered in and around Saigon's markets. The Vietnamese use a modest cut of meat, but I like to take the dish uptown by using tenderloin tips, (which cost considerably less than filet mignon). You could also use thinly sliced sirloin or New York strip.

1 pound beef tenderloin tips
Aromatic Lemongrass Marinade (recipe follows)
1 to 2 tablespoons vegetable oil, for basting
¼ cup finely chopped dry-roasted peanuts, for garnish (optional)

1. Cut the beef into strips 4 inches long, 1 inch wide, and ¼ inch thick and place in a nonreactive baking dish. Add the marinade and toss the beef to coat thoroughly. Cover and let marinate, in the refrigerator, for 30 to 60 minutes.

2. Preheat the grill to high.

3. Weave the beef strips lengthwise onto the skewers. When ready to cook, oil the grill grate. Arrange the skewers on the hot grate, baste with the oil, and grill, turning once with tongs (baste again), until the meat is cooked to taste, 1 to 2 minutes per side (2 to 4 minutes in all) for medium (the Vietnamese-preferred doneness for this dish). Serve at once, sprinkled with peanuts, if desired.

Serves 4 as an appetizer or snack, 2 as an entrée

Aromatic Lemongrass Marinade

This marinade demonstrates the universal appeal of one of the oddest and most ancient food pairings: anchovies with beef. The Romans did it when they seasoned their meats with liquamen (pickled anchovy sauce). Italians carry on the tradition with their steak *pizzaiola* (garnished with anchovies and tomatoes). The Vietnamese version features a highly aromatic marinade based on *nuoc mam* (fish sauce), a malodorous but highly tasty condiment made with pickled anchovies.

3 stalks fresh lemongrass, trimmed and coarsely chopped, or 3 strips lemon zest (each 2 x ½ inches; removed with a vegetable peeler)
2 large shallots, coarsely chopped
5 cloves garlic, coarsely chopped
3 tablespoons sugar
5 tablespoons Asian fish sauce
3 tablespoons fresh lime juice
1 teaspoon freshly ground black pepper

Combine the lemongrass, shallots, garlic, and sugar in a mortar and pound to a coarse paste with the pestle. Work in the fish sauce, lime juice, and pepper. If you don't have a mortar and pestle, combine all the ingredients in a blender and process to a smooth purée.

Makes about 1 cup; enough for 1½ pounds beef, chicken, or fish

The Argentinian Grill

To say that Argentinians love meat would be the understatement of the year. This nation of 31 million consumes beef on a scale our own country hasn't seen since the 1950s. Buenos Aires fairly bulges with *parrillas* (grills), *asado* restaurants, and chop houses. Statistics are hard to come by (misplaced, I was told, during the last change of government), but a casual poll of the people I met suggests that the average Argentinian eats meat 10 to 12 times a week.

Actually, Argentina offers two very different grilled meat experiences: *asado* and *parrilla* (pronounced "par-EE-yha"). The former is traditional ranch-style barbecue: whole baby goats, suckling pigs, sides of beef ribs, and briskets roasted upright on stakes in front of a fire.

The *parrilla* corresponds to what we would call a steakhouse in North America. Sausages, innards, and belly-bludgeoning steaks are the specialty of *parrilla* cooking, and in contrast to *asado,* the meats are cooked to order. If you like kid, pork, or beef ribs roasted to fall-off-the-bone tenderness, your best bet is an *asado.* If succulent steaks served sizzling and rare are your fancy, head for a *parrilla.* If you can't make up your mind, don't worry—many restaurants serve both.

GAUCHOS AND GRILLED MEAT

Argentina's love affair with grilled meats began with the gauchos, rugged cowboys who herded cattle on the grassy plains of the Pampas. The arrival in Buenos Aires of the first refrigerated ship from Europe in 1876 ushered in a golden age for cattlemen. The *estancieros* (ranchers) became millionaires selling Argentinian beef to Europe. By 1910, Buenos Aires was the largest city in South America, and in the Western hemisphere second in size and affluence only to New York. Beef money built the wide avenues, graceful plazas, and extravagant buildings that make Buenos Aires the Paris of South America.

There's a tendency to romanticize the gauchos. The real gauchos, often *mestizos* (of mixed Spanish and Indian heritage), lived a considerably less glamorous life. Yes, they wore *boinas* (berets) and *rastras* (coin-studded leather belts; the coins were a way of showing off their wages) festooned with *faccas* (South American bowie knives). Yes, they congregated at *pulperias,* a combination of a country store, warehouse, and saloon. Yes, they danced the *malambo,* a solitary male dance that imitates the motions of a horse. Still, they lived a lonely existence, on the margins of society, with little or no female contact.

But it was the gauchos who developed *asado.* To experience the phenomenon first hand, I signed up for a bus tour of a ranch called Estancia La Cinacina. An hour outside of Buenos Aires, the land becomes flat and spacious, with clumps of trees punctuating the grasslands. There, we turned in at a cluster of white-washed stone buildings near the town of San Antonio de Rico.

Cinacina is owned by the Ramirez family, three generations of ruggedly handsome gauchos decked out in berets, bandanas, and riding boots. For the next three hours, they entertained us with carriage rides, gaucho music, handkerchief dancing, and demonstrations of equestrian prowess. Eventually, we piled into a mess hall for a communal cowboy lunch.

In an adjacent courtyard was a circular fire pit, where one of the Ramirezes worked as an *asador* (pit master) tending a bonfire that was started early that morning. By the time we arrived, whole rib sections of beef and *vacios* (a cut that corresponds to the breast and brisket) had been tied to cruciform metal stakes and stood before the fire. The stakes were angled slightly away from the flames, so that the juices dripped on the ground, not the coals. The roasting lasted 2 to 3 hours, and when the meat was removed from the stakes, it was tender enough to eat with a spoon. The only seasoning was salt and fresh air. It was the only seasoning needed.

Cinacina's *asado* came with the traditional accompaniments: salad, *salsa criollo* (onion and tomato relish), and a vinaigrette-like condiment called *chimichurri.* The latter is Argentina's national steak sauce, and there are probably as many different versions as there are individual pit masters. At its simplest, *chimichurri* consists of olive oil flavored with a little dried oregano, hot pepper flakes, salt, and pepper. This is the sort of *chimichurri* served at Cinacina.

In the cities, one finds a more elaborate *chimichurri:* fresh parsley, garlic, olive oil, and wine vinegar puréed to a pesto-like paste, sometimes with hot peppers. There's even a red *chimichurri* made from tomatoes and bell peppers.

LA CABANA

Once back in Buenos Aires, I set out to investigate the other branch of the barbecue family tree: *parrilla*. My destination was the grandaddy of Argentinian steakhouses: the venerable La Cabaña. Founded in 1935, La Cabaña is to the kingdom of barbecue what Windsor Castle is to the royal family of England. As you enter the restaurant, you pass by an ancient wooden meat locker and a wood-burning grill with a gleaming copper hood. The dining room has the grandeur of a Tudorian hunting lodge. Wrought-iron chandeliers the size of Volkswagen Beetles hang from ceilings 30 feet high. The dignified waiters in their black jackets and ties seem to have worked here forever.

You can warm up with crusty *mollejas* (grilled sweetbreads). Meltingly tender *riñones* (kidneys). Creamy *chinchulin* (intestines). Handsome coils of *longaniza* (spicy Calabrian-style sausage). Crisp-skinned *morcillas* (raisin-studded sweet blood sausages that taste a lot better than they sound). And that's just for starters. These and other items—all, I can assure you, are absolutely delicious—are commonly served together as a *parrillada* (mixed grill) on a table-top hibachi stoked with blazing coals to keep them hot. But the specialty here is clearly the beef. A ranch in the Junin district west of Buenos Aires supplies La Cabaña with specially raised steers, each weighing half a ton. A *bife de lomo* (filet mignon) at La Cabaña would prob-

ably dwarf a grapefruit. A single *costilla* (bone-in rib steak) tips the scale at more than $3\frac{1}{2}$ pounds.

Accompanying the beef is one of the most unusual *chimichurris* I sampled in South America: a tangy red paste brewed from garlic, peppers, anchovies, canned tuna, and tomato sauce. The addition of anchovies suggests parentage with two other of the world's great steak sauces: A-1 and Worcestershire. The presence of tuna recalls Italy's great *tonnato* sauce, which is traditionally served with cold roast veal.

Here, as at most Argentinian steak houses, dessert is a simple affair. A wood-fired oven-baked apple. Or perhaps a flan with *dulce de leche*—dark, thick milk caramel—whose burnt-sugar flavor echos the smokiness of charcoal seared meat. Dinner is an event—you eat late, long, and a lot.

A VISIT TO COSTANERA NORTE

Today the epicenter of this style of grilling is an area called the Costanera Norte, about 15 minutes from downtown Buenos Aires. Thirty years ago, there was nothing there, save a seawall along the Plata River. The Costanera lies on the road city dwellers would take driving back to Buenos Aires from weekend trips to the country and seaside. About 30 years ago, a few enterprising cooks began setting up makeshift grills and serving steak dinners out of the backs of their cars.

Today, the Costanera is lined with dozens of stylish restaurants, with names like Happening and Los Años Locos. The decors vary from retro to modern, but the bill of fare is pretty

much the same. Which is to say every imaginable type of steak and organ meat expertly grilled and served without artifice. Well-dressed customers flock here from Buenos Aires for lunch on the weekends.

I was able to find one establishment that still maintains a sense of what the Costanera must have been like in the old days. It's located in a nearby port area, where a couple of young men have set up a grill shack called El Potro. Here, under the shadow of a huge derrick, amid thick clouds of smoke, men in sweaty red jackets grill an astonishing assortment of meats.

The grill consists of a metal table piled with glowing coals surmounted by a chain-link grate. It is a set up popular throughout South America. The grate slopes gently upward from front to back, offering a range of cooking temperatures. Meats are seared on the hotter front part of the grill, then moved back to finish cooking at a lower temperature. I could make a meal on the aroma alone. At El Potro, salads are dished up without ceremony from plastic tubs. Guests get to eat on a rickety terrace overlooking a power plant. The entertainment takes the form of a soccer game on a small black-and-white TV.

As you've probably guessed by now, Argentina can be a forbidding place for a vegetarian. In recent years many generally health-conscious North Americans have come to regard meat with suspicion if not downright contempt, but while I consider myself as nutritionally correct as the next guy, nonetheless I feel obliged to note that after a week of restaurant hopping in Buenos Aires, I was one happy fella.

KOREAN GRILLED SHORT RIBS
Kalbi Kui

METHOD:
Direct grilling

ADVANCE PREPARATION:
3 hours for marinating the meat

Mention *kalbi* to a Korean and watch his mouth water. Beef short ribs are something of a national treasure here, served braised to fall-off-the-bone tenderness or savored in the delicate soups and soulful stews for which the Land of Morning Calm is famous. But the most popular way to eat *kalbi* is grilled (*kui*). Korean chefs have developed an ingenious method for handling this flavorful but hard-to-eat cut of beef: the meat is sliced and butterflied to create a long, paper-thin strip, which is grilled right on the bone.

Dine at a restaurant in Korea and the waitress will set a charcoal-filled brazier in the center of the table. Each person cooks his *kalbi* to taste, and then the meat is wrapped in lettuce leaves (so the fingers aren't soiled) and dipped in a sweet-salty Asian pear sauce.

FOR THE RIBS AND MARINADE:
2 pounds beef short ribs, cut into
    2-inch lengths and butterflied
    (see box, facing page)
½ Asian pear or regular pear, peeled
    and cored
2 cloves garlic, peeled
2 scallions, both white and green
    parts, trimmed
¼ cup soy sauce
2 tablespoons Asian (dark)
    sesame oil
2 tablespoons honey
2 tablespoons sake or dry sherry
1 tablespoon sugar
½ teaspoon freshly ground black
    pepper

FOR SERVING:
1 head romaine lettuce, separated
    into leaves, rinsed, and spun dry
**Asian Pear Dipping Sauce
    (page 486)**

1. Place the butterflied ribs in a large nonreactive baking dish.

2. Roughly chop the Asian pear, the garlic, and the scallions and combine in a blender with the remaining ingredients for the marinade. Process to a smooth purée. Pour the marinade over the ribs in the baking dish, cover, and let marinate, in the refrigerator, for 3 hours.

3. Preheat the grill to high.

4. When ready to cook, oil the grill grate. Arrange the butterflied short ribs on the hot grate and grill, turning with tongs, to taste, 2 to 3 minutes per side (4 to 6 minutes in all) for well done (as Koreans tend to like their short ribs).

5. To eat, cut the meat off the bone of each short rib and wrap it in a romaine lettuce leaf. Dip the beef and lettuce in the dipping sauce and pop it into your mouth. Don't forget to gnaw on the bone, which may well be the best part of *kalbi kui!*

Serves 4

How to Butterfly Short Ribs for Korean-Style Grilling

*H*ave your butcher cut the short ribs into 2-inch lengths. (You can butterfly the longer ribs sold at the supermarket, but it will be a little more difficult.)

1. Lay one short rib section at the lower right corner of the cutting board, cut side (sawn bone end) facing you, thick (meaty part of the rib) on top. If you're lefthanded, position the rib on the lower left corner of the cutting board and follow the directions in reverse.

2. Use a small, sharp knife, holding the blade parallel to the cutting board and, working from right to left, slide the knife through the meat along the top of the bone, almost to the left edge to free it from the bone. Don't cut all the way through; you want to leave the meat attached to the bone. Fold the meat flap over to the left to make a flat rectangle of meat attached to the bone.

3. Now, holding your knife parallel to the cutting board, make another cut through the meat two thirds of the way down, again almost to the left edge, and open this flap up, too. You'll have a strip of meat whose left half is twice as thick as the right.

4. Make a final cut through that thicker section on the left, this time through the center, to but not through the left edge. Again, the knife should be parallel to the cutting board. Open up this last flap of meat. You should wind up with a very thin strip of meat 4 to 5 inches long and 2 inches wide, with the bone attached at the right end.

5. The last step is to tenderize the meat. Place the strip flat on the cutting board and score it slightly by tapping it with the back of a heavy knife on the diagonal—first in one direction, then in the other—to make a crosshatch pattern.

This sounds a good deal more complicated than it really is. Cutting and unfolding the beef is quite similar to unrolling a flattened roll of paper towels.

DINOSAUR RIBS

U.S.A.

METHOD:
Indirect grilling

*B*eef ribs play second fiddle to pork ribs—at least in North America. (Indeed, it's often difficult to find them.) A very different mind-set exists in Asia, where grilled short ribs are the national dish of Korea (*kalbi kui*—Korean

ADVANCE
PREPARATION:
*1 to 6 hours for
marinating the
meat*

SPECIAL
EQUIPMENT:
*2 cups wood
chips, soaked for
1 hour in cold
water to cover
and drained*

Grilled Short Ribs, see Index) and where braised beef ribs are popular in China. The following recipe merges East and West, featuring a rub based on traditional Chinese five-spice powder and a sweet, sticky glaze made with hoisin sauce. The cooking method—long, slow, smoke-grilling—is a hundred percent American. The mammoth size of these ribs led a young friend of mine to call them "dinosaur ribs." So dinosaur ribs they remain at our house.

FOR THE RIBS:
2 racks beef ribs (2½ to 3 pounds each; see Note)
4 teaspoons Chinese five-spice powder
1 tablespoon coarse (kosher or sea) salt
1 tablespoon freshly ground black pepper
2 teaspoons garlic powder

FOR THE BASTING MIXTURE/SAUCE:
⅔ cup hoisin sauce
¼ cup rice wine, sake, or dry sherry, or more if needed
2 tablespoons honey
2 cloves garlic, minced
2 teaspoons grated fresh ginger

1. Rinse the ribs under cold running water and blot dry with paper towels. Combine the five-spice powder, salt, pepper, and garlic powder in a small bowl. Place the ribs in a large baking dish and rub all over with the mixture. Cover and let marinate, in the refrigerator, for at least 1 hour, ideally 4 to 6 hours.

2. Combine the hoisin sauce, rice wine, honey, garlic, and ginger in a bowl and whisk to mix. Add rice wine as needed to thin the sauce to basting consistency. Set aside about ½ cup to use for serving.

3. Set up the grill for indirect cooking (see page 14 or 16), placing a drip pan in the center. *If using a charcoal grill,* preheat to medium.

If using a gas grill, place all the chips in the smoker box and preheat the grill to high. When smoke appears, lower the heat to medium.

4. When ready to cook, if using charcoal, toss half the wood chips on the coals. For both gas and charcoal, oil the grill grate. Place the ribs on the hot grate over the drip pan and cover the grill. Cook the ribs for 1 hour. If using a charcoal grill, add 10 to 12 fresh coals per side and toss the remaining wood chips on the fire. Continue cooking the ribs until done, 30 minutes to 1 hour longer. The ribs are done when the meat is very tender and it has shrunk back from the ends of the bones. Start basting the ribs with the hoisin mixture the last 30 minutes. (Baste several times, giving the ribs one final brushing just before serving.) Serve the ribs accompanied by the reserved sauce.

Serves 4

Note: The sort of ribs I use for this recipe are the long beef ribs sold in racks measuring 6 to 8 inches high and 10 to 12 inches wide, each rack containing 7 ribs. These racks are what remain after the butcher cuts the rib roast off the bones. At first glance, they may not look very meaty, but they're incredibly succulent and there's really quite a bit of meat between the bones.

MONTEVIDEAN-STYLE SWEETBREADS
Mollejas Asadas

URUGUAY

METHOD:
Direct grilling

This is the simplest way I know to cook sweetbreads, and it's certainly one of the best. It requires only two ingredients: sweetbreads and salt. (I've added optional pepper.) You'll find it on the grills at Montevideo's Mercado del Puerto and at Buenos Aires steak houses, too. The grilling produces a crispy, crusty exterior, while leaving the interior soft and moist. The blanching, poaching, and pressing recommended by French chefs (which can take several hours) is omitted entirely. Sweetbreads, by the way, are the thymus glands of calves.

Serve with one of the Argentinian *chimichurris* (see Index).

1½ pounds veal sweetbreads
Coarse (kosher or sea) salt
Coarsely ground black pepper, to taste
    (optional)
Lemon wedges, for serving

1. Preheat the grill to high.

2. Rinse the sweetbreads under cold running water, drain, and blot dry with paper towels. Trim off any pieces of vein or sinew, then butterfly the sweetbreads, that is, cut them horizontally almost in half through the narrow side and open out like a book (see Note).

3. When ready to cook, oil the grill grate. Sprinkle the sweetbreads generously on both sides with salt and pepper (if using). Place the sweetbreads, cut side down to start with, on the hot grate and grill, turning with tongs, until crusty and browned, 6 to 8 minutes per side (12 to 16 minutes in all). Taste for seasoning, adding salt if necessary. Serve immediately, with lemon wedges.

Serves 6 to 8 as an appetizer, 4 as an entrée

Note: Lamb sweetbreads would be prepared the same way.

ARGENTINIAN VEAL AND CHICKEN KEBABS

ARGENTINA

METHOD:
Direct grilling

I first sampled these belt-loosening kebabs at La Estancia (literally "The Ranch"), a boisterous steak house on the equally boisterous street, the Lavalle pedestrian mall in downtown Buenos Aires. The combination of sweet (the prunes) and salty (the meat and bacon) is a savory common thread in Latin American cooking.

Serve accompanied by Argentinian

**SPECIAL
EQUIPMENT:**
*4 long metal
skewers*

Tomato Relish (see Index) or a *chimichurri*, one of the classic Argentinian garlic and parsley sauces (see Index).

1 pound boneless veal loin cut into
    1½-inch chunks
1 pound skinless, boneless chicken breasts
    or thighs, cut into 1½-inch chunks
6 ounces thick-sliced pancetta or
    slab bacon (rind removed),
    cut into 1½-inch pieces
1 medium red bell pepper, stemmed,
    seeded, and cut into 1-inch pieces
1 medium onion, cut into 1-inch pieces
16 large pitted prunes
2 lemon wedges
¼ cup olive oil
Coarse (kosher or sea) salt and freshly
    ground black pepper, to taste

1. Preheat the grill to high.

2. Thread the veal, chicken, pancetta, pepper, onion, and prunes onto the skewers, alternating the ingredients (see Note).

3. Squeeze the lemon wedges into the oil in a small bowl. Drop in the rinds and set aside.

4. When ready to cook, oil the grill grate. Arrange the kebabs on the hot grate and grill, turning with tongs, until the veal and chicken are cooked through, 3 minutes per side (12 minutes in all). Brush the kebabs with the lemon oil as they cook. Season with salt and pepper and serve at once.

Serves 4

Note: Try to place the pancetta next to the pieces of veal and chicken; the melting fat will help keep the meats from drying out as they cook.

GRILLED OXTAILS
Kare Kare

PHILIPPINES

METHOD:
Direct grilling

**ADVANCE
PREPARATION:**
*1½ hours for
boiling the
oxtails*

Every nation has its comfort foods—hearty, uncomplicated dishes that are enjoyed without fuss or culinary pretense. A Filipino favorite is *kare kare*, oxtails. Traditionally, the oxtails would be stewed, but chef Romy Dorotan likes the smoky flavor achieved by finishing the meat on the grill. Orotan is the Luzon-born owner-chef of the restaurant Cendrillon in New York's Soho, where he presents innovative remakes of Filipino dishes.

Cooks seem divided into two camps when it comes to oxtails. There are those, like me, who love their soulful, meaty flavor—and there are those who are afraid to try them. If you belong to the latter group,

please know that oxtails are amazingly flavorful, ridiculously inexpensive, and probably available at your local supermarket. Try them—I bet you'll like them.

Finally, to be strictly authentic, you should garnish the oxtails with *bagoong* (Filipino fermented shrimp). If you're feeling adventurous, you can find this tangy, salty ingredient at Filipino and Asian markets, but you should be warned that *bagoong* can be pretty robust tasting. I find that a splash of fish sauce or a diced anchovy or two works just as well, with much less fuss.

FOR THE OXTAILS:

2 pounds oxtails, cut into 1½-inch slices
1 medium onion, cut in quarters
3 cloves garlic, peeled
1 bay leaf
Salt and freshly ground black pepper, to taste

FOR THE TOMATO-PEANUT SAUCE:

1 tablespoon olive oil
1 small onion, finely chopped
1 clove garlic, chopped
¾ cup tomato purée, fresh or canned
¾ cup broth from cooking oxtails
3 tablespoons chunky peanut butter
3 tablespoons minced fresh Italian (flat-leaf)
    parsley
Salt and freshly ground black pepper, to taste

TO FINISH:

1 tablespoon olive oil, for basting
Salt and freshly ground black pepper,
    to taste
2 to 3 teaspoons *bagoong,* chopped
    anchovies, or Asian fish sauce, for garnish
    (optional)

1. Place the oxtails in a large, heavy pot with cold water to cover by 4 inches. Add the onion, garlic, bay leaf, salt, and pepper and bring to a boil over medium-high heat, skim-

ming off any foam that rises to the surface. Reduce the heat to low and simmer the oxtails gently, uncovered, until tender, 1 to 1½ hours, skimming the broth from time to time to remove any fat. Let the oxtails cool in the broth, then transfer to a plate. Reserve ¾ cup broth for the sauce; save the remainder for soups or stews (see Note).

2. Preheat the grill to high.

3. Meanwhile, prepare the sauce. Heat the oil in a nonstick skillet. Add the onion and garlic and sauté over medium heat until softened but not brown, about 3 minutes. Add the tomato purée and bring to a boil. Stir in the oxtail broth and peanut butter and simmer until the sauce is thick (the consistency of heavy cream) and richly flavored, about 5 minutes. Add the parsley and cook for 1 minute more. Remove from the heat and season with salt and pepper, then keep warm over low heat.

4. Lightly brush the oxtails with oil and season with salt and pepper. When ready to cook, oil the grill grate. Arrange the oxtails on the hot grate and grill, turning with tongs, until heated thoroughly, 2 to 4 minutes per side (4 to 8 minutes in all). Rotate the oxtails 90 degrees after 1 to 2 minutes, to create an attractive crosshatch of grill marks. Spoon the sauce on plates or a platter and set the oxtails on top. If desired, place a spoonful of *bagoong* or chopped anchovies or a splash of fish sauce on each serving and serve immediately.

Serves 4

Note: The recipe can be prepared a day, or even several, ahead to this point.

High on Hog

This South American cookout lends new meaning to the words "pit barbecue."

Every May, tens of thousands of barbecue buffs from around the world flock to Memphis, Tennessee, for a three-day orgy of barbecuing and feasting known as the Memphis in May World Championship Barbecue Cooking Contest. The imaginative names of the teams at this self-proclaimed "Barbecue Super Bowl"—Patio Porkers, Sultans of Swine, Jurassic Pork—indicate loud and clear the preferred meat of these grill maestros: pork.

Pork is just about the perfect meat for barbecuing and grilling. Blessed with a generous marbling, the meat keeps moist during prolonged cooking and has a robust flavor that stands up to fiery chiles, lively Chinese five-spice powder, and dulcet barbecue sauce.

Americans aren't the only ones who like to live high off the hog. A survey of the world's great barbecue dishes would surely include Jamaican Jerk Pork Tenderloin, Bali's *babi guling* (Balinese Roast Pork), and Mexico's *cecina adobada* (Chile-Marinated Pork in the Style of Oaxaca). I even found pork satés in a primarily Muslim country—Indonesia—the legacy of Chinese merchants who settled in the Old Port district of Jakarta.

So stir up the barbecue sauce and get ready to make a perfect hog of yourself.

Pork Grilling Chart*

CUT	METHOD	HEAT	DONENESS	
			MEDIUM (160°F)	WELL-DONE (170°F)
CHOPS/STEAKS			4–6 MIN/SIDE	6–8 MIN/SIDE
ROASTS				
LOIN (2–3 LBS)	INDIRECT	MEDIUM	1–1½ HRS	1½–2 HRS
SHOULDER (5–6 LBS)	INDIRECT	MED TO MED-LOW		4–6 HRS
FRESH HAM (18–20 LBS)	INDIRECT	MED TO MED-LOW		6–10 HRS
RIBS	INDIRECT	MED TO MED-LOW		1½–2 HRS

*This chart is offered as a broad guideline to cooking times for the various cuts of meat. Remember, grilling is an art, not a science. When in doubt, refer to times in the individual recipes.

ELIZABETH KARMEL'S NORTH CAROLINA–STYLE PULLED PORK

U.S.A.

METHOD:
Indirect grilling

ADVANCE PREPARATION:
3 to 8 hours for marinating the meat (optional); also, leave yourself 4 to 6 hours for cooking the meat

SPECIAL EQUIPMENT:
6 cups hickory chips, soaked for 1 hour in cold water to cover and drained

Barbecue means different things to different people in different parts of the country. In North Carolina it means pork, or more precisely smoked pork shoulder, that has been grilled using the indirect method until fall-off-the-bone tender, then pulled into meaty shreds with fingers or a fork. Doused with vinegar sauce and eaten with cole slaw on a hamburger bun, it's one of the most delicious things on the planet, and it requires only one special ingredient: patience.

My friend and barbecue buddy, Elizabeth Karmel, makes the best pork shoulder I've tasted. Elizabeth comes from Greensboro, North Carolina, where she grew up on pulled pork. Her secret is to cook the pork to an internal temperature of 195°F—higher than is recommended by most books. But this is the temperature needed for the pork to separate easily into the fine, moist, tender shreds characteristic of true Carolina barbecue. Elizabeth doesn't use a rub, although many of her compatriots do. (I personally like a rub, but I've made it optional in the recipe.)

A true pork shoulder includes both the Boston butt (the upper part of the leg with the shoulder blade) and the picnic ham (the actual foreleg), a cut of meat that weighs 14 to 18 pounds in its entirety and is used chiefly at professional barbecue competitions. The following recipe calls solely for Boston butt (5 to 6 pounds), which, thanks to its generous marbling, gives you superb barbecue. The appropriate beverage for all this? Cold beer or Cheerwine (a sweet red soda pop).

FOR THE RUB (optional; see Note):
1 tablespoon mild paprika
2 teaspoons firmly packed light brown sugar
1½ teaspoons hot paprika
½ teaspoon celery salt
½ teaspoon garlic salt
½ teaspoon dry mustard
½ teaspoon freshly ground black pepper
½ teaspoon onion powder
¼ teaspoon salt

FOR THE BARBECUE:
1 Boston butt (bone-in pork shoulder roast;
    5 to 6 pounds), covered with a layer (½
    to 1 inch thick) of fat
Vinegar Sauce (recipe follows)
10 to 12 hamburger buns
North Carolina–Style Coleslaw (page 156)

1. If using the rub, combine all the ingredients in a bowl and toss with your fingers to mix. Wearing rubber or plastic gloves if desired, rub this mixture into the pork shoulder on all sides, then wrap in plastic and refrigerate for at least 3 hours, but preferably 8.

2. Set the grill up for indirect grilling (see page 14 or 16), placing a drip pan in the center.

If using a gas grill, place all the wood chips in the smoker box and preheat the grill to high; when smoke appears, lower the heat to medium-low.

If using a charcoal grill, preheat to medium-low and adjust the vents to obtain a temperature of 325°F.

3. When ready to cook, if using charcoal, toss 1 cup wood chips on the coals. Place the pork shoulder, fat side up, on the hot grate over the drip pan. Cover the grill and smoke-cook the pork shoulder until fall-off-the-bone tender and the internal temperature on an instant-read thermometer reaches 195°F, 4 to 6 hours. (The cooking time will depend on the size of the piece of meat and heat of the grill.) If using charcoal, add 10 to 12 fresh coals per side every hour, and toss more wood chips on the fresh coals, adding about 1 cup chips (½ cup per side) every time you replenish the coals. With gas, all you need to do is be sure that you start with a full tank of gas.

4. Transfer the cooked pork roast to a cutting board, tent with aluminum foil, and let rest for 15 minutes. After the resting period, wearing heavy-duty rubber gloves if desired, pull off and discard any skin from the meat, then pull the pork into pieces, discarding any bones or fat. Using your fingertips or a fork, pull each piece of pork into shreds 1 to 2 inches long and ⅛ to ¼ inch wide. This requires time and patience, but a human touch is needed to achieve the perfect texture. If patience isn't one of your virtues, you can finely chop the pork with a cleaver. (Many respected North Carolina barbecue joints serve chopped 'cue.) Transfer the shredded pork to a nonreactive roasting pan. Stir in 1 to 1½ cups of the vinegar sauce, enough to keep the pork moist, then cover the pan with foil and place on the grill for up to 30 minutes to keep warm.

5. To serve, mound the pulled pork on the hamburger buns, and top with coleslaw. Let each person add vinegar sauce to taste.

Serves 10 to 12

Note: If not using the rub, generously season the pork all over with coarse (kosher or sea) salt and freshly ground black pepper; you can start cooking immediately.

Vinegar Sauce

This peppery, piquant vinegar sauce is the preferred condiment of eastern North Carolina. In the western part of the state, the sauce becomes more tomatoey, while in southern parts of the Carolinas, mustard sauce reigns supreme.

2 cups cider vinegar

1⅓ cups water

½ cup plus 2 tablespoons ketchup

¼ cup firmly packed brown sugar, or
   more to taste

5 teaspoons salt, or more to taste

4 teaspoons hot red pepper flakes

1 teaspoon freshly ground black
   pepper

1 teaspoon freshly ground white
   pepper

Combine the vinegar, water, ketchup, brown sugar, salt, hot pepper flakes, and peppers in a nonreactive medium-size bowl and whisk until the sugar and salt are dissolved. Taste for seasoning, adding sugar or salt as necessary; the sauce should be piquant but not quite sour.

Makes about 4 cups

North Carolina–Style Coleslaw

This is coleslaw at its simplest and best. No onions. No carrots. No peppers. No mayonnaise. Just cabbage and peppery barbecue sauce.

1 small or ½ large head green cabbage
   (about 2 pounds), cored
1 cup Vinegar Sauce, or to taste (recipe above)
Salt (optional)

1. Chop the cabbage fine by hand or shred on a mandoline or using the shredding disk of a food processor.

2. Place the cabbage in a large bowl and stir in the vinegar sauce. Let stand for 10 minutes, then reseason, adding sauce or salt as needed.

Makes about 6 cups

CUBAN CHRISTMAS EVE "PIG"

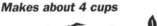

Lechon Asado

METHOD:
Indirect grilling

ADVANCE PREPARATION:
8 to 48 hours for marinating the meat; also, leave yourself 6 to 8 hours for cooking the meat

Pit-roasted pig is the traditional centerpiece of a Cuban Nochebuena, or Christmas Eve supper, a holiday that stirs the same sort of emotions—and digestive juices—in a Cuban heart that Thanksgiving does in ours. Come Christmas Eve day in Miami, the sky fills with fragrant smoke, as thousands of backyard barbecue buffs—everyone from bricklayers to bankers—cook whole young pigs that have been mari-

nating overnight in tangy *adobo,* a garlic–sour orange marinade flavored with cumin and oregano. This recipe calls for a cut of meat of a more manageable size—a fresh (uncured) ham, which has the advantage of being both more widely available than a whole pig and able to fit in your refrigerator.

Cubans don't generally go in for smoke flavor, but you could certainly add a couple of cups of soaked wood chips to the coals or the smoker pan while the pork cooks. If you are using a gas grill, be sure to start with a full tank of gas.

1 whole fresh ham (18 to 20 pounds; see Note)
2 heads garlic, broken into cloves and peeled
2 tablespoons coarse (kosher or sea) salt
1 tablespoon dried oregano
1 tablespoon ground cumin
1 tablespoon freshly ground black pepper
2 cups fresh sour orange juice or 1½ cups fresh lime juice plus ½ cup fresh regular orange juice
¼ cup olive oil
1 cup dry sherry
2 large onions, thinly sliced
4 bay leaves
2 recipes Cuban Mojo (recipe follows)

1. Using the tip of a sharp paring knife, make shallow slits in both the skin and meat sides of the ham, spacing them about 1½ inches apart. Set aside while you prepare the marinade.

2. Combine the garlic, salt, oregano, cumin, and pepper in a mortar and pound to a smooth paste with the pestle, then work in 1 cup of the juice and the oil. If you don't have a mortar and pestle, combine all these ingredients in a blender. Rub this mixture all over the ham, forcing it into the slits. Place the ham in a large plastic bag (such as a garbage bag) with the remaining 1 cup juice, the sherry, onions, and bay leaves. Marinate overnight or even up to 48 hours, turning several times.

3. Set up the grill for indirect grilling (see page 14 or 16), placing a drip pan in the center, and preheat to high. When ready to cook, place the ham, meat side down, on the hot grate over the drip pan and cover the grill.

4. Cook the ham until the skin is well browned and very crisp and the meat is fork-tender. When tested with an instant-read meat thermometer, the internal temperature should register about 190°F. (Cubans like their pork more well done than we do.) If using charcoal, add 10 to 12 fresh coals per side after each hour of cooking. The whole process will take 6 to 8 hours. If the skin browns too much, drape a sheet of aluminum foil loosely over it.

5. Transfer the ham to a cutting board and let rest for 15 minutes. Cut the meat off the bone and chop with a cleaver or thinly slice (be sure to include a little skin). Splash the meat with the Cuban Mojo and serve immediately.

Serves 16 to 20

Note: You can also prepare a pork loin (2 to 3 pounds) or shoulder (4 to 6 pounds) the same way. You'd need only half as much marinade, and the cooking time would be 4 to 6 hours for the pork shoulder, 1 to 2 hours for the loin.

Cuban Mojo

No, it's not pronounced "mo-jo." *Mojo* ("mo-ho") is Cuba's barbecue sauce, a sort of cumin and fried garlic vinaigrette that's splashed over every imaginable dish, from *palomilla* (Cuban steak) to the above roast pork. Cubans make their *mojo* with sour orange juice. Sour oranges can be found at Hispanic grocery stores, but excellent *mojo* can be made with fresh lime juice mixed with a little regular orange juice for sweetness. Serve the *mojo* in a jar or bottle with a tight-fitting lid, so you can shake it up before pouring. This recipe is easily doubled; if you are making *lechon asado,* you will need to do so. Just make sure you use a saucepan deep enough to safely accommodate a cup of boiling oil.

½ cup olive oil

8 large cloves garlic, cut into paper thin slices or finely chopped

⅔ cup fresh sour orange juice or ½ cup fresh lime juice plus 3 tablespoons fresh regular orange juice

½ cup water

1 teaspoon ground cumin

1 teaspoon dried oregano

1 teaspoon salt, or to taste

1 teaspoon freshly ground black pepper, or to taste

3 tablespoons chopped fresh cilantro or Italian (flat-leaf) parsley

1. Heat the oil in a deep saucepan over medium heat. Add the garlic and cook until fragrant and pale golden brown, 1 to 2 minutes. Do not let brown too much, or the garlic will become bitter.

2. Stir in the sour orange juice, water, cumin, oregano, 1 teaspoon salt, and 1 teaspoon pepper. Stand back; the sauce may sputter. Bring the sauce to a rolling boil. Taste for seasoning, adding salt and pepper. Let cool to room temperature, then stir in the cilantro. Transfer the *mojo* to a jar or bottle with a tight-fitting lid. Serve in the jar and shake well before serving.

Makes about 1½ cups

BALINESE ROAST PORK
Babi Guling

INDONESIA

METHOD:
Rotisserie or indirect grilling

SPECIAL EQUIPMENT:
Rotisserie (optional)

*B**abi guling* (spiced roasted pig) is the most famous dish in Bali. Traditionally, *babi guling* is made with a whole suckling pig that has been stuffed with a fragrant *bumbu* (spice paste) and spit-roasted over a barbecue. Lemongrass, turmeric, galangal, and coriander make this one exquisitely flavorful pork dish.

The following recipe comes from one lingah Kepidana, Balinese pit master extraordinaire, who showed me how to pound the ingredients for the spice paste in a tub-size mortar with a pestle the size of a baseball bat. Kepidana cooks his *babi guling* over fire in a half 55-gallon drum, turning the rickety spit by hand.

I've retooled the recipe to be made with boneless pork shoulder. Long Bean Salad with Fresh Coconut and Balinese Yellow Rice (see Index) make great accompaniments.

1 boneless pork shoulder roast (about 3 pounds)

4 large shallots, peeled

4 to 8 Thai chiles or 2 to 4 jalapeños

4 cloves garlic, peeled

2 tablespoons chopped fresh ginger

1 tablespoon chopped fresh turmeric or ½ teaspoon ground turmeric

1 tablespoon chopped fresh galangal or additional ginger

3 stalks fresh lemongrass, trimmed and finely chopped (about ¼ cup), or 3 strips lemon zest (each 2 x ½ inches; removed with a vegetable peeler)

1½ teaspoons ground coriander

1 teaspoon finely ground black pepper

2 tablespoons fresh lime juice

1 tablespoon firmly packed light brown sugar

2 teaspoons salt

5 tablespoons vegetable oil, or more as needed

1. Using a sharp, heavy knife, cut a deep pocket in one side of the roast, starting and ending about ¾ inch from each end and cutting almost all the way through to the other side. Set the roast aside while you prepare the spice paste.

2. Combine the shallots, chiles, garlic, ginger, turmeric, galangal, lemongrass, coriander, pepper, lime juice, sugar, and salt in a mortar and pound to a smooth paste with the pestle. If you don't have a mortar and pestle, combine all the ingredients in a food processor or mini chopper and process to a smooth paste.

3. Heat 3 tablespoons of the oil in a wok or small nonstick skillet over medium heat. Add the spice paste and sauté until fragrant and shiny, about 5 minutes, stirring occasionally (see Frying Chiles). Remove from the heat and cool to room temperature, about 15 minutes.

4. Spread half the cooled spice paste into the pocket you cut in the side of the pork roast. Tie the roast, using butcher's string at 1-inch intervals, or pin the opening shut with metal skewers. Using a rubber spatula, spread the remaining paste over the entire surface of the roast and set aside while you prepare the grill.

5. *Rotisserie method:* Set up the grill for the rotisserie (see page 20) and preheat the grill to high. When ready to cook, skewer the roast lengthwise on the rotisserie spit and let it rotate on the grill until nicely browned on all sides and cooked through, 1 to 1½ hours, brushing with the remaining oil as needed. (If using charcoal, add 10 to 12 fresh coals per side after 1 hour.) When tested with an instant-read meat thermometer, the internal temperature should read 190°F for very well done. (This is the way Indonesians prefer their pork.)

Indirect grilling method: Set up the grill for indirect grilling (see page 14 or 16), placing a drip pan in the center, and preheat to medium. When ready to cook, oil the grill grate. Place the roast on the hot grate over the drip pan, cover, and cook until nicely browned on all sides and the internal temperature is 190°F, 1½ to 2 hours, basting with the remaining oil occasionally. (Here, too, if using charcoal, add fresh coals, as per above.)

6. Transfer the roast to a cutting board or platter, removing it from the spit first, if necessary, and let stand for 10 minutes, then remove the string or skewers and cut the roast into thin crosswise slices to serve.

Serves 6 to 8

ROSEMARY GRILLED PORK LOIN

For sixteen years Aiello Rosario and his wife, Luccia D'Ambrosio, of Florence, Italy, have turned their spotless white truck into a rotisserie. Their specialty is a whole pig that has been artfully boned, stuffed with a pungent paste of garlic and rosemary, and roasted over smoldering oak. I met the couple at the weekly market in the medieval town of San Gimignano near Siena. There, lines quickly formed for their herb-scented, meltingly tender pork and spit-roasted chicken sandwiches.

I've done the recipe using both the rotisserie and indirect method. It's the next best thing to spending an afternoon in the Tuscan countryside.

**SPECIAL
EQUIPMENT:**
*Rotisserie
(optional)*

6 cloves garlic, peeled
1 bunch fresh rosemary, stemmed
   (about ¼ cup leaves)
1 tablespoon coarse (kosher or sea) salt
1 tablespoon freshly ground black pepper
2 tablespoons extra-virgin olive oil
1 boneless pork loin roast (about 2 pounds)

1. Combine the garlic, rosemary, salt, and pepper in a mortar and pound to a smooth paste with the pestle, then work in the oil. If you don't have a mortar and pestle, combine all the ingredients in a spice mill or mini chopper and process to a purée.

2. Using a long, sharp knife, cut the pork roast almost in half lengthwise, starting at one side, as directed in the box on butterflying on page 163. Open out the meat as you would a book, then cut a lengthwise pocket down the center of each side, starting and ending about ½ inch from each end and cutting almost all the way through to the other side. Spread half the herb paste over the surface and into the pockets of the opened-out roast, then bring the sides together so the meat resumes its original shape. Tie the roast at 1-inch intervals with butcher's string, then spread the remaining herb paste over the entire surface. If desired, loosely cover the roast with plastic wrap, and let marinate, in the refrigerator, for 2 to 4 hours, bringing it to room temperature while you preheat the grill.

3. *Rotisserie method:* Set up the grill for the rotisserie (see page 20) and preheat the grill to high. When ready to cook, skewer the roast lengthwise on the rotisserie spit and let it rotate on the grill until well browned on all sides and cooked through, about 1 hour. The internal temperature should register at least 160°F when an instant-read meat thermometer is inserted.

Indirect grilling method: Set up the grill for indirect grilling (see page 14 or 16), placing a drip pan in the center, and preheat to medium. When ready to cook, oil the grill grate. Place the roast on the hot grate over the drip pan, cover the grill, and cook until the internal temperature registers as above, 1 to 1½ hours.

4. Transfer the roast to a cutting board or platter, removing it from the spit first if necessary, and let stand for 5 minutes, then remove the string and cut the roast into thin crosswise slices. Serve hot, warm, or (as they do in Italy) at room temperature.

Serves 4

Pork the Italian Way

*H*ere's how Luccia D'Ambrosio explains the preparation of her rosemary-roasted pork loin, which is popular throughout Tuscany and Umbria.

"Every Friday, Aiello buys three whole young pigs, each weighing sixty pounds, which he bones through the belly, using a razor-sharp knife. It's my job to prepare the spice mix, a fragrant paste of garlic, salt, pepper, and fresh rosemary, which I pound in a mortar with a pestle. I stuff the cavity of the pig with this mixture, tucking it into all the nooks and crannies, then sew the pig up with a giant needle and string. The meat marinates overnight with the herb mixture—the salt both flavors and cures the meat.

"The next day, Aiello builds a fire of Tuscan oak and lets it die down to glowing red coals. The pigs are roasted for three to four hours, and when they're finished, they're tender enough to cut with a fork."

CHILE-MARINATED PORK IN THE STYLE OF OAXACA

Cecina Adobada

MEXICO

METHOD:
Direct grilling

ADVANCE PREPARATION:
4 to 6 hours for soaking the chiles and marinating the meat

SMOKY GRILLED PORK
You can prepare a smoky version of the Oaxacan-style pork. Simply proceed with the recipe as directed, substituting chipotle chiles (smoked jalapeños) for the guajillos.

Variations of this dish turn up all over Mexico. The Oaxacan version (*cecina adobada*) refers to broad, thin slices of pork that have been marinated in an aromatic (but not particularly fiery) paste of dried chiles, vinegar, garlic, and spices. *Cecina* is a popular item in the restaurants of Oaxaca, but the best place to eat it is at one of the grill stalls in the December 20th Food Market. In fact, this recipe was inspired by the fare featured at stall #189 at the market, manned by a shy woman (and 18-year barbecue veteran) who would only give her first name: Laura.

The only remotely tricky part of this recipe is butterflying the pork to make the thin sheets that are traditionally used for grilling. The idea is to obtain what looks like pork scaloppine.

Cecina adobada is traditionally served with guacamole and a spicy salsa, and warm corn tortillas for wrapping everything up.

FOR THE PORK AND ADOBO:
6 guajillo chiles or ¼ cup pure
    chile powder
½ cup distilled white vinegar
4 cloves garlic
1 teaspoon salt
1 teaspoon freshly ground
    black pepper
1 teaspoon dried oregano
½ teaspoon ground cinnamon
¼ teaspoon ground cloves
1 piece (1½ pounds) boneless pork loin,
    tenderloin, or chops

FOR SERVING:
8 corn tortillas (6 inches)
Oaxacan-Style Guacamole (page 449)
Salsa Mexicana (page 174)

1. If using the chiles, tear them open and remove the veins and seeds. Soak the chiles in the vinegar for 30 minutes, or until soft.

2. Combine the chiles (or chile powder), vinegar, garlic, salt, pepper, oregano, cinnamon, and cloves in a blender and process to a smooth, wet paste.

3. Cut the pork loin into 4 broad, thin (¼ inch thick) sheets, using the butterflying technique on page 163. Spread each piece of pork with the adobo mixture and stack in a nonreactive baking dish. Cover and let marinate, in the refrigerator, for 4 to 6 hours.

4. Preheat the grill to high.

5. When ready to grill, oil the grill grate. Arrange the slices on the hot grate and grill, turning with tongs, until nicely browned and cooked through, 2 to 3 minutes per side.

6. Serve immediately, accompanied by the tortillas, the guacamole, and salsa, wrapping the pork and condiments in the tortillas.
Serves 4

GRILLED PORK WITH FIERY SALSA
Poc Chuc

MEXICO

METHOD:
Direct grilling

ADVANCE PREPARATION:
15 minutes for brining the meat

SOUR ORANGE

Sour orange is one of the defining flavors in Yucatecan and Caribbean grilling, essential for marinades and for squeezing over finished dishes.

The juice of the bumpy, roundish, greenish-orange, irregularly sized fruit is sharply acidic, like lime juice, with just a hint of orange flavor. If you live in an area with a large Hispanic or West Indian community, you may be able to find sour oranges. The flavor can be approximated by combining 3 or 4 parts fresh lime juice with 1 part fresh regular orange juice.

There are many reasons people visit the Yucatán. To explore the Mayan ruins at Uxmal and Chichén Itzá. To lounge on the beaches of Cozumel and Cancún. I came to this peninsula on the southeastern coast of Mexico for the purpose of eating *poc chuc*.

Poc chuc is one of the world's great pork dishes—and best-kept secrets. Unless you've visited the Yucatán, you've probably never heard of it. The name suggests that *poc chuc* is an ancient dish: *poc* is the Mayan word for "to grill"; *chuc* means "burning embers." Fire charring is an important element, not only for the meat, but for the salsa and pickled onions.

Poc chuc originated in the villages of central Yucatán, where *campesinos* (farmers) would cure pork in salt water to prevent it from spoiling in the hot sun. The seasoning was equally simple and flavorful: fire-charred onions marinated in sour orange juice and a salsa—called *salsa chiltomate*—made of charred tomatoes at their reddest and ripest and local habanero chiles.

Poc chuc is easy to make, dramatic to serve, and astonishingly tasty. But you need all three components—the cured pork, the grilled pickled onions, and charred tomato sauce—to achieve the full effect.

Serve this grilled pork with plenty of warm corn tortillas for wrapping and eating the meat.

FOR CURING THE PORK:
1 piece (1½ pounds) boneless pork loin, tenderloin, or chops
3 tablespoons coarse (kosher or sea) salt
1 cup water

FOR THE PICKLED ONION:
1 large red onion, peeled, root end left intact
1 cup fresh sour orange juice or ¾ cup fresh lime juice plus ¼ cup fresh regular orange juice
2 teaspoons salt

FOR THE SALSA CHILTOMATE:
2 fresh, ripe medium tomatoes
1 to 3 habanero or scotch bonnet chiles
1 clove garlic, minced
¼ cup chopped fresh cilantro
3 tablespoons fresh sour orange juice or 2½ tablespoons fresh lime juice plus ½ tablespoon fresh regular orange juice
½ teaspoon salt, or to taste

8 tortillas (6 inches or larger), for serving

1. To obtain 4 broad sheets of meat about ¼ inch thick, butterfly the pork according to the directions for butterflying pork tenderloin (see box, facing page).

2. Combine the salt and water in a shallow bowl and whisk until the salt is dissolved. Add the pork pieces to the brine, cover, and let marinate for 15 minutes, turning the pieces once or twice to make sure all are equally exposed to the brine. Drain and refrigerate until ready to cook.

3. Preheat the grill to high.

4. Cut the onion into 8 wedges. Do not trim away the root end on each wedge; it will help hold the wedge together as it grills. When ready to cook, oil the grill grate. Arrange the wedges on the hot grate and grill, turning with tongs, until nicely charred on both sides, about 4 minutes per side.

How to Butterfly Pork or Beef

Various recipes in this book call for butter-flied pork and beef. Here's how to do it.

■ To obtain broad, thick (1 inch) sheets from pork or beef loin or tenderloin, place the meat on a cutting board so one end is facing you. Holding a long, slender, sharp knife parallel to the cutting board, cut the loin or tenderloin horizontally in half, starting on one long side (at the right if you are righthanded and at the left if you're lefthanded) and cutting almost all the way through to the opposite side, stopping about 1 inch from the edge. Open the piece of meat as you would a book, then place it between two sheets of plastic wrap and pound it gently with the side of a heavy cleaver or with a rolling pin to make a rectangle uniformly about 1 inch thick.

■ To obtain broad, thin (¼ inch thick) sheets of loin or tenderloin (for dishes like *pamplona* and *poc chuc*), first cut the tenderloin crosswise in half, then place each half on a cutting board so one end is facing you. Holding a long, slender, sharp knife parallel to the cutting board, cut each tenderloin half horizontally in half, starting on one long side (at the right if you are righthanded and at the left if you're lefthanded) and cutting almost all the way through to the opposite side, stopping about ½ inch from the edge. Open out the piece of meat as you would a book, then place it between two sheets of plastic wrap and pound it gently with the side of a heavy cleaver or with a rolling pin to make a rectangle uniformly about ¼ inch thick.

■ To butterfly a boneless pork chop or vertical slice of pork loin, cut it almost in half through one side, stopping about ¼ inch from the edge. Open the chop as you would a book, then place it between two sheets of plastic wrap and pound it gently with the side of a heavy cleaver or with a rolling pin to achieve a uniform thickness of ¼ inches.

make a horizontal cut in the tenderloin

opened-out tenderloin

make a cut in the boneless chop

opened-out boneless chop

5. Trim off the root ends of the onions and transfer them to a small serving bowl; stir in the sour orange juice and salt. Let the onions marinate at least 10 minutes.

6. Meanwhile, arrange the tomatoes and chiles on the grate and grill, turning with tongs, until nicely charred on all sides, about 8 to 12 minutes in all. The idea is to char the skins without cooking the vegetables through. Transfer the tomatoes and chiles to a plate to cool, 5 minutes.

7. Combine the cooled tomatoes and chiles with the garlic in a blender or food processor and process to a coarse purée.

Add the cilantro, sour orange juice, and salt and process just to mix. Transfer the salsa to a serving bowl.

8. Just before serving, oil the grill grate and add 20 fresh coals, if necessary, to bump up the heat. Arrange the pork on the hot grate and grill, turning with tongs, until cooked through, 2 to 3 minutes per side. Press the pieces against the grate with the back of a metal spatula to make well-defined grill marks. Transfer the pork to a platter. Place the tortillas on the grate, just to warm, about 20 seconds per side. Serve the pork, accompanied by the grilled pickled onions, salsa, and a basket of warmed tortillas.

Serves 4

BRAZILIAN PORK ROLLATINI

BRAZIL

METHOD:
Direct grilling

IF DOING AHEAD

The rollatini can be prepared several hours ahead of time. Refrigerate the rolls, loosely covered with plastic wrap, until ready to grill. Brush with the oil and sprinkle with cheese just before grilling.

These tangy pork rolls come from Rio's legendary Porção restaurant chain, where they're cooked on a spit. I like to think of them as Brazilian rollatini. For the sake of authenticity, I should note that the mustard and cornichons are my contributions to the recipe. Their flavors contrast perfectly with the flavor of the Gruyère. Because you want these rollatini lean, it's best to start with trimmed pork.

**1¼ pounds boneless pork loin,
   trimmed**
**Salt and freshly ground black pepper,
   to taste**
**½ cup finely grated Gruyère or
   Parmesan cheese**
3 tablespoons Dijon mustard
**1 slice smoked or cooked ham
   (about 2 ounces and ¼ inch thick),
   cut into pencil-thin strips**
1 small onion, cut into 12 wedges
12 cornichon pickles (optional)
2 tablespoons olive oil, for brushing

1. Cut the pork loin crosswise into 12 thin slices, or have your butcher do it. (It helps to partially freeze the pork before slicing.) Each slice should be about 4 inches long, 3 inches wide, and ¼ inch thick; if the slices are too thick, you can pound them between sheets of plastic wrap, using the side of a heavy cleaver or a rolling pin. Season the slices with salt and pepper.

2. Spread the grated cheese in a shallow bowl. Dip each slice of pork in grated cheese, turning to lightly coat both sides and shaking off the excess. Lay the pork slices flat on your work surface and spread the surface of each lightly with mustard. Place a strip of ham, an onion wedge, and a cornichon (if using) at one narrow end of each slice, then roll the pork tightly around the filling to form a compact roll. Tie each roll in the center with butcher's string or pin shut with toothpicks. Brush the rolls with oil, put on a plate, and sprinkle with any remaining cheese (see If Doing Ahead).

3. Preheat the grill to medium-high.

4. When ready to grill, oil the grate. Arrange the pork rolls on the hot grate and grill, turning with tongs, until nicely browned on all sides and just cooked through (firm to the touch), 8 to 12 minutes in all. Remember to remove the strings or toothpicks before serving.

*Makes 12 rolls; serves 6 as an appetizer,
4 as an entrée*

JAMAICAN JERK PORK TENDERLOIN

JAMAICA

METHOD:
Direct grilling

**ADVANCE
PREPARATION:**
*At least 4 hours
for marinating
the meat*

**SPECIAL
EQUIPMENT:**
*2 cups hickory
or oak chips,
soaked for 1 hour
in cold water to
cover and
drained*

Traditional Jamaican jerk would be made with a whole pig, boned and spread open like a book, marinated with fiery jerk seasoning, and smoke-grilled over smoldering allspice wood. (See page 166 for a complete description of jerk.) Here's a home version that can be made with pork tenderloin. To achieve the right flavor, you must use scotch bonnet chiles or their Mexican cousins, habaneros. If you can't find either, use fresh jalapeño chiles and a few tablespoons of a scotch bonnet–based hot sauce, like Busha Browne's Pukka Sauce, Coyote Cocina Howlin' Hot Sauce, or Matouk's Hot Pepper Sauce. If you have sensitive skin, wear rubber gloves when handling scotch bonnets. I've suggested a range of chiles: tender-tongues should start with 2 to 4; fiery food buffs can use the full amount.

The traditional accompaniments to jerk pork are Jamaican Fry Bread and Fire-Roasted Breadfruit (see Index).

**2 pounds pork tenderloin (3 to 4 tenderloins;
  see Notes)**
**2 to 16 scotch bonnet chiles (for a milder
  jerk, seed the chiles)**
**2 bunches scallions, both white and green
  parts, trimmed and cut into 1-inch pieces**
½ medium onion, cut into 1-inch pieces
1 piece (1 inch) fresh ginger, thinly sliced
3 cloves garlic, peeled
1 tablespoon fresh thyme or 2 teaspoons dried
2½ teaspoons ground allspice
½ teaspoon freshly ground black pepper
½ teaspoon freshly grated nutmeg
¼ teaspoon ground cinnamon
¼ cup distilled white vinegar
3 tablespoons soy sauce
2 tablespoons vegetable oil
3 tablespoons coarse (kosher or sea) salt
1 tablespoon firmly packed light brown sugar
1 to 2 tablespoons vegetable oil, for basting

1. Butterfly the tenderloins as directed in the box on page 163, for 1-inch-thick sheets. Then, using the tip of a paring knife, make holes ¼ inch deep all over each sheet of meat. Place the tenderloins in a large nonreactive baking dish and set aside while you prepare the seasoning.

2. Combine the chiles, scallions, onion, ginger, and garlic in a food processor and process until finely chopped. Add the thyme, allspice, pepper, nutmeg, cinnamon, vinegar, soy sauce, oil, salt, and sugar and process to a smooth purée (see Notes).

3. Using a rubber spatula, spread the seasoning mixture over the tenderloins, stuffing it into the holes. Cover and let marinate, in the refrigerator, for at least 4 hours, turning the meat several times.

4. *If using a charcoal grill,* preheat it to medium.

If using a gas grill, place the wood chips in the smoker box and preheat the grill to high; when smoke appears, lower the heat to medium.

5. When ready to cook, if using charcoal, toss the wood chips on the coals. Oil the grill grate. Arrange the sheets of pork on the hot grate and grill, turning with tongs and brushing occasionally with oil, until nicely browned on both sides and cooked through, 16 to 20 minutes in all. When not turning the meat, keep the grill covered to hold in the smoke.

6. Transfer the pork to a cutting board and let rest for 5 minutes, then cut into thin diagonal slices and serve immediately.

Serves 4 to 6

Notes: Jerk pork is usually prepared with the pork fat left on, but you can certainly trim it off, if you wish.

■ You can make the marinade in a blender; if you do, add all the ingredients at once.

Jerk: The Jamaican Barbecue

I have eaten Jamaica's national dish and I can tell you this much: It hurts. Smoke stings your eyes and scotch bonnet chiles scorch the gullet. I experienced my first real fiery jerk pork in Boston Beach on the northeastern coast of Jamaica. After making it through one order, I wiped my brow . . . and promptly ordered seconds!

Jerk is Jamaican barbecue. Like its North American counterpart, jerk is simultaneously a dish, a cooking method, and a way of life. It turns up at rugged roadside eateries and respectable restaurants from one end of Jamaica to the other. To make jerk, the meat (usually pork or chicken) is washed with lime juice or vinegar, marinated in a fiery paste of scotch bonnet chiles and other spices, and smoke-cooked over smoldering hardwood.

Some people cook jerk on a barbecue grill, others in a steel drum or over a pit. As for the seasoning, as the jerk marinade is called, there are probably as many different formulas as there are individual cooks in Jamaica. And, in recent years, the traditional jerk pork and jerk chicken have given way to such newfangled creations as jerk snapper, jerk lobster, even jerk pasta.

Historically, jerk is associated with the Maroons, runaway slaves who settled in the St. Thomas highlands in eastern Jamaica in the late seventeenth century. To preserve meats while on the run from British soldiers, the Maroons rubbed wild boar with a fiery paste of salt, spices, and scotch bonnet chiles, then smoked it over smoldering wood.

Actually, the preparation probably dates back to the region's first inhabitants, the Arawak Indians. After all, the raw materials for jerk—the incendiary scotch bonnet chile, the pimiento berry (allspice), thyme, wild cinnamon, and scallions—have existed in Jamaica for centuries. The very term "barbecue" seems to have come from an Arawak word, a grill made of green branches called *barbacoa*.

According to Winston Stoner, charismatic director of the Busha Browne Company (which manufactures a popular line of Jamaican seasonings), the term "jerk" is derived from a Jamaican patois word, *juk,* meaning "to stab" or "stick with a sharp implement." "The first thing to be jukked was the wild boar," Stoner explained to me at his office in a Kingston warehouse. "Today it's a tame pig." Once dressed, the meat would be jukked a second time to speed the absorption of the spice mix. "But to really understand Jamaican jerk," insisted Stoner, "you've got to go to Boston Beach."

Twist my arm. This tiny seaside community, a 20-minute drive from the city of Port Antonio in northeastern Jamaica, has the sort of serene horseshoe-shaped beach you dream about on a cold winter night. Brightly painted canoes dot the golden sands, which are lapped by the turquoise Caribbean. Named for the Boston Fruit Company, which had a Jamaican outpost, Boston Beach was once a center of the banana trade. Today, it's renowned for another gastronomic specialty: jerk. Although jerk is served all over Jamaica, Boston Beach is the best place to find traditional jerk pits.

For, like the barbecue of the American South and the bean hole beans of New England, jerk is born quite literally from a hole in the ground. Even the fanciest steel drum rig (and there are some fancy ones in Jamaica) can't compete with the elemental flavor of meat cooked over an open pit.

A jerk pit consists of a shallow trough, framed on either side by a row of cinderblocks. Arranged across these blocks is a sort of grate made of inch-thick sticks cut from green pimiento (allspice tree). Spaced 1 inch apart, the sticks literally burn up during the cooking process and must be replaced every few hours. As the sticks burn, they impart a smoky flavor that is unique to Jamaican jerk.

WHAT'S IN A NAME?

To call Sufferer's Jerk Pork Front Line No. 1 a restaurant might be stretching it a bit. The dining room is a rickety pavilion made of bamboo slats with four mismatched tables. An American health inspector would wince at the sight of the open-air kitchen, with its dirt floor, corrugated tin roof, concrete work table, and cutting board made from an old tree stump. There are only three basic items on the menu: jerk chicken, jerk pork, and jerk sausage. But to come to Jamaica without visiting Sufferer's (or one of the other jerk purveyors in Boston Beach) would be to miss one of the most intense gastronomic experiences in the world.

Prince Duncan Sufferer doesn't know the origins of his restaurant. The serious, soft-spoken man took over from his parents in 1975. Today, he's assisted by a half dozen young men at an operation that begins at 6 A.M. and doesn't finish until 7 or 8 at night.

When I arrived at 11 A.M., the crew had been working for hours. A wiry young man named Darrick Minot has the painful task of puréeing 24 pounds of scotch bonnet chiles in a hand-cranked meat grinder. When you stop to consider that the scotch bonnet is the world's hottest chile—up to 50 times hotter than a jalapeño—painful is the operative word here. "Don't touch your eyes when doing this," Minot warned, as the stinging pepper fumes swirled all around us. I guess it's not for nothing that he works at a place called Sufferer's.

The tongue-torturing chile paste that emerges from the meat grinder forms the backbone of the seasoning. But it's not until 21 different spices and condiments are added that the marinade is complete. The spices include wild cinnamon sticks, whole nutmegs, and fistfuls of pungent allspice berries. The bittersweet flavor of the latter is one of the defining flavors of jerk.

Other essential seasonings include bushy branches of thyme, antler-shaped clusters of ginger, and escallions (Caribbean chives), which taste like a cross between a North American scallion and a shallot. Garlic powder, soy sauce, brown sugar, vinegar, and a generous measure of sea salt are added to the marinade, which is mixed in a plastic bucket. The resulting mixture is so hot, it would probably qualify for regulation by the Atomic Energy Commission.

Pit master William Gallimore, a tall black man dressed in a battered blue shirt and shoes that literally fall off his feet, tends the four pits where the jerk is cooked. The first is a ground-level barbecue grill, where thick coils of homemade sausage sizzle over blazing embers. The second holds split chickens on a wire grill, with a sheet of metal over them to keep in the fragrant smoke. The third is a round hole in the ground where whole breadfruits roast among blazing pimiento wood. The fourth pit is the rallying point for all this activity, for it is here that a whole pig is transformed into meltingly tender jerk pork.

According to Gallimore, the secret to great jerk is the slow cooking over low heat. Every half hour, he shovels fresh coals under the pork. It takes about an hour to cook a chicken and 5 hours to cook a pig. The pork is turned every 30 minutes, an operation that plunges the pit master into dense clouds of eye-stinging smoke. The lengthy cooking produces pork of astonishing succulence, meltingly tender, richly flavored, subtly smoky, spicy but not unbearably hot. The slow cooking seems to attenuate the bite of the chiles.

The service of jerk is as simple as the cooking process is complex. You order it by the pound. The pit master hacks off pieces with a cleaver and serves them to you in a sheet of waxed paper. That's it.

The traditional accompaniments to jerk pork include festival and breadfruit. The former is a cigar-shaped fritter made from flour, cornmeal, and sugar. The latter, a tropical fruit brought to the West Indies by Captain Bligh himself, tastes a little like a baked potato. If you ever tasted breadfruit and thought it bland, you haven't tasted Sufferer's. To wash down this princely repast, there are icy bottles of Red Stripe Beer, dark sweet Dragon Stout, or for the teetotaler, a refreshing grapefruit soda called Ting.

In the last ten years, jerk has spread far beyond the shores of Jamaica. I've eaten jerk at a strip mall in Ft. Lauderdale, a boisterous bar in Boston, Massachusetts, and a trendy restaurant in SoHo, New York. My neighborhood eatery in Miami serves jerk scrambled eggs for breakfast and jerk chicken Caesar salad for lunch. But to taste the real McCoy, you must make a pilgrimage to Boston Beach in northern Jamaica. Which isn't the worst assignment—especially as winter approaches!

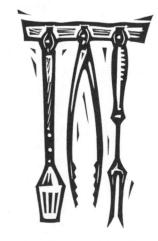

URUGUAYAN GRILLED STUFFED, ROLLED PORK

Pamplona de Puerco

URUGUAY

METHOD:
Direct grilling

A *pamplona* is a stuffed rolled roast that is grilled over a gentle fire. This specialty of the grill stalls and restaurants at Montevideo's Mercado del Puerto is made with few ingredients, but the peppers and provolone fill the pork with flavor, and the resulting mosaic of color makes the dish pretty to look at, too. Uruguayans would serve a whole *pamplona* per person—as an appetizer! (Then again, South Americans eat a lot more meat than do their North American neighbors.) Don't be intimidated: This recipe is really quite easy—even if you've never butterflied a roast before.

If desired, serve one of the *chimichurris* (see Index) as an accompaniment.

2 pork tenderloins (about 1½ pounds
   in all)
Salt and freshly ground black pepper,
   to taste
1 large red bell pepper
2 slices (¼ inch thick) provolone
   cheese (2 ounces each)
1 to 2 tablespoons olive oil, for
   basting

1. Trim the tenderloins of any excess fat and sinew, then cut each crosswise in half. Butterfly each piece according to the directions for ¼-inch-thick sheets in the box on page 163. You will have four 7-inch squares. Season with salt and pepper.

2. Stem and seed the pepper and cut it lengthwise into ¼-inch strips. Cut each slice of cheese into ¼-inch strips. Arrange 4 to 5 strips each of pepper and cheese lengthwise across each piece of pork, alternating pepper and cheese and leaving a ½-inch border on each side. Roll up the first piece of the pork to enclose the filling and form a compact cylinder. Tie the roll in several places with butcher's string or pin it shut with small metal skewers. Assemble the other *pamplonas* the same way (see Note).

3. Preheat the grill to medium-high.

4. When ready to cook, brush the *pamplonas* lightly with oil and season with salt and pepper. Arrange them on the hot grate and grill, turning with tongs, until the pork is browned on all sides and is cooked through, 16 to 20 minutes in all. When tested with an instant-read meat thermometer, the internal temperature should register at least 160°F.

5. Transfer the *pamplonas* to a platter and remove the butcher's string or skewers. Let rest for 5 minutes before slicing. Traditionally the roll would be served whole on a plate, but I like to cut it crosswise into ½-inch slices, fanning the slices out on the plate to create a pinwheel effect.

Serves 6 as an appetizer, 4 as an entrée

Note: The *pamplonas* may be prepared to this point up to 6 hours ahead of time. Cover loosely with plastic wrap and refrigerate if planning to wait more than 30 minutes.

SUSUR LEE'S CHINESE BARBECUED PORK

CHINA

METHOD:
Direct grilling

ADVANCE PREPARATION:
1 to 2 days for marinating the meat

Susur Lee, Hong Kong–born owner of the restaurant Lotus in Toronto, is one of Canada's fastest-rising culinary stars. This recipe takes an East-meets-West approach to classic Chinese barbecue. Actually, "barbecue" is something of a misnomer, seeing as the Chinese roast and/or fry their barbecued pork, but almost never resort to grilling. In this exception, pork's natural affinity for sweet flavorings shines through. It is as simple and easy to make as the results are delicious.

1½ pounds pork tenderloin (2 to 3 tenderloins)
1 medium rib celery, finely chopped
1 medium carrot, finely chopped
1 medium onion, finely chopped
1 tablespoon minced fresh ginger
5 strips fresh tangerine or orange zest (each 2 x ½ inches; removed with a vegetable peeler)
⅔ cup rice wine or dry sherry
⅓ cup soy sauce
⅓ cup pure maple syrup
2 tablespoons Asian (dark) sesame oil

1. Trim the tenderloins of any excess fat or sinew. Combine the celery, carrot, onion, ginger, tangerine zest, sherry, soy sauce, maple syrup, and 1 tablespoon of the sesame oil in a nonreactive baking dish and stir to mix. Add the tenderloins, turning to coat. Cover and let marinate, in the refrigerator, for 24 to 48 hours, turning occasionally.

2. Preheat the grill to medium-high.

3. Remove the tenderloins from the marinade and blot dry with paper towels. Strain the marinade into a small nonreactive saucepan and bring to a boil over medium-high heat. Boil the marinade until thick and syrupy, 5 to 8 minutes.

4. When ready to cook, brush the tenderloins with the remaining 1 tablespoon sesame oil. Arrange the tenderloins on the hot grate and grill, turning with tongs, until the pork is browned on all sides and cooked through, 16 to 20 minutes in all. Start brushing the tenderloins with the reduced marinade after 10 minutes. When tested with an instant-read meat thermometer, the temperature should register at least 160°F when the pork is done.

5. Transfer the tenderloins to a cutting board and let rest for 5 minutes. Cut each tenderloin on the diagonal into ½-inch slices. Fan the slices out on plates or a platter and serve with any remaining marinade.

Serves 4 to 6

PORK WITH MOORISH SEASONINGS
Pinchos Morunos

SPAIN

METHOD:
Direct grilling

I've always been fascinated by the dishes that result from the clash of two cultures. Consider the following kebabs, a popular tapa in Spain. The Spanish name for the dish means, literally, "Moorish kebabs," and the seasonings—cumin,

ADVANCE PREPARATION: 4 to 8 hours for marinating the meat

SPECIAL EQUIPMENT: 8 long metal skewers

coriander, and hot pepper flakes—are certainly characteristic of North African cooking. But no self-respecting Muslim would prepare this dish with what is probably Spain's most popular meat: pork. Here, then, is a dish born of two cultures and continents. Serve with Spanish Grilled Vegetable Salad and Catalan Tomato Bread (see Index).

2 pounds boneless pork loin or tenderloin
1 medium onion, finely diced
3 cloves garlic, minced
3 tablespoons minced fresh Italian (flat-leaf) parsley
1 tablespoon paprika, preferably Spanish
½ teaspoon hot red pepper flakes
½ teaspoon ground cumin
½ teaspoon ground coriander
½ teaspoon dried oregano
¼ teaspoon saffron threads, crumbled
4 tablespoons extra-virgin olive oil

2 tablespoons red wine vinegar
2 tablespoons dry sherry or white wine
1 teaspoon salt
½ teaspoon freshly ground black pepper

1. Cut the pork into ¾-inch cubes. Combine all the remaining ingredients except 2 tablespoons oil in a large nonreactive baking dish. Add the meat and toss thoroughly to coat, then marinate, covered, in the refrigerator for 4 to 6 hours or as long as overnight.

2. Preheat the grill to high.

3. When ready to cook, thread the pork cubes onto the skewers. Oil the grill grate, then arrange the kebabs on the hot grate. Grill until the pork is browned on all sides and cooked through, 2 to 3 minutes per side, 8 to 12 minutes in all, brushing occasionally with the reserved 2 tablespoons oil. Serve immediately.

Serves 8 as an appetizer, 4 as an entrée

SWEET PORK SATE
Saté Babi Manis

INDONESIA

METHOD: Direct grilling

ADVANCE PREPARATION: 1 hour for marinating the meat

This may seem like a straightforward saté recipe, but it's also a profound comment on religious tolerance in modern Indonesia. Like most of the Indonesian archipelago, Java is a Muslim island, yet here's a pork kebab from a bustling hawkers' center in the heart of Batavia (the port section of Jakarta). The explanation is simple: Batavia was Jakarta's Chinatown (although the current Chinese community is a fraction of what it once was), and the Chinese love pork.

This recipe comes from the Saté Babi Sop Bakut Shop in the Pecenongan district, near the Radisson Hotel. If you have the time and you're feeling adventurous, dinner here makes a fun outing. (Come late to avoid Jakarta's hellish traffic.) You'll sit under an awning with fluorescent lights and oilcloth-covered tables, to be served satés—sizzling hot from the grill—on red plastic plates.

GALANGAL

Galangal is a root in the ginger family with a peppery, aromatic flavor. Look for it ground in Asian markets and gourmet shops. Sometimes it's sold under the name of **laos.**

1 pound boneless pork loin or
    shoulder, with some fat,
    cut into ½-inch dice
⅔ cup sweet soy sauce (ketjap manis)
    or ⅓ cup each regular soy sauce
    and molasses
2 cloves garlic, minced
2 shallots, thinly sliced
1 cucumber, peeled and seeded,
    (see box page 89), then
    cut into ½-inch dice
1 tablespoon ground dried galangal
    4 kaffir limes or key limes, or 2 Persian
    limes, cut into wedges
Mixed Vegetable Achar (page 443; optional)

1. Thread the pork onto the skewers, 5 to 6 pieces per skewer. Combine ⅓ cup of the soy sauce, the garlic, and shallots in a plate and roll the satés around in the mixture. Cover and let marinate, in the refrigerator, for 1 hour, turning the skewers occasionally to ensure even marinating.

2. Preheat the grill to high.

3. Meanwhile, set out 4 dinner plates. On one side of each plate place a mound of diced cucumbers, a small pool of the remaining soy sauce, a small pile of the galangal powder, and a few lime wedges.

4. When ready to cook, oil the grill grate. Arrange the satés on the hot grate and grill, turning with tongs, until the meat is nicely browned and cooked through, about 8 minutes in all.

5. To eat, skewer a piece of cucumber on the end of the skewer. Dip the saté first into soy sauce, then into the galangal powder. Squeeze a little lime juice over all, then pop the saté into your mouth. Eat the Shallot Achar (if using) to cleanse the palate between satés.

Serves 4 as an appetizer, 2 to 3 as an entrée

SWEET AND GARLICKY PORK CHOPS

THAILAND

METHOD:
Direct grilling

ADVANCE PREPARATION:
1 to 2 hours for marinating the meat

One of the constants in the world of barbecue is the pairing of grilled meats with garlic. Another is the use of a sugar- or honey-based marinade to counterpoint the richness of a meat like pork. Put them together and you get this Thai-style barbecue, which is made here with pork chops but could also be used for pork tenderloin or loin. I like to use 1-inch-thick loin chops for this recipe, but you can also use twice as many of the more widely available thin chops. Jasmine Rice (see Index) would make a good accompaniment.

4 thick (1 inch) or 8 thin (½ inch) pork
    chops (about 2 pounds in all)
1 head garlic, broken into cloves and peeled
3 tablespoons sugar
⅓ cup Asian fish sauce or soy sauce
3 tablespoons honey
3 tablespoons rice wine
2 tablespoons Asian (dark) sesame oil
1 tablespoon grated fresh ginger
2 teaspoons salt
1 teaspoon freshly ground black pepper

1. Make 1 or 2 cuts in the fat side of each pork chop to keep it from curling during grilling. Arrange the chops in a baking dish and set aside.

2. Combine the garlic and sugar in a mini chopper or food processor and process to a paste, or pound to a paste in a mortar using the pestle. Work in the fish sauce, honey, rice wine, sesame oil, ginger, salt, and pepper. Using a rubber spatula, spread the mixture over both sides of the chops. Cover and let marinate, in the refrigerator, for 1 to 2 hours.

3. Preheat the grill to high.

4. When ready to cook, oil the grill grate.

Arrange the chops on the hot grate and grill until nicely browned on both sides and cooked through, 6 to 8 minutes per side for thick chops (half that amount of time for thin). When tested with an instant-read thermometer, the internal temperature should register 160°F. Transfer the chops to a platter and serve immediately.

Serves 4

ROMY'S RIBS WITH FILIPINO SEASONINGS

PHILIPPINES

METHOD:
Indirect grilling

ADVANCE PREPARATION:
8 hours for marinating the ribs

SPECIAL EQUIPMENT:
2 cups wood chips, soaked for 1 hour in cold water to cover and drained

Romy Dorotan is a man with a mission: to introduce New Yorkers to the soulful flavors of his native Philippines. His Mercer Street restaurant, Cendrillon, has the industrial look of the Soho gallery scene (bare brick walls, exposed heating ducts), but his food hums with complex flavors and his painterly plate presentations enchant the eye. Romy's ribs are a cross-cultural triumph, fragrant with citrus and Sichuan peppercorns. He cooks the ribs in what he calls a Chinese smoker. (Actually, it's more like a steamer.) I adapted them to cook on the grill using the indirect grilling method.

The ribs can be served as is, but for a

truly amazing experience, try painting them with Ginger-Plum Barbecue Sauce (see Index).

FOR THE PORK AND MARINADE:
4 racks baby back pork ribs (3 to 4 pounds)
½ cup soy sauce
Juice and grated zest of 1 orange
Juice and grated zest of 1 lemon
Juice and grated zest of 1 lime
2 stalks fresh lemongrass, trimmed and thinly sliced (optional)
1 tablespoon minced fresh ginger
2 cloves garlic, minced

FOR THE RUB:
1 tablespoon paprika
2 teaspoons Sichuan peppercorns
2 teaspoons coriander seeds
2 teaspoons cumin seeds
2 teaspoons mustard seeds
1 teaspoon fennel seeds
1 dried hot red chile or ½ teaspoon cayenne pepper
2 teaspoons firmly packed light brown sugar
2 teaspoons salt

1. Remove the thin, papery skin from the back of each rack of ribs by pulling it off in a sheet with your fingers, using one corner of a towel to gain a secure grip, or with pliers. Place the ribs in a nonreactive roasting pan.

2. Combine all the ingredients for the marinade in a blender and process to a smooth purée. Pour the marinade over the ribs, turning to coat both sides. Cover and let marinate 8 hours, in the refrigerator, turning once or twice.

3. Combine all the ingredients for the rub in a spice mill or blender and grind to a fine powder (see Note).

4. Set up the grill for indirect cooking (see page 14 or 16), placing a large drip pan in the center. *If using a charcoal grill*, preheat it to medium.

If using a gas grill, place the wood chips in the smoker box and preheat the grill to high; when smoke appears, reduce the heat to medium.

5. When ready to cook, remove the ribs from the marinade and blot dry with paper towels. Rub the spice mix over the ribs on both sides. If using charcoal, toss half the wood chips on the coals. Then arrange the ribs on the hot grate, over the drip pan. Cover the grill and smoke-cook the ribs until the meat is very tender and it has shrunk back from the ends of the bones, 1½ to 2 hours. If using a charcoal grill, after 1 hour add 10 to 12 fresh coals per side and the remaining 1 cup wood chips.

Serves 4

Note: For extra flavor, you can toast the spices in a dry skillet over medium heat until fragrant, about 3 minutes, before grinding.

OAXACAN-STYLE PORK RIBS

MEXICO

METHOD:
Direct grilling

ADVANCE PREPARATION:
Up to 24 hours for marinating the ribs

La Capilla (The Chapel) plays to the sort of nostalgia city dwellers everywhere have for the countryside. Located about a half hour outside Oaxaca, the restaurant offers its patrons the opportunity to spend an afternoon in the country, dining at communal tables under open-air thatch-roofed huts, serenaded by a mariachi band, and surrounded by wooden ox carts and caged farm animals. You sip locally brewed mescal and feast on simply grilled meats, cooked the old-fashioned way—in an open kitchen over a blazing charcoal fire. And after you've eaten—an activity that seems to take a couple of hours—there are hammocks for a siesta. It is, in short, the perfect way to spend an afternoon in the country.

La Capilla's chef is a short, serious woman named Manuela Martinez Torres,

and her pork ribs would do a Kansas Citian proud. The first thing I noticed about them was that the bones of each rack were neatly cracked in the center. This allows the adobo (spice paste) to penetrate the meat on all sides, explains Torrez, and it also releases the marrow and juices from the bones, adding flavor and succulence to the meat. If you have a cooperative butcher, ask him to do this for you.

The second curious thing about her ribs is the adobo itself, a dark green paste of dried herbs and vinegar made without chiles (unusual for these parts). The preparation has the rare virtue of seeming to intensify the flavor of the meat without masking or altering it.

The third surprise is the cooking method: direct grilling over charcoal, not the slow, smoky, indirect cooking method used by most barbecue joints in the U.S. If you like a rib that has some chew to it (not everyone likes 'em fall-off-the-bone tender), these are the ribs for you. And they're great served with tortillas, Oaxacan-Style Guacamole (see Index), and the Salsa Mexicana that follows this recipe.

Note that Martina uses spareribs. You could certainly use loin ribs or baby back ribs.

2 racks pork spareribs (about 4 pounds)
6 cloves garlic, peeled
1 tablespoon dried thyme
1 tablespoon dried oregano
1 tablespoon dried marjoram
2 teaspoons salt
1 piece (½ inch) cinnamon stick or
    ½ teaspoon ground cinnamon
2 allspice berries or ⅛ teaspoon ground
    allspice
2 whole cloves or ⅛ teaspoon ground cloves
¼ cup distilled white vinegar
3 tablespoons water, or more if needed
Salsa Mexicana (recipe follows)

1. Remove the thin, papery skin from the back of each rack of ribs by pulling it off in a sheet with your fingers, using one corner of a kitchen towel to gain a secure grip, or with pliers. Place the ribs in a roasting pan.

2. Combine the garlic, thyme, oregano, marjoram, 2 teaspoons salt, the cinnamon stick, allspice berries, cloves, vinegar, and 3 tablespoons water in a blender or spice mill and process to a smooth paste, adding more water, if needed. Rub this paste over the ribs on both sides, cover, and let marinate, in the refrigerator, at least overnight and up to 24 hours.

3. Preheat the grill to medium.

4. When ready to cook, season the ribs with salt. Oil the grill grate, then arrange the ribs on the hot grate, meaty side down. Grill the ribs until nicely browned and cooked through, 30 to 40 minutes in all, turning once or twice with tongs (see Note).

5. Cut the racks into sections of 2 or 4 ribs for serving. Pass the Salsa Mexicana.

Serves 4

Note: You'll probably get flare-ups—especially as the fat melts in the beginning. Control them by moving the ribs around on the grate or by squirting the fire a few times with a water pistol.

Salsa Mexicana

This simple salsa is a constant on Mexico's culinary landscape. The name changes from region to region (*pico de gallo* in the north; *salsa mexicana* in the south), but the basic elements—crisp white onions, fiery green chiles, and tomatoes so luscious and red that eating them is almost carnal—remain the same.

2 fresh, ripe medium tomatoes
1 medium or ½ large white onion
2 to 8 serrano or jalapeño chiles
¼ cup chopped fresh cilantro
3 tablespoons fresh lime juice, or more if
    needed
½ teaspoon salt, or more if needed

1. Cut the tomatoes, onion, and chiles into ¼-inch dice. (You can soften the bite of the chiles by scraping out the veins and seeds.) Combine in a serving bowl.

2. Add the cilantro, lime juice, and salt and toss to mix. Correct the seasoning, adding lime juice or salt to taste.

Makes about 2 cups

MEMPHIS-STYLE RIBS

METHOD:
Indirect grilling

ADVANCE PREPARATION:
4 to 8 hours for marinating the ribs

SPECIAL EQUIPMENT:
2 cups wood chips (preferably hickory), soaked for 1 hour in cold water to cover and drained

It never fails to amaze me how one simple idea can give birth to so many great regional variations. Consider ribs. The pork rib is one of the most perfect morsels ever to grace a dinner plate. The meat is generously marbled, which keeps it moist during the prolonged cooking. As the fat melts, it crisps the meat fibers and bastes the meat naturally. The bones impart a rich meaty flavor (meat next to the bone always tastes best), while literally providing a physical support—a gnawable rack on which to cook the meat. Yet depending on whether you eat ribs in Birmingham or Kansas City, or Bangkok or Paris for that matter, you'll get a completely different preparation.

I've always been partial to Memphis-style ribs. Memphians don't mess around with a lot of sugary sauces. Instead, they favor dry rubs—full-flavored mixtures of paprika, black pepper, and cayenne, with just a touch of sugar for sweetness. The rubs are massaged into the meat the night before cooking, by way of a marinade, then sprinkled on the ribs at the end of cooking. This double application of spices creates incredible character and depth of flavor, while at the same time preserving the natural taste of the pork. Sometimes a vinegar-and-mustard-based sauce—aptly called a "mop" sauce—is swabbed over the ribs (with said mop) during cooking; I've included one here, for you to use if you like.

You can use any type of rib for this recipe: baby back ribs, long ends, short ends, rib tips, you name it (for more on these cuts, see Index for The Four Styles of American Barbecue). Times are approximate. The ribs are done when the bones extrude and the meat is fork tender.

FOR THE RIBS AND RUB:
6 racks pork ribs (4 to 6 pounds baby back ribs or 6 to 8 pounds spareribs)
¼ cup paprika
1½ tablespoons freshly ground black pepper
1½ tablespoons firmly packed dark brown sugar
1 tablespoon salt
1½ teaspoons celery salt
1½ teaspoons cayenne pepper
1½ teaspoons garlic powder
1½ teaspoons dry mustard
1½ teaspoons ground cumin

FOR THE MOP SAUCE (OPTIONAL):
2 cups cider vinegar
½ cup yellow (ballpark) mustard
2 teaspoons salt

1. Remove the thin, papery skin from the back of each rack of ribs by pulling it off in a sheet with your fingers, using the corner of a kitchen towel to gain a secure grip, or with pliers. Combine the ingredients for the rub in a small bowl and whisk to mix. Rub two thirds of this mixture over the ribs on both sides, then transfer the ribs to a roasting pan. Cover and let marinate, in the refrigerator, 4 to 8 hours.

2. Set up the grill for indirect grilling (see page 14 or 16), placing a large drip pan in the center. *If using a charcoal grill,* preheat it to medium.

If using a gas grill, place the wood chips in the smoker box and preheat the grill to high; when smoke appears, reduce the heat to medium.

3. When ready to cook, if using charcoal, toss half the wood chips on the coals. Oil the grill grate. Arrange the ribs on the hot grate over the drip pan. Cover the grill and smoke-cook the ribs for 1 hour.

4. Meanwhile, prepare the mop sauce (if using). Mix together the mustard, vinegar, and salt in a bowl and set aside.

5. When the ribs have cooked for an hour, uncover the grill and brush the ribs with the mop sauce (if using). If using a charcoal grill, toss the remaining wood chips on the fire. Continue cooking the ribs until tender and almost done, 1/2 to 1 hour longer for baby back ribs, somewhat longer for spareribs. If using charcoal, after 1 hour add 10 to 12 fresh coals per side to the grill. The ribs are done when the meat is very tender and it has shrunk back from the ends of the bones. Fifteen minutes before the end, season the ribs with the remaining rub, sprinkling it on.

6. To serve, cut the racks in half, or for a plate-burying effect, just leave them whole.

Serves 6

Note: I like my ribs served dry, in the style of Memphis's legendary barbecue haunt, the Rendezvous. If you want to serve them with a sauce, see the Index.

RASTA RIBS

JAMAICA

METHOD:
Indirect grilling

ADVANCE PREPARATION:
5 hours for marinating the ribs

SPECIAL EQUIPMENT:
2 cups wood chips (preferably oak or hickory), soaked for 1 hour in cold water to cover and drained

Memphis meets Montego Bay in this rib recipe, a takeoff on Jamaican jerk. To make it, I replace the traditional wet jerk seasoning with a dry rub made with Jamaican spices. The method—applying the rub in two stages, once before cooking, once before serving—is Memphis barbecue at its best. The scotch bonnet chile and its cousin, the habanero, are two of the world's hottest chiles, so don't use more of the powder than you mean to. Neophytes should make the rub with 2 teaspoons of the powder. Masochists can use the whole 2 tablespoons. Good accompaniments would be Two-Tone Potato Salad, Jamaican Fry Bread, and Haitian Slaw (see Index).

FOR THE RIBS:
4 racks baby back pork ribs (3 to 4 pounds)
2 cups dark rum

FOR THE DRY JERK SEASONING:
2 teaspoons to 2 tablespoons scotch bonnet or habanero chile powder, or more to taste
2 tablespoons freeze-dried chives
1 tablespoon dried onion flakes
1 tablespoon dried garlic flakes
1 tablespoon coarse (kosher or sea) salt
2 teaspoons ground coriander
2 teaspoons ground ginger
1 teaspoon freshly ground black pepper
1 teaspoon ground allspice
1/2 teaspoon ground cinnamon
1/4 teaspoon ground cloves
1/4 teaspoon freshly grated nutmeg

1. Remove the thin, papery skin from the back of each rack of ribs by pulling it off in a sheet with your fingers, using one corner of a kitchen towel to gain a secure grip, or with pliers. Place the ribs in a nonreactive roasting pan and pour the rum over them, turning the ribs to coat completely. Cover and let marinate, in the refrigerator, for 4 hours, turning occasionally.

2. Meanwhile, combine all the ingredients for the jerk seasoning in a spice mill or blender and grind to a fine powder.

3. Drain the ribs and blot dry with paper towels. Rub half the jerk mixture over the ribs on both sides, cover, and let marinate, in the refrigerator, for 1 hour.

4. Set up the grill for indirect grilling (see page 14 or 16), placing a large drip pan in the center. *If using a charcoal grill,* preheat it to medium.

If using a gas grill, place the wood chips in the smoker box and preheat the grill to high; when smoke appears, reduce the heat to medium.

5. When ready to cook, if using charcoal, toss half the wood chips on the coals. Arrange the ribs on the hot grate, over the drip pan. Cover the grill and smoke-cook the ribs until the meat is very tender and it has shrunk back from the ends of the bones, $1\frac{1}{2}$ to 2 hours. If using a charcoal grill, after 1 hour add 10 to 12 fresh coals per side and the remaining 1 cup wood chips.

6. Transfer the ribs to a platter and season with the remaining rub, sprinkling it on. Serve immediately.

Serves 4

A Little Lamb

"Don't think—cook!"

—LUDWIG WITTGENSTEIN

Lamb is the preferred meat for grilling on a huge stretch of the world's barbecue trail. You could start enjoying it in Morocco and eat your way east through North Africa, the Middle East, Turkey, Central Asia, and the Indian subcontinent to Indonesia, Australia, and New Zealand.

Throughout the Arab world, birthdays, weddings, and other happy occasions are celebrated with a pit-roasted lamb called *mechouie,* and no Greek holiday feast would be complete without a lamb that's been whole spit-roasted. As for Australians, well, you'd expect great grilled lamb in a country where sheep are said to outnumber humans by twenty to one.

In this chapter you'll find familiar favorites, such as shish kebab and lamb Provençal, as well as many exotic new ways to grill lamb, including Afghan lamb chops marinated in onion water and Mexican *barbacoa* (chile-marinated leg of lamb wrapped in avocado leaves). Did I mention Senegalese lamb with mustard sauce, Indian tandoori lamb with chickpea flour, and Capetown grilled leg of lamb with a brown-sugar and two-mustard crust?

When you travel the world's barbecue trail, a little lamb quickly becomes a lot of lamb. And that's good news for so many of us who love this flavorful meat.

A kebabi man carves donner kebab in Turkey.

Lamb Grilling Chart *

CUT	METHOD	HEAT	DONENESS		
			RARE (140°F)	MEDIUM (160°F)	WELL-DONE (170°F)
CHOPS	DIRECT	HIGH (450°F)			
½ INCH THICK			1–2 MIN/SIDE	2–3 MIN/SIDE	3–4 MIN/SIDE
1 INCH THICK			2–4 MIN/SIDE	4–6 MIN/SIDE	6–8 MIN/SIDE
1½ INCHES THICK			4–6 MIN/SIDE	6–8 MIN/SIDE	8–10 MIN/SIDE
RACKS	INDIRECT	MEDIUM	30–40 MIN	40–50 MIN	50–60 MIN
LEG (4–6 LBS, BONELESS)	INDIRECT	MEDIUM	1 HR	1–1½ HRS	1½–2 HRS
LEG (6–8 LBS, BONE-IN)	INDIRECT	MEDIUM	1½–2 HRS	2–2½ HRS	2½–3 HRS

This chart is offered as a broad guideline to cooking times for the various cuts of meat. Remember, grilling is an art, not a science. When in doubt, refer to times in the individual recipes.

MOROCCAN BARBECUED LAMB
Mechouie

NORTH AFRICA

METHOD:
Direct grilling

Mechouie is North African barbecued lamb. Traditionally, a whole lamb would be gutted, spitted, rubbed with butter and spices, and cooked over an open pit fire. The quality of the local lamb, coupled with the intensity of Moroccan spices and the heady scent of wood smoke, makes this one of the most memorable, flavorful dishes you'll find anywhere on the planet. Here's an easy, satisfying, home version made with a more manageable leg of lamb that captures the open-air drama of the original. Serve with A Simple Harissa, Moroccan Shallot Relish,

Moroccan Eggplant Salad (see Index), and pita bread.

There are three options for grilling the lamb. The closest to the original would be on a rotisserie over the fire. Alternatively, you could use the indirect grilling method in a covered grill (see page 14 or 16). In the third method (the least traditional, but the most unabashedly delicious, which is why I have chosen it here), a butterflied leg of lamb is grilled directly over the fire. Your butcher will bone and butterfly the lamb for you.

FOR THE LAMB AND SPICED BUTTER:

1 leg of lamb, boned and butterflied (3½ to 4
   pounds after boning), trimmed of any
   papery skin

Salt and freshly ground black pepper,
   to taste

8 tablespoons (1 stick) salted butter,
   at room temperature

4 cloves garlic, minced

16 fresh mint leaves, minced, or
   1 tablespoon dried

1 teaspoon ground coriander

1 teaspoon sweet paprika

½ teaspoon ground cumin

FOR THE SAUCE:

3 tablespoons salted butter

1 onion, finely chopped

2 cloves garlic, minced

3 tablespoons distilled white vinegar or
   fresh lemon juice, or more to taste

16 fresh mint leaves, thinly slivered,
   or 3 tablespoons mint jelly

2 cups chicken broth, homemade or low-
   sodium canned, or water

Salt, to taste

Ground cumin, for serving

1. Preheat the grill to medium-high.

2. Open out the butterflied leg of lamb on your work surface so the inside is up and season with salt and pepper. Set aside while you prepare the spice butter.

3. Combine the butter, garlic, mint leaves, coriander, paprika, and cumin in a food processor and process to a smooth paste.

4. When ready to cook, spread about one third of the butter mixture over the inside of the lamb. Spread about 1 tablespoon more over the outside surface of the lamb. Arrange the lamb, outer side down, on the hot grate and grill, turning with tongs, until cooked to taste, 15 to 20 minutes per side. If the lamb starts to burn, lower the heat to medium (if gas) or move the lamb to a cooler section of the grill (if charcoal). Every 5 minutes, spread the top with some of the remaining spiced butter.

5. Meanwhile, prepare the sauce. Melt the butter in a small, heavy saucepan over medium heat. Add the onion and garlic and sauté until lightly browned, about 5 minutes. Add 3 tablespoons vinegar and the mint and bring to a boil, then stir in the chicken broth. Bring to a boil, then reduce the heat to medium-low and simmer until richly flavored and slightly reduced, about 5 minutes. Remove from the heat and taste for seasoning, adding salt or vinegar as necessary.

6. Transfer the lamb to a cutting board and let stand for 10 minutes before slicing. Serve the lamb with the sauce and tiny bowls of salt and cumin on the side for seasoning.

Serves 8

ROTISSERIED LEG OF LAMB WITH LEMON AND BUTTER

GREECE

METHOD:
Direct grilling

Lamb is the preferred meat of Greeks—especially at Easter. It's hard to imagine an Easter celebration in Athens (not to mention in Chicago, Boston, or Astoria, New York), without a fire pit where whole lambs are spit-roasted to the color

**ADVANCE
PREPARATION:**
*4 to 6 hours for
marinating the
meat*

**SPECIAL
EQUIPMENT:**
Rotisserie

of mahogany and the crispness of cellophane. This recipe calls for butterflied leg of lamb, which can easily be cooked on a backyard barbecue grill. The turning motion of a rotisserie will give you the best results, but you can also cook the lamb using the indirect grilling method over medium heat (see page 14 or 16); this will take 1½ to 2 hours. Have your butcher bone and butterfly the lamb.

FOR THE LAMB AND MARINADE:

1 tablespoon coarse (kosher or sea)
    salt
1 tablespoon freshly ground white
    pepper
1 tablespoon dried oregano,
    preferably Greek
1 leg of lamb, boned and butterflied (3½ to 4
    pounds after boning), trimmed of any
    papery skin
1 lemon, cut in half
6 tablespoons (¾ stick) unsalted butter,
    at room temperature

FOR THE BASTING MIXTURE:

½ cup olive oil
¼ cup fresh lemon juice
¼ cup dry white wine
2 cloves garlic, minced
2 teaspoons dried oregano, preferably
    Greek
1 teaspoon freshly ground black
    pepper

1. Combine the salt, pepper, and oregano in a small bowl. Open out the butterflied leg of lamb on your work surface so the inside is up and sprinkle with one third of the spice mixture. Squeeze the juice from one lemon half over the meat, then cut the used lemon half into quarters. Set the pieces aside while you rub the

surface of the lamb with 3 tablespoons of the butter, then scatter the pieces on top. Fold the lamb back into its original cylindrical shape and tie it at 1-inch intervals with butcher's string. Place on a baking sheet, cover loosely with plastic wrap, and let marinate, in the refrigerator, for 4 to 6 hours.

2. Set up the grill for rotisserie cooking (see page 20) and preheat to high.

3. When ready to cook, skewer the lamb roast lengthwise on the spit and rub all over with the cut side of the second lemon half and the remaining 3 tablespoons butter. Add another generous sprinkling of the spice mixture. Attach the spit to the rotisserie mechanism, cover, and let the meat start rotating.

4. Meanwhile, prepare the basting mixture. Combine the oil, lemon juice, wine, garlic, oregano, and pepper in a medium-size nonreactive bowl and whisk to mix.

5. After the meat has been rotating 15 minutes, restir the basting mixture and brush it all over the lamb, using a long-handled basting brush. Cook the lamb until crusty and brown on the outside and done to taste, 1 to 1½ hours; an instant-read thermometer inserted in the thickest part of the roast will register 170°F for medium (see Note). Uncover the grill to brush the lamb every 15 minutes with the basting mixture. Reseason with spice mix from time to time. If using a charcoal grill, you'll need to add 10 to 12 fresh coals per side after 1 hour.

6. Transfer the roast, on the spit, to a cutting board. Extract the spit and let the roast rest for 10 minutes. Remove the string before slicing.

Serves 8

Note: As the lamb fat melts, it may cause flare-ups. Snuff these out by flattening the coals with a metal spatula or with a few squirts from a water pistol.

A Traditional Barbacoa

Barbacoa helped build at least one Mexican mom-and-pop eatery into a multimillion dollar restaurant that serves up to 5,000 guests a day. Arroyo, founded in 1940 in the Mexico City suburb of Coyoacán (about 40 minutes south of downtown), has become a gustatory amusement park. Occupying a city block, it is complete with roving orchestras and a private bullfighting ring.

Jesus Arroyo Bergeyre is the third-generation owner of the restaurant and a passionate spokesman for the cultural traditions it strives to preserve. I began my tour of the restaurant in a garden of maguey cactus. The leaves are an essential part of barbacoa, not to mention home to the *gusano,* a cactus worm that is a beloved delicacy in Mexico (it's enjoyed crisply fried).

Next, Bergeyre led me to the focal point and pride of the restaurant, a row of *barbacoa* pits, six kettle-shaped holes built into a raised brick dais. Each pit was so deep, I could have stood in one and still barely seen over the edge. The evening before, the pits were loaded with wood and ignited. It's only when the wood burns down to glowing coals that the cooking of the *barbacoa* begins.

A cook appeared with a huge steel kettle filled with water, beans, vegetables, garlic, and bunches of cilantro and epazote. This would become the *consommé de cordeiro* (lamb soup, flavored with the drippings) and it, too, is an essential part of *barbacoa.* The pot was lowered into the pit on top of the coals. Meanwhile, whole hindquarters or shoulders of lamb were wrapped and tied in flame-scorched maguey cactus leaves. The cook positioned the lamb on a metal rack over the kettle. The pit was then closed with a metal lid whose edges were sealed the old-fashioned way: with dirt.

The *barbacoa* will roast "underground," as it were, for 8 to 10 hours. When it emerges from the pit, it will be tender enough to pull apart with fingers. The herbal-tequilla taste of the cactus leaves, the herb-scented steam from the soup kettle, and the smoke from the wood will combine to produce a lamb with an extraordinary flavor—a lamb unique in the world of barbecue.

MEXICAN PIT-BARBECUED LAMB
Barbacoa

MEXICO

METHOD:
Indirect grilling

Mexico's answer to barbecue, *barbacoa* (see box): It is intriguingly delicious and easy to adapt for the backyard barbecue grill. I've chosen a recipe for Oaxacan-style *barbacoa,* featuring a guajillo chile marinade and a wrapping of avocado leaves. The latter can be found dried at Mexican markets and gourmet shops and impart a pleasant anise-like flavor. But don't worry if you can't find avocado leaves, because the lamb will still be quite delectable barbecued without a wrapping.

Barbacoa is served in two courses: first the soup (flavored with lamb drippings), then the lamb, which is eaten with tortillas.

ADVANCE PREPARATION: *4 to 8 hours for marinating the lamb, plus about 4 hours cooking time*

SPECIAL EQUIPMENT: *8 to 10 fresh or dried avocado leaves (optional; dried leaves soaked for 20 minutes in cold water to cover)*

CHILE NOTES

Guajillo chiles are smooth-skinned, mild, sweet, dried chiles whose taste is similar to sweet paprika. If they are unavailable, use ¼ cup pure chile powder.

Chipotles are smoked jalapeño chiles. If using canned chipotles for the soup, simply chop them. If using dried chipotles, soak them in hot water for 20 minutes, then chop.

FOR THE ADOBO (SPICE PASTE) AND LAMB:

6 guajillo chiles (see Chile Notes)
5 cloves garlic, coarsely chopped
¼ medium onion, coarsely chopped
½ teaspoon dried oregano
2 whole cloves
2 whole allspice berries
1 small piece (½ inch) cinnamon stick or ½ teaspoon ground cinnamon
1 teaspoon salt
¼ cup distilled white vinegar
¼ cup water
½ bone-in leg of lamb (4 to 5 pounds), trimmed of any papery skin

FOR THE CONSOMME:

1 medium onion, cut into ½-inch dice
2 carrots, peeled and cut into ½-inch dice
1 zucchini, scrubbed and cut into ½-inch dice
1 piece (12 ounces) calabaza (West Indian pumpkin) or butternut squash, peeled and cut into ½-inch dice
½ small green cabbage, cored and cut into ½-inch dice
1 large fresh, ripe tomato, cut into ½-inch dice
1 medium potato, peeled and cut into ½-inch dice
1 ear corn, shucked and cut into ½-inch rounds (optional)
2 bay leaves, 2 sprigs cilantro, and 2 sprigs epazote (optional), tied in a piece of cheesecloth
8 to 10 cups water
¼ cup finely chopped fresh cilantro leaves
1 chipotle chile, minced (see Chile Notes)
Salt and freshly ground black pepper, to taste

FOR SERVING:

Warm tortillas
Salsa Mexicana (page 174)

1. Prepare the *adobo.* Stem the chiles, tear open, and remove the veins and seeds.

Soak in water to cover until soft and pliable, about 20 minutes. Drain the chiles and place in a blender with the garlic, onion, oregano, cloves, allspice berries, cinnamon, salt, vinegar, and water. Process to a smooth paste.

2. Using the tip of a paring knife, make a series of slits in the lamb, ¼ inch deep and 1 inch apart. Smear the chile paste all over the lamb, working it into the slits, cover loosely with plastic wrap, and let marinate, in the refrigerator, for 4 to 8 hours (the longer the better).

3. Set up the grill for indirect grilling (see page 14 or 16) and preheat to medium-low.

4. Assemble the consommé. Combine the onion, carrots, zucchini, calabaza, cabbage, tomato, potato, corn (if using), herb bundle, and water in a large fire-proof pot.

5. You're now ready to assemble the *barbacoa.* Place the consommé pot in the center of the grate that holds the charcoal, or if using gas, the grill grate (away from the heat). Place a metal rack, like a sturdy cake rack, on top and layer with half the avocado leaves, if using (see Special Equipment); if not using, oil the rack. Place the lamb on top of the leaves, fat side up, and carpet it with the remaining avocado leaves. Cover the grill tightly.

6. Cook the *barbacoa* until the lamb is fall-off-the-bone tender, 3 to 4 hours. If using a charcoal grill, you'll need to add 10 to 12 fresh coals per side every hour. When the lamb is done, the internal temperature will be about 170°F.

7. To serve the *barbacoa,* discard the top layer of avocado leaves and transfer the lamb and bottom layer of leaves to a platter. Let sit for 5 minutes, then thinly slice the meat or cut it into chunks. Remove the herb bundle from the consommé, then, using a ladle, skim off any fat floating on the surface of the soup. Stir in the chopped cilantro, chipotle, and salt and pepper; the soup should be highly seasoned. Serve the consommé first, then the meat. Accompany both with tortillas and salsa.

Serves 8

CAPETOWN LAMB

SOUTH AFRICA

METHOD:
Indirect grilling

**ADVANCE
PREPARATION:**
*3 to 8 hours for
marinating the
meat*

This recipe is simplicity itself, and it makes a pleasant switch from the usual lamb with mint sauce. The preparation reflects the ecumenism of the South African kitchen. Asia is represented by the use of ginger, soy sauce, and Chinese mustard. A British influence can be seen in the Worcestershire sauce and brown sugar. Put them together and you get an energizing jolt of flavor—sweet, sour, and spicy—that will give you a whole new perspective on lamb. I like to serve this lamb with equally ecumenical accompaniments: *naan* (Tandoori-Baked Flat Breads), Persian-Style Steamed Rice, and Pineapple Achar (see Index).

FOR THE LAMB:
1 bone-in leg of lamb (6 to 8 pounds),
    trimmed of any papery skin
6 cloves garlic, cut into thin slivers
6 thin slices fresh ginger, cut into
    thin slivers

FOR THE GLAZE:
¼ cup Worcestershire sauce
¼ cup soy sauce
¼ cup firmly packed brown sugar
3 tablespoons Dijon mustard
2 tablespoons hot Chinese-style mustard
    or 1 tablespoon dry mustard
3 tablespoons fresh lemon juice
3 tablespoons vegetable oil
3 cloves garlic, minced
1 tablespoon minced fresh ginger
Salt and freshly ground black pepper,
    to taste

1. Using the tip of a sharp paring knife, make slits about an inch deep all over the surface of the lamb, spacing them about an inch apart. Insert a sliver each of garlic and ginger into each slit. Place the lamb in a non-reactive roasting pan and set aside while you prepare the glaze.

2. Combine the Worcestershire sauce, soy sauce, sugar, both the mustards, lemon juice, oil, garlic, and ginger in a small, heavy saucepan and bring to a boil over medium heat, stirring to dissolve the sugar. Cook until thick and syrupy, about 3 minutes, stirring frequently to prevent sticking. Remove from the heat and taste for seasoning, adding salt and pepper as necessary. Let cool to room temperature.

3. Pour half the cooled glaze over the lamb in the roasting pan, brushing to coat on all sides. Cover and let marinate, in the refrigerator, for 3 to 8 hours (the longer the better).

4. Set up the grill for indirect grilling (see page 14 or 16), placing a large drip pan in the center, and preheat to medium.

5. When ready to cook, place the lamb on the hot grate over the drip pan and brush with more glaze. Cover the grill and cook the lamb until done to taste, 2 to 2½ hours; an instant-read meat thermometer inserted in the thickest part of the leg (but not touching the bone) will register 160°F for medium. Brush the leg with glaze two or three times during cooking. If using a charcoal grill, add 10 to 12 fresh coals per side every hour.

6. Transfer the lamb to a cutting board and brush one last time with glaze, then let stand for 10 minutes before carving. While the lamb stands, heat any remaining glaze to serve as a sauce with the lamb.

Serves 12

LEG OF "MUTTON" WITH SAFFRON AND ROSEWATER

INDIA

METHOD:
Indirect grilling

ADVANCE PREPARATION:
4 hours for draining the yogurt, plus 6 hours for marinating the meat

This is one of the most remarkable tandoori dishes I had anywhere in India. "Mutton" is what Indians call baby goat. Here its haunting flavor comes from a marinade perfumed with rosewater, mace, and saffron, seasonings that suggest the Persian roots of this dish. (Don't forget, the Mogul rulers of northern India were descended from Persians.) Muhammad Farooq, master chef of the Mughal Sheraton in Agra, uses goat so young that a whole leg is about the size of a turkey leg!

Baby goat tastes like a cross between lamb and veal. You may be able to order it from a specialty butcher, but leg of lamb is perfectly delicious here.

This recipe may sound a little involved, but actually it's a series of simple steps. The only challenging part is remembering to drain the yogurt ahead of time. By the way, the liquid you drain from the yogurt can be made into the refreshing Afgan Yogurt Drink (see Index). Chickpea flour, or *besan*—which imparts a nutty taste—is available at Indian markets and natural foods stores. Indian-style basmati rice and Pineapple Chutney (see Index) would make good accompaniments.

1½ cups plain whole-milk yogurt
¼ teaspoon saffron threads
1 teaspoon rosewater
½ cup chickpea flour (besan; optional)
1 green cardamom pod
1 black cardamom pod (optional)
½ teaspoon black peppercorns
2 blades mace or ¼ teaspoon freshly grated nutmeg
½ teaspoon salt
½ teaspoon cayenne pepper

1 teaspoon grated fresh ginger
1 clove garlic, minced
1 tablespoon unsalted butter, at room temperature
½ leg of lamb (about 4 pounds bone-in), preferably shank end (see Note), trimmed of any papery skin

1. Set a yogurt strainer, or a regular strainer lined with a double layer of dampened cheesecloth, over a small bowl. Add the yogurt to the strainer and let drain, in the refrigerator, until a firm "cheese" forms, about 4 hours; you should have about 1 cup.

2. When ready to marinate the lamb, place the saffron in a small bowl and grind to a fine powder with a pestle or the end of a wooden spoon. Add the rosewater, stir, and let stand for 10 minutes.

3. Meanwhile, cook the chickpea flour (if using) in a dry skillet over medium heat until lightly toasted and aromatic, about 3 minutes, shaking the pan occasionally. Remove from the heat and transfer the toasted flour to a medium-size bowl. Add the green and black cardamom pods, the peppercorns, and mace to the skillet and toast over medium heat until aromatic, about 2 minutes, shaking the pan once or twice. Remove from the heat and let cool, then grind the spices in a spice mill or clean coffee grinder and add to the chickpea flour.

4. Using a wooden spoon, mash the yogurt cheese into the chickpea flour to blend thoroughly, then add the dissolved saffron, the salt, cayenne, ginger, garlic, and melted butter. Stir with the spoon or knead the mixture with your fingers until blended and smooth; it will be a thick paste.

5. Using a sharp paring knife, make slits about ¾ inch deep all over the lamb and rub in the paste. Place the meat in a deep bowl, cover, and let marinate, in the refrigerator, for 6 hours.

6. Set up the grill for indirect grilling (see page 14 or 16), placing a large drip pan in the center, and preheat to medium.

7. When ready to cook, place the lamb on the hot grate, then cover the grill and cook the lamb until done to taste, 1¼ to 1¾ hours for fall off-the-bone tender (Indians like their lamb—and kid—well done); an

instant-read thermometer inserted in the thickest part of the leg (but not touching the bone) will register 170°F for well-done. If using a charcoal grill, add 10 to 12 fresh coals per side after 1 hour.

8. Transfer the lamb to a cutting board and let stand for 10 minutes before carving and serving.

Serves 4

Notes: If you can get kid, use two 1½-pound legs, trimmed of fat and sinews, instead of the lamb. Cook as above but reduce the time to about 1 hour.

AUSTRALIAN LAMB STEAKS WITH SICHUAN PEPPER RUB

METHOD:
Direct grilling

For centuries, lamb was Australia's preferred meat—in many places its only meat—a legacy of the vast sheep farms that represented the continent's first industry. Even today, no Down Under cookout would be complete without lamb.

My choice for this dish would be steaks cut from the leg of lamb. If you have a butcher who will do this, you will be richly rewarded with an uncommonly flavorful piece of meat. Otherwise, use chops from the shoulder, loin, or rib.

Coriander and Sichuan peppercorns may not seem like traditional seasonings, but the proximity of this former British colony to Southeast Asia has made Australia one of the epicenters of Pacific Rim cuisine. The Sichuan peppercorns lend the lamb a clean, woodsy flavor that is unexpected but right on the money.

1 tablespoon Sichuan peppercorns
1 tablespoon black peppercorns
1 tablespoon coriander seeds
1 tablespoon coarse (kosher or sea) salt
4 lamb steaks, cut from the leg
   or shoulder (each about 8 ounces and
   ¾ inch thick; see Note)

1. Combine the Sichuan and black peppercorns, the coriander seeds, and salt in a dry skillet. Cook the spices over medium heat until the peppercorns are toasted and very fragrant, about 3 minutes, stirring or shaking the pan occasionally. Transfer the mixture to a spice mill and grind to a powder (you can also grind the spices in a mortar with a pestle).

2. Rub as much of this mixture as you wish over both sides of the lamb steaks. Place the steaks on a platter and let marinate, at room temperature, while you light the grill.

3. Preheat the grill to high.

4. When ready to cook, oil the grill grate. Arrange the lamb steaks on the hot grate and grill, turning with tongs, until cooked to taste, 3 to 4 minutes per side for medium-rare.

5. Remove the steaks to serving plates or a platter. Season with a little more rub, if any remains, and serve at once.

Serves 4

Note: If desired, substitute 8 loin or 12 rib lamb chops for the steaks. Each loin chop should be about 4 ounces and $1\frac{1}{2}$ inches thick (grill about 6 minutes per side for medium-rare); each rib chop, about 3 ounces and 1 inch thick (grill about 4 minutes per side for the same doneness).

RACK OF LAMB CIRAGAN PALACE

TURKEY

METHOD:
Direct grilling

ADVANCE PREPARATION:
24 hours for marinating the meat

The Ciragan Palace (pronounced "Chee-raan") is one of the world's most celebrated hotels, an 11-acre pleasure palace (former summer home of Sultan Abdül Aziz) located on the banks of the Bosporus on the outskirts of Istanbul. There you can get an exquisite Ottoman meal at the hotel's Turkish restaurant, Tugra, for about the same price that you'd pay at a bistro in New York.

I'd spent the week sampling grilled lamb at kebab parlors and street stalls. What a nice change of pace it was to enjoy it in a formal dining room surrounded by chandeliers and sweeping views of the Bosporus. The chef starts with the most expensive of all cuts of lamb—tenderloin—which he marinates overnight in a mixture of olive oil, milk, and fresh onion juice. A sauce made of charred eggplant and yogurt reinforces the smoky flavor of the lamb. To be strictly authentic, you would use lamb tenderloin, but, since this costs a Sultan's fortune, I've retooled the recipe for more affordable and readily available rack of lamb.

My marinating the lamb in tightly sealed plastic bags is untraditional but effective. It keeps the onion aroma from permeating the refrigerator.

FOR THE LAMB AND MARINADE:
2 racks of lamb (3 to 4 pounds in all)
1 large white onion, finely chopped (enough to make $\frac{1}{2}$ cup juice)
1 cup whole milk or half-and-half
1 cup extra-virgin olive oil
1 teaspoon freshly ground black pepper

FOR THE EGGPLANT SAUCE:
1 cup plain whole-milk yogurt
2 long, slender eggplants (about 1 pound in all)
1 small green bell pepper
1 clove garlic, minced
2 tablespoons unsalted butter, at room temperature
1 teaspoon fresh lemon juice, or more to taste
Salt and freshly ground black pepper, to taste

1. Trim most of the fat off the lamb, then scrape the rib bones clean with a sharp paring knife (or have your butcher do it). Place each rack in a large, heavy-duty plastic bag with a zip-lock closing and set aside while you prepare the marinade.

2. Process the onion in a blender or food processor to a smooth purée, then strain through a strainer lined with a double layer of dampened cheesecloth into a medium-size bowl; you should have about ½ cup juice. Whisk in the milk, oil, and pepper. Pour half the mixture over each rack of lamb in its plastic bag, then seal the bags and turn over several times so the racks are coated with the marinade. Place in the refrigerator for 24 hours, turning the bags several times.

3. About 4 hours ahead of time, set a yogurt strainer, or a regular strainer lined with a double layer of dampened cheesecloth, over a small bowl. Add the yogurt to the strainer and let drain, in the refrigerator, until a firm "cheese" forms.

4. When ready to continue with the sauce, preheat the grill to high.

5. Arrange the eggplants on the hot rack and grill, turning with tongs, until charred all over and the flesh is very soft, 20 to 30 minutes. About 20 minutes before the eggplant is done, add the pepper to the grate and grill, turning with tongs as necessary, until charred all over and soft. Transfer the charred vegetables to a plate and let cool.

6. Using a paring knife, scrape the skin off the cooled eggplant and pepper; stem and seed the pepper. Combine the vegetables in a food processor with the garlic, yogurt cheese, butter, 1 teaspoon lemon juice, and salt and pepper. Process to a smooth purée, then transfer to a small, heavy saucepan. Bring to a simmer over low heat and cook

until thick and creamy, about 2 minutes, stirring occasionally. Remove from the heat and taste for seasoning, adding salt or lemon juice as necessary; the sauce should be highly seasoned. Keep the sauce warm, covered (see Note).

7. *If using a gas grill,* reduce the heat to medium-high; *if using charcoal,* the grill should now be at medium-high. If not, bump up the heat with 20 to 24 fresh coals.

8. When ready to cook, drain the lamb, reserving the marinade. Season each rack generously with salt, then oil the grill rack. Arrange the lamb on the hot grate, bone side up. Grill until nicely browned and cooked to taste, 10 to 15 minutes per side, turning with tongs as needed to prevent burning; at the end, stand each rack upright to grill the ends. Baste the racks with the reserved marinade during the first 15 minutes of cooking only.

9. Transfer the racks to a cutting board and let stand 5 minutes before carving. Spread the warm sauce over serving plates or a platter. Carve each rack into chops and arrange on top of the sauce. Serve immediately.

Serves 4

Note: The sauce may be made up to 24 hours ahead of time. Refrigerate, covered, then reheat in a small saucepan over low heat on the stovetop, or on a corner of the grill grate, just before serving.

GRILLED LAMB WITH HERBES DE PROVENCE

FRANCE

METHOD:
Direct grilling

This recipe is about the easiest and best way I know to cook lamb chops. You find it everywhere in Provence, from backyard cookouts to country inns and roadside restaurants. The basic seasoning is *herbes de Provence,* a fragrant mixture of rosemary, thyme, majoram, savory, basil, bay leaf, and—for a touch of sweetness—fennel and lavender. *Herbes de Provence* is sold in most gourmet shops, often in decorative jars at inflated prices. But it's easy to make your own for a lot less money.

12 rib lamb chops (each 3 to 4 ounces and
   1 inch thick)
2 lemons
¼ cup extra-virgin olive oil
Salt and freshly ground black pepper,
   to taste
3 tablespoons Herbes de Provence
   (page 492)

1. Preheat the grill to high.

2. Arrange the chops in a nonreactive baking dish large enough to hold them in a single layer. Cut one lemon in half and squeeze the juice from both halves into the oil in a small bowl; whisk to blend. Brush the lamb chops on both sides with the mixture, using about half, and season with salt and pepper. Sprinkle the chops with 2 tablespoons *herbes de Provence* and let marinate, at room temperature, for 10 minutes.

3. When ready to cook, oil the grill grate. Arrange the lamb chops on the hot grate and grill, turning with tongs, until cooked to taste, about 4 minutes per side for medium-rare. Rotate each chop 60 degrees after 1 minute on each side to create an attractive crosshatch of grill marks. Baste the lamb chops from time to time with the remaining oil mixture as they cook.

4. Transfer the chops to a platter and season with the remaining *herbes de Provence.* Serve at once, accompanied by the remaining lemon, cut into wedges.
   Serves 4

LAMB WITH ONION-MUSTARD SAUCE
Dibi

SENEGAL

METHOD:
Direct grilling

As a rule, West Africans favor stews and boiled dishes over grilled fare. But *dibi* (grilled lamb) is so popular in Senegal, it could qualify as an official state dish. You'll find it being served at sidewalk stalls and roadside eateries throughout Dakar almost any time of day or night. All manner of lamb cuts hang in sanguine glory from the walls of the stall—chops, shoulders, legs, and organ meats. Customers simply point to the cut they want and the vendor cooks it on a simple grill, then slathers it with oniony mustard sauce. This princely repast is served up in foil or newspaper, and it's so good you want to lick your fingers when you're fin-

ished. The popularity of grilled lamb here can be explained by religion: Senegal is 95 percent Muslim. Arab traders brought the art of grilling, not to mention the love of lamb, to this West African nation.

8 loin lamb chops (each about 4 ounces and
   1½ inches thick) or 12 rib lamb chops
   (each about 3 ounces and 1 inch thick)
1 tablespoon plus ¼ cup vegetable oil
Salt and freshly ground black pepper,
   to taste
1 medium onion, finely chopped
¼ cup grainy French mustard
3 to 4 tablespoons water
½ teaspoon sugar (optional)

1. Preheat the grill to high.

2. Brush the lamb chops lightly on both sides with 1 tablespoon oil and season with salt and pepper. Place on a platter and let marinate while you prepare the sauce.

3. Combine the chopped onion, the ¼ cup oil, and the mustard in a small, heavy saucepan and bring to a boil, stirring. Reduce the heat to low and simmer gently until the onion is soft and lightly browned, about 10 minutes, stirring frequently. Thin the mixture to sauce consistency with 3 tablespoons water, adding up to 1 tablespoon more, if needed. Remove from the heat and taste for seasoning, adding salt and pepper to taste, or the sugar if the sauce tastes too tart. Remove from the heat and cover to keep warm.

4. When ready to cook, oil the grill grate. Arrange the chops on the hot grate and grill, turning with tongs, until cooked to taste, 6 to 8 minutes per side for medium.

5. Transfer the chops to serving plates or a platter and spoon the onion mustard sauce on top. Serve immediately.

Serves 4

EXOTIC YOGURT AND SAFFRON MARINATED LAMB CHOPS
Shishlik

IRAN

METHOD:
Direct grilling

ADVANCE PREPARATION:
24 to 48 hours for marinating the meat

Shishlik is one of the most sumptuous dishes in the Iranian repertoire, double-thick lamb chops cut from the rack, marinated in a saffron-scented mixture of yogurt, garlic, and lemon juice. Don't trim away too much fat—you need it to melt and baste the lamb as the chops cook. This recipe comes from Iranian cooking authority Najmieh Batmanligj, who adds home-made candied orange peel for a touch of sweetness. I've had good results with both commercial candied peel and strips of orange zest.

For equally delicious results, try the marinade with chicken and use the basting sauce while grilling chicken, veal, and other cuts of lamb.

Serve the lamb with Persian-Style Steamed Rice (see Index).

FOR THE LAMB AND MARINADE:
½ teaspoon saffron threads
1 tablespoon warm water
2 cups plain whole-milk yogurt
½ cup fresh lemon juice
1 medium onion, finely chopped
8 cloves garlic, finely chopped
2 tablespoons cracked black peppercorns
2 tablespoons chopped candied orange peel, or 4 strips orange zest (each 2 x ½ inches)
8 double rib lamb chops (each about 5 to 6 ounces and 2 inches thick)

FOR THE SAFFRON BASTING SAUCE:
¼ teaspoon saffron threads
1 tablespoon warm water
3 tablespoons salted butter
3 tablespoons fresh lemon juice
Salt and freshly ground black pepper, to taste

1. Prepare the marinade. Place the saffron in a large, deep nonreactive bowl and grind to a fine powder with a pestle or the end of a wooden spoon. Add the warm water, stir, and let stand for 10 minutes.

2. Add the yogurt, lemon juice, onion, garlic, peppercorns, and orange peel to the dissolved saffron and stir to mix. Add the lamb chops and make sure they are completely submerged in the marinade. Cover the bowl with plastic wrap and let marinate, in the refrigerator, for 24 to 48 hours (the longer the better).

3. Preheat the grill to high.

4. Meanwhile, prepare the saffron basting sauce. Place the saffron in a small, heavy nonreactive saucepan and grind it to a fine powder with a pestle or the end of a wooden spoon. Add the warm water, stir, and let stand for 10 minutes. Add the butter and lemon juice to the dissolved saffron and stir over low heat until the butter is melted and the mixture is blended and heated through. Remove from the heat and set aside.

5. When ready to cook, remove the chops from the marinade, season with salt and pepper. Oil the grill grate, then arrange the chops on the hot grate. Grill, turning with tongs, until cooked to taste, 8 to 10 minutes per side for medium-well, which is how Iranians like their lamb ("It's more tender that way," explains Najmieh). Brush the chops several times as they cook with the saffron basting sauce.

6. Transfer the chops to serving plates or a platter and serve immediately.

Serves 4

"ONION WATER" LAMB CHOPS
O Be Peyaz

AFGHANISTAN

METHOD:
Direct grilling

ADVANCE PREPARATION:
2 hours for marinating the meat

The Afghan name of this dish—*o be peyaz*—means, literally, "onion water." The lamb chops are marinated in an intensely flavored mixture of onion juice, saffron, turmeric, and chiles. Most Afghan meats are marinated for several days prior to cooking, but these chops can be grilled after a couple of hours. The recipe was inspired by the Khyber Pass restaurant in New York City. The onion juice has a tenderizing and aromatizing effect on the lamb, and it's used throughout the Islamic world. Serve with pita bread, Quick-Cook Basmati Rice, and Persian Yogurt Drink (see Index).

8 loin lamb chops (each 4 to 5 ounces and 1½ inch thick)
¼ teaspoon saffron threads
1 tablespoon warm water
1½ pounds onions, peeled and quartered
1 to 3 serranos or other hot chiles, minced
1 teaspoon ground turmeric
2 teaspoons salt
1 teaspoon freshly ground black pepper

1. Trim most of the excess fat off the lamb chops.

2. Place the saffron in a small bowl and grind it to a fine powder with a pestle or the end of a wooden spoon. Add the warm water, stir, and let stand for 5 minutes.

3. Place the onions in a food processor and process, in batches if necessary, until the onions are puréed and quite watery. Transfer the contents of the workbowl to a fine-meshed strainer and set over a large, deep nonreactive bowl and drain, pressing the solids with the back of a rubber spatula or wooden spoon to extract the juice; you should have about 2 cups. Discard the contents of the strainer.

4. Add the chile, turmeric, salt, pepper, and the dissolved saffron to the onion juice. Whisk until the salt is dissolved. Add the lamb chops and turn to coat thoroughly. Cover and let marinate, in the refrigerator, for 2 hours, turning several times.

5. Preheat the grill to high.

6. When ready to cook, remove the chops from the marinade and blot dry with paper towels. Oil the grill grate, then arrange the chops on the hot grate and grill, turning with tongs, until cooked to taste, about 6 minutes per side for medium.

7. Transfer the chops to serving plates or a platter and serve immediately.

Serves 4

LAMB CHOPS STALL #26

MOROCCO

METHOD:
Direct grilling

SPECIAL EQUIPMENT:
4 long metal skewers

The lamb chops served at the stall of Muhammad Moutawakel in the Jema al-Fna probably aren't any better than those served at a hundred other eateries in Marrakesh. They just taste that way, served as they are under the open sky, amid the carnivalesque surroundings of the liveliest public square in North Africa.

This recipe is extremely simple to prepare, but to get the full effect you need all three simple components: the grilled lamb, the tomato sauce, the shallot relish.

12 rib lamb chops (each about 3 ounces and 1 inch thick)
1 tablespoon coarse (kosher or sea) salt
1 teaspoon ground cumin
1 teaspoon garlic powder
1 teaspoon freshly ground black pepper
4 pita breads
Moroccan Tomato Sauce (recipe follows)
Moroccan Shallot Relish (page 441)

1. Preheat the grill to high.

2. Lay three lamb chops flat on a cutting board in a row, ribs on the diagonal, pointing in the same direction. Run a metal skewer through the meat of each chop at a 60-degree angle to the bones. Skewer the remaining chops the same way.

3. Combine the salt, cumin, garlic powder, and pepper in a small bowl. Using some of this mixture, season the lamb chops on both sides. Place the remaining mixture in tiny bowls for serving and set aside.

4. When ready to cook, oil the grill grate. Arrange the skewers on the hot grate and grill, turning with tongs, until the lamb is cooked to taste, 4 to 6 minutes per side for medium.

5. Fold a pita around the meat on each skewer and pull out the skewer. Accompany the chops with a hefty dollop of tomato sauce, a spoonful of relish, and a generous pinch of seasoned salt.

Serves 4

Moroccan Tomato Sauce

There are probably as many versions of this sauce as there are individual grill jockeys in Morocco. This one offers the refreshing taste of fresh mint.

2 large fresh, ripe tomatoes
   (about 1 pound)
1 large shallot or ½ small onion, peeled
3 tablespoons chopped fresh mint or
   Italian (flat-leaf) parsley
1 tablespoon fresh lemon juice
Salt and freshly ground black pepper,
   to taste

Cut the tomatoes in half crosswise. Grate the tomatoes through the large holes of a four-sided grater into a shallow bowl. Grate in the shallot or onion the same way. Stir in the mint, lemon juice, and salt and pepper and serve immediately.

Makes about 1½ cups

THE REAL TURKISH SHISH KEBAB

TURKEY

METHOD:
Direct grilling

ADVANCE PREPARATION:
24 hours for marinating the meat

SPECIAL EQUIPMENT:
6 long metal skewers, including 2 flat ones for the vegetables

Shish kebab is Turkey's most celebrated kebab (although the average Turk eats it far less often than ground lamb kebabs). There are probably as many versions in Turkey as there are individual cooks. This one—from the restaurant Develi in Istanbul—owes its tangy flavor to a 24-hour soak in olive oil and yogurt.

Contrary to American versions of the dish, Turkish shish kebab rarely comes with vegetables on the same skewer as the meat. Rather, the vegetables are grilled on separate skewers, so each can be cooked the proper length of time.

For the tenderest possible kebabs, use lamb tenderloin or loin. You can also use leg or shoulder, but the kebabs will be a little tougher. It doesn't hurt to intersperse lean pieces of lamb with a few fatty pieces; the fat will tenderize the lean meat as it melts. See pages 230 and 232 for notes on sumac and Aleppo pepper.

1 cup plain whole-milk yogurt
¼ cup extra-virgin olive oil
2 cloves garlic, minced
2 teaspoons Aleppo pepper flakes or
   1 teaspoon hot red pepper flakes
1 teaspoon salt
1 teaspoon freshly ground black pepper
1½ pounds boneless loin or shoulder
   of lamb, cut into 1-inch cubes
   (include some fatty pieces)
8 fresh, ripe plum tomatoes or small round
   tomatoes
12 bull's horn peppers (see Glossary),
   stemmed
2 tablespoons ground sumac, for serving
   (optional)
4 pita breads

1. Combine the yogurt, oil, garlic, pepper flakes, salt, and pepper in a nonreactive bowl. Add the lamb and toss to coat thoroughly. Cover and let marinate, in the refrigerator, for 24 hours, stirring once or twice.

2. Preheat the grill to high.

3. When ready to grill, remove the lamb from the marinade and thread onto the thin skewers, alternating lean and fatty pieces. Thread the tomatoes onto a separate, flat skewer and the peppers onto another flat skewer. Oil the grill grate, then arrange all the kebabs on the hot grate, and grill, turning with tongs, until the skins on the vegetables are blistered and browned and the lamb is browned and done to taste, 8 to 12 minutes in all) for well-done.

4. Using a pita to protect your hand, unskewer the lamb and vegetables onto serving plates, dividing the vegetables evenly. Serve immediately, accompanied by sumac (if using) for sprinkling.

Serves 4

MOROCCAN LAMB KEBABS

MOROCCO

METHOD:
Direct grilling

ADVANCE PREPARATION:
30 minutes to 8 hours for marinating the meat

SPECIAL EQUIPMENT:
4 to 6 long metal skewers

There is nothing exotic about the flavorings here, they just happen to produce exceptionally tasty lamb. Kebabs are a culinary common denominator in Morocco, found at palatial restaurants, open-air cook shops, and just about everywhere in between. The secret to good kebabs is to intersperse the lean meat with cubes of fatty meat or lamb fat—preferably from the tail. I've given a range of marinating times: 30 minutes will give you tasty lamb for a week-night supper; 8 hours will give you incredibly rich flavored lamb for a special occasion. Serve with Grilled Zucchini Salad (see Index).

1 medium onion, grated
3 tablespoons chopped fresh Italian (flat-leaf) parsley
3 tablespoons chopped fresh cilantro
½ teaspoon ground cumin
½ teaspoon paprika
½ teaspoon freshly ground white or black pepper
½ teaspoon salt
1 tablespoon olive oil
1½ to 2 pounds boneless leg or shoulder of lamb, cut into 1-inch cubes (include some fatty pieces)
4 pita breads

1. Combine the onion, herbs, spices, salt, and oil in a large bowl and stir to mix. Add the lamb cubes and toss thoroughly to coat, then cover and let marinate, in the refrigerator, at least 30 minutes and up to 8 hours (the longer the better).

2. Preheat the grill to high.

3. When ready to grill, oil the grill grate. Remove the lamb from the marinade and thread onto the skewers, dividing evenly and alternating lean and fatty pieces. Arrange the kebabs on the hot grate and grill, turning with tongs, until nicely browned and cooked to taste, 8 to 12 minutes in all, for well done (as the Moroccans tend to like their lamb).

4. Fold a pita around the meat on each skewer and pull out the skewer. Serve immediately.

Serves 4

The Moroccan Grill

Marrakesh. Everything you've heard about this legendary red city at the foot of the Atlas Mountains lives up to its reputation: the splendor, the squalor, the stately mosques, the labyrinthine souks, the kaleidoscopically colorful markets bursting with everything from robes to rugs to rosewater.

As for the food, well, it's easy to see why chefs from all over the world take inspiration from Morocco. The cuisine of this Arab kingdom combines the refinement of France (its former colonial ruler) with the exoticism of Africa and the Middle East. Moroccan cooking is exotic enough to challenge your taste buds, but familiar enough to be comfort food. It's a cuisine of intense flavors, built on a lavish use of spices and an intricate interplay of textures and tastes.

This is certainly the case of the kebabs, sausages, chops, roasts, organ meats, and seafood that constitute the Moroccan grill. Grilling occupies a central position in Morocco's culinary life, practiced in public squares and crowded markets, at sidewalk cafés and waterfront restaurants. Almost anywhere you turn, you will smell the sweet scent of lamb roasting over charcoal. Look skyward at dusk and the sky will be filled with plumes of smoke rising from a thousand cook shacks and push-cart grills.

Interestingly, Moroccan haute cuisine relies mainly on wet cooking methods such as stewing, steaming, and deep-frying. Think of Morocco's most famous dishes: couscous, *tagine, bisteeya.* None are cooked on a grill. Grilled fare is the popular food of Morocco, what people eat when they're in a hurry, on a budget, or in the mood for casual dining. And they eat it with gusto.

JEMA AL-FNA

This quickly became apparent my first day in Marrakesh, at my first stop, the Jema al-Fna. This fabled piazza, the entryway to the old city, offers a total immersion in everything that is exotic and wondrous about Morocco: the shrill trumpets of the snake charmers (those are real cobras coiled on the blankets), the singsong shouts of the story-tellers, the cries of the hustlers and beggars. The din is positively cacophonous, and it continues from morning to midnight.

Come nightfall, the Jema al-Fna fills with open-air cook stalls, like the immaculate Stall #26, run by a ruggedly handsome man in a crisp white paper cap named Muhammad Moutawakel. Each evening, around 5 o'clock, he sets out white enamel trays piled high with couscous, hand-cut french fries, and shiny salads of peppers, carrots, and other vegetables. But the star attraction here is the lamb chops and kebabs sizzling away on his grill.

The secret to a great kebab, explained Muhammad, is to intersperse the cubes of meat with pieces of lamb tail fat. The fat melts during grilling, basting the lamb, keeping it moist and tender. Unlike many American backyard grillers, Muhammad is not afraid of the flare-ups that explode when drops of melting fat hit the fire. "Flare-ups are the best way to give the meat a charred, smoky flavor," he said.

Muhammad seasons his lamb with a mixture of cumin, salt, and garlic powder. The accompaniments, variations of which I experienced throughout Morocco, include a spicy fresh tomato sauce, a tangy shallot and parsley relish, and a wedge of a crusty flat Moroccan bread called *chobs.* You dine under the stars, surrounded by the circus-like swirl of activity in the Jema al-Fna. Barbecue just doesn't get any better.

BANI MARINE STREET

Well, actually, it's not half bad on Bani Marine Street, a few blocks away from the Jema, either. Bani Marine Street is one of the many "barbecue lanes" found in the newer quarters of Marrakesh. The crowded street is lined with simple storefront grill restaurants. You don't really need a menu, since the bill of fare is displayed in the window: stacks of lamb chops, trays of liver, coils of *merguez* sausage (reddened with paprika and cayenne), and decoratively sculpted mounds of *koefta* (ground spiced lamb).

There are plenty of items Americans would relish, like the lamb steaks, chops, and shish kebabs. To combat the toughness of Moroccan beef, cooks cut the meat for kebabs into cubes as small as your thumbnail. There are also plenty of items most

Americans wouldn't eat, like lamb's brains, testicles, and spleen. The latter comes stuffed with chopped onions and parsley and tastes like tough, spongy, strong-flavored liver. In the interest of science, I tried it, but it seems to be one of those foods you have to have been brought up on to enjoy.

A meal at one of the Bani Marine Street restaurants is a simple but soul-satisfying experience: a dish of olives, a plate of kebabs, served with fire-toasted bread, shallot relish, and fiery *harissa,* the North African hot sauce made with cayenne pepper and puréed tomatoes. The shallot relish is a rather ingenious concoction: The parsley in it is a natural mouthwash that neutralizes the pungency of the shallots. You also get a tiny dish of salt and ground cumin.

THE MECHOUIE MYSTIQUE

At least one Moroccan grilled meat dish has made the leap from street food to the stratosphere of haute cuisine: *mechouie.* Like American barbecue or Brazilian *churrasco, mechouie* refers simultaneously to a single dish, a style of cooking, and a kind of meal. The original *mechouie* was a whole lamb, stuffed with herbs, rubbed with butter and spices, and roasted on a spit over an open pit fire. You can still find this style of *mechouie* in villages in the countryside.

As *mechouie* moved from the country to the city, cooks abandoned the open fire for a wood-fired underground oven. My next stop took me to the heart of the souk, that Ali Baba–esque labyrinth of shops and alleyways that constitutes the main market of Marrakesh. My destina-

tion was the *mechouie* shop of Housseine Admov. A wiry man with a salt and pepper mustache, wearing a black *djellaba,* Housseine has owned this tiny shop, in the center of the souk, for 40 years. He proudly showed me his trade license—#E67830—qualifying him as a "master rôtisseur."

Actually, when I arrived, there wasn't much to look at. Four white-tile walls. A bare earthenware floor from which rose a rickety cast-iron stovepipe. It turned out that the action at a *mechouie* parlor takes place not above ground, but beneath it. Under the floor is an urn-shaped clay oven, 9 feet deep, 5 feet across, and tapering to an opening perhaps 14 inches wide in the center of the floor. The *mechouie* pit resembles a giant underground tandoor (Indian barbecue oven).

Twice a day Housseine builds a roaring fire in the underground oven, letting the logs burn down to embers. Twice a day he spits whole, freshly slaughtered lambs on thick wooden poles and lowers them into the oven. The lambs are seasoned with salt, pepper, and cumin, then smoke-roasted in the underground oven for two to three hours. The meat that emerges is fall-off-the-bone tender, with buttery-crisp skin and a subtle smoky flavor that made me think of American barbecue. It is nothing short of sublime.

Over the next two days I spent a fair amount of time at Housseine's shop. I watched him build the fires: one at 5:00 A.M. (for the noon lambs), one at 2:30 P.M. (for the night lambs), using discarded cardboard boxes for kindling. I watched him lower the lambs into the oven, haul them out, and line them up, like soldiers, against the white-tile wall, to be packaged in plastic garbage bags and sent home with their owners.

Housseine collects 50 dirham (about $6) for each lamb. He doesn't actually sell the lambs; he levies a fee for roasting them. The pit can accommodate up to 10 lambs, so when it's full for both the noon and night shifts, he turns a tidy profit. Of course, the pit requires regular maintenance. Once a month, Housseine hires a dwarf to climb down into the oven and clean it. Once every 20 years, he digs the oven up and replaces it with a new one.

Owning a *mechouie* pit is an upbeat occupation. Because *mechouie* is a rich man's dish or a ceremonial treat served on happy occasions, such as birthdays and weddings, people who order *mechouie* from Housseine generally have something to celebrate. Even the shop next door benefits from his commerce. It specializes in roasted sheep heads—a much-prized delicacy in these parts.

Not that you need an underground pit to make great *mechouie.* Restaurants in Marrakesh roast them on rotisseries or in the oven. A North American–style kettle grill produces a great *mechouie.* Leg of lamb gives you the spirit of the dish in proportions that don't require a whole community to enjoy (see page 180).

How to Unskewer Shish Kebabs

Shish kebab is one of the most world's most beloved methods for cooking meats, especially lamb. But unskewering the meat can be challenging—as anyone knows who's tried to unskewer too vigorously and sent cubes of meat sailing across the dining room.

Cooks in the Near East and Central Asia have developed an ingenious method for unskewering kebabs. They hold the end of the skewer in one hand and grab the meat with the other, using a piece of pita bread or a sheet of lavash as a pot holder. They pull the meat toward them a tiny bit to loosen it from the skewer, then slide it off the skewer onto the plate.

SOUVLAKI FLAMBEED WITH METAXA

GREECE

METHOD:
Direct grilling

ADVANCE PREPARATION:
6 to 24 hours for marinating the meat

SPECIAL EQUIPMENT:
4 long metal skewers

Souvlaki is the Greek version of shish kebab, a popular street food consisting of lamb bathed in a tangy marinade of olive oil, lemon juice, garlic, and bay leaves and grilled over blazing coals. The retsina (a Greek wine flavored with resin) isn't strictly traditional, nor is flambéeing the souvlakis with Metaxa (Greek brandy). But both beverages would be served at a Greek barbecue, and both add flavor and drama to the meat. The purist could omit them. Serve the souvlaki with pita bread, Yogurt-Cucumber Salad with Mint, and A Different Greek Salad (see Index).

¼ cup extra-virgin olive oil, preferably Greek
¼ cup retsina wine or dry red wine
¼ cup fresh lemon juice
4 bay leaves
3 cloves garlic, minced
1 teaspoon dried oregano, preferably Greek
1 teaspoon salt, or more to taste
1 teaspoon freshly ground black pepper, or more to taste

1½ pounds boneless leg or shoulder of lamb, cut into 1-inch cubes (include some fatty pieces)
1 medium onion, cut into 1-inch pieces
⅓ cup Metaxa (Greek brandy) or other brandy
Lemon wedges, for serving
4 pita breads, for serving

1. Combine the oil, wine, and lemon juice in a large nonreactive bowl and whisk to blend. Stir in the bay leaves, garlic, oregano, salt, and pepper. Add the lamb and toss to coat thoroughly, then cover and let marinate, in the refrigerator, for at least 6 hours and up to 24 hours.

2. Preheat the grill to high.

3. When ready to grill, remove the lamb from the marinade, reserving the marinade, and thread onto the skewers, alternating with onion pieces. Oil the grill grate, then arrange the kebabs on the hot grate and grill, turning with tongs, until nicely browned and cooked to taste, 8 to 12 minutes in all, for well done (as Greeks tend to like their lamb).

Brush the kebabs as they cook with the reserved marinade (but not during the last 3 minutes), and season with salt and pepper.

4. Transfer the souvlakis to a heatproof platter. Warm the brandy in a small saucepan over very low heat; do not allow it to boil or even become hot. Remove from the heat and then, making sure your sleeves are rolled up and hair is tied back, light a long match and use it to ignite the brandy, averting your face as you do so. Very carefully pour the flaming brandy over the souvlakis and serve immediately, accompanied by lemon wedges and pitas.

Serves 4

ALEXANDRE DUMAS'S GEORGIAN-STYLE LAMB KEBABS

REPUBLIC OF GEORGIA

METHOD:
Direct grilling

ADVANCE PREPARATION:
1 to 8 hours for marinating the meat

SPECIAL EQUIPMENT:
4 long metal skewers

Alexandre Dumas was one of the most prolific and beloved novelists of the nineteenth century, writing such classics as *The Count of Monte Cristo* and *The Man in the Iron Mask*. What you may or may not know is that he was also a passionate trencherman, and in addition to penning a volume entitled *Grand dictionnaire de cuisine*, he wrote extensively about food encountered during his travels.

The following recipe was inspired by Dumas's travels through the Caucasus Mountains in 1859. Concerning the cooking equipment, he imparts some curious advice, quoted in Darra Goldstein's fine book *The Georgian Table*: "Even if you don't have a skewer or happen to be traveling in a place where skewers are unknown, you can always substitute something else. Throughout my travels the cleaning-rod of my rifle served as a skewer, and I didn't notice any harm to the worthiness of my weapon from using it in this humble role."

Amen!

I've embellished his original recipe, adding a traditional Georgian spice mix called *khmeli-suneli*. I think you'll find the results incredibly aromatic; the ground marigold is available at markets specializing in Russian products, and see page 230 for a description of sumac.

Serve these kebabs with grilled tomatoes, Georgian Pickled Plum Sauce, and Georgian Pickles (see Index).

½ teaspoon ground coriander
½ teaspoon dried dill
½ teaspoon dried basil
½ teaspoon dried mint
½ teaspoon ground marigold (optional)
Salt and freshly ground black pepper, to taste
1½ pounds boneless leg of lamb, cut into 1-inch cubes (Dumas calls them "walnut size")
1 medium onion, finely chopped
1 cup red wine vinegar
2 tablespoons olive oil, for basting
2 tablespoons ground sumac, for serving (optional)

1. Combine the coriander, dill, basil, mint, ground marigold (if using), 1 teaspoon salt, and ½ teaspoon pepper in a large bowl. Add the lamb and toss thoroughly to coat. Cover and let marinate, in the refrigerator, for 30 minutes.

2. Add the onion and vinegar to the lamb, tossing again to mix well. Re-cover and

let marinate, in the refrigerator, for at least another 30 minutes and up to 8 hours (the longer you marinate the lamb, the tangier it will be).

3. When ready to cook, thread the lamb onto the skewers. Oil the grill grate, then arrange the kebabs on the hot grate and grill, turning with tongs, until nicely browned and cooked to taste, 8 to 12 minutes in all, for well done. Brush the kebabs several times as they cook with oil and season with salt and pepper.

4. Unskewer the lamb onto serving plates and serve immediately, accompanied by ground sumac (if using) for sprinkling.

Serves 4

LAMB AND TOMATO KEBABS

FRANCE

METHOD:
Direct grilling

SPECIAL EQUIPMENT:
4 long metal skewers

A rresting in their simple beauty, these kebabs caught my eye in a shop window on the Rue de la Huchette in Paris. This area, a warren of medieval lanes on the Left Bank has become the Plaka of Paris, lined with dozens of Greek restaurants and grill joints. I love the idea of putting whole lamb chops on kebabs—you get to gnaw the bones after you eat the meat. Serve the chops with Grilled Polenta (see Index).

FOR THE KEBABS:
1 large onion, peeled
1 large green bell pepper
12 rib lamb chops (each about 3 ounces and 1 inch thick)
8 fresh, ripe plum tomatoes

FOR THE SPICE MIXTURE:
1 tablespoon coarse (kosher or sea) salt
1 teaspoon freshly ground black pepper
1 teaspoon dried mint
1 teaspoon dried oregano
1 teaspoon dried rosemary

3 tablespoons extra-virgin olive oil, or as needed, for brushing
4 pita breads

1. Cut the onion into eight wedges and break each wedge into segments. Stem and seed the bell pepper and cut into strips 1½ inches long and ½ inch wide.

2. Thread the ingredients for the kebabs onto the skewers in the following sequence: a lamb chop, a piece of onion, a piece of bell pepper, a tomato (skewered crosswise), a piece of onion, a piece of bell pepper, another lamb chop, more onion and pepper, another tomato, more onion and pepper, and another lamb chop. Run a metal skewer through the meat of each chop at a 60-degree angle to the bone. Arrange the kebabs on a platter or baking sheet, cover loosely with plastic wrap, and set aside, in the refrigerator, until ready to grill.

3. Preheat the grill to high.

4. When ready to grill, prepare the spice mixture. Combine the salt, pepper, mint, oregano, and rosemary in a small bowl, crumbling the rosemary between your fingers.

5. Brush the chops and vegetables on each skewer all over with oil and season generously with the spice mixture. Oil the grill grate, then arrange the kebabs on the hot grate and grill, turning with tongs, until the lamb is cooked to taste, about 12 minutes in all for medium. As the kebabs cook, brush with oil and season with more of the spice mix.

6. Fold a pita around the meat on each skewer and pull out the skewer. Serve immediately.

Serves 4

ARMENIAN SHISH KEBAB

**REPUBLIC OF
ARMENIA**

METHOD:
Direct grilling

**ADVANCE
PREPARATION:**
*8 hours to 1 day
for marinating
the meat*

**SPECIAL
EQUIPMENT:**
*4 long metal
skewers*

Shish kebab is common currency in the cuisines of the Middle and Near East and Central Asia. The Armenian version owes its richness to the addition of tomato paste to the marinade—a tangy mixture of red wine, wine vinegar, and olive oil. This recipe is equally delicious with beef. Either goes well with lavash and bulgur, and with Grilled Eggplant, Tomato, and Pepper Salad, and Onion Relish with Pomegranate Molasses (see Index).

½ cup dry red wine
¼ cup tomato paste
¼ cup extra-virgin olive oil
2 tablespoons red wine vinegar
1 medium onion, finely chopped
1 clove garlic, finely chopped
1 teaspoon dried marjoram or summer
    savory
1 teaspoon salt
½ teaspoon freshly ground black pepper
½ teaspoon hot red pepper flakes
¼ teaspoon ground allspice
1½ pounds boneless shoulder of lamb,
    cut into 1-inch cubes (include
    some fatty pieces)

24 pearl onions, peeled and cut in half, or
    2 medium onions, cut into 1-inch pieces
2 green bell peppers, stemmed, seeded,
    and cut into 1-inch pieces
Lavash (flat bread), for serving

1. Combine the wine, tomato paste, oil, and vinegar in a large nonreactive bowl and whisk to blend. Stir in the onion, garlic, marjoram, salt, black pepper, hot pepper flakes, and allspice. Add the lamb and toss to coat thoroughly, then cover and let marinate, in the refrigerator, for at least 8 hours and up to 24 hours.

2. Preheat the grill to high.

3. When ready to cook, remove the lamb from the marinade and thread onto the skewers, alternating with pearl onion halves and bell pepper pieces. Oil the grill grate, then arrange the kebabs on the hot grate and grill, turning with tongs, until nicely browned and cooked to taste, 8 to 12 minutes in all, for well-done.

4. Using a piece of lavash to protect your hand, unskewer the lamb and vegetables onto serving plates and serve immediately.

Serves 4

Ground Meat,
BURGERS, AND SAUSAGES

This butcher shop in Greece has all the sausages for grilling that you could wish for.

The hamburger is the U.S.'s most famous contribution to the world of barbecue. And while we may think that nothing can beat the succulence of a thick, hand-patted burger expertly charred over fire, grill jockeys around the world offer some stiff competition, elevating lowly ground meat to the level of art.

Bulgarians have earned bragging rights for their *kufteh* (cumin-scented veal and pork burgers). Romanians deserve raves for their *mititei* (spicy pork and lamb sausages). And Croatians should be proud of their *cevapcici* (three-meat burgers flavored with coriander). Moving east, the burger gives way to a sort of skinless sausage, molded and cooked on a flat metal skewer, called *kofta kebab* in the Middle East, *lyulya kebab* in Azerbaijan, and *seekh kebab* in India.

As for actual sausages, there is no shortage on the barbecue trail, from the chorizo of Spain and Latin America to the *kupati* (beef sausage studded with pomegranate seeds) of the Republic of Georgia.

The recipes may seem a long way from hamburgers and hot dogs. Yet the appeal of grilled ground meats is universal.

A Special Word About the Recipes in This Chapter

The recipes in this chapter are easy, but they do involve some special care.

■ First, a word about grinding. The kebabi and saté men I met on the barbecue trail grind their own meat from scratch, and time permitting I like to do the same. But I know that perfectly delicious results can be obtained with a lot less fuss and time by using preground meat, so that is what I call for in the recipes.

■ If you do grind your own meat (see page 211), use a fairly fatty cut (unless otherwise instructed), like shoulder (for lamb and pork) or chuck (for beef). Put it through the fine plate of the meat grinder (the plate with $\frac{1}{8}$-inch holes).

■ Sometimes I call for kneading the kebab mixture by hand, either over a low heat or at room temperature. Kneading (especially over heat) creates a smooth, tightly knit, almost spongy texture much prized by Central Asians. There is no need to knead unless instructed to do so in a recipe.

■ Some of the recipes call for molding the ground meat onto skewers. In general, chilling the meat before molding it will make the task easier. If it is necessary to chill the meat, I note that in the recipe. I also like to chill the molded kebabs for 1 to 2 hours before grilling. This makes the meat less likely to fall off the skewers. Note that chilling is a luxury not available to many kebab and saté chefs in the Third World, who have no refrigeration. If you're pressed for time, most of the *koftas,* kebabs, and satés in this chapter can be assembled and grilled without chilling. If you're preparing the meat ahead of time, always refrigerate it until you're ready to grill.

■ The ground meat should go on flat skewers (available at Middle Eastern and Iranian markets; see Mail-Order sources). Ideally the skewers will be $\frac{1}{2}$ inch wide, but you can get away with using a $\frac{1}{4}$-inch-wide skewer. Use slender metal or bamboo skewers only as a last resort; the meat is more likely to fall off them.

■ Because ground meat satés are fairly fragile, I suggest arranging them on a baking sheet lined with plastic wrap as they are prepared. When I prepare larger kebabs, I rest both ends of the skewers on the sides of a roasting pan so that the meat is suspended. This prevents the kebabs from flattening out.

■ I also recommend grilling ground meat kebabs "without a grate," a procedure in which the ends of the skewers rest on bricks or metal pipe so they are raised above the grate. This makes the kebabs less likely to stick and fall apart than if they're placed directly on the grate. (For an explanation of grateless grilling, see page 21).

If you're in a hurry or you don't have bricks or pieces of pipe, you can cook directly on the grate. Just remember to oil it well before adding the kebabs.

■ Use tongs for turning the kebabs. (Try to hold the ends of the skewers, rather than the meat part, when turning.)

■ To unskewer a ground meat kebab, do as an Iranian kebabi man does: Use a piece of pita bread or lavash as a pot holder. Gently pull the portion of meat toward you to loosen it, then push it away from you to unskewer.

THE GREAT AMERICAN HAMBURGER

U.S.A.

METHOD:
Direct grilling

What makes a great hamburger? First there's the meat. You want to use a flavorful cut, like sirloin (for uptown burgers), or chuck or round (if you're feeling more democratic). The meat should be ground twice—first through the coarse plate of the grinder, then through the fine plate. And it shouldn't be too lean. Fifteen to 20 percent fat is ideal.

I adhere to the "less is more" school when it comes to making hamburgers. Namely, the fewer ingredients you add to the meat, the better. Oh, I know how tempting it is for cooks to want to season the meat with onion, garlic, spices, and condiments. But to taste a burger at its best, keep it utterly simple. The garnishes will add all the flavor you need.

One final bit of advice: Handle the meat as little as possible: a few pats to form it into a patty. Anything more will rob the burger of its juiciness and primal flavor.

FOR THE BURGERS:
2¼ pounds ground round, chuck, or sirloin
2 tablespoons unsalted butter, melted,
      or olive oil
Salt and freshly ground black pepper, to taste
6 hamburger buns
6 slices (½ inch thick) Vidalia or other
      sweet onion (optional)

FOR THE TOPPINGS (ANY OR ALL):
Iceberg lettuce leaves
Sliced fresh, ripe tomatoes
Sliced dill pickles or sweet pickles
Cooked bacon (2 strips per burger)
Ketchup
Mustard
Mayonnaise

1. Preheat the grill to high.
2. Divide the meat into 6 equal portions.

Lightly wet your hands with cold water, then form each portion of meat into a round patty, 4 inches across and of even thickness (see Note).

3. When ready to cook, oil the grill grate.

4. Brush one side of the patties and the onion slices (if using) lightly with melted butter and season with salt and pepper. Arrange both the burgers and onion slices, butter side down, on the hot grate and grill until nicely browned, about 4 minutes. Brush the other side lightly with more melted butter and season with more salt and pepper. Turn with a spatula and continue grilling until nicely browned and cooked to taste, about 4 minutes for medium. Brush the cut sides of the buns with the remaining melted butter and place, cut sides down, on the grill the last 2 minutes.

5. Set out the toppings. Place the burgers and onion slices on the buns and serve.

Serves 6

Note: If not planning on cooking the burgers immediately, place on a large plate, cover loosely with plastic wrap, and refrigerate.

Cheeseburgers

In addition to the ingredients in the main recipe, you'll need:

6 slices (¼ inch thick) sharp
      Cheddar cheese, Swiss cheese,
      or 6 pieces Roquefort

Follow the instructions through cooking the first side of the burgers in step 4. After you flip them, place a piece of cheese on top.

Cover the grill and cook the burgers until the cheese is melted and the meat is done to taste. Check after 3 minutes.

Serves 6

Bacon and Smoked-Cheese Burger

In addition to the ingredients in the main recipe you'll need:

12 thin slices bacon
6 slices (¼ inch thick) smoked mozzarella or other smoked cheese

In step 2, wrap each patty with 2 strips of bacon. The bacon strips should be placed perpendicular to each other. Cook the burg-

ers as described in the main recipe. Place on buns and top with the cheese. The heat of the burgers will melt the cheese.

Serves 6

Avocado, Sprout, and Salsa Burger

Instead of the toppings suggested in the main recipe you'll need:

1 large ripe avocado, peeled, pitted, and cut into ¼-inch slices
1½ cups alfalfa sprouts
1½ cups Salsa Mexicana (page 174)

Cook the burgers as described in the main recipe. Place them on buns and top with avocado slices, sprouts, and salsa.

Serves 6

Cooking Hamburgers

When I was growing up, a salmonella outbreak was a freak occurrence. Today you can hardly pick up the newspapers these days without reading about some sort of mass food contamination.

Ground meats seem to be particularly susceptible to contamination. In order to kill salmonella (or other bacteria), you need to cook hamburgers (and other meats) to an internal temperature of 160°F. That's the temperature of medium-done meat.

Here are some other procedures that can help make hamburgers safer:

■ Buy your meat at a top-notch butcher shop where the meat is ground daily. If possible, choose your meat before it's ground and have the butcher grind it while you wait.

■ Store the meat in the refrigerator until you're ready to cook it.

■ Wash any cutting board you've cut meat on with very hot water and plenty of soap immediately after each use.

BULGARIAN BURGERS
Kufteh

BULGARIA

METHOD:
Direct grilling

Kufteh (aka *kafta, kofta, koefta*) gener-ally refers to grilled ground lamb kebabs or meatballs popular through-out the Arab world. But in Bulgaria, the term describes a meat patty similar to a hamburger. The lamb used in Muslim countries gives way to ground pork and veal in Bulgaria—an exceptionally flavor-ful combination of meats. *Kufteh* and *kebabche* (the same mixture formed into a sausage shape) are popular enough to qualify as the national snack in Bulgaria, where they're served with crusty rolls or country-style bread and tomato salad (see Index for Tomato Salad with Feta Cheese).

8 ounces ground veal
8 ounces ground pork
1 small onion, minced
3 tablespoons minced fresh parsley
1 teaspoon salt, or more to taste
Generous ½ teaspoon ground cumin, or
    more to taste
½ teaspoon freshly ground black pepper, or
    more to taste

1. Preheat the grill to high.

2. Combine all the ingredients in a mix-ing bowl and stir to mix with a wooden spoon. To test the mixture for seasoning, sauté a teaspoon of it in a nonstick skillet until cooked through, then taste, adding salt, pepper, or cumin to the remaining mix-ture as necessary; the mixture should be highly seasoned.

3. Divide the meat into 4 equal portions. Lightly wet your hands with cold water, then form each portion into a patty 3 inches across and about ¾ inch thick (see Note).

4. When ready to cook, oil the grill grate. Arrange the burgers on the hot grate and grill, turning with a spatula, until nicely browned on both sides and cooked through, about 4 minutes per side. Serve immediately.

Serves 4

Note: If not planning to cook immediate-ly, place on a large plate, cover loosely with plastic wrap, and refrigerate.

"SLIPPER" BURGERS
Chapli Kebab

PAKISTAN

METHOD:
Direct grilling

His name was Mohammed Bashir and he wore a powder blue *shilwar* (pan-taloon) and *kamiz* (tunic). I met him not in his home town of Faisalabad, Pakistan, but in a taxi in Philadelphia. As is my wont with cabbies wherever I travel, I asked him about the barbecue of his homeland. He told me about a dish with the curious name of *chapli kebab*, literally "slipper" or "sandal" patties.

From Hamburg to Hoboken: A Brief History of the Hamburger

The hamburger ranks as one of the most popular dishes in the world. At least, if you figure by numbers. According to Jeffrey Tennyson, author of *Hamburger Heaven: The Illustrated History of the Hamburger,* Americans consume more than 38 billion burgers a year—three burgers a week for each American man, woman, and child. Add foreign consumption and you've got a food phenomenon unique in human history.

The hamburger's history begins, logically enough, in Hamburg, Germany, which in the eighteenth century was the largest port in Europe. According to Tennyson, German seafarers acquired a taste for chopped beef In Russia, where steak tartare had been a staple for centuries. Tartare takes its name from the Tartary (or Tatary) plains in Central Asia, home to the nomadic warriors known as the Mongols. Mongol horsemen, so the legend goes, enjoyed their beef raw, tenderizing it by placing it under their saddles.

(The riding action reduced it to a tender pulp.)

History neglects to tell us whether it was a Mongol, Russian, or German who first had the idea to cook the chopped beef. We do know that by the time the hamburger reached North America, with German immigrants, it was cooked—and beloved and respected. The first North American restaurant to propose hamburger on its menu was the legendary Delmonico's in New York, which in 1834 offered "hamburger steaks" for the princely sum of 10 cents—twice the price of roast beef or veal cutlet.

As the hamburger became more familiar, the price dropped. By the turn of the century, hamburgers had become the food of the masses, sold at horse-drawn lunch wagons, soda fountains, and newly invented luncheonettes. Somewhere along the line, the tomatoes and pickles were added—and the patty was placed on a bun, making the hamburger the ultimate convenience food you could eat on the run.

ADVANCE PREPARATION:
1 hour for chilling the patties

(The word kebab is used here in the original sense of "meat," not "food on a skewer.")

To make *chapli kebab,* ground meat is shaped in a large, flat patty that looks like the sole of a slipper or sandal. *Chapli kebab* is a specialty of the town of Peshawar on the India-Pakistan border—Muslim country, so you can use either beef or lamb for the patties. Pakistani restaurants in the U.S. tend to serve the *chapli kebab* pan-fried. But I like the patties grilled—the way I imagine they're made in Peshawar—with *naan* (Tandoori-Baked Flat Breads, see Index) alongside.

1 pound ground lamb (see Ground Lamb, page 221) or beef
½ medium onion, minced
2 cloves garlic, minced
1 to 2 serrano or other hot chiles, minced (for milder patties, seed the chiles)
¼ cup finely chopped fresh cilantro
1 tablespoon grated fresh ginger
2 teaspoons ground or crushed coriander seeds
1 teaspoon salt, or more to taste
½ teaspoon freshly ground black pepper, or more to taste
½ teaspoon cayenne pepper
½ teaspoon ground cumin

1. Preheat the grill to high.

2. Combine the lamb or beef, onion, garlic, chiles, cilantro, ginger, coriander seeds, 1 teaspoon salt, ½ teaspoon pepper, the cayenne, and cumin in a large bowl. Knead and squeeze the mixture with your hands until thoroughly blended, 3 to 4 minutes. To test the mixture for seasoning, sauté a small amount of it in a nonstick skillet until cooked through, then taste, adding salt or pepper to the remaining mixture as necessary; the mixture should be highly seasoned.

3. Line a large plate with plastic wrap. Divide the meat mixture into 4 equal portions. Lightly wet your hands with cold water, then form each portion of meat into an oval patty about 5 inches long and ¾ inch thick. Place each patty as it is made on the prepared plate. Cover loosely with plastic wrap and refrigerate for 1 hour.

4. When ready to cook, oil the grill grate. Arrange the patties on the hot grate and grill, turning with a spatula, until nicely browned on both sides and cooked to taste, 4 to 5 minutes per side for medium. Serve immediately.

Serves 4

BOSNIAN THREE-MEAT PATTIES
Cevapcici

BOSNIA

METHOD:
Direct grilling

ADVANCE PREPARATION:
1 hour for chilling the patties

Cevapcici (pronounced "che-VAP-chee-chee") are one of the many grilled ground meat patties popular in the Balkans; compare them with the *mititei* (Romanian Pork and Lamb Sausages) and *kufteh* (Bulgarian Burgers) in this chapter. This version calls for an equal amount of beef, veal, and pork, but *cevapcici* are also made with just lamb or any combination of these meats. The resulting flavor is so richly complex it tastes like a hamburger that's gone to finishing school. The addition of baking soda helps to make the mixture light.

Note that the meat shouldn't be too lean; 15 percent fat is ideal.

FOR THE PATTIES:
8 ounces ground beef chuck
8 ounces ground pork butt
8 ounces ground veal or lamb
½ medium onion, grated
3 tablespoons chopped fresh Italian (flat-leaf) parsley
1½ teaspoons salt, or more to taste
½ teaspoon ground coriander
½ teaspoon freshly ground black pepper, or more to taste
½ teaspoon baking soda
⅓ cup beef broth, homemade or reduced-sodium canned, or water

FOR SERVING:
1 medium onion, finely chopped
1 fresh, ripe tomato, finely chopped
1 red bell pepper, stemmed, seeded, and finely chopped, or 3 tablespoons chopped pickled peppers
4 crusty rolls

1. Combine the beef, pork, veal, onion, parsley, 1½ teaspoons salt, the coriander, ½ teaspoon pepper, and the baking soda in a large bowl. Knead and squeeze the mixture with your hands until thoroughly blended, 3 to 4 minutes. Knead in the broth. To test the mixture for seasoning, sauté a small amount of it in a nonstick skillet until cooked through, then taste, adding salt or pepper to the remaining mixture as necessary; it should be highly seasoned.

2. Lightly oil a large plate. Divide the mixture into 8 equal portions. Lightly wet your hands with cold water, then roll each portion between your palms to form a sausage shape about 1 inch in diameter and 2 inches long. Place the *cevapcici* as they are made on the prepared plate. Cover loosely with plastic wrap and refrigerate them for 1 hour. Place the onion, tomato, and bell pepper in sepa-

rate serving bowls. Cover and set aside until ready to serve.

3. Preheat the grill to high.

4. When ready to cook, oil the grill grate. Arrange the *cevapcici* on the hot grate and grill, turning with a spatula, until nicely browned and cooked through, 6 to 8 minutes in all.

5. Serve the *cevapcici* on crusty rolls (2 per roll), topped with spoonfuls of onion, tomato, and bell pepper.

Makes 8 patties; serves 4

ROMANIAN PORK AND LAMB SAUSAGES
Mititei

ROMANIA

METHOD:
Direct grilling

ADVANCE PREPARATION:
2 to 4 hours for chilling the patties

Mititei are skinless sausages popular in Romania. Legend credits La Iordachi restaurant in Bucharest as their birthplace. One particularly busy night, the story goes, the kitchen ran out of regular sausages, so ground pork and lamb were mixed and patted into short, stubby sausage shapes (*mititei* means "little" in Romanian) and grilled without casings. The blend of spices used, including caraway, allspice, and cloves, makes this one of the most interesting ground meat dishes around. Some people like to use beef instead of pork; in either case, the meat shouldn't be too lean.

12 ounces ground pork or beef
12 ounces ground lamb shoulder
1 small onion, minced as fine as possible
2 cloves garlic, minced as fine as possible
1 tablespoon olive oil
1½ teaspoons salt, or more to taste
1 teaspoon baking soda

1 teaspoon hot or sweet paprika, preferably imported
½ teaspoon dried marjoram
½ teaspoon caraway seeds
½ teaspoon freshly ground black pepper, or more to taste
¼ teaspoon ground allspice
Tiny pinch of ground cloves

1. Combine the pork, lamb, onion, garlic, oil, 1½ teaspoons salt, the baking soda, paprika, marjoram, caraway seeds, ½ teaspoon pepper, the allspice, and cloves in a large bowl. Knead and squeeze the mixture with your hands until thoroughly blended, 3 to 4 minutes. To test the mixture for seasoning, sauté a small amount of it in a nonstick skillet until cooked through, then taste, adding salt or pepper to the remaining mixture as necessary; it should be highly seasoned.

2. Lightly oil a large plate. Divide the meat mixture into 8 equal portions. Lightly

Grinding It Out

Somewhere in the recesses of my grandmother's cellar is an ancient hand-crank meat grinder. I am reminded of this because it's a piece of equipment I saw often on the barbecue trail, and when it comes to grinding meat for burgers and *koftas*, nothing can beat it (or its motorized cousins).

The reason is simple. Inside the meat grinder is a cross-shaped blade that rotates against a perforated metal plate. Together, they function like a knife on a cutting board. The grinder cleanly chops the meat into tiny pieces, just as a well-wielded knife or cleaver would do.

Hard-core grill buffs may wish to invest in their own motorized or hand-crank meat grinder or a meat grinder attachment for another appliance, such as a KitchenAid mixer.

How different is the food processor, today's high-tech answer to the meat grinder. A food processor tears and mashes the meat instead of chopping it. The result tends to be mushy and stringy, with a spongy, uneven texture.

GRINDING IN A FOOD PROCESSOR

If you wish to grind your own meat, and must use a food processor, be sure it's fitted with a metal chopping blade. First cut the meat into ½-inch dice. Do not fill the processor bowl more than one quarter full. Run the machine in short bursts. Following these three simple steps will give you ground meat, not mush

THE FAT FACTOR

Two other factors determine the flavor and succulence of your grilled ground meat: the cut of meat and the fat content. In general, you want to use a flavorful cut of meat: shoulder when it comes to pork or lamb; chuck, round, or sirloin for beef.

You need a certain amount of fat to keep ground meat succulent. Turks use as much as 30 percent fat in their ground lamb kebabs. This may seem excessive to health-conscious North Americans, but remember that fat carries flavor and it bastes the meat as it cooks (and some of the fat will melt out during cooking). For the recipes in this chapter, I recommend a fat content of 15 to 20 percent to keep ground meat dishes moist and tender.

The fat content of ground beef is usually marked on the package at the supermarket (ground sirloin is leaner than ground round or chuck). When in doubt about fat content, ask your butcher.

By the way, in Turkey, Azerbaijan, and other Near East countries, the preferred fat for making kebabs is lamb tail fat. If you live near a neighborhood with a Muslim butcher, you may be able to buy this flavorful fat.

wet your hands with cold water, then roll each portion between your palms to form sausage shapes about 1 inch in diameter and 3½ inches long. Place the *mititei* as they are made on the prepared plate. Cover loosely with plastic wrap and refrigerate them for 2 to 4 hours.

3. Preheat the grill to high.

4. When ready to cook, oil the grill grate. Arrange the *mititei* on the hot grate and grill, turning with a spatula, until nicely browned and cooked through, 6 to 8 minutes in all. Serve immediately.

Makes 8 sausages; serves 4

Ground Meats Grilling Chart*

CUT	METHOD	HEAT	DONENESS	
			MEDIUM* (160°F)	WELL (170°F)
BURGERS	DIRECT	HIGH	4–5 MIN/SIDE	6–7 MIN/SIDE
SAUSAGES	DIRECT	MED TO MED-HIGH		16–20 MINUTES IN ALL
KOFTAS & LULAS	DIRECT	HIGH		6–8 MINUTES IN ALL
SATES	DIRECT	HIGH	2–4 MIN/SIDE	4–6 MIN/SIDE

*To eliminate the risk of bacterial contamination, cook all ground meats to at least 160°F.

SAMBA DOGS

BRAZIL

METHOD:
Direct grilling

I tasted these unusual hot dogs at a samba school in Rio. From midnight to 4 A.M., the cavernous concrete hall reverberates with the thunderous rhythm of samba. An army of street vendors stands by to assuage the hunger of the dancers and I was particularly intrigued by the hot dog stand: The vendor crowned her hot dogs with a luscious relish of corn, tomatoes, peas, black and green olives, and hard-cooked eggs.

1 large egg, hard-cooked, peeled, and cut into ¼ inch dice
1 fresh, ripe medium tomato, seeded (see box, page 62) and finely chopped
¼ cup corn kernels, freshly cooked or drained canned
¼ cup cooked fresh or frozen green peas or drained canned petits pois
¼ cup pimiento-stuffed green olives, cut into ¼-inch dice
¼ cup pitted black olives, cut into ¼-inch dice
¼ cup diced red onion
3 tablespoons extra-virgin olive oil

1½ tablespoons red wine vinegar, or more to taste
Salt and freshly ground black pepper, to taste
8 best-quality frankfurters
8 best-quality hot dog buns, split

1. Preheat the grill to high.

2. Combine the eggs in a medium-size bowl with the tomato, corn, peas, olives, onion, oil, 1½ tablespoons vinegar, and salt and pepper and toss gently but thoroughly to mix. Taste for seasoning, adding vinegar or salt and pepper as necessary; the mixture should be highly seasoned.

3. When ready to cook, oil the grill grate. Arrange the frankfurters on the hot grate and grill, turning with tongs, until crusty and nicely browned all over, 6 to 8 minutes in all. While the frankfurters cook on the second side, add the buns, cut side down, to the grate and toast lightly.

4. Serve the frankfurters on the buns, topped with the relish.
Serves 8

SPICY CHORIZOS

S P A I N

METHOD:
Direct grilling

**ADVANCE
PREPARATION:**
*1 hour for
soaking the
sausage casing*

**SPECIAL
EQUIPMENT:**
*Sausage stuffer
(optional)*

To judge by geographic distribution, chorizo is the world's most popular sausage. Born in Spain, this spicy reddish-orange link is found throughout Spain's former colonies, from the Caribbean to South America to the Philippines and beyond. The paprika, garlic, and vinegar give it loads of flavor, while the black and hot pepper impart a deliciously fiery bite. As always, I give a range of hot peppers.

7 feet of sausage casing (see Notes)
**2½ pounds ground pork (about
    20 percent fat)**
⅓ cup red wine vinegar
¼ cup ice water
**3 tablespoons sweet paprika, preferably
    imported**
**1 tablespoon hot paprika, preferably
    imported, or ancho chile powder**
1 to 2 tablespoons hot red pepper flakes
**1 tablespoon coarse (kosher or sea) salt,
    or more to taste**
2 teaspoons dried oregano
2 teaspoons ground cumin
2 teaspoons ground coriander
5 cloves garlic, minced
1 tablespoon sugar
**1 teaspoon freshly ground black pepper,
    or more to taste**
**1 to 2 tablespoons vegetable oil,
    for brushing the sausages**
Crusty rolls, for serving (optional)

1. Soak the sausage casing in a large bowl of cold water for 1 hour, changing the water several times.

2. Combine the ground meat, vinegar, water, sweet and hot paprikas, 1 tablespoon hot pepper flakes, 1 tablespoon salt, the oregano, cumin, coriander, garlic, sugar, and 1 teaspoon black pepper in a large mixer bowl. Beat the mixture with a mixer fitted with the paddle or dough hook. Alternatively, you can mix with a wooden spoon. To test the mixture for seasoning, sauté a small amount of it in a nonstick skillet until cooked through, then taste, adding hot pepper flakes, salt, or black pepper to the remaining mixture as necessary; it should be highly seasoned.

3. Follow the instructions in the box on page 214 for stuffing and tying the casing, first removing the casing from the soaking water and rinsing out the insides as directed (see Notes).

4. Preheat the grill to high.

5. When ready to cook, prick each sausage in several places with a needle or toothpick and brush lightly with oil. (Make sure the needle doesn't wind up in the sausage.) Arrange the sausages on the hot grate and grill, turning with tongs, until nicely browned all over and cooked through (a metal skewer inserted in one will come out very hot to the touch), 16 to 20 minutes in all.

6. Serve the chorizos, hot dog style, on crusty rolls; or cut them into pieces and serve on small skewers or toothpicks.

Makes twelve 5-inch links; serves 6

Notes: If you do not wish to make sausages in casings, mold the sausage mixture onto flat skewers as in step 2 of Oasis Kebabs (page 220), then proceed to cook the kebabs as directed in that recipe.

■ If you're not planning to cook the prepared sausage immediately, cover loosely with plastic wrap and refrigerate.

How to Stuff Sausages Like a Pro

Making sausage at home isn't difficult, but you do need some special equipment. The traditional tool is a sausage funnel, a slender, tapering tube that fits over the end of a meat grinder. The casing is pulled over the tube, which extrudes the sausage mixture inside.

Some modern mixers, such as KitchenAid, have both meat grinder and sausage stuffer attachments. There's also a more elaborate stuffer that looks like a large elbow pipe with a tapered tube at one end and a hand-pumped piston at the other. Lowering the piston forces the sausage mixture through the tube into the waiting casing. Such devices can be ordered by mail from the Richard S. Kutas Co., 1067 Grant Street, Buffalo, New York 14207. In a pinch you can use a piping bag filled with a large round tip for stuffing sausage.

SAUSAGE CASINGS: These are available at butcher shops, ethnic markets, and some supermarkets. To prepare them for use: Soak for 1 hour in several changes of cold water. Drain, then pull one end of the casing over the end of the faucet in your kitchen sink. Gently ease the cold water tap on and let the running water rinse out the inside of the casing for 5 minutes.

TO STUFF THE SAUSAGE CASING: Attach the sausage-stuffing tube to your meat grinder and fill it with the meat mixture; or fill whatever sausage-stuffing device you are using. Remove the casing from the faucet and, starting at one end, gather it onto the nozzle of the sausage stuffer (much as a woman might gather a stocking as she prepares to put it on); make sure the casing isn't twisted. When only 2 or 3 inches of the casing are left dangling, knot the end tightly. Holding onto the casing so the flow of the meat mixture into the casing is controlled, pump the handle or crank the meat grinder to force the mixture into the casing, packing the casing firmly but not to the bursting point; after every 4 to 6 inch-

es, give the casing a couple of tight twists to make individual links. If air pockets form, you can deflate them by piercing the casing with the point of a sharp needle (just be careful the needle doesn't end up in a sausage!). When the filling is used up and/or the casing is filled, remove the end of the casing from the sausage stuffer and either tie a knot in it or tie it closed with a short length of string.

IF YOU ARE USING A PIPING BAG: This method will take longer, and you might find it a bit awkward at first, but it will get the job done. Remove the casing from the faucet and cut it into 20-inch lengths. Knot one end. Fit a large piping bag with a ½-inch round tip. Place some of the meat mixture in the bag (don't fill it too full) and pull the open end of the casing up over the tip, gathering it as much as possible. Squeeze the bag with one hand, holding the top of the casing with the other; the sausage mixture will flow neatly into the casing. Refill the bag as necessary. Make 3 to 4 individual links and finish off the casing as described above. Repeat with the remaining casing.

PORK AND POMEGRANATE SAUSAGES
Kupati

METHOD:
Direct grilling

**ADVANCE
PREPARATION:**
*1 hour for
soaking the
sausage casing
(optional)*

**SPECIAL
EQUIPMENT:**
*Sausage stuffer
(optional)*

The pairing of meats with fruit is one of the hallmarks of the cuisines of the Caucasus Mountains. A case in point: these sausages, a popular breakfast dish in the Republic of Georgia, especially in the fall, when fresh pomegranates are in season. The meat mixture is traditionally stuffed into sausage casings, but excellent *kupati* can be cooked in free-form patties or molded on flat skewers in the form of *kofta* (see page 220).

There are several ways these sausages can be enjoyed. You can cut them into inch-long pieces to be served at the end of toothpicks for hors d'oeuvres, or you can serve them on rolls or Georgian bread for a different kind of sandwich. I think you'll find the combination of pomegranate, dill, cilantro, and cinnamon a delectable addition to pork.

**7 feet of sausage casing (optional; see box,
      facing page)**
1 large pomegranate
1½ pounds ground pork (not too lean)
2 cloves garlic, chopped
**2 tablespoons chopped fresh dill or
      1 tablespoon dried**
2 tablespoons chopped fresh cilantro
1½ teaspoons salt, or more to taste
1 teaspoon freshly ground pepper
¼ teaspoon ground cinnamon, or more to taste
**1 to 2 tablespoons vegetable oil, for brushing
      the sausages**

1. If using the sausage casing, soak it in a large bowl of cold water for 1 hour, changing the water several times.

2. Meanwhile, break the pomegranate into quarters and seed; set aside.

3. Place the pork in a large bowl and stir in the pomegranate seeds, garlic, dill, cilantro, 1½ teaspoons salt, the pepper, and ¼ teaspoon cinnamon. Knead and squeeze the mixture with your hands until blended 3 to 4 minutes. To test the mixture for seasoning, sauté a small amount of it in a nonstick skillet until cooked through, then taste, adding salt or cinnamon to the remaining mixture as necessary; it should be highly seasoned.

4. Line a baking sheet with plastic wrap. *If making sausages in casings,* follow the instructions in the box on the facing page for stuffing and tying the casing, first removing the casing from the soaking water and rinsing out the insides as directed.

If making sausage patties, divide the mixture into 8 equal portions, then lightly wet your hands with cold water and form each portion into a patty 3 inches across and about ½ inch thick.

Place sausages as they are made on the prepared baking sheet (see Note).

5. Preheat the grill to high.

6. When ready to cook, oil the grill grate. If the sausages are in casings, prick each one in several places with a needle or toothpick and brush lightly with oil. (Make sure the needle doesn't wind up in the sausage.) Arrange the sausages, in whatever your chosen form, on the hot grate. Grill, turning with tongs, until the sausages in casings are nicely browned and cooked through (a metal skewer inserted in one will come out very hot to the touch), 16 to 20 minutes in all; the patties will need 4 minutes a side. Serve immediately.

***Makes twelve 4-inch stuffed sausages or
3-inch patties; serves 4***

Note: If not planning to cook immediately, cover loosely with plastic wrap and refrigerate.

SAMBA SAUSAGES
Choriçou

BRAZIL

METHOD:
Direct grilling

SPECIAL EQUIPMENT:
4 long bamboo skewers, soaked for 1 hour in cold water to cover and drained

This simple recipe is the perfect symbol of Brazil's sensuality and scintillating spirit. Grilled sausages are, of course, common currency among the world's street foods, but it's only in Brazil that street vendors take the time to make tiny slits in the sausages, fill them with minutely diced onions and bell peppers, and lovingly baste them with olive oil as they cook. The "grill" of the vendor who gave me his version was the charcoal-filled hubcap of an old car.

Virtually any type of cooked sausage could be prepared this way. I've called for chorizos, but kielbasa, knockwurst, or even hot dogs would work well, too.

4 cooked chorizos, homemade (page 213) or store-bought, or other cooked sausages (each 1 inch thick and 4 to 5 inches long)
½ small onion, minced very fine
½ medium red or green bell pepper, stemmed, seeded, and minced very fine
2 cloves garlic, minced
2 tablespoons olive oil

1. Preheat the grill to medium-high.

2. Push a skewer lengthwise through each sausage. Make a series of diagonal parallel slits, ¼ inch deep and ½ inch apart in one side of each sausage. Turn the sausage over and make a similar set of slits going the opposite direction.

3. Combine the onion, pepper, and garlic in a small bowl, then stuff some of the mixture into the slits in the sausages.

4. When ready to cook, oil the grill grate. Arrange the sausages on the hot grate and grill, turning with tongs, until lightly browned on all sides and heated through, turning as necessary, 5 to 8 minutes in all. As the sausages cook, drizzle oil over the slits.

5. Serve the sausages right on the skewers and eat them like Popsicles, with any remaining onion mixture.
Serves 4

BEEF SATES WITH CORIANDER
Saté Age

INDONESIA

METHOD:
Direct grilling

This lovely coriander-scented beef saté, *saté age*, which comes from Solo in central Java, is traditionally served on a flat bamboo skewer that looks like an ice-cream pop stick. The closest thing to a *saté age* skewer here is a Popsicle stick—an item easy enough to find at most supermarkets. Otherwise, try using tongue depressors or two bamboo skewers for each saté.

These aromatic satés are also good made with lamb or a mixture of beef and lamb.

1 pound lean ground beef chuck or sirloin
3 tablespoons chopped fresh cilantro
2 shallots, minced
1 clove garlic, minced
4 teaspoons ground coriander
1 teaspoon salt, or more to taste
1 teaspoon freshly ground black pepper,
    or more to taste
⅔ cup sweet soy sauce (ketjap manis)
    or ⅓ cup each regular
    soy sauce and molasses

1. Combine the ground beef, cilantro, shallots, garlic, 2 teaspoons of the coriander, and 1 teaspoon each salt and pepper in a food processor and process until well blended. To test for seasoning, sauté a small amount of the mixture in a nonstick skillet until cooked through, then taste, adding salt and pepper to the remaining mixture as necessary.

2. Line a baking sheet with plastic wrap. Lightly wet your hands with cold water. Take a handful (3 to 4 tablespoons) of the meat mixture and mold it onto a skewer or Popsicle stick to form a flat sausage shape about 3 inches long, ¾ inch wide, and ½ inch thick. Continue until all the mixture is used up, placing the satés as they are made on the prepared baking sheet (see Note).

3. Prepare a glaze by stirring the sweet soy sauce and remaining 2 teaspoons coriander in a shallow dish. Set aside.

4. Preheat the grill to high.

5. When ready to cook, oil the grill grate. Arrange the satés on the hot grate and grill, turning with tongs, for 2 minutes per side (4 minutes in all). Remove them from the grill and roll them lightly in the sweet soy glaze, then return to the grill and continue cooking until nicely browned on the outside and cooked through, an additional 1 to 2 minutes per side. Serve immediately.

Serves 4 to 6 as an appetizer, 2 as an entrée

Note: If not planning to cook immediately, cover loosely with plastic wrap and refrigerate.

FLYING FOX SATES
Saté Kalong

This beef and garlic saté takes its curious name from the nocturnal mammal called the flying fox. The squirrel-like creature comes out at dusk, sailing from tree to tree on folds of skin that extend, parachute-like, from the sides of its body. That's precisely the time of day that saté vendors traditionally set up shop in the town of Cirebon in northwestern Java.

Saté kalong is one of Indonesia's most delicate kebabs, traditionally measuring 3 inches long and a mere ¼ inch wide. (Lacking the patience of an Indonesian saté maker, I tend to make them a bit larger.) The pairing of sugar and garlic with beef may seem odd—until you stop to think about the sweet sauces that accompany American barbecue.

SPECIAL EQUIPMENT:
16 long bamboo skewers, soaked for 1 hour in cold water to cover and drained

10 ounces ground beef chuck or sirloin

5 cloves garlic, minced

3 tablespoons palm sugar or firmly packed light brown sugar, or more to taste

½ teaspoon salt, or more to taste

½ teaspoon freshly ground black pepper

1. Combine the beef, garlic, 3 tablespoons sugar, ½ teaspoon salt, and the pepper in a large bowl, then knead and squeeze the mixture with your hands until thoroughly blended, 3 to 4 minutes. To test the mixture for seasoning, sauté a small amount of it in a nonstick skillet until cooked through, then taste, adding salt or sugar to the remaining mixture as necessary; the mixture should be both savory and a little sweet.

2. Line a baking sheet with plastic wrap.

Divide the meat mixture into 16 portions. Lightly wet your hands with cold water, then mold each portion around a skewer, preferably in the traditional shape: a strip about 5 inches long, ½ inch wide, and ⅛ inch thick. To achieve the requisite flatness, pinch the meat between your thumb and forefinger. Place each saté as it is made on the prepared baking sheet, then cover loosely with plastic wrap and refrigerate for 1 to 2 hours.

3. Preheat the grill to high.

4. When ready to cook, oil the grill grate. Arrange the satés on the hot grate and grill, turning with tongs, until nicely browned on both sides and cooked through, 3 to 6 minutes in all. Serve immediately.

Makes 16 satés; serves 4 as an appetizer, 2 as a light entrée

LAMB SATE WITH TAMARIND SAUCE

Saté Buntel

INDONESIA

METHOD:
Direct grilling

ADVANCE PREPARATION:
1 hour for chilling the satés

SPECIAL EQUIPMENT:
4 short bamboo skewers (if using caul fat) or 4 Popsicle sticks, soaked for 1 hour in cold water to cover and drained

This largest of all Indonesian satés (at least of the ones I sampled) is a sausage-size kebab of ground lamb that takes four skewers to hold. I first tasted it at a simple but spotless eatery called Asli, in Jakarta. The saté originated in the city of Solo in Java, explains Asli's owner, Mr. Budiyanto, whose grandparents came from Solo and founded the restaurant in 1949. The Solo influence is apparent in the sweet-sour tamarind sauce used for basting and serving.

To be strictly authentic, you'll need one special ingredient: caul fat (a lacy membrane from the belly of a pig used in sausage making). Ask for it at a specialty butcher. But don't worry if you can't find caul fat, for free-form *saté buntel* is easy to make and equally delicious.

FOR THE LAMB:

1 pound ground lamb (see Ground Lamb, page 221)

1 teaspoon ground coriander

1 teaspoon salt

1 teaspoon freshly ground black pepper

4 squares (each 6 inches) caul fat (optional)

FOR THE MARINADE/SAUCE:

1 cup Tamarind Water (recipe follows) or frozen tamarind purée, thawed

⅓ cup firmly packed light brown sugar

1 tablespoon sweet soy sauce (ketjap manis) or 1½ teaspoons each regular soy sauce and molasses

FOR GARNISHING:

1 cucumber, peeled and thinly sliced

1 large or 2 medium shallots, thinly sliced

1. Combine the lamb, coriander, salt, and pepper in a medium-size bowl and stir to blend. Divide into 4 equal portions.

2. *If using caul fat,* lay the 4 pieces on a work surface. Place one portion of the lamb mixture on each piece and roll the caul fat around the meat to form a sausage about 4 inches long and 1 inch thick. Push a skewer into one end of each sausage. Carefully transfer the sausages to a plate, cover, and refrigerate for 1 hour.

If making free-form satés, lightly oil a plate. Lightly wet your hands with cold water. Take a portion of lamb mixture and mold it onto a Popsicle stick to form a sausage-like kebab 4 inches long and 1 inch thick. Place the satés on the prepared plate, cover, and refrigerate for 1 hour.

3. Preheat the grill to medium-high.

4. Make the marinade. Combine the Tamarind Water, sugar, and sweet soy sauce in a small nonreactive saucepan and boil, stirring to dissolve the sugar, until thick and syrupy, about 3 minutes. Let cool completely. Pour half the mixture into one or more small bowls and set them aside for serving.

5. When ready to cook, oil the grill grate. Arrange the satés on the hot grate and grill, turning with tongs, until the lamb is nicely browned and cooked through, 8 to 12 minutes in all. Halfway through the cooking process, begin brushing the satés with the remaining tamarind sauce. Transfer the satés to a platter and brush one final time with tamarind sauce. Garnish the satés with the sliced cucumber and shallots. Serve the reserved sauce on the side for dipping.

Serves 4 as an appetizer, 2 as an entrée

Tamarind Water

Tamarind is the fruit of a tall tropical tree, a fava bean–shaped pod filled with a fruity, orange-brown, sweet-sour pulp. The fruit takes its name from the Arabic words *tamr hindi,* literally "Indian date." Actually, tamarind tastes more like prune than date—prune mixed with lime juice and a drop of liquid smoke.

This distinctive sweet-sour flavor has endeared tamarind to cooks all along the world's barbecue trail, from Asia to the Caribbean. You've probably tasted it, for tamarind is a key flavoring in Worcestershire sauce and A-1 steak sauce.

You can buy fresh tamarind pods in Caribbean and Asian markets. (Look for fleshy, heavy pods with cracked skins that reveal the sticky brown pulp inside; tamarind with unbroken skins is underripe.) Peeling fresh tamarind is time consuming, so most ethnic markets and many supermarkets sell peeled tamarind pulp, which is quicker and easier to use.

Stringy and full of seeds, tamarind is rarely used in its natural state. The first step is to transform the sticky flesh into tamarind water, also known as tamarind purée. This is done by puréeing the pulp from peeled tamarind pods with boiling water.

If you live in an area with a large Hispanic community, you may be able to find frozen tamarind purée, which eliminates the need to make this recipe.

8 ounces tamarind pods (8 to 10 pods), or
    ½ cup peeled tamarind pulp
1¾ cups hot water

1. If using tamarind pods, peel the skin off with a paring knife. Break the pulp into 1-inch pieces and place in a blender with 1 cup of the hot water. Let the tamarind soften for 5 minutes.

2. Run the blender in short bursts at low

speed for 15 to 30 seconds to obtain a thick brown liquid. Don't overblend, or you'll break up the seeds. Pour the resulting liquid through a strainer, pressing hard with a wooden spoon to extract the juices, scraping the underneath side of the strainer with a spatula.

3. Return the pulp in the strainer to the blender and add the remaining ¾ cup hot water. Blend again and pour the mixture through the strainer, pressing well to extract the juices. Store in a tightly covered container in the refrigerator for up to 5 days; or freeze for several months (I like to freeze it in plastic ice-cube trays, so I have convenient pre-measured portions).

Makes about 1½ cups

Note: Indian markets sell plastic jars of smooth, dark, syrupy tamarind extract. This product has an interesting flavor, but you can't use it to make tamarind water.

OASIS KEBABS
Kofta

MIDDLE EAST

METHOD:
Direct grilling

ADVANCE PREPARATION:
1 hour for chilling the meat

SPECIAL EQUIPMENT:
8 flat, wide, long metal skewers

Kofta (also called *koefta, kafta,* and *kufte*) describes a sort of skinless sausage enjoyed throughout North Africa, the Balkans, and the Middle East. Depending on where you eat it, the meat will be lamb or beef (in the Arab world), pork or veal (in the Balkans), or a mixture of meats. The seasonings reflect local taste preferences, too, ranging from the onion-garlic-parsley triumvirate of the Balkans to the cinnamon and mint of the Middle East.

These kebabs are easy to make, but there are a few things to watch for. First, since there's no casing to seal in the juices, it's best to use a fairly fatty meat— 15 to 20 percent—to keep them moist. Also, it's essential to use wide, flat skewers (see Mail-Order Sources); the meat will fall off the slender metal skewers used for traditional shish kebab.

Here, then, is a *kofta* in the style of the Middle East. The cinnamon and mint add an unexpected sweet touch. Serve it with Moroccan Eggplant Salad (see Index).

FOR THE MEAT:
1½ pounds ground beef, lamb
    (see Ground Lamb on facing page), or
    a mixture of the two
1 large onion, very finely chopped
1 cup finely chopped fresh Italian
    (flat-leaf) parsley
½ cup chopped fresh mint or
    1 tablespoon dried
1 teaspoon ground cinnamon
1½ teaspoons salt, or more
    to taste
1 teaspoon freshly ground black pepper,
    or more to taste

FOR SERVING:
Pita bread or lavash
Finely chopped onion
Ground sumac (optional; see box,
    page 230)

1. Combine the beef, onion, parsley, mint, cinnamon, 1½ teaspoons salt, and 1 teaspoon pepper in a large bowl, then knead and squeeze the mixture with your hands

GROUND LAMB

I*f you can't buy lamb already ground, buy bone- less lamb shoulder in the amount you need, cut into 1-inch cubes, and have your butcher grind it, or grind it yourself through the fine (⅛ inch) plate of a meat grinder; then proceed with the recipe as directed.*

until thoroughly blended, 3 to 4 minutes. To test the mixture for seasoning, sauté a small amount of it in a nonstick skillet until cooked through, then taste, adding salt or pepper to the remaining mixture as necessary.

2. Divide the meat mixture into 8 equal portions. Lightly wet your hands with cold water, then, starting about 1 inch from the tip of a skewer, mold each portions around the skewer to form a flattish sausage about 10 inches long and 1 inch wide. To keep from flattening the meat, place each *kofta* as it is made on a baking pan so the ends of the skewers rest on the sides of the pan. Cover loosely with plastic wrap and refrigerate for 1 hour.

3. If desired, set up the grill for grate- less grilling (see box, page 21). Preheat the grill to high.

4. When ready to cook, if not using the grateless method, generously oil the grate. Arrange the *koftas* on the grill as described in the grateless method or arrange directly on the hot oiled grate. Grill, turning with tongs, until nicely browned and cooked through, 6 to 8 minutes in all).

5. Use a pita bread to protect your hand as you slide each *kofta* off its skewer onto a plate. Serve the *koftas* sprinkled with chopped onion and, if desired, ground sumac, and accompanied by pita breads.

Makes 8** koftas; **serves 4 as an entrée

Of Koftas, Lyulyas, and Seekh Kebabs

Arabs call them *koftas*. Iranians call them *kubideh*. Afghanis and Azerbaijanis know them as *lula* (or *lyulya kebab*), while Indians and Pakistanis call them *seekh kebabs*. Whatever you call them, ground meat molded on a skewer and grilled is one of the world's most popular treats.

Kofta country begins in Morocco and stretches as far east as Bangladesh. Perhaps even further— you could certainly argue that Indonesia's ground beef and lamb satés are actually a sort of *kofta*. The name, main ingredients, and flavorings change along the way, but the result remains the same. That result is a sort of skinless sausage. The secret is to mold a sausage-shaped span of meat on a flat metal skewer and cook it over a grateless grill.

At its simplest, *kofta* consists merely of ground lamb or beef flavored with onion, garlic, and parsley. Sometimes egg or cracked wheat is added to give the kebab a firmer consistency.

Sometimes the meat is kneaded by hand in a pan over a low flame to create the close-knit texture of fine fabric. Cooks in the Balkans and Iran add baking soda or selzer water to make their *mititels* and *cevapcicis* (the Balkan *kofta*) light.

The spicing, too, reflects the country of ori- gin. As you move east, the cumin and paprika pop- ular in Morocco give way to cinnamon and mint in the Middle East. Kebabi men in Central Asia flavor their *lula kebab* with hot peppers, dill, and cilantro. Indians turn to the evocative flavors of ginger, cumin, and turmeric to give their *seekh* (ground lamb) *kebab* pizzazz.

In this chapter, you'll find many variations on a theme of ground meat grilled on a stick. To be strictly authentic, you'd cook these kebabs using the grateless grilling technique on page 21. If you're careful and you oil the grate well, you can also cook the kebabs directly on the grate.

SPICED LAMB AND BEEF KEBABS
Lula Kebab

AFGHANISTAN

METHOD:
Direct grilling

**ADVANCE
PREPARATION:**
*1 to 8 hours for
chilling the
kebabs*

**SPECIAL
EQUIPMENT:**
*8 flat, wide, long
metal skewers*

Here's the Afghan version of a ground meat kebab known elsewhere in the Muslim world as *kofta, kubideh,* and *lyulya.* The spicing reflects Afghanistan's unique location at Asia's crossroads: The cilantro and dill are characteristic of Central Asian cooking; the chiles and turmeric of the Indian subcontinent. Made with both lamb and beef, *lulas* are some of the most flavorful ground meat kebabs ever to grace a skewer. Serve them with pita bread, accompanied by Afghan Coriander Sauce and Central Asian Pickles (see Index).

1 pound lean ground lamb (see Ground Lamb, page 221)
1 pound lean ground beef, such as round or sirloin
1 small onion, grated
1 to 2 bird or serrano chiles, minced (for milder kebabs, seed the chiles)
1 large egg
3 tablespoons minced fresh dill
3 tablespoons minced fresh cilantro
2 teaspoons salt, or more to taste
1 teaspoon freshly ground black pepper
1 teaspoon ground cumin, or more to taste
¼ teaspoon ground turmeric

1. Combine the lamb, beef, onion, chile, egg, dill, cilantro, 2 teaspoons salt, the pepper, 1 teaspoon cumin, and the turmeric in a large bowl. Knead and squeeze the mixture with your hands until thoroughly blended, 3 to 4 minutes. Transfer the mixture to a large heavy skillet and set over very low heat. Cook just until the mixture is warmed through, stirring constantly with a wooden spoon. Remove from the heat and let stand until completely cooled.

2. To test the mixture for seasoning, sauté a small amount of it in a nonstick skillet until cooked through, then taste, adding salt or cumin to the remaining mixture as necessary; it should be highly seasoned.

3. Line a baking sheet with plastic wrap. Divide the mixture into 8 equal portions. Lightly wet your hands with cold water, then, starting about 1 inch from the tip of a skewer, mold each portion around the skewer to form a flattish sausage 11 to 12 inches long and 1 inch wide. Using the fore- and middle fingers of one hand in scissors fashion, make a series of shallow ridges the length of the sausage, perpendicular to the skewer. Place each kebab as it is made on the prepared baking sheet, then cover loosely with plastic wrap and refrigerate at least 1 hour or as long as overnight.

4. If desired, set up the grill for grateless grilling (see box, page 21). Preheat the grill to high.

5. When ready to cook, if not using the grateless method, generously oil the grate. Arrange the kebabs on the grill as described in the grateless method, or arange directly on the hot oiled grate. Grill, turning with tongs, until nicely browned on both sides and cooked through, 6 to 8 minutes in all. Serve immediately.

Makes 8 kebabs; serves 8 as an appetizer, 4 as an entrée

PERSIAN LAMB AND BEEF KEBABS
Kubideh

IRAN

METHOD:
Direct grilling

ADVANCE PREPARATION:
1 to 2 hours for chilling the kebabs

SPECIAL EQUIPMENT:
8 wide, flat, long metal skewers

Ground lamb and beef kebabs (*kubideh*) are the truest test of the competency of an Iranian kebabi man. When properly prepared (*kubideh* is the Persian word for "chopped" or "mashed"), these kebabs are moist, succulent, and feather light—no small feat considering that the principle ingredients are beef and lamb, and rather fatty (at least 25 percent) beef and lamb at that. The following recipe requires a little work, but the results are astonishing. Serve it, unskewered, on a mound of Persian Rice with a Golden Crust (see Index).

Be sure you grate or purée the onion just prior to adding it to the meat; this will keep it from getting too strong (the longer it remains in contact with air, the stronger it becomes).

1 pound ground lamb (see Ground Lamb, page 221)
1 pound ground beef round or sirloin
2 teaspoons salt, or more to taste
1 teaspoon freshly ground black pepper, or more to taste
½ teaspoon baking soda
1 large onion, peeled
Lavash or pita bread

1. Place the lamb, beef, 2 teaspoons salt, 1 teaspoon pepper, and the baking soda in a large bowl and stir to blend. Transfer the mixture to a large heavy saucepan. Set the saucepan over very low heat and knead the mixture with your hands until it's warmed through and very smooth, about 5 minutes. Remove from the heat.

2. Cut the onion into 1-inch chunks, then grate it through the next-to-smallest holes of a four-sided hand grater or process it in a food processor; you should have about 1 cup grated onion. Add the onion to the meat mixture in the saucepan and knead again, this time off the heat, until the onion is thoroughly mixed in, another 5 minutes.

3. To test the mixture for seasoning, sauté a small amount of it in a nonstick skillet until cooked through, then taste, adding salt or pepper to the remaining mixture as necessary.

4. Line a baking sheet with plastic wrap. Divide the mixture into 8 equal portions. Lightly wet your hands with cold water, then, starting about 1 inch from the tip of a skewer, mold each portion around the skewer to form a flattish sausage 11 to 12 inches long and 1 inch wide. Using the fore- and middle fingers of one hand in scissors fashion, make a series of shallow ridges the length of the sausage, perpendicular to the skewer. Place each kebab as it is made on the prepared baking sheet, then cover loosely with plastic wrap and refrigerate for 1 to 2 hours.

5. If desired, set up the grill for grateless grilling (see box, page 21). Preheat the grill to high.

6. When ready to cook, if not using the grateless method, generously oil the grate. Arrange the kebabs on the grill as described in the grateless method, or arrange directly on the hot oiled grate. Grill, turning with tongs, until nicely browned and cooked through, 6 to 8 minutes in all.

7. Use a lavash to protect your hand as you slide each *kubideh* off its skewer onto a plate. Serve accompanied by lavash.

Makes 8 kubideh; serves 8 as an appetizer, 4 as an entrée

The Turkish Grill

You probably won't find the name Imam Cagdas—or Gazientep—in your typical Turkish guide book. But mention either place to a Turk and you'll get the sly, conspiratorial look reserved not for tourists but insiders. Imam Cagdas (pronounced "ee-mam cha-dahsh"), which is also the name of the owner, is arguably the most famous kebab house in Turkey, a boisterous, two-story storefront founded by Imam's great-grandfather in 1887. The day of my visit, guests included the city mayor and the commander of the local army base, not to mention 700 other hungry customers. And it was slow season!

Turkish gastronomes have the sort of reverential regard for Gazientep that Americans have for New Orleans. Gazientep is the sixth largest city in Turkey, a booming, dusty metropolis located 30 miles west of the Euphrates River near the Syrian border in south central Turkey. The few American businessmen I met here know it as a center for textiles and machine-made carpets. Foodies know it as the pistachio capital of Turkey, not to mention a city whose collective fondness for chile peppers would rival Santa Fe.

But the stars of the show are the kebabs, which are stacked in towering piles on metal trays in Imam Cagdas's open kitchen. The variety bears testimony to the Turkish culinary imagination. There is *sogar kebab*—skewers of ground lamb and whole shallots that are seasoned with a few drops of pomegranate molasses before serving. There is *semit kebab,* springy sausages of ground lamb and bulgur wheat spiced up with fresh mint and allspice. For sheer visual appeal you can't beat *sedzeli kebab:* shiny purple chunks of eggplant spit-roasted with ground lamb. And that's just in winter. Imam Cagdas varies the half dozen kebabs it serves on a typical day according to the seasons.

Gazientep might seem like an odd place to begin a story on Turkish grilling. It's not particularly easy to get to and it's certainly not on the tourist circuit, but the love of barbecue here is evident even before you land at the airport. A few years ago, an airline pilot passing over Gazientep radioed the fire department to report a forest fire. Closer investigation revealed the thick cloud of smoke to be the output of thousands of portable grills brought to the woods by families for holiday picnics.

Almost every restaurateur worth his salt in Turkey claims to have a chef from Gazientap—as I was to discover on my next stop: the restaurant Develi in Istanbul.

WHEN IN ISTANBUL

Develi is the sort of restaurant I came to love so much in Turkey: fancy enough to have tablecloths, but relaxed enough for men to pass the evening drinking *raki* (anise liquor) and eating *mezze* (appetizers) with their buddies after work. The night I was there, I saw no women and no foreigners. According to its fifth-generation owner, Ali Develier, Develi was opened in 1912 by a camel trader from Gazientep. Today, the four-story restaurant seats 450.

I started with *pilaki,* a variety of

dips and salads seasoned with fruity Turkish olive oil. *Lamejun,* Turkish ground lamb pizza, came next, followed by freshly baked *pida,* a Turkish bread that tastes like a cross between *focaccia* and pita. In short order, I was served the house specialty, ground lamb and pistachio nut kebabs, followed by lemony *shish kebab* and *Ali Nasik kebab,* a sausage of ground lamb served on a bed of puréed grilled eggplant and yogurt. (The idea of pairing grilled meat and puréed eggplant is suppose to have originated with a Bursa grill jockey whose name means "Gentle Al.") Desserts are exquisite pastry confections doused with butter, syrup, and rosewater.

STREET KEBABS

I don't mean to give the impression that grilled fare is solely restaurant food. Indeed, Turkey's most popular "barbecue" is a street food known as *donner kebab. Donner* means "twirling" or "turning" in Turkish; the kebab in question consists of thin flat strips of spiced lamb (or sometimes chicken), layered and stacked to make a giant roast that turns on a vertical spit in an upright rotisserie.

The genius of *donner kebab* is that each portion comes off the roast freshly grilled and delicately crusty. (Good *donner kebab* is like a prime rib with nothing but end cuts.) *Donner* is always

carved from the bottom up to allow the dripping fat from the top to baste the meat. Actually, there are two types of *donner: yaprak* (literally "leaf" *donner*) made with whole lamb and *kyma,* made with ground lamb. I prefer the former.

The sliced *donner* is rolled in a piece of pita bread or a sheet of lavash with sliced lettuce and tomatoes and yogurt sauce. It's fresh, hot, and succulent, and a serving costs less than a dollar.

SHORT-ORDER KEBABS

My last night in Turkey, I wandered the streets of the Beyolu (a lively neighborhood in istanbul that reminds me of the Latin Quarter in Paris). I came upon a smoky grill restaurant tucked away amid the area's taverns and cafés. No one spoke English, but it really didn't matter, for the menu was self explanatory. In the center of the restaurant stood a troughlike brazier perhaps 12 feet long and 2 feet wide, crowned by a hand-hammered copper hood decorated with scenes of Turkish country life. Around the brazier ran a marble counter with seats for a dozen guests. It reminded me of a sushi bar that specialized in grilled lamb instead of raw fish.

Kiyi's (for such was the name of the restaurant) pit master is Murat Dademir, a big, gracious man in his thirties, from Adana in southern Turkey,

who tilts his head in a kindly way when you ask him a question. When I met him, he was making *adana kebab,* molding ground lamb spiced with fiery Aleppo chiles onto flat metal skewers by hand. In rapid succession he turned out some of Turkey's most popular grilled dishes: *iskander kebab,* thinly sliced ground lamb served over diced *pida* with yogurt, hot tomato sauce, and melted butter. Next came *durum*—thinly sliced grilled lamb wrapped with lettuce, tomato, onion, and yogurt in a sheet of lavash.

When Murat learned of my interest in Turkish grilling, he offered to make me a special salad called *ezmeli.* He laid a skewer of bull's horn peppers directly on the coals until the skins were charred and blistered. Tomatoes and slender Turkish eggplants were charred the same way. He scraped off the burnt skin (or most of it—a little was left on for flavor), then cut the vegetables into bite-size pieces. He tossed them with chopped parsley, fruity Turkish olive oil, and freshly squeezed lemon juice—exquisitely delicious proof that even a vegetarian can eat great grilled fare in Turkey.

In the end, I didn't have a favorite grill joint in Turkey. I enjoyed kebabs in a wide range of settings, at street stalls and restaurants on every level of the socioeconomic scale. That is to say, I ate like a Turk!

SHALLOT KEBABS WITH POMEGRANATE MOLASSES
Sogar Kebab

METHOD:
Direct grilling

SPECIAL EQUIPMENT:
8 flat, wide, long metal skewers

A specialty of the Imam Cagdas restaurant in Gaziantep, Turkey, this simple kebab is made with a small, red-skinned onion that looks like the familiar shallot. I've used both shallots and pearl onions with equal success. One unexpected touch: After grilling, the lamb and onions and a few drops of pomegranate molasses are placed in a covered dish for a few minutes. This steams the onions, imparting an incredible sweet-sour flavor to the meat.

1 pound ground lamb (see Ground Lamb, page 221)
1 clove garlic, minced
1 teaspoon salt, or more to taste
½ teaspoon ground cumin, or more to taste
½ teaspoon freshly ground black pepper, or more to taste
20 large shallots or pearl onions
Pita breads, for serving
2 to 3 teaspoons Pomegranate Molasses (recipe follows)

1. If desired, set up the grill for grateless grilling (see box, page 21). Preheat the grill to high.

2. Combine the lamb, garlic, 1 teaspoon salt, ½ teaspoon cumin, and ½ teaspoon pepper in a large bowl. Knead and squeeze the mixture with your hands until thoroughly blended, 3 to 4 minutes. To test the mixture for seasoning, sauté a small amount of it in a nonstick skillet until cooked through, then taste, adding salt, cumin, or pepper to the remaining mixture as necessary.

3. Peel the shallots and cut each lengthwise in half. Starting on the round sides, thread 5 shallot halves onto each skewer, leaving about 1 inch between each.

4. Line a baking sheet with plastic wrap. Divide the meat mixture into 32 equal portions. Lightly wet your hands with cold water, then take one portion of the meat and mold it around a skewer, between 2 shallot halves, making it as much as possible the same size. Repeat with the remaining portions of meat so each skewer contains 5 shallot halves alternating with 4 portions of meat. Place each kebab as it is made on the prepared baking sheet (see Note).

5. When ready to cook, if not using the grateless method, generously oil the grate. Arrange the kebabs on the grill as described in the grateless method, or arrange directly on the hot grate. Grill, turning with tongs, until the shallots are nicely browned and soft and the meat is browned as well and cooked through, about 12 minutes in all.

6. Use a pita to protect your hand as you slide the meat and shallots off their skewers into a serving bowl. Toss with the Pomegranate Molasses, cover, and let stand for 3 minutes. Divide the meat and shallots among serving plates and serve immediately, accompanied by the pita.

Makes 8 kebabs, serves 8 as an appetizer, 4 as an entrée

Note: If not planning to cook immediately, cover loosely with plastic wrap and refrigerate.

Pomegranate Molasses
Narshrab

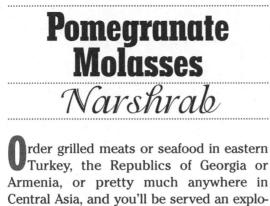

Order grilled meats or seafood in eastern Turkey, the Republics of Georgia or Armenia, or pretty much anywhere in Central Asia, and you'll be served an explosively flavorful, sweet-sour condiment that looks like liquid tar. Often it's drizzled on the food before it is served, as well. Known locally as *narshrab,* and as pomegranate molasses in the West, it consists of fresh pomegranate juice boiled down to a thick, perfumed syrup. A few drops drizzled over chops or kebabs has an amazing way of bringing out the flavor of grilled meats. Bottled *narshrab* can be found at Middle Eastern and Armenian markets (see Mail-Order Sources). Here's how to make it from scratch.

8 to 10 pomegranates (for 4 cups juice)
¼ cup sugar

1. Cut the pomegranates in half; juice them on a citrus reamer. You should have 4 cups. Strain the juice into a large, wide, heavy saucepan and add the sugar.

2. Bring the juice to a boil, reduce the heat and cook the pomegranate juice at a brisk simmer until dark, thick, syrupy, and reduced by two-thirds, 15 to 20 minutes. Transfer the pomegranate syrup to a sterile bottle or jar. It will keep for 2 months in the refrigerator.

Makes about 1½ cups

LAMB AND PISTACHIO KEBABS

TURKEY

METHOD:
Direct grilling

ADVANCE PREPARATION:
2 hours for chilling the meat

SPECIAL EQUIPMENT:
4 flat, wide, long metal skewers

These lovely ground lamb kebabs—flecked with crunchy green bits of pistachio nuts—are a specialty of the popular Develi restaurant in Istanbul. The restaurant's founder came from Gaziantep, Turkey's culinary capital near the Syrian border. In addition to its spicy cooking, Gaziantep is famed for its pistachios, which have an intense flavor and supernaturally bright green color. The nuts lend the meat a wonderful texture and flavor. For the best results, use Turkish pistachios, which are available at Middle or Near Eastern markets. Turkish Radish Salad, Onion Relish with Pomegranate Molasses (see Index), and pita bread would make great accompaniments.

1 pound ground lamb (see Ground Lamb, page 221)
½ cup shelled pistachio nuts, preferably Turkish, coarsely chopped by hand or in a food processor
¼ cup minced red onion
1 clove garlic, minced
1 teaspoon salt, or more to taste
1 teaspoon ground or flaked Aleppo pepper (see box, page 232) or pure chile powder
½ teaspoon ground cumin
½ teaspoon freshly ground black pepper, or more to taste
Pita bread, for serving

1. Combine the lamb, pistachios, onion, garlic, 1 teaspoon salt, the Aleppo pepper, cumin, and ½ teaspoon pepper into a large bowl. Knead and squeeze the mixture with your hands until thoroughly blended, 3 to 4 minutes. To test the mixture for seasoning, sauté a small amount of it in a nonstick skillet until cooked through, then taste, adding salt or pepper to the remaining mixture as necessary. Cover and refrigerate the meat mixture for 2 hours.

2. If desired, set up the grill for grateless grilling (see box, page 21). Preheat the grill to high.

3. Line a baking sheet with plastic wrap. Divide the meat mixture into 4 equal portions. Lightly wet your hands with cold water, then, starting about 1 inch from the tip of a skewer, mold each portion of the mixture around the skewer to form a flattish sausage about 11 inches long and ½ inch wide. Place each kebab as it is made on the prepared baking sheet.

4. When ready to cook, if not using the grateless method, generously oil the grate. Arrange the kebabs on the grill as described in the grateless method, or arrange directly on the hot grate. Grill, turning with tongs, until nicely browned and cooked through, 6 to 8 minutes in all.

5. Use a pita to protect your hand as you slide each sausage off its skewer onto a serving plate. Serve immediately.

Makes 4 sausages; serves 4 as an entrée

THE ORIGINAL KARIM'S SEEKH KEBAB

INDIA

METHOD:
Direct grilling

ADVANCE PREPARATION:
1 hour for chilling the meat

SPECIAL EQUIPMENT:
4 flat, wide, long metal skewers

Seekh kebab is the Indian version of sausage, ground spiced meat (or vegetables) molded onto square or flat skewers and grilled over charcoal. Sometimes the kebabs are cooked in the extremely high heat of a tandoor oven (especially at fancy restaurants), but traditionally they're grilled on a brazier. Flat skewers (at least ½ inch wide) work well, too, but don't use slender metal skewers or the meat will fall off.

There are probably as many versions of *seekh kebab* as there are grill jockeys in India. This one comes from the venerable Karim restaurant in New Delhi. Note the addition of *dal* (cooked split peas), which gives these kebabs a unique earthy flavor and texture. Don't be bashful about the fat in this recipe—the meat should have at least 20 percent—you need it to keep the kebabs moist. Besides, much of it melts out during the cooking. Accompany these succulent kebabs with an Indian bread (*naan*—Tandoori-Baked Flat Bread—is my first choice) and Afghan Coriander Sauce (see Index).

½ cup dried yellow split peas
¼ teaspoon ground turmeric
1 pound ground lamb (see Ground Lamb, page 221)
1 clove garlic, minced
2 scallions, both white and green parts, trimmed and minced
2 tablespoons chopped fresh cilantro
2 teaspoons grated fresh ginger
1 teaspoon salt, or more to taste
½ teaspoon cumin seeds, toasted (see box, page 93)
½ teaspoon freshly ground black pepper, or more to taste
¼ teaspoon cayenne pepper, or more to taste
1 small red onion or large shallot, very thinly sliced, for serving
Lemon wedges, for serving

1. Combine the split peas and turmeric in a medium-size saucepan with water to cover. Bring to a boil over high heat, then reduce the heat to medium and simmer the peas, uncovered, until just tender but not mushy, 12 to 15 minutes; you should be able to crush a properly cooked pea between your thumb and forefinger. Drain the peas in a colander and let cool.

2. Grind the cooled peas to a coarse meal in a food processor. Stir the peas into the lamb in a large bowl along with the garlic, scallions, cilantro, ginger, 1 teaspoon salt, the cumin seeds, $\frac{1}{2}$ teaspoon pepper, and $\frac{1}{4}$ teaspoon cayenne, then knead and squeeze the mixture with your hands until thoroughly blended, 3 to 4 minutes. To test the mixture for seasoning, sauté a small amount of it in a nonstick skillet until cooked through, then taste, adding salt, pepper, or cayenne to the remaining mixture as necessary; it should be highly seasoned. Cover and refrigerate the meat mixture for 1 hour.

3. If desired, set up the grill for grateless grilling (see box, page 21). Preheat the grill to high.

4. Line a baking sheet with plastic wrap. Divide the meat mixture into 4 equal portions. Lightly wet your hands with cold water, then, starting about 1 inch from the tip of a skewer, mold one portion of the mixture around the skewer to form a sausage about 10 inches long and 1 inch in diameter. Place each kebab as it is made on the prepared baking sheet (see Note).

5. When ready to cook, if not using the grateless method, generously oil the grate. Arrange the kebabs on the grill as described in the grateless method, or arrange directly on the hot oiled grate. Grill, turning with tongs, until nicely browned and cooked through, 6 to 8 minutes in all.

6. Slide each sausage off its skewer onto a serving plate (if serving with *naan,* use it to protect your hand as you remove the sausages). Serve accompanied by sliced onion and lemon wedges.

Makes 4 sausages; serves 4 as an entrée

Note: If not planning to cook immediately, cover loosely with plastic wrap and refrigerate.

LAMB IN LAVASH
Lyulya Kebab

AZERBAIJAN

METHOD:
Direct grilling

SPECIAL EQUIPMENT:
8 flat, wide, long metal skewers

Ground lamb kebabs are enjoyed throughout the Muslim world, from Sumatra to Marrakech, but they reach their apotheosis in Turkey, Iran, and the former Soviet republics of Central Asia. *Lyulya* is the Azerbaijani version, and the use of fragrant fresh basil and sweet-sour pomegranate seeds make it unique among the ground meat kebabs. This particular rendition, which comes from the restaurant in the Hyatt Regency in Baku, is served wrapped with fresh herbs in thin sheets of the paper-like Middle and Near Eastern flat bread called lavash. (Lavash is widely available in Middle Eastern markets and even many supermarkets.) The lavash —a sort of edible napkin—makes these kebabs perfect finger fare for a cookout.

FOR THE KEBABS:

1½ pounds ground lamb (see Ground Lamb, page 221)

1 small onion, finely chopped

2 tablespoons whole-wheat flour

¼ cup coarsely chopped fresh Italian (flat-leaf) parsley

¼ cup thinly slivered fresh basil leaves

1½ teaspoons salt, or more to taste

½ teaspoon freshly ground black pepper, or more to taste

FOR SERVING:

2 large lavash or 4 pita breads

24 fresh basil leaves

24 Italian (flat-leaf) parsley sprigs

4 scallions, both white and green parts, trimmed and thinly sliced

1 large pomegranate, broken into seeds

3 tablespoons ground sumac (optional; see box)

1. Place the lamb and onion in a food processor and process until the onion is ground very fine. Add the flour, chopped parsley, slivered basil, 1½ teaspoons salt, and ½ teaspoon pepper and process briefly to combine. To test the mixture for seasoning, sauté a small amount of it in a nonstick skillet until cooked through, then taste, adding salt or pepper to the remaining mixture as necessary; it should be highly seasoned. Transfer to a large bowl, cover, and refrigerate for 20 minutes.

2. If desired, set up the grill for grateless grilling (see box, page 21). Preheat the grill to high.

3. Line a baking sheet with plastic wrap. Divide the meat mixture into 8 equal portions. Lightly wet your hands with cold water, then mold each portion around a skewer to form a sausage about 12 inches long and ¾ inch wide. Place each kebab as it is made on the prepared baking sheet (see Note).

Sumac

Whenever you sit down to a meal of kebabs or *kofta* in the Middle East and Central Asia, you will be offered a dish of purplish red powder with a tart, lemony, almost sour plum flavor. This is sumac. Made from a Middle Eastern berry and available at Middle and Near Eastern and Armenian markets, sumac is used throughout the region as a seasoning for grilled meats and seafood. If unavailable, use a squeeze of lemon juice.

4. When ready to cook, if not using the grateless grill method, generously oil the grate. Arrange the kebabs as described in the grateless method, or arrange directly on the hot oiled grate. Grill, turning with tongs, until nicely browned on both sides and cooked through, 6 to 8 minutes in all.

5. Remove the kebabs to a platter and arrange the lavash in one layer on the grill grate. Grill just until warm and pliable, about 20 seconds per side. Remove from the grill and cut into 5 × 4 inch strips.

6. Use a strip of lavash to protect your hand as you slide each sausage off its skewer onto a platter. Cut each sausage into three 4-inch pieces. Wrap each piece, along with a whole basil leaf and a sprig of parsley, in a strip of lavash. Arrange the bundles on a serving platter and sprinkle with the sliced scallions and pomegranate seeds. Serve accompanied, if desired, by ground sumac.

Makes 24 pieces; serves 8 to 12 as an appetizer, 4 to 6 as an entrée

Note: If not planning to cook immediately, cover loosely with plastic wrap and refrigerate.

LAMB AND EGGPLANT KEBABS
Sedzeli Kebab

METHOD:
Direct grilling

SPECIAL EQUIPMENT:
8 flat, wide, long metal skewers

This colorful skewer is one of the most popular kebabs in Turkey, and given the mild, sweet flavor of Turkish eggplants, it's easy to see why. As the kebabs cook, the eggplant absorbs the lamb juices, creating one luscious combination. Another plus for health-conscious eaters is the high proportion of vegetables to meat. Choose eggplants that are rather long and narrow: Asian eggplants work well. Serve these kebabs with Onion Relish with Pomegranate Molasses and Turkish Radish Salad (see Index).

1 pound ground lamb (see Ground Lamb, page 221)
¼ cup minced red onion
1 clove garlic, minced
3 tablespoons finely chopped fresh Italian (flat-leaf) parsley
1 teaspoon salt, or more to taste
½ teaspoon ground cumin
½ teaspoon freshly ground black pepper, or more to taste
8 Asian or other long slender eggplants (each 6 to 7 inches long and 1½ inches wide)
Lavash or pita bread, for serving

1. If desired, set up the grill for grateless grilling (see box, page 21). Preheat the grill to high.

2. Place the lamb in a large bowl and mix in the onion, garlic, parsley, 1 teaspoon salt, the cumin, and ½ teaspoon pepper. Knead and squeeze the mixture with your hands until thoroughly blended, 3 to 4 minutes. To test the mixture for seasoning, sauté a small amount of it in a nonstick skillet until cooked through, then taste, adding salt or pepper to the remaining mixture as necessary; it should be highly seasoned.

3. Trim the ends off the eggplants and discard; cut each eggplant crosswise into 1½-inch rounds. Thread each round, through the cut sides, on a skewer, 4 to a skewer, spacing about 1½ inches apart.

4. Line a baking sheet with plastic wrap. Divide the meat mixture into 24 equal portions. Lightly wet your hands with cold water, then take one of the portions of meat and mold it around a skewer, between 2 eggplant rounds, making it as much as possible the same size and shape as the eggplant. Repeat with the remaining portions of meat so each skewer contains 4 eggplant rounds alternating with 3 portions of meat. Place each kebab as it is made on the prepared baking sheet (see Note).

5. When ready to cook, if not using the grateless method, generously oil the grate. Arrange the kebabs on the grill as described in the grateless method, or arrange directly on the hot oiled grate. Grill, turning with tongs, until nicely browned and cooked through, 12 to 16 minutes in all.

6. Use a lavash to protect your hand as you slide the meat and eggplant off their skewers onto serving plates. If desired, trim away the charred eggplant skin before eating. Serve accompanied by lavash.
Serves 4
Note: If not planning to cook immediately, cover loosely with plastic wrap and refrigerate.

CRACKED WHEAT AND LAMB KEBABS
Semit Kebab

TURKEY

METHOD:
Direct grilling

ADVANCE PREPARATION:
2 hours for soaking the bulgur

SPECIAL EQUIPMENT:
6 flat, wide, long metal skewers

The combination of lamb and bulgur (cracked wheat) is a popular one in the Near and Middle East. My favorite variation on this theme of grain and meat is Turkish *cig kofte,* a fiery pâté of chile-spiced bulgur and uncooked lean ground lamb. From this pâté, it's not much of a leap to *semit kebab* (bulgur kebab), a highly unusual and amazingly tasty kebab that's a specialty at the restaurant Cagdas in Gaziantep, Turkey. Bulgur gives the kebabs a firm, chewy texture, the mint and allspice reinforce the sweet flavor of the wheat, while the Aleppo pepper and hot paprika turn up the heat.

½ cup fine bulgur
1 pound ground lamb (see Ground Lamb, page 221)
1 small onion, minced
1 clove garlic, minced
2 teaspoons dried mint
1 teaspoon Aleppo pepper (see box this page) or hot paprika, or more to taste
1 teaspoon salt, or more to taste
½ teaspoon freshly ground black pepper, or more to taste
½ teaspoon hot red pepper flakes
¼ teaspoon ground allspice
Lavash or pita bread, for serving

1. Place the bulgur in a bowl with cold water to cover by 1 inch and let soak for 2 hours.

2. If desired, set up the grill for grateless grilling (see box, page 21). Preheat the grill to high.

3. Place the meat in a large bowl. Drain the bulgur in a strainer, then squeeze it

Aleppo Pepper

The Aleppo pepper is a small, round, reddish brown chile hailing from Syria and eastern Turkey. Usually sold powdered or in flakes, it has a clean, tart, almost metalic, ancho-like flavor with considerable heat. Look for it in Middle Eastern grocery stores or see Mail-Order Sources.

between your fingers to wring out all the water. Add the bulgur to the ground meat along with the onion, garlic, mint, 1 teaspoon Aleppo pepper, 1 teaspoon salt, ½ teaspoon black pepper, the hot pepper flakes, and allspice. Knead and squeeze the mixture with your hands until thoroughly blended, 3 to 4 minutes. To test the mixture for seasoning, sauté a small amount of it in a nonstick skillet until cooked through, then taste, adding Aleppo pepper, salt, or black pepper to the remaining mixture as necessary; it should be highly seasoned.

4. Line a baking sheet with plastic wrap. Divide the meat mixture into 6 equal portions. Lightly wet your hands with cold water, then mold each portion of the mixture around a skewer to form a sausage 11 to 12 inches long and 1 inch in diameter. Place each kebab as it is made on the prepared baking sheet (see Note).

5. When ready to cook, if not using the grateless method, generously oil the grate. Arrange the kebabs as described in the grateless method, or arrange directly on the hot oiled grate. Grill, turning with tongs, until nicely browned and cooked through, about 8 minutes in all.

6. Use a lavash to protect your hand as you slide each sausage off its skewer onto a serving plate. Serve immediately, accompanied by lavash.

Serves 4 to 6

Note: If not planning to cook immediately, cover loosely with plastic wrap and refrigerate.

"GENTLE AL" KEBABS WITH FIRE-CHARRED EGGPLANT AND YOGURT

VIETNAM

METHOD:
Direct grilling

ADVANCE PREPARATION:
1 to 2 hours for chilling the kebabs

SPECIAL EQUIPMENT:
4 flat, wide, long metal skewers

This is one of the most popular kebabs in Turkey—a glory of smoke and fire featuring two of the best ingredients ever to hit a barbecue grill: lamb and eggplant. Legend credits its invention to a kebab maker named Ali Nasik ("Gentle Al") from the city of Bursa. Gentle Al's brainstorm was to serve grilled, spiced ground lamb kebabs over a tangy purée made from fire-charred eggplant and yogurt. Today, you find the kebabs all over Turkey. For the sake of convenience, the eggplant purée can be prepared ahead. (I like to grill it the day before.) For a really great tasting purée, use whole-milk yogurt from a Middle Eastern market. Note that the dill in the lamb isn't strictly traditional, but I like the way it rounds out the flavor.

FOR THE KEBABS:
1 pound ground lamb (see Ground Lamb, page 221)
3 tablespoons minced onion
1 clove garlic, minced
1 tablespoon chopped fresh dill or 1½ teaspoons dried (optional)
1 teaspoon salt
½ teaspoon ground cumin
½ teaspoon freshly ground black pepper

FOR THE EGGPLANT PUREE
2 Asian or other long slender eggplants (about 10 ounces each)
2 cloves garlic, minced
1 to 1¼ cups whole-milk yogurt
1 tablespoon fresh lemon juice, or more to taste
1 teaspoon salt, or more to taste
½ teaspoon freshly ground black pepper, or more to taste

FOR FINISHING:
Pita bread
1 cup whole-milk yogurt
2 tablespoons chopped fresh Italian (flat-leaf) parsley

1. Combine the lamb, onion, garlic, dill (if using), salt, cumin, and pepper in a large bowl. Knead and squeeze the mixture with your hands until thoroughly blended, 3 to 4 minutes. To test the mixture for seasoning, sauté a small amount of it in a nonstick skillet until cooked through, then taste, adding salt or pepper to the remaining mixture as necessary.

2. Line a baking sheet with plastic wrap. Divide the meat mixture into 4 equal portions. Lightly wet your hands with cold water, then mold each portion around a skewer to form a sausage about 11 inches long and 1 inch in diameter. Place each kebab as it is made on the prepared baking sheet. Cover and refrigerate the kebabs for 1 to 2 hours.

3. Preheat the grill to high.

4. When ready to cook, place the eggplants on the hot grate and grill, turning with tongs, until the skin is charred on all sides and the flesh is soft, 20 to 30 minutes. Transfer the eggplants to a plate and let cool.

5. Scrape off as much of the charred skin as possible (it's not necessary to remove every bit). Cut the eggplant into chunks and process in a food processor until puréed. Transfer to a bowl and stir in the garlic, 1 cup yogurt, 1 tablespoon lemon juice, 1 teaspoon salt, and the pepper. The purée should be quite loose; add the remaining $\frac{1}{4}$ cup yogurt as needed. Correct the seasoning, adding lemon juice, salt, and pepper to taste; the mixture should be highly seasoned. Cover and set aside.

6. If necessary, add 20 to 24 fresh coals to bump up the grill heat to high. If desired, set up the grill for grateless grilling (see box, page 21).

7. When ready to cook, if not using the grateless method, generously oil the grate. Arrange the kebabs on the grill as described in the grateless method, or arrange directly on the hot oiled grate. Grill, turning with tongs, until nicely browned and cooked through, 6 to 8 minutes in all.

8. Meanwhile, warm the eggplant purée on one side of the grill in an uncovered medium-size saucepan.

9. Use a pita to protect your hand as you slide each sausage off its skewer onto a platter, then cut the sausages into 2-inch pieces. To serve, spoon the warmed eggplant purée into the center of 4 serving plates. Top each portion with $\frac{1}{4}$ cup of the yogurt and arrange a cut-up sausage on the yogurt. Sprinkle with parsley and serve immediately with the pita.

Makes 4 kebabs; serves 4

FOUR-PEPPER CHICKEN KEBABS
Kafta

IRAQ

METHOD:
Direct grilling

SPECIAL EQUIPMENT:
4 flat, wide, long metal skewers

Kafta (with its myriad other spellings) refers to a huge family of ground meat kebabs found as far east as India and as far west as Morocco. The traditional meat for *kafta* is lamb, often fatty lamb at that. Imagine my delight in finding a *kafta* made with America's favorite low-fat meat—boneless chicken breast. This recipe was inspired by a dish I had in Detroit's Fendi restaurant, which is owned by Caldeans, Iraqi Christians. These kebabs may be low in fat, but they're long on flavor, thanks to the colorful addition of paprika and the bell peppers. For milder *kafta,* use sweet paprika; for spicier, use hot. Serve with Central Asian Pickles, Persian-Style Steamed Rice, or Persian Rice with a Golden Crust (see Index).

1 pound skinless, boneless chicken breasts, trimmed of visible fat or sinews and cut into 1-inch cubes
1 clove garlic, minced
1 teaspoon salt, or more to taste
½ teaspoon freshly ground white pepper, or more to taste
½ teaspoon hot or sweet paprika, or more to taste
½ teaspoon ground cumin, or more to taste
3 tablespoons finely chopped Italian (flat-leaf) parsley
3 tablespoons minced green bell pepper
3 tablespoons minced red bell pepper
1 tablespoon olive oil, for brushing

1. Preheat the grill to high.

2. Combine the chicken, garlic, 1 teaspoon salt, ½ teaspoon each white pepper, paprika, and cumin in a food processor and process just to a coarse paste. Mix in the parsley and bell peppers, running the machine in short bursts; don't overgrind, or the parsley and peppers will make the mixture a drab color. To test the mixture for seasoning, sauté a small amount of it in a nonstick skillet until cooked through, then taste, adding salt, white pepper, paprika, or cumin to the remaining mixture as necessary; the mixture should be highly seasoned.

3. Line a baking sheet with plastic wrap. Divide the chicken mixture into 4 equal portions. Lightly wet your hands with cold water, then take one portion of the mixture and mold it onto a skewer to form a flattish sausage about 12 inches long and ¾ inch thick. Place each kebab as it is made on the prepared plate (see Note).

4. When ready to cook, brush the kebabs lightly with some of the oil. Arrange the kebabs on the hot grate, oiled side down, and grill until nicely browned on the first side, 2 to 4 minutes. Brush the tops of the kebabs with the remaining oil, turn with tongs, and continue cooking until cooked through, 2 to 4 minutes more. Serve immediately.

Makes 4 kebabs; serves 4

Note: If not planning to cook immediately, cover loosely with plastic wrap and refrigerate.

Bird Meets Grill

I'm standing at a rotisserie at a market in Provence, where rows of chickens slowly rotate on spits in front of a wall of fire. I could just as easily be in Turkey or Bali or Tuscany or the West Indies. Grilled chicken ranks among the world's most popular barbecue. The diversity of its preparation is limited only by the imagination of the world's grill jockeys.

In this chapter you'll learn how to grill all forms of chicken and other poultry, from quick-cook cuts like wings and breasts to whole chickens, ducks, and turkeys, which take advantage of the indirect method to achieve smoky, fall-off-the-bone tender-

Grilling chicken for a crowd is a venerable tradition in the American South.

ness. I'll tell you how to avoid the dual perils of serving under-cooked chicken and burning the highly flammable skin.

The variety of grilled chicken dishes from around the world is mind-boggling. During my travels I discovered fiery Portuguese Piri-Piri Chicken, fragrant game hens grilled with Moroccan spices, Pakistani Sea Captain's Chicken Tikka (marinated with yogurt and cardamom), and—a favorite on the American barbecue circuit Beer Can Chicken (a bird smoke-grilled on an open can of beer).

So pop the tops of your favorite six-pack and get ready to cook the perfect bird on the grill.

DIMPLES' BARBECUED CHICKEN

METHOD:
Indirect grilling

ADVANCE PREPARATION:
12 to 24 hours for marinating the chicken

SPECIAL EQUIPMENT:
1 cup oak or fruit wood chips, soaked for 1 hour in cold water to cover and drained

Jerk, especially jerk pork, is so famous in Jamaica, it's easy to forget that the island has other barbecued dishes. Among them is this incredibly flavorful, fall-off-the-bone-tender chicken, which I enjoyed by flickering torchlight at a riverside eatery called Boar Hill outside Kingston. The chef, although she would blush to be identified as such, was a pretty, short, shy woman named Fastina Sherman. Compliment her on her cooking, or simply ask her a question, and she would break into an embarrassed, deep-dimpled smile. No wonder everyone called her Dimples!

FOR THE CHICKEN:
1 whole chicken (3½ to 4 pounds)
1 bunch scallions, both white and green parts, trimmed and finely chopped
2 cloves garlic, minced
½ to 1 scotch bonnet chile, seeded and finely chopped, or ½ to 1 teaspoon scotch bonnet–based hot sauce
1 tablespoon sweet paprika
1 teaspoon fresh thyme or ½ teaspoon dried
½ teaspoon salt
½ teaspoon freshly ground black pepper
1½ tablespoons soy sauce
1 tablespoon vegetable oil

FOR THE BARBECUE SAUCE:
1 cup ketchup
⅓ cup soy sauce
4 scallions, both white and green parts, trimmed and minced
2 cloves garlic, minced
2 tablespoons minced fresh ginger
¼ to ⅓ cup firmly packed dark brown sugar, or more to taste
¼ cup distilled white vinegar, or more to taste
2 tablespoons dark rum

1. Remove and discard the fat just inside the body cavities of the chicken. Remove the package of giblets and set aside for another use. Rinse the chicken, inside and out, under cold running water, then drain and blot dry, inside and out, with paper towels. Set aside while you prepare the seasoning.

2. Combine the scallions, garlic, chile, paprika, thyme, salt, pepper, soy sauce, and oil in a small bowl and stir to mix or, for a richer flavor, combine the ingredients in a blender or mini processor and process to a smooth purée. Spoon half the mixture into the neck and body cavities of the chicken, then rub the remainder over the skin (or under it; see box, page 243) to cover completely. Place the chicken in a large, heavy-duty plastic bag with a zip-lock closing. Seal the bag and let the chicken marinate, in the refrigerator, for 12 to 24 hours, turning the bag over several times.

3. Prepare the barbecue sauce. Combine the ketchup, soy sauce, scallions, garlic, ginger, sugar, and vinegar in a medium-size nonreactive saucepan and bring to a boil over medium heat, stirring until the sugar is dissolved. Reduce the heat to low and simmer, uncovered, until thick and richly flavored, 10 to 12 minutes. Stir in the rum the last 2 minutes, then remove from the heat. You should have about 2 cups of sauce.

4. Set up the grill for indirect grilling (see page 14 or 16), placing a drip pan in the center. *If using a charcoal grill,* preheat it to medium.

If using a gas grill, place all the wood chips in the smoker box and preheat the grill to high; then, when smoke appears, lower the heat to medium.

5. When ready to cook, if using charcoal, toss half the wood chips on the coals. Oil the grill grate. Remove the chicken from the plastic bag and place, breast side up, on the hot grate over the drip pan. Cover the grill and cook the chicken for 45 minutes.

6. Uncover the grill and brush the chicken liberally with barbecue sauce. Cover again and continue grilling the chicken until the skin is mahogany brown and the juices run clear when the tip of a skewer or sharp knife is inserted in the thickest part of a thigh (see Note), 30 to 45 minutes more. If using charcoal, add 10 to 12 fresh coals per side and the remaining wood chips after 1 hour.

Continue to brush the chicken with sauce as it cooks.

7. Transfer the chicken to a cutting board or platter and let stand for 5 minutes before carving. Save accompanied by the remaining barbecue sauce. Save any leftover sauce in the refrigerator for up to 2 weeks.

Serves 2 to 4

Note: An instant-read meat thermometer inserted in the inner muscle of a thigh, not touching the bone, should register 180°F.

Poultry Grilling Chart*

CUT	METHOD	HEAT	DONENESS
			(WELL; 180°F)
CHICKEN			
WHOLE	INDIRECT	MEDIUM	1¼–1½ HRS
WHOLE	ROTISSERIE	HIGH	1–1¼ HRS
WHOLE (SPATCHCOCKED)	DIRECT	MED-HIGH	40 TO 60 MIN
BONELESS BREAST	DIRECT	HIGH	4–6 MIN/SIDE
BONE-IN BREAST	DIRECT	MED-HIGH	8–10 MIN/SIDE
WINGS	DIRECT	MED-HIGH	6–8 MIN/SIDE
LEGS	DIRECT	MED-HIGH	8–10 MIN/SIDE
GAME HEN			
WHOLE (SPATCHCOCKED)	DIRECT	MEDIUM	8–10 MIN/SIDE
DUCK			
WHOLE	ROTISSERIE	MED-HIGH	1½–2 HRS
WHOLE	INDIRECT	MEDIUM	2–2½ HRS
TURKEY			
WHOLE	INDIRECT	MEDIUM	15–20 MIN/LB

This chart is offered as a guideline to cooking times for the various types of poultry. Remember, grilling is an art, not a science. When in doubt, refer to times in the individual recipes.

How to Grill the Perfect Whole Chicken

*I*n my estimation, if you really want to cook the perfect whole chicken, you need to equip your grill with a rotisserie.

Why is spit-roasting over or next to an open flame such a perfect way to cook chicken? I have a few theories. First, the slow rotation in front of a live fire provides a gentle, even heat that cooks the legs through without drying out the breast meat. Second, as the bird cooks, the fat under the skin melts, basting the meat continuously. Third, the steady, even exposure to the flame crisps the skin without burning it.

GRILLING ON A ROTISSERIE

1. Start with a good chicken, preferably grain fed, free range, and organic. Remove and discard the fat just inside the body cavities of the chicken. Remove the package of giblets and set aside for another use. Rinse the chicken, inside and out, under cold running water, then drain and blot dry, inside and out, with paper towels.

2. Generously salt and pepper the bird, inside and out. For extra flavor you can put a peeled garlic clove, bay leaf, strip of lemon zest, and/or a sprig of rosemary inside the body and neck cavities. (My editor, Suzanne, inserts slices of garlic under the skin.)

3. Tightly truss the bird, using either butcher's string and a trussing needle or skewers. Trussing helps the meat cook evenly and it gives the bird an attractive shape for serving.

4. Set up the grill for rotisserie cooking (see page 20). If using charcoal, light 50 to 60 coals and let them burn down until glowing red and covered with a thin coat of ash. Rake one row of coals just in front of the place the chicken will be turning and one row just behind it. Place a drip pan directly under where the chicken will be.

If using a gas grill, turn the front and rear burners on high and leave the middle burner off. Put the drip pan in the center.

5. Place the chicken on the spit according to the rotisserie manufacturer's directions, then set the spit in place on the grill and turn the rotisserie on. Cook, covered if possible, until the chicken skin is gorgeously browned and the flesh is cooked through, 1 to 1¼ hours. Every 15 minutes or so, baste the rotating bird with the juices that accumulate in the drip pan. When cooked, the bird's internal temperature will read 180°F on an instant-read meat thermometer inserted in the inner muscle of one thigh, not touching the bone. Another test is to pierce the thickest part of the thigh with the tip of a skewer or sharp knife; the juices should run clear. Unspit the chicken and transfer it to a cutting board or platter. Let stand for 5 minutes before carving. Remove the trussing strings (or skewers) and get ready for great eating.

GRILLING WITHOUT A ROTISSERIE

You can also make a delicious chicken using the indirect grilling method. As above, you must start with a good chicken and season and truss it.

1. Set up the grill for indirect grilling (see page 14 or 16), placing a drip pan in the center of the grill, under the grate, and preheat to medium. Place the chicken, breast side up, on the hot grate over the drip pan.

2. Cover the grill and cook the chicken until the skin is nicely browned and the meat is cooked through (as determined above), 1¼ to 1½ hours. Baste the bird with the pan drippings every 20 minutes or so as it cooks. If using a charcoal grill, add 10 to 12 fresh coals per side per hour. Let the chicken stand for 5 minutes before carving and serving.

PIRI-PIRI CHICKEN

SOUTH AFRICA

METHOD:
Indirect grilling

ADVANCE PREPARATION:
4 to 12 hours for marinating the chicken

Piri-piri is the Portuguese name for a hot sauce made with tiny fiery chiles and vinegar. The chile was a New World food, of course, and the Portuguese seafarers of the fifteenth and sixteenth century deserve credit for introducing it to the rest of the world. You still find the sauce in Portugal and former Portuguese colonies of Brazil, Macao, Goa, Angola, and Mozambique. The South African love of *piri-piri* no doubt comes from the two last, its northern neighbors.

Note that at Brazilian markets, *piri-piri* goes by the name of *molho malagueta* (malagueta pepper sauce). For a mail-order source, see one of the hot sauce companies listed in the Mail-Order section. In a pinch you could use Tabasco sauce or even a Caribbean scotch bonnet chile–based hot sauce, but if you do, add a tablespoon or two of vinegar to the marinade.

2 whole chickens (3½ to 4 pounds each)
½ cup extra-virgin olive oil
8 tablespoons (1 stick) salted butter, melted
⅓ cup fresh lemon juice
3 to 4 tablespoons Portuguese Hot Sauce (page 478), malagueta pepper sauce, or other hot sauce (as much as you and your guests can bear)
1 tablespoon sweet paprika
1 teaspoon ground coriander
3 cloves garlic, peeled
3 scallions, both white and green parts, trimmed and sliced
3 tablespoons coarsely chopped fresh Italian (flat-leaf) parsley
1 piece (1 inch) fresh ginger, thinly sliced
2 bay leaves, crumbled
½ teaspoon salt
½ teaspoon freshly ground black pepper

1. Remove and discard the fat just inside the body cavities of the chickens. Remove the packages of giblets and set aside for another use. Rinse the chickens, inside and out, under cold running water, then drain and blot dry, inside and out, with paper towels. Spatchcock the chickens (see page 244), then place in a large, nonreactive bowl or baking dish and set aside while you prepare the marinade/sauce.

2. Combine the oil, melted butter, lemon juice, Portuguese Hot Sauce, paprika, coriander, garlic, scallions, parsley, ginger, bay leaves, salt, and pepper in a blender and process to a smooth purée. Pour half this sauce over the chickens in the bowl and coat the chickens with it, using your hands. Set aside the remaining mixture to serve with the chickens. Cover and let the chickens marinate, in the refrigerator, for 4 to 12 hours (the longer the better); transfer the remaining sauce to a small bowl and refrigerate, covered, until serving time. Bring the sauce to room temperature before serving.

3. Set up the grill for indirect grilling (see page 14 or 16), placing one large or two smaller drip pans in the center, and preheat to medium (see Note).

4. When ready to cook, oil the grill grate. Place the chickens, skin side up, on the hot grate, reserving any marinade in the bowl. Brush the chickens with the marinade, then cover the grill and cook for 30 minutes. Uncover and brush the chickens with any remaining marinade. Cover again and continue grilling the chickens until the juices run clear when the tip of a skewer or sharp knife is inserted in the thickest part of a thigh or an instant-read meat thermometer inserted in the inner muscle of a thigh registers 180°F, 30 to 45 minutes more. If a crisp skin is desired, place the chickens, skin side down, on the grill grate directly over the fire for the last 5 to 10 minutes.

5. Using long spatulas, carefully transfer the chickens to a cutting board or platter and let stand for 5 minutes before carving. Serve accompanied by the reserved sauce.

Serves 4 to 8

Note: For a smokier flavor, you can cook the chickens using the direct method rather than the indirect method. Preheat the grill to medium, oil the grate, and add the chickens to the hot grate skin side down. Grill, uncovered, for 15 to 20 minutes per side, turning the birds very carefully with long spatulas so they stay in one piece.

BEER CAN CHICKEN

U.S.A.

METHOD:
Indirect grilling

SPECIAL EQUIPMENT:
1½ cups mesquite chips, soaked in cold water to cover for 1 hour and drained

This odd recipe makes some of the most moist, succulent, flavorful barbecued chicken I've ever tasted. The secret: an open can of beer is inserted into the cavity of the bird, which is cooked upright on the grill. Besides being incredibly tender, the bird makes a great conversation piece. The recipe was inspired by the Bryce Boar Blazers, a barbecue team from Texas I met at the Memphis in May World Championship Barbecue Cooking Contest. The proper beverage? Beer, of course.

1 large whole chicken (4 to 5 pounds)
3 tablespoons Memphis Rub (page 490) or your favorite dry barbecue rub
1 can (12 ounces) beer

1. Remove and discard the fat just inside the body cavities of the chicken. Remove the package of giblets, and set aside for another use. Rinse the chicken, inside and out, under cold running water, then drain and blot dry, inside and out, with paper towels. Sprinkle 1 tablespoon of the rub inside the body and neck cavities, then rub another 1 tablespoon all over the skin of the bird. If you wish, rub another ½ tablespoon of the mixture between the flesh and skin (see box, facing page). Cover and refrigerate the chicken while you preheat the grill.

2. Set up the grill for indirect grilling (see page 14 or 16), placing a drip pan in the center. *If using a charcoal grill,* preheat it to medium.

If using a gas grill, place all the wood chips in the smoker box and preheat the grill to high; then, when smoke appears, lower the heat to medium.

3. Pop the tab on the beer can. Using a "church key"–style can opener, make 6 or 7 holes in the top of the can. Pour out the top inch of beer, then spoon the remaining dry rub through the holes into the beer. Holding the chicken upright, with the opening of the body cavity down, insert the beer can into the cavity.

4. When ready to cook, if using charcoal, toss half the wood chips on the coals. Oil the grill grate. Stand the chicken up in the center of the hot grate, over the drip pan. Spread out the legs to form a sort of tripod, to support the bird.

5. Cover the grill and cook the chicken until fall-off-the-bone tender, 2 hours. If using charcoal, add 10 to 12 fresh coals per side and the remaining wood chips after 1 hour.

6. Using tongs, lift the bird to a cutting board or platter, holding a large metal spatula underneath the beer can for support. (Have the board or platter right next to the bird to make the move shorter. Be careful not to spill hot beer on yourself.) Let stand for 5 minutes before carving the meat off the upright carcass. (Toss the beer can out along with the carcass.)

Serves 4 to 6

A Marinating Tip

From time to time, pit masters are required to perform feats of surgery. Consider the strange process of placing a rub or marinade under the skin of a chicken or other bird before grilling.

As far as seasonings are concerned, at least, chicken skin is not the permeable membrane you'd expect it to be. Spices simply can't get through it. But put the rub or marinade *under* the skin and the meat will soak up the flavorings like a sponge. And the skin seals in the juices. Here's how to do it.

1. Gently loosen the skin from the body of the bird. To do so, start at the neck and tunnel your fingers, then your whole hand, under the skin to separate it from the breast meat. Slide your hand in deeper to loosen the skin over the thighs, drumsticks, and back. Work carefully so as not to tear the skin. This may feel a little weird at first, but it gets easier with practice.

2. Spread the rub or marinade under the skin with your fingers or a spoon. Place the bird on a platter or in a roasting pan, cover, and let marinate, in the refrigerator, for several hours or as long as the recipe instructs.

3. Use the same technique to flavor halved or quartered birds as well as whole breasts.

BAHAMIAN GRILLED CHICKEN

BAHAMAS

METHOD:
Direct grilling (two-tiered)

ADVANCE PREPARATION:
30 minutes to 2 hours for marinating the chicken

On most of the islands of the Caribbean, it's common to rinse chicken and meats in lime juice before cooking. The practice probably originated in the days before refrigeration, when the citrus juice served as both a flavoring and disinfectant. Today we prize the lime juice for the tart, tangy flavor it imparts to the chicken.

Serve with Bahamian Peas and Rice (see Index).

1 chicken (3½ to 4 pounds), quartered, or 4 bone-in chicken breast halves with skin
1 cup fresh lime juice
1 small onion, thinly sliced
2 cloves garlic, minced
½ to 2 scotch bonnet or other hot chiles, thinly sliced
2 teaspoons chopped fresh thyme or 1 teaspoon dried
2 tablespoons vegetable oil
1 tablespoon paprika
1 teaspoon salt
½ teaspoon freshly ground white pepper

1. Rinse the chicken pieces under cold running water, then drain and blot dry with paper towels. Place the pieces in a nonreactive bowl or baking dish and pour in the lime

juice; turn the pieces to coat. Let marinate, at room temperature, for 15 minutes, turning the pieces once or twice.

2. Pour off and discard the lime juice, then add the onion, garlic, chile, thyme, oil, paprika, salt, and pepper and turn the chicken pieces to coat thoroughly. Let the chicken marinate in this mixture for at least 15 minutes or as long as 1 to 2 hours (the longer the better), covering and refrigerating if marinating the longer time.

3. Preheat the grill, using the two-tiered method (see page 14).

4. When ready to cook, oil the grill grate. Using a rubber spatula, scrape any bits of onion or garlic off the chicken pieces. Arrange the pieces, skin side down, on the grate over the hotter section of the grill and cook for 3 to 5 minutes, then finish cooking as directed in steps 3 and 4 in the box on page 246.

5. Transfer the chicken pieces to serving plates or a platter and serve.

Serves 4

How to Spatchcock a Chicken or Game Hen

A chicken or game hen that has been spatchcocked has been partially boned and butterflied (spread open). This speeds up the cooking process and enables you to cook a whole chicken using the direct grilling method, since you expose a lot more of the surface area of the meat to the flames.

Spatchcocking may seem intimidating the first time you do it, but you'll get the hang of it quickly.

1. Remove and discard the fat just inside the body cavities of the chicken or game hen; rinse the bird, inside and out, under cold running water, then drain and blot dry, inside and out, with paper towels. Place the bird, breast side down, on a cutting board. Using poultry shears, cut through the flesh and bone along both sides of the backbone. Cut from the tail end to the head end and completely remove the backbone.

2. Open out the bird, like opening a book, by gently pulling the halves apart. Using a sharp paring knife, lightly score the top of the breastbone. Run your thumbs along and under the sides of the breastbone and attached cartilage and pop them out. Spread the bird out flat.

3. Turn the bird over. Using a sharp knife, make a slit in the skin between the lower end of the breastbone and the leg, on each side, 1 inch long for a chicken, ½ inch for a game bird. Stick the end of the drumstick on that side through the slit. (This step is optional, but it gives you a more attractive bird.)

CHICKEN WITH LEMON MUSTARD SAUCE

Yassa

SENEGAL

METHOD:
*Direct grilling
(two-tiered)*

**ADVANCE
PREPARATION:**
*2 to 12 hours for
marinating the
chicken*

I first encountered this dish at a Senegalese restaurant in Washington, D.C. It was a fairly mild version of a dish that can be quite fiery, flavored as it traditionally is with the African equivalent of a scotch bonnet chile. The recipe is unusual by Western barbecue standards, but quite typical of Africa, in that the meat is grilled first, then simmered in sauce.

FOR THE CHICKEN AND SPICE PASTE:
1 chicken (3½ to 4 pounds), quartered
8 cloves garlic, peeled
1 to 2 scotch bonnet chiles (for a milder
     marinade, seed the chiles)
1½ teaspoons salt
1 teaspoon freshly ground black pepper
3 tablespoons vegetable oil

FOR THE LEMON MUSTARD SAUCE:
1 large onion, finely chopped
     (about 2 cups)
1 cup grainy French mustard
½ cup vegetable oil
¼ cup fresh lemon juice
12 green olives, pitted and thinly sliced
1 bay leaf
½ to 1 scotch bonnet chile (for a
     milder sauce, seed the chiles)
Salt and freshly ground black pepper,
     to taste

1. Rinse the chicken pieces under cold running water, then drain and blot dry with paper towels. Make 1 or 2 deep slashes, to the bone, in each piece, then place in a nonreactive baking dish large enough to hold the pieces in a single layer. Set aside while you prepare the spice paste.

2. Combine the garlic, chiles, salt, and pepper in a mortar and pound to a paste with the pestle, then work in the oil; or combine the oil with the other ingredients in a blender and process until smooth. Using your fingers, stuff half the spice paste into the slashes in each piece of chicken, then spread the remainder over the skin. Cover and let marinate, in the refrigerator, for 2 to 12 hours (the longer the better).

3. Preheat the grill, using the two-tiered method (see page 14).

4. Meanwhile, prepare the sauce. Select a heavy nonreactive saucepan or flameproof casserole large enough to hold the chicken and in it combine the onion, mustard, oil, lemon juice, olives, bay leaf, chile, and salt and pepper. Stir well to mix and bring to a boil over medium heat, then reduce the heat to low. Simmer, uncovered, stirring frequently, until the onion is soft and the sauce is thick and creamy and the oil has started to separate out, about 15 minutes. Remove from the heat and taste for seasoning, adding salt and pepper to taste. Discard the bay leaf and chile. Set the sauce aside, covered.

5. When ready to cook the chicken, oil the grill grate. Arrange the chicken pieces, skin side down, on the grate over the hotter section of the grill and cook as directed in steps 3 and 4 on page 246.

6. Transfer the chicken to the saucepan with the sauce and bring to a simmer over low heat, spooning the sauce over the chicken to coat. Cover and cook until the chicken is well flavored by the sauce, 4 to 5 minutes.

7. Transfer the chicken pieces to serving plates or a platter, spoon the sauce over, and serve.
Serves 4

How to Grill Perfect Chicken Halves and Quarters

Chicken is one of the most popular foods to grill, yet it causes more trouble than any other grilled fare. More often than not, people serve birds that are burnt on the outside and raw in the center. It's understandable: A halved or quartered chicken with the skin on presents a twofold challenge.

The first problem is that the fat in the skin melts and causes flare-ups. The second problem is that, because it contains bones, chicken takes longer to cook than, say, steaks or burgers. And because of food safety issues, you don't want to eat chicken anything less than well done.

To cook chicken halves or quarters to perfection, use the two-tiered method, which will enable you to control the heat by moving the birds back and forth over hotter and cooler sections of the grill:

1. *If using charcoal:* When you build your fire, pile the coals in a double layer on one side of the grill and in a single layer on the other.

If using a gas grill: Preheat one side to high, the other to medium. In either case, leave yourself plenty of room, so you can move the birds around to avoid flare-ups.

2. Season the chicken pieces with salt, pepper, or any other seasonings you plan to use.

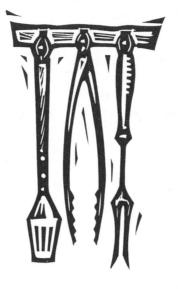

3. After oiling the grill grate, place the pieces, skin side down, on the hotter section of the grill. Cook until the skin starts to brown, 3 to 5 minutes. Move the pieces to the cooler section of the grill and continue grilling until the skin is thoroughly browned, 5 to 7 minutes more. Watch carefully and use tongs to move the pieces away from flare-ups.

4. Turn the pieces and move them back to the hotter section of the grill. Brown the second side well (3 to 5 minutes), then move the pieces back to the cooler side of the grill to finish cooking. The total cooking time will be 16 to 24 minutes. When ready, the chicken will be crisp and golden-brown outside and the juices will run clear when the meat is pierced.

5. If the recipe calls for basting and you are using an oil- or wine-based marinade, you can brush the chicken continuously. If using a sugar-based marinade, start brushing it on during the last 5 minutes of grilling.

FOR THE CHICKEN-HEARTED: BIRD WITHOUT FLAMES

You can avoid the risk of flare-ups entirely by grilling halved or quartered chickens using the indirect method. Set up the grill for indirect grilling (see page 14 or 16), placing a drip pan in the center, under the grate, and preheat to medium. When ready to cook, oil the grill grate. Place the chicken pieces, skin side down, on the hot grate, over the pan. Cover the grill and cook until the juices run clear, about 40 minutes for halved birds, 30 to 40 minutes for chicken quarters. (In general, breast pieces require less cooking time than leg pieces.) The advantage of this method is that it's absolutely failproof; the disadvantage is that the bird will lack the charred flavor you get cooking over direct flames.

BRAZILIAN BEER CHICKEN

BRAZIL

METHOD:
*Direct grilling
(two-tiered)*

**ADVANCE
PREPARATION:**
*6 hours to 2 days
for marinating
the chicken*

The United States isn't the only place where beer and barbecue are inextricably interwoven. In Rio de Janeiro, I came across this savory grilled chicken, which owes its exceptional succulence to a two-day bath in beer. Try, if possible, to find a Brazilian beer if you can: Antarctica (a pilsener-style brew) will produce a mild-flavored chicken; Xingu Black Beer (a dark bitter stout) will produce a bird with a rich, malty flavor.

Serve with Crazy Rice or Brazilian Black Beans with Bacon (see Index).

2 cups beer
½ cup vegetable oil
½ cup Dijon mustard
1 tablespoon sweet paprika
**1 teaspoon freshly ground black
   pepper**
1 medium onion, thinly sliced
12 cloves garlic, thinly sliced
2 bay leaves
**1 chicken (3½ to 4 pounds),
   quartered**
Coarse (kosher or sea) salt

1. Combine the beer, oil, mustard, paprika, and pepper in a large nonreactive bowl and whisk thoroughly to blend. Stir in the onion, garlic, and bay leaves.

2. Rinse the chicken pieces under cold running water, then drain and blot dry with paper towels. Add to the marinade in the bowl and turn to coat. Cover and let marinate, in the refrigerator, for 6 hours or up to 2 days (the longer the better), turning the pieces occasionally.

3. Preheat the grill, using the two-tiered method (see page 14).

4. When ready to cook, remove the chicken pieces from the marinade, reserving the marinade, and blot dry. Season the pieces generously with salt. Oil the grill grate and arrange the chicken, skin side down, on the grate over the hotter section of the grill and cook as directed in steps 3 and 4 in the box on the facing page. During the first 10 minutes only, brush several times with the reserved marinade.

5. Transfer the chicken pieces to serving plates and serve immediately.
Serves 4

BALINESE GRILLED CHICKEN WITH APPLE-MACADAMIA CHILE SAUCE

INDONESIA

METHOD:
*Direct grilling
(two-tiered)*

I first tasted this sweet-spicy grilled chicken at the Amandari Resort in Ubud, Bali. It was so good I all but ate the bones. Amandari is a luxurious hotel perched on the top tier of a rice paddy. You stroll out onto your terrace and observe a method of agriculture that's as ageless as Bali itself.

ADVANCE
PREPARATION:
*4 to 12 hours for
marinating the
chicken*

The original recipe calls for wonderful-sounding exotic ingredients, including candlenuts and *kencur* (lesser galangal). To make the recipe more user friendly, I've substituted macadamia nuts and ginger, but if you can find these ingredients, by all means make the authentic recipe. And to make the recipe more health conscious, I've substituted vegetable oil for the original coconut oil. Tamarind water is exotic, but it's easy to prepare and I've included a recipe for it in this book. Balsamic vinegar makes a readily available substitute. Serve with Balinese Yellow Rice (see Index).

FOR THE CHICKEN AND MARINADE:
½ cup Tamarind Water (page 219), or
　　¼ cup balsamic vinegar
2 tablespoons vegetable oil
2 cloves garlic, minced
1½ teaspoons salt
½ teaspoon freshly ground black pepper
1 chicken (3½ to 4 pounds), quartered,
　　or 4 bone-in chicken breast halves
　　with skin

FOR THE SAUCE:
2 tablespoons vegetable oil
2 shallots, minced
2 cloves garlic, minced
1 to 2 fresh hot red chiles, minced
　　(for a milder sauce, seed
　　the chiles)
1 tablespoon minced fresh ginger
½ teaspoon ground turmeric
5 macadamia nuts, coarsely
　　chopped
1 large Granny Smith apple, peeled,
　　cored, and finely chopped
1 cup chicken broth, homemade or
　　canned low-sodium
2 teaspoons Asian fish sauce or
　　soy sauce, or to taste
1 teaspoon fresh lime juice, or more
　　to taste
Salt and freshly ground black pepper,
　　to taste

1. Combine the Tamarind Water, oil, garlic, salt, and pepper in a large nonreactive bowl and whisk to mix. Rinse the chicken pieces under cold running water, then drain and blot dry with paper towels. Add the pieces to the mixture in the bowl and turn to coat. Cover and let marinate, in the refrigerator, for 4 to 12 hours (the longer the better).

2. Preheat the grill, using the two-tiered method (see page 14).

3. Meanwhile, prepare the sauce. Heat the oil in a medium-size nonreactive saucepan over medium heat. Add the shallots, garlic, chile, and ginger and sauté until lightly browned, about 4 minutes. Stir in the turmeric, macadamia nuts, and apple and sauté until the apple is soft, 3 to 5 minutes. Add the broth, 2 teaspoons fish sauce, and the teaspoon of lime juice and bring to a boil. Boil, uncovered, for 3 minutes, stirring occasionally. Remove from the heat and transfer the mixture to a blender. Process to a smooth purée, then return to the pan and simmer, uncovered, over low heat until thick and richly flavored, 3 to 5 minutes longer. Remove from the heat and taste for seasoning, adding fish sauce, lime juice, and salt and pepper as necessary; the sauce should be highly seasoned. Keep warm, covered (see Note).

4. When ready to cook, oil the grill grate. Remove the chicken pieces from the marinade; discard the marinade. Arrange the pieces, skin side down, on the grate over the hotter section of the grill and cook for 3 to 5 minutes, then finish cooking as directed in steps 3 and 4 on page 246.

5. Transfer the chicken pieces to serving plates or a platter and spoon the sauce on top, to serve.

Serves 4

Note: The sauce can be prepared up to 48 hours ahead of time. Refrigerate, covered, and reheat before serving.

TANDOORI CHICKEN
Tandoori Murgh

METHOD:
Direct grilling

**ADVANCE
PREPARATION:**
*4 hours for
making the
yogurt cheese
(optional), plus
4 hours for
marinating the
chicken*

**SPECIAL
EQUIPMENT:**
*2 or 3 long metal
skewers*

Tandoori chicken is the most popular of all Indian barbecue dishes—exquisite to eat by itself and a starting point for many more sophisticated dishes, including Grilled Chicken Salad with Indian Spices (see Index). The bird owes its extraordinary moistness, tenderness, and flavor to a double marinade—first a tenderizing bath of lemon juice and chile powder, then a flavorful paste of ginger, garlic, saffron, and yogurt.

If you have the time to drain the yogurt, as called for in step 1, you'll get a richer tandoori. If you're in a hurry, use 1 cup undrained yogurt. I've given a range for the cayenne: 1 teaspoon will give you gently spicy tandoori; 3 teaspoons will produce a bird that bites back. I've made the orange food coloring optional, but most Indian chefs would use it. This recipe calls for a cut-up whole chicken, but you could certainly make chicken tandoori with boneless breasts. For the latter, cut the marinating times in half and cook as directed on page 262.

Serve with *naan* (Tandoori-Baked Flat Breads), Quick-Cook Basmati Rice, and Afghan Coriander Sauce (see Index).

FOR THE YOGURT MARINADE:
1½ cups plain whole-milk yogurt
¼ teaspoon saffron threads
3 to 4 tablespoons warm water
5 cloves garlic, sliced
1 piece fresh ginger (2 inches), sliced
1 teaspoon salt
½ teaspoon freshly ground black pepper
½ cup heavy cream or sour cream
1 teaspoon Quick Garam Masala (page 499)
1 to 2 drops orange food coloring (optional)

FOR THE CHICKEN:
1 chicken (3½ to 4 pounds), cut into
    8 pieces (see box, page 255)
1 to 3 teaspoons cayenne pepper
1½ teaspoons salt
½ teaspoon freshly ground black pepper
½ cup fresh lemon juice
3 tablespoons unsalted butter,
    melted

1. Set a yogurt strainer, or regular strainer lined with a double layer of dampened cheesecloth, over a bowl. Add the yogurt to the strainer and let drain, in the refrigerator, for 4 hours.

2. When ready to finish the marinade, place the saffron in a small bowl and crush to a power with a pestle or the end of a wooden spoon. Stir in 3 tablespoons warm water and let stand for 2 minutes; then combine with the garlic and ginger in a blender or spice mill and process to a smooth paste, adding more water if necessary.

3. Remove the drained yogurt from the refrigerator and discard the liquid. Transfer the yogurt to a large bowl and stir in the saffron mixture, salt, pepper, cream, and *garam masala* until thoroughly blended and smooth. If desired, stir in food coloring to the desired tint. Set the marinade aside while you prepare the chicken.

4. Rinse the chicken pieces under cold running water and remove and discard the skin. Then drain and blot dry with paper towels. Make 2 deep slashes, to the bone, in the fleshy side of each piece. Place the pieces in a nonreactive baking dish large enough to hold the pieces in one layer. Combine the cayenne, salt, and black pepper in a small bowl, then sprinkle the mixture over the chicken, rubbing it in thoroughly with your fingers, making sure it gets into the slashes. Add the lemon juice and turn the pieces to coat. Let marinate, at room temperature, for 15 minutes.

5. Drain the chicken and add to the yogurt marinade, stirring to coat the pieces completely. Cover and let marinate, in the refrigerator, for 4 hours, turning the pieces occasionally.

6. Preheat the grill to high.

7. When ready to cook, remove the chicken from the marinade and thread onto skewers, leaving 2 inches between each piece to allow for better heat circulation. Oil the grill grate and arrange the skewers on the hot grate. Grill, turning with tongs, until browned but not fully cooked, about 4 min-

utes per side (8 minutes in all). Transfer the skewers to a large platter (see Note).

8. Brush the chicken pieces generously on all sides with melted butter and return the skewers to the grate. Grill until the chicken is nicely charred on the outside and the juices run clear when the tip of a skewer or sharp knife is inserted in the thickest part of a thigh and the breast meat near the bone shows no trace of pink, 2 to 4 more minutes per side, 4 to 8 more minutes in all.

9. Unskewer the chicken pieces onto serving plates or a platter and serve.

Serves 4

Note: Many Indian chefs cook the chicken ahead of time to this point, finishing it at the last minute to order. If you decide to do this, refrigerate the chicken, covered, if you are going to wait longer than 30 minutes.

BUCCANEER CHICKEN
Poulet Boucanée

GUADELOUPE

METHOD:
Indirect grilling

ADVANCE PREPARATION:
24 hours for marinating the chicken

When the Europeans first came to the wilds of Hispaniola, they observed a singular style of cooking. The Carib Indians would cure wild boar and other game with salt and spices, then dry it over a smoky fire. The Carib word for this technique sounded to European ears like "boucan." As for the first Europeans to practice this style of cooking, they were shipwrecked sailors and religious iconoclasts, who hid out in the wilds of what is now northwestern Haiti. They became known as the buccaneers. *Poulet boucanée* (buccaneer-style chicken) remains popular in the French West Indies.

This recipe may seem a little involved, but actually it's a series of simple steps. The only tricky part will be finding sugarcane, and thanks to exotic produce companies, like Frieda's Finest, fresh cane can be found at many supermarkets and specialty produce shops. Other good outlets include Hispanic and Asian markets.

The following recipe is designed for a charcoal or gas barbecue grill. If you have a patio-style smoker, you can smoke the chicken in it, using sugarcane instead of wood chips. For any type of cooker, if you can't find sugarcane, use the chips.

2 chickens (each 3½ to 4 pounds),
    quartered
3 limes
8 cloves garlic, crushed
1 bunch scallions, both white and green
    parts, trimmed and coarsely chopped
1 small onion, finely chopped
½ cup chopped fresh Italian (flat-leaf) parsley
1 to 3 scotch bonnet chiles or other hot
    peppers, thinly sliced (for a milder
    marinade, seed the chiles)
1 tablespoon chopped fresh thyme or
    1½ teaspoons dried
1 tablespoon whole cloves
2 teaspoons black peppercorns
2 teaspoons allspice berries
1 cinnamon stick (3 inches long)
1 whole nutmeg
6 cups water
1 cup dark rum
1 tablespoon red wine vinegar
3 tablespoons salt
2 tablespoons firmly packed brown sugar

1. Rinse the chicken pieces under cold running water, then drain and blot dry with paper towels. Set aside while you prepare the marinade.

2. Cut the limes in half and squeeze the juice into a large nonreactive bowl. Toss in the lime rinds, then add the remaining ingredients and stir until the salt and sugar are dissolved. Add the chicken pieces and turn to coat with the marinade, then cover and let marinate, in the refrigerator, for 24 hours.

3. Set up the grill for indirect grilling (see page 14 or 16), placing a drip pan in the center. *If using a charcoal grill,* preheat it to medium.

If using a gas grill, place the sugarcane in the smoker box and preheat the grill to high; then, when smoke appears, lower the heat to medium.

4. When ready to cook, if using charcoal, toss all the sugarcane on the coals. Remove the chickens from the marinade, discarding the marinade, and blot dry. Oil the grill grate, then arrange the chicken pieces, skin side down, on the hot grate over the drip pan. Cover the grill and cook the chicken until the juices run clear when the tip of a skewer or sharp knife is inserted in the thickest part of a thigh and the breast meat near the bone shows no trace of pink, 1 to 1½ hours (see Note). If using charcoal, add 10 to 12 fresh coals per side after 1 hour.

5. Transfer to serving plates or a platter and serve immediately; or refrigerate, covered, to serve cold later.

Serves 8

Note: Because the chicken is smoked rather than grilled, the meat near the joints may remain a little pink, even when the chicken is fully cooked.

BAXTER ROAD GRILLED CHICKEN

Baxter Road at midnight is one of the highlights of a food lover's tour of Barbados. I doubt many visitors make it to this rough-and-tumble row of cook stalls that spring up nightly along an equally rough-and-tumble street on the outskirts of Bridgetown. The chicken owes its exceptional succulence and flavor to Barbados's national marinade, which is called, simply, "seasonin'." A tangy paste based on garlic, chives, peppers, and thyme, "seasonin'" is considerably milder than Jamaican jerk, which makes it ideal for people who can't stand chile hellfire.

ADVANCE PREPARATION: 4 to 12 hours for marinating the chicken

1 chicken (3½ to 4 pounds), quartered
4 cloves garlic, peeled
3 shallots, peeled
1 bunch of chives or scallions, trimmed
1 medium green bell pepper, stemmed, seeded, and coarsely chopped
1 medium rib celery, coarsely chopped
1 scotch bonnet chile or 2 jalapeño chiles, seeded and minced (for a milder marinade, seed the chiles)
3 tablespoons chopped fresh Italian (flat-leaf) parsley
2 teaspoons chopped fresh thyme or 1 teaspoon dried
2 tablespoons fresh lime juice, or to taste
2 tablespoons soy sauce
2 tablespoons olive oil
Salt and freshly ground black pepper, to taste

1. Rinse the chicken pieces under cold running water, then drain and blot dry with paper towels. Place in a large nonreactive bowl or baking dish and set aside while you prepare the marinade.

2. Combine the garlic, shallots, chives, bell pepper, celery, chile, parsley, and thyme in a food processor and process to a smooth paste. Add 2 tablespoons lime juice, the soy sauce, and oil and process until blended and smooth. Taste for seasoning and add salt, pepper, and lime juice as needed; the mixture should be highly seasoned. Pour the mixture over the chicken in the bowl and turn the pieces to coat. Cover and let marinate, in the refrigerator, for 4 to 12 hours (the longer the better).

3. Preheat the grill, using the two-tiered method (see page 14).

4. When ready to cook, oil the grill grate. Remove the chicken pieces from the bowl, reserving any marinade that has drained off. Arrange the pieces, skin side down, on the grate over the hotter section of the grill and cook as directed in steps 3 and 4 on page 246. Brush the pieces once or twice with the reserved marinade, but not during the last 5 minutes.

5. Transfer the chicken pieces to serving plates or a platter and serve.

Serves 4

SEA CAPTAIN'S CHICKEN TIKKA

PAKISTAN

METHOD: Direct grilling

ADVANCE PREPARATION: 6 to 12 hours for marinating the chicken

This recipe demonstrates the ambassadorial powers of barbecue. I got it from a Pakistani sea captain, one Mushtaque Ahmad, whom I met on a Singapore Airlines flight from Singapore to Bangkok. (The captain was on his way home to Karachi after seven months at sea.) Our conversation began about the O. J. Simpson trial and eventually led to cooking. Here's how the captain prepares a spicy, yogurt-marinated Pakistani favorite: chicken *tikka*.

1 chicken (3½ to 4 pounds) cut into 8 pieces (see box, page 255)
Salt
3 whole cardamom pods
3 cloves garlic, coarsely chopped
3 tablespoons finely chopped fresh ginger
1 cup plain whole-milk yogurt
3 tablespoons fresh lemon juice
1 teaspoon freshly ground black pepper
½ to 1 teaspoon cayenne pepper, to taste
1 to 2 drops orange food coloring (optional)
1 onion, thinly sliced lengthwise, for serving

1. Rinse the chicken pieces under cold running water and remove and discard the skin. Then drain and blot dry with paper towels. Place the chicken pieces in a large non-reactive bowl. Sprinkle with 1 teaspoon salt and toss to mix. Let stand for 5 minutes.

2. Meanwhile, crush the cardamom pods in a mortar, using the pestle, then add the garlic and ginger and pound to a coarse paste; or process the ingredients to a paste in a mini chopper or spice mill. Transfer the mixture to a small bowl and stir in the yogurt, lemon juice, black pepper, cayenne, food coloring (if using), and salt to taste. Pour the marinade over the chicken in the bowl and turn the pieces to coat. Cover and

let marinate, in the refrigerator, for 6 to 12 hours (the longer the better).

3. Preheat the grill to high.

4. When ready to cook, oil the grill grate. Remove the chicken pieces from the marinade and arrange them on the hot grate. Grill, turning with tongs, until nicely browned and the juices run clear when the tip of a skewer or sharp knife is inserted in the thickest part of a thigh and the breast meat near the bone shows no trace of pink, 6 to 8 minutes per side.

5. Transfer the chicken to serving plates or a platter and serve topped with the sliced onion.

Serves 4

ANGUILLAN ROAST CHICKEN

BRITISH WEST INDIES

METHOD:
Direct grilling (two-tiered)

ADVANCE PREPARATION:
12 hours for marinating the chicken

SPECIAL EQUIPMENT:
1 to 2 cups wood chips of choice, soaked for 1 hour in cold water to cover and drained

Anguilla is a tiny island in the British West Indies, located a five-minute plane ride from St. Martin. Its long, low-lying profile inspired Columbus to call it Anguilla, which is the Spanish word for "eel." In keeping with the island's small scale, barbecue grills here are made not from 50-gallon drums, but from empty propane tanks that are cut in half and propped up on spidery welded legs. The following recipe was inspired by a fine Anguillan cook, octogenarian Allyne Hazel Guichard, mother of the catering director of the stunning Cap Juluca resort.

Allyne cooks her chicken Anguillan style, over sea grape wood. To achieve a similar smoke flavor, I like to toss a cup of soaked and drained apple, cherry, or maple wood chips on the coals. Smoke flavor, combined with a rum and scotch bonnet chile–based marinade and hot sauce, conspire to make this one of the tastiest

chicken preparations in the Caribbean. Serve with Bahamian Peas and Rice (see Index).

1 chicken (3½ to 4 pounds), cut into
    8 pieces (see box, page 255)
1 bunch scallions, both white and green
    parts, trimmed and coarsely chopped
1 shallot, coarsely chopped
4 cloves garlic, coarsely chopped
1 small onion, coarsely chopped
½ to 2 scotch bonnet chiles, chopped
    (for a milder seasoning, seed the chiles)
2 teaspoons salt, or more to taste
2 teaspoons chopped fresh thyme or
    1 teaspoon dried
½ teaspoon freshly ground black pepper
2 bay leaves, crumbled
½ cup olive oil
¼ cup rum, preferably 151 proof
**Anguillan Barbecue Sauce
    (recipe follows)**

1. Rinse the chicken pieces under cold running water, then drain and blot dry with paper towels. Place the chicken in a large nonreactive bowl. Combine the scallions, shallot, garlic, onion, chiles, 2 teaspoons salt, thyme, pepper, and bay leaves in a food processor and process to a paste. Add the oil and rum and process until blended and smooth. Taste for seasoning, adding salt as necessary; the mixture should be highly seasoned. Pour the marinade over the chicken in the bowl and turn the pieces to coat thoroughly. Cover and let marinate, in the refrigerator, for 12 hours.

2. Preheat the grill, using the two-tiered method (see page 14). *If using a charcoal grill*, preheat to medium.

If using a gas grill, place the wood chips in the smoker box and preheat the grill to high; then, when smoke appears, lower the heat to medium.

3. When ready to cook, if using charcoal, toss the wood chips on the coals. Oil the grill grate. Remove the chicken from the marinade and place, skin side down, on the grate over the hotter section of the grill. Cook as directed in steps 3 and 4 on page 246. The last 5 minutes, brush the chicken with a small amount of the barbecue sauce.

4. Transfer the chicken to a serving platter and serve with the sauce on the side. Reserve any leftover sauce for another use.

Serves 4

Anguillan Barbecue Sauce

Here's a barbecue sauce full of island flavor. Half of a scotch bonnet will give you a gentle heat; culinary pyromaniacs can certainly leave the seeds in or add more chiles.

This makes much more barbecue sauce than you need for a single chicken. It keeps well in the refrigerator.

3 tablespoons olive oil
1 medium onion, finely chopped
2 cloves garlic, minced
½ to 2 scotch bonnet chiles, seeded and minced
3 pounds fresh, ripe tomatoes, peeled and seeded (see box, page 62), then chopped
¼ cup tomato paste
¼ cup commercial barbecue sauce
2 tablespoons Anguillan or other Caribbean hot sauce
¼ cup cider vinegar, or more as needed
¼ cup firmly packed dark brown sugar, or more as needed
¼ cup dark rum
¼ cup water, or more as needed
1 teaspoon dried oregano
1 teaspoon chopped fresh thyme or ½ teaspoon dried
Salt and freshly ground black pepper, to taste

1. Heat the oil in a large saucepan over medium heat. Add the onion, garlic, and chile and sauté until just beginning to brown, about 5 minutes. Stir in the tomatoes and cook until most of the liquid has evaporated, 5 to 7 minutes.

2. Stir in the tomato paste, barbecue sauce, hot sauce, ¼ cup each vinegar and sugar, the rum, ¼ cup water, the oregano, thyme, salt, and pepper and bring to a boil, stirring to dissolve the sugar. Reduce the heat to low and simmer, uncovered, until thick and richly flavored, 20 to 30 minutes, stirring occasionally.

3. Remove from the heat and taste for seasoning, adding salt, vinegar, or sugar as necessary; the sauce should be highly seasoned. Add water if the sauce seems too thick.

4. Any unused sauce may be stored, covered, in the refrigerator for 2 to 3 weeks.

Makes 3 to 4 cups

How to Cut Up a Chicken

Many recipes in this book call for cut-up chickens. Sure, you can buy already-cut chicken, but it's handy to know how to cut up a whole chicken. One advantage is that you can do a French cut, which isn't available commercially. Another advantage is that you get to keep the backbone for making stock. Use good-quality knives with sharp edges for the best results.

THE AMERICAN CUT

My version of the American cut leaves a piece of breast meat attached to each wing. This makes for a more equitable division of the chicken.

1. Remove and discard the fat just inside the body cavities of the chicken. Remove the package of giblets and set aside for another use. Rinse the chicken, inside and out, under cold running water, then drain and blot dry, inside and out, with paper towels. Lay the bird on a cutting board on its side. Insert the knife between the top leg and the carcass and cut off the leg. When you get to the joint connecting the thigh to the body of the bird, pop it out of the hip socket and cut through it to remove the

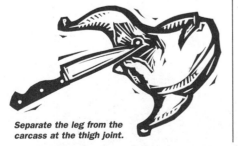
Separate the leg from the carcass at the thigh joint.

entire leg. Cut the leg in half at the knee joint to separate the thigh from the drumstick. Repeat on the other side.

Separate the drumstick from the thigh.

2. Place the bird, back side down so the neck end of the breast is facing you. Make a downward diagonal cut to remove the wing on each side, including a 2-inch piece of breast meat with each wing. When the knife comes to the wing joint, simply cut through it.

Remove the wing and a piece of breast meat.

3. Cut the breast section off the backbone, following the yellow line of fat that runs between the wing joint and the bottom of the rib cage. Cut the breast section in half crosswise through the breastbone. You should have 8 pieces of chicken (plus the backbone), each about the same size.

Cut the breast section in half.

THE FRENCH CUT

The French cut produces a piece of chicken called a *suprême,* a boneless half breast with the first joint of the wing attached.

1. Remove and discard the fat just inside the body cavities of the chicken. Remove the package of giblets and set aside for another use. Rinse the chicken, inside and out, under cold running water, then drain and blot dry, inside and out, with paper towels. Place the bird, back side down, on a cutting board so the rear end of the breast is facing you. Starting at the neck end, make a clean lengthwise cut through the meat and along the right side of the breastbone. Continue cutting, keeping your knife pressed against the breastbone and the rib cage to remove the breast meat on that side in a solid strip. When the knife reaches the wing, cut through the joint, leaving the wing attached to the meat. Repeat this procedure to remove the meat on the other side of the breast. Cut off the 2 end sections of each wing at the joint, leaving only the mini-drumstick attached.

2. Finish cutting up the bird as described in step 1 of the American Cut, but don't separate the drumsticks and thighs; you will have 4 pieces of chicken. Leave the rib cage attached to the backbone; save it, along with the wing tips, for stock.

GRILLED CHICKEN WITH SAFFRON
Joojeh Kebab

METHOD:
Direct grilling (two-tiered)

ADVANCE PREPARATION:
24 hours for marinating the chicken

This will be one of the easiest and most delectable recipes you will ever prepare. The yogurt and lemon juice tenderize the chicken, while the saffron perfumes the flavor. In an Iranian restaurant, the chicken would be cooked kebab style on skewers, breast pieces on one skewer, thighs on another, drumsticks on a third, and so on. This allows the chef to cook each part for the exact amount of time it needs. There is no reason why you couldn't do that with this recipe if it makes things easier for you.

Serve with lavash and Central Asian Pickles (see Index).

FOR THE CHICKEN AND MARINADE:
½ teaspoon saffron threads
1 tablespoon warm water
1½ cups plain whole-milk yogurt
1 large onion, finely chopped
    (about 2 cups)
½ cup fresh lemon juice
2 teaspoons salt
1 teaspoon freshly ground black pepper
2 chickens (3½ to 4 pounds each),
    each cut into 8 pieces (see box,
    page 255)

FOR THE BASTING MIXTURE:
¼ teaspoon saffron threads
1 tablespoon fresh lemon juice
3 tablespoons unsalted butter

1. Prepare the marinade. Place the saffron in a medium-size bowl and crush to a powder with a pestle or the end of a wooden spoon. Stir in the warm water and let stand for 5 minutes, then stir in the yogurt, onion, lemon juice, salt, and pepper.

2. Rinse the chicken pieces under cold running water, then drain and blot dry with paper towels. Place the chicken in a very large nonreactive bowl or baking dish and pour the marinade over them, turning the pieces to coat thoroughly. Cover and let marinate, in the refrigerator, for 24 hours, turning the pieces occasionally.

3. Preheat the grill, using the two-tiered method (see page 14).

4. Prepare the basting mixture. Place the saffron in a small bowl and crush to a powder with a pestle or the end of a wooden spoon. Stir in the lemon juice and let stand for 5 minutes. Melt the butter in a small saucepan over low heat, then remove from the heat and stir in the saffron mixture.

5. When ready to cook, oil the grill grate. Remove the chicken pieces from the marinade and arrange, skin side down, on the grate over the hotter section of the grill. Cook as directed in steps 3 and 4 on page 246. Brush the pieces once or twice as they cook with the basting mixture, watching them to see that they don't burn. Season with salt and pepper.

6. Transfer the chicken pieces to serving plates or a platter and serve.
Serves 8

YAKITORI

JAPAN

METHOD
Direct grilling

SPECIAL EQUIPMENT:
16 short bamboo skewers, soaked for 1 hour in cold water to cover and drained, or more as needed

Yakitori (literally "grilled chicken") is Japan's most popular snack—enjoyed daily at innumerable yakitori parlors, where office workers gather after work for drinks, eats, and camaraderie. (To read about a quintessential yakitori parlor in Tokyo, see page 388.) Traditionally, the chicken is skewered with *negi,* a member of the green onion family that's thicker than a scallion but thinner than a leek. If you can find slender young leeks, use them for the following recipe; otherwise, use scallions. Also, to be strictly authentic use chicken thighs, which the Japanese believe to be more flavorful than breast meat. For speed and convenience, use boneless breasts, my first choice here. Serve with Grilled Rice Cakes, Spicy Japanese Bean Sprout Salad, or Sesame Spinach (see Index).

2 pounds skinless, boneless chicken
　　breasts or thighs
2 pounds slender young leeks
　　(8 or 9 in all, see Notes)
½ cup soy sauce
½ cup sake
½ cup mirin (sweet rice wine) or
　　cream sherry
3 tablespoons sugar
3 slices fresh ginger (each ¼ inch thick)
3 cloves garlic, smashed
3 scallions, both white and green parts,
　　trimmed and coarsely chopped

1. Rinse the chicken breasts or thighs under cold running water, then drain and blot dry with paper towels. Cut crosswise into pieces 2 inches long and both ½ inch wide and thick. Set aside while you prepare the leeks.

2. Cut off and discard the green parts of the leeks. Cut the white parts that remain in half lengthwise as far as the roots. Rinse the leeks carefully under cold running water, then drain, cut off the roots, and cut each leek half crosswise into 2-inch pieces.

3. Thread the chicken pieces crosswise on the skewers, alternating with pieces of leek; you should be able to get 4 pieces of chicken on each skewer. Arrange the skewers on a platter and cover loosely with plastic wrap. Refrigerate until ready to grill, up to 6 hours.

4. Preheat the grill to high.

5. Prepare the yakitori sauce. Combine the soy sauce, sake, mirin, sugar, ginger, garlic, and scallions in a small, heavy saucepan and bring to a boil over medium heat, stirring until blended and the sugar is dissolved. Reduce the heat to low and simmer, uncovered, until the sauce is glossy and syrupy and reduced to ¾ cup, about 5 minutes. Remove from the heat and strain into a bowl (see Notes).

6. When ready to cook, oil the grill grate. Arrange the skewers on the hot grate and grill, turning with tongs, until the chicken is nicely browned and cooked through, 3 to 5 minutes per side (6 to 10 minutes in all). Brush the yakitori generously with the sauce at least once on each side while cooking, but not during the last 3 minutes.

7. Transfer the skewers to serving plates or a platter and serve immediately.

Serves 4 to 6

Notes: If young leeks are not available, substitute 2 bunches thick scallions. Trim off the roots and cut the white parts into 2-inch pieces; cut the scallion greens into 4-inch pieces and fold them in half.

■ The sauce can be made up to 6 hours ahead. Cover and refrigerate until ready to use.

PALESTINIAN CHICKEN

MIDDLE EAST

METHOD:
*Direct grilling
(two-tiered)*

**ADVANCE
PREPARATION:**
*4 to 12 hours for
marinating the
chicken*

In the course of writing this book, I've acquired recipes from every imaginable source: not just chefs and pit masters. The following came from a phone-in caller to the *Miami Herald* on a day when I was invited to answer readers' questions. This woman, originally from the West Bank, wanted to discuss a problem with her crème caramel, but we soon found ourselves chatting about grilling. She gave me this recipe for a typical Palestinian chicken favorite. The traditional way to prepare this dish would be with boneless breast meat on kebabs, but I like to use whole, bone-in chicken breasts. (I like the extra flavor added by the bones). The cinnamon and cardamom add an unexpected touch of sweetness. Serve with grilled or fresh pita, rice, and Charred Tomato Sauce with Pomegranate Molasses (see Index).

2 whole, bone-in chicken breasts with skin
    (12 to 16 ounces each), split
1 cup plain whole-milk yogurt
3 tablespoons fresh lemon juice
6 cloves garlic, minced
1 teaspoon salt
½ teaspoon ground cinnamon
½ teaspoon freshly ground black pepper
¼ teaspoon ground cardamom
⅛ teaspoon ground cloves

1. Rinse the chicken breasts under cold running water, then drain and blot dry with paper towels. Arrange the breasts in a nonreactive baking dish large enough to hold them in one layer and set aside.

2. Combine the yogurt, lemon juice, garlic, salt, cinnamon, pepper, cardamom, and cloves in a small nonreactive bowl and whisk to blend. Pour the mixture over the chicken in the baking dish and spread it over the breasts to cover completely, using your fingers. Cover and let marinate, in the refrigerator, 4 to 12 hours (the longer the better).

3. Preheat the grill, using the two-tiered method (see page 14).

4. When ready to cook, oil the grill grate. Remove the chicken breasts from the baking dish and arrange, skin side down, on the grate over the hotter section of the grill. Cook as directed in steps 3 and 4 in the box on page 246.

5. Transfer the chicken breasts to serving plates or a platter and serve.
Serves 4

MONTEVIDEAN CHICKEN BREASTS
Pamplona de Pollo

URUGUAY

METHOD:
Direct grilling

The term *pamplona* refers to stuffed, rolled, grilled meats popular at Uruguayan steak houses and barbecues. Almost any meat is a candidate for stuffing, especially chicken, pork, and veal. (Beef is considered so noble, it's generally cooked by itself.) The fillings are limited only by your imagination. This recipe was inspired by a Mercado del Puerto restaurant called El Talero (named for the leather truncheon that's part of a cowboy's equipment). The prunes, ham, pepper, and egg make this a particularly colorful stuffing. The juxtaposition of sweet prunes and salty ham gives an orchestral range of flavor.

In Montevideo, these rolls would be wrapped and cooked in caul fat, a lacy membrane of fat from the belly of a pig. Caul fat is often used in charcuterie for wrapping sausages and pâtés. If you want to try using it here, ask for it at butcher shops. Caul fat doesn't have much of a flavor, but as it cooks the fat bastes the meat. The olive oil in the recipe below supplies a similar moistness.

Don't be intimidated by the prospect of making stuffed roll-ups; this one can literally be assembled in 5 minutes—even if you've never stuffed a chicken breast before. It's a failproof recipe, and the results will look like a million bucks.

Each whole skinless, boneless chicken breast called for here must be in one piece—breast halves just won't do.

Serve with one of the *chimichurris* in the sauce chapter (see Index).

2 whole skinless, boneless chicken breasts
    (12 to 16 ounces each)
Salt and freshly ground black pepper
1 teaspoon dried oregano
½ medium red bell pepper, stemmed
    and seeded
1 slice (¼ inch thick) cooked or
    smoked ham (about 1½ ounces)
1 hard-cooked egg, peeled
12 pitted prunes
2 to 3 tablespoons olive oil,
    for brushing

1. Rinse the chicken breasts under cold running water, then drain and blot dry with paper towels. Spread the breasts open, smooth side down and with one long side facing you, on your work surface. Cut out the fillets (the long, slender strip of meat on each half breast) and set aside for another use (see Note). Season the breasts with salt, pepper, and ½ teaspoon of the oregano.

2. Cut the bell pepper lengthwise into ¼-inch strips. Cut the ham into ¼-inch strips; cut the hard-cooked egg into 6 lengthwise wedges. Arrange the pepper and ham strips, flat on the opened breasts. Place the egg wedges and prunes lengthwise on top, leaving a ½-inch border on each side.

3. Starting at the side facing you, roll each breast up to form a compact cylinder. Pin the rolls closed with short metal skewers or tie with butcher's string as follows: Tie the string around one end of each roll and then wrap it around the roll until you reach the other end; tie the ends to secure. Rub the outsides of the rolls with the oil and season with salt, pepper, and the remaining ½ teaspoon oregano. Place the *pamplonas* on a platter, cover loosely with plastic wrap, and refrigerate until ready to grill, up to 6 hours.

4. Preheat the grill to medium-high.

5. When ready to cook, oil the grill grate. Arrange the *pamplonas* on the hot grate and grill, turning with tongs and basting with a small amount of the oil, until nicely browned, firm to the touch, and a skewer inserted in the center of each comes out very hot to the touch, 20 to 30 minutes in all.

6. Transfer the *pamplonas* to a cutting board. Traditionally, *pamplonas* are served whole on plates, but I like to cut them crosswise into ½-inch slices, fanning the slices out on serving plates or a platter to create a mosaic effect. Let rest for 5 minutes before removing the skewers or string.

Makes 2 pamplonas; serves 6 as an appetizer, 2 to 4 as an entrée

Note: One good use for the fillets would be any of the satés in this book; see the Index.

Uruguay's Mercado Del Puerto

"Where's the beef?" asked a popular TV commercial a few years back. Where, indeed! Virtually everyone I know in North America is cutting back on meat consumption or eliminating it entirely.

How different life is south of the equator, where meat remains the bedrock of the Latin American diet. This truth became apparent to me the moment I landed in Montevideo, Uruguay.

"Beef is cheaper here than chicken," explained my taxi driver, pointing out the profusion of butcher shops (one every couple blocks) on the way to my hotel. During my stay, the Montevideans I met proudly admitted to eating meat between 10 and 12 times a week.

If this seems like a cultural flashback, just a stroll through the old quarter of Montevideo proves it out. Studebakers, panel trucks, even Model-T Fords ply the tree-lined avenues and cobblestone streets. Laundry hangs on the wrought-iron balconies of moldering eighteenth-century townhouses. Here, in the old quarter of the capital of the smallest nation in South America, time seems to have stood still.

Time has surely stood still at the Mercado del Puerto. Montevideans flock to this once-stately covered market for a carnivorian orgy of grilled steaks, sausages, roasts, roulades, and organ meats.

Built in 1868, the Mercado del Puerto is a soaring temple of girders and glass. Access to the block-long market is gained through grandiose iron gates, and a three-story-high skylight, blackened with smoke and age, towers over an ornate clock tower whose hands are frozen at 4:30 P.M. The dilapidated stone floor gives the Mercado a slightly seedy feel—which is what a proper market should have. And one thing's for sure: The beef is definitely here.

FOLLOW YOUR NOSE

As you walk through the old town, you can smell the market before you actually see it. It's a common aroma in South America—a comforting blend of fire-seared meat and wood smoke. Formerly Montevideo's main food market, the Mercado of today is its barbecue headquarters, home to more than a dozen bare-bones restaurants specializing in grilled meats. Take a seat at one of the counters and you'll taste some of the best barbecue in South America—as well as parts of animals you never knew you could eat.

Consider the Estancia del Puerto (Port Ranch), a lively grill founded more than a quarter century ago by Antonio and Marono Fraga. The latter is a short, bald, bespectacled man who remembers when the Mercado was a working food market with only one or two simple eateries. The boom came in the 1980s, when gentrification turned most of the food stalls into restaurants. The Estancia alone will serve 500 people a day, going through more than a ton of beef a week.

Patrons, many of them regulars since the restaurant opened, take their seats at black marble counters surrounding the kitchen. (There's also a separate seating area with proper tables and chairs.) Some are office workers, while others are city employees or dock hands, although the crowd is dressier than you'd expect for the portside location. There's no doubt that the focal point of the restaurant is the massive grill, where pork, lamb, chicken, and especially beef are charred to smoky perfection.

The Uruguayan grill has two working parts. The first is a U-shaped metal basket that holds blazing hardwood logs. As the logs disintegrate, the glowing coals are raked under the *parilla,* a large, rectangular metal grate that serves as the actual grill. The grate slopes gently upward in the back: The front (the part closest to the coals) is used for searing the meat; the rear is used for roasting and warming.

The *asador* (grill man) is recognizable by his white coat and *gorra* (short-brimmed cap). He remains in constant motion, now adding a log to the fire box, now raking a fresh load of coals under the grate, now moving meats from hot spots to cool spots or back again. When not actually grilling meats, he may be boning a chicken to make a *pamplona* (or stuffed roast), or rolling carrots, peppers, hard-cooked eggs, and flank steak into a belt-loosening roast called *matambre,* literally "hunger-killer."

The first thing that strikes you at a Montevidean grill is how limited the North American notion is of what makes suitable barbecue. No part of the animal is overlooked by a Montevidean grill master. A typical meal might start with *mollejas* (grilled sweetbreads), *choto* (a crispy roll of sheep's small intestines coiled around large intestines that tastes better than it sounds), *chinchulin* (buttery, crescent-shaped spirals of lamb's small intestine), or *riñones* (veal kidneys).

Uruguayans are also great fans of sausage—a love they may have acquired from the German immigrants who settled here in the early part of this century. Chorizo is the most famous Latin American sausage. To most North Americans, chorizo means the spicy Mexican variety. Uruguayan chorizo, on the other hand, is salty and garlicky, but not in the least bit spicy. It's rather like kielbasa.

Another tasty sausage is *salchicha,* which comes in a slender, tightly coiled casing. *Morcilla* is blood sausage, recognizable by its shiny black, crackling-crisp casing. It, too, tastes a lot better than it sounds. There are, in fact, two different types of *morcilla* in Uruguay, savory and sweet. The latter is flavored with sugar and raisins and is absolutely delicious. I wish I could find it at home.

Uruguayan beef cuts will be equally unfamiliar to most North Americans. The most popular is *asado de tira*—a long, thin cross section of rib roast that literally buries the plate. The noises of the market are punctuated by the high-pitched whine of the meat saw, cutting sides of beef into *asados.* The generous marbling makes the meat incredibly succulent, while the rib bones provide extra flavor. Another popular cut is the *pulpa,* smokily charred "breast," which is similar to brisket.

NO-FRILLS DINING

Whatever you order, know that it will be served with the utmost simplicity. The plate is cheap stamped metal. The accompaniments are limited to a parsley and garlic sauce called *chimichurri* (think of it as South American pesto) and a tomato, onion, and pepper relish known as *salsa criolla.* Some restaurants follow the example of Uruguay's northern neighbor, Brazil, serving *farofa* (toasted manioc flour) for sprinkling over the meat to absorb the juices.

To round out your meal, you might have a baked potato or simple salad of lettuce, tomato, and onions. Desserts are usually packaged confections that are as intensely sugary as the espresso served after the meal.

Another popular lunch spot is Don Garcia, named for its jovial proprietor, who runs the restaurant with his dark-eyed wife, Alicia. This tiny eatery has no tables, and you'll probably have to wait a while for a seat at the red granite counter. However long it takes, don't miss it, for Don Garcia serves some of the best, most reasonably priced food at the Mercado. Two could eat themselves silly for 63 pesos (about $12) by ordering the *parillada* (mixed grill). You'll be presented with a sizzling-hot plate heaped with chorizo, *morcilla, salchicha,* several types of innards, and even a steak. Another of the Don's specialties is grilled bread, which Garcia slathers with oil and garlic. To wash it down there's a sort of Uruguayan sangria made with ginger ale and red wine.

The Mercado del Puerto is mainly a lunch spot: Most of the grills close by 6:00 P.M. At least one restaurant reopens for dinner: El Palenque. Founded in 1964, this popular eatery straddles the east wall of the market. At lunchtime, patrons line up at its marketside counter. At night, there's a streetside dining room with country hams hanging from the rafters and a terrace with plastic café chairs.

El Palenque serves the sort of staunchly carnivorous fare found throughout the Mercado del Puerto, but there are two house specialties that will delight nonmeat eaters. The first is *provolone asado,* grilled slabs of provolone cheese sprinkled with olive oil, oregano, and pimientos. The second are grilled sardines—among the rare seafood I saw at the market.

El Palenque's owner, Emilio Gonzales Portela, came to work here in the 1960s as a humble grill man. Today he owns the restaurant, which serves 400 customers a day. I guess you could call it the American dream—Montevidean style.

How to Grill Perfect Chicken Breasts

Skinless, boneless breasts are the easiest part of the chicken to grill. Because they're so lean, you don't get the flare-ups associated with whole chicken or legs and you can grill them directly over high flames. But the lack of fat can also be a drawback: Chicken breasts must be generously basted with oil or melted butter during grilling to keep them from drying out.

1. Preheat the grill to high.

2. Rinse and drain the chicken breasts under cold running water, then drain and blot dry with paper towels.

3. When ready to cook, oil the grate. For extra smoke flavor, toss a few soaked wood chips on the coals, lava stones, or inverted V bars before grilling. Arrange the breasts all going in the same direction on the hot grate. Grill for 2 minutes, then, using tongs, rotate the breasts 45 degrees and grill for 2 to 4 minutes more. This creates an attractive crosshatch of grill marks. Generously baste the breasts with oil, melted butter, or marinade as they cook. (However, if using a sugar-based barbecue sauce, apply it only during the last 2 minutes of grilling on each side.)

4. Turn the breasts with tongs and grill the other side, again rotating each breast 45 degrees after 2 minutes. The total cooking time for a skinless, boneless chicken breast will be 4 to 6 minutes per side.

BADEMIYA'S JUSTLY FAMOUS CHILE-CORIANDER CHICKEN

INDIA

METHOD:
Direct grilling

The Taj Mahal Hotel is the most famous hotel in Bombay. But for me the real attraction of the neighborhood is a food stall called Bademiya, located on tiny Tulloch Road behind the venerable Taj. Founded by Muhammad Yaseen in the 1940s and now run by his 30-year-old jean- and Nike-clad son Jamal, this sidewalk eatery attracts Bombay barbecue buffs of all castes and classes for its fiery grilled chicken, meltingly succulent *seekh* (minced lamb) kebabs, and grilled lamb's udder. (The latter tastes like chewy liver and is for adventurous eaters only.) The original version of this dish is hot, hot, hot. For the full effect, use 1 entire tablespoon of cayenne. For a milder but highly flavorful rendition, use 1 to 2 teaspoons cayenne, or substitute hot paprika which isn't quite as fiery. To round out your meal at Bademiya, two fulltime bakers work nonstop tossing paper-thin disks of dough onto charcoal-fired metal domes to make freshly cooked *ruoomali* ("handkerchief" bread). Since these are difficult to make, I suggest serving this chicken with either of

ADVANCE PREPARATION:
4 to 6 hours for marinating the chicken

two thoroughly non-Indian but definitely satisfactory alternatives, flour tortillas or lavash. Afghan Coriander Sauce and Tamarind Dipping Sauce (see Index) make great accompaniments.

4 whole chicken legs or 1 whole chicken (3½ to 4 pounds), cut into 8 pieces (see box, page 255)
1½ tablespoons coriander seeds
2 teaspoons whole black peppercorns
1 teaspoon cumin seeds
6 cloves garlic, peeled
1 piece (2 inches) fresh ginger, thinly sliced
3 tablespoons vegetable oil
¼ cup water, or as needed
2 tablespoons fresh lemon juice
1 tablespoon cayenne pepper or hot paprika, or to taste
1½ teaspoons salt
½ cup chopped fresh cilantro
Thinly sliced red onion, for garnish
Wedges of limes or lemons, for garnish

1. Remove and discard the skin from the chicken legs, then rinse under cold running water. Drain and blot dry with paper towels. Place the legs in a baking dish large enough to hold them in one layer and set aside while you prepare the seasoning paste.

2. Heat a dry skillet over medium heat and add the coriander seeds, peppercorns, and cumin seeds. Toast the spices until fragrant, 2 to 3 minutes, shaking the skillet occasionally. Let cool, then transfer to a spice mill and grind to a fine powder. Combine the ground spices in a blender or mini chopper with the garlic, ginger, oil, ¼ cup water, lemon juice, cayenne, and salt. Process to a smooth paste, adding more water if necessary to obtain a pourable consistency. Add the cilantro and process just to mix.

3. Using your fingers, spread the seasoning paste over the chicken legs to coat on both sides, then cover and let marinate, in the refrigerator, for 4 to 6 hours.

4. Preheat the grill to high.

5. When ready to cook, oil the grill grate. Remove the chicken legs from the baking dish and arrange on the hot grate. Grill, turning with tongs, until the juices run clear when the tip of the skewer or sharp knife is inserted in the thickest part of a thigh, 6 to 10 minutes per side (12 to 20 minutes in all).

6. Transfer the chicken legs to serving plates or a platter and serve immediately garnished with sliced red onion and lime or lemon wedges.

Serves 4

Bombay Tikka "Taco"

Bademyia also serves a version of chicken *tikka* that uses the seasoning paste from the recipe for Chile-Coriander Chicken. To make it, rinse 1½ pounds skinless, boneless chicken breasts under cold running water, then drain and blot dry with paper towels. Cut the breasts into 2-inch squares. Prepare the seasoning paste as directed in the recipe, then spread it over the chicken pieces in a baking dish. Cover and let marinate, in the refrigerator, for 1 to 2 hours. Preheat the grill to high, and when ready to cook, thread the chicken pieces on 4 long metal skewers, dividing evenly. Oil the grill grate and grill until nicely browned and cooked through, 3 to 5 minutes per side. To serve, heat 4 flour tortillas or lavash on the grill until soft and pliable, about 30 seconds per side. Unskewer the chicken onto the tortillas and top each serving with sliced red onion and drizzles of Afghan Coriander Sauce and Tamarind Dipping Sauce (see Index). Roll the tortillas up tightly for eating. This, too, serves 4.

The Splendid Restaurant Karim

A trip to the famous restaurant Karim in New Delhi, India, will take you through a National Geographic-esque warren of narrow lanes teeming with veiled women and white-robed men, noisy street merchants and swarming beggers, wandering cows and nose-tweaking aromas.

The lanes are too narrow for a taxi to take you directly to the restaurant, but a squadron of turbaned *sieks* in red livery, positioned every 30 yards, will guide you. After a short walk, you arrive at the last place you'd expect to find in this colorful neighborhood: a proper restaurant with air conditioning, wood paneling, coffered ceilings, and nattily set, tableclothed tables.

Karim's founder was Hazi Amliudine Ahmed (Karim was his nickname), scion of a long line of royal chefs and chef himself to one of the region's last kings, Bahadur Shah Zafar. Like the chefs of the Ancienne Régime in France, Karim found himself unemployed when changing socio-economic conditions forced the closure of the palace kitchen. So in 1913 he opened a restaurant in the shadow of the Jamma Masjid Mosque outside the walls of the Red Fort.

The original Karim's still stands in the courtyard of a small building. Over the years half a dozen dining rooms have been added, including one where men can dine with their families (the bulk of the clientele is male). We're in Muslim territory now, and I was reminded of this by the sight of Karim's 27-year-old great-grandson (also a chef) who wears a white skull cap and sits cross-legged before a bank of pots simmering over charcoal, like a potentate surveying his fiefdom. As in most Muslim neighborhoods, the restaurant doesn't get busy until after sundown.

The original Karim's specializes in the butter- and cream-enriched stews of the Moguls. Indeed, there's only one grilled meat on the menu: *seekh kebab.* You can watch these ground lamb kebabs being cooked on rectangular metal braziers over charcoal that an electric fan blows to bright red. What comes off these heavy skewers is a sort of tubed-shaped sausage that's perfumed with spices, extraordinarily succulent, and in its own way fully as splendid as the famous mosque.

In 1970, the family opened a second restaurant in another colorful Muslim neighborhood, Nizamuddin. Endowed with a larger kitchen and fancier dining room, the Nizamuddin Karim offers a wider selection of grilled dishes, including *tandoori bakra,* a whole goat stuffed with dried fruits, hard-cooked eggs, and a basmati rice preparation called *biryani.* I succumbed to *tandoori barra* (lamb ribs), *seekh kebab,* and an astonishing variety of grilled breads. But the one dish I still dream about is Karim's Afghani *murgh,* Afghan-Style Chicken, and to try to get the recipe, I asked for a tour of the kitchen.

The good news is that the food prep area here was as immaculate as the dining room. (Lord knows, this isn't always the case in this part of the world.) The cooks wore gray jumpsuits, which made them look a little like convicts. Two sat barefoot and cross-legged before a pair of giant tandoors, where the meats and breads were cooked. Marinades were mixed in flat metal pans on a floor clean enough to eat off.

The bad news is that the family keeps tight wraps on its recipes—to the point where the spice mixes used to flavor the lamb marinades are blended in a separate location. So not even the chef knows the full recipe. In the *murgh,* I was able to detect the tangy presence of yogurt cheese and lemon juice, with a generous dose of puréed garlic and ginger. A taste of the raw marinade also revealed the heat of cayenne and the pungency of cumin. Curiously, the overall effect reminded me of Hungarian liptauer cheese, and the results can be found on the facing page.

AFGHAN-STYLE CHICKEN
Murgh

INDIA

METHOD:
Direct grilling

ADVANCE PREPARATION:
4 to 6 hours for marinating the chicken, plus 4 to 6 hours for making the yogurt cheese

SPECIAL EQUIPMENT:
4 short metal skewers

Despite the name, this recipe comes from India, not Afghanistan (although it may have originated in the latter country). It's the specialty of New Delhi's famous Karim restaurant. In the eighteenth and nineteenth centuries, the borders of the countries we now know as Afghanistan, Pakistan, and India were considerably more fluid. Recipes and culinary philosophies traveled with merchandise and politics along a trade route known as the Silk Road. So it's not surprising to find Karim's chefs serving a yogurt and chile marinade characteristic of Afghanistan—it is an electrifying paste of flavors. Hopefully you'll experience the restaurant's slogan when you taste it:

The secret of a good mood . . .
Taste Karim's food!

FOR THE CHICKEN AND MARINADE:
3 cups plain whole-milk yogurt
6 cloves garlic, minced
2 tablespoons grated fresh ginger
1 small onion, minced
3 tablespoons fresh lemon juice
$\frac{1}{2}$ to 1 tablespoon cayenne pepper
2 teaspoons salt
1 teaspoon freshly ground black pepper
1 teaspoon cumin seeds, toasted
   (see box, page 93)
6 chicken legs (2 to $2\frac{1}{2}$ pounds total) cut
   into drumsticks and thigh sections

FOR THE GARNISH:
Sliced red onion
Sliced tomato
Sliced cucumber
Sliced radishes
Lemon wedges

1. Set a yogurt strainer, or regular strainer lined with a double layer of dampened cheesecloth, over a bowl. Add the yogurt to the strainer and let drain, in the refrigerator, for 4 to 6 hours.

2. Remove the drained yogurt from the refrigerator (it will be quite thick) and discard the liquid. Transfer the yogurt to a large nonreactive bowl. Add the garlic, ginger, onion, lemon juice, cayenne, salt, black pepper, and cumin seeds and whisk to blend. Set aside while you prepare the chicken.

3. Remove and discard the skin from the chicken pieces, then rinse the pieces under cold running water. Drain and blot dry with paper towels. Make 2 or 3 deep slashes, to the bone, in each piece. Add the chicken to the marinade in the bowl and turn the pieces to coat. Cover and let marinate, in the refrigerator, for 4 to 6 hours.

4. Preheat the grill to high (see Note).

5. When ready to grill, oil the grill grate. Remove the chicken from the marinade and arrange on the hot grate. Grill, turning with tongs, until nicely browned on the outside and the juices run clear when the tip of a skewer or sharp knife is inserted in the thickest part of a drumstick or thigh, 8 to 10 minutes per side (16 to 20 minutes in all).

6. Transfer the chicken to serving plates or a platter and serve immediately, garnished with onion, tomato, cucumber, and radish slices and lemon wedges.

Serves 6

Note: For best results, use charcoal.

THAI CHICKEN SATES SERVED IN LETTUCE LEAVES

THAILAND

METHOD:
Direct grilling

ADVANCE PREPARATION:
20 minutes to 2 hours for marinating the chicken

SPECIAL EQUIPMENT:
16 long bamboo skewers, soaked for 1 hour in cold water to cover and drained

Satés originated in Indonesia, but Thais and Malaysians adopted these tiny kebabs with passion. Along the way, the seasoning changed from Indonesia's sweet soy–based marinade to the fish sauce so prized in Thai cooking. I like to serve satés the way they are commonly eaten in Southeast Asia—wrapped in lettuce leaves.

FOR THE CHICKEN AND MARINADE:
1 pound skinless, boneless chicken breasts
¼ cup coconut milk, canned or homemade (page 522)
2 tablespoons Asian fish sauce
2 tablespoons fresh lime juice
2 teaspoons honey or sugar
2 cloves garlic, minced
½ teaspoon ground turmeric

FOR SERVING:
Thai Peanut Sauce (page 472)
1 head Boston lettuce, separated into leaves, rinsed, and trimmed

1. Rinse the chicken breasts under cold running water, then drain and blot dry with paper towels. Cut the breasts lengthwise (with the grain) into 16 strips, each 4 inches long, ½ inch wide, and ¼ inch thick. Set aside while you prepare the marinade.

2. Combine the coconut milk, fish sauce, lime juice, honey, garlic, and turmeric in a medium-size nonreactive bowl and whisk to blend. Add the chicken to the marinade and toss thoroughly to coat. Cover and let marinate, in the refrigerator, 20 minutes to 2 hours (the longer the better).

3. Preheat the grill to high.

4. Weave the chicken strips lengthwise onto the skewers.

5. When ready to cook, oil the grill grate. Arrange the satés on the hot grate and grill, turning with tongs, until lightly browned and cooked through, 1 to 3 minutes per side (2 to 6 minutes in all).

6. Transfer the satés to serving plates and serve, accompanied by tiny bowls of the peanut sauce. To eat, place a saté on a lettuce leaf and top the chicken with a spoonful of the sauce; wrap the lettuce around the saté and pull out the skewer.

Makes 16 satés; serves 4 as an appetizer, 2 as an entrée

MALAYSIAN CHICKEN SATES

MALAYSIA

METHOD:
Direct grilling

Satés are enjoyed throughout Southeast Asia, where each country boasts that it makes the best. The Malaysian version is particularly aromatic, thanks to the fragrant paste of shallots, lemongrass, turmeric, coriander, and peanuts in which the meat is marinated. A Malaysian would use fresh turmeric. As this is difficult to find in North America, I've substituted fresh ginger and turmeric powder.

ADVANCE PREPARATION:
1 hour for marinating the chicken

SPECIAL EQUIPMENT:
About 40 short bamboo skewers, soaked in cold water for 1 hour and drained

1 stalk fresh lemongrass, untrimmed

Asians prefer the rich flavor of dark-meat chicken (chicken thighs or drumsticks). For ease in preparation, I've called for boneless breasts, but you could certainly use dark meat. Beef, lamb, or shrimp satés would be made the same way.

FOR THE CHICKEN AND MARINADE:
1½ pounds skinless, boneless chicken breasts
4 large or 6 medium shallots, quartered
2 stalks fresh lemongrass, trimmed and cut into ½-inch pieces, or 2 strips lemon zest (each 2 × ½ inch; removed with a vegetable peeler)
1 tablespoon chopped fresh ginger
3 tablespoons dry-roasted peanuts
6 tablespoons vegetable oil
2 tablespoons fresh lemon or lime juice, or more to taste
1 tablespoon soy sauce
1 teaspoon salt, or more to taste
1 teaspoon ground turmeric
1 teaspoon ground cumin
1 teaspoon ground coriander
¼ teaspoon ground cinnamon
½ teaspoon freshly ground black pepper
Dutch West Indian Peanut Sauce
(see page 473)

1. Rinse the chicken under cold running water, then drain and blot dry with paper towels. Cut the meat lengthwise (with the grain) into strips the size of your little finger. Place the strips in a large bowl and set aside while you prepare the marinade.

2. Combine the shallots, the lemongrass pieces, the ginger, peanuts, 3 tablespoons of the oil, 2 tablespoons lemon juice, the soy sauce, 1 teaspoon salt, and the ground spices in a blender and process to a smooth paste. Taste for seasoning, adding salt or lemon juice to taste; the mixture should be highly seasoned. Add the mixture to the chicken in the bowl, stirring to coat completely. Cover and let marinate, in the refrigerator, for 1 hour, stirring once or twice.

3. Preheat the grill to high.

4. Weave the chicken strips lengthwise onto the skewers.

5. When ready to cook, oil the grill grate. Arrange the satés on the hot grate and grill, turning with tongs, until lightly browned and cooked through, 1 to 3 minutes per side (2 to 6 minutes in all). Using the whole lemongrass stalk as a brush, baste the satés with the remaining oil once or twice as they cook.

6. Transfer the satés to serving plates or a platter and serve with the peanut sauce.
Serves 8 as an appetizer, 4 as an entrée

SRI LANKAN SATES

SRI LANKA

METHOD:
Direct grilling

Most people associate satés (aka satays) with Southeast Asia, particularly with Indonesia, Malaysia, or Singapore. Imagine my surprise at finding them on the menu of Taprobane, a Sri Lanken restaurant in Manhattan. (Taprobane was an early name of the island.) The notion isn't as far fetched as it might seem. The principle of kebabs seems to have arrived in Indonesia with Arab traders in the twelfth century A.D. Sri Lanka certainly could have been a stopping point on the way.

This Sri Lankan version of saté features a lively marinade of coriander and paprika. It comes with an equally lively

ADVANCE PREPARATION:
30 minutes to 6 hours for marinating the chicken

SPECIAL EQUIPMENT:
40 to 50 short bamboo skewers, soaked for 1 hour in cold water to cover and drained

sauce, gilded with turmeric and enriched with coconut milk. I like the bite provided by hot paprika, but sweet paprika is easier on the taste buds.

FOR THE CHICKEN:

1½ pounds skinless, boneless chicken breasts
1 tablespoon sweet or hot paprika
2 teaspoons ground coriander
1 teaspoon salt
1 teaspoon freshly ground black pepper
2 cloves garlic, minced
3 tablespoons vegetable oil

FOR THE SAUCE:

3 tablespoons vegetable oil
1 large onion, thinly sliced
1 tablespoon minced fresh ginger
2 cloves garlic, minced
1 teaspoon ground cumin
1 teaspoon ground coriander
½ teaspoon hot paprika or cayenne pepper
½ teaspoon ground turmeric
Salt and freshly ground black pepper, to taste
1 cup coconut milk, canned or homemade (page 522)
2 teaspoons distilled white vinegar, or more to taste

1. Rinse the chicken breasts under cold running water, then drain and blot dry with paper towels. Cut the breasts lengthwise (with the grain) into 2½-inch-long strips and place in a large bowl. Add the paprika, coriander, salt, and pepper, and garlic rubbing into the meat with your fingers. Stir in the oil to coat thoroughly, cover, and let marinate, in the refrigerator, for 30 minutes or up to 6 hours (the longer the better).

2. Meanwhile, prepare the sauce. Heat the oil in a medium-size saucepan over high heat. Add the onion, ginger, garlic, cumin, coriander, ½ teaspoon paprika, the turmeric, and salt and black pepper. Sauté for 1 minute, stirring to coat the onion with the seasonings. Reduce the heat to medium and cook the onion, stirring occasionally, until very soft and a deep golden brown, 15 to 20 minutes. Stir in the coconut milk and 2 teaspoons vinegar. Simmer until you have a thick, spoonable sauce, about 5 minutes. Taste for seasoning, adding salt or vinegar as necessary; the mixture should be highly seasoned. Remove from the heat and set aside.

3. Preheat the grill to high.

4. Weave the chicken strips lengthwise onto the skewers.

5. When ready to cook, oil the grill grate. Arrange the satés on the hot grate and grill, turning with tongs, until lightly browned and cooked through, 1 to 3 minutes per side (2 to 6 minutes in all).

6. Transfer the satés to serving plates or a platter and spoon a little sauce over each. Serve immediately.

Makes 40 to 50 satés, enough to serve 6 as an appetizer, 4 as an entrée

SCHOOLYARD CHICKEN SATES

THAILAND

METHOD:
Direct grilling

The same impulse that sends American schoolchildren rushing out to Pizza Hut and McDonald's when the lunch bell rings has the uniformed youngsters of Nat Monekugrasae High School in Bangkok heading to the saté stand of Suay and Pong Pochana. The Pochana sisters are just two among the twenty or so vendors who fill the stalls in the parking lot across the street from the school, but it's their satés

ADVANCE PREPARATION:
1 to 2 hours for marinating the chicken

SPECIAL EQUIPMENT:
About 40 short bamboo skewers, soaked for 1 hour in cold water to cover and drained

that the children seem to prefer above everything else. Pong sits cross-legged on a raised dias, threading the meat of chicken legs on skewers, while Suay fans a narrow brazier to heat the coconut shell charcoal used for grilling. Saté originated in Indonesia, of course (see page 444), but the coconut milk in the marinade and tangy Tamarind Dipping Sauce the satés are served with are distinctly Thai. The latter, thanks to the smoky tartness of the tamarind, is one of the tastiest sweet-and-sour sauces ever to grace grilled chicken.

Serve also with Jasmine Rice (see Index).

1 pound skinless, boneless chicken breasts or leg meat
3 cloves garlic, minced
1 piece (1 inch) fresh ginger, thinly sliced
1 tablespoon sugar
1 teaspoon salt
2 tablespoons Asian fish sauce
½ cup coconut milk, canned or homemade (see page 522)
Tamarind Dipping Sauce (page 484)

1. Rinse the chicken under cold running water, then drain and blot dry with paper towels. Cut the meat lengthwise (with the grain) into 2½-inch strips (the size of your little finger). Place the strips in a large bowl and set aside while you prepare the marinade.

2. Combine the garlic, ginger, sugar, and salt in a mortar and pound to a coarse paste with the pestle, then work in the fish sauce and coconut milk; if you don't have a mortar and pestle, process the ingredients, all at once, in a blender. Add the mixture to the chicken in the bowl, turning the strips to coat. Cover and let marinate, in the refrigerator, for 1 to 2 hours (the longer the better), stirring occasionally.

3. Preheat the grill to high.

4. Remove the chicken strips from the marinade, reserving the marinade, and weave lengthwise onto the skewers.

5. When ready to cook, oil the grill grate. Arrange the satés on the hot grate and grill until lightly browned and cooked through, 1 to 3 minutes per side (2 to 6 minutes in all). Brush the satés once or twice before turning with the reserved marinade.

6. Transfer to serving plates or a platter and serve immediately, accompanied by small bowls of the Tamarind Dipping Sauce.

Serves 4 as an appetizer, 2 as an entrée

JAKARTA CHICKEN SATE
Saté Ayam

INDONESIA

METHOD:
Direct grilling

This is probably the most popular saté in Jakarta, the street food equivalent of, say, a hot dog in New York. This particular recipe comes from Nurul Phamid, a willowy young man with a faint mustache, who sells satés from a pushcart on Jabang Street. Phamid loads his satés with chicken livers and chicken skin, as well as dark chicken meat. For the sake of simplicity, I make the liver and skin optional; you certainly could add either or both, if you wish. What really makes Phamid's satés so succulent is what he uses for basting: chicken fat!

SPECIAL EQUIPMENT: *About 28 short bamboo skewers, soaked for 1 hour in cold water to cover and drained*

1 pound boneless chicken breasts or leg meat, with skin if desired

4 ounces chicken livers, trimmed (optional)

⅔ cup sweet soy sauce (ketjap manis) or ⅓ cup each regular soy sauce and molasses

¾ cup Thai Peanut Sauce (page 472)

3 tablespoons finely chopped onion

1 tablespoon fresh lime juice

2 tablespoons rendered chicken fat (see box) or unsalted butter, melted

1 tablespoon chile paste (sambal ulek) or your favorite hot sauce, for serving

1. Preheat the grill to high.

2. If the chicken has skin and you plan to use it in the recipe, remove it from the chicken and reserve; otherwise, discard it. Rinse the chicken, chicken skin (if using), and chicken livers (if using) under cold water. Then drain and blot dry with paper towels. Cut the chicken and livers into ½-inch dice and the skin into ½-inch squares. Thread the pieces alternately on the skewers; each saté should be about 3 inches long. Place on a platter, cover loosely with plastic wrap, and refrigerate while you prepare the marinade.

3. Combine ¼ cup of the sweet soy sauce, ¼ cup of the peanut sauce, the onion, and lime juice in a shallow dish and stir to mix. Roll the satés in the marinade to coat thoroughly.

4. When ready to grill, oil the grill grate. Arrange the satés on the hot grate and grill, turning with tongs, until lightly browned

To Render Chicken Fat

Remove the large pieces of fat from just inside the main body cavity of the bird. Place them in a small skillet over medium heat and cook until the fat renders out, 5 to 10 minutes. Strain the fat into a jar and cover. The main cavity of an average chicken will contain 1 to 2 ounces of fat. This will yield 1 to 2 tablespoons rendered fat. You can render this amount or, alternatively, save lumps of fat in the freezer and render a cup or two at a time. (The lumps of fat will keep, frozen, for about 2 months.) Rendered chicken fat will keep in the refrigerator for several weeks.

and cooked through, 1 to 3 minutes per side (2 to 6 minutes in all). Brush once or twice with the chicken fat as the satés cook.

5. To serve, place the remaining ½ cup peanut sauce in a small bowl and spoon the remaining 2 tablespoons sweet soy sauce and the chile paste into the center (the motion of dipping the satés into this sauce will mix the ingredients together). Transfer the satés to serving plates or a platter and serve accompanied by the sauce.

Serves 4 as an appetizer, 2 as an entrée

TURKEY PASTRAMI

U.S.A.

METHOD: *Indirect grilling*

Pastrami is truly a dish of three continents. Most Americans associate this cured meat with delicatessens. The first delicatessens were opened by Jews from Eastern Europe to provide immigrants with the beloved foods they left behind in Germany, Russia, and Poland.

Actually, pastrami seems to have originated in Central Asia (particularly in eastern Turkey and Armenia), where it goes by the name of *basturma*. *Basturma* can be made with a variety of different meats, including beef, horse, and even camel. The meat is cut into 2-foot-long strips, which are cured in salt, garlic, paprika, and other spices.

As for turkey pastrami, well, that's a uniquely North American invention—designed to be high in flavor, low in fat, and requiring only 1 day instead of the traditional 2 weeks, curing time needed to make beef pastrami.

2 pounds skinless, boneless turkey breast
1 tablespoon coriander seeds
2 teaspoons cracked black peppercorns
1½ tablespoons coarse (kosher or sea) salt
2 teaspoons firmly packed dark brown sugar
2 teaspoons sweet paprika
1½ teaspoons mustard seeds
1 teaspoon ground ginger
3 cloves garlic, minced

1. Rinse the turkey breast under cold running water, then drain and blot dry with paper towels. Set aside while you prepare the spice rub.

2. Coarsely crush the coriander seeds and pepper in a spice mill or under the edge of a cast-iron skillet. Combine the crushed spices in a bowl and whisk in the salt, sugar, paprika, mustard seeds, ginger, and garlic. Using your fingers, pat the mixture over the entire surface of the turkey breast and rub in thoroughly. Wrap the breast in plastic wrap or place in a large zip-lock plastic bag and let the turkey cure in the refrigerator for 24 hours.

3. Set up the grill for indirect grilling (see page 14 or 16), placing a drip pan in the center. *If using a charcoal grill,* preheat it to medium.

If using a gas grill, place all the wood chips in the smoker box and preheat the grill to high; then, when smoke appears, lower the heat to medium.

4. When ready to cook, if using charcoal, toss the wood chips on the coals. Unwrap the turkey and oil the grill grate. Place the turkey on the hot grate over the drip pan. Cover the grill and cook the turkey until an instant-read thermometer inserted in the thickest part of the breast registers 180°F, 1 to 1½ hours. If using charcoal, add 10 to 12 fresh coals per side after 1 hour of cooking.

5. Transfer the turkey pastrami to a rack to cool, then refrigerate, covered, until cold. To serve, cut the pastrami into thin slices across the grain.

Serves 4 to 8

ADVANCE PREPARATION: 24 hours for marinating the turkey

SPECIAL EQUIPMENT: 1 cup wood chips, soaked for 1 hour in cold water to cover and drained

ANNATTO-SPICED GRILLED TURKEY

U.S.A.

METHOD: Indirect grilling

ADVANCE PREPARATION: 4 hours for marinating the turkey

This certainly isn't like the turkey grandmother used to make! Unless grandmother wore cowboy boots and hailed from Santa Fe, New Mexico. Southwestern cooking mogul Mark Miller marinates his turkey in a tangy tincture of citrus juice, marjoram, and annatto seeds. The latter (also known as *achiote*) are a rust-colored spice native to Central America, with an earthy, iodine-like flavor. Annatto comes to the Southwest cooking via the Yucatán and can be found in Hispanic markets and many supermarkets. Cascabel chiles are fiery round dried chiles that rattle like sleighbells when you shake them. If unavailable, use 2 small hot dried red peppers.

**SPECIAL
EQUIPMENT:**
*3 cups wood
chips, soaked for
1 hour in cold
water to cover
and drained*

For extra flavor and moistness, I like to loosen the skin from the bird and place some of the marinade underneath it. If this seems too tricky, omit step 3.

If you like, you can prepare the marinade the day before. This will deepen the flavor.

1 turkey (10 to 12 pounds)
Salt and freshly ground black pepper,
    to taste
3 cascabel chiles or 2 small dried hot red
    peppers
1 tablespoon annatto seeds
1 cup water
1 bunch fresh marjoram or
    1 tablespoon dried
2 cups fresh orange juice
3 tablespoons fresh lime juice
4 cloves garlic, minced
½ teaspoon ground cumin
1 tablespoon olive oil,
    for brushing

1. Remove and discard the fat from just inside the body cavities of the turkey. Remove the package of giblets and set aside for another use. Rinse the turkey, inside and out, under cold running water, then drain and blot dry, inside and out, with paper towels. Season the turkey inside and out with salt and pepper; cover and refrigerate while you prepare the marinade.

2. Combine the cascabel chiles, annatto seeds, and water in a small saucepan and bring to a boil over medium-high heat. Cook, uncovered, until the chiles have softened and all liquid has been absorbed, 5 to 10 minutes. Transfer the chiles and annatto seeds to a blender and add the marjoram, orange juice, lime juice, garlic, cumin, 1 teaspoon salt, and ¼ teaspoon pepper. Process until smooth. Pour the mixture into a strainer set over a medium-size bowl and press it through with a wooden spoon. Taste for seasoning, adding salt and pepper as necessary; the mixture should be highly seasoned.

3. If you wish to put some of the marinade between the skin and flesh of the turkey, follow the directions in the box on page 243 for loosening the skin.

4. Spoon a few tablespoons of the marinade into the body cavity of the turkey and a tablespoon into the neck cavity. Brush the outside of the bird with additional marinade, liberally if you didn't put in under the skin, and a little oil. Place the turkey in a roasting pan and cover loosely with plastic wrap. Let marinate, in the refrigerator, for 4 hours.

5. Set up the grill for indirect grilling (see page 14 or 16), placing a large drip pan in the center. *If using a charcoal grill,* preheat it to medium.

If using a gas grill, place as many of the wood chips as possible in the smoker box and preheat the grill to high; then, when smoke appears, lower the heat to medium.

6. When ready to cook, if using charcoal, toss 1 cup of the wood chips on the coals. Oil the grill grate. Remove the turkey from the roasting pan and place on the hot grate over the drip pan. Cover the grill and cook until the juices run clear when the tip of a skewer or sharp knife is inserted in the thickest part of a thigh and the legs wiggle freely in the joint (see Note), about 3 hours (figuring on 15 to 20 minutes per pound). If using charcoal, add 10 to 12 fresh coals and ½ cup wood chips per side every hour.

7. Transfer the turkey to a cutting board or platter and let stand, loosely covered with aluminum foil, for 15 minutes before carving.
Serves 10 to 12
Note: An instant-read thermometer inserted in the inner muscle of a thigh, not touching the bone, should register 180°F.

GRILLED GAME HENS WITH MOROCCAN SPICES

MOROCCO

METHOD:
Direct grilling (two-tiered)

ADVANCE PREPARATION:
1 to 8 hours for marinating the chicken

For the most part in Morocco, grilled fare means lamb, but here's a dish for poultry lovers that's fairly bursting with Moroccan spice flavors. Cumin, ginger, paprika, and cilantro combine to transform a commonplace bird into a flame-cooked triumph.

4 game hens (each about 1 pound)
1 medium onion, grated
2 tablespoons chopped fresh Italian (flat-leaf) parsley
2 tablespoons chopped fresh cilantro
3 tablespoons fresh lemon juice
2 tablespoons olive oil
1 teaspoon salt
½ teaspoon ground cumin
½ teaspoon hot or sweet paprika
½ teaspoon ground ginger
½ teaspoon freshly ground white pepper
Lemon wedges, for garnish

1. Remove and discard thc fat just inside the body cavities of the game hens. Remove the packages of giblets (if any) and set aside for another use. Rinse the hens, inside and out, under cold running water, then drain and blot dry, inside and out, with paper towels. Spatchcook the game hens (see page 244) or cut each one lengthwise in half with poultry shears. Place the birds in a large, deep nonreactive bowl or baking dish and set aside while you prepare the marinade.

2. Combine the onion, parsley, cilantro, lemon juice, oil, salt, cumin, paprika, ginger, and pepper in a small bowl and whisk to mix. Pour the mixture over the game hens in the large bowl and turn the birds to coat thoroughly. Cover and let marinate, in the refrigerator, for 1 to 8 hours (the longer the better), turning the birds occasionally.

3. Preheat the grill, using the two-tiered method (see page 14).

4. When ready to cook, oil the grill grate. Remove the game hens from the marinade and arrange, skin side down, on the grate over the hotter section of the grill and cook as directed in steps 3 and 4 in the box on page 246. The total cooking time will be 25 to 35 minutes.

5. Transfer the hens to serving plates or a platter and serve immediately, garnished with lemon wedges.
Serves 4

AFGHAN-STYLE GAME HENS

AFGHANISTAN

METHOD:
Direct grilling

Afghans are some of the world's best grill masters, and this recipe proves it. The marinade uses familiar ingredients that you probably have on hand, but the birds come out so exotic tasting, succulent, and flavorful that your guests will think they're dining in a great ethnic restaurant. You can get away with marinating for only 8 hours, but after the full 24 hours, the hens will taste their best.

ADVANCE PREPARATION:
8 to 24 hours for marinating the hens

SPECIAL EQUIPMENT:
Rotisserie (optional; see Note)

4 game hens (each about 1 pound)
¾ cup extra-virgin olive oil
¾ cup plain whole-milk yogurt
⅓ cup fresh lemon juice
1 tablespoon paprika
1 teaspoon ground cumin
2 teaspoons salt
1 teaspoon freshly ground black pepper
3 medium onions, thinly sliced
8 cloves garlic, thinly sliced
1 lemon, thinly sliced
1 to 4 bird peppers or jalapeño chiles, thinly sliced

1. Remove and discard the fat just inside the body cavities of the game hens. Remove the packages of giblets (if any) and set aside for another use. Rinse the hens, inside and out, under cold running water, then drain and blot dry with paper towels, inside and out. Place the hens in a large, deep nonreactive bowl or baking dish and set aside while you prepare the marinade.

2. Combine the oil, yogurt, lemon juice, paprika, cumin, salt, and black pepper in a medium-size bowl and whisk to blend. Stir in the onions, garlic, sliced lemon, and bird peppers, then pour the mixture over the game hens in the larger bowl, turning the birds to coat. Cover and let marinate, in the refrigerator, 8 to 24 hours (the longer the better), turning the hens occasionally.

3. Set up the grill for rotisserie cooking (see page 20).

4. When ready to cook, place the hens on the spit and set the spit in place on the grill. Turn on the rotisserie and cook until the birds are nicely browned and the juices run clear when the tip of a skewer or sharp knife is inserted in the thickest part of a thigh, 20 to 35 minutes if the grill is covered, somewhat longer uncovered.

5. Unspit the hens and transfer to a cutting board or platter. Let rest 5 minutes before serving.

Serves 4

Note: If desired, you may cook the hens directly on the grill. Spatchcook the birds (see page 244) or cut lengthwise in half with poultry shears, then marinate as directed in step 2 and grill as directed in the preceding recipe.

AFGHAN GRILLED QUAIL

AFGHANISTAN

METHOD:
Direct grilling

ADVANCE PREPARATION:
2 to 3 hours for draining the yogurt, 12 to 24 hours for marinating the quail

If you've always found quail to be a little on the dry side, this recipe is for you. The spiced yogurt marinade makes the birds exceptionally moist and succulent. The only difficult thing about the recipe is remembering to drain the yogurt ahead of time. By the way, even if you don't like quail, you can enjoy this dish. The marinade makes a wonderful dip for crudités. This recipe was inspired by the Khyber Pass restaurant in New York.

4 cups plain whole-milk yogurt
2 teaspoons hot or sweet paprika
1 teaspoon salt, or more to taste
1 teaspoon ground coriander
½ teaspoon cayenne pepper, or more to taste
½ teaspoon curry powder
½ teaspoon ground cumin
½ teaspoon ground turmeric
½ teaspoon freshly ground black pepper
8 quail (about 2 pounds in all)

1. Set a yogurt strainer, or regular strainer lined with a double layer of dampened cheesecloth, over a bowl. Add the yogurt to the strainer and let drain, in the refrigerator, for 2 to 3 hours.

2. Remove the drained yogurt from the refrigerator and discard the liquid. Transfer the yogurt (it will be semifirm but not dry), to a large nonreactive bowl or baking dish. Add the paprika, 1 teaspoon salt, the coriander, ½ teaspoon cayenne, the curry powder, cumin, turmeric, and black pepper and whisk to blend. Taste for seasoning, adding salt and cayenne as necessary; the mixture should be highly seasoned. Set aside while you prepare the quail.

3. Remove and discard the fat just inside the body cavities. Rinse the quail inside and out, under cold running water, then drain and blot dry with paper towels. Spatchcock the quail following the directions on page 244.

4. Add the quail to the bowl with the marinade, turning to coat thoroughly. Cover and let marinate, in the refrigerator, 12 to 24 hours, turning the birds occasionally.

5. Preheat the grill to high.

6. When ready to grill, oil the grate. Remove the quail from the marinade and place them, skin side down, on the hot grate. Cook until nicely browned and the juices run clear when the tip of a skewer or sharp knife is inserted in the thickest part of a thigh, 4 to 6 minutes per side (8 to 12 minutes in all).

7. Transfer the quail to serving plates or a platter, and serve immediately.

Serves 4

GRILLED QUAIL SANTORINI

GREECE

METHOD:
Direct grilling

ADVANCE PREPARATION:
1 to 2 hours for marinating the quail

Santorini is one of the most heartachingly beautiful of the Greek islands, a collapsed shell of volcano on whose steep sides cling whitewashed villas and churches. The island has given its name to an equally romantic restaurant in Chicago's Greektown, a softly lit, split-level dining room where guests dine amid copper cookware, rustic wicker chairs, baskets hanging from the rafters, and a blazing fireplace. Quail is a house specialty here, and despite the simplicity of the preparation, this is one of the best ways I know to prepare the tiny bird.

8 quail (about 2 pounds in all)
½ cup red wine vinegar, more to taste
½ cup fresh lemon juice
1½ tablespoons crumbled dried oregano (see Greek Oregano, page 276)
2 teaspoons salt, or more to taste
2 teaspoons freshly ground black pepper, or more to taste
¾ cup extra-virgin olive oil, preferably Greek

1. Remove and discard the fat just inside the body cavities and rinse the quail, inside and out, under cold running water, then drain and blot dry with paper towels. Spatchcock the quail following the directions on page 244. Arrange the quail, skin side down, in a nonreactive baking dish and set aside while you prepare the vinaigrette marinade.

2. Combine ½ cup vinegar, the lemon juice, oregano and 2 teaspoons each salt and pepper in a large bowl and whisk until the salt is dissolved. Whisk in the oil to blend. Taste for seasoning, adding salt, pepper, or vinegar as necessary; the mixture should be highly seasoned. Pour half the vinaigrette over the quail, turning the birds to coat thoroughly. Cover and let marinate, in the refrigerator, for 1 to 2 hours, turning once or twice. Reserve the remaining vinaigrette until serving time.

3. Preheat the grill to high.

4. When ready to cook, oil the grill grate.

Remove the quail from the marinade and arrange them skin side down, on the hot grate. Grill until nicely browned and the juices run clear when the tip of a skewer or sharp knife is inserted in the thickest part of a thigh, about 4 to 6 minutes per side (8 to 12 minutes in all).

5. Transfer the quail to serving plates or a platter and serve immediately, accompanied by the reserved vinaigrette.

Serves 4

SPICED GRILLED QUAIL

UZBEKISTAN

METHOD:
Direct grilling

ADVANCE PREPARATION:
4 hours for marinating the quail

This recipe comes from what I call the barbecue belt of the former Soviet Union. Grilling plays a central role in the cuisines of the Caucasus republics of Georgia, Armenia, Azerbaijan, and Uzbekistan. The following quail are popular in Uzbekistan, where, according to Caucasus culinary authority Darra Goldstein, the birds would be wrapped in pumpkin leaves and roasted in hot ashes. As pumpkin leaves are not widely available, I suggest using grape leaves. But even if you omit using leaves, the garlic, cumin, and coriander marinade creates complex layers of flavor. You'll be amazed how such a tiny bird can have such a big taste.

Goldstein, author of the *The Georgian Feast,* has adopted a more streamlined method for cooking the quail—splitting, marinating, and grilling them over direct flames. You'll find both methods in the following recipe.

8 quail (about 2 pounds in all)
2 teaspoons coarse (kosher or sea) salt
2 teaspoons cumin seeds
2 teaspoons coriander seeds
2 teaspoons whole black peppercorns
2 cloves garlic, chopped
2 tablespoons olive oil

1. Remove and discard the fat just inside the body cavities and rinse the quail, inside and out, under cold running water, then drain and blot dry with paper towels. Spatchcock the quail following the directions on page 244. Place the quail in a large bowl or baking dish and set aside while you prepare the spice paste.

2. Combine the salt, cumin and coriander seeds, and peppercorns in a mortar and crush to a powder with the pestle, then work in the garlic and oil; or grind the salt and spices to a powder in a spice mill and combine with the garlic and oil in a small bowl. Using your fingers, rub this paste over the quail to coat thoroughly. Cover and let marinate, in the refrigerator, for 4 hours.

3. Preheat the grill to high.

4. When ready to cook, oil the grate. Arrange the quail, skin side down, on the hot grate and grill until nicely browned and the juices run clear when the tip of a skewer or sharp knife is inserted in the thickest part of a thigh, 4 to 6 minutes per side (8 to 12 minutes in all).

5. Transfer the quail to serving plates or a platter and serve immediately.

Serves 4 as an entrée

Uzbekistani Quail Grilled in Grape Leaves

Intrigued by the traditional recipe, I tried wrapping the quail in grape leaves (different from pumpkin leaves, of course, but more widely available in this country) and roasting them in the embers. The results were delectable. In order to cook the quail using this method, you need to have a charcoal grill.

40 grape leaves packed in brine
8 quail (about 2 pounds in all)
Spice paste as prepared in Spiced Grilled Quail (step 2, above)

1. Rinse the grape leaves under cold running water, then let soak in a bowl of cold water to cover for 1 hour, changing the water several times.

2. Preheat a charcoal grill to medium-high.

3. Remove and discard the fat just inside the body cavities of the quail, rinse the quail inside and out, under cold running water, then drain and blot dry, inside and out, with paper towels. Leave the quail whole. Place a little spice paste in the cavity of each bird; rub the remaining spice paste on the skin.

4. Drain the grape leaves and blot dry. Wrap each quail in 5 grape leaves and tie securely with kitchen string.

5. Nestle the wrapped quail in the ashes. Roast until the birds are cooked, 15 to 20 minutes, turning the quail from time to time with tongs. To test for doneness, insert the tip of a metal skewer or sharp knife into the thickest part of a thigh. It should come out very hot to the touch.

6. Serve the quail in the leaves, but since they've been in the ashes, the leaves will be inedible, so should be removed before the quail are eaten.

Serves 4

GRILLED DUCK WITH GARLIC AND GINGER

U . S . A .

METHOD:
Indirect grilling

I'm about to make an extravagant claim: There is no better way to cook duck than on a grill. This may sound iconclastic coming from a cook who was trained in France, where duck is almost always roasted in the oven and where it is served fashionably rare, like steak.

The truth is that the ducks we get in North America taste best cooked long and slow to tenderize the meat and melt out the fat. And indirect grilling is about the best way I know to produce crackling crisp skin and well-done meat that is virtually fat free and fall-off-the-bone tender. Besides, it takes the mess of cooking a fatty bird, like duck, outside your kitchen.

Here's a basic recipe for grilled duck, flavored by slivers of garlic and ginger inserted in slits in the flesh. The slits perform a second function, the same as the pricks made all over the skin by a fork: They allow the fat to drain off, crisping the skin in the process. If you like a smoke flavor with duck, throw a cupful of soaked wood chips on the coals (or into the smoker box of a gas grill). Fruit woods, like apple and cherry, go particularly well with duck. The duck is wonderful served with one of the sauces that follow. Then again, it's pretty outrageous eaten just by itself.

1 duck (4½ to 5 pounds), thawed if frozen
2 cloves garlic, quartered lengthwise
2 slices (each ¼-inch thick) fresh ginger,
    cut into ¼-inch slivers
Salt and freshly ground black pepper, to taste
Cinnamon Cherry or Orange Sauce for Duck
    (recipes follow)

1. Set the grill up for indirect grilling (see page 14 or 16), placing a large drip pan in the center, and preheat to medium-low.

2. Remove and discard the fat just inside the body cavities of the duck. Remove the package of giblets and set aside for another use. Rinse the duck inside and out, under cold running water, then drain and blot dry, inside and out, with paper towels.

3. Place the duck on its breast so the back side is up. Using the tip of a sharp, slender knife, make 1 slit in the fatty part of the duck under each wing and 1 slit in the underside of each thigh. Insert a sliver of garlic and a sliver of ginger into each slit, then place the remaining garlic and ginger in the body cavity. Prick the duck skin all over with a fork, being careful not to pierce the meat; then season the duck, inside and out, very generously with salt and pepper.

4. Place the duck, breast side up, on a rack over the drip pan. Cover the grill and cook the duck for 1½ hours.

5. At this point, turn the bird on its end over a bowl to drain off any juices that accumulate in the cavity; discard the juices. Continue cooking the duck until the skin is mahogany brown and crackling crisp and the meat is well done and tender, another 30 to 60 minutes. An instant-read thermometer inserted in the inner muscle of a thigh, not touching the bone, should register 170°F. If using a charcoal grill, add 10 to 12 fresh prelighted coals per side after each hour of cooking.

6. Transfer the duck to a platter and let sit for 5 minutes before carving. Serve with either of the suggested sauces on the side.

Serves 2 as an entrée

Cinnamon Cherry Sauce for Duck

Duckling à la Montmorency is a classic of French cuisine. I've made the sauce with both sweet and tart cherry varieties and both fresh and canned fruit. Fresh are obviously better, but canned pitted cherries are certainly convenient and still quite tasty. (Be sure to use canned fruit, not the thick pie filling that also comes in cans.) Adjust the sugar accordingly. To reinforce the cinnamon flavor, place a cinnamon stick in the cavity of the duck before grilling.

12 ounces fresh cherries or 1 can
    (15 ounces) cherries packed in light
    syrup, drained
¼ cup sugar, or as needed
3 tablespoons water
¼ cup red wine vinegar
½ cup port wine
1 tablespoon fresh lemon juice
¼ teaspoon grated fresh lemon zest
1 cup rich duck or chicken stock, or canned
    low-sodium chicken broth
1 stick (3 inches) cinnamon
1½ teaspoons cornstarch or arrowroot
1 tablespoon kirsch
Salt and freshly ground black pepper, to taste
1 teaspoon honey or sugar (optional)

1. If using fresh cherries, stem and rinse them under cold running water, then drain. Pit the cherries with a cherry pitter; you should have about 1½ cups. If using canned cherries, drain, rinse, and drain again. Set the cherries aside.

2. Combine the sugar and water in a small, deep, heavy saucepan. Cover, set over high heat, and cook for 2 minutes. Uncover the pan, reduce the heat to medium high, and cook until the sugar caramelizes (turns a deep golden brown), gently swirling the pan to ensure even cooking. This should take 6 to 8 minutes, but watch carefully—it can burn quickly. Remove the pan from the heat and add the vinegar. (Stand back: The sauce will emit a Vesuvian hiss, releasing eye-stinging vinegar vapors.) Return the mixture to low heat and simmer, whisking until the caramel is completely dissolved, 2 to 3 minutes.

3. Stir the port, lemon juice, and lemon zest into the caramel mixture and bring to a boil over medium heat. Cook, uncovered, for 2 minutes. Add the stock and cinnamon and cook until reduced slightly, about 5 minutes. Reduce the heat to low, add the cherries, and simmer gently until the cherries are soft but not mushy, about 5 minutes for fresh cherries, 2 minutes for canned. Remove and discard the cinnamon stick.

4. Dissolve the cornstarch in the kirsch and whisk this mixture into the sauce. Boil until the sauce thickens slightly, about 1 minute. Remove from the heat and taste for seasoning, adding salt and pepper; if additional sweetness is desired, whisk in the honey. Serve or cover and refrigerate for up to 5 days.

Makes about 2 cups, enough for 2 ducks

Orange Sauce for Duck

Duckling à l'orange was one of the first dishes I learned to make at the La Varenne cooking school in Paris; it is another French classic. The sauce owes its unique sweet-sour-caramel flavor to the *bigarade,* a mixture of burnt sugar and vinegar. The traditional preparation calls for oranges, but I also like the exotic flavor you get with tangerines. To reinforce the orange flavor, place a few strips of the orange zest in the cavity of the duck before grilling.

2 large oranges, preferable navels
¼ cup sugar
3 tablespoons water
¼ cup red wine vinegar
1½ cups rich duck or chicken stock or
    canned low-sodium chicken broth
1 tablespoon orange marmalade
1½ teaspoons cornstarch
2 tablespoons Grand Marnier or other orange
    liqueur
Salt and freshly ground black pepper, to taste

1. Finely grate enough zest off one of the oranges to make 1 teaspoon. Cut the remaining rind and all the white pith off this orange to expose the flesh. Working over a bowl to catch any juices, and using a sharp paring knife, make V-shaped cuts between the membranes to release neat segments. Set the segments aside, first removing any seeds with a fork. Juice the second orange: You should have about ⅔ cup juice in all.

2. Combine the sugar and water in a small, deep, heavy saucepan. Cover, set over high heat, and cook for 2 minutes. Uncover the pan, reduce the heat to medium-high, and cook until the sugar caramelizes (turns a deep golden brown), gently swirling the pan to ensure even cooking. This should take 6 to 8 minutes, but watch carefully—it can burn quickly. Remove the pan from the heat and add the vinegar. (Stand back: The sauce will emit a Vesuvian hiss, releasing eye-stinging vinegar vapors.) Return the mixture to low heat and simmer gently, whisking steadily, until the caramel is completely dissolved, 2 to 3 minutes.

3. Stir the orange juice and stock into the caramel mixture and bring to a boil over medium heat. Cook, uncovered, to reduce by half, 10 to 15 minutes. Reduce the heat to low and whisk in the orange marmalade. Simmer

Grating Citrus Peel

*T*he next time you grate oranges or other citrus fruit on a conventional grater, press a sheet of parchment paper or waxed paper onto the side of the grater before grating. When you're finished, the zest will be on the paper, not stuck in the teeth of the grater.

until melted, about 1 minute. Dissolve the cornstarch in the Grand Marnier and whisk this mixture into the sauce. Cook until the sauce thickens slightly, about 1 minute. Add the orange segments and remove from the heat. Season with salt and pepper. Serve or cover and refrigerate for up to 5 days.

Makes about 2 cups, enough for 2 ducks

PEKING DUCK

MACAO

METHOD:
Indirect grilling

ADVANCE PREPARATION:
24 hours for drying the duck skin

Peking duck is one of the glories of Chinese gastronomy. I never thought of it as barbecue until I visited Macao. This tiny Portuguese enclave, located an hour south of Hong Kong by hydrofoil, boasts some of the best food in Asia. (That's what happens when you marry two cultures who love to eat: the Portuguese and the Chinese.)

You won't find Lam Yam Wing in any of the guidebooks, but to come to Macao without visiting the restaurant would be to miss a major gastronomic experience. The real pride and joy of the house is Peking duck, which has been brushed with honey and roasted to the color of mahogany. The waiter carves the skin into crackling crisp shards and serves it with silver dollar–size scallion pancakes. (No papery Peking pancakes here, but velvety, delicate, thin crêpes.) The actual meat of the duck is returned to the kitchen, to be stir-fried with shallots and garlic. This recipe is inspired by Lam Yam Wing.

Cooking duck in a covered grill using the indirect method produces a succulent and crisp duck without a lot of mess and work. Leaving the duck to dry uncovered in the refrigerator overnight crisps the skin even more.

Here, then, is a not strictly traditional, but eminently tasty Peking duck cooked on the grill. Don't be intimidated by the length of the recipe—the actual preparation time is minimal. I've included a recipe for scallion crêpes, which you can make while the duck cooks. If you're in a hurry, you could use packaged Peking pancakes or even flour tortillas, but neither is as delicate as the crêpes.

FOR THE DUCK:

1 duck (5 pounds), thawed if frozen
Salt and freshly ground black pepper, to taste
1 teaspoon Chinese five-spice powder
1 clove garlic, peeled
1 scallion, both white and green parts, trimmed
3 thin slices fresh ginger
1 tablespoon Asian (dark) sesame oil

FOR THE SAUCE:

1 cup hoisin sauce
¼ cup honey
¼ cup soy sauce
¼ cup rice wine or sake
3 cloves garlic, minced
1 tablespoon minced fresh ginger

FOR SERVING:

16 Scallion Crêpes (recipe follows) or 12 Peking pancakes or flour tortillas
16 scallion brushes (see box, page 282)

1. The day before you're serving, remove and discard the fat just inside the body cavities of the duck. Remove the package of giblets and set aside for another use. Rinse the duck, inside and out, under cold running water, then drain and blot dry, inside and out, with paper towels. Place the duck in a roasting pan and let stand, uncovered, in the refrigerator overnight to dry out the skin.

2. Set the grill up for indirect grilling (see page 14 or 16), placing a large drip pan in the center, and preheat to medium-low.

3. Season the body cavity with salt, pepper, and half the five-spice powder. Place the garlic, scallion, and ginger slices in the body cavity, then turn the duck over on its breast so the back side is up. Using the tip of a sharp, slender knife, make 1 small slit in the fatty part of the duck under each wing and 1 slit on the underside of each thigh. Prick the duck skin all over with a fork, being careful not to pierce the meat. Brush the duck all over the outside with sesame oil and season by rubbing the skin all over with the remaining five-spice powder and salt and pepper.

4. When ready to cook place the duck, breast side up, on the hot grill grate over the drip pan. Cover the grill and cook the duck for 1½ hours.

5. Meanwhile, prepare the sauce. Combine the hoisin sauce, honey, soy sauce, rice wine, garlic, and ginger in a small, heavy saucepan and bring to a simmer over low heat. Simmer gently, uncovered, until well flavored and syrupy, about 5 minutes.

6. After 1½ hours, turn the bird on its end over a bowl to drain off any juices that accumulate in the cavity; discard the juices. Reprick the skin with a fork and make fresh slits under the wings and thighs to encourage draining. Continue cooking the duck until the skin is mahogany brown and crackling crisp and the meat is well done and tender, another 30 to 60 minutes. An instant-read meat thermometer inserted in the inner muscle of a thigh, not touching the bone, should register 170°F. If using a charcoal grill, add 10 to 12 fresh coals per side after each hour of cooking.

7. Transfer the duck to a platter. Present it to your guests, then, using a sharp knife, carve the skin and meat off the bones. (You may want to do this in the kitchen.) Spoon the sauce into small bowls or ramekins, one per guest. Arrange the duck meat and skin on one platter, the crêpes and scallion brushes on another. Have each guest brush a crêpe with sauce, using a scallion brush. Place a slice of duck skin and meat on the crêpe (and a scallion brush, if desired) and roll it into a cone for eating.

Serves 4

Scallion Crêpes

These crêpes are much more delicate than Peking pancakes or tortillas. You can make them up to 24 hours ahead and store, wrapped in plastic in the refrigerator.

2 large eggs
½ teaspoon sugar
½ teaspoon salt
¾ cup milk
½ cup water, or as needed
1 cup unbleached all-purpose flour
3 tablespoons very finely chopped
    trimmed scallion greens
1 tablespoon Asian (dark) sesame oil
Nonstick cooking spray, melted
    butter, or more sesame oil
    for oiling the pans

How to Make Scallion Brushes

Cut the roots and green tops off 16 scallions, reserving the latter for crêpes. You want to wind up with 3-inch pieces of scallion white. Make a series of 1-inch lengthwise cuts in each end, gradually rotating the scallion, to form the individual "bristles" of the brush. Soak the scallions in a bowl of ice water for a couple of hours to curl the ends of the brushes.

1. Whisk the eggs, sugar, and salt in a bowl until the sugar and salt are dissolved. Whisk in the milk and ½ cup water to blend well, then add the flour and whisk just to mix. If the batter looks lumpy, strain it into another bowl. Whisk in the scallions and sesame oil. The batter should be the consistency of heavy cream. If too thick, thin it with a little more water.

2. Lightly spray a 5-inch crêpe pan with oil (or brush with a little more sesame oil) and heat over a medium heat. (When the pan is the proper temperature, a drop of water will evaporate in 2 to 3 seconds.) Off the heat, add 2 tablespoons crêpe batter to the pan all at once. Gently tilt and rotate the pan to form a thin, 4-inch round pancake.

3. Return the pan to the heat and cook the crêpe until lightly browned on both sides, 1 to 2 minutes per side, turning with a spatula. As the crêpes are done, stack them on a plate on top of one another. For best results, spray the pan lightly with oil between crêpes.

Makes about sixteen 4-inch crêpes

The Macanese Grill

As a frequent and fervent traveler, I am fascinated by crossroads cuisines. The meeting—and sometimes clash—of two cultures along a narrow geographic interface has produced some of the world's most interesting food.

If you don't believe me, visit Macao. This tiny Portuguese enclave on the southeastern coast of China is the very embodiment of what contemporary American chefs have come to call "fusion cuisine." Except that in this case the fusion has been going on for more than 400 years, merging two cultures from opposite ends of the earth.

Macao is a tiny snippet of land in the mouth of China's Pearl River estuary. Tiny? Its population of 450,000 lives on two small islands and a peninsula only 2.5 square miles in size. Macao has been a Portuguese colony since 1557, when Iberian traders established an outpost here to serve as mercantile go-betweens to the Chinese and Japanese.

Portugal is one of the smallest countries in Europe, but in the seventeenth century it projected its sphere of influence around the world. Macao was the easternmost outpost of an empire that stretched from Brazil to Angola and Mozambique to Goa in India and Timor.

Today, only 5 percent of the mostly Chinese population speaks Portuguese, but you still find Baroque churches, markets selling salt cod and olive oil, and pastry shops specializing in Portuguese pastries. This is also one of the few places in China (or soon to be China, as the colony will revert to the Mainland in 1999), where grilling is widespread, for the Portuguese brought grilling to China, a country whose complex cuisine is remarkable, and surprising, for its lack of live-fire cooking. In other words, you have a fusion of Chinese and Portuguese culinary cultures—known locally as Macanese cuisine.

Like most of the million-plus tourists who come here each year, I arrived on a jet foil from Hong Kong. The ride took less than an hour, but it took me decades back in time. At first glance, Macao looks like any emerging Asian city—relentless construction, hellish traffic, high-rise apartments, and casinos crowding the waterfront. But step onto a side street, like the Rua de la Felicidade (the appropriately named "street of happiness" that once served the colony's red light district), and you could be in prewar China.

Merchandise spills from storefronts onto rickety tables lining the sidewalks. Vendors cook sheets of *au jok kohn,* a sort of sweet, salty, and deliciously fatty pork jerky, over braziers filled with blazing charcoal. Restaurants specialize in foods you didn't know you could eat: snakes slither in the window of one establishment; another boasts cages of a small tapir-like mammal that are empty at the end of the evening. Come nightfall, the street fills with the heady aroma of cooking, as locals converge here for doorsill dining and outdoor socializing.

You'd expect to find grilling at Macao's Portuguese restaurants and you will. Consider Fernando's, opened by an Azores Islander and located on the most tranquil of Macao's islands, Coloane. In the center of Fernando's open-air kitchen stands a barbecue pit, where sardines, salt cod, even cuttlefish are grilled over burning charcoal. In true Portuguese fashion, grilled seafoods and meats are served with a tomato, bell pepper, and olive oil "salsa" and fiery *piri-piri* sauce.

Many of Macao's Chinese have adopted live-fire cooking. My next stop was a roadside barbecue joint called Lam Yam Wing on the island of Taipa. Run by four brothers, Lam Yam Wing is the farthest thing from a tourist trap. Instead the place is hopping with locals, who come here for Chinese barbecue.

The focal point of the restaurant is the grill, a 20-foot-long metal trough with half a dozen different cooking zones. There's a rotisserie area, where whole chickens (with heads still intact) spin on mechanized turnspits. There's a gridiron on which sizzle chicken wings, sea crabs, and fat, buttery local eels. The cooking technique may be Portuguese, but the flavorings are pure Chinese: soy sauce, sesame oil, rice wine, ginger, and scallions. The food is cut into bite-size pieces, so you can eat it with chopsticks. But many customers have adopted the Western practice of eating the 'cue with their hands.

TUSCAN GRILLED PHEASANT

ITALY

METHOD:
Direct or indirect grilling

SPECIAL EQUIPMENT:
Rotisserie (optional)

ADVANCE PREPARATION:
30 minutes for soaking the bread

Da Delfina, in the village of Artimino near Florence, is the just sort of restaurant you want to wind up at after a long day on the barbecue trail. You drive up progressively narrower roads to a village perched atop a precipitously steep Tuscan hilltop. You come to a dining establishment that feels less like a restaurant than a private home. You're in Chianti country now, and Da Delfina has a terrace where, weather permitting, you can dine with an almost extraterrestrial view of the manicured vineyards below you.

The first thing you see when you enter the restaurant is an open kitchen with a massive hearth equipped with a multi-spit rotisserie and wood-burning grill. Cords of Tuscan oak lie stacked on the floor and in the courtyard below. The white-haired woman shelling cannellini beans at a table by the door is none other than Delfina Cioni herself, who founded the restaurant, after a stint as a private chef for a nearby countess, in 1961. Today the restaurant is run by her son, Carlo.

According to Carlo, it makes sense to cook game on the grill. After all, it wasn't so long ago that our hunter-gatherer forebears caught their own food and cooked it over communal campfires. Nonetheless, when grilling game, you have to keep its inherent dryness in mind. Game is much leaner than domesticated animals; as a result, it tends to dry out during cooking. The best way to avoid this is to wrap the game in pancetta, bacon, or caul fat.

I was the only person at my table eating pheasant the day I dined at Delfina, so they served me a boned, stuffed pheasant leg. This recipe calls for a whole pheasant, which you can bone if you're feeling ambitious (see below). But the pheasant will be perfectly delicious even if you don't bone it.

Note that if you can't find pheasant, chicken and game hen are delicious prepared in this fashion.

1 pheasant (about 2¼ pounds)
1 cup milk
4 thick slices stale country-style white bread, crusts removed
8 ounces Swiss chard leaves, trimmed
Salt, to taste
1 clove garlic, minced
⅓ cup freshly grated Parmesan cheese
Freshly ground black pepper, to taste
8 thin slices pancetta
4 sprigs fresh rosemary

1. Rinse the pheasant, inside and out, under cold running water, then drain and blot dry, inside and out, with paper towels. If you're feeling ambitious, partially bone the pheasant. Start at the neck opening. Using the tip of a sharp paring knife, cut the flesh away from the rib cage. When you get to the wing joints, cut right through them. As you bone the bird, pull the flesh back over the rib cage, the way you would peel off a glove. Continue boning until you get to the leg joints. Cut through them as well. Cut out the thigh bones. Pull out the rib cage and turn the pheasant back inside in (like turning an inside-out sock back to right side out). This sounds a good deal more complicated and messy than it really is. You can certainly stuff and cook the pheasant without removing the bones. Refrigerate the bird, covered, while you prepare the stuffing.

2. Pour the milk over the bread in a shallow bowl and let soak for 30 minutes.

3. Meanwhile, cook the Swiss chard in a large pot of rapidly boiling salted water until tender, about 5 minutes. Refresh under cold water, drain well, and blot dry with paper towels. Chop the Swiss chard as fine as possible and squeeze it in your hands to wring out any water. Place in a medium-size bowl.

4. Squeeze the bread to wring out the milk. Add the bread to the chard in the bowl along with the garlic and cheese and mix well, adding salt and pepper. Spoon this mixture into the pheasant and sew or skewer the bird shut.

5. Salt and pepper the pheasant on the outside. Wrap the bird in strips of pancetta, tucking sprigs of rosemary beneath them. Use kitchen string to tie the pancetta in place.

6. There are two ways to cook the pheasant. One is on a spit on a rotisserie over a high heat. The other is by indirect grilling.

Rotisserie method: Set up the grill for rotisserie cooking (see page 20). When ready to cook, place the pheasant on the spit and set the spit in place on the grill. Turn on the rotisserie and cook, covered, until the bird is nicely browned and the tip of a metal skewer or sharp knife inserted into the thickest part of the thigh comes out very hot to the touch, 40 to 60 minutes.

Indirect grilling method: Set up the grill for indirect grilling (see page 14 or 16) placing a drip pan in the center, and preheat to medium. When ready to cook, oil the grill grate. Place the pheasant on the hot grate over the drip pan. Cover the grill and cook until the bird tests done as above, about 1 hour.

7. To serve, remove the trussing string. Let the bird stand for 10 minutes, then cut in half and serve.

Serves 2

Grilled Pheasant Legs

The Italian preparation for whole pheasant also works well with pheasant or chicken legs.

4 pheasant legs (about 2 pounds in all)
Stuffing from Tuscan Grilled Pheasant
    (recipe above)
8 thin slices pancetta
4 sprigs fresh rosemary

1. Partially bone the pheasant legs by cutting out each thigh bone, working from the inside of the top of the leg. Prepare the stuffing as described, then stuff the pheasant legs with the stuffing and tie or sew the openings shut, or pin shut with toothpicks. Wrap each pheasant leg in 2 strips of pancetta with a sprig of rosemary underneath. Tie the pancetta in place with butcher's string.

2. Preheat the grill to medium-high.

3. When ready to cook, oil the grill grate. Arrange the pheasant legs on the hot grate and grill, turning with tongs, until the skin is nicely browned and the tip of a skewer or sharp knife comes out very hot, 8 to 12 minutes per side. Move the legs as needed to avoid flare-ups from the dripping pancetta fat. Untruss the legs before serving.

Serves 2

Water Meets Fire:
FISH ON THE GRILL

"Food is meant to tempt as well as nourish, and everything that lives in water is seductive."

—JEAN-PAUL ARON

There's no shortage of good grill choices at this fish market in Naples.

Fish live in water. But they acquire their maximum flavor from fire. This truth is not lost on grill jockeys around the world, who grill everything imaginable, from tiny sardines to spectacular whole flamed sea bass, from Turkish and Brazilian swordfish kebabs to chile-laced Bahamian-style snapper. Grilling was probably the first way man cooked fish and, as my travels suggest, it remains the best.

This chapter covers the fine points of grilling fish, from steaks and fillets to dramatically presented whole sea creatures. Have you ever had a problem with fish falling apart or sticking to the grill? Here's where I explain how to avoid these pitfalls. I also explore some of the ingenious techniques grilling experts have evolved for keeping fish moist and flavorful, including wrapping and grilling it in grape leaves, in the style of the Republic of Georgia, or cooking it on lemongrass skewers in the manner of Bali. You'll be amazed how luscious grilled fish can taste.

For many people, the subject of grilling fish begins and ends with simple salmon or tuna steaks. Journey with me on the barbecue trail and you'll discover a whole new, thrilling world of grilled seafood.

WHOLE GRILLED SNAPPER WITH SOUTH AFRICAN SPICES

Fish Brai

METHOD:
Indirect grilling

**ADVANCE
PREPARATION:**
*3 to 8 hours for
marinating the
fish*

Brai is the South African word used to describe a barbecue. You may be surprised by the Indian/Malaysian flavorings (curry, ginger, and coconut milk) in this recipe, but not once you know that South Africa has large Indian and Malaysian communities. I find that the curry and coconut milk have a wonderful way of bringing out the sweetness of fish.

Cooking a whole fish on the grill always presents a challenge. If you cook it directly over live fire, you run the risk of burning the skin before the center of the fish is cooked. You also face the tricky task of inverting the fish without having it fall apart. South Africans solve the problem by using the indirect grilling method, so you don't need to turn the fish.

**1 whole snapper, bluefish, sea bass, or other
    large fish (3½ to 4 pounds), cleaned and
    trimmed of fins, head and tail left on**
**Salt and freshly ground black pepper,
    to taste**
1½ teaspoons ground cumin
1 tablespoon curry powder
**1 tablespoon hot paprika or 1 to 2
    teaspoons cayenne**
3 tablespoons vegetable oil
3 tablespoons canned coconut milk
2 tablespoons fresh lemon juice
**1 bunch scallions, both white and green
    parts, trimmed and finely chopped**
5 cloves garlic, crushed
**1 piece (½ inch) fresh ginger, peeled and
    thinly sliced**
¾ cup coarsely chopped fresh cilantro leaves

1. Rinse the fish, inside and out, under cold running water, then drain and blot dry with paper towels. Make 4 diagonal slashes, to the bone, in each side of the fish. Season the fish, inside and out (including the side slashes), with salt and pepper. Place the fish in a roasting pan and set aside while you prepare the spice paste.

2. Combine the cumin, curry powder, paprika, oil, coconut milk, lemon juice, scallions, garlic, ginger, and cilantro, 1 teaspoon salt, and ½ teaspoon pepper in a blender or food processor and process to a smooth paste. Taste for seasoning, adding salt and pepper as necessary; the mixture should be highly seasoned.

3. Spoon half the mixture into the cavity and under the gills of the fish. Spread the remaining mixture over the outside of the fish, working it into the slashes in the sides of the fish. Cover and let marinate, in the refrigerator, for at least 3 hours, or, for a richer flavor, overnight.

4. Set up the grill for indirect grilling (see page 14 or 16) and preheat to high.

5. When ready to cook, oil the grill grate. Place the fish on the hot grate and cover the grill. Grill the fish until it breaks into firm flakes when pressed with a finger, 45 minutes to 1 hour.

6. Using two long spatulas, carefully transfer the fish to a serving platter. At the table, fillet the fish as described on page 293 and serve at once.
Serves 4

How to Grill the Perfect Whole Fish

A beach. A campfire. A glistening fish—minutes out of the water—cooked on a stick or grate over blazing coals. It's a scene that's almost as old as mankind itself and as enjoyable as perfect beach weather. And it serves to remind us that fish never tastes better than when cooked over open fire.

That's the good news. The bad news is that most of us either burn fish to a crisp, serve it raw in the center, or leave half the fish sticking to the grate of the grill.

Fortunately, there are three methods for grilling a perfect whole fish every time. But before you even start your fire, choose the right kind of fish for grilling whole. Flat fish, like snappers, pompano, black bass, sole, trout, porgies, and grunts are ideal for grilling whole. You can also grill large whole fish, like salmon, using the indirect method.

The fish should be impeccably fresh. The eyes should be shiny and clear; the gills should be red; and the fish should be utterly free of a fish smell. Ask your fishmonger to gut and scale the fish before you take it home.

Make 3 or 4 deep diagonal slashes in each side of the fish to the bone. This allows the marinade and basting mixture to penetrate the flesh and speeds up the cooking time.

You may want to invest in a fish grilling basket. These hinged, fish-shaped devices keep the fish off the grate (where it can stick), enabling you to turn the fish without having it slide off a spatula. Essential? Of course not. But fish baskets can make the process a whole lot easier.

THE MEDIUM FLAME METHOD

1. Preheat the grill to medium.

2. Generously oil the grate or hinged fish grilling basket. Brush both sides of the fish with oil or melted butter. Place the fish on the hot grate directly over the heat and grill until the skin is dark and crisp and the flesh is cooked through to the bone, 6 to 15 minutes per side, depending on the size of the fish. Turn the fish, using a long spatula or by inverting the basket, and cook the other side the same way.

3. To test for doneness, press the fish with your finger. When properly cooked, the area around where you pressed will break into firm flakes. It should pull away easily from the bones.

4. Use a long crook-handled spatula to gently slide the fish off the grate (or remove the basket from the grate) and onto a platter.

THE INDIRECT METHOD

This method is particularly well suited to large fish, like whole salmon.

1. Set up the grill for indirect cooking (see page 14 or 16) and preheat to medium. You don't really need a drip pan because fish is so lean, but if you wish, set one in place.

2. Generously oil the grate or hinged fish grilling basket and brush the fish on both sides with oil or melted butter. Place the fish in the center of the grate, away from the heat, cover, and grill until cooked through, 30 to 60 minutes (sometimes more), depending on the size of the fish.

3. Follow steps 3 and 4 in The Medium Flame Method for testing for doneness and removing the fish from the grate.

THE BANANA LEAF METHOD

This method from Southeast Asia is the easiest way to grill a 1- to 2-pound whole fish. A fresh or frozen banana leaf will keep the fish from drying out. It can be purchased at an Asian or Hispanic market. The banana leaf should be cut into a rectangle a little larger than the size of the fish you will be grilling. In a pinch, you can make a high-tech banana leaf by cutting 4 to 6 sheets of aluminum foil slightly larger than the fish and stacking them in layers.

1. Preheat the grill to high.

2. Generously oil the grate. Brush both sides of the fish with oil or melted butter. Place the fish on the hot grate directly over the heat and grill until the skin is dark and crisp, 6 to 12 minutes, depending on the size of the fish.

3. Place the banana leaf on the grate next to the fish and invert the fish onto it. Cook until the fish is cooked through to the bone, 6 to 12 minutes, depending on the size of the fish.

4. Follow steps 3 and 4 in The Medium Flame Method for testing the fish for doneness and removing it from the grate. Discard the banana leaf before serving.

Fish Grilling Chart*

CUT	METHOD	HEAT	DONENESS
WHOLE FISH			
1–1½ LBS	DIRECT	MED-HIGH	COOKED THROUGH; 6–10 MIN/LB
2–5 LBS	INDIRECT	MEDIUM	COOKED THROUGH; 12–15 MIN/LB
FILLETS			
½ INCH THICK	DIRECT	HIGH	COOKED THROUGH; 2–4 MIN/SIDE
1 INCH THICK	DIRECT	HIGH	COOKED THROUGH; 3–6 MIN/SIDE
STEAKS			
½ INCH THICK	DIRECT	HIGH	COOKED THROUGH; 2–4 MIN/LB
1 INCH THICK	DIRECT	HIGH	COOKED THROUGH; 4–6 MIN/LB

*This chart is offered as a broad guideline to cooking times for the various cuts of fish. Remember, grilling is an art, not a science. When in doubt, refer to times in the individual recipes.

BAHAMIAN-STYLE WHOLE GRILLED SNAPPER

BAHAMAS

METHOD:
Indirect grilling

ADVANCE PREPARATION:
30 minutes for marinating the fish

This recipe comes from a cook shack in Nassau in the Bahamas, but it typifies the way fish is cooked throughout the Caribbean. There they start with a whole fish so fresh it was still swimming a few hours earlier. They rub it with goat peppers and marinate it in a piquant mixture of fresh lime juice, garlic, ginger, and pepper. Then it's grilled using the indirect method or directly over a low flame. When served, the lucky diner can't help but marvel at how something so simple can taste so good.

I can't think of a more dramatic showpiece for a summery Caribbean-style cook-out. No sweat on the advance preparation, which takes a couple of minutes and can be done several hours ahead. No sweat on the cooking—fish grilled using the indirect method eliminates the burning worry. For maximum drama, I like to use one large fish—a 4- to 5-pound snapper or pompano, for example, which will serve 4 people. Good northern fish to prepare this way include striped bass, sea bass, and porgy.

Goat peppers are the Bahamian version of a scotch bonnet. The tender of tongue could use a milder chile, but the flavor won't be strictly authentic. (Don't worry—goat peppers and scotch bonnets lose a lot of their heat during cooking.) I like to cook the fish on a banana leaf or piece of aluminum foil. This is not strictly traditional, but it retains some of the juices and keeps the fish from sticking to the grate. Serve it with Bahamian Peas and Rice (see Index).

1 whole snapper, pompano, or other large fish (4 to 5 pounds), cleaned and trimmed of fins, head and tail left on
3 goat peppers, scotch bonnet chiles, or habanero chiles
4 large, juicy limes
Salt and freshly ground black pepper, to taste
1 piece (2 inches) fresh ginger, peeled and thinly sliced
2 cloves garlic, thinly sliced
1 to 2 tablespoons olive oil (not traditional, but I like it)

1. Rinse the fish, inside and out, under cold running water, then drain and blot dry with paper towels. Make 4 or 5 diagonal slashes, to the bone, in each side of the fish. Set the fish aside.

2. Thinly slice 2 of the chiles; cut the other chile lengthwise in half. Cut one of the limes in half lengthwise, then into thin crosswise slices. Cut the second lime in half crosswise. Juice the remaining limes.

3. Rub the fish all over with the cut chile and lime. Sprinkle salt and pepper in the cavity and into the slashes in the sides of the fish. Place a slice each of chile, lime, ginger, and garlic in each slit and under each gill, then place the remaining slices in the cavity. Place the fish on the banana leaf or foil on a large platter. Pour the lime juice over the fish and season again with salt and pepper, then drizzle with oil, if using. Cover and let the fish marinate, in the refrigerator, for 30 minutes or so while you preheat the grill.

4. Set up the grill for indirect cooking (see page 14 to 16) and preheat to high.

5. When ready to cook, place the fish, on its banana leaf, in the center of the grill away from the heat. Cover the grill, and cook the fish until the flesh breaks into firm flakes when pressed with a finger, 1 to 1½ hours. If using a charcoal grill, you'll need to add 10 to 12 fresh coals after 1 hour.

6. Using two long spatulas, carefully transfer the fish to a serving platter. At the table, fillet the fish as described on page 293 and serve at once.

Serves 4

FENNEL-GRILLED BASS FLAMBEED WITH PERNOD

Loup de Mer au Fenouil Flambé

FRANCE

METHOD:
Direct grilling

Here's a dish for cooks with a penchant for theatrics. Freshly caught *loup de mer* (literally, "wolf of the sea," corre- sponding to our sea bass) grilled over burning fennel stalks and dramatically flambéed at the tableside is the ultimate

ADVANCE PREPARATION:
24 hours to dry the fennel stalks, if used

culinary showpiece of the French Riviera. It's easy to make and impressive to serve. There are only two remotely challenging aspects to the recipe: finding whole fennel stalks and remembering to dry them ahead of time.

Fennel, a bulbous green-white vegetable with the flavor of licorice and the crunch of celery grows wild in Provence, in the south of France. My wife, Barbara, and I often found it on roadside picnics. Once considered exotic in the U.S., it can now be found at most supermarkets, but to get fennel with the stalks attached, you may need to go to a farm stand, an Italian market, or specialty greengrocer (although there are supermarket produce departments that do carry untrimmed fennel). Once you find it, cut off the stalks and dry as described in the box on this page. (The dried stalks will keep for months.)

Here's the authentic recipe for *loup de mer au fenouil flambé* from the Auberge des Glycines on the tiny island of Porquerolles. Use the bulbs to prepare Grilled Fennel (see Index). An alternative recipe, for people who can't find fennel stalks, follows the main recipe.

**2 whole sea bass (each about 2 pounds),
   cleaned and trimmed of fins, heads
   and tails left on (see Note)**
**Salt and freshly ground black pepper,
   to taste**
**10 to 12 dried fennel stalks (see box,
   this page)**
3 tablespoons extra-virgin olive oil
¼ cup Pernod or other anise-flavored liqueur
Lemon wedges, for serving

1. Preheat the grill to medium-high.

2. Rinse the fish, inside and out, under cold running water, then drain and blot dry with paper towels. Make 3 diagonal slashes, to the bone, in each side of each fish. Season the fish, inside and out (including the side slashes), with salt and pepper. Place 2 dried

How to Dry Fennel Stalks

Preheat the oven to 200°F. Take 2 to 3 bulbs of fennel with stalks and leaves attached and cut the stalks off flush with the bulbs; reserve the bulbs for another use. Cut away the leaves and arrange the stalks in one layer on a baking sheet. Bake in the low oven for 3 hours. Turn off the heat and let stay in the oven overnight to finish drying. (Alternatively, you can tie the fennel stalks together and hang them upside down in a cool, dry place until brittle and dry, 1 to 2 weeks.) If not using immediately, store the stalks in a zip-lock plastic bag for up to 3 months.

fennel stalks in each cavity. Brush the fish on both sides with the oil and season again with salt and pepper.

3. When ready to cook, arrange 6 fennel stalks on a serving platter and set aside. Place the remaining fennel stalks directly on the hot coals and oil the grill grate. If you're worried about the fish sticking, use hinged fish grilling baskets (see page 289); otherwise, place both fish directly on the hot grate and grill until the skin on the first side is dark and crisp and the flesh is cooked through to the bone on that side, 10 to 15 minutes. Turn each fish carefully with a long spatula and cook on the second side until the flesh breaks into firm flakes when pressed with a finger, another 10 to 15 minutes. During the last 2 or so minutes of cooking, warm the Pernod in a heavy saucepan at the side of the grill; don't let it boil, or even get too warm to touch.

4. Using the spatula, transfer each fish

carefully to the fennel stalk–lined platter. Pour the warmed Pernod over the fish and then, making sure your hair is tied back and your sleeves are rolled up, avert your face and ignite the liqueur carefully with a long match. Carefully bring the flaming fish to the table, then, when the flame dies out, fillet the fish as described below and serve at once, with lemon wedges.

Serves 4

Note: *Loup de mer* is a long, slender, dark gray fish with a fine-flavored, tender white flesh. While it corresponds most closely to North American sea bass, snapper, striped bass, or sea trout could be substituted here.

Fennel-Grilled Bass Flambéed with Pernod II

Prepare as described in the main recipe, substituting a bulb of fresh fennel, trimmed, for the dried stalks. Cut the fennel into thin lengthwise slices. Place a few slices in the cavity of each fish and toss a few strips on the coals before grilling the fish. Brush the remaining fennel slices with olive oil and season with salt and pepper, then grill, along with the fish, until tender and nicely browned, about 4 minutes per side, turning with tongs. Arrange the grilled fennel slices on the serving platter and place the grilled fish on top. Flambé as described above and serve. (The advantage of this method is that you can eat the grilled fennel.)

How to Fillet a Whole Grilled Fish

Maître d's do it at the tony restaurants on the Côte d'Azur. You, too, can fillet a whole grilled fish at tableside, and with a little practice, you'll display the panache of a pro. First, you'll need a large serving fork and spoon and a second platter for disposing of the fish bones.

Using the fork and spoon, carefully peel off the skin from the top side of the fish (if desired) and set it on the refuse platter. Using the side of the spoon, make a lengthwise cut down the back of the fish, just above the backbone. Gently ease the spoon into the cut, loosening the fish from the bones along the entire side of the fish frame.

Using the spoon and fork, transfer the top half of the fish to the side of the platter.

Now, using the side of the spoon, make a lengthwise cut down the back of the fish, just below the backbone. Slide the spoon under the backbone. Using the spoon and fork, lift the backbone, frame, and head and transfer them to the refuse platter.

Carefully lift the bottom section of the fish and turn over; peel off and discard the skin (if desired). Don't worry if the fish breaks into large pieces. Just cover the breaks with strategically placed lemon slices. Cut the fillets into individual portions and transfer to your guests' plates.

A New French Paradox

This is a story about a French paradox. Not the one that explains how the French can consume endless quantities of butter and foie gras—without gaining excess weight or keeling over from heart disease. (The solution to that paradox, seemingly, lies in drinking lots of red wine.)

No, the paradox puzzling me has to do with how a nation that reputedly has the world's greatest cuisine can do without what is arguably the world's most basic, primal, and universal cooking method: grilling.

That's right, grilling. Thumb through any of the great reference books on French cuisine—from Escoffier to Bocuse—and you'll find few if any recipes for grilling. Dine at a Michelin-starred restaurant in Paris and you'd be hard pressed to find a single dish that is grilled. Sautéed? Yes. Roasted? Yes. Baked. Broiled. Fried. Even steamed. But grilling simply isn't a part of the classic French culinary repertory.

So does this mean that the French don't like barbecue? Not on your life. It turns out that the French are ardent grillers. Just not at their high-profile restaurants.

So where do you find French grilling? Well, first of all, in the countryside. Especially in Provence. This most Mediterranean of French provinces is the epicenter of grilling, featuring casual grill eateries and country inns where embers blaze away in fireplaces. Traditionally, live-fire cooking was done indoors over the hearth, and it remains as much an activity done in winter as in summer.

One such establishment bears the evocative name of La Grillade au Feu de Bois (The Wood Fire Grill). Located in an eighteenth-century Provençal farmhouse in the hamlet of Flassons-Sur-Issole, the restaurant–country inn features simple lamb chops and massive rib steaks grilled over blazing vine trimmings in an ancient stone fireplace. As in most French grilling, the seasonings are simple: olive oil, salt, pepper, and a sprinkling of *herbes de Provence.*

Seafood restaurants are another source of live-fire cooked French fare—especially on the coast. One of the most famous dishes of the Côte d'Azur is sea bass flamed with fennel. The fish is grilled over dried fennel stalks and flambéed—theatrically at tableside—with an anise-flavored liqueur, like Pernod.

Less well known but no less delectable is *raito*, a dish of grilled tuna served with a red wine, olive, and caper sauce that I first tasted at an inn on a remote Mediterranean island called Porquerolles.

The French also do a lot of grilling at home. One of a Frenchman's favorite social gatherings bears the curious name of *mechouie.* The term comes from North Africa, where it refers to a whole spit-roasted lamb. It's interesting to note that the French had to borrow a term from another language to describe a backyard barbecue.

Some years ago, I attended a *mechouie* with friends at a farmhouse in the Champagne region. A huge fire had been built, using vine stalks. The fare ranged from grilled lamb to sanguine sirloin steaks to pork chops. The only remotely North African element in this *mechouie* was a spicy Algerian sausage called *merguez.* This lurid red sausage has become a fixture on the French culinary landscape.

But with a little persistence, you don't even need to leave Paris to find great live-fire cooking. In fact, in most cases you don't have to go much farther than a neighborhood charcuterie. The French do all things culinary well, but no one can beat them at spit-roasted chicken.

The French rotisserie is an awesome contraption, a tall vertical hearth with horizontal rows of mechanical turnspits that spin in front of what looks like a wall of flame. (Said wall of flame is created by rows of horizontal gas burners.) Fresh chickens are placed on the top turnspit, and as they turn, the dripping fat bastes the more cooked birds below. Sure, the quality of the poultry helps. But equally important is cooking method: the high, even heat of the wall of flames.

So, barbecue buffs, when you visit France, don't despair of finding great grilling—you just have to know where to look for it. Which just goes to show that even a Frenchman knows a good paradox when he sees one.

GRILLED SEA BASS WITH FRESH ARTICHOKE SALAD

Loup de Mer Grillé aux Artichauts

FRANCE

METHOD:
Direct grilling

My wife and I arrived in Nice in June, just in time for the first of the season's *artichauts violets*. These purple-tinged baby artichokes are so mild-flavored and tender, you needn't even bother to cook them. Rather, the tough outside leaves are pulled off and discarded (there's no hairy choke to remove), then the artichokes are sliced paper thin on a mandoline to be enjoyed raw. Their softly crunchy texture and delicate licorice flavor are a revelation.

Baby artichokes are usually served in salads, but at least one restaurant in Nice serves them atop grilled sea bass—a combination that is as unforgettable as it is unexpected.

The traditional fish for this recipe is *loup de mer* (sea bass), but you can also use whole snappers, porgies, striped bass, or even 1½ to 2 pounds of a steak fish, like swordfish or tuna.

FOR THE FISH AND MARINADE:
2 whole sea bass (each about 2 pounds), cleaned and trimmed of fins, heads and tails left on
Coarse (kosher or sea) salt and freshly ground black pepper, to taste
2 tablespoons extra-virgin olive oil, plus additional for brushing

FOR THE ARTICHOKE SALAD:
16 baby artichokes (see Note)
2 tablespoons fresh lemon juice
1 large or 2 small fresh, ripe tomatoes, peeled and seeded (see box, page 62), then cut into ¼-inch dice
8 fresh basil leaves, thinly slivered
2 tablespoons finely chopped fresh chives or scallion greens
1 small clove garlic, minced
1 canned anchovy fillet, drained and finely chopped, or 1 teaspoon anchovy paste (optional)
¼ cup extra-virgin olive oil
Salt and freshly ground black pepper, to taste

1. Preheat the grill to medium-high.

2. Rinse the fish, inside and out, under cold running water, then drain and blot dry with paper towels. Make 3 diagonal slashes, to the bone, in each side of each fish. Season the fish, inside and out (including the side slashes), with salt and pepper and brush both sides with 2 tablespoons oil. Set aside to marinate for 20 minutes.

3. Meanwhile, prepare the artichoke salad. Tear the green outer leaves off the artichokes and cut off the ends of the stems using a sharp knife. Cut the artichokes into paper-thin slices, preferably on a mandoline, or by hand. Toss them with the lemon juice in a nonreactive bowl.

4. Add the tomato, basil, chives, garlic, anchovy (if using), and oil to the artichokes and toss gently but thoroughly to mix. Add salt and pepper to taste; the mixture should be highly seasoned. Set aside.

5. When ready to cook, brush each fish lightly on both sides with additional oil and sprinkle with more salt and pepper. If you're worried about the fish sticking, use hinged fish grilling baskets (see page 289); otherwise, oil the grate and place both fish directly on it. Grill until the skin on the first side is dark and crisp and the flesh is cooked through to the bone on that side, 8 to 10 minutes. Turn each fish carefully with a long spatula and cook on the second side until the flesh breaks into firm flakes when pressed with a finger, another 8 to 10 minutes.

6. Using the spatula, carefully transfer the fish to a serving platter. Fillet the fish as described on page 293, then spoon the artichoke salad over the fish to serve.

Serves 4

Note: Baby artichokes are available in May and June at Italian markets, specialty greengrocers, and many supermarkets. If you can't find them, use one 10-ounce package frozen artichoke hearts, prepared according to package directions, then thinly sliced and tossed with lemon juice. In a real pinch, you can use canned artichoke hearts; just make sure you rinse and drain them well before slicing.

PORTUGUESE GRILLED SARDINES

PORTUGAL

METHOD:
Direct grilling

ADVANCE PREPARATION:
30 to 60 minutes for salting the sardines

Grilled fresh sardines are as popular in Portugal as hot dogs and hamburgers are in North America. People devour them by the dozen from street vendors, in informal seaside fish houses and proper restaurants, and at backyard cookouts. So beloved are sardines in Portugal that they turn up in Portuguese outposts and former colonies all over the world. I've enjoyed this popular Portuguese dish in Macao, Brazil, and my former home of Cambridge, Massachusetts, where there is a large Portuguese-American community.

If your experience with sardines is limited to the canned variety, you're in for a revelation. The only challenge is where to find fresh sardines. If you live in an area with a large Iberian or Italian population, you may be able to find fresh sardines at an ethnic fishmonger—especially in the warmer months. (The best time of year to eat sardines is between May and October, when the fish fatten for spawning.) Alternatively, you may have to settle for frozen sardines.

The salting that's done here gives the sardines extra flavor—almost like a cured fish.

In Macao, grilled sardines are served with Argentinian Tomato Salsa (see Index) and crusty Portuguese or corn bread.

24 fresh sardines, cleaned, heads and tails left on
1 cup coarse (kosher or sea) salt
2 tablespoons extra-virgin olive oil
Freshly ground black pepper, to taste (optional)
Lemon wedges, for serving

1. Rinse the sardines under cold running water, then drain and blot dry with paper towels. Sprinkle a third of the salt in the bottom of a baking dish. Arrange half the sardines on top and sprinkle with half the remaining salt. Add another layer of sardines and sprinkle the remaining salt over all. Cover and let cure in the salt, in the refrigerator, for 30 to 60 minutes.

2. Preheat the grill to high.

3. When ready to cook, rinse the salt off the sardines and blot dry with paper towels. Brush the sardines with the oil and season with pepper, if desired. If you're worried about the fish sticking, use a hinged fish grilling basket (see page 289); otherwise, oil the grate and arrange the fish directly on it. Grill the sardines until their skins are lightly charred and the flesh is cooked to flakiness, 3 to 6 minutes per side. Remove to a platter with a long spatula and serve at once. Let diners remove the head and tail, and bones, too. Serve with lemon wedges for squeezing.

Serves 6 as an appetizer, 3 to 4 as an entrée

GRILLED FISH WITH SAUCE VIERGE

FRANCE

METHOD:
Direct grilling

One of the best seafood restaurants on the Côte d'Azur bears the unlikely name of Bacon. This has less to do with a smoked meat that, on occasion, is used to enhance grilled fish than with the location of the restaurant, Bacon Point, on the Cap d'Antibes, overlooking the medieval city. Simplicity is the name of the game at Bacon (as it is at all great fish houses), and to this day I can still remember the taste of the perfectly grilled John Dory fish I had there served with a simple but equally perfect *sauce vierge*.

The sauce takes its name (literally, "virgin sauce"), it is said, from the fact that none of its ingredients are cooked—which is about the closest the French get to salsa. John Dory (or St. Pierre, as it is called, in French) is a delicate, white-fleshed fish found throughout the Mediterranean. You rarely find it in the U.S. (unless you know someone in the airfreight business). But almost any mild white fish (whole, steak, or fillet) will be enhanced by this preparation. Good candidates include striped bass, sea bass, halibut, cod, snapper, or mahimahi.

This recipe calls for small whole fish; for steak and fillet how-to's, see pages 317 and 324.

FOR THE FISH:
4 small whole fish (each about 1 pound), cleaned and trimmed of fins, heads and tails left on
2 tablespoons extra-virgin olive oil
Salt and freshly ground black pepper, to taste

FOR THE SAUCE VIERGE:
2 large fresh, ripe tomatoes, peeled and seeded (see box, page 62), then diced
2 cloves garlic, minced
20 fresh basil leaves, thinly slivered
½ cup extra-virgin olive oil
2 tablespoons fresh lemon juice, or more to taste
2 teaspoons red wine vinegar
Salt and freshly ground black pepper, to taste

1. Preheat the grill to medium-high.

2. Place the fish in a nonreactive baking dish. Brush all sides with some of the oil and season with salt and pepper, then set aside to marinate while you prepare the sauce.

3. Combine the tomatoes, garlic, basil leaves, oil, 2 tablespoons lemon juice, vinegar, and salt and pepper in a nonreactive bowl and toss gently to mix. Taste for seasoning, adding salt, pepper, and lemon juice as necessary; the sauce should be highly seasoned.

4. When ready to cook, brush each fish lightly on both sides with more oil and sprinkle with more salt and pepper. If you're worried about the fish sticking, use hinged fish grilling baskets (see page 289); otherwise, oil the grill grate and place the fish directly on it. Grill until the skin on the first side is dark and crisp and the flesh is cooked through to the bone on that side, 6 to 10 minutes. Turn each fish carefully with a long spatula and cook on the second side until the flesh breaks into firm flakes when pressed with a finger, another 6 to 10 minutes.

5. Using the spatula, carefully transfer the fish to a serving platter. Fillet the fish as described on page 293 (if desired) and serve immediately, topping each serving with a generous spoonful of the sauce.

Serves 4

GRILLED FISH GURNEY DRIVE

MALAYSIA

METHOD:
Direct grilling

Charcoal Grill Seafood is one of the many open-air cook stalls lining scenic bay-front Gurney Drive in Penang, Malaysia. One of many, but certainly not average. There, nothing is served that isn't at its freshest. A bank of aquariums keeps eels and prawns alive until the moment of cooking. Other fish—that swam in the Andaman Sea just hours earlier—are displayed under a thatched roof on a bed of banana leaves in a miniature wooden dingy.

I ordered something called *ikan tumone,* a small fish that looks like a tiny mackerel. My waitress cleaned it on the spot and handed it to a grill man, who stuffed it with a fragrant paste of lemongrass, shallots, and chiles. He fanned the coconut-shell charcoal fire until it glowed red and basted the fish with coconut milk. What came off the grill was one of the tastiest fish I had anywhere, East or West.

There are lots of possibilities for fish to use here. The spice paste is designed to counterpoint the oiliness of a fatty fish like mackerel. You could also use whole porgies, grunts, or pompanos; steak fish, like salmon or swordfish; or even a fillet fish, like bluefish. And because it keeps well, you might think about doubling the spice paste to have on hand whenever you get that urge to grill; I've used it to coat just about everything—chicken, beef, pork, and even tofu.

FOR THE SPICE PASTE
2 large shallots, coarsely chopped
6 cloves garlic, coarsely chopped
2 large or 6 small stalks fresh lemongrass, trimmed and coarsely chopped
1½ tablespoons chopped fresh ginger
2 serrano chiles, coarsely chopped (for a milder dish, seed the chiles)
2 tablespoons peanut oil
2 tablespoons soy sauce
2 tablespoons fresh lime juice
Salt, to taste

FOR THE FISH AND BASTING MIXTURE:
4 small whole fish, such as mackerel, porgies, or grunts (each about 1 pound), cleaned and trimmed of fins, heads and tails left on
2 tablespoons canned coconut milk
2 tablespoons unsalted butter, melted

1. Prepare the spice paste. Combine the shallots, garlic, lemongrass, ginger, and chiles in a mortar and pound to a smooth paste with the pestle, then work in the oil, soy sauce, lime juice, and salt; or use a blender, processing all the ingredients at once. Transfer the paste to a small nonstick skillet and cook over medium heat until richly flavored and shiny with oil, 5 to 10 minutes, stirring frequently to prevent sticking. Remove from the heat and let cool (see Note).

2. Preheat the grill to medium-high.

3. Meanwhile, rinse the fish, inside and out, under cold running water, then drain and blot dry with paper towels. Using a thin, sharp knife, cut a pocket in each side of each fish from front to back. Setting half the spice paste aside for later use, spoon the remainder first into the cavities of the fish, then into the pockets on the sides, dividing the paste evenly.

4. When ready to cook, combine the coconut milk and melted butter in a small bowl and whisk to blend; brush over each fish on both sides. Oil the grill grate. If you're worried about the fish sticking, use hinged fish grilling baskets (see page 289); otherwise, place the fish directly on the hot grate and grill until the skin on the first side is dark and crisp and the flesh is cooked through to the bone on that side, 6 to 10 minutes. Turn each fish carefully with a long spatula and brush first with any remaining coconut milk mixture; spoon on the remaining spice paste. Cook on the second side until the fish breaks into firm flakes when pressed with a finger, another 6 to 10 minutes.

5. Using the spatula, carefully transfer the fish to a platter. Bring it to the table, then fillet them as described on page 293 (if desired) and serve immediately.

Serves 4

Note: The spice paste can be prepared ahead of time. Refrigerate in a tightly covered container for up to 1 week.

THAI GRILLED FISH WITH SWEET-SOUR TAMARIND SAUCE
Pla Pow

THAILAND

METHOD:
Direct grilling

I encountered this dish, not in Thailand, but at the stunning Amanusa Resort at Nusa Beach in Bali. (It turned out that the chef worked for many years in Thailand.) We don't usually serve sweet sauces with seafood in the West, but this sweet-sour tamarind sauce is great with the charcoaled flavor of grilled fish. Try it with small whole fish such as porgies or small snappers. You could also use fish steaks, such as swordfish or tuna (see page 317). Serve with Balinese Cucumber Salad and Jasmine Rice (see Index).

ADVANCE PREPARATION:
30 minutes for marinating the fish

FOR THE FISH:

4 small whole fish, such as porgies or small snappers (each about 1 pound), cleaned and trimmed of fins, heads and tails left on
5 tablespoons Asian fish sauce
5 tablespoons fresh lemon juice
1 lemon, thinly sliced
1 teaspoon freshly ground black pepper

FOR THE SWEET-SOUR TAMARIND SAUCE:

¾ cup palm sugar or firmly packed light brown sugar
⅔ cup Tamarind Water (page 219)
⅓ cup Asian fish sauce

TO FINISH THE SAUCE:

1 cup peanut oil for frying
3 shallots, very thinly sliced
6 cloves garlic, very thinly sliced
4 jalapeño or serrano chiles, thinly sliced
2 tablespoons fresh lemon juice

1. Rinse the fish, inside and out, under cold running water, then drain and blot dry with paper towels. Make 3 or 4 diagonal slashes, to the bone, on each side of each fish. Place the fish in a nonreactive baking dish or roasting pan just large enough to hold them in a single layer. Combine the fish sauce and lemon juice in a small bowl and whisk to blend, then pour the mixture over the fish. Turn the fish once or twice to coat, then sprinkle with the lemon slices and pepper. Cover and let marinate in the refrigerator for 30 minutes.

2. Preheat the grill to medium-high.

3. While the fish marinates, prepare the sauce. Combine the sugar, Tamarind Water, and fish sauce in a small, heavy saucepan and bring to a boil over medium heat, stirring to dissolve the sugar. Reduce the heat to low and simmer gently, uncovered, until thick and well flavored, 5 to 10 minutes, stirring occasionally.

4. Meanwhile, heat the oil to 350°F in a small, heavy skillet over medium-high heat. Add the shallots and fry until crisp, 1 to 2 minutes. Using a wire skimmer, remove the shallots from the oil to paper towels to drain. Add the sliced garlic to the hot oil and fry until crisp, 1 to 2 minutes, then remove with the skimmer to paper towels. Add the sliced chiles to the hot oil and fry until crisp, another 1 to 2 minutes, then transfer with the skimmer to paper towels. Set the oil aside to cool.

5. Remove the sugar mixture from the heat and stir in the lemon juice and half each of the fried shallots, garlic, and chiles, setting the remainder aside for garnish. Cover the sauce and set aside to keep warm.

6. When ready to cook, remove the fish from the marinade and blot dry with paper towels. Brush each fish on both sides with the reserved frying oil. If you're worried about the fish sticking, use hinged fish grilling baskets (see page 289); otherwise, oil the grill grate and place each fish directly on it. Grill until the skin on the first side is dark and crisp and the flesh is cooked through to the bone on that side, 6 to 10 minutes. Turn each fish carefully with a long spatula and cook on the second side until the fish breaks into firm flakes when pressed with a finger, another 6 to 10 minutes.

7. Using the spatula, carefully transfer the fish to a platter. Bring them to the table and fillet as described on page 293, then spoon half the sauce over the fillets and sprinkle with the remaining fried shallots, garlic, and chiles. Serve immediately, accompanied by the remaining sauce.

Serves 4

The Most Famous Fish House in Indonesia

Sunda Kelapa is one of the best restaurants in Jakarta, but you'd sure never guess it by the neighborhood. The ride there took me through a dilapidated stretch of the port section of Batavia, past derelict warehouses, down trash-strewn streets lined with shanties.

Then I turned into a walled compound guarded by attendants in paramilitary garb and began to see why this fish house has fetched rave reviews in dozens of languages in publications all over the world: The sheer variety of seafood offered was amazing.

I had come to Indonesia as a globe-trotting student of barbecue. I wasn't disappointed. This sprawling country comprised of thousands of islands—and the world's fourth largest population—is home to some of the most interesting grilling in the world. When most people think of Indonesian grilling, what comes to mind is a tiny kebab called saté. It's true that the saté is Indonesia's national snack and there are dozens if not hundreds of different types to choose from. But saté is only part of Indonesia's barbecue story, as I quickly learned at Sunda Kelapa.

Sunda Kelapa is the brainchild of Sri Rosilowati, a short, stylishly dressed woman from western Java. In 1972 Mrs. Rosilowati opened a fish shack adjacent to the harbor to feed the crews of the wooden freighters from the island of Sulawesi.

Mrs. Rosilowati's concept was simple: Serve impeccably fresh fish, grilled simply over charcoal, in clean, unpretentious surroundings. it was a winning formula, to say the least! Today Mrs. Rosilowati and her daughter Suripah preside over 120 employees and two cavernous dining rooms that must seat 500.

The warehouse-sized kitchen is an immaculate jumble of blazing grills, stainless-steel work tables, and plastic barrels filled with Indonesian seafood with unfamiliar names—*baronangs* (rabbit fish), *ikan grapu* (a sort of grouper), and *gourame* (a large flat fish that reminds me of pompano), to list a few. The grills are stoked with Indonesia's favorite fuel, coconut shell charcoal, and young boys fan the grills with rattan flags to make the embers glow. Sunlight filters through the slat walls and ceiling, illuminating the smoke rising from the grills. The overall effect is less that of a restaurant kitchen than of cooking over a campfire in the woods.

What fascinates me most about Sunda Kelapa are the techniques used by the grill cooks. If you've ever tried to grill a whole fish, you know how it has a tendency to burn on the outside, remain raw on the inside, and generally dry out during the grilling. Sunda Kelapa uses three popular Indonesian techniques to obtain perfectly cooked fish every time: brine marinating, double basting, and grill-roasting on banana leaves.

The marinade—called a *bumboo*—is a tangy mixture of lime juice, water, and brine-strength quantities of salt. The fish is slashed to the bone to allow the mixture (and heat) to penetrate the flesh. The brine both moisturizes and slightly cures the fish. The marinating time is brief and most of the *bumboo* drips into the coals.

To further moisturize the fish, it is basted as it grills with the *bumboo* and also with a mixture of melted butter flavored generously with garlic, shallots, and turmeric.

To cook the fish through without burning it, the cook sears it on one side directly over the fire, then inverts it onto a rectangle of banana leaf to finish cooking. The banana leaf shields the fish from the flames, preventing it from drying out and over cooking.

Sunda Kelapa serves its grilled fish with a *lalapan*, a plate of herbs and raw vegetables that include lemon balm, parsley, basil, sliced cucumber, tomato and cabbage wedges, and boiled long beans. You'll also get bowls of *achar* (a sort of mango and shallot pickle) and *chobal*, a painfully hot relish made from chiles, shallots, and shrimp paste, named for the small black stone mortar in which these ingredients are traditionally pounded and served. I've included recipes for all these in this book; now fire up the grill and enjoy. Oh, and to be like the locals, eat the fish with your fingers!

GRILLED FISH SUNDA KELAPA

INDONESIA

METHOD:
Direct grilling

ADVANCE PREPARATION:
30 minutes for marinating the fish

SPECIAL EQUIPMENT:
2 to 4 banana leaves (see box, page 289), cut to the size and shape of the fish or 4 to 6 layers of aluminum foil, folded to the size and shape of the fish

One of my favorite ways to cook seafood comes from a fish house in Jakarta called Sunda Kelapa. Sometimes it's tricky to adapt a cooking technique from halfway around the world to the North American kitchen, but Sunda Kelapa's grilling techniques are perfectly suited to cooking fish on an American grill (see page 301).

This recipe is ideal for grilling whole fish. Good candidates in this country, depending on where you live, include porgies, small snappers, scup, mackerel, pompano, redfish, or small bluefish. You can also cook your favorite steak fish this way (see page 317); fresh tuna prepared in this manner is absolutely delicious.

If you're lucky enough to live in a city with a large Asian or Hispanic community, you may be able to find fresh or frozen banana leaves for this. Otherwise use aluminum foil.

FOR THE FISH AND BUMBOO (SEASONING MIXTURE):

4 small whole fish, such as pompano
    or small snappers (each about 1 pound),
    cleaned and trimmed of fins,
    heads and tails left on
1 cup fresh lime juice
1 cup water
½ cup coarse (kosher or sea)
    salt

FOR THE SPICED BUTTER:

6 tablespoons (¾ stick) unsalted
    butter
1½ tablespoons fresh lime juice
1 tablespoon soy sauce
3 cloves garlic, minced
1 large shallot, minced
2 teaspoons minced fresh ginger
½ teaspoon ground turmeric

1. Rinse the fish, inside and out, under cold running water, then drain and blot dry with paper towels. Make 3 or 4 diagonal slashes, to the bone, in each side of each fish. Place the fish in a nonreactive baking dish large enough to hold them in one layer and set aside while you prepare the *bumboo*.

2. Combine the lime juice, water, and salt in a medium-size bowl and whisk until the salt is dissolved. Pour the mixture over the fish in the baking dish, turn once or twice to coat, then cover and let marinate, in the refrigerator, for 30 minutes.

3. Preheat the grill to medium-high.

4. Meanwhile, prepare the spiced butter. Melt the butter in a small, heavy saucepan over low heat, then stir in the lime juice, soy sauce, garlic, shallot, ginger, and turmeric. Simmer until fragrant but not brown, about 5 minutes, then remove from the heat.

5. When ready to grill, drain the fish, reserving the *bumboo*. Brush each fish on both sides with the spiced butter. Generously oil the grill grate and arrange the fish on it. Brush the fish lavishly with the reserved *bumboo*. Grill until the undersides of the fish are nicely browned, 6 to 10 minutes, brushing with additional spiced butter and *bumboo* as the fish cook.

6. Using a long spatula, carefully invert each fish onto a banana leaf or foil rectangle. Brush again with spiced butter and continue grilling until the fish are nicely browned on their second sides and the flesh breaks into firm flakes when pressed with a finger, 6 to 10 minutes more; brush once more with the butter as the fish finish cooking.

7. Using the spatula, carefully transfer the fish to a serving platter. Bring them to the table and fillet as described on page 293 and serve, or serve whole, to be eaten with fingers.

Serves 4

GUADELOUPEAN GRILLED SNAPPER WITH CUCUMBER SAUCE

GUADELOUPE

METHOD:
Direct grilling

ADVANCE PREPARATION:
2 to 4 hours for marinating the fish

The night I stopped at Agoupa, a popular eatery in the resort community of Gosier in Guadeloupe, the first-year anniversary party was in full swing. Souk music blared from the sound system, bodies swayed in the heat, and the rum flowed like water. This open-air eatery (located just outside Pointe-à-Pitre) draws tourists and locals alike for this exuberant ambience and reasonable prices. (*Agoupa* means "something extra" in Creole, a little like *lagniappe* in Cajun French.) From a distance, the steel-drum barbecue grills blaze like blast furnaces in the night.

The sauce for this fish dish is a sort of gazpacho made with cucumbers and green tomatoes. It's very original and very tasty. Don't be put off by the seemingly large number of ingredients. Most you'll have on hand already, and the actual preparation time is only 15 or 20 minutes. Serve the snappers with Bahamian Peas and Rice (see Index).

FOR THE FISH AND MARINADE:
4 whole small snappers (each about
   1 pound), cleaned and trimmed
   of fins, heads and tails left on
2 bunches fresh chives or scallions,
   both white and green parts,
   trimmed and finely chopped
1 head garlic, cut in half
1 medium onion, thinly sliced
2 bay leaves
1 scotch bonnet or other hot chile, cut in
   half (for a milder dish, seed the chiles)
4 cups water
⅔ cup fresh lime juice
¼ cup dark rum
3 tablespoons salt

FOR THE CUCUMBER SAUCE:
1 cucumber, peeled and seeded
   (see box, page 89)
1 green (unripe) tomato, cored and
   peeled, or 4 tomatillos, husked,
   cored, and peeled (see box, page 62)
¼ cup diced onion
3 scallions, both white and green parts,
   trimmed and finely chopped
¼ cup chopped fresh Italian (flat-leaf)
   parsley
3 tablespoons white wine vinegar
   or distilled white vinegar, or
   more to taste
3 tablespoons extra-virgin olive oil, plus
   additional for brushing
Salt and freshly ground black pepper,
   to taste

1. Rinse the fish, inside and out, under cold running water, then drain and blot dry with paper towels. Make 3 or 4 diagonal slashes, to the bone, on each side of each fish. Place the fish in a nonreactive baking dish or roasting pan just large enough to hold them in a single layer. Scatter the chives, garlic, onion slices, bay leaves, and chile over the fish and set aside while you prepare the marinade.

2. Combine the water, lime juice, rum, and salt in a medium-size bowl, stirring until the salt is dissolved. Pour the mixture over the fish, then cover and let marinate, in the refrigerator, for at least 2 hours and up to 4.

3. Preheat the grill to medium-high.

4. When almost ready to grill, prepare the cucumber sauce. Combine the cucumber, green tomato, onion, scallions, parsley, 3 tablespoons vinegar, the oil, and salt and pepper in a blender and process to a smooth purée. Taste for seasoning, adding vinegar or salt as necessary; the sauce should be highly seasoned.

5. When ready to cook, remove the fish from the marinade and blot dry with paper towels; reserve the marinade. Brush each fish lightly on both sides with additional oil. If you're worried about the fish sticking, use hinged fish grilling baskets (see page 289); otherwise, oil the grill grate and place the fish directly on it. Grill, basting once or twice with the reserved marinade, until the skin on the first side is dark and crisp and the flesh

is cooked through to the bone on that side, 6 to 10 minutes. Turn each fish carefully with a long spatula and cook on the second side until the flesh breaks into firm flakes when pressed with a finger, another 6 to 10 minutes, again basting with the marinade.

6. Using the spatula, carefully transfer the fish to a platter. Bring them to the table, then fillet as described on page 293 (if desired) and serve immediately, accompanied by the cucumber sauce.

Serves 4

GRILLED FISH WITH ESARN SEASONING

THAILAND

METHOD:
Direct grilling

ADVANCE PREPARATION:
1 to 2 hours for marinating the fish

Here's a simple, but amazingly flavorful way to prepare fish, from the Esarn region in northeast Thailand. To be strictly authentic, you'll need cilantro roots, which taste like a cross between cilantro and celery root. Asian and Hispanic markets sell cilantro with the roots intact, but if you can't find the whole plant, cilantro leaves produce a highly tasty spice mix, too.

I like to use small whole fish, like sea bass or snappers, for this recipe. Serve the grilled fish with Jasmine Rice and Lemon Honey Sauce with Garlic (see Index).

FOR THE FISH AND SPICE PASTE:
4 small whole fish, such as sea bass or small snappers (each about 1 pound), cleaned and trimmed of fins, heads and tails left on
12 cloves garlic, crushed
½ cup chopped cilantro roots or leaves, roots rinsed well and drained before chopping
1 tablespoon salt
2 teaspoons ground coriander
2 teaspoons freshly ground white pepper

FOR THE BASTING SAUCE:
3 tablespoons Asian fish sauce
3 tablespoons vegetable oil
3 tablespoons fresh lime juice
1½ tablespoons sugar

1. Rinse the fish, inside and out, under cold running water, then drain and blot dry with paper towels. Make 3 or 4 diagonal slashes, to the bone, on each side of each fish. Set aside while you prepare the spice paste.

2. Combine the garlic, cilantro, salt, coriander, and pepper in a mortar and pound to a paste with the pestle, or process in a food processor. Stuff half the spice paste into the slashes in the sides of the fish, dividing evenly, then spread the remainder in the cavities and over the surface of the fish. Arrange the fish in a baking dish. Cover and let marinate, in the refrigerator, for 1 to 2 hours.

3. Preheat the grill to medium-high.

4. While the fish marinate, prepare the basting sauce. Combine the fish sauce, oil, lime juice, and sugar in a small bowl and stir until the sugar is dissolved.

5. When ready to cook, if you're worried about the fish sticking, use hinged fish grilling baskets (see page 289); otherwise, oil the grill grate and place the fish directly on it. Grill, brushing continuously with the basting sauce, until the skin on the first side is dark and crisp and the flesh is cooked through to the bone on that side, 6 to 10 minutes. Turn each fish carefully with a long spatula and cook on the second side, brushing continuously again with the sauce, until the flesh breaks into firm flakes when pressed with a finger, another 6 to 10 minutes.

6. Using the spatula, carefully transfer the fish to a platter. Bring them to the table, then fillet as described on page 293 (if desired) and serve immediately.

Serves 4

GRILLED SNAPPER WITH FRENCH WEST INDIAN CAPER SAUCE

GUADELOUPE

METHOD:
Direct grilling

ADVANCE PREPARATION:
1 hour for marinating the fish

Here's how fish is served at the open-air cook stalls lining the beaches of Guadeloupe. The marinade features the four essential flavors of the French Antilles: lime juice, scotch bonnet chiles, garlic, and fresh thyme. Pair them with a caper sauce invigorated with more chile pepper and you get a dish your taste buds won't soon forget. This recipe calls for snappers, but any whole fish would work. (For that matter, you could use fish steaks; see page 317.) The larger the fish, the lower the heat you'll have to work over, so as to cook the fish through without burning.

FOR THE FISH AND MARINADE:
4 whole small snappers (each about 1 pound), cleaned and trimmed of fins, heads and tails left on
3 cloves garlic, peeled
1 to 2 scotch bonnet chiles, seeded and chopped (for a spicier fish, leave the seeds in)
2 teaspoons salt
1 teaspoon freshly ground black pepper
1 teaspoon chopped fresh thyme or ½ teaspoon dried
½ cup fresh lime juice

FOR THE CAPER SAUCE:
1 clove garlic, minced
1 shallot, minced
2 tablespoons minced fresh Italian (flat-leaf) parsley
2 tablespoons drained capers
½ scotch bonnet chile, seeded and minced
1 to 2 tablespoons fresh lime juice
1 tablespoon red wine vinegar
½ cup extra-virgin olive oil, plus 2 tablespoons for brushing
Salt and freshly ground black pepper, to taste

1. Rinse the fish, inside and out, under cold running water, then drain and blot dry with paper towels. Make 3 to 4 diagonal slashes, to the bone, on each side of each fish. Set aside while you prepare the marinade.

2. Combine the garlic, chiles, salt, pepper, and thyme in a mortar and pound to a paste with the pestle, then work in the lime juice; or use a food processor, processing all the ingredients at once. Pour the mixture over the fish, turning the fish to coat and working the mixture into the slashes in the sides. Arrange the fish in a nonreactive baking dish or roasting pan, then cover and let marinate, in the refrigerator, for 1 hour, turning once or twice.

3. Preheat the grill to medium-high.

4. While the fish marinate, prepare the caper sauce. Combine the garlic, shallot, parsley, capers, chile, lime juice, and vinegar in a small bowl and whisk to mix. Whisk in the $\frac{1}{4}$ cup oil and salt and pepper; the sauce should be highly seasoned (see Note).

5. When ready to cook, blot the fish dry with paper towels and brush generously on both sides with 2 tablespoons oil. If you're worried about the fish sticking, use hinged fish grilling baskets (see page 289); otherwise, oil the grill grate and place the fish directly on it. Grill until the skin on the first side is dark and crisp and the flesh is cooked through to the bone on that side, 6 to 10 minutes. Turn each fish carefully with a long spatula and cook on the second side until the flesh breaks into firm flakes when pressed with a finger, another 6 to 10 minutes.

6. Using the spatula, carefully transfer the fish to a platter. Bring them to the table, then fillet as described on page 293 (if desired). Spoon some of the caper sauce on top of the fish and serve immediately, accompanied by the remaining sauce.

Serves 4

Note: For a smoother sauce, you can process the ingredients in a food processor or blender.

SEAFOOD MIXED GRILL IN THE STYLE OF ESSAOUIRA

MOROCCO

METHOD:
Direct grilling

Essaouira is a port town on the northwest coast of Morocco. Here, on the concrete wharf where the fishing boats tie up, seafood fanciers will find a most remarkable fish barbecue. To get to this spot, you must navigate a tangled web of fishing nets, a gauntlet of touts (each one attempting to drag you to the stall of his employer), and a disconcerting cloud of flies. Take courage, because once you are seated, you will enjoy impeccably fresh seafood the way it is meant to be served: in sight of the bobbing fishing boats and the blue, blue ocean from which it was taken only a few hours earlier. Talk about fresh—the vendors clean the fish the moment you order it. Seasoned by the sea breeze and served under the whirling gulls in the wide blue sky, there's nothing that can beat it.

This feast is elemental in its simplicity: grilled fish, tangy tomato salad, crusty bread. I've written the recipe as a mixed grill, based on the most commonly served seafoods in Essaouira. Feel free to vary the selection based on whatever looks freshest in your area.

In Essaouira, the shrimp would be served with the heads on, grilled in the shells.

FOR THE FISH:

2 pounds shrimp, ideally in the shell

16 fresh sardines, cleaned and trimmed of fins, heads and tails left on

8 whole whiting, cleaned and trimmed of fins, heads and tails left on

2 pounds squid, cleaned (see Note)

¾ cup extra-virgin olive oil, or as needed

Coarse (kosher or sea) salt and freshly ground black pepper, to taste

FOR THE TOMATO SALAD:

8 fresh, ripe tomatoes, seeded (see box, page 62) and finely chopped

2 large red onions, finely chopped

½ cup chopped fresh Italian (flat-leaf) parsley

½ cup extra-virgin olive oil

¼ cup fresh lemon juice, or more to taste

2 teaspoons red wine vinegar

Salt and freshly ground black pepper, to taste

FOR SERVING:

Moroccan bread or pita bread

Lemon wedges

1. Preheat the grill to high.

2. Leaving the shrimp shells on, if desired, devein the shrimp according to the instructions on page 349. Rinse the shrimp and remaining seafood under cold running water, then drain and blot dry with paper towels. Brush the shrimp, fish, and squid on both sides with some of the oil and season with salt and pepper. Set aside while you make the salad.

3. Combine the tomatoes, onion, parsley, oil, ¼ cup lemon juice, and the vinegar in a large bowl and toss gently but thoroughly to mix. Taste for seasoning, adding salt, pepper, and additional lemon juice if needed. Set aside.

4. When ready to cook, oil the grill grate. Arrange the seafood on the hot grate and grill, turning the whole fish with a long spatula and the shrimp and squid with tongs, until nicely browned and cooked through, 4 to 8 minutes per side for the whole fish (the flesh will break into firm flakes when pressed with a finger), 1 to 2 minutes per side for the shrimp and squid. After turning, brush the seafood again with the oil, and reseason with salt and pepper.

5. Divide the seafood among 8 serving plates. Serve immediately, accompanied by the salad, Moroccan or pita breads, and lemon wedges.

Serves 8

Note: The squid pieces for this recipe should be large—whole bodies and whole tentacles. If you can only get squid that's been cut into rings or chunks, thread them on a skewer to grill.

GRILLED FISH WITH BRAZILIAN GARLIC MARINADE

BRAZIL

METHOD:
Direct grilling

Marius Fontana is one of the most celebrated restaurateurs in Rio de Janeiro, a charismatic guy with shoulder-length brown hair and a stratospheric energy level. Marius created this garlic marinade for fish kebabs, but I've discovered that it also works great on fish steaks or small whole fish. Swordfish, tuna, or salmon steaks, or small whole snappers or black bass all work well. Serve up Brazilian Daiquiris beforehand and Crazy Rice alongside (see Index).

4 tuna, swordfish, or salmon steaks (each 6 to 8 ounces and 1 inch thick)
6 cloves garlic, peeled
½ medium onion, quartered
½ medium red bell pepper, stemmed, quartered, and seeded
¼ cup olive oil
¼ cup dry white wine
2 tablespoons ketchup
2 tablespoons sweet paprika
1 teaspoon salt
½ teaspoon freshly ground black pepper
¼ cup finely chopped fresh cilantro

1. Rinse the tuna steaks under cold running water, then drain and blot dry with paper towels. Place in a nonreactive baking dish just large enough to hold them flat in a single layer and set aside while you prepare the marinade.

2. Combine the garlic, onion, bell pepper, oil, wine, ketchup, paprika, salt, and black pepper in a blender and process to a smooth purée. Add the cilantro and pulse just to mix. Pour the mixture over the fish in the baking dish, turning the steaks to coat. Cover and let marinate, in the refrigerator, for 1 hour.

3. Preheat the grill to high.

4. When ready to cook, oil the grill grate. Remove the tuna steaks from the marinade and arrange, facing in the same direction, on the hot grate. If using tuna, grill until cooked to taste, 3 to 4 minutes per side for medium-rare, turning over carefully with a long spatula (see Note). For an attractive crosshatch of grill marks, rotate the steaks 90 degrees after the first 2 minutes on each side.

5. Transfer the steaks to serving plates or a platter and serve immediately.
Serves 4
Note: If using swordfish or salmon, cook the steaks until opaque in the center when pierced with a knife, 4 to 6 minutes per side.

GRILLED SHARK AND BAKE

One of the most popular dishes in Trinidad is shark and bake, a shark steak marinated in "seasoning" (a tangy tincture of chiles and West Indian herbs), then deep-fried and served on a puffy pillow of fried bread, called a "bake." The combination is so flavorful, Trinidadians eat it for breakfast, lunch, dinner, and between-meal snacks.

Much as I enjoyed the traditional preparation, I couldn't help thinking it would be tasty—and healthier—if the ingredients were grilled. After all, the firm texture of shark makes it ideal for grilling. And grilled bread is a part of Indian cooking, which certainly inspired many Trinidadian dishes.

FOR THE FISH AND MARINADE:

4 shark steaks, such as mako
    (each 6 to 8 ounces and about
    ¾ inch thick)
½ bunch chives or scallions, trimmed
2 shallots or ½ small onion, coarsely
    chopped
2 cloves garlic, peeled and coarsely
    chopped
1 medium rib celery, coarsely chopped
¼ cup fresh cilantro leaves
¼ cup fresh Italian (flat-leaf) parsley
    leaves
2 tablespoons fresh mint leaves
2 teaspoons fresh thyme leaves or
    1 teaspoon dried
½ scotch bonnet chile, seeded and
    deveined, or ¼ cup chopped
    green bell pepper
¾ cup water
¼ cup fresh lime juice, or more
    to taste
2 teaspoons salt, or more to taste
½ teaspoon freshly ground black pepper

FOR THE "BAKES":

1 tablespoon active dry yeast
1 tablespoon sugar
1¼ cups warm water
2½ cups unbleached all-purpose flour,
    plus more as needed
2 teaspoons baking powder
1¼ teaspoons salt

2 to 3 tablespoons vegetable oil,
    for brushing
Salt and freshly ground black pepper
Garlic Sauce (page 482)
Matouk's, Bushe Browne's, or other
    Caribbean hot sauce, for serving

1. Rinse the shark steaks under cold running water, then drain and blot dry with paper towels. Place in a nonreactive baking dish just large enough to hold them flat in a single layer and set aside while you prepare the marinade.

2. Combine the chives, shallots, garlic, celery, cilantro, parsley, mint, thyme, chile, water, ¼ cup lime juice, 2 teaspoons salt, and the pepper in a blender or food processor and purée. Taste for seasoning, adding lime juice or salt as necessary; the mixture should be highly seasoned. Pour the mixture over the steaks in the baking dish, turning to coat. Cover and let marinate, in the refrigerator, for 2 to 4 hours.

3. At least 2 hours ahead of time, prepare the dough for the bakes. Combine the yeast, sugar, and ½ cup of the warm water in a large bowl and stir until the yeast and sugar are dissolved. Let the mixture stand until foamy, 5 to 10 minutes, then stir in the remaining water. Sift in the 2½ cups flour, the baking powder, and salt. Stir the mixture with the wooden spoon to form a stiff but moist dough, adding flour as necessary. The dough will be moister than conventional bread dough, but not so wet that you can't roll it (see Note). Knead the dough in the bowl until smooth and elastic, 5 minutes.

4. Cover the bowl with plastic wrap, place it in a warm, draft-free spot, and let the dough rise until doubled in bulk, 1 to 2 hours.

5. Preheat the grill to medium-high.

6. Punch the dough down by stirring with the wooden spoon. Divide the dough into 4 equal pieces and roll each piece into a ball. Dust the balls with flour. Working on a liberally floured work surface with an equally liberally floured rolling pin, roll each dough ball out to a circle 6 to 7 inches in diameter and ¼ inch thick.

7. When ready to grill the bakes, oil the grill grate. Lightly brush the bakes with oil and arrange them on the hot grill grate. Grill them until blistered and lightly browned, 2 to 4 minutes per side, turning them with a long spatula. Keep the breads warm in a bread basket lined with a towel.

8. When ready to cook the steaks, remove from the marinade and blot dry with paper towels. Brush lightly on both sides with oil, sprinkle with salt and pepper, and arrange, facing in the same direction, on the hot grate. Grill until cooked through in the center when pierced with a knife, 3 to 5 minutes per side, turning over carefully with a long spatula. For an attractive crosshatch of grill marks, rotate the steaks 90 degrees after 2 minutes on each side.

9. Using the spatula, carefully transfer the steaks to serving plates or a platter. To eat, fold a piece of shark in a bake, pouring on garlic and hot sauce to taste.

Serves 4

Note: The dough can also be made in a mixer with a dough hook.

A Few Shark and Bake Tips

Several varieties of shark are marketed in the U.S., including mako, blue shark, and black tip. All three have a firm, white, mild-flavored flesh that belies the predatory fierceness of their source. Mako tastes quite similar to swordfish; blue shark has a whiter flesh and more delicate flavor; black shark shares these qualities, but tends to be a little dry.

Although shark may seem exotic, even weird to many Americans, it's more commonplace than you think. A fair amount of what passes for swordfish in this country is actually shark. Anxious to avoid unpleasant connotations, though, many fishmongers market shark by the benign name of dogfish; a rather strange choice considering the idea was to make the fish sound more attractive.

There's another reason to love shark, besides its fine-flavored flesh: It's virtually boneless. Endowed with a cartilaginous backbone, shark lacks the tiny bones found in ordinary fish.

As for the seasoning, fresh herbs, including chives, parsley, thyme, mint leaves, and *culantro* are basic. (The latter is a sawtooth-leafed herb that tastes like strong cilantro.) These herbs grow in profusion in Paramin, a hilltop community a half hour north of Port of Spain.

To round out the seasoning, you'd ideally add a Trinidadian chile, called a seasoning pepper, that tastes like a scotch bonnet without the heat. Possible substitutes in this country include green bell pepper, cachucha pepper (a small, pattypan squash–shaped pepper sometimes called *chile rocotillo* or *aji dulce*), or even a seeded, deveined scotch bonnet.

The recipe included here is a North American's take on a Trinidadian classic—inspired by one of the best places to eat shark and bake: Natalie's Shark and Bake Shop at Maracas Bay on Trinidad's north coast. If you're in a hurry, you could omit the "bakes," substituting grilled slices of your favorite prepared bread, instead. This recipe also works well with swordfish.

GRILLED SWORDFISH EN PIPIAN

MEXICO

METHOD:
Direct grilling

**ADVANCE
PREPARATION:**
*1 hour for
marinating the
fish*

Pipián refers to a family of Mexican sauces made with *pepitas,* hulled green pumpkin seeds. The toasted, ground seeds serve as both a flavoring and thickener. *Pipián* is found all over Mexico, but especially in the southwestern province of Guerrero, where it goes by the name of *mole verde* (green sauce). It's relative mildness makes it heaven sent for seafood. This recipe pairs the sauce with swordfish, but you can also serve it with salmon, snapper, shrimp, or one of my favorite fishes, pompano. For that matter, grilled pork or chicken would be delicious with pumpkin seed sauce.

The recipe includes two special ingredients: tomatillos and epazote. The former are a small, green tomatolike fruit in the gooseberry family recognizable by their papery husks. Canned tomatillos will work fine for this recipe and are widely available. Epazote is a jagged-leafed herb with a pungent smell and flavor. Known as pigweed in English, it's available at Mexican markets and is often found growing in vacant lots. I've made the epazote optional; the sauce will be quite delicious if not strictly authentic without it.

As I do throughout the book, I've given a range of chiles. The larger amount is the more authentic. (Remember, the chiles lose some of their heat when blanched.) Don't be intimidated by the number of ingredients—the sauce is quite quick and easy to make—but if you want to simplify things, you can omit the marinade and just brush the steaks with oil, seasoning with a little salt and pepper before grilling. The sauce itself can be made up to 3 days in advance and may even be frozen.

FOR THE FISH AND MARINADE:
6 swordfish steaks (each 6 to 8 ounces and
    about 1 inch thick)
2 to 6 jalapeño or serrano chiles, thinly sliced
    (for a milder sauce, seed the chiles)
¼ cup coarsely chopped fresh cilantro
3 tablespoons fresh lime juice
3 tablespoons extra-virgin olive oil
Salt and freshly ground black pepper,
    to taste

FOR THE SAUCE:
1 cup hulled pumpkin seeds
2½ cups fish stock, bottled clam broth,
    chicken broth, or water
8 fresh tomatillos (see Note)
4 to 6 fresh jalapeño chiles, 6 to 10 serrano
    chiles, or 1 poblano chile, cut in half
    lengthwise and seeded (for a spicier
    sauce, leave the seeds in)
½ small onion
4 cloves garlic, peeled
2 scallions, both white and green parts,
    trimmed and cut into 1-inch pieces
½ cup coarsely chopped fresh cilantro,
    plus a few tablespoons for garnish
2 tablespoons coarsely chopped fresh Italian
    (flat-leaf) parsley
2 romaine lettuce leaves, cut crosswise
    into 1-inch slices
1 tablespoon fresh lime juice, or more
    to taste
¼ teaspoon ground cumin
2 tablespoons lard or olive oil
2 sprigs epazote, finely chopped (optional)
Salt, to taste

1. Rinse the swordfish steaks under cold running water, then drain and blot dry with paper towels. Place the steaks in a nonreactive baking dish just large enough to hold them flat in a single layer. Combine the chiles, cilantro, lime juice, oil, and salt and pepper in a small bowl and whisk briefly to blend the liquids. Pour the mixture over the steaks in the baking dish. Cover and let marinate, in the refrigerator, for 1 hour, turning once or twice.

2. Prepare the sauce. Roast the pumpkin seeds in a dry skillet over medium heat until they begin to brown and pop, 3 to 5 minutes. Shake the pan as you cook the seeds and do not let them burn. Transfer the pumpkin seeds to a shallow bowl to cool. Setting 3 tablespoons seeds aside for garnish, grind the remainder to a fine powder in a blender or mini chopper. Stir in 1 cup of the stock and set aside.

3. Discard the papery husks from the tomatillos and place in a small saucepan with water to cover. Add the chiles and bring to a boil over medium heat. Reduce the heat to low and gently simmer until the tomatillos are soft, about 5 minutes. Drain the tomatillos (both softened and canned, if using) and place in a blender with the chiles, remaining 1½ cups stock, the onion, garlic, scallions, ½ cup cilantro, the parsley, lettuce, 1 tablespoon lime juice, and the cumin and process to a smooth purée.

4. Heat the lard or oil in a large deep saucepan over medium heat. Add the pumpkin seed mixture and fry until dark, thick, and fragrant, about 5 minutes, stirring frequently to prevent splattering. Stir in the tomatillo mixture and continue cooking the sauce until thick and richly flavored, 15 to 20 minutes, stirring often. The last 5 minutes, stir in the epazote (if using). Remove from the heat and taste for seasoning, adding salt or lime juice as necessary; the mixture should be highly seasoned. Set aside and keep warm.

5. Preheat the grill to high.

6. When ready to cook, oil the grill grate. Remove the steaks from the marinade and arrange, facing in the same direction, on the hot grate. Grill until cooked through when pierced by a knife, 4 to 6 minutes per side, turning over carefully with a long spatula. For an attractive crosshatch of grill marks, rotate the steaks 90 degrees after the first 2 minutes on each side.

7. Using the spatula, carefully transfer the steaks to a serving platter and spoon the sauce over. Sprinkle with the reserved whole pumpkin seeds and additional chopped cilantro and serve at once.

Serves 6

Note: If fresh tomatillos are not available, one 28-ounce can, drained, rinsed, and drained again, can be substituted; it is not necessary to cook them before adding to the blender.

STURGEON SHASHLYK

AZERBAIJAN

METHOD:
Direct grilling

ADVANCE PREPARATION:
30 minutes to 2 hours for marinating the fish

Azerbaijan is an oil-rich former Soviet republic located to the east of the world's sturgeon capital, the Caspian Sea. *Shashlyk* is the Russian (and former Soviet Republic's) term for a shish kebab. You could certainly grill the fish on spits in this recipe, but here I've called for it to be marinated and cooked as steaks. The sour cream has both a tenderizing and enriching effect. Sweet-tart pomegranate molasses can be bought commercially at Middle Eastern markets or made fresh following the recipe I've included in this book (see Index). Sumac is a sour red spice served as a seasoning for grilled meats throughout the Near East; it, too, can be found in Middle Eastern markets and speciality food stores.

FOR THE FISH AND MARINADE:

4 fresh sturgeon, monkfish, or swordfish steaks (each 6 to 8 ounces and ¾ to 1 inch thick)

2 tablespoons vegetable oil

Salt and freshly ground black pepper, to taste

1 cup sour cream

3 tablespoons fresh lemon juice

2 tablespoons chopped fresh dill or 1 tablespoon dried

1 clove garlic, minced

FOR SERVING:

4 scallions, both white and green parts, trimmed and thinly sliced

1 fresh, ripe tomato, cut into wedges

Lemon wedges

1 cucumber, thinly sliced

2 to 3 tablespoons Pomegranate Molasses (page 227)

3 tablespoons ground sumac

1. Rinse the sturgeon steaks under cold running water, then drain and blot dry with paper towels. Brush the steaks on both sides with the oil and season with salt and pepper, then place in a nonreactive baking dish just large enough to hold them flat in a single layer.

2. Combine the sour cream, lemon juice, dill, and garlic in a small bowl and pour over the steaks, turning the steaks to coat completely. Cover and let marinate, in the refrigerator, for at least 30 minutes and up to 2 hours, turning the steaks occasionally.

3. Preheat the grill to high.

4. When ready to cook, oil the grill grate. Remove the steaks from the marinade and arrange, facing in the same direction, on the hot grate. Grill until cooked through in the center when pierced with a knife, 3 to 6 minutes per side, turning over carefully with a long spatula. For an attractive crosshatch of grill marks, rotate the steaks 90 degrees after 2 minutes on each side.

5. Using the spatula, carefully transfer the steaks to a serving platter. Sprinkle with the sliced scallions and garnish with the tomato and lemon wedges and cucumber slices. Serve immediately, accompanied by the Pomegranate Molasses and ground sumac.

Serves 4

FISH YASSA

SENEGAL

METHOD:
Direct grilling

ADVANCE PREPARATION:
1 to 2 hours for marinating the fish

The term *yassa* refers to a family of dishes popular in West Africa, especially in Senegal. The basic preparation centers on a tangy sauce of onions, mustard, and lemon juice. Traditionally, the onions are fried in palm oil, a richly flavored, reddish oil sold at African and Brazilian markets. It is also high in saturated fat, so here I approximate its color and flavor by cooking regular vegetable oil with a spoonful of paprika. There are lots of possibilities for fish here: The traditional choice would be a dark, rich fish, like kingfish or bluefish, but salmon is also delectable prepared in this fashion. Serve accompanied by a pitcher of Ginger Pineapple Punch (see Index) and steamed white rice.

FOR THE FISH:
4 fish steaks, such as salmon,
    (each 6 to 8 ounces and
    about 1 inch thick)
Salt and freshly ground black pepper, to taste
¼ cup fresh lemon juice
2 tablespoons vegetable oil

FOR THE SAUCE:
¼ cup canola oil
1 teaspoon paprika
4 medium onions, cut into ¼-inch wedges
    (about 3 cups)
1 medium carrot, peeled and thinly sliced
½ to 2 scotch bonnet chiles, seeded and
    thinly sliced (for a spicier sauce, leave
    the seeds in)
⅓ cup water
¼ cup fresh lemon juice, or more to taste
¼ cup grainy French mustard, or more
    to taste
2 tablespoons distilled white vinegar
Salt and freshly ground black pepper, to taste

1. Rinse the steaks under cold running water, then drain and blot dry with paper towels. Season the fish with salt and pepper and place in a baking dish just large enough to hold them flat in a single layer. Whisk the lemon juice and oil in a small bowl to blend and pour over the fish. Turn the steaks once or twice to coat, then cover and let marinate, in the refrigerator, for 1 to 2 hours.

2. Preheat the grill to high.

3. When almost ready to grill, prepare the sauce. Heat the oil in a nonstick skillet over medium heat. Stir in the paprika, then add the onions, carrot, and chile and sauté until the onion is translucent, 3 to 4 minutes. Add the water, ¼ cup each lemon juice, and mustard, and the vinegar and bring to a boil. Reduce the heat to low and simmer the sauce until reduced, thick, and richly flavored, about 15 minutes, stirring often; the onions should remain a little crisp. Remove from the heat and taste for seasoning, adding salt, pepper, mustard, or lemon juice as necessary; the sauce should be highly seasoned. Cover and keep warm.

4. When ready to cook the steaks, oil the grill grate. Remove the steaks from the marinade and arrange, facing in the same direction, on the hot grate. Grill until cooked through in the center when pierced with a knife, 4 to 6 minutes per side, turning over carefully with a long spatula. For an attractive crosshatch of grill marks, rotate the steaks 90 degrees after the first 2 minutes on each side.

5. Using the spatula, carefully transfer the steaks to serving plates or a platter and spoon the sauce on top. Serve immediately.
Serves 4

TUNA STEAKS, MADEIRA-STYLE

PORTUGAL

METHOD:
Direct grilling

ADVANCE PREPARATION:
3 to 4 hours for marinating the fish

Readers of my books will know of my love for Portugal and Portuguese cooking. I would venture to say that Portugal is the best-kept culinary secret in Europe—and this includes their outdoor cooking. The following preparation comes from Portuguese-owned Madeira, a volcanic island off the coast of Africa, which is famed for its fortified wine, tropical flowers, and vertiginously steep terraced hillsides. I suppose it's no accident that grilling should be popular in Madeira. The island was once covered with trees that were used for making charcoal.

Serve these tuna steaks with crusty Portuguese bread or cornbread.

4 cloves garlic, peeled
1 tablespoon coarse (kosher or sea) salt
1 tablespoon dried oregano leaves
1 tablespoon dried basil leaves
1 teaspoon freshly ground black pepper
½ cup extra-virgin olive oil, preferably Portuguese, or as needed
4 tuna steaks (each 6 to 8 ounces and about 1 inch thick)
8 bay leaves

1. Combine the garlic, salt, oregano, basil, and pepper in a mortar and pound to a paste with the pestle, then work in enough oil to achieve a spreading consistency, 1 to 2 tablespoons (see Note).

2. Rinse the tuna steaks under cold running water, then drain and blot dry with paper towels. Using your fingers or a spatula, spread the spice paste on both sides of each of the steaks, then place in a baking dish just large enough to hold them flat in a single layer. Pour another ¼ cup of the oil over the fish and turn the steaks once or twice to coat. Place a bay leaf under each steak and one on top, then cover and let marinate, in the refrigerator, for 3 to 4 hours, spooning the oil over the steaks occasionally.

3. Preheat the grill to high.

4. When ready to cook, oil the grill grate. Remove the tuna steaks from the marinade. Rinse and blot dry with paper towels, then brush on both sides with another 1 to 2 tablespoons oil. Arrange the steaks, facing in the same direction, on the hot grate and grill until cooked to taste, 4 to 6 minutes per side for medium well (the Portuguese like their tuna on the medium side of medium well), turning over carefully with a long spatula. For an attractive crosshatch of grill marks, rotate the steaks 90 degrees after the first 2 minutes on each side.

5. Transfer the steaks to serving plates or a platter and serve at once.

Serves 4

Note: If you don't have a mortar and pestle, mash the ingredients together in a bowl using the back of a wooden spoon, or process in a mini chopper or blender, adding the oil gradually.

GRILLED TUNA WITH RED WINE, CAPER, AND OLIVE SAUCE
Thon Grillé au Jus de Raïto

FRANCE

METHOD: *Direct grilling*

I first tasted this dish (or one very nearly like it) on the end of a barely inhabited island located a few miles off the Côte d'Azur. The Isle de Porquerolles is where to go when you want to escape the crowds and traffic of the Riviera. Immortalized by the mystery writer Georges Simenon, the island has a single town you can cross on foot in about 10 minutes, set amid acres of national parkland. The people who live there have the good sense to ban cars from the mainland.

But you never get so remote in France that you can't find a good meal—in this case at a gracious, Michelin one-star restaurant in the hotel Mas de Langoustier.

Chef Joël Guillet takes a contemporary approach to Provençal cooking, but there was one dish on his menu that may date all the way back to the Phoenicians.

According to local lore, the red wine, olive, and caper sauce known as *raïto* originated in Greece and was brought to Massilia (as Marseilles was known in ancient times) by Phoenician sailors. Provence is the only place in France where you find it, and it's rooted deeply enough to have acquired several names, including *rayte* and *raïte*. Whatever its origins, it's a sauce richly rooted in the Mediterranean, with a deep flavor that goes well with grilled tuna. The following recipe was inspired by the dish at the Mas de Langoustier.

FOR THE FISH:
4 tuna steaks (each 6 to 8 ounces and
about 1 inch thick)
2 tablespoons extra-virgin olive oil
Salt and freshly ground black pepper,
to taste

FOR THE RAITO:
⅓ cup extra-virgin olive oil
1 medium onion, finely chopped
3 cloves garlic, minced
1 small fresh, ripe tomato, peeled and
seeded (see box, page 62), then
finely chopped
2 cups dry red wine
1 tablespoon tomato paste
1 sprig fresh thyme or ¼ teaspoon
dried
1 bay leaf
¼ cup black olives, preferably tiny
Niçoise, pitted
2 tablespoons drained capers
Salt and freshly ground black pepper,
to taste

1. Brush the tuna steaks on both sides with the oil and season with salt and pepper. Place in a baking dish, cover, and let marinate, in the refrigerator, for 30 minutes.

2. Preheat the grill to high.

3. While the steaks marinate, prepare the *raïto*. Heat 3 tablespoons of the oil in a large saucepan over medium-high heat. Add the onion and garlic and cook until golden brown, about 5 minutes. Add the tomato and cook for 2 minutes. Stir in the wine, tomato paste, thyme, bay leaf, olives, and capers and bring to a boil. Reduce the heat to medium and simmer briskly until the mixture is reduced by half, about 10 minutes.

4. Remove the sauce from the heat and discard the thyme sprig and bay leaf. Whisk in the remaining oil and salt and pepper; the mixture should be highly seasoned (see Note). Cover and keep the sauce warm.

5. When ready to cook, oil the grill grate. Arrange the steaks, facing in the same direction, on the hot grate and grill until cooked to taste, 3 to 4 minutes per side for medium rare, turning over carefully with a long spatula. For an attractive crosshatch of grill marks, rotate the steaks 90 degrees after the first 2 minutes on each side.

6. Transfer the steaks to serving plates or a platter and serve immediately, with the sauce spooned on top.

Serves 4

Note: Chef Guillet likes the refinement of puréeing the sauce in a blender, adding the olives and capers at the end instead of before the sauce is reduced; he returns the sauce to the pan just to heat the olives and capers through. Being a robust sort of guy, I like the gutsiness of an unstrained sauce, but purée it, if you so fancy.

How to Grill the Perfect Fish Steak

Steaks cut from firm, meaty fish like salmon, swordfish, and tuna are delicious when grilled. You cook them pretty much as you would beef steaks. Actually, this isn't completely true. I cover the grill when cooking thick fish steaks. Restaurant chefs invert a metal pie pan over each. Both methods help speed up the cooking process.

1. Start with the freshest possible fish. Tuna, for example, should be sushi quality. If you like it rare in the center, cut the steak 1 to 2 inches thick. If you like it cooked through, cut the steaks ½ inch thick. Swordfish can be cut ½ to 1 inch thick. When grilling salmon steaks, leave the bones in. They help hold the fish together.

2. Preheat the grill to high.

3. When ready to cook, brush the fish steaks on both sides with oil or melted butter and season with salt and pepper. If you've marinated the fish in a mixture rich with oil, butter, or coconut milk, it is unnecessary to either blot dry, further oil, or season. The grate should be oiled, however; the fish can go on the grate right after you've done that.

4. Arrange the fish steaks on the hot grate, all facing the same direction. Cover the grill and cook the fish steaks on one side for about 2 minutes for a steak ½ inch thick; 4 to 6 minutes for one an inch or more thick. If desired, after 2 minutes, using a long spatula, rotate the steaks 90 degrees. This creates an attractive crosshatch of grill marks.

5. Carefully turn the steaks over, using the spatula, and cook the other side the same way, rotating the steaks 90 degrees after 2 minutes and covering the grill again. Tuna tastes best served rare or pink in the center; swordfish and salmon should be cooked through.

6. To test steaks that should be cooked through for doneness, gently pierce the steak in the center with a knife; it should look cooked through. Or, press the fish with your finger. When properly cooked the area around where you pressed will break into firm flakes. If there is a center bone, the fish should pull away easily.

SPANISH GUINEAN FISH GRILL WITH THREE SAUCES

EQUATORIAL GUINEA

METHOD: *Direct grilling*

The Claris is one of the smartest hotels in Barcelona, an ultramodern hideaway whose quiet, luxurious rooms nestle behind the ornate facade of a nineteenth-century mansion. It's an odd place, to be sure, to begin an account of a fish barbecue from Equatorial Guinea. But it was here that I met Arsenio Pancho Sobe,

**ADVANCE
PREPARATION:**
*1 hour for
marinating
the fish*

doorman extraordinaire and passionate barbecue buff. Sobe is one of the 100,000 or so Guineans living in Spain, the former colonial ruler of Guinea.

Sobe comes from Malabo, the capital of Equatorial Guinea, located on the tiny island of Bioko, off the coast, where seafood is grilled over coconut logs and served with a triumvirate of spicy sauces. The first is an irresistible peanut sauce flavored with dried shrimp; the second, an intriguing green sauce made with a spinach-like edible leaf called *machea*; the third, a tangy avocado sauce.

All three sauces owe their firepower to the large, bright red Guinea pepper, a cousin of the habanero. If you live near a West African market, you may be able to find Guinea peppers; if not, use habaneros or scotch bonnets. As for fish, a Guinean would use a full-flavored, dark-fleshed fish like kingfish or mackerel. I've had equal success with bluefish, tuna steaks (which I suggest here), and whole snappers.

Although this may seem like an imposing recipe, it's actually just a series of simple steps. A couple of things can make it even easier. First, you could cook a smaller amount of fish and just prepare one of the sauces. In this case, I'd go with the peanut sauce, which is the most unusual. Second, the sauces keep well, so you could prepare them ahead and use them later or as needed—the sauces are what make the dish Guinean.

8 fish steaks, such as tuna or kingfish
    (each 6 to 8 ounces and about
    1 inch thick)
Salt and freshly ground black pepper,
    to taste
3 cloves garlic, crushed
½ to 2 Guinea peppers or scotch bonnet
    chiles, seeded and minced
    (optional)
1 cup fresh lime juice
2 to 3 tablespoons coconut oil or other
    vegetable oil, for brushing
Peanut Sauce (facing page)
Spinach Sauce (facing page)
Avocado Sauce (page 320)

1. Rinse the fish steaks under cold running water, then drain and blot dry with paper towels. Season the steaks generously on both sides with salt and pepper and place in a nonreactive baking dish just large enough to hold them flat in a single layer. Add the garlic and chiles. Pour the lime juice over the steaks and turn once or twice to coat, then cover and let marinate, in the refrigerator, for 1 hour, turning once or twice.

2. Preheat the grill to high (see Note).

3. When ready to cook, remove the tuna steaks from the marinade. Blot dry, then brush on both sides with oil and season with salt and pepper. Oil the grill grate, then arrange the steaks, facing in the same direction, on the hot grate and grill until cooked to taste, 3 to 4 minutes per side for medium-rare, turning over carefully with a long spatula. (If using steaks other than tuna, cook 4 to 6 minutes per side.) For an attractive crosshatch of grill marks, rotate the steaks 90 degrees after the first 2 minutes on each side.

4. Transfer the steaks to serving plates and serve at once, with the sauces.

Serves 8

Note: If you're using a charcoal grill and you have coconut-shell charcoal or husks left over from a fresh coconut, so much the better. Make sure the husks are really dry before throwing them on the grill.

Peanut Sauce

Dried shrimp aren't a particularly popular flavoring in North America—which is a shame, because their sweet, briny flavor is delectable—but they turn up widely in Africa, Asia, the Caribbean, and Brazil. Brazilians, in fact, boast a dish very similar to this one, a stew based on dried shrimp and peanuts called *vatapá*, from the state of Bahia in northern Brazil. If you can't find dried shrimp, use fresh instead.

1½ cups water
½ cup finely chopped onion
2 cloves garlic, minced
1 large fresh, ripe tomato, finely chopped, with juices
½ to 2 Guinea peppers or scotch bonnet chiles, seeded and minced (for a hotter sauce, leave the seeds in)
2 teaspoons minced fresh ginger
1 bay leaf
1 ounce (3 to 4 tablespoons) dried shrimp, coarsely chopped, or 4 ounces fresh shrimp, shelled and deveined (see page 349), then coarsely chopped
½ cup chunky peanut butter
3 to 4 tablespoons minced fresh cilantro (optional)
Salt and freshly ground black pepper, to taste

1. Combine the water, onion, garlic, tomato, Guinea pepper, ginger, bay leaf, and shrimp in a saucepan and bring to a boil over medium heat. Reduce the heat to low and simmer gently until the shrimp are soft, about 5 minutes.

2. Remove from the heat and discard the bay leaf, then whisk in the peanut butter, cilantro (if using), and salt and pepper. Return to low heat and continue simmering until the sauce is thick and richly flavored, about 5 minutes. Transfer to a small bowl, cover, and refrigerate until ready to serve.

Makes about 2 cups

Spinach Sauce

This sauce is traditionally made with an edible green leaf called *machea*. Spinach gives a pretty close approximation in this country. Palm oil has a distinctive orange color and sourish flavor. Look for it in African or Brazilian markets, but if you can't find it, or have health concerns (palm oil is high in saturated fat), use olive oil instead. Add some paprika to give the olive oil a touch of reddish color.

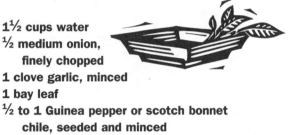

1½ cups water
½ medium onion, finely chopped
1 clove garlic, minced
1 bay leaf
½ to 1 Guinea pepper or scotch bonnet chile, seeded and minced
½ teaspoon salt, or more to taste
½ package frozen chopped spinach (about 5 ounces), thawed, or 4 cups stemmed fresh leaf spinach, rinsed well, drained, and chopped
1 tablespoon palm oil or olive oil
Freshly ground black pepper, to taste
1 to 2 teaspoons lime juice (optional)

1. Combine the water, onion, garlic, bay leaf, Guinea pepper, and ½ teaspoon salt in a large, heavy saucepan and bring to a boil over medium heat. Cook, uncovered, until the onion is tender, about 5 minutes.

2. Remove and discard the bay leaf, then add the spinach and boil until tender, about 2 minutes. Stir in the palm oil, then remove from the heat. Transfer the mixture to a blender or food processor and process to a coarse purée. Transfer the purée to a small bowl and taste for seasoning, adding salt, pepper, and lime juice, if desired. Cover and refrigerate until ready to serve.

Makes about 2 cups

Avocado Sauce

This sauce, too, finds an analog on the other side of the Atlantic: the avocado sauces of Mexico, also served with grilled fish.

1 ripe Hass avocado, peeled, pitted,
   and cut into ¼-inch dice
1 tablespoon fresh lime juice, or
   more to taste
½ cup finely chopped onion
2 cloves garlic, minced
1 bay leaf
½ to 1 Guinea pepper or scotch bonnet chile,
   seeded and minced
¼ cup finely chopped fresh Italian (flat-leaf)
   parsley
½ cup water, or more as needed
¼ cup finely chopped fresh cilantro
1 large, fresh, ripe tomato, seeded
   (see box, page 62) and finely diced
Salt and freshly ground black pepper, to taste

1. Combine the avocado and lime juice in a nonreactive small, heavy saucepan and toss to mix. Stir in the onion, garlic, bay leaf, Guinea pepper, parsley, and ½ cup water. Bring to a simmer over low heat and cook until the avocado and onion are soft, about 5 minutes. Stir in the cilantro, tomato and salt and pepper and simmer for 1 minute more.

2. Remove from the heat and taste for seasoning, adding salt or lime juice as necessary; add a little water as necessary if the sauce is too thick. Remove the bay leaf before serving. Transfer to a small bowl, cover, and refrigerate until ready to serve.

Makes about 2 cups

How to Skin and Bone Fish Fillets

Fish fillets can be grilled with or without the skin. Some skin is even exquisitely tasty (I'm thinking salmon) brushed with oil, sprinkled with salt, and grilled over a medium-high flame until crisp. But if a recipe calls for the skin to be removed, here's how to do it.

Lay the fillet, skin side down, on a cutting board at the edge of the board closest to you, tail (or narrow end) to the left (or right, if you're left-handed). Holding the tail with your left (or right) hand, and using a long, slender knife, make a cut through the tail meat but not through the skin. The cut should be made about ½ inch in from the end so you have a small piece to hold on to. Gradually bring the knife blade parallel to the cutting board and cut toward the head end of the fillet, using a sawing motion, pinching the skin between the knife and the cutting board. The fillet will come cleanly away from the skin.

It's always a good idea to check a fillet for any remaining bones. Run your fingers over the top of the fillet, feeling for bones. Pull out any you may find with a needlenose pliers, tweezers, or strawberry huller.

YUCATAN-STYLE GRILLED FISH
Tikin Xik

MEXICO

METHOD:
Direct grilling

**ADVANCE
PREPARATION:**
*30 minutes for
marinating the
fish*

**SPECIAL
EQUIPMENT:**
*1 banana leaf
(see box, page
289), cut into
4 rectangles
a little larger
than the pieces
of fish, or 4
rectangles of
aluminum foil,
each 4 to 6
layers thick;
a fish or
vegetable grate
(optional)*

Le Saint Bonnet is just the sort of restaurant you want to wind up at after a long, hot morning driving the monotonously straight roads of the Yucatán. Its open-air dining area, shaded by a thatched roof and cooled by sea breezes, overlooks the blue-green waters of the Gulf of Mexico. It's the kind of place where ordering a beer brings you half a dozen tiny plates of *botanas* (cocktail snacks) and where you can easily spend three hours over lunch.

The restaurant's founder was French, which accounts for both the restaurant's name. French heritage notwithstanding, it was here that I learned to make the most famous fish dish in the Yucatán: *tikin xik* (pronounced "tee-ken-SHEEK"). As the Mayan-sounding name suggests, *tikin xik* is one of the oldest dishes in the Yucatán, predating the arrival of the Spanish. *Xik* is the Mayan word for "marinated fish"; *tikin,* "something that is turned or rotated." And though *tikin xik* is not actually on the restaurant's menu, regulars know how to ask for it, and chef Miguel Angel Canto-Ruiz is always happy to oblige.

At the restaurant, as is traditional, a whole fish is cleaned and boned through the back (a fairly complicated process), spread open like a book and marinated with a special *recado*, a bright orange spice paste made with annatto seeds, garlic, and sour orange juice. The day I tried it, it was a freshly caught grouper that underwent the process, but other traditional fish for *tikin xik* include snapper and pompano. Because the boning of the whole fish is so complicated, I suggest using fish fillets, but if you wish to try a whole fish, see the box on page 322 for a simple version.

FOR THE FISH AND RECADO:
4 mahimahi fillets (each 6 to 8 ounces)
1 teaspoon annatto seeds
½ teaspoon black peppercorns
2 allspice berries
2 whole cloves
½ teaspoon ground cinnamon
**2 tablespoons fresh sour orange juice or
    1½ tablespoons fresh regular orange
    juice plus ½ tablespoon lime juice**
2 tablespoons fresh regular orange juice
2 tablespoons distilled white vinegar
2 cloves garlic, minced
1 bay leaf
Salt
¼ cup water, or more as needed
**2 to 4 tablespoons vegetable oil or melted
    unsalted butter, for brushing**
Freshly ground black pepper

FOR COOKING THE FISH (OPTIONAL):
1 small white onion, cut into ¼-inch wedges
**1 large fresh, ripe tomato, cut into
    ¼-inch wedges**
4 sprigs epazote (optional)

FOR SERVING:
Shredded lettuce
Cucumber and tomato slices
Lime slices
Fresh Italian (flat-leaf) parsley sprigs
"Dog's Nose" Salsa (page 453)

1. Rinse the mahimahi fillets under cold running water, then drain and blot dry with paper towels. Place the fillets in a nonreactive baking dish just large enough to hold them flat in a single layer. Set aside while you prepare the *recado*.

2. Combine the annatto seeds, peppercorns, allspice, cloves, and cinnamon in a spice mill or clean coffee mill and grind to a fine powder. Transfer the powder to a small bowl and add the sour orange juice, regular orange juice, vinegar, garlic, bay leaf, and 1 teaspoon salt. Stir until the salt is dissolved and the mixture is well blended, then taste and add enough water to take out the sharpness. Pour the *recado* over the fish in the baking dish, turning the fillets to coat. Cover and let marinate, in the refrigerator, for 30 minutes.

3. Preheat the grill to high.

4. When ready to cook, preheat a fish or vegetable grate (if using) for 5 minutes. Drain the fillets and blot dry with paper towels. Brush both sides of the fillets with oil and season with salt and pepper. Generously oil the fish or vegetable grate or grill grate, then arrange the fillets on it. Grill 3 to 4 minutes. Using a long spatula, carefully turn the fillets, inverting each one onto a banana leaf rectangle (see Note). Arrange the onion and tomato wedges and the epazote (if using) on top of the fillets and grill until the fish breaks into firm flakes when pressed with a finger, 3 to 4 minutes more.

5. Using the spatula, carefully transfer the fillets to a serving platter. Surround the fish with the lettuce and the cucumber, tomato, and lime slices, and top with parsley sprigs. Serve immediately, accompanied by the salsa.

Serves 4

Note: You can omit the banana leaf, if you like, and just turn the fillets over onto the fish grate, but the fish won't be quite as moist.

Whole Fish, Tikin Xik Style

1. For the fish fillets in the recipe above substitute 1 large whole fish, such as snapper, grouper, or pompano, trimmed of fins and cleaned, head and tail left on. Rinse the fish, inside and out, under cold running water. Drain and blot dry with paper towels. Make 5 or 6 deep diagonal slashes, to the bone, in each side of the fish. Place the fish in a nonreactive roasting pan while you prepare the marinade as directed in the main recipe. Pour the marinade over the fish, using your fingers to spread it over both sides of the fish, working it into the slashes as well. Cover and let marinate, in the refrigerator, for 1 to 3 hours.

2. Set up the grill for indirect cooking (see page 14 or 16); preheat to high. It is not necessary to use a drip pan.

3. When ready to cook, set the fish on a piece of banana leaf or 4 to 6 layers of aluminum foil cut just larger than the fish and place in the center of the grill grate, away from the flame. Cover the grill and cook until the fish flakes easily when pressed with a finger, 40 to 60 minutes. Arrange the onion, tomato wedges, and epazote (if using) on top of the fish 5 minutes before the ending of the cooking time.

4. Using two long spatulas, carefully remove the fish to a serving platter. Garnish as directed and serve with the "Dog's Nose" Salsa (page 453), filleting the fish as directed on page 293.

Serves 4

BARRAMUNDI IN ASIAN SPICED COCONUT MILK

METHOD:
Direct grilling

ADVANCE PREPARATION:
2 hours for marinating the fish

SPECIAL EQUIPMENT:
Fish or vegetable grate (optional)

Barramundi, one of the most beloved fish in Australia, is a gold-flecked beauty with a firm, sweet, white flesh that forms large meaty flakes when cooked. You probably won't be able to find barramundi in this country (do try it when you go to Australia), but sea bass, grouper, and especially tilapia make good substitutes.

The Southeast Asian roots of this recipe are obvious. You'll love the haunting flavors of the lemongrass and kaffir lime leaves, not to mention the wonderful way the coconut milk moisturizes and enriches the fish. This recipe was inspired by the Bathers Pavillion restaurant on Balmoral Beach in Sydney.

4 barramundi, sea bass, grouper, or
   tilapia fillets (each 6 to 8 ounces
   and about ¾ inch thick), checked
   over for bones
1 large shallot, finely chopped
3 cloves garlic, minced
2 stalks fresh lemongrass, trimmed and
   minced (see Note)
1 piece (1 inch) fresh ginger, minced
1 piece (1 inch) fresh galangal, minced
   (see Note)
2 Thai or serrano chiles, minced
   (for a milder sauce, seed the chiles)
2 tablespoons vegetable oil, preferably
   peanut
½ teaspoon shrimp paste (see Note)
2 cups coconut milk, canned or fresh
   (see page 522)
3 tablespoons Asian fish sauce
1 tablespoon fresh lime juice
1 teaspoon palm sugar or light brown sugar
2 kaffir lime leaves, cut crosswise into
   hair-thin slivers (see Note)

1. Rinse the fillets under cold running water, then drain and blot dry with paper towels. Place the fillets in a nonreactive baking dish just large enough to hold them flat in a single layer. Set aside while you prepare the marinade/sauce.

2. Combine the shallot, garlic, lemongrass, ginger, galangal, and chiles in a mortar and pound to a thick paste with the pestle (or process in a food processor). Set aside.

3. Heat the oil in a wok or large, heavy skillet over medium heat. Add the shrimp paste and sauté until fragrant, about 1 minute. Add the shallot paste and sauté, stirring constantly, until brown and fragrant, about 10 minutes. Stir in the coconut milk, fish sauce, lime juice, sugar, and half the kaffir lime leaves. Increase the heat to medium-high and bring to a boil, then reduce the heat to medium and simmer the mixture until thick and richly flavored, about 5 minutes. Remove from the heat and cool to room temperature.

4. Pour half of the cooled sauce over the fish in the baking dish, refrigerating the remainder, covered, until just before serving. Turn the fish once or twice to coat, then cover, and let marinate, in the refrigerator, for 2 hours, turning the pieces occasionally so they marinate evenly.

5. Preheat the grill to high.

6. When ready to cook, preheat a fish or vegetable grate for 5 minutes (if using), then oil it or the grill grate. Remove the fish fillets from the marinade and arrange on the hot grate. Grill 3 to 6 minutes, then turn over carefully with a long spatula and grill until the fish breaks into firm flakes when pressed with a finger, 3 to 6 minutes more. While the fish cooks, heat the reserved sauce in a saucepan on the side burner of the grill, if you have one, or over low heat on the stovetop.

7. Using a spatula, transfer the fillets to serving plates or a platter and spoon the sauce over them. Garnish each piece of fish with a tuft of shredded kaffir lime leaves and serve at once.

Serves 4

Note: You'll need a few special ingredients for this recipe, all of which are defined in the Glossary and can be found at Asian markets. But don't be discouraged if you can't find fresh lemongrass, galangal, shrimp paste, or kaffir lime leaves. Substitute 2 strips lemon zest (each $2 \times \frac{1}{2}$ inches) for the lemongrass, 1 tablespoon more of minced fresh ginger for the galangal, an anchovy, chopped, for the shrimp paste, and a couple of strips of lime zest (each $2 \times \frac{1}{2}$ inches) for the kaffir lime leaves. Even with these stand-ins, you'll have a voluptuously flavorful dish.

How to Grill Perfect Fish Fillets

Fillets are the hardest cut of fish to grill, yet people like them because they're free of bones and the broad surface area readily absorbs charcoaled flavors. The problem is that fish fillets tend to stick to the grate and crumble when turned.

The secret is to use a fish or vegetable grate, a porcelain or enamel-coated metal plate, with lots of small holes, that fits on top of the grill. This holds the fillets flat, so pieces won't fall between the bars when you turn them. If you don't have a fish or vegetable grate, and are a big fan of grilled fish, you owe it to yourself to get one.

SKINLESS FILLET METHOD

1. Preheat the grill to high.

2. When ready to cook, place the fish grate (if using) on the grill and preheat it for 5 minutes. Brush the fish fillets with oil or melted butter and season with salt and pepper. Generously oil the fish grate or the grill grate. Arrange the fillets on the grate and cook until browned on the bottom and starting to turn opaque on the top, 3 to 6 minutes.

3. If the fillets are really fragile, like sole or flounder, avoid turning them. Instead, cook with the grill covered. For other, more sturdy fillets, brush with oil or melted butter, turn carefully with a long spatula and cook until browned on the second side, 3 to 6 minutes more. When done, the fish should break into firm flakes when pressed with a finger.

SKIN-ON METHOD

This works well for fillets of oily fish, like bluefish and salmon.

1. Preheat the grill to medium-high.

2. When ready to cook the fish, brush the skin of the fish with oil or melted butter. Place the fillets, skin side down, on the grate. Cover the grill. Cook the fish until the skin is darkly browned and crackling crisp and the meat flakes easily when pressed with a finger, 6 to 12 minutes. If the skin starts to burn before the fish is cooked, pull the fillets onto a piece of aluminum foil. The top side will cook by the trapped-in heat.

SALMON GRILLED IN GRAPE LEAVES
Kolheeda

REPUBLIC OF GEORGIA

METHOD:
Direct grilling

ADVANCE PREPARATION:
20 minutes for soaking the grape leaves

One of the most intriguing grilled fish dishes I've ever enjoyed is a Georgian specialty called *kolheeda*. Named for a mythical gold mine in the Caucasus Mountains, *kolheeda* features a boned whole salmon trout stuffed with walnuts and dill, wrapped in grape leaves, and grilled. The grape leaves impart a delectable tartness to the fish, while offsetting the richness of the walnuts. They also keep the fish from drying out.

This recipe was inspired by Nancy and Gogetidze Gelody of the Pearl Café in Brighton Beach, Brooklyn, New York. I've called for salmon fillets, which are easier to get than salmon trout in most parts of the country, but do use salmon trout, if you can find it. Grape leaves preserved in brine are available in jars at Middle Eastern markets and most supermarkets

Kolheeda makes an excellent introduction to Georgian cuisine, not to mention a dramatic dish for entertaining.

16 to 24 grape leaves packed in brine, drained

4 salmon fillets (each about 6 ounces and ¾ inch thick), skinned and checked over for bones (see box, page 322)

Salt and freshly ground black pepper, to taste

1 cup shelled walnuts

2 cloves garlic, chopped

2 tablespoons chopped fresh dill or 1 tablespoon dried

2 tablespoons chopped fresh cilantro or Italian (flat-leaf) parsley

1 tablespoon fresh lemon juice, or more to taste

4 paper-thin lemon slices

1. Rinse the grape leaves thoroughly under cold running water, then place in a bowl with cold water to cover and let soak for 20 minutes, changing the water once or twice. Drain the grape leaves and blot dry with paper towels.

2. Meanwhile, rinse the fillets under cold running water, then drain and blot dry with paper towels. Place the fillets on a cutting board. Holding the knife parallel to the cutting board, cut a deep pocket in one long side of each fillet, starting and ending about 1 inch from each end and cutting almost but not quite through to the other side. Season the fillets, inside and out, with salt and pepper, then set aside while you prepare the stuffing.

3. Combine the walnuts, garlic, dill, cilantro, and 1 tablespoon lemon juice in a food processor and process to a coarse paste. Taste for seasoning adding salt, pepper, and lemon juice as necessary; the mixture should be highly seasoned. Spoon the stuffing into the pockets in the salmon, dividing evenly.

4. Working with one piece of fish at a time, arrange 2 or 3 grape leaves on a work surface to form a rectangle 2 inches larger than the piece of fish; the grape leaves should overlap slightly. Place the piece of fish on the grape leaves. Place a lemon slice on top of each piece of salmon. Cover the fish with the remaining grape leaves, tucking the ends under (see Note).

5. Preheat the grill to high.

6. When ready to cook, oil the grill grate. Place the wrapped fish on the hot grate. Grill the fish until the grape leaves are nicely browned and the fish is cooked through, 3 to 6 minutes per side, testing for doneness by inserting a thin metal skewer into the thickest part of the fish; if it comes out very hot to the touch, the fish is cooked.

7. Using a spatula, transfer the fish to plates or a platter and serve at once. Unwrap and discard the grape leaves before eating.

Serves 4

Note: The recipe can be prepared to this point several hours ahead of time; refrigerate, covered.

GRILLED SALMON KIEV

UKRAINE

METHOD:
Direct grilling

**ADVANCE
PREPARATION:**
*1 hour to 2 days
for chilling the
butter*

**SPECIAL
EQUIPMENT:**
*Fish or vegetable
grate (optional)*

Okay, okay, I know this dish is traditionally made with chicken, not salmon, and it's supposed to be deep-fried, not grilled. But I can think of few experiences more pleasurable than cutting into a smokily grilled piece of fish to release the fragrant squirt of melted herb butter inside.

4 tablespoons (½ stick) unsalted butter,
    at room temperature
2 tablespoons minced fresh Italian
    (flat-leaf) parsley
1 clove garlic, minced (optional)
½ teaspoon grated lemon zest
2 teaspoons fresh lemon juice, or more
    to taste
Salt and freshly ground black pepper, to taste
4 salmon fillets (each 6 to 8 ounces and
    ¾ to 1 inch thick), skinned and checked
    over for bones (see box, page 322)
1 tablespoon extra-virgin olive oil or
    melted unsalted butter

1. Combine the butter, parsley, garlic (if using), lemon zest, 2 teaspoons lemon juice, salt, and pepper in a small bowl and whisk until smooth and creamy. Taste for seasoning, adding salt or lemon juice as necessary. Place the butter on a large piece of plastic wrap and shape into a cylinder. Refrigerate the mixture until hard, at least 1 hour and up to 2 days.

2. Preheat the grill to high.

3. Rinse the salmon fillets under cold running water, then drain and blot dry with paper towels. Place the fillets on a cutting board. Holding a thin, sharp knife parallel to the cutting board, cut a pocket about 2 inches long in the center of one side of each piece of fish, stopping about ½ inch from the opposite end. Cut the hardened Kiev butter into 4 equal pieces and stuff one piece into the pocket in each piece of fish. Pin each pocket shut with a long toothpick or small skewer, then transfer the fish pieces to a plate and brush on both sides with oil or butter. Season both sides with salt and pepper and set aside.

4. When ready to cook, preheat a fish or vegetable grate (if using) for 5 minutes, then oil it or the grill grate. Arrange the salmon pieces on the hot grate and grill 3 to 6 minutes. Using a long spatula, carefully turn the pieces over and grill until a skewer inserted into a salmon piece comes out very hot to the touch, 3 to 6 minutes longer. If desired, after 2 minutes of grilling on each side, rotate the fish 45 degrees with the spatula to create an attractive crosshatch of grill marks.

5. Using the spatula, carefully transfer the salmon pieces to serving plates or a platter. Remove the toothpicks and serve the salmon immediately.

Serves 4

PINO'S GRILLED SALMON WITH BASIL CREAM

ITALY

METHOD:
Direct grilling

SPECIAL EQUIPMENT:
Fish or vegetable grate (optional)

Salmon has a natural affinity for basil, especially when paired with the following basil cream sauce. It is an invention of my friend Pino Savarino, a fine chef from Italy who works in Miami.

FOR THE FISH:
4 salmon fillets (each 6 to 8 ounces and
   ¾ to 1 inch thick), skinned and checked
   over for bones (see box, page 322)
2 tablespoons olive oil
2 tablespoons fresh lemon juice
Salt and freshly ground black pepper,
   to taste

FOR THE SAUCE:
20 fresh basil leaves
⅓ cup dry white wine
2 cloves garlic
1 cup heavy cream
1 tablespoon fresh lemon juice
2 tablespoons unsalted butter
Salt and freshly ground black pepper, to taste

1. Preheat the grill to high.
2. Rinse the salmon fillets under cold running water, then drain and blot dry with paper towels. Place the fillets on a platter and brush on both sides with the oil. Season both sides with lemon juice and salt and pepper, then set aside while you prepare the sauce.

3. Combine the basil, wine, and garlic in a blender and process to a smooth purée. Transfer the purée to a small, heavy saucepan and stir in the cream. Bring to a simmer over medium heat and cook until reduced by half, about 15 minutes, stirring frequently. Whisk in the lemon juice and butter. When the butter is incorporated, remove from the heat and season with salt and pepper. Keep warm, covered.

4. When ready to cook, preheat a fish or vegetable grate (if using) for 5 minutes, then oil it or the grill grate. Arrange the salmon fillets on the hot grate and grill 3 to 6 minutes. Using a long spatula, carefully turn the fillets over and grill until the fish breaks into firm flakes when pressed with a finger, 3 to 6 minutes more.

5. Using the spatula, carefully transfer the fillets to serving plates or a platter. Spoon the basil sauce on top and serve.

Serves 4

SOLE WITH CATALAN FRUITS AND NUTS

SPAIN

METHOD:
Direct grilling

Grilling isn't particularly prevalent in Spain, but live-fire cooking lends itself to a number of Spanish preparations. Consider the following specialty from La Cuineta, a restaurant in Barcelona's Barri Gòtic (medieval district) that positively oozes charm. The chef uses sole (Dover sole, that is), which is

ADVANCE PREPARATION:
30 minutes for marinating the fish

SPECIAL EQUIPMENT:
Fish or vegetable grate (optional)

much firmer and meatier than what passes for sole in this country. If you live in a large city, you may be able to find fresh Dover sole or halibut, but any grillable fish will work—I often make this dish with mahimahi. The contrast of sweet with savory (currants and sugar, in this case, with pine nuts and seafood) is quite typical of Catalan cooking.

FOR THE FISH:

4 pieces (each 6 to 8 ounces)
   Dover sole or mahimahi fillet,
   checked over for bones
   (see box, page 320)
Salt and freshly ground black pepper,
   to taste
2 tablespoons olive oil
2 tablespoons fresh orange juice
1 clove garlic, minced

FOR THE SAUCE:

2 tablespoons unsalted butter
½ cup minced shallots
1 tablespoon all-purpose flour
2 tablespoons brandy
¾ cup fresh orange juice, or more
   to taste
1 tablespoon sugar, or more
   to taste
½ cup heavy cream
3 tablespoons currants
3 tablespoons pine nuts, toasted
   (see box, page 93)
Salt and freshly ground black pepper,
   to taste
Fresh lemon juice, to taste
   (optional)

1. Rinse the fish under cold running water, then drain and blot dry with paper towels. Season the fish on both sides with salt and pepper and place in a nonreactive baking dish just large enough to hold the pieces in a single layer. Drizzle with the oil and orange juice and sprinkle with the garlic, turning the pieces a few times to coat. Set

aside to marinate for 30 minutes.

2. Preheat the grill to high.

3. While the fish marinates, prepare the sauce. Melt the butter in a small, heavy saucepan over medium heat. Add the shallots and sauté until soft and translucent but not browned, about 2 minutes. Stir in the flour and cook, stirring, for 1 minute. Remove from the heat and whisk in the brandy and ¾ cup orange juice, then return to medium heat and bring to a boil. Add 1 tablespoon sugar and the cream, stirring until the sugar dissolves. Simmer until thick and rich-flavored, 5 to 10 minutes. Remove from the heat and stir in the currants, pine nuts, and salt and pepper (see Note). Taste for seasoning, adding salt or sugar as necessary; the sauce should be a little sweet. If more acidity is desired, add a little more orange juice or even a drop of lemon juice. Keep warm, covered.

4. When ready to cook, preheat a fish or vegetable grate (if using) for 5 minutes, then oil it or the grill grate. Arrange the fish pieces on the hot grate and grill for 3 to 6 minutes, basting with any leftover marinade. Using a long spatula, carefully turn the pieces over and grill until the fish breaks into firm flakes when pressed with a finger, 3 to 6 minutes more.

5. If desired, spoon the sauce onto 4 serving plates, dividing evenly. Using the spatula, carefully transfer the fish pieces to the plates, on top of the sauce. Or serve the sauce separately, to accompany the fish. In any case, serve immediately.

Serves 4

Note: If you're feeling fancy, you can strain the sauce through a fine-meshed strainer before adding the currants and pine nuts. I'm a rustic kind of guy, and I like a rustic kind of sauce with the shallot pieces still in it.

GRILLED SKATE WINGS WITH NONYA SWEET-AND-SOUR SAUCE

MALAYSIA

METHOD:
Direct grilling

SPECIAL EQUIPMENT:
Fish or vegetable grate (optional)

Meltingly tender, buttery, and crisp, these skate wings are the specialty of Mrs. Goh Choi Eng, owner of a cook stall on Gurney Drive in Penang. The fish receive a double barrage of flavor—first from a tangy basting sauce made from aromatic, locally grown cloves, then from a Malaysian sweet-and-sour sauce redolent of lemongrass, shallots, and chiles. If skate is impossible to find in your neighborhood, this is also delicious with bluefish, swordfish, and mahimahi.

Nonya is the Malay word for "grandmother." It refers to a hybrid style of cooking developed in the nineteenth century in Singapore and Malaysia. The Nonyas were local women (usually Muslims) who married immigrant Chinese laborers. The latter immigrated to the Malaysian peninsula to work—often for the British. The Nonyas adopted Chinese seasonings, like soy sauce and five-spice powder, and Chinese cooking techniques, like stir-frying, while retaining their passion for such Malay ingredients as lemongrass and fiery chiles. The frying of the spice paste is another Nonya technique.

2 pounds skate wings
1 tablespoon ground coriander
2 teaspoons curry powder
¼ teaspoon ground cloves
1 to 2 serrano or other hot chiles, seeded and minced (for a hotter mixture, leave the seeds in)
6 tablespoons water
2 tablespoons Worcestershire sauce
Salt and freshly ground black pepper, to taste
½ cup Nonya Sweet-and-Sour Sauce (recipe follows), or as needed
1 to 2 tablespoons vegetable oil, for brushing

1. Preheat the grill to high.

2. Cut the skate wings crosswise (in the same direction as the bones) into 1-inch strips. Butterfly each strip by cutting it in half lengthwise as far as, but not through, the bottom piece of skin. Spread the halves open, then set the strips aside while you prepare the basting mixture.

3. Combine the coriander, curry powder, cloves, chile, water, Worcestershire sauce, salt, and pepper in a bowl and whisk until smooth (see Note).

4. When ready to cook, preheat a fish or vegetable grate (if using) for 5 minutes, then oil it or the grill grate. Arrange the skate pieces on the hot grate and grill until nicely browned on the bottom, 2 to 4 minutes. Using a long spatula, carefully turn the pieces over and brush each with 1 to 2 tablespoons of the Nonya Sweet-and-Sour Sauce. Grill until browned on the second side and the meat flakes easily when pressed with a finger, 2 to 4 minutes longer.

5. Using the spatula, transfer the skate to serving plates or a platter and serve immediately.

Serves 4

Note: This makes a wonderful basting liquid for any type of seafood; it will keep for weeks in the refrigerator.

Nonya Sweet-and-Sour Sauce

This sauce bears the name "sweet-and-sour," but I promise you it's unlike any sweet-and-sour sauce you've ever tasted. Garlic and shallots give it pungency and lemongrass provides fragrance, while chiles instill a gentle heat. To be strictly authentic, you'd thin the spice paste to a spreadable consistency with oil, but I like to use another popular Nonya ingredient, coconut milk. Also, a Nonya would probably add a teaspoon of MSG (which of course you can do, too).

8 ounces shallots, coarsely chopped
6 to 8 jalapeños or other hot chiles,
    seeded and coarsely chopped
    (for a hotter sauce, leave the seeds in)
3 to 4 large stalks fresh lemongrass,
    trimmed and coarsely chopped, or
    3 strips lemon zest (each 2 x ½ inches;
    removed with a vegetable peeler)
2 heads garlic, peeled
½ cup vegetable oil
⅓ cup fresh lime juice, or more to taste
2 tablespoons fresh orange juice or
    additional lime juice
2 tablespoons sugar, or more to taste
1½ tablespoons soy sauce, or more
    to taste
1 teaspoon salt, or more to taste
½ teaspoon ground turmeric
½ cup coconut milk, canned or fresh
    (see page 522)

1. Combine the shallots, chiles, lemongrass, garlic, oil, ⅓ cup lime juice, the orange juice, 2 tablespoons sugar, 1½ tablespoons soy sauce, 1 teaspoon salt, and the turmeric in a blender and process until almost smooth; the sauce should remain a little chunky.

2. Transfer the mixture to a small, heavy saucepan and cook over medium heat until slightly reduced, nicely browned, and richly flavored, 15 to 20 minutes, stirring frequently. Stir in the coconut milk and simmer the sauce until thick and creamy, about 5 minutes longer. Remove from the heat and taste for seasoning, adding salt, sugar, soy sauce, or lime juice as necessary; the sauce should be a little sweet, a little tart, and very aromatic.

3. If not using immediately, cool the sauce to room temperature, then transfer to a clean jar and store, tightly covered, in the refrigerator. It will keep for several weeks.

Makes 1½ to 2 cups

GRILLED SALT COD

PORTUGAL

METHOD:
Direct grilling

There's an old saying in Portugal, the gist of which is that a woman isn't ready to get married until she knows 365 ways to prepare *bacalhao* (salt cod). Hyperbole (and a touch sexist), perhaps, but the dictum serves to remind us of the important role salt cod plays in Portuguese cuisine and culture.

One of the most original salt cod preparations I've ever experienced is grilled salt cod, or *bacalhao grelhado*. The fish is soaked for a day to soften and desalinate it, then it's grilled and topped with sizzling fried garlic and olive oil. You can make a meal on the aroma alone! When buying salt cod, choose a 1-inch-thick center cut of the whitest fish you can find. (Yellowish salt cod and thin, stringy tail pieces are inferior.) The best place to buy salt cod is at a Portuguese, Spanish, Italian, or Hispanic market.

2 pounds salt cod
⅔ cup extra-virgin olive oil
8 cloves garlic, thinly sliced
½ teaspoon cracked or coarsely ground
　　black pepper
Lemon wedges, for serving

1. Place the salt cod in a large bowl and pour in enough cold water to cover by 1 inch. Cover with plastic wrap and place in the refrigerator to soak for 24 hours. (If the cod has skin on it, soak it skin side up.) Change the water 3 or 4 times to make the cod less salty.

2. Drain the salt cod, then rinse under cold running water. Drain again and pat dry with paper towels. Cut the cod into 4 equal parts and remove any skin.

3. When ready to cook, preheat a fish or vegetable grate (if using) for 5 minutes. Meanwhile, lightly brush each piece of cod with some of the oil, using 1½ to 2 tablespoons. Oil the grate as well, then arrange the pieces of cod on the hot grate and grill until nicely browned on the bottom, 3 to 6 minutes. Using a long spatula, carefully turn the pieces over and grill until browned on the second side and flaky and piping hot in the center, 3 to 6 minutes more. While the fish finishes cooking, place the remaining oil in a small saucepan and heat almost to smoking on the side burner of the grill, if you have one, or over medium heat on the stovetop.

4. Using the spatula, transfer the fish to a heatproof platter. Divide the garlic slices among the fish pieces, concentrating them in the center; sprinkle with the coarse pepper. Pour the hot oil over the fish, especially where the garlic is (the garlic should sizzle and brown). Serve immediately, accompanied by lemon wedges.

Serves 4

PERUVIAN FISH KEBABS
Anticuchos de Pescado

The idea for this recipe comes from a charming Peruvian-Italian restaurant in Coral Gables, Florida, called Tito's Place. It's a refined version of Peru's most popular street food (traditional *anticuchos* are made with beef hearts). Here in Miami we use mahimahi, but swordfish, halibut, or even shark are all good choices.

To be strictly authentic, you would use a chile powder or paste called *aji amarillo* (literally, "yellow pepper") in the glaze. If you live in a city with a large Peruvian community, you may be able to find it at a Hispanic grocery store, but if not, the flavor can be approximated by combining hot paprika with a pinch of turmeric. Don't be put off by the seemingly large quantity of salt; most of it drains onto the coals.

**SPECIAL
EQUIPMENT:**
4 long metal
skewers

Serve with Peruvian Potato Mixed Grill (see Index).

FOR THE FISH
1½ pounds firm white fish, such as mahimahi, swordfish, or halibut (about 1 inch thick)
1½ teaspoons salt
2 red bell peppers, stemmed and seeded

FOR THE MARINADE:
6 cloves garlic, peeled
½ teaspoon fresh ground black pepper
1 teaspoon ground cumin
⅓ cup distilled white vinegar
⅓ cup fresh lemon juice

FOR THE GLAZE:
3 tablespoons vegetable oil
1 tablespoon aji amarillo powder or paste, ancho chile powder, or hot paprika
¼ teaspoon ground turmeric (optional)
2 teaspoons salt
1 teaspoon freshly ground black pepper

Lemon wedges, for serving

1. Rinse the fish under cold running water, then drain and blot dry with paper towels. Cut the fish into 1-inch cubes and toss with the salt in a medium-size bowl. Let stand for 5 minutes. Meanwhile, cut the bell peppers into 1-inch squares and set aside.

2. Prepare the marinade. Combine the garlic, pepper, cumin, vinegar, and lemon juice in a blender and process until blended and smooth. Pour this mixture over the fish and toss to coat. Cover and let marinate, in the refrigerator, for 30 minutes.

3. Preheat the grill to high.

4. While the fish marinates, prepare the glaze. Heat the oil in a small skillet or saucepan over medium-low heat. Add the *aji amarillo,* turmeric (if using), salt and pepper. Gently cook the mixture, stirring with a wooden spoon, until red and fragrant, about 5 minutes. Set aside to cool (see Note).

5. When ready to cook, thread the fish cubes onto the skewers, alternating with squares of bell pepper. Oil the grill grate, then arrange the skewers on the hot grate and brush with half of the glaze. Grill, turning with tongs, until the fish cubes are nicely browned on the outside and cooked through in the center, 2 to 4 minutes per side. Brush with the remaining glaze after turning. Serve immediately with lemon wedges.

Serves 4

Note: You can also simply mix the ingredients for the glaze in a bowl without cooking them. The result will still be very flavorful, but not quite as flavorful as it would be if you cooked them first.

BRAZILIAN SWORDFISH KEBABS WITH WITH COCONUT MILK

BRAZIL

METHOD:
Direct grilling

This recipe comes from the most unlikely of sources, a Rio de Janeiro meat emporium called Porcão (Big Pig). Like most *churrascarias* (barbecue restaurants), Porcão specializes in an astonishing assortment of grilled meats presented on swordlike spits and carved directly onto your plate at the table. Conspicuous consumption is the name of the game: The waiters keep bringing food until you expressly ask them to stop.

The following kebabs caught my eye (and taste buds) precisely because they weren't meat. Porcão makes them with *surubinho,* a giant mild, sweet freshwater fish from the Amazon. The closest equivalent in North America would be halibut—which you could use—as well as tuna, sea bass, or any firm, meaty fish. I usually make the recipe with swordfish.

Coconut milk is a traditional ingredient in northern Brazilian cooking. Its high fat content keeps the fish moist and flavorful. Be sure to use unsweetened coconut milk: reliable brands include A Taste of Thai, which is available at most supermarkets. For additional flavor, Porcão's chef bastes the kebabs with garlic butter as they cook. The fish will have plenty of flavor without this step, but it does offer added richness.

Crazy Rice (see Index) makes a good accompaniment.

FOR THE FISH AND MARINADE:
1½ **pounds swordfish steaks
(about 1 inch thick)**
1 **cup coconut milk, canned or homemade
(see page 522)**
2 **tablespoons olive oil**
6 **cloves garlic, coarsely chopped**
1 **medium onion, quartered**
½ **medium green bell pepper, stemmed,
seeded, and quartered**
1 **teaspoon salt, or more to taste**
1 **teaspoon freshly ground black pepper**
¼ **cup chopped fresh Italian (flat-leaf)
parsley**

FOR THE BASTING MIXTURE (optional)**:**
2 **tablespoons salted butter**
1 **clove garlic, minced**

FOR THE KEBABS:
1 **medium onion, quartered**
1 **red bell pepper, stemmed, seeded, and cut
into 1-inch squares**
1 **green bell pepper, stemmed, seeded, and
cut into 1-inch squares**

1. Trim the skin off the fish steaks. Rinse the fish under cold running water, then drain and blot dry with paper towels. Cut into 1-inch cubes and place in a medium-size nonreactive bowl. Set aside while you prepare the marinade.

2. Combine the coconut milk, oil, garlic, onion, green pepper, 1 teaspoon salt, and the black pepper in a blender and process to a smooth purée. Add the parsley and blend for 30 seconds. Taste for seasoning, adding salt as necessary; the mixture should be highly seasoned. Pour the mixture over the fish cubes in the bowl and toss to coat. Cover and let marinate, in the refrigerator, for at least 1 hour and up to 4 hours (the longer the better), stirring occasionally.

3. Preheat the grill to high.

4. If using the basting mixture, place the butter in a saucepan and melt over low heat, either on the burner attachment of your grill, if you have one, or on the stovetop. Stir in the garlic and remove from the heat.

5. When ready to cook, break the onion quarters into individual layers. Remove the fish cubes from the marinade and thread onto the skewers, placing a piece of onion and a pepper square between each and dividing evenly. Oil the grill grate, then arrange the kebabs on the hot grate and grill, turning with tongs, until the fish cubes are nicely browned on the outside and cooked through in the center, 8 to 12 minutes in all. Brush the kebabs with the garlic butter (if using) during the last minute of cooking.

6. Transfer the kebabs to serving plates or a platter and serve immediately.

Serves 4

RUSSIAN STURGEON KEBABS

RUSSIA

METHOD:
Direct grilling

**ADVANCE
PREPARATION:**
*4 to 8 hours for
marinating the
fish*

**SPECIAL
EQUIPMENT:**
*4 long metal
skewers*

Russians often grate onions for marinades rather than chop them. This exposes more of the onion to air, producing a stronger flavor. The sweet-sour trickle of pomegranate molasses is a hallmark of the soulful cooking of the Republic of Georgia.

1½ pounds fresh sturgeon,
  monkfish, or swordfish steaks
  (about 1½ inches thick)
1 onion, coarsely grated
½ cup dry white wine
¼ cup vegetable oil
3 tablespoons fresh lemon juice
1 tablespoon sweet paprika
1½ teaspoons salt
1 bay leaf, crushed
½ teaspoon freshly ground black
  pepper
1 to 2 tablespoons vegetable oil,
  for brushing
2 to 3 tablespoons Pomegranate
  Molasses (page 227), for
  serving
Lemon wedges, for serving

1. Trim the skin off the fish steaks and cut the meat off the bones, if necessary. Rinse the fish under cold running water, then drain and blot dry with paper towels. Cut the meat into 1½-inch cubes and set aside while you prepare the marinade.

2. Combine the onion, wine, oil, lemon juice, paprika, salt, bay leaf, and pepper in a large bowl and stir to mix. Add the fish cubes and toss to coat. Cover and let marinate, in the refrigerator, for at least 4 hours and up to 8 hours, stirring occasionally.

3. Preheat the grill to high.

4. When ready to cook, remove the fish cubes from the marinade and thread onto the skewers, dividing evenly. Oil the grill grate, then arrange the skewers on the hot grate and brush generously with oil, then grill, turning with tongs, until nicely browned on the outside and opaque in the center, 8 to 12 minutes in all, brushing again with oil after turning.

5. Serve the kebabs with Pomegranate Molasses drizzled on top and accompanied by lemon wedges.

Serves 4

Sturgeon

Most people think of sturgeon as the source of fine caviar or as smoked fish for bagels. But in the former Soviet Union, this whiskered, prehistoric-looking fish is a popular item for grilling, as I quickly discovered during a day of restaurant-hopping in the Brighton Beach area of Brooklyn, New York's "Little Odessa." Sturgeon has a mild sweet flavor and firm, almost gelatinous consistency, and its dense texture makes it ideal for grilling on skewers, as here, or as steaks (see page 312). If you live in an area with a large Russian community (in the Pacific Northwest or in Minnesota), you may be able to find it fresh. Monkfish has a similar texture. Another possibility is swordfish, which has a much softer consistency but tastes equally delicious prepared in this fashion.

PANDELI SWORDFISH KEBABS

TURKEY

METHOD:
Direct grilling

ADVANCE PREPARATION:
30 minutes for marinating the kebabs

SPECIAL EQUIPMENT:
4 large metal skewers

Pandeli is a landmark restaurant located on the second floor of the entryway into Istanbul's Spice Bazaar. It has the most famous staircase in Istanbul, with shimmering blue and white tiles that line an ancient passageway. But to come to Pandeli solely for the visual virtuosity of its stairway would be to overlook a bill of fare so appealing and tasty that modern Turkey's founder, Kemal Atatürk, made the restaurant his regular lunch spot. If you arrive early enough, you may be able to get a seat at a table overlooking the spice market or the Bosporus. But wherever you sit, be sure to order the seafood *mezze* (a sampler of cured Black and Caspian Sea seafoods) and these swordfish kebabs.

Turkish cooks paint with a simple but powerful palette, so while there may not seem to be anything extraordinary about this recipe, I think you'll find, as I do, the results are exceedingly tasty. See the Index for A Griller's Guide to the World's Chiles for a description of bull's horn peppers.

1½ pounds swordfish steaks (about 1 inch thick)
12 bull's horn peppers or 2 large green bell peppers (see Note)
12 bay leaves
2 large, fresh, ripe tomatoes, each cut into 6 wedges
1 large lemon, cut into ¼-inch slices (12 slices in all)
Salt and freshly ground black pepper
¼ cup extra-virgin olive oil
3 tablespoons fresh lemon juice
1 bunch fresh Italian (flat-leaf) parsley, stemmed, half coarsely chopped, half broken into large sprigs
Lemon wedges, for serving

1. Trim the skin off the fish steaks. Rinse the fish under cold running water, then drain and blot dry with paper towels. Cut into 2-inch squares and thread onto the skewers alternately with the peppers, bay leaves, tomato wedges, and lemon slices, dividing all the ingredients evenly among the skewers. Season the kebabs with salt and pepper.

2. Place the kebabs in a large nonreactive baking dish. Combine the oil and lemon juice in a small bowl and whisk to blend, then pour over the kebabs. Sprinkle with the chopped parsley. Let marinate, at room temperature, for 30 minutes, turning once or twice.

3. Preheat the grill to high.

4. When ready to cook, remove the kebabs from the baking dish, reserving whatever marinade is left. Oil the grill grate, then arrange the kebabs on the hot grate. Grill, turning with tongs, until the vegetables and swordfish are nicely browned and the fish is opaque in the center, 4 to 5 minutes per side. As the kebabs cook, baste with any remaining marinade, but not during the last 3 minutes.

5. Transfer the kebabs to serving plates or a platter and serve immediately, accompanied by lemon wedges and strewn with parsley sprigs.

Serves 4

Note: If using bull's horn peppers, leave whole and stem but do not seed. If using green peppers, stem and seed them, then cut into 2 × 1-inch strips.

BALINESE FISH MOUSSE SATES
Saté Lilit

METHOD:
Direct grilling

ADVANCE PREPARATION:
2 hours for chilling the mousse

SPECIAL EQUIPMENT:
24 stalks fresh lemongrass, each trimmed to 6 inches long (see Notes), or 24 Popsicle sticks, soaked for 1 hour in cold water to cover and drained

Saté lilit rank among the most exquisite of Indonesia's satés. Their birthplace is Bali, where they are used in and served at religious festivals. To make them, delicate mousse is flavored with explosively aromatic spices, then enriched with coconut milk and grilled on fragrant lemongrass stalks. The mousse can be made of fish, shrimp, chicken, duck, and even turtle.

Even if you can't find a few of the special ingredients, you can still prepare *saté lilit*. Kaffir lime leaves, electrifying with their perfumed lime flavor, can be found fresh or frozen at Asian markets, but if none is available, a little grated lime zest will work. Shrimp paste (*trassi*) is a strong-smelling seasoning made from pickled shrimp. Substitutes include Asian fish sauce or anchovy paste.

Don't be frightened by the long list of ingredients. These satés are easy to make and aren't as time consuming as they seem. The results are truly dazzling.

FOR THE SPICE PASTE:
4 large shallots, sliced
4 macadamia nuts
3 cloves garlic, sliced
1 to 3 Thai or serrano chiles, sliced
1 piece (1 inch) galangal or fresh ginger, peeled and sliced
2 teaspoons ground coriander
½ teaspoon freshly ground black pepper
½ teaspoon ground turmeric
1 teaspoon shrimp paste or anchovy paste, or 1 tablespoon Asian fish sauce
½ teaspoon salt
1½ tablespoons vegetable oil

FOR THE FISH MOUSSE:
12 ounces firm white fish fillets, such as snapper, mahimahi, bass, or catfish
8 ounces shrimp, peeled and deveined
¼ cup canned coconut milk
1 large egg white
1 tablespoon fresh lime juice, or to taste
2 kaffir lime leaves, cut into hair-thin slivers, or ½ teaspoon grated lime zest
4 teaspoons palm sugar or firmly packed light brown sugar
Salt, to taste (optional)

1. Prepare the spice paste. Combine the shallots, macadamia nuts, garlic, chile, galangal, coriander, pepper, turmeric, shrimp paste or anchovy paste (see Notes), and salt in a food processor and process to a smooth paste. Heat the oil in a small, heavy skillet over medium heat. Add the spice paste and sauté until dark and fragrant, 5 to 10 minutes, stirring constantly. Remove from the heat and transfer to a small bowl to cool.

2. Prepare the fish mousse. Combine the fish and shrimp in the food processor and process to a smooth purée. Add the cooled spice paste, coconut milk, egg white, 1 tablespoon lime juice, kaffir lime leaves, and sugar and process until thoroughly blended. To test the mixture for seasoning, sauté a small amount of it in a nonstick skillet until cooked through, then taste, adding lime juice and salt to the remaining mixture as necessary; it should be highly seasoned. Refrigerate the mixture, covered, for 2 hours.

3. Divide the mousse mixture into 24 equal portions. Lightly wet your hands with cold water, then take each portion of mousse mixture and mold it around the bulbous part of a lemongrass stalk to make a sausage shape about 3 inches long; place the satés as they are finished on a baking sheet lined with plastic wrap. Cover with more plastic wrap and refrigerate until ready to cook, up to 6 hours.

4. Preheat the grill to high.

5. When ready to cook, oil the grill grate. Arrange the satés on the oiled grate and grill until nicely browned on the outside and cooked through, 3 to 4 minutes per side. If the fish mixture sticks to the grate, use a long spatula to help turn the satés.

6. Using the spatula, carefully transfer the satés to serving plates or a platter. Serve immediately.

Serves 4 to 6 as an appetizer, 2 as an entrée

Notes: If you can buy large lemongrass stalks (about 12 inches long with bases ½ inch in diameter), the tops may be thick enough to use as skewers; then, because you'll be cutting the stalks crosswise in half, you'll need only 12 stalks.

■ If using fish sauce, add it to the mousse mixture along with the spice paste in step 2.

SWORDFISH SOUVLAKI

GREECE

METHOD:
Direct grilling

ADVANCE PREPARATION:
30 minutes for marinating the fish

SPECIAL EQUIPMENT:
4 long metal skewers

My friend Patsy Jamieson, test kitchen director for the magazine *Eating Well*, prepares fish kebabs the same way *souvlaki* (the Greek version of shish kebab) is prepared, using the traditional Greek flavorings of olive oil, lemon, garlic, oregano, and bay leaves. Patsy uses fresh tuna; I like swordfish, but any firm steak fish—or even shrimp or scallops—will do.

Couscous, rice, or warmed pita bread would make a good accompaniment.

FOR THE FISH AND MARINADE:
1½ pounds swordfish or tuna steaks about 1½ inches thick)
3 tablespoons olive oil
3 tablespoons fresh lemon juice
3 tablespoons dry white wine
2 cloves garlic, minced
1 tablespoon chopped fresh oregano or 1½ teaspoons dried
1 teaspoon grated lemon zest
1 teaspoon salt, or more to taste
½ teaspoon freshly ground black pepper

FOR THE KEBABS:
24 bay leaves
1 medium onion, quartered

Lemon wedges, for serving

1. Trim the skin, if any, off the fish steaks. Rinse the fish under cold running water, then drain and blot dry with paper towels. Cut into 1½-inch cubes and set aside while you prepare the marinade.

2. Combine the oil, lemon juice, wine, garlic, oregano, lemon zest, 1 teaspoon salt, and the pepper in a large nonreactive bowl and whisk until blended and the salt is dissolved. Taste for seasoning, adding salt as necessary; the mixture should be highly seasoned. Add the fish and turn to coat. Let marinate, at room temperature, for 30 minutes, turning occasionally. Soak the bay leaves in a bowl of cold water for 20 minutes.

3. Preheat the grill to high.

4. When ready to cook, break the onion quarters into individual layers. Drain the bay leaves. Remove the fish cubes from the bowl, reserving whatever marinade is left, and thread onto the skewers, placing a piece of onion and a bay leaf between each and dividing evenly. Oil the grill grate, then arrange the kebabs on the hot grate and grill, turning with tongs, until the fish cubes are nicely browned on the outside and opaque in the center, 2 to 3 minutes per side, (8 to 12 minutes in all). As the kebabs cook, baste with any remaining marinade, but not during the last 2 minutes.

5. Transfer the kebabs to serving plates or a platter and serve immediately, accompanied by lemon wedges.

Serves 4

FLORIDA SNAPPER BURGERS

U.S.A.

METHOD:
Direct grilling

ADVANCE PREPARATION:
30 minutes to 6 hours for chilling the fish

Here's a "meatless" burger from one of the pioneers of the new Floridian style of cooking, Allen Susser of Chef Allen's in North Miami Beach. Susser uses red snapper; in areas of the country where snapper isn't available, you could use mahimahi or halibut (you need a fish that contains a lot of gelatin). The texture of these burgers is rather like that of fish mousse, which the fish sauce and fresh dill make exceptionally flavorful. In keeping with the tropical theme, Chef Allen's serves this burger with a mango ketchup Susser bottles and distributes nationally. If you can't find it, try the recipe for Mark Militello's Mango Barbecue Sauce. Susser suggests serving the burgers on crusty French bread topped with spinach.

1¼ **pounds skinless fresh red snapper fillets,** cut into 1-inch pieces
3 **large egg whites, lightly beaten**
1 **tablespoon Thai fish sauce**
1 **teaspoon coarse (kosher or sea) salt,** or more to taste
¼ **teaspoon freshly ground black pepper,** or more to taste
¼ **teaspoon cayenne pepper, or more** to taste
2 **tablespoons chopped scallions, both white** and green parts
2 **tablespoons chopped fresh dill**
3 to 4 **tablespoons fresh bread crumbs**
2 **tablespoons olive oil**
1 **loaf French bread (about 16 inches long),** cut in half lengthwise, then each half cut crosswise into 4 equal pieces
12 **fresh spinach leaves, rinsed and** patted dry
½ **cup Mark Militello's Mango Barbecue** Sauce (optional; page 461)

1. Run your fingers over the snapper fillets, feeling for bones, then use needlenose pliers or tweezers to remove any you may find. Transfer the snapper to a food processor and process, in short bursts, just until finely chopped. Do not overprocess; you don't want a purée (see Note). Still processing in short bursts, work in the egg whites, fish sauce, 1 teaspoon salt, ¼ teaspoon pepper, and ¼ teaspoon cayenne. Add the scallions, dill, and enough bread crumbs to bind the mixture together (start with 3 tablespoons). To test the mixture for seasoning, sauté a small amount of it in a nonstick skillet until cooked through, then taste, adding salt or pepper to the remaining mixture as necessary; it should be highly seasoned.

2. Divide the mixture into 4 equal portions. Lightly wet your hands with cold water and form each portion into a patty 3½ inches across and about ½ inch thick. Place the patties on a generously oiled plate, cover, and refrigerate for at least 30 minutes and up to 6 hours.

3. Preheat the grill to high.

4. When ready to cook, brush the tops of the patties generously with oil. Oil the grill grate, then arrange the patties, oiled side down, on the hot grate. Grill, turning with tongs, until nicely browned on both sides and cooked through, 3 to 4 minutes per side, adding the French bread pieces, cut sides down, to the grill when you turn the patties. Do not overcook the burgers.

5. Serve the burgers on the French bread, topped with spinach leaves and barbecue sauce, if desired.

Serves 4

Note: Alternatively, chop the fish by hand with a cleaver or sharp, heavy knife and transfer to a bowl, working in the remaining ingredients by hand.

Hot Shells:
LOBSTERS, SHRIMP, SCALLOPS & CLAMS

"Many shrimps, many flavors; many men, many whims."

—MALAYSIAN PROVERB

Lobster fresh out of the water and ready for the grill.

I've often pondered how early man figured out how to eat oysters. Certainly not with an oyster knife! I like to think he placed them on the coals of a campfire and let the smoky heat open the shells. And while you may not think of the grill when it comes to cooking shellfish, grilling remains one of the best methods I know for cooking clams, mussels, shrimp, and even lobster.

This chapter will introduce you to the world of grilled shellfish, from Greek grilled octopus to Caribbean shrimp grilled on skewers made of sugar cane. You'll find out how Australians cook their famous shrimp "on the barbie," not to mention their beloved Morton Bay "bugs" (rock lobsters).

Grilling is a great way to cook lobster. It keeps shrimp moist and soft-shell crabs crackling crisp. Broaden your repertoire with the likes of Bombay Flaming Prawns, Penganese Grilled Shrimp with Painfully Hot Salsa, and Bahamian Grilled Conch.

Shellfish never tasted so good!

MORTON BAY "BUGS" WITH GINGER-MINT BUTTER

METHOD:
Direct grilling

I love the affectionate disrespect fishermen everywhere seem to have for Neptune's noblest creature. That is, whether you buy lobsters from a fisherman on the coast of Maine or in Morton Bay, Australia, you're likely to hear them called "bugs." The Morton Bay "bug" is one of Australia's most prized shellfish, a clawless crustacean similar to a Florida (or rock or spiny) lobster. I call for lobster tails in the following recipe, but you could also use Maine lobster; spot prawns or even jumbo shrimp would take to this preparation as well. Ginger, lime, and mint create an explosively flavorful butter that is brushed on the lobster during grilling. The preparation is simple, but powerfully good.

4 lobster tails (8 to 9 ounces each), thawed if frozen, or 4 live Maine lobsters (1¼ to 1½ pounds each)
8 tablespoons (1 stick) unsalted butter
2 tablespoons chopped fresh mint or 1½ teaspoons dried
1 tablespoon minced fresh ginger
1 clove garlic, minced
1 teaspoon grated lime zest
3 tablespoons Asian fish sauce or soy sauce
2 tablespoons fresh lime juice
Salt and freshly ground black pepper, to taste

1. Preheat the grill to high.
2. If using lobster tails, cut them in half lengthwise with kitchen scissors or a sharp, heavy knife; use a fork to remove the intestinal vein running the length of the tail. If using

When You're Feeling Less Than Brave

The parboiling technique described below is for those of you who don't take too well to the idea of dispatching a lobster with a knife.

Bring 8 quarts of water (enough for 4 lobsters) to a boil in a large pot with a lid. Add the lobsters, cover the pot tightly, and boil for 2 minutes. Using tongs, transfer the lobsters to a platter and let cool. Then cut in half and grill as directed.

live lobsters, kill each by inserting a sharp knife in the back of the head between the eyes; this will dispatch them instantly (or see box above). Cut the lobsters in half lengthwise and remove the vein and the papery gray sac from the head. Break off the claws and crack with a nutcracker. Set the lobsters or tails aside while you prepare the ginger-mint butter.
3. Melt the butter in a small, heavy saucepan over low heat. Add the mint, ginger, garlic, and lime zest and increase the heat to medium. Cook until the mixture is fragrant but not brown, about 3 minutes. Stir in the fish sauce and lime juice and bring to a

boil, then remove from the heat.

4. Brush the cut sides of the lobster tails or lobsters with the ginger-mint butter and sprinkle with salt and pepper.

5. When ready to cook, oil the grill grate. Arrange the lobster halves or tails and claws (if any), cut sides down, on the hot grate and grill for 6 to 8 minutes. Turn, using tongs, and grill on the shell sides until the flesh is firm and white, 6 to 8 minutes more, brushing generously several times with the butter as the lobsters cook.

6. Transfer the lobsters to serving plates or a platter and pour any remaining butter over them. Serve immediately.

Serves 4

GRILLED SPINY LOBSTER WITH BASIL BUTTER

FRENCH WEST INDIES

METHOD:
Direct grilling

This imposing dish is the speciality of a New Age inn called Hostellerie des Trois Forces in St. Barthélemy. Astrologer-chef Hubert Delamotte makes it with spiny lobster, which has a broad tail and fiercely barbed carapace, but no claws. If you live in Florida or Texas, the equivalent would be a "Florida" lobster. Maine lobster can be prepared the same way. Whichever lobster you use, you'll surely enjoy the way the fragrance of the basil brings out the sweetness of the lobster meat. Serve with Grilled Polenta (see Index).

4 lobster tails (8 to 9 ounces each), thawed if frozen, or 4 live Maine lobsters (1¼ to 1½ pounds each)
8 tablespoons (1 stick) salted butter, melted
Salt and freshly ground black pepper, to taste
½ cup coarsely chopped fresh basil
1 to 2 limes, halved

1. Preheat the grill to high.

2. If using lobster tails, cut them in half lengthwise with kitchen scissors or a sharp, heavy knife; use a fork to remove the intestinal vein running the length of the tail. If using live lobsters, kill each by inserting a sharp knife in the back of the head between the eyes; this will dispatch them instantly (or see box, facing page). Cut the lobsters in half lengthwise and remove the vein and the papery gray sac from the head. Break off the claws and crack with a nutcracker.

3. Brush the cut sides of the lobster tails or lobsters with some of the melted butter and season with salt and pepper. Add the chopped basil to the remaining butter.

4. When ready to cook, oil the grill grate. Arrange the tails or lobster halves and claws (if any), cut sides down, on the hot grate and grill for 6 to 8 minutes. Turn, using tongs, and grill on the shell sides until the flesh is firm and white, 6 to 8 minutes more, squeezing lime juice over the lobsters as they cook and brushing generously several times with the basil butter.

5. Transfer the lobsters to serving plates or a platter and serve immediately, accompanied by the remaining basil butter in ramekins on the side.

Serves 4

Shellfish Grilling Chart*

TYPE	METHOD	HEAT	COOKING TIME
CLAMS (IN SHELL)	DIRECT	HIGH	UNTIL SHELLS OPEN, 6–8 MIN
LOBSTER			
HALF LOBSTERS	DIRECT	HIGH	COOKED THROUGH, 6–8 MIN/SIDE
TAILS	DIRECT	HIGH	COOKED THROUGH, 6–8 MIN/SIDE
OYSTERS (IN SHELL)	DIRECT	HIGH	UNTIL SHELLS OPEN, 6–10 MIN
SCALLOPS	DIRECT	HIGH	COOKED THROUGH, 1–3 MIN/SIDE
SHRIMP	DIRECT	HIGH	COOKED THROUGH, 1–3 MIN/SIDE

*This chart is offered as a broad guideline to cooking times for the various types of shellfish. Remember, grilling is an art, not a science. When in doubt, refer to times in the individual recipes.

SPINY LOBSTER WITH CREOLE SAUCE

FRENCH WEST INDIES

METHOD:
Direct grilling

My wife and I first tasted this dish on our honeymoon in Saint Barthélemy in 1990. The place was a tiny beach restaurant called the Marigot Bay Club, run by a fisherman friend named Michel Ledée. The lobster had emerged from the water about an hour before we ate it. To enjoy it any fresher, we'd have had to have dined in bathing suits!

Michel's Creole Sauce has complex layers of flavor: the bass tones of garlic and scallions, the brassy notes of thyme and lime juice, and the shrill accent of scotch bonnet–based hot sauce.

As I write this recipe, I note with sadness that Michel died tragically while rescuing his daughter from a swimming accident. This recipe is dedicated to his memory.

4 lobster tails (8 to 9 ounces each), thawed
if frozen, or 4 live Maine lobsters
(1¼ to 1½ pounds each)

4 tablespoons lard (see Note)
½ cup finely chopped shallots
4 scallions, both white and green parts,
trimmed and finely chopped
3 cloves garlic, minced
3 tablespoons chopped fresh Italian
(flat-leaf) parsley
2 teaspoons chopped fresh thyme or
1 teaspoon dried
1 cup ketchup
⅔ cup water
2 tablespoons fresh lime juice, or
more to taste
1 teaspoon hot pepper sauce,
preferably a scotch bonnet–based
sauce such as Inner Beauty or
Matouk's, or more to taste
Salt and freshly ground black pepper,
to taste

1. Preheat the grill to high.

2. If using lobster tails, cut them in half lengthwise with kitchen scissors or a sharp, heavy knife; use a fork to remove the intestinal vein running the length of the tail. If using live lobsters, kill each by inserting a sharp knife in the back of the head between the eyes; this will dispatch them instantly (or see box, page 342). Cut the lobsters in half lengthwise and remove the vein and the papery gray sac from the head. Break off the claws and crack with a nutcracker. Set aside, covered in the refrigerator, while you prepare the Creole sauce.

3. Melt 2 tablespoons of the lard in a medium-size saucepan over medium heat. Add the shallots, scallions, garlic, parsley, and thyme and sauté until the shallots and scallions are lightly browned, 3 to 5 minutes. Stir in the ketchup, water, 2 tablespoons lime juice, and 1 teaspoon hot pepper sauce and bring to a boil. Reduce the heat to low and simmer gently, uncovered, until the sauce is thickened and nicely flavored, about 5 minutes. Remove from the heat and taste for seasoning, adding salt and pepper, lime juice, or hot pepper sauce as necessary; the sauce should be highly seasoned.

4. Melt the remaining 2 tablespoons lard in a small saucepan over low heat and brush over the cut sides of the lobster tails or lobsters.

5. When ready to cook, oil the grill grate. Arrange the lobsters with the claws (if any), cut sides down, on the hot grill grate and grill for 6 to 8 minutes. Turn, using tongs, and spoon on the Creole sauce, dividing evenly. Grill the lobsters on the shell sides until the flesh is firm and white, 6 to 8 minutes more.

6. Transfer the lobster tails or lobsters to serving plates or a platter and serve immediately.

Serves 4

Note: Lard may seem like a strange, even off-putting ingredient, but it's often used for basting at French barbecues. Here it is used as a base for Caribbean lobster seasoning. You can certainly substitute melted butter or oil.

SOUTH AFRICAN GRILLED ROCK LOBSTER

SOUTH AFRICA

METHOD:
Indirect grilling

South Africans have an ingenious way of preparing rock lobster for grilling. They snip open the thin shell covering the bottom of the tail. The lobster is then cooked in the shell, belly side up, using the indirect method. This keeps the lobster moist and tender—ideal for rock or spiny lobsters.

There is nothing flashy about the basting sauce used with the lobsters, but the butter, wine, and Worcestershire add a world of flavor without masking the pristine taste of the lobster.

4 live spiny or rock lobsters (1¼ to 1½ pounds each), or 4 lobster tails (8 to 9 ounces each), thawed if frozen
4 tablespoons (½ stick) unsalted butter
3 tablespoons extra-virgin olive oil
2 tablespoons Worcestershire sauce
2 tablespoons fresh lemon juice
2 tablespoons dry white wine
2 cloves garlic, minced
3 tablespoons minced fresh (flat-leaf) Italian parsley
½ teaspoon cayenne pepper, or to taste
Salt and freshly ground black pepper, to taste

1. Set up the grill for indirect grilling (see page 14 or 16); it is not necessary to use a drip pan, but set one in place if you wish. Preheat the grill to medium.

2. If using live lobsters, kill each by inserting a sharp knife in the back of the head between the eyes; this will dispatch them instantly (or see box, page 342). Then, using kitchen scissors or poultry shears, make 4 cuts, 2 lengthwise and 2 crosswise, in the "belly" side of the tail; remove the thin shell. If using lobster tails, cut them in half lengthwise, through the flesh but not through the back shell with kitchen scissors or a sharp, heavy knife. Open out the tails like a butterfly. Using a fork, remove the intestinal vein running the length of the tail. Set the lobsters or tails aside while you prepare the basting/serving sauce.

3. Melt the butter in a small, heavy saucepan over medium-low heat. Add the oil, Worcestershire sauce, lemon juice, wine, garlic, parsley, and cayenne pepper and simmer gently until the garlic is fragrant and has lost its raw edge, 3 to 5 minutes. Remove from the heat and add salt and cayenne and black pepper. Set half aside for serving.

4. When ready to cook, place the lobsters or lobster tails (see Note) in the center of the grate, belly side up, and brush generously with the basting sauce. Cover the grill and cook until the lobster flesh is firm and white, about 30 to 40 minutes for lobsters and 20 to 30 minutes for tails. Brush the exposed meat once or twice with the basting sauce during cooking.

5. Transfer the lobsters to serving plates or a platter and serve immediately, accompanied by the reserved sauce in ramekins for dipping.

Serves 4

Note: The lobster tails may also be grilled over direct heat. Preheat the grill to high and cook the tails cut sides down for 6 to 8 minutes to sear the meat. Using tongs, turn the tails over and cook, cut sides up, until the flesh is firm and white, 6 to 8 minutes. Brush the flesh with the basting sauce as they cook and again just before serving.

GUADELOUPEAN GRILLED "CRAYFISH" WITH CURRY BEURRE BLANC

GUADELOUPE

METHOD:
Direct grilling

ADVANCE PREPARATION:
30 minutes to 1 hour for marinating the shellfish

Guadeloupe is famous throughout the Caribbean for a large, sweet-fleshed shellfish known as *oassou* (pronounced "wa-sou"). Although commonly translated as crayfish, the *oassou* is actually a type of prawn. The preferred cooking method is grilling: The shellfish are skewered, heads and all, and roasted over glowing coals. *Oassous* are not available in the U.S. (at least not yet), but the spot prawns found in Hawaii and the Pacific Northwest have a similar flavor. Jumbo shrimp can be prepared the same way.

In Guadeloupe (this is France, after all), the *oassou* would be accompanied by a *beurre blanc* (butter sauce) flavored with a French West Indian curry powder called

**SPECIAL
EQUIPMENT:**
*4 long metal
skewers*

colombo, available in West Indian markets. My version of the sauce offers you the option of using *colombo* or a standard (though good-quality) curry powder.

FOR THE BROCHETTES AND MARINADE:

20 spot prawns or jumbo shrimp in
    the shell
1 onion, halved lengthwise and each
    half cut into 6 to 8 wedges
1 red bell pepper, stemmed, seeded, and
    cut into 1-inch squares
3 tablespoons fresh lime juice
3 tablespoons extra-virgin olive oil
2 cloves garlic, minced
Salt and freshly ground black pepper,
    to taste

FOR THE BEURRE BLANC:

1 cup dry white wine
¼ cup white wine vinegar
¼ cup minced shallots
1½ teaspoons colombo powder,
    homemade (page 493) or store-bought,
    or good-quality regular
    curry powder, or more to taste
¼ cup heavy cream
8 tablespoons (1 stick) cold unsalted
    butter, cut into ½-inch pieces
Salt and freshly ground black pepper,
    to taste

1. Rinse the prawns under cold running water, then drain and blot dry with paper towels. Thread the prawns lengthwise onto the skewers, dividing evenly and threading a chunk of onion and a piece of pepper between each. Place the brochettes on a platter and set aside while you prepare the marinade.

2. Combine the lime juice, oil, garlic, and salt and pepper in a small bowl and whisk to mix. Brush some of the mixture over the brochettes and reserve the remainder for brushing on later. Cover the brochettes loosely with plastic wrap and let marinate, in the refrigerator, 30 minutes to 1 hour.

3. Preheat the grill to high.

4. While the brochettes marinate, prepare the *beurre blanc.* Combine the wine, vinegar, shallots, and *colombo* powder in a small, heavy saucepan over medium-high heat, stirring to mix in the *colombo* powder. Boil this mixture, uncovered, until only ¼ cup liquid remains, 6 to 8 minutes. Add the cream and boil, uncovered, until only ¼ cup liquid remains, another 2 to 4 minutes. Reduce the heat to medium. Add the butter, one piece at a time, whisking continuously to obtain an emulsified sauce. Wait until each piece is thoroughly incorporated before adding the next. Once all the butter is incorporated, remove the pan from the heat; do not allow the sauce to boil or it may curdle. Taste for seasoning, adding salt, pepper, or curry powder as necessary; the sauce should be highly seasoned. Set the sauce aside until serving time, keeping it warm on a shelf over the stove or in a pan of hot (not boiling) water. Do not place it over direct heat or it may curdle.

5. When ready to cook, oil the grill grate. Arrange the brochettes on the hot grate and grill, turning with tongs, until the shells on the prawns turn bright red and the meat is opaque, 4 to 6 minutes per side. Brush the brochettes with the reserved marinade once or twice during grilling.

6. Using a fork, slide the prawns and vegetables off the skewers onto serving plates and serve immediately, accompanied by the *beurre blanc.*

Serves 4

GRILLED SOFT-SHELL CRABS WITH SPICY TARTAR SAUCE

U.S.A.

METHOD:
Direct grilling

Like all crustaceans, crabs periodically shed their shells to make room for future growth. Soft-shell crabs are freshly molted blue crabs. The molted crab is eaten carapace and all and is in season from May through August. Most recipes call for soft-shells to be pan-fried or deep-fried. Grilling produces great-tasting crabs, with a fraction of the fat. You still get the wonderful soft-shell crab flavor and texture: briny as the ocean and potato-chip crisp.

The crabs should be live when you buy them. Ask your fishmonger to clean them for you, and always cook them the same day you buy them. Serve with Grilled Garlic Bread Fingers and Your Basic Slaw (see Index).

FOR THE TARTAR SAUCE:
1 cup good-quality mayonnaise
1 to 2 fresh or pickled jalapeño chiles, seeded and finely chopped
1 tablespoon Dijon mustard
1 tablespoon fresh lime juice, or more to taste
1 tablespoon capers, drained and chopped
1 tablespoon chopped fresh chives or trimmed scallion greens
1 tablespoon chopped sour pickles, preferably cornichons
1 tablespoon chopped fresh tarragon or basil
Salt, to taste (optional)

FOR THE CRABS:
½ cup unsalted butter, melted, or olive oil
1 tablespoon fresh lemon juice
12 soft-shell crabs, cleaned
Salt and freshly ground black pepper, to taste

1. Preheat the grill to high.

2. Prepare the tartar sauce. Combine the mayonnaise, chiles, mustard, 1 tablespoon lime juice, the capers, chives, pickles, and tarragon in a small bowl and whisk thoroughly to mix. Taste for seasoning, adding salt or lime juice as necessary; the mixture should be highly seasoned. Set aside until serving time (see Note).

3. Combine the melted butter and lemon juice in a small bowl and whisk to blend. Brush the crabs on both sides with some of the mixture and season generously with salt and pepper.

4. When ready to grill, oil the grill grate. Arrange the crabs on the hot grate and grill, turning with tongs, until the shells are bright red, 3 to 6 minutes per side. Brush the crabs with the remaining butter mixture once or twice as they cook.

5. Transfer the crabs to serving plates or a platter and serve immediately, accompanied by the tartar sauce.

Serves 4 to 6

Note: The sauce can be made up to 2 days ahead of time. Refrigerate, covered.

How to Peel and Devein Shrimp

Shrimp is delectable grilled both in and out of the shell—leaving the shell on keeps the meat moist and flavorful—but sooner or later that shell has got to come off, as does, at least in the larger shrimp we use for grilling, the black intestinal vein that runs down the back.

Cookware shops and fish markets sell a simple device that makes peeling and deveining raw shrimp a snap. The shrimp peeler looks like a red plastic knife with a long, slender, arched, flexible tip. To use it, hold an unpeeled shrimp as straight as possible in one hand. Insert the slender end of the peeler into the vein at the head end of the shrimp with your other hand and push. The wedge-shaped blade of the peeler will cut cleanly through the shell and remove the vein. If you want to remove the shell now, it will be a simple matter of pulling the shrimp free of it, through the open back.

TO PEEL A RAW SHRIMP BY HAND: Pull off the legs, which will open up the shell on the underside. Loosen the shrimp from the shell with your fingers, then pull it free. The shell may break as you work, since It tends to cling to the flesh of the shrimp; if so, make sure you find and remove any stray pieces. The only part of the shell you might want to leave on, for aesthetic reasons, is the feathery tail.

TO DEVEIN AN UNPEELED SHRIMP BY HAND: Make a lengthwise cut along the back of the shell, using kitchen scissors. Scrape out the exposed vein with the tine of a fork or the tip of a paring knife.

TO DEVEIN A PEELED SHRIMP BY HAND: The classic way is to cut a V-shaped groove down the back of the shrimp; the groove should be just deep enough to include the vein. Remove the wedge of flesh and the vein will come with it.

There's a lightning-quick method for deveining a peeled shrimp, one taught to me by a Louisianan. Insert the tine of a fork in the back of the shrimp, midway between the head and tail. Pull the fork gently away from the shrimp and the vein will come with it.

TO BUTTERFLY A SHRIMP: Carry the vein-removing procedure described in either of the two methods above a step further. Once the vein is removed, make a deeper cut in the flesh, almost but not quite entirely through it, lengthwise almost to the tail.

HONEY SESAME SHRIMP "ON THE BARBIE"

AUSTRALIA

METHOD:
Direct grilling

Shrimp "on the barbie" (grill) is Australia's most famous culinary export. Even if you know nothing else about Down Under cooking, you're surely aware of how much Australians love grilling—especially seafood. If the truth be told, shrimp is something of a misnomer, as most Australians would say "prawns."

ADVANCE PREPARATION:
30 to 60 minutes for marinating the shrimp

The Chinese roots of this dish are obvious—a legacy of the huge influx of Asian immigrants to Australia in the 1970s and 80s. I love the way the sweetness of the honey and five-spice powder play off the nuttiness of the sesame seeds and oil and the brininess of the shrimp and soy sauce.

1½ pounds jumbo shrimp, peeled and
    deveined (see box, page 349)
5 tablespoons Asian (dark) sesame oil
3 tablespoons rice wine, sake, or
    dry sherry
3 tablespoons soy sauce
1½ tablespoons honey
1½ tablespoons sesame seeds
1 tablespoon Thai sweet chile sauce
    (optional; see Note)
½ teaspoon Chinese five-spice powder
2 cloves garlic, crushed with the side
    of a cleaver
2 slices (¼ inch thick) fresh ginger
2 scallions, trimmed, white part
    flattened with the side of a cleaver,
    green part finely chopped and
    set aside for garnish

1. Rinse the shrimp under cold running water, then drain and blot dry with paper towels. Set aside while you prepare the marinade.

2. Combine 3 tablespoons of the sesame oil, the rice wine, soy sauce, honey, sesame seeds, chile sauce (if using), and five-spice powder in a large bowl and whisk to blend. Stir in the garlic, ginger, scallions, and shrimp to coat, then cover and let marinate, in the refrigerator, for 30 to 60 minutes.

3. Preheat the grill to high.

4. Using a slotted spoon, remove the shrimp from the marinade to a bowl and toss with the remaining 2 tablespoons sesame oil. Pour the marinade into a saucepan; remove and discard the garlic, ginger, and scallion whites, using the slotted spoon. Bring the marinade to a boil over medium-high heat and cook, uncovered, to a thick, syrupy glaze, about 3 minutes. Remove from the heat and set aside.

5. When ready to cook, oil the grill grate. Arrange the shrimp on the hot grate and grill, turning with tongs, until nicely browned on the outside and firm and pink inside, about 2 minutes per side. Brush the shrimp with the glaze as they cook.

6. Transfer the shrimp to serving plates or a platter and sprinkle with the scallion greens. Serve immediately.

Serves 4

Note: Sweet chile sauce is the Thai version of ketchup. One good brand to look for is Siriacha. If not available, simply omit.

PRAWNS WITH KETJAP BUTTER

INDONESIA

METHOD:
Direct grilling

Prawns the size of lobsters, grilled crackling crisp in the shells, basted with a succulent, sweet-salty mixture of butter and sweet soy sauce—this is one of the specialties of Jakarta's famous fish house, Sunda Kelapa, and it is delicious enough to eat with your hands, which is what most of the customers do. We can't get those huge prawns here, but if you live in the Pacific Northwest or Hawaii, try making this recipe with spot prawns; otherwise, use jumbo shrimp in the shells. Serve with Javanese Salad Plate and Shallot Sambal (see Index), and steamed rice.

3 tablespoons unsalted butter
3 tablespoons sweet soy sauce
   (ketjap manis), or 1½ tablespoons
   each regular soy sauce and molasses
1 tablespoon fresh lime juice
1½ pounds spot prawns or jumbo shrimp,
   shells left on but deveined and
   butterflied (see box, page 349)

1. Preheat the grill to high.
2. Melt the butter in a small saucepan. Remove from the heat and stir in the sweet soy sauce and lime juice. Brush the cut sides of the prawns with the mixture.

3. When ready to cook, oil the grill grate. Arrange the prawns, cut sides down, on the hot grate and grill until lightly browned on that side, about 2 minutes. Brush the shell sides with the butter mixture and turn the prawns over, using tongs. Continue to grill until lightly browned on the second side and firm and pink inside, 2 to 4 minutes, brushing once or twice with the butter mixture.

4. Transfer the prawns to serving plates or a platter, pour over any remaining butter mixture, and serve immediately.
Serves 4

SALT AND PEPPER GRILLED SHRIMP

VIETNAM

METHOD:
Direct grilling

Like much grilled fare, this recipe is simplicity itself, but the addition of three commonplace seasonings to shrimp grilled in the shells makes an irresistible combination. I first heard about the preparation from my friend, travel correspondent Jane Wooldridge. Sure enough, when I tasted it in Saigon, I understood Jane's enthusiasm. In Vietnam the shrimp would be grilled with the heads and shells intact and this, indeed, enhances the flavor. If you live in a coastal region, you may be lucky enough to find shrimp with heads on. At very least, try to use shrimp in the shells.

1½ pounds jumbo shrimp (2 pounds
   if using shrimp with the heads on),
   shells left on but deveined
   (see box, page 349)
3 tablespoons fresh lime juice
3 teaspoons coarse salt, preferably
   sea salt
3 teaspoons freshly ground white pepper
1 large, juicy lime

1. Preheat the grill to high.
2. Rinse the shrimp under cold running water, then drain and blot dry with paper towels. Place the shrimp in a nonreactive baking dish and sprinkle with the lime juice and 1 teaspoon each salt and pepper. Toss to coat, then let marinate, at room temperature, 10 minutes.
3. Meanwhile, cut the lime into 4 lengthwise wedges. Place 1 wedge in each of 4 tiny shallow bowls or dishes. Place a small mound of salt (½ teaspoon) on one side of the lime wedge and a mound of pepper (½ teaspoon) on the other. Set aside.
4. When ready to cook, oil the grill grate. Arrange the shrimp, in their shells, on the hot grate and grill, turning with tongs, until the meat is firm and pink, about 2 minutes per side.
5. Transfer the shrimp to serving plates. To eat, squeeze the lime wedge over the salt and pepper and stir two or three times with chopsticks; peel the shrimp and dip in the lime mixture.
Serves 4

The Brazilian Grill

Let the Turks have their shish kebab, Indonesians their saté. I raise my fork for *churrasco,* Brazil's version of barbecue. *Churrasco* makes a prodigious meal and an evening's entertainment. *Churrasco* (pronounced "shoe-HRA-skoo") is served with belt-loosening largesse by a ceremonious procession of waiters bearing swordlike spits to carve at your table. And no one does it better than Marius Fontana.

Marius is the owner of three upscale *churrascarias* (grills) in Rio de Janeiro. You'd never guess it to meet him. Tasseled loafers. Designer jeans. Meticulously combed shoulder-length hair. He looks more like a movie star than a pit jockey. But ask a Carioca (a Rio resident) where to go for *churrasco* and you're almost sure to be told Marius. The night I arrived at his restaurant in the fashionable Ipanema district, the 400 seats were packed.

Churrasco is a method of cooking, but it's also a way of life. This rustic style of eating originated in Brazil's cattle country, Rio Grande do Sul. The traditional cooking equipment for *churrasco* was simple enough: an open fire, a sword for skewering meats, and a razor-sharp knife for carving them. The seasonings were even simpler: coarse sea salt and fresh air. For the better part of four centuries the cowboys of southern Brazil enjoyed *churrasco* in this fashion.

More recently, *churrasco* spread from Rio Grande to the rest of Brazil. As it moved north, it evolved from rustic cookout to a culinary extravaganza. Baptisms, birthdays, sporting events, even political rallies are celebrated over *churrasco.* Today, some of the fanciest restaurants in Rio are *churrascarias.*

Consider Marius (the restaurant). The sleekly contemporary dining room boasts polished wood paneling, frosted glass partitions, brass rails, and coffered ceilings with recessed pin spots. It's a long way from a cowboy campfire! So is the clientele, which includes an air-kissing crowd of moguls, movie stars, and tourists from three continents.

The large portions of a traditional *churrasco* have evolved into a curious display of conspicuous consumption. You're not simply handed a cocktail menu. The waiter rolls a portable bar right to your table. The hors d'oeuvre course is nothing less than a personal buffet that includes *pão de queijo* (tiny steaming cheese buns), crisply fried manioc, hard-cooked quail eggs, and a dozen other Brazilian appetizers. Come time for the main course, well, all I can say is that it's a good thing they supply you with the "sign."

The "sign" is a fixture at most Brazilian *churrascarias.* It enables you to control the pace of what is otherwise a relentless assault on your waistline. The miniature signpost at Marius comes with three panels: normal, *lento* ("slow"), and *suspenso* ("stop"). (Elsewhere, you may get a wheel with an arrow that points to the particular cut of meat you want more of or a placard that reads "stop.")

A squadron of waiters circulates through the dining room, each one bearing a different cut of meat. One staggers under the weight of whole spit-roasted prime rib. Others bear coils of *linguiça* (Portuguese sausage), *picanha* (spit-roasted sirloin), *cupim* (steer hump), chicken hearts, mint-glazed lamb kebabs—perhaps twenty different items in all. And as long as the "normal" sign is in place, each and every waiter will make a trip to your table. The only way to ward them off is to flip the sign to *suspenso.*

Each item arrives at the table sizzling hot off the grill. To learn how this amazing feat is achieved, I asked if I might visit the kitchen. Built into one wall is a giant stainless-steel rotisserie with motorized spits. The fatty cuts of meat are placed on the highest level, so that the melting fat bastes the leaner cuts roasting below. Ingenious. The waiters carry the spits to the dining room, carve off the cooked portion, then return the spits to the kitchen for more cooking.

A meal at a Brazilian *churrascaria* probably sounds like a relentlessly carnivorian experience. It *is* a relentlessly carnivorian experience, but Brazil's *churrascarias* serve some pretty amazing seafood dishes as well—see Grilled Fish with Brazilian Garlic Marinade (page 307) and Shrimp Kebabs with Bahian Peanut Sauce (facing page).

Whatever you order, I promise you won't go hungry!

SHRIMP WITH BAHIAN PEANUT SAUCE

BRAZIL

METHOD:
Direct grilling

ADVANCE PREPARATION:
30 minutes for marinating the shrimp

SPECIAL EQUIPMENT:
12 long bamboo skewers, soaked for 1 hour in cold water to cover and drained

This recipe takes its inspiration from Bahia in northern Brazil. Bahia has been called the New Orleans of Brazil. Nowhere are African influences on Brazilian cooking more evident or more delicious. Coconut milk, cilantro, fiery chiles, and peanuts are cornerstones of Bahian cooking. They come together here to provide a rich, hauntingly flavorful sauce for grilled shrimp.

FOR THE SHRIMP AND MARINADE:
1½ pounds jumbo shrimp, peeled and deveined (see box, page 349)
¾ cup coconut milk, homemade (page 522) or canned
¼ cup fresh lime juice
2 cloves garlic, minced
1 teaspoon salt
½ teaspoon freshly ground black pepper

FOR THE SAUCE:
2 tablespoons extra-virgin olive oil
4 cloves garlic, minced
1 bunch scallions, both white and green parts, trimmed and minced
1 tablespoon minced fresh ginger
½ medium green bell pepper, stemmed, seeded, and finely chopped
½ medium red bell pepper, stemmed, seeded, and finely chopped
2 fresh, ripe tomatoes, peeled and seeded (see box, page 62), then finely chopped
1¼ cups coconut milk, canned or homemade (page 522)
½ cup creamy peanut butter
3 tablespoons fresh lime juice
½ cup chopped fresh cilantro
Salt and freshly ground black pepper, to taste
¼ teaspoon cayenne pepper, or to taste

¼ cup chopped peanuts, toasted (see box, page 93), for garnish

1. Rinse the shrimp under cold running water, then drain and blot dry with paper towels. Set aside while you prepare the marinade.

2. Combine the coconut milk, lime juice, garlic, salt, and pepper in a large nonreactive bowl and stir to blend. Add the shrimp and toss to coat. Cover and let marinate, at room temperature, for 30 minutes.

3. Preheat the grill to high.

4. While the shrimp marinate, prepare the sauce. Heat the oil in a medium-size saucepan over medium heat. Add the garlic, scallions, ginger, and bell peppers and sauté until lightly browned, about 5 minutes. Add the tomatoes, increase the heat to high, and cook for 1 minute to evaporate some of the tomato liquid.

5. Stir in the coconut milk, peanut butter, lime juice, and half the cilantro. Reduce the heat to low and simmer gently, uncovered, until the mixture is well flavored and slightly thickened, 5 to 10 minutes. Taste for seasoning, adding salt, black pepper, and cayenne as necessary; the sauce should be highly seasoned. Keep warm, covered.

6. Drain the shrimp and thread them onto the skewers.

7. When ready to cook, oil the grill grate. Arrange the kebabs on the hot grate and grill, turning with tongs, until the shrimp are nicely browned on the outside and firm and pink inside, about 2 minutes per side. Brush the shrimp with some of the peanut sauce after turning.

8. Spoon the sauce onto serving plates, dividing evenly. Using a fork, slide the shrimp off the skewers onto each portion of sauce. Sprinkle with the chopped peanuts and remaining cilantro and serve immediately.

Serves 6 to 8 as an appetizer, 4 as an entrée

BALINESE PRAWN SATES
Saté Udang

INDONESIA

METHOD:
Direct grilling

ADVANCE PREPARATION:
1 hour for marinating the shrimp

SPECIAL EQUIPMENT:
12 thin stalks fresh lemongrass, trimmed of roots, tips, and outer leaves, or 12 long bamboo skewers, soaked in cold water for 1 hour and drained

Balinese shrimp satés owe their extraordinary fragrance to the skewers on which they're cooked: fresh lemongrass stalks. When buying lemongrass, try to choose slender stalks. But don't worry too much if you can't find lemongrass—satés cooked on bamboo skewers will still have plenty of flavor.

24 extra-large shrimp (about 1½ pounds), peeled and deveined (see box, page 349)
¼ cup sweet soy sauce (ketjap manis) or 2 tablespoons each regular soy sauce and molasses
3 cloves garlic, minced
1½ teaspoons ground coriander
2 tablespoons fresh lime juice
2 tablespoons palm sugar or firmly packed light brown sugar
3 tablespoons vegetable oil

1. Rinse the shrimp under cold running water, then drain and blot dry with paper towels. Set aside while you prepare the marinade.

2. Combine the soy sauce, garlic, coriander, lime juice, sugar, and 1 tablespoon of the oil in a large bowl and whisk until blended and the sugar is dissolved. Add the shrimp and toss to coat. Cover and let marinate, in the refrigerator, for 1 hour.

3. Preheat the grill to high.

4. Drain the shrimp. If using the lemongrass stalks as skewers, make a "starter" hole in each shrimp with a metal skewer. Thread the shrimp on the stalks, or on the bamboo skewers, 2 shrimp to each.

5. When ready to cook, oil the grill grate. Arrange the satés on the hot grate and grill, turning with tongs, until the shrimp are nicely browned on the outside and firm and pink inside, about 2 minutes per side. Brush once or twice with the remaining oil as the shrimp cook.

6. Transfer the satés to serving plates or a platter and serve immediately.

Serves 6 to 8 as an appetizer, 4 as an entrée

GRILLED SHRIMP WITH TARATOOR

LEBANON

METHOD:
Direct grilling

This is another favorite grilled shrimp dish around my house. It's quick, easy, and wonderfully exotic. What sets the recipe apart is the dipping sauce that accompanies the lightly marinated shrimp. *Taratoor* is a creamy, nutty, lemony white sauce made from sesame paste and lemon.

Tahini (sesame paste) is widely available at Middle Eastern markets, natural food stores, and in many supermarkets.

For a pretty presentation, arrange the shrimp on a platter, cut side up, and spoon the sauce on top. In this case, I'd sprinkle the shrimp with a little chopped parsley.

ADVANCE PREPARATION:
30 minutes for marinating the shrimp

SPECIAL EQUIPMENT:
About 40 short bamboo skewers, soaked for 1 hour in cold water to cover and drained

FOR THE SHRIMP:

1½ pounds jumbo shrimp, in their shells
2 tablespoons olive oil
2 tablespoons fresh lemon juice
1 clove garlic, minced
Salt and freshly ground black pepper, to taste

FOR THE TARATOOR:

½ cup tahini
2 cloves garlic, minced
½ cup fresh lemon juice, or more to taste
3 tablespoons minced fresh Italian (flat-leaf) parsley
3 to 5 tablespoons warm water
Salt and freshly ground white pepper, to taste

Pita bread, for serving

1. Cut each shrimp in half lengthwise, starting at the underside and cutting to but not through the top shell. Fold the shrimp open and devein, then rinse under cold running water. Drain and blot dry with paper towels. Place the shrimp in a nonreactive baking dish and sprinkle with the oil, lemon juice, garlic, and salt and pepper. Cover and let marinate, in the refrigerator, for 30 minutes, turning occasionally.

2. Preheat the grill to high.

3. While the shrimp marinate, prepare the *taratoor*. Combine the tahini, garlic, ½ cup lemon juice, and parsley in a small bowl and whisk to mix, then whisk in enough warm water to obtain a pourable sauce. Taste for seasoning, adding lemon juice and salt and pepper as necessary; the sauce should be highly seasoned. Transfer the sauce to 4 ramekins, dividing evenly, and set aside until serving time.

4. Remove the shrimp from the baking dish, reserving any marinade. Lay each shrimp flat and pin open crosswise with 2 skewers, one each, top and bottom.

5. When ready to cook, oil the grill grate. Arrange the shrimp, cut side down, on the hot grate and grill, turning with tongs, until nicely browned on the outside and firm and pink inside, about 2 minutes per side. Brush once or twice with any reserved marinade while cooking.

6. Protecting your hands with a pita bread, unskewer the shrimp onto serving plates or a platter and serve accompanied by the *taratoor* for dipping.

Serves 4

TANDOORI PRAWNS

INDIA

METHOD:
Direct grilling

ADVANCE PREPARATION:
2 hours for marinating the shrimp

SPECIAL EQUIPMENT:
4 long metal skewers

I landed in New Delhi after an 18-hour flight from New York. My reason for coming was simple: I wanted to sample tandoori (Indian barbecue) in its land of birth. Fortunately, I didn't have to travel much farther: India's most famous barbecue restaurant, Bukhara, was located in my hotel. One look at the exhibition kitchen, with its blazing tandoors and hammered copper walls hung with barbecue skewers, and I knew that I'd struck pay dirt.

A tandoor is a cross between a barbecue pit and an oven. The waist-high, urn-shaped clay vessel holds a charcoal fire in the bottom. Seafood, meats, even vegetables are roasted on vertical spits over the coals, while breads are baked directly on the tandoor's walls.

At Bukhara, the following recipe would be made with huge, juicy prawns from the Bay of Bengal. In this country I've used both shrimp and lobster tails. Whichever shellfish you use, the exotic ginger, cream,

**GOING
GRATELESS**

*T*o simulate the
type of grilling
done in an Indian
tandoor, use
the grateless
grilling method
outlined on page
23 to cook these
shrimp.

and spice marinade makes this some of the most succulent and explosively flavorful fare you'll taste on the world's barbecue trail. You'll need to know about two special ingredients: chickpea flour (*besan*), which is available at Indian and some Italian markets and natural foods stores. In a pinch you could substitute whole-wheat flour in place of *besan* or simply omit it. *Garam masala* is an Indian spice mix. I included a recipe for it in this book, but you can also use a commercial blend.

1½ pounds jumbo shrimp, peeled and
    deveined (see box, page 349)
3 tablespoons coarsely chopped fresh ginger
6 cloves garlic, sliced
1 teaspoon salt, or more to taste
2 tablespoons fresh lemon juice, or more
    to taste
⅔ cup heavy cream or plain whole-milk
    yogurt
1 large egg
3 tablespoons chickpea flour (optional)
½ teaspoon cayenne pepper
½ teaspoon ground turmeric
½ teaspoon ground cumin
½ teaspoon Quick Garam Masala (page 499)
    or a commercial blend
½ teaspoon freshly ground white pepper
2 to 3 tablespoons melted salted butter,
    for brushing
Lemon wedges, for serving

1. Rinse the shrimp under cold running water, then drain and blot dry with paper towels. Set aside while you prepare the marinade.

2. Combine the ginger, garlic, and 1 teaspoon salt in a mortar and pound to a paste with the pestle, then work in the 2 tablespoons lemon juice and 2 tablespoons of the cream; or process the ingredients, all at once, to a smooth paste in a blender or spice mill.

3. Transfer the ginger-garlic paste to a large nonreactive bowl and whisk in the remaining cream, egg, chickpea flour (if using), cayenne, turmeric, cumin, *garam masala*, and white pepper. Taste for seasoning, adding lemon juice or salt as necessary; the mixture should be highly seasoned. Add the shrimp and toss to cook. Cover and let marinate, in the refrigerator, for 2 hours.

4. Preheat the grill to high. Remove the shrimp from the bowl and thread onto the skewers.

5. When ready to cook, oil the grill grate. Arrange the kebabs on the hot grate and grill, turning with tongs, until nicely browned on the outside and firm and pink inside, about 2 minutes per side. Brush the shrimp with the melted butter once or twice as they cook. Using a fork, slide the shrimp off the skewers onto serving plates or a platter and serve immediately with lemon wedges.
Serves 4

FLAMING PRAWNS

INDIA

METHOD:
Direct grilling

Muhammad Ishtiyaque Qureshi comes from a long line of Indian master chefs. To look at him, you'd think he was straight out of California. A ponytail peeps out from under his toque. A gold earring gleams in one ear. Ishtiyaque is the chef of the Indian Harvest restaurant at the Leela Hotel in Bombay, and his penchant for theatrics certainly extends to his cooking. Every few minutes, the dining room erupts with a volcanic roar and tower of flames from a sizzling platter of

ADVANCE PREPARATION:
1 hour for marinating the shrimp

dahakte jhinga, "flaming prawns." The show is designed to delight Japanese and Western businessmen (and their Indian hosts), but according to Ishtiyaque, there is a tradition of serving flambéed food in India. After all, Indian barbecue originated with the Mogul rulers from Persia, and Ishtiyaque claims that they seasoned their grilled fare with flaming wine.

Ishtiyaque's prawns come from the Bay of Bengal and are the size of small lobsters. Their flavor is reinforced by a two-stage marinating process: first in vinegar, then in yogurt. In North America, either jumbo shrimp or lobster tails work well. To be strictly authentic, you'd marinate the prawns in a fruity black vinegar made from an Indian berry called *jamun.* I approximate its flavor by combining cider vinegar with apricot nectar. Ishtiyaque uses yogurt cheese for his marinade, but plain yogurt will produce tasty results, too.

FOR THE SHRIMP AND VINEGAR MARINADE:
1½ pounds jumbo shrimp, in their shells (see Note)
3 tablespoons cider vinegar
2 tablespoons apricot nectar
2 tablespoons lemon juice

FOR THE YOGURT MARINADE:
1 cup plain whole-milk yogurt
1 to 3 teaspoons cayenne pepper or hot paprika
3 cloves garlic, minced
1 tablespoon grated fresh ginger
¼ teaspoon ground cloves
1 teaspoon salt

2 to 3 tablespoons melted butter, for brushing
¼ cup rum, preferably 151 proof, for flambéing

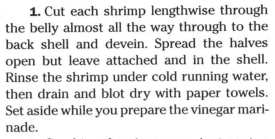

1. Cut each shrimp lengthwise through the belly almost all the way through to the back shell and devein. Spread the halves open but leave attached and in the shell. Rinse the shrimp under cold running water, then drain and blot dry with paper towels. Set aside while you prepare the vinegar marinade.

2. Combine the vinegar, apricot nectar, and lemon juice in a nonreactive baking dish large enough to hold the shrimp in one layer. Add the shrimp, cut side down, and let marinate, at room temperature, for 15 minutes.

3. Meanwhile, prepare the yogurt marinade: Combine the yogurt, cayenne, garlic, ginger, cloves, and salt in a large nonreactive bowl and whisk to blend. Add the shrimp, turning to coat, then cover and let marinate, in the refrigerator, for 1 hour.

4. Preheat the grill to high.

5. When ready to cook, oil the grill grate. Remove the shrimp from the marinade, discarding the marinade, and arrange the shrimp, cut sides down, on the hot grate. Grill for 2 minutes, then turn, using tongs, and grill until nicely browned on the outside and firm and pink inside, 2 to 4 minutes more. Brush the shrimp once or twice with the melted butter as they cook.

6. Transfer the shrimp to a platter. Make sure the area is clear of flammable material and that no one is standing too close. Roll back your sleeves and tie back your hair if necessary. Gently warm the rum, over very low heat, in a small saucepan; do not let it boil or even get hot. Remove the pan from the heat and, averting your face and using a long match, ignite the rum. Very carefully pour it over the shrimp and serve immediately.

Serves 4

Note: Lobster tails also work well in this recipe. Prepare 4 lobster tails as directed for the shrimp in step 1 and marinate as directed, first in the vinegar mixture and then in the yogurt. Grill as directed, 6 to 8 minutes per side.

PLANTATION SHRIMP

CARIBBEAN

METHOD:
Direct grilling

ADVANCE PREPARATION:
1 hour for marinating the shrimp

SPECIAL EQUIPMENT:
1 piece (12 inches) fresh sugarcane

You won't actually find this dish in the Caribbean, although it's made with some of the most typical ingredients of the West Indies: sugarcane (hence the "plantation" in the name), rum, allspice, and nutmeg. I created the recipe for a Caribbean restaurant in Hong Kong that bore the name of my book *Miami Spice*.

You're not really meant to eat the sugarcane (it's much too tough). The idea is to chew the cane skewers as you eat the shrimp to release the sweet juices.

If you're in a hurry, simply marinate the shrimp in the honey-soy mixture and grill them. They'll be amazing—even without the sugarcane and glaze. Serve with Bahamian Peas and Rice (see Index).

FOR THE SHRIMP AND MARINADE:
24 extra-large shrimp (1½ pounds), peeled and deveined (see box, page 349)
2 cloves garlic, minced
2 scallions, both white and green parts, trimmed and minced
1 tablespoon minced fresh ginger
½ scotch bonnet chile or 1 jalapeño, seeded and minced
2 tablespoons soy sauce
2 tablespoons honey
2 tablespoons peanut oil

FOR THE RUM GLAZE:
⅓ cup plus 1 tablespoon dark rum
2 tablespoons tomato paste
2 tablespoons firmly packed dark brown sugar
1 tablespoon honey
1 tablespoon distilled white vinegar
1 tablespoon Worcestershire sauce
1½ teaspoons Tabasco or other hot sauce
⅛ teaspoon ground allspice
⅛ teaspoon ground cloves
Salt and freshly ground black pepper, to taste

1. Rinse the shrimp under cold running water, then drain and blot dry with paper towels. Set aside while you prepare the marinade.

2. Combine the garlic, scallions, ginger, chile, soy sauce, honey, and peanut oil in a large bowl and whisk to mix. Add the shrimp, tossing to coat. Cover and let marinate, in the refrigerator, for 1 hour.

3. Preheat the grill to high.

4. While the shrimp marinates, prepare the sugarcane skewers. Peel the piece of sugarcane, using a sharp knife, then cut crosswise into 3-inch sections. Cut each section into 8 lengthwise strips, each about ¼ inch wide (this will make 24 strips in all). Cut one end off each strip at an angle to make a sharp point. Set aside while you prepare the glaze.

5. Combine the ⅓ cup rum, the tomato paste, sugar, honey, vinegar, Worcestershire sauce, Tabasco, allspice, and cloves in a small, heavy saucepan and bring to a boil over medium-high heat, stirring until blended and the sugar is melted. Reduce the heat to medium and simmer to a syrupy glaze, 3 to 5 minutes. Remove from the heat, stir in the remaining 1 tablespoon rum, and taste for seasoning, adding salt and pepper as necessary.

6. Remove the shrimp from the bowl and make a "starter" hole through the center of each with a metal skewer, since the sugarcane strips are not stiff enough. Thread the shrimp on the cane strips, starting with the pointed end, 1 shrimp to each.

7. When ready to cook, oil the grill grate. Arrange the shrimp on the hot grate and grill, turning with tongs, until nicely browned on the outside and firm and pink inside, about 2 minutes per side. Brush the shrimp with the glaze as they cook.

8. Transfer the shrimp to serving plates or a platter and serve immediately.

Serves 6 to 8 as an appetizer, 4 as an entrée

EMERIL LAGASSE'S NEW ORLEANS–STYLE BARBECUED SHRIMP

U.S.A.

METHOD:
Direct grilling

ADVANCE PREPARATION:
1 hour for marinating the shrimp

You may be surprised to find a New Orleans–style recipe in this book: After all, grilling isn't traditionally associated with Louisianan cooking. Indeed, the first time I tasted this dish, the shrimp were sautéed, not grilled. But grilling works great here—I love the way the smoky, charcoaled flavor of the shrimp counterpoints the lemony richness of the cream-based barbecue sauce.

2 pounds jumbo shrimp
3 tablespoons olive oil
3 tablespoons Cajun Rub, (page 491)
    or a commercial brand of
    Cajun seasoning
1 small onion, finely chopped
2 tablespoons minced fresh garlic
3 bay leaves
2 lemons, peeled, cut into thin
    crosswise slices, and
    seeded
2 cups bottled clam broth or water
½ cup Worcestershire sauce
¼ cup dry white wine
2 cups heavy cream
2 tablespoons unsalted butter
Salt and freshly ground black pepper,
    to taste

1. Peel and devein the shrimp (see box, page 349), leaving the feathery tail shells intact and reserving the shells. Rinse the shrimp under cold running water, then drain and blot dry with paper towels.

2. Place the shrimp in a large bowl and sprinkle with 2 tablespoons of the oil and 1½ tablespoons of the Creole seasoning. Rub the oil and seasonings into the shrimp with your hands to coat well, then cover and let marinate, in the refrigerator, for 1 hour.

3. Preheat the grill to high.

4. While the shrimp marinates, prepare the barbecue sauce. Heat the remaining 1 tablespoon oil in a large saucepan over high heat. Add the onion and garlic and sauté until just beginning to brown, about 3 minutes. Add the reserved shrimp shells, the remaining 1½ tablespoons Creole seasoning, the bay leaves, lemon slices, clam broth, Worcestershire sauce, and wine. Bring to a boil, stirring, then reduce the heat to medium and simmer, uncovered, until only about 1½ cups liquid remain; this will take 20 to 30 minutes.

5. Strain the mixture into a second saucepan and place over high heat. Boil, uncovered, stirring often to prevent scorching, until thick, syrupy, and dark brown, about 15 minutes; you should have about ½ cup. Whisk in the cream and bring to a boil. Reduce the heat slightly and cook the mixture until only about 2 cups liquid remain; this will take 5 to 10 minutes. Remove from the heat and whisk in the butter until melted. Taste for seasoning, adding salt and pepper as necessary; the sauce should be highly seasoned. Set ½ cup sauce aside for basting. Keep the remaining sauce warm, covered, for serving.

6. When ready to cook, oil the grill grate. Arrange the shrimp on the hot grate and brush with some of the ½ cup barbecue sauce. Grill until nicely browned on the outside and firm and pink inside, about 2 minutes per side. Brush the shrimp liberally with the barbecue sauce once or twice as they cook.

7. Transfer the shrimp to a serving platter and serve immediately, topped with the remaining barbecue sauce.

Serves 6 to 8 as an appetizer, 4 as an entrée

PENGANESE GRILLED SHRIMP WITH PAINFULLY HOT SALSA

METHOD:
Direct grilling

SPECIAL EQUIPMENT:
8 long bamboo skewers, soaked for 1 hour in cold water to cover and drained

The mere mention of Penang is enough to make most Malaysians' mouths water. This tropical island off the northeastern coast is reputed to have some of the best food in Asia—a reputation easily verified by visiting the food stalls on Gurney Drive.

You'd expect the fiendishly hot *nam choh* (shallot "salsa") in this recipe to overpower the delicate butter and coconut milk–basted shrimp, but in fact it does just the opposite: The heat seems to sensitize your taste buds to the mild, sweet flavor of the shrimp.

You'll need to know about one special ingredient to prepare this recipe: shrimp paste (called *belacan* in Malaysian and *trasi* in Indonesian), a pungent paste made from pickled shrimp and salt. Despite its off-putting aroma, shrimp paste adds a complex and pleasing flavor that has endeared it to chefs from one end of Southeast Asia to another. Toasting helps mellow the nose-jarring smell of the paste. It can be found at Asian markets and in some gourmet shops. In a pinch you can use a dab of anchovy paste or a teaspoon or two of fish sauce (omitting the toasting, of course). Malaysians use shrimp with the heads still on, which are not that easy to find in this country. If you can get them, by all means use them here.

1½ pounds jumbo shrimp (2 pounds if using shrimp with the heads on), shells left on
2 tablespoons salted butter, at room temperature
¼ teaspoon shrimp paste
3 tablespoons fresh lime juice, or more to taste
1 teaspoon sugar, or more to taste
¾ teaspoon salt, or more to taste
¾ cup thinly sliced shallots
6 to 8 Thai or serrano chiles, thinly sliced (for a milder salsa, seed the chiles)
1 cup coconut milk, canned or homemade (page 522), for brushing

1. Preheat the grill to high.

2. Devein the shrimp (see box, page 349), then run a knife along the top of each to make the slit deeper, since you will be stuffing the shrimp with butter. Rinse the shrimp under cold running water, then drain and blot dry with paper towels. Spread the butter inside the slits in the shrimp, then thread the shrimp lengthwise on the skewers so both ends are caught. Place on a platter and set aside while you prepare the *nam choh.*

3. Place the shrimp paste on the end of one tine of a grill fork. Hold it over the fire until lightly toasted and aromatic, about 2 minutes. Transfer to a small bowl and add 3 tablespoons lime juice, 1 teaspoon sugar, and ¾ teaspoon salt. Stir until blended and the sugar and salt are dissolved, then stir in the shallots and chiles. Taste for seasoning, adding lime juice, sugar, or salt as necessary; the sauce should be highly seasoned. Set aside until serving time.

4. When ready to cook, oil the grill grate. Brush the shrimp with coconut milk and arrange the skewers on the hot grate. Grill, turning with tongs, until the shrimp are nicely browned on the outside and firm and pink inside, about 2 minutes per side.

Brush with the coconut milk once or twice during cooking.

5. Transfer the skewers to serving plates or a platter and serve immediately, accompanied by tiny bowls of the *nam choh*.
Serves 4

GULF COAST SHRIMP

U.S.A.

METHOD:
Direct grilling

ADVANCE PREPARATION:
2 to 4 hours for marinating the shrimp

CANE SYRUP
Cane syrup can be found in stores specializing in Southern products or by mail order (see Mail-Order Sources); one popular brand is Steen's. If you can't find it, you can always substitute dark corn syrup, such as Karo.

Hot, sweet, and smoky are these Gulf Coast Shrimp, which have jumped from the proverbial frying pan to the fire, since traditionally the shrimp would be sautéed, not grilled. Put tradition aside for these—they're great!

1½ pounds jumbo shrimp, peeled and deveined, shells reserved (see box, page 349)
1 cup bottled clam broth, chicken broth, or water
8 tablespoons (1 stick) unsalted butter
6 cloves garlic, minced
4 scallions, both white and green parts, trimmed and finely chopped
1 to 2 tablespoons Tabasco or other Louisiana-style hot sauce
1 tablespoon Worcestershire sauce
2 bay leaves
2 teaspoons cayenne pepper
2 teaspoons sweet paprika
2 teaspoons dried thyme
2 teaspoons dried oregano
1½ teaspoons salt
1 teaspoon freshly ground black pepper
¾ cup dark cane syrup (see Cane Syrup)

1. Combine the shrimp shells and clam broth in a medium-size saucepan and bring to a boil. Reduce the heat to low and simmer, uncovered, until slightly reduced and well flavored (the shrimp shells will turn orange),

10 to 15 minutes. Strain the broth into another medium-size saucepan; you should have about ¾ cup.

2. To the shrimp broth add the butter, garlic, scallions, Tabasco, Worcestershire sauce, bay leaves, cayenne, paprika, thyme, oregano, salt, black pepper, and syrup. Bring to a boil over medium heat and cook, uncovered, until thick, syrupy, and richly flavored, about 10 minutes. Remove from the heat and let cool to room temperature.

3. Meanwhile, rinse the shrimp under cold running water, then drain and blot dry with paper towels.

4. Add the shrimp to the cooled marinade in the saucepan and toss to coat. Cover and let marinate, in the refrigerator, for 2 to 4 hours.

5. Preheat the grill to high.

6. When ready to cook, oil the grill grate. Remove the shrimp from the marinade, reserving the marinade. Arrange the shrimp on the hot grate and grill, turning with tongs, until nicely browned on the outside and firm and pink inside, about 2 minutes per side. Brush the shrimp with 2 to 3 tablespoons of the reserved marinade while cooking.

7. Transfer the shrimp to a serving platter. Bring the remaining marinade to a boil in its saucepan over medium heat. Pour over the shrimp and serve immediately.
Serves 6 to 8 as an appetizer, 4 as an entrée

LATIN QUARTER SHRIMP KEBABS

GREECE·FRANCE

METHOD:
Direct grilling

SPECIAL EQUIPMENT:
4 long metal skewers

The prettiest kebabs I've ever seen were prepared on the Rue de la Huchette in the Latin Quarter of Paris. This warren of narrow streets—one of the oldest neighborhoods in Paris—is home to dozens of Greek restaurants, each one vying to outdo the next with the drama of its shish kebabs. Everything is fair game for a skewer—lamb, beef, tightly coiled *merguez* (Moroccan sausage), seafoods ranging from oval, bright orange salmon steaks to jumbo prawns with their heads still attached. The kebabs are composed with the precision of a Swiss watchmaker and a painterly eye to form and color. Subtle variations distinguish the kebabs of one establishment from another. The following kebabs feature an aromatic rub of oregano, thyme, and rosemary. You're not actually meant to eat the grilled lemon but it sure imparts a great flavor.

FOR THE SPICE MIXTURE:
1 tablespoon coarse (kosher or sea) salt
1 teaspoon freshly ground white pepper
1 teaspoon dried oregano
1 teaspoon dried rosemary
1 teaspoon dried thyme

FOR THE KEBABS:
12 jumbo shrimp or spot prawns, ideally with the heads attached, shells left on but deveined (see box, page 349)
2 medium onions, peeled
1 large green bell pepper, stemmed, seeded, and quartered lengthwise
1 lemon, cut into 8 wedges
12 large cherry tomatoes
3 tablespoons extra-virgin olive oil, or as needed for brushing

Pita bread, for serving

1. Combine the ingredients for the spice mixture in a bowl, crumbling the rosemary between your fingers. Set aside.

2. Rinse the shrimp under cold running water, then drain and blot dry with paper towels. Cut each onion into 4 wedges and cut each wedge crosswise in half. Cut each pepper quarter crosswise into 4 equal pieces.

3. Preheat the grill to high.

4. Arrange the ingredients for the kebabs on a cutting board. Here's a sequence I like (but feel free to follow any you desire): a lemon wedge (cut edge toward you), a piece of bell pepper, a piece of onion, a shrimp (underside facing you) with a cherry tomato placed in the hollow space formed by the curve, another piece of pepper and onion, another shrimp with a tomato, more pepper and onion, another shrimp with a tomato, more pepper and onion, and, finally, another lemon wedge (cut edge *away* from you). Run a skewer through these ingredients to make an attractive kebab, then thread the remaining kebabs the same way (see Note).

5. When ready to cook, brush the kebabs on both sides with oil and sprinkle with the spice mixture. Arrange the kebabs on the hot grate and grill until the shrimp flesh is firm and pink and the tomatoes and onions are lightly charred, 3 to 6 minutes per side. Brush the kebabs once or twice with additional oil and season liberally with the spice mixture as they cook.

6. Protecting your hands with pita bread, unskewer the kebabs onto serving plates.

Serves 4

Note: The kebabs may be prepared up to 6 hours ahead of time. Refrigerate, loosely covered with plastic wrap.

SCALLOP KEBABS WITH PANCETTA, LEMON, AND BASIL

U.S.A.

METHOD:
Direct grilling

ADVANCE PREPARATION:
30 minutes for marinating the scallops

SPECIAL EQUIPMENT:
8 long bamboo skewers, soaked in cold water for 1 hour and drained

These kebabs are as easy to make as anyone could wish for and they are full of flavor. The salty pancetta (Italian bacon) and the piguant lemon combine to deliver a tangy punch. If you live on the East Coast, in the winter you may be able to find true bay scallops, small, meaty nuggets of incredible sweetness. But larger sea scallops will work, too, provided you cut them down to size. Most scallops come with a crescent-shaped muscle on one side, which should be removed before cooking. (It is noticeably tougher than the rest of the shellfish.) Serve with buttered noodles.

1½ pounds bay or sea scallops
3 tablespoons extra-virgin olive oil
3 tablespoons fresh lemon juice
4 strips lemon zest (each 2 x ½ inches; removed with a vegetable peeler)
Plenty of freshly ground black pepper
1 bunch fresh basil, stemmed
8 thin slices pancetta (Italian bacon) or regular bacon, cut into 1-inch pieces

1. Using your fingers, pull off and discard the small, half moon–shaped muscle from the side of any scallop that has one. If using sea scallops, cut any large ones in quarters, mediums in half, so that all the pieces are the same size. Rinse the scallops under cold running water, then drain and blot dry with paper towels. Set aside while you prepare the marinade.

2. Combine the oil, lemon juice, lemon zest, and pepper in a medium-size bowl and whisk to mix. Add the scallops and toss to coat. Cover and let marinate, at room temperature, for 30 minutes.

3. Preheat the grill to high.

4. Remove the scallops from the marinade, reserving the marinade. Thread the scallops on the skewers, inserting a basil leaf and a piece of pancetta between each.

5. When ready to cook, oil the grill grate. Arrange the kebabs on the hot grate and grill until the scallops are just firm and white, 1 to 2 minutes per side. Brush the scallops once or twice with the reserved marinade as they cook.

6. Using a fork, push the scallops off the skewers onto serving plates or a platter and serve immediately.

Serves 4

GRILLED CLAMS WITH COLOMBO BUTTER

FRENCH WEST INDIES

METHOD:
Direct grilling

Clams are probably the last thing to come to mind when most of us think of grilled seafood. But grilling over or in the coals of a fire was most likely the first way man cooked bivalves, and the tradition survives in many regions, including the French West Indies, one of the birthplaces of barbecue. *Colombo* is a French

West Indian curry powder made with rice as well as spices. Its nutty, spicy, aromatic flavor has an uncanny way of bringing out the sweetness of the clams. I've included a recipe, but commercially made *colombo* can be found in West Indian markets or a good curry powder can be substituted.

8 tablespoons (1 stick) salted butter
3 cloves garlic, minced
2 teaspoons colombo powder, homemade
    (see page 493) or store-bought, or
    good-quality regular curry powder,
    or more to taste
Freshly ground black pepper,
    to taste
2 dozen littleneck or cherrystone clams
    (see Note), scrubbed

1. Preheat the grill to high.

2. Melt the butter in a small, heavy saucepan over medium heat. Add the garlic and 2 teaspoons *colombo* powder and sauté until very fragrant and the garlic is softened but not browned, about 2 minutes. Remove from the heat and taste for seasoning, adding *colombo* powder and pepper as necessary; the mixture should be highly seasoned.

3. If you have a fish or vegetable grate, preheat it on the grill grate for 5 minutes, then arrange the clams on it. Otherwise, arrange the clams directly on the grate. Grill until the shells open, 6 to 8 minutes.

4. Transfer the clams to serving plates or a platter, discarding any clams that did not open. Spoon a little of the *colombo* butter into each shell and serve immediately.

Serves 4 to 6 as an appetizer, 2 to 3 as an entrée

Note: Clams are graded by size, littlenecks being the smallest. For best results, do not use clams wider than 2 inches across for this recipe, or they will be too tough.

GRILLED MUSSELS
Éclade

FRANCE

METHOD:
Direct grilling

*É*clade is one of the world's most distinctive styles of barbecuing, consisting of cooking mussels under a blazing pile of dry pine needles. (The name may come from the French verb, *éclore,* "to open.") This not only sounds like the way our prehistoric ancestors cooked shellfish, it probably *is* the way. To this day, *éclade* remains popular picnic fare in the Cognac region of France.

Unless you live in the country, your access to dry pine needles may be limited. Fortunately, mussels grilled over charcoal have very nearly as fine a flavor—with a lot less fuss.

The mussels taste best eaten hot off the grill, which means the shells may burn your fingers a little. That's why another name for this dish is *moules-brûlés-doigts* ("finger burners")!

4 pounds mussels
¾ cup (1½ sticks) unsalted butter
3 cloves garlic, minced
⅓ cup minced fresh Italian (flat-leaf) parsley
Salt and freshly ground black pepper, to taste

1. Preheat the grill to high.

2. Scrub the mussels under cold running water, discarding any with cracked shells or shells that fail to close when tapped. Using a needlenose pliers, pull out and discard any clumps of threads that gather at the hinges of the mussels.

3. Melt the butter in a small, heavy saucepan over medium heat. Add the garlic, parsley, salt, and pepper and sauté until the garlic is softened but not browned, about 2 minutes. Remove from the heat and transfer the garlic-parsley butter to 4 small bowls, one for each person for dipping.

4. If you have a fish or vegetable grate, preheat it on the grill grate for 5 minutes, then arrange the mussels on it, rounded side down (see Note). Otherwise, arrange the mussels directly on the grate. Grill until the shells open, 2 to 5 minutes if you cover the grill, somewhat longer if you don't.

5. Transfer the mussels to serving bowls, discarding any that didn't open. To eat, remove the mussels from the shells with your fingers or a small seafood fork and dip them into the garlic-parsley butter. Provide a platter or plates for the discarded shells.

Serves 4

Note: If you look at a mussel closely, you will see it has a rounded and a flat side.

BAHAMIAN GRILLED CONCH

BAHAMAS

METHOD:
Direct grilling

CONCH

If you live in Florida or Louisiana, you may be able to find fresh or at least thawed frozen conch at your local fishmonger. Elsewhere in the country, you'll have to settle for frozen conch. Fortunately, conch freezes well. Thaw the conch in the refrigerator.

Conch (pronounced "konk") is the whitest, sweetest, most delicately flavored of all shellfish. Although it's not well known in North America, it's virtually the national dish of the Bahamas. Stroll along the Potters Cay market beneath the bridge to Paradise Island or along the Arawak Cay recreation area (a popular local hangout) and you'll find dozens of stalls specializing in the preparation of this giant sea snail. After you've had fiery conch salad (the most popular way to eat conch) and "cracked" (fried) conch, you'll be ready for the most delicious preparation of all: grilled conch.

The basic procedure is to grill the conch wrapped in foil with onions, garlic, chiles, and butter. To enhance the smoke flavor, Nassau chef Basil Dean chars the conch directly over the coals before wrapping. By the way, any white fish fillets can be prepared in this fashion (omitting the tenderizing), with delectable results.

1½ pounds trimmed, cleaned conch
   (4 large or 8 small steaks; see Conch)
Salt and freshly ground black pepper, to taste
⅔ cup very finely chopped onion
2 cloves garlic, minced
½ to 1 bird pepper, or other hot chile, minced
   (for a milder dish, seed the chiles)
2 tablespoons fresh lime juice
4 tablespoons (½ stick) salted butter
4 lime wedges, for serving

1. Preheat the grill to high.

2. Tenderize the conch steaks by pounding them with a meat mallet or rolling pin to a ¼-inch thickness. Season on both sides with salt and pepper.

3. When ready to cook, oil the grill grate. Arrange the steaks on the hot grate and quickly grill, turning with tongs, about 1 minute per side. (The idea here is to leave grill marks on the conch and impart a charcoaled flavor.) Transfer the steaks to a platter to cool.

4. Cut four 12 × 8-inch sheets of heavy-duty aluminum foil. Place 1 large or 2 small conch steaks in the center of each piece.

5. Combine the onion, garlic, and chile in a bowl, then place 3 to 4 tablespoons of this mixture on top of each steak. Drizzle each steak with ½ tablespoon lime juice and top with 1 tablespoon butter. Bring the sides of the foil up over the top and pleat to make an airtight package. Wrap the remaining conch steaks the same way.

6. When ready to cook, arrange the foil packages on the hot grate and grill until the conch is cooked through and tender, about 5 minutes (a metal skewer inserted into the conch through the foil will be very hot when withdrawn).

7. Open the foil packages and slide the conch steaks, with their topping, onto plates. (Or let everyone unwrap their own bundle. But warn them to avoid the escaping steam.) Serve the conch steaks with wedges of lime for squeezing.

Serves 4

OYSTERS WITH HORSERADISH CREAM

U.S.A.

METHOD:
Direct grilling

Oysters possess a natural affinity for horseradish—a fact appreciated by anyone who has passed an hour or two at a raw bar. In this recipe the horseradish is folded into unsweetened whipped cream, which melts as it hits the hot oysters. Nothing can beat the pungency of freshly grated horseradish, but the bottled product will produce highly delicious results, too.

1 cup heavy cream
1 tablespoon grated plain horseradish,
   drained if bottled, or more to taste
1 tablespoon chopped fresh chives or
   scallion greens
1 teaspoon grated lemon zest
2 teaspoons fresh lemon juice, or
   more to taste
Salt and freshly ground black pepper, to taste
2 dozen oysters in the shell, scrubbed

1. Preheat the grill to high.

2. Beat the cream to soft peaks in a chilled medium-size bowl, then fold in 1 tablespoon horseradish, the chives, lemon zest, 2 teaspoons lemon juice, and salt and pepper. Taste for seasoning, adding horseradish and lemon juice as necessary; the mixture should be highly seasoned.

3. If you have a fish or vegetable grate, preheat it on the grill grate for 5 minutes, then arrange the oysters on it, rounded side down (see Note). Otherwise, arrange the oysters directly on the grate. Grill until the shells open, 6 to 10 minutes.

4. Transfer the oysters to serving plates or a platter, discarding any top shells or oysters that did not open. Place a spoonful of horse-radish cream on each oyster and serve immediately.

Serves 4 to 6 as an appetizer, 2 to 3 as an entrée

Note: If you look at an oyster closely, you will see that one side is more rounded than the other.

GRILLED OCTOPUS

Khtapothi Sti Skhara

GREECE

METHOD:
Direct grilling

OUZO AND OCTOPUS

The traditional beverage to drink with grilled octopus is ouzo, Greece's national anise-flavored spirit. Pour a few fingers of ouzo in a glass and fill the glass with water. The ouzo will turn the color of milk. Ouzo goes down with astonishing ease. Make sure you have a designated driver!

If I were to pick the quintessential taste of the Greek islands, it would be this popular *mezze* (appetizer). Octopus is one of those foods that seems to have been put on earth expressly for grilling: The fire brings out the sweetness of the delicate white meat, which in turn absorbs the flavors of the olive oil, oregano, and charcoal without surrendering its own. The cleaning and tenderizing of an octopus can be an intimidating process: Fortunately, virtually all the octopus sold in North America is cleaned and tenderized already. This leaves you with the easy task of grilling the octopus (preferably over charcoal) until nicely charred on all sides, without quite being burnt. Octopus is available frozen at Greek markets, Japanese markets, and specialty seafood shops. Squid or shrimp could be prepared in a similar fashion.

This recipe is unusual in the world of grilled seafood in that the octopus is grilled dry, then marinated. Serve with New Greek Salad (see Index).

2 pounds cleaned, trimmed octopus
2 tablespoons red wine vinegar, or more to taste
2 tablespoons fresh lemon juice
2 teaspoons dried oregano, preferably Greek
1 teaspoon coarse (kosher or sea) salt, or more to taste
½ teaspoon freshly ground black pepper
6 to 8 tablespoons extra-virgin olive oil
¼ cup finely chopped fresh Italian (flat-leaf) parsley
Lemon wedges, for serving

1. Preheat the grill to high.

2. Using a paring knife, peel or scrape any reddish skin off the octopus. (You probably won't need to do this, as most octopus comes already cleaned.) Leave the legs whole, but cut the body in quarters. Rinse the octopus under cold running water, then drain and blot dry with paper towels.

3. When ready to cook, oil the grill grate. Arrange the octopus pieces on the hot grate and grill, turning with tongs, until nicely charred (but not quite burnt) on all sides, 3 to 6 minutes per side, (6 to 12 minutes in all).

4. Transfer the octopus to a cutting board and cut it into bite-size pieces. Place the pieces in a serving bowl.

5. Combine 2 tablespoons vinegar, the lemon juice, oregano, 1 teaspoon salt, the pepper, oil, and parsley in a small bowl and whisk to mix, then pour over the octopus and toss to coat. Let marinate for at least 5 minutes and up to 30 (the octopus can be served warm or at room temperature). Taste for seasoning, adding salt or vinegar as necessary; the octopus should be highly seasoned. Serve accompanied by lemon wedges for squeezing.

Serves 4 to 6

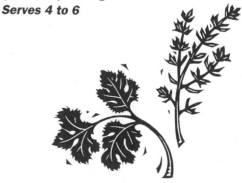

GRILLED SQUID DURBAN

SOUTH AFRICA

METHOD:
Direct grilling

**ADVANCE
PREPARATION:**
*1 to 2 hours for
marinating the
squid*

You probably know that South Africa's culinary roots go back to England, Holland, and, of course, Africa. What you may not realize is that many cities, like the east coast port of Durban, boast large Indian and Malaysian communities—a throwback to the days when Asian laborers were brought here to work in the gold and diamond mines. These grilled squid have the gustatory fireworks you'd associate with India or Southeast Asia.

The scoring of the surface of the squid prior to marinating is optional, but it will give you a dramatic presentation.

2 pounds cleaned squid, including tentacles
2 teaspoons coriander seeds
1 teaspoon cumin seeds
3 cloves garlic, peeled
½ small onion, peeled
1 piece (1-inch) fresh ginger
**3 stalks fresh lemongrass, trimmed and
   thinly sliced, or 3 strips lemon zest
   (each 2 x ½ inches; removed with a
   vegetable peeler)**
**1 to 3 serrano or jalapeño chiles
   (for milder squid, seed the chiles)**
**¾ cup coconut milk, canned or homemade
   (page 522)**
½ teaspoon salt, or more to taste
**½ teaspoon freshly ground black pepper,
   or more to taste**
1 cup fresh cilantro leaves
Lime wedges, for serving

1. Rinse the squid under cold running water, then drain and blot dry with paper towels. Make a lengthwise cut in one side of the bodies to open them up into broad, thin sheets. If desired, lightly score the outside of each piece in a crosshatch pattern with a sharp knife, cutting about halfway through the squid. Leave the tentacle sections whole. Place in a large bowl and set aside in the refrigerator while you prepare the marinade.

2. Heat a dry small skillet over medium heat. Add the coriander and cumin seeds and cook until toasted and fragrant, about 3 minutes, shaking the pan occasionally. Remove from the heat and let cool, then place the spices in a blender and grind to a coarse powder (see Note). Add the garlic, onion, ginger, lemongrass, chiles, coconut milk, and ½ teaspoon each salt and pepper and process to a smooth paste. Taste for seasoning, adding salt and pepper as necessary; the mixture should be highly seasoned. Stir in half the cilantro, then pour the mixture over the squid in the bowl and toss to coat. Cover and let marinate, in the refrigerator, for 1 to 2 hours, turning the pieces occasionally.

3. Preheat the grill to high.

4. If you have a fish or vegetable grate, preheat it 5 minutes before you're ready to cook, then oil. Otherwise, just oil the regular grill grate. Arrange the squid pieces on the hot grate and grill, turning with tongs, until just firm and white, 1 to 2 minutes per side.

5. Transfer the squid to serving plates or a platter and sprinkle with the remaining cilantro. Serve immediately, accompanied by lime wedges.

Serves 4

Note: If you're in a hurry, you can omit the whole seeds and toasting procedure and use ground spices instead.

FERNANDO'S GRILLED CUTTLEFISH WITH MACANESE "SALSA"

METHOD:
Direct grilling

ADVANCE PREPARATION:
30 minutes for marinating the cuttlefish

Fernando Gomes knows a good thing when he sees it. When the Azores Islander landed in the Portuguese colony of Macao (soon to be part of China) in the early 1980s, it was love at first sight—and bite. So he did what many Portuguese do in Macao: He opened a restaurant. Behind a funky brick storefront is a spacious courtyard, where guests dine under whirling paddle fans in an open air pavilion. Fernando's is located on the quietest of Macao's islands, Coloane, and it backs up to Hac Sa Beach. The grilled cuttlefish alone is worth the trip.

Cuttlefish is a larger, wider, fleshier, somewhat sweeter cousin of squid. If you live in an area with a large Asian, Iberian, or Italian community, you may be able to find cuttlefish at an ethnic fish market. Squid also works well for this recipe and is much more widely available.

If possible, use charcoal for grilling here.

1½ to 2 pounds cleaned cuttlefish or squid, with tentacles
⅔ cup extra-virgin olive oil
3 tablespoons red wine vinegar, or more to taste
1 small onion, finely chopped
¼ cup finely chopped fresh Italian (flat-leaf) parsley
½ teaspoon salt, or more to taste
½ teaspoon freshly ground black pepper
1 fresh, ripe medium tomato, seeded (see box, page 62) and diced

1. Rinse the cuttlefish under cold running water, then rinse and blot dry with paper towels. Place in a nonreactive baking dish and set aside while you prepare the marinade.

2. Combine the oil, 3 tablespoons vinegar, the onion, parsley, ½ teaspoon salt, and pepper in a nonreactive bowl and whisk to mix. Taste for seasoning, adding salt or vinegar as necessary; the mixture should be highly seasoned. Pour half the mixture over the cuttlefish in the dish, then cover and let marinate, in the refrigerator, for 30 minutes. Transfer the remaining mixture to an attractive bowl and stir in the tomato. Set this sauce aside.

3. Preheat the grill to high.

4. If using a fish or vegetable grate, preheat it for 5 minutes before you're ready to cook, then oil. Otherwise, when ready to cook, oil the grill grate. Remove the cuttlefish from the marinade, reserving the marinade. Arrange on the hot grate and grill, turning with tongs, until nicely charred and just firm, 2 to 3 minutes per side (4 to 6 minutes in all). Brush the cuttlefish once or twice with the remaining marinade as it cooks.

5. Transfer the cuttlefish to serving plates or a platter. Serve immediately, accompanied by the reserved sauce.

Serves 4

Vegetables:
GREENS MEET GRILL

"What was paradise but a garden full of vegetables."

—WILLIAM LAWSON

This produce market in Sicily is a vegetable griller's paradise.

When I was growing up, barbecue meant meat. Especially steak. The idea of grilling a bell pepper or a portobello mushroom would have seemed as strange as landing a man on the moon.

Well, we did land a man on the moon and we have discovered grilled vegetables. In fact, North Americans may be newcomers to a wide range of grilled vegetables, but we've embraced the cause with religious fervor. Why is this? Because no other cooking method produces a better taste. Grilling evaporates some of the water in a vegetable, concentrating the flavor. High, dry heat caramelizes natural plant sugars, heightening a vegetable's sweetness. Unlike boiling, which removes flavor from vegetables, grilling seems to intensify their natural taste. Add a whiff of smoke (from wood chips or chunks) and you'll have vegetables with an astonishing depth of flavor.

This chapter offers a mouthwatering tour of the world of grilled vegetables, from Korean grilled oyster mushrooms to tandoori cauliflower fragrant with Indian spices. Along the way, you'll learn how to grill corn, fennel, long beans, and even breadfruit. If you had trouble eating your vegetables when you were a kid, it's probably because they weren't grilled.

How to Grill Perfect Vegetables Every Time

*I*n general, vegetables benefit from a direct, high-heat grilling method. The exceptions are dense root vegetables, like potatoes and turnips, that are best cooked by the indirect method or by parboiling and finishing over the fire.

ASPARAGUS, OKRA, GREEN BEANS, AND OTHER LONG, SKINNY, FIBROUS VEGETABLES: Snap or cut off the ends of the vegetables and lay 4 to 6 vegetables side by side on a work surface. Skewer them crosswise with slender bamboo skewers. Brush with olive oil or sesame oil and sprinkle with salt and pepper. Grill over high heat until nicely browned on both sides. Cook asparagus 6 to 8 minutes in all. Okra cook in 8 to 10 minutes, green beans, too, in 8 to 10 minutes. Scallions need a total time of 4 to 8 minutes.

CORN: There are two schools of thought on this one. The easiest way is

simply to toss unshucked ears on the grill and cook over high heat until the husks are completely charred. Scrape off the charred husks with paper towels (the silk will come off with them). You'll need about 15 to 18 minutes in all. The corn will be sweet and mildly smoky.

My favorite way to grill corn is to start with shucked ears, which I generously brush with melted butter or olive oil and generously season with salt and pepper. I grill the corn over high heat, directly over the flames, until the kernels are darkly browned and starting to pop. This will take 8 to 12 minutes in

all. The advantage of this method is that the corn acquires a wonderful smoke flavor.

EGGPLANTS: Choose eggplants that are long and slender. Preheat the grill to high. Grill the eggplant until the skin is black and charred on all sides and the flesh is soft. (Test it by gently poking the top.) You're supposed to burn the skin; that's what gives the eggplant its smoky flavor. Turn the eggplant with tongs as it cooks: The whole process will take 20 to 30 minutes. Transfer the eggplant to a plate and let cool, then scrape off the charred skin. (You don't have to remove all the burnt pieces; they add a terrific flavor.) The eggplant is now ready for chopping to make salads or puréeing to make dips.

Note that some recipes in this book call for Asian eggplants, which are about 1 inch in diameter and about

6 inches long. They cook in 9 to 12 minutes.

MUSHROOMS: Mushrooms tend to get somewhat dry if grilled plain, so it's best to marinate them for a few hours in an oil-based marinade or slather them with an herb or flavored butter during grilling. Thread small mushrooms on skewers so that they lie flat on the grill grate, for easy grilling and turning. Grill over high heat. Cook 3 to 6 minutes per side (6 to 12 minutes in all). When grilling portobellos, cook cap side down first, then invert. Cook portobellos 4 to 6 minutes per side (8 to 12 minutes in all). Grill stuffed mushroom caps, rounded side down, 15 to 20 minutes, using the indirect method. All mushrooms should be generously basted as they cook.

ONIONS: Cut onions in quarters, but leave the root intact on each piece. Peel back the skin to the root end. (The root holds the onion together during cooking.) Brush the onion quarters with oil or melted butter. Grill over a high flame until nicely charred on the outside and cooked through, turning to ensure even cooking. You'll need 10 to 12 minutes in all. Scrape off the burnt skin before serving.

PEPPERS (this works for both bell peppers and chile peppers): Choose peppers that are rotund and smooth, with relatively few depressions or crevasses. Preheat the grill to high. Place the whole peppers on the grill and cook until darkly charred on all sides, 4 to 5 minutes per side (16 to 20 minutes in all) for larger peppers; the smaller chiles will take less time. Don't forget to grill the top and bottom; if necessary, hold the peppers with tongs if they won't balance properly on either end. This is another food you're supposed to burn. Transfer the grilled peppers to a large bowl and cover with plastic wrap or place in a closed paper or plastic bag. This creates steam, which makes it easy to remove the skin. When the pepper is cool enough to handle, scrape off the skin with a paring knife. Cut out the stem and remove the seeds.

Another way to grill peppers is to brush them lightly with olive oil and grill until nicely browned but not burnt. In this case, you wouldn't bother peeling the peppers.

RADICCHIO OR KALE AND OTHER LEAFY VEGETABLES: Cut radicchio in quarters, wedges, or thick slices. Grill kale leaves whole. Grill over high heat until the leaves start to brown. Cook 2 to 4 minutes per side. Watch carefully; do not allow the leaves to burn to a crisp.

TOMATOES: Thread small or plum tomatoes on a wide, flat skewer and grill over high heat, turning, until the skins are browned and blistered all over. Grill individual tomatoes the same way, turning with tongs. To grill really large tomatoes (such as beefsteaks), cut them crosswise into 1-inch-thick slices. Brush with olive oil, season with salt and pepper, and grill over high heat. Cook small or plum tomatoes 8 to 12 minutes in all. Larger, whole tomatoes take twice as long, and tomato slices take 2 to 4 minutes per side.

ZUCCHINI AND SUMMER SQUASH: Cut the vegetables lengthwise into $\frac{1}{4}$- or $\frac{1}{2}$-inch-thick slices. Brush each side with olive oil or walnut oil. Season with salt and pepper and grill over high heat. Cook 4 to 6 minutes per side.

Vegetable Grilling Chart*

VEGETABLE	METHOD	HEAT	COOKING TIME
ARTICHOKES	DIRECT	MED-LOW	1–1¼ HRS
ASPARAGUS	DIRECT	HIGH	6–8 MIN IN ALL
CORN	DIRECT	HIGH	8–12 MIN IN ALL
EGGPLANT (WHOLE)			
ASIAN	DIRECT	HIGH	9–12 MIN/COOKED THROUGH
REGULAR (LONG SLENDER)	DIRECT	HIGH	20–30 MIN/COOKED THROUGH
GREEN BEANS	DIRECT	HIGH	8–10 MIN/SIDE
MUSHROOM CAPS			
PORTOBELLO	DIRECT	HIGH	4–6 MIN/SIDE
REGULAR	DIRECT	HIGH	3–5 MIN/SIDE
ONIONS			
QUARTERED	DIRECT	HIGH	10–12 MIN/SIDE
SLICED	DIRECT	HIGH	4–8 MIN/SIDE
PEPPERS (WHOLE)	DIRECT	HIGH	16–20 MIN (LET SKIN BURN)
SQUASH, SLICED			
(YELLOW AND ZUCCHINI)	DIRECT	HIGH	4–6 MIN/SIDE
TOMATOES			
SLICED	DIRECT	HIGH	2–4 MIN/SIDE
WHOLE	DIRECT	HIGH	8–24 MIN IN ALL

* This chart is offered as a broad guideline to cooking times for various vegetables. Remember, grilling is an art, not a science. When in doubt, refer to times in the individual recipes.

GEORGIAN VEGETABLE KEBABS

REPUBLIC OF GEORGIA

METHOD:
Direct grilling

SPECIAL EQUIPMENT:
4 long, flat metal skewers

These colorful vegetable kebabs turn up at any Republic of Georgia barbecue. Their simplicity makes a nice counterpoint to the complex flavors of Georgian marinated meats. Georgian Pickled Plum Sauce (see Index) makes a good accompaniment, but they're also delicious plain. Choose tomatoes that are ripe but still a little firm, so they won't fall off the skewers. A Georgian would use a flat, wide steel skewer (see Mail-Order Sources).

8 small green bell peppers
6 fresh, ripe plum tomatoes
16 large white mushrooms, stemmed, caps wiped clean with dampened paper towels
3 tablespoons olive oil
Coarse (sea or kosher) salt and freshly ground black pepper, to taste
1 lemon, cut in half

1. Preheat the grill to high.

2. Thread the vegetables on the skewers, alternating bell peppers and tomatoes, placing mushrooms between each. Brush the kebabs with olive oil and season with salt and pepper.

3. When ready to cook, arrange the kebabs on the hot grate and grill, turning with tongs, until nicely browned, 4 to 6 minutes per side (8 to 12 minutes in all), brushing with olive oil. Squeeze lemon juice over the vegetables and serve immediately.

Serves 4

JAPANESE VEGETABLE MIXED GRILL
Robatayaki

JAPAN

METHOD:
Direct grilling

SPECIAL EQUIPMENT:
50 to 60 bamboo skewers (assorted lengths), soaked for 1 hour in cold water to cover and drained

Robatayaki refers to a theatrical, upscale style of Japanese grilling you can read all about on page 388. Traditionally the foods were grilled over a prized Japanese charcoal called *bincho*, and in certain sections of Tokyo—among the eateries near the Yurakucho train station, for example—you still find restaurants with charcoal grills. Others take a more contemporary approach, cooking food over high-tech gas grills. This mixed vegetable grill has many virtues, not the least of which is that it's the very best way I know of to cook okra.

1 pound okra (see Note, page 391)
1 pound sugar snap peas, stems and strings removed
1 pound thick asparagus, fibrous ends removed, stalks trimmed to matching lengths

12 ounces fresh shiitake or large white mushrooms, stemmed, caps wiped clean with dampened paper towels
1 bunch scallions, both white and green parts, trimmed and cut into 2-inch pieces
1 tablespoon coarse (kosher or sea) salt
2 teaspoons freshly ground white pepper (optional)
2 tablespoons Asian (dark) sesame oil

1. Preheat the grill to high.

2. Trim the tips off the stems of the okra, but do not cut into the pods. This would expose the insides to air, making the okra slimy. Lay 4 or 5 okra side by side in a neat row on a cutting board. Stick a bamboo skewer through each end of each piece. The idea is to hold them flat for grilling. Transfer the skewered okra to a large platter. Skewer the sugar snap peas the same way and transfer to the okra platter.

3. Cut the asparagus stalks in half crosswise. Thread these halves on skewers at a 90-degree angle to the skewers, 4 to 5 pieces to a skewer, alternating tip halves and stalk pieces. Transfer the asparagus to the platter with the other vegetables.

4. Cut any large shiitakes in half or quarters; leave small ones whole. Thread the shiitake caps onto skewers, 4 caps to a skewer, alternating with pieces of scallion. The caps should be threaded on so they will lie flat on the grill. Transfer the shiitake skewers to the platter. Mix the salt and pepper (if using) in a small bowl. Brush the vegetables with the sesame oil and sprinkle with salt and pepper.

5. When ready to cook, arrange the okra, sugar snap peas, asparagus, and shiitakes on the hot grate and grill, turning with tongs, until lightly browned and tender, 3 to 6 minutes per side, depending on the vegetable. Serve the various skewers as soon as they're ready. Don't worry about serving everything at once. It's more fun if the food arrives sequentially.

Serves 4 to 6

GRILLED VEGETABLES IN THE STYLE OF SANTA MARGHERITA

ITALY

METHOD:
Direct grilling

SPECIAL EQUIPMENT:
Vegetable grate (optional)

After two grueling weeks on the barbecue trail, the town of Santa Margherita on the Italian Riviera appeared like an oasis in the desert. Imagine a spectacularly craggy cove surrounding a harbor filled with bobbing yachts and fishing boats. Trompe l'oeil painted houses. Cafés crowded with chic young Italians. Come lunchtime, it was impossible to ignore a buffet served on a bluff overlooking the bay—especially the centerpiece of that buffet, an enormous platter of grilled vegetables.

In keeping with the Italian understatement when it comes to grilling, the vegetables were cooked without the benefit of a marinade and with only a drizzle of olive oil and squirt of lemon juice by way of a sauce. But I guarantee you'll never taste better grilled vegetables, nor feast your eyes on a prettier platter. Use the following ingredient list as a starting point, substituting whatever vegetables look freshest.

2 medium red bell peppers
2 medium yellow bell peppers
2 Belgian endives
1 pound fresh cremini or regular white mushrooms, stemmed, caps wiped clean with dampened paper towels
4 small eggplants or zucchini
½ cup extra-virgin olive oil
Coarse (kosher or sea) salt and freshly ground black pepper, to taste
1 pound thick asparagus, fibrous ends removed
8 small fresh, ripe tomatoes
2 tablespoons balsamic vinegar (optional)
8 lemon wedges, for serving

1. Preheat the grill to high.

2. Stem, halve, and seed the bell peppers, then cut each half into 3 lengthwise strips. Cut the endives lengthwise in quarters, leaving the stem ends attached. Cut the mushrooms in half and the eggplants or zucchini in half lengthwise.

3. When ready to cook, preheat a vegetable grate (if using) for 5 minutes. Lightly brush the bell pepper pieces with olive oil, season with salt and black pepper, and arrange on the hot grate. Grill until lightly charred on both sides, leaving the skins intact, 4 to 6 minutes per side. Transfer to a platter. Oil, season, and grill the endive, asparagus, tomatoes, porcini, and eggplants the same way. Each vegetable should be nicely charred on the outside and soft and tender inside; depending on the vegetable, this will take 3 to 6 minutes per side. Brush all the vegetables lightly with oil and season with salt and pepper once or twice as they cook.

4. Arrange the grilled vegetables in rows on a platter, varying color and shape. Drizzle the remaining oil on top of the hot vegetables and let cool.

5. Just before serving, season the vegetables again with salt and pepper. If you like, drizzle a little balsamic vinegar on top. Serve lemon wedges on the side for squeezing over the vegetables.

Serves 8

WEST INDIAN GRILLED VEGETABLES
Choka

TRINIDAD

METHOD:
Direct grilling

In general, Trinidadians aren't big grillers, preferring the deep-fat frying of their British heritage or the stewing of their African forebears. That's not to say that you don't see a lot of charcoal fires at roadside stalls in Port of Spain. But by and large, they are used to heat bubbling stockpots and fryers, not for direct grilling. One exception are the *chokas* enjoyed by the Indian community. A *choka* is a fire-roasted vegetable that is chopped and seasoned with oil. The traditional vegetable for *choka* is eggplant, but you can also use tomatoes, potatoes, even pumpkin. It is traditionally served with *sada roti* (flat bread)—often for breakfast. In this country, use pita bread or any of the grilled breads featured in this book (see Index). Here's a *choka* inspired by the stylish Port of Spain restaurant Monsoon.

FOR THE CHOKA:
2 smallish eggplants (10 to 12 ounces each)
6 cloves garlic, peeled and cut in half lengthwise
2 fresh, ripe medium tomatoes
1 medium green bell pepper
1 large onion, peeled and cut into quarters (leave the root ends intact)
1 tablespoon vegetable oil
Salt and freshly ground black pepper, to taste

FOR THE SPICE MIXTURE:
2 tablespoons vegetable oil
2 teaspoons mustard seeds, preferably black
1 medium onion, finely chopped
2 cloves garlic, minced
1 tablespoon finely chopped fresh ginger
½ to 1 scotch bonnet chile, seeded and minced
2 tablespoons fresh lime juice

¼ cup chopped fresh cilantro, for garnish

1. Preheat the grill to high.

2. Make 6 randomly placed slits around each eggplant with the tip of a paring knife. Insert a half clove of garlic in each slit. Lightly brush the eggplants, tomatoes, bell pepper, and onion with oil and season with salt and black pepper.

3. When ready to cook, arrange the vegetables on the hot grate and grill, turning with tongs, until the skins are charred, about 20 minutes for the eggplant (the flesh should be very soft as well) and bell pepper, and about 12 minutes for the tomatoes and onion quarters. Transfer the vegetables to a plate and let cool.

4. Scrape most of the charred skin off the vegetables. Cut the eggplant and tomatoes into 1-inch dice. Stem, seed, and finely dice the bell pepper. Thinly slice the onion crosswise. Transfer the vegetables to a shallow heatproof serving bowl and stir to mix, adding salt and pepper to taste.

5. Just before serving, prepare the spice mixture. Heat the oil in a small, heavy skillet over medium-high heat. Add the mustard seeds, onion, garlic, ginger, and chile and sauté until fragrant and golden brown, about 5 minutes. Add the lime juice, let boil, then pour the hot spice mixture over the vegetables. Toss gently to mix, sprinkle with cilantro, and serve warm or at room temperature

Serves 8

CATALAN GRILLED ARTICHOKES

SPAIN

METHOD:
Direct grilling

La Tomaquera is a one-room chop-house in a working-class neighborhood in Barcelona. It's the sort of place that takes pride in not serving Coca-Cola; the sort of place that closes early when there's a soccer game on TV. For about $25, you could eat yourself into oblivion in this lively restaurant. For me that meant snails in a rich gravy, followed by an assortment of grilled beef, lamb, and other meats.

What most captivated me was an unusual vegetable dish, grilled artichokes—one of the best things I have eaten in my life. The long, low-heat grilling process renders the leaves so crisp, you can almost eat them whole. I know of only one other dish that makes artichokes so delectably crisp—Rome's *carciofi alla Giudia,* artichokes in the Jewish style.

For best results, choose medium-size artichokes; you want ones with the leaves fairly spread open. You could also use baby artichokes, but if you do, cook them for a shorter amount of time. Avoid the dense jumbo globe artichokes, which are delicious boiled, but difficult to grill.

8 medium artichokes
½ lemon
1 cup (2 sticks) unsalted butter
6 cloves garlic, minced
¼ cup minced fresh Italian (flat-leaf)
 parsley
Coarse (kosher or sea) salt
Lots of cracked or coarsely ground black
 pepper

1. Preheat the grill to medium-low.

2. Cut the stems off the artichokes so they stand upright. Rub the bottoms with the lemon to prevent discoloring. Trim the spiny tips off the leaves with a scissors. Using your fingers, gently push the leaves apart to open the artichoke like a flower.

3. Melt the butter in a small, heavy saucepan over low heat, then add the garlic and parsley, increase the heat to medium, and bring to a simmer. Simmer until the garlic loses its rawness, about 3 minutes. Brush the artichokes all over with a generous amount of the butter mixture and sprinkle with salt and pepper. Pour a spoonful of the mixture over the top of each artichoke, letting it drip into the leaves.

4. When ready to cook, arrange the artichokes on the hot grate, stem sides down, and grill until the bottoms are a deep golden brown, rotating often with tongs to ensure even cooking. Baste often with the butter mixture and season generously with salt and pepper. You'll need about 30 minutes to brown the bottoms.

5. Starting in the center, working with tongs, again spread the artichoke leaves out to open each artichoke like a flower. Baste with more garlic butter and season with more salt and pepper. Invert the artichokes and cook until a deep golden brown, 30 to 40 minutes more. The leaves should be crisp and should pull out easily; the heart should be tender (test it for doneness by inserting a skewer). If using a charcoal grill, add 25 fresh coals after 1 hour.

6. Turn the artichokes again (the bottoms should now be on the grate) and baste and season again. Cook a few more minutes to rewarm the bottoms. Drizzle the artichokes with any remaining garlic butter and serve immediately.

Serves 8

FIRE-ROASTED BREADFRUIT

JAMAICA

METHOD:
Direct or indirect grilling

Breadfruit was brought to the Caribbean from the South Pacific by the infamous Captain Bligh and has become one of the classic accompaniments to Jamaica's jerk pork. Sufferer's restaurant in Jamaica has a special charcoal pit for roasting breadfruits, which are buried in the embers. Char-roasting is one of the best ways to cook this large, round (think bowling ball), pebbly and green-skinned fruit, whose chief characteristic is its mild flavor (some people might say utter blandness)—perfect for taming the blast furnace heat of jerk pork! Breadfruit may be fruit, botanically speaking, but it's usually served as a vegetable or starch. Charring imparts a smoky flavor that is readily absorbed by the starchy, white flesh. The most authentic way to cook it is on a charcoal grill, but you can also char it on a gas grill using either the direct or indirect method. Breadfruit can be found at West Indian markets and specialty green-grocers. Choose a firm, unblemished specimen and ripen at room temperature until it just begins to yield when pressed with your thumb. It should still be rather firm.

1 breadfruit (3 to 4 pounds)
4 tablespoons ($\frac{1}{2}$ stick) salted butter,
    for serving
Salt and freshly ground black pepper,
    for serving

1. *If using a charcoal grill (direct method),* preheat it to high. When ready to cook, nestle the breadfruit in the coals, raking the latter around it to cover as much of the fruit as possible. Cook the breadfruit until the skin is charred and the flesh is very soft. This will take 40 to 60 minutes, depending on the size and ripeness of the breadfruit. To test for doneness, insert a metal skewer; the breadfruit should be soft in the center.

If using a gas grill (direct method), preheat to medium. When ready to cook, place the breadfruit on the hot grate and grill until the skin is charred and the flesh is very soft (see above for timing and test for doneness).

If using a gas grill (indirect method), preheat to medium-high. When ready to cook, place the breadfruit in the center of the grill, away from the heat, and roast until well browned on the outside and soft in the center, 1 to 1½ hours. (I prefer the direct method, because you actually char the skin, but the indirect method requires less intervention.)

2. To serve, cut or break the breadfruit into wedges and trim away the burnt part. Spread a little butter over the breadfruit, season with salt and pepper, mash with a fork, and eat.

Serves 4 to 6

TANDOORI CAULIFLOWER

INDIA

METHOD:
Indirect grilling

ADVANCE PREPARATION:
2 hours for marinating the cauliflower

SPECIAL EQUIPMENT:
8 long metal skewers

When it comes to barbecue, few Westerners would think of cauliflower. Not so in India. There cauliflower (*gobi*) is appreciated for its ability to absorb smoke and spice flavors and maintain its firm texture. You'll need to know about two special ingredients for this recipe: *besan* (chickpea flour) and *ajwain* (carum seeds, also known as lovage seeds). Both are available at Indian markets, and the former can also be found at natural foods stores and many gourmet shops. If unavailable, whole-wheat flour makes an acceptable substitute. I've made the *ajwain* optional, as it's somewhat more difficult to find. The cauliflower will still be plenty flavorful without it.

2 cups plain whole-milk yogurt (see Note)
1 whole cauliflower (about 1½ pounds)
3 cloves garlic, minced
1½ tablespoons grated fresh ginger
¼ cup vegetable oil
1 tablespoon sweet paprika
1 teaspoon cayenne pepper
1 teaspoon salt
½ teaspoon freshly ground black pepper

½ teaspoon ajwain (optional)
½ teaspoon ground cumin
2 teaspoons fresh lemon juice
**¾ cup chickpea flour (besan) or
    ¼ cup whole-wheat flour, or
    as needed**
**3 tablespoons unsalted butter, melted,
    for brushing**

1. Set a yogurt strainer, or a regular strainer lined with a double layer of dampened cheesecloth, over a medium-size bowl. Add the yogurt and drain, in the refrigerator, for 4 hours. You should wind up with about 1¼ cups

2. Cut the cauliflower into florets, leaving about 1 inch of stem on each floret. Prick each floret 8 to 10 times with a trussing needle or carving fork to allow the marinade to penetrate to the center.

3. Combine the garlic, ginger, and oil in a spice mill or mini chopper and process to a smooth paste. Alternatively, grind the garlic and ginger to a paste in a mortar with the pestle, then work in the oil. Transfer the paste to a large nonreactive bowl. Whisk in the paprika, cayenne, salt, pepper, *ajwain* (if

using), cumin, yogurt, lemon juice, and enough chickpea flour to make a smooth mixture. Stir in the cauliflower, cover, and let marinate, in the refrigerator, for 2 hours.

4. Set up the grill for indirect grilling (see page 14 or 16), placing a drip pan in the center, and preheat to high.

5. Thread the cauliflower florets crosswise through the stems onto the skewers. (The flower ends should all be pointing up.)

6. When ready to cook, spoon any remaining marinade over the cauliflower and arrange the skewers on the hot grate over the drip pan. Cover and grill for 10 minutes, then brush the florets with a little melted butter and continue grilling until nicely browned and tender, 10 to 20 minutes more. Move the skewers directly over the flames for the last 2 to 3 minutes to lightly brown the cauliflower. Brush the cauliflower with the remaining butter and unskewer onto plates or a platter. Serve immediately.

Serves 6 to 8

Note: If you prefer not to drain the yogurt, you will need only 1½ cups.

GRILLED CORN WITH SHADON BENI BUTTER

TRINIDAD

METHOD:
Direct grilling

Despite the wide use of charcoal as a cooking fuel, Trinidadians aren't particularly keen on grilling. One exception is corn. Stroll through Queen's Park Savannah in Port of Spain at dusk and you'll find large crowds at the corn vendors. They line up for crackling crisp ears of a mature variety of corn that most Americans would consider too large, old, and dried out for eating. But it's these very defects that make the corn so munchable crisp and delicious.

Traditionally, the cooked ears are brushed with melted butter and sprinkled with salt and pepper. Inspired by a popular Trinidadian herb, I've come up with a more interesting topping: *shadon beni* butter. *Shadon beni* (literally "false cilantro") is a dark green, thumb-shaped, sawtooth-edged herb with a taste similar to cilantro. It's generally sold in North America by its Hispanic name, *culantro*. (Look for it in Hispanic and West Indian markets.) But don't despair if you can't find *shadon beni*: cilantro makes an equally delicious butter. By the way, you can use *shadon beni* as a great topping for other simply grilled vegetables and seafood.

8 ears of corn (the larger and older, the better)
8 tablespoons (1 stick) salted butter, at room temperature
3 tablespoons finely chopped fresh culantro or cilantro
2 scallions, both white and green parts, trimmed and minced
1 clove garlic, minced
Freshly ground black pepper, to taste

1. Preheat the grill to high.

2. Shuck the corn and set aside while you prepare the *shadon beni* butter.

3. Place the butter, *culantro,* scallions, garlic, and pepper in a food processor and process until smooth. Transfer to a bowl. Alternatively, if the herbs and garlic are minced really fine, you can stir them right into the butter in the bowl.

4. When ready to cook, oil the grill grate. Arrange the corn on the hot grate and grill, turning with tongs, until nicely browned all over, 8 to 12 minutes. As the corn cooks, brush it occasionally with the butter. Remove from the grill and brush once more with the butter. Serve immediately.

Serves 8

GRILLED EGGPLANTS WITH MISO "BARBECUE" SAUCE

JAPAN

METHOD:
Direct grilling

Grilled eggplant might seem like an odd bar snack to Westerners, but it's a best seller in the teriyaki bars near the train stations in Tokyo. I like to think of it as a vegetarian hot dog. The "barbecue sauce" used to glaze the eggplants is a sweet-salty mix made from miso (cultured soy bean paste). White miso, the most common variety, can be found in the refrigerator case of natural foods stores and in many large supermarkets. For this recipe, the eggplant of choice would be a slim Asian variety. The advantage to a small eggplant is that it cooks quickly and can be eaten in a couple of bites.

6 Asian eggplants (about 4 ounces each)
⅓ cup white miso
1 tablespoon sake
1 tablespoon mirin (sweet rice wine) or cream sherry
1 tablespoon sugar
1 tablespoon mayonnaise
1 tablespoon Asian (dark) sesame oil, for brushing
1 teaspoon black sesame seeds or toasted regular sesame seeds (see box, page 93)

1. Preheat the grill to high.

2. Cut the eggplants in half lengthwise. Using a sharp knife, make shallow crisscrosses on the flesh and skin sides of each half eggplant. The cuts should be ⅛ inch deep and ⅛ inch apart.

3. Combine the miso, sake, mirin, sugar, and mayonnaise in a bowl and whisk until smooth.

4. Brush the eggplants on both sides with sesame oil. Arrange the eggplants, flesh side down, on the hot grate and grill until nicely browned, 3 to 4 minutes. Turn the eggplants with tongs and spread a generous spoonful of miso sauce over the flesh side of each. Continue grilling until the undersides are nicely browned and the flesh is soft, 6 to 8 minutes more. To test for doneness, gently squeeze the sides of the eggplant; they should be softly yielding. Sprinkle the sesame seeds on top and serve immediately.

Serves 6 as a side dish, 3 as a light entrée

Grate Expectations: Some Tips on Grilling Vegetables

You know the scenario: You love grilled vegetables, but as you go to turn those mushrooms, scallions, and onion wedges sizzling away on the grill, they fall between the bars of the grate into the fire.

To avoid this problem, savvy grill buffs use a vegetable grate—an auxiliary grate that goes on top of the main grate. Often made of porcelain- or Teflon-coated metal, the vegetable grate has small holes that allow the flames and smoke flavor to reach the vegetables but keep them from falling into the fire.

A variation on the vegetable grate is the vegetable basket, a hinged wire basket into which you can put loose mushrooms, cherry tomatoes, summer squash and zucchini slices, and other small pieces of vegetables. Instead of trying to turn each piece on the grill grate, you simply invert the basket.

Vegetable grates and baskets are sold at cookware shops and via mail order (see Mail-Order Sources). If you use one, you should preheat it on the regular grill grate for about 5 minutes before adding the vegetables.

Barbecue buffs are divided on whether or not to oil the grate—regular or vegetable—before grilling vegetables. Vegetables don't tend to stick to the bars of the grate as much as meats and seafood do (it's the proteins in the latter that do the sticking). But if you want the better grill marks that oiling the grate gives you, and if you feel it's better to be safe than sorry, go ahead and oil your grate right before grilling—after it has been preheated.

And please don't feel that you can't grill vegetables if you don't have a vegetable grate. I traveled the barbecue train on five continents and only on one—North America—did I find cooks using vegetable grates.

ARGENTINIAN GRILLED EGGPLANT

ARGENTINA

METHOD:
Direct grilling

Argentinians don't generally dilute their staunchly carnivornian meals with superfluous side dishes or vegetables. However, grilled eggplant has become part of the steak house repertoire. The eggplant of choice is a small (4 inches long) Italian variety—the sort you'd find in an Italian market or gourmet shop. Larger eggplants can be cooked this way, too. (If using large eggplant, cut crosswise into ½-inch-thick slices and grill 3 to 5 minutes per side.)

3 small (4 to 6 ounces each) Italian
    eggplants
2 cloves garlic, minced
3 tablespoons olive oil
1 teaspoon dried oregano
1 teaspoon dried basil
½ teaspoon dried thyme
1 teaspoon sweet or hot paprika
½ teaspoon hot red pepper flakes (optional)
Salt and freshly ground black pepper,
    to taste

1. Preheat the grill to high.

2. Cut the eggplants in half lengthwise; do not trim off the stem ends. Mix the garlic and oil in a small bowl. Brush the mixture over the cut sides of the eggplants. Combine the herbs and spices in a small bowl and set aside.

3. When ready to cook, arrange the eggplants, cut sides down, on the hot grate and grill until nicely browned, 3 to 4 minutes.

Lightly brush the skin sides of the eggplants with the oil mixture. Turn the eggplants with tongs and brush the tops with the remaining oil. Sprinkle with the dried herb mixture and salt and black pepper to taste. Continue cooking the eggplants, cut sides up, until the flesh is soft, 6 to 8 minutes more. Serve immediately.

Serves 6

GRILLED FENNEL

ITALY

METHOD:
Direct grilling

ADVANCE PREPARATION:
2 hours for marinating the fennel

You've probably seen it in the produce section of the supermarket: the weird vegetable with the fern-like, feathery leaves, crisp green stalks, and bulbous, green-white bottom. The taste of fresh fennel might well be described as licorice-flavored celery. Grilling seems to bring out its sweetness. Add a sweet-sour balsamic vinegar marinade and you have a vegetable you're not likely to soon forget. It can be served at room temperature as an antipasto or hot as a vegetable side dish. The balsamic vinegar marinade doubles as the dressing.

4 small or 2 large fennel bulbs (1½ to
    2 pounds)
⅓ cup olive oil
⅓ cup balsamic vinegar
2 tablespoons honey
2 cloves garlic, minced
2 small shallots, minced
3 tablespoons chopped fresh tarragon
    or basil
Salt and freshly ground black pepper,
    to taste

1. Cut the stalks and outside leaves off the fennel. (Reserve the stalks for another use, such as the Fennel-Grilled Bass, see

Index.) Cut each bulb lengthwise into ½-inch-wide slices through the narrow side.

2. Combine the oil, vinegar, honey, garlic, shallots, and tarragon in a large nonreactive bowl and whisk to mix. Add the fennel and toss to coat thoroughly. Cover and let marinate for 2 hours, not necessarily in the refrigerator.

3. Preheat the grill to high.

4. When ready to cook, remove the fennel slices from the marinade, arrange on the hot grate, and grill, turning with tongs until just tender, 8 to 16 minutes in all, seasoning with salt and pepper. Toss the grilled fennel with any remaining marinade and serve warm or at room temperature.

Serves 4

GARLIC KEBABS

KOREA

METHOD:
Direct grilling

SPECIAL EQUIPMENT:
8 large toothpicks (no soaking necessary)

These tiny kebabs traditionally accompany Korean grilled meats, like Korean Sesame-Grilled Beef (*bool kogi*; see Index). The grilling imparts a delicate charcoal flavor, while the foil covering prevents the garlic cloves from burning.

2 to 3 heads garlic (for 24 large cloves)
1 tablespoon Asian (dark) sesame oil
Salt and freshly ground black pepper, to taste

1. Preheat the grill to high.
2. Break the heads of garlic into cloves. Peel each clove (see Note). Skewer the garlic cloves crosswise on toothpicks, 3 cloves to a toothpick. Brush the cloves with sesame oil and season with salt and pepper. Loosely wrap each kebab in aluminum foil.

3. When ready to cook, arrange the packets on the hot grate and grill the garlic until tender, about 5 minutes per side, turning with tongs to ensure even cooking. Remove the foil the last few minutes to allow the garlic to brown lightly.
Serves 4 to 8
Note: To loosen the skin, gently flatten the clove using the side of a cleaver. Or use a flexible tube-shaped garlic peeler.

GRILLED LONG BEANS

CARIBBEAN

METHOD:
Direct grilling

SPECIAL EQUIPMENT:
Vegetable grate (optional)

Long beans (aka yard-long beans) are a traditional Chinese vegetable. Shaped like green beans, but up to 18 inches long, they found their way to the Caribbean via the Chinese indentured laborers who came to Trinidad in the mid 1800s. Long beans taste similar to green beans but are a little earthier. Perhaps the niftiest thing about them is that they are so long, you can tie them into decorative knots.

1 pound long beans or green beans
2 tablespoons sesame oil
Salt and freshly ground black pepper, to taste
1 tablespoon sesame seeds, toasted (see box, page 93)

1. Preheat the grill to high.

2. Bring a large pot of salted water to a boil and cook the beans until crisp-tender, about 3 minutes. Refresh under cold running water and drain well. Cut each bean into 8- to 9-inch lengths and tie each into a loose knot (see Note). Let dry on paper towels.

3. When ready to cook, preheat a vegetable grate (if using) for 5 minutes. Brush the knotted beans with sesame oil and sprinkle with salt and pepper. Arrange on the hot grate and grill, turning with tongs, until nicely browned, 4 to 6 minutes in all. Transfer the long beans to plates or a platter, sprinkle with the sesame seeds, and serve immediately.
Serves 4
Note: If using regular beans, thread them, 4 or 5 at a time, crosswise on short bamboo skewers that have been soaked in cold water for 1 hour and drained. Young, slender green beans don't need to be parboiled.

KOREAN GRILLED MUSHROOM AND SCALLION KEBABS

KOREA

METHOD:
Direct grilling

ADVANCE PREPARATION:
1 to 2 hours for marinating the kebabs

SPECIAL EQUIPMENT:
12 long bamboo skewers (or as needed), soaked for 1 hour in cold water to cover and drained

Mushrooms are the perfect vegetable for grilling. The high heat caramelizes the exterior of the mushrooms, intensifying their flavor. The high water content keeps them moist. These virtues aren't lost on Koreans, who enjoy a wide variety of grilled mushroom dishes. These kebabs are vegetarian, but Koreans will often grill mushrooms with strips of chicken or beef.

12 ounces fresh cremini or shiitake mushrooms, stemmed, caps wiped clean with dampened paper towels
2 bunches large scallions, both white and green parts, trimmed
1 medium yellow bell pepper, stemmed, seeded, and cut into 1½ x ½-inch strips
¼ cup soy sauce
3 tablespoons sugar
1 tablespoon Asian (dark) sesame oil
4 cloves garlic, minced
2 tablespoons sesame seeds, toasted (see box, page 93)
½ teaspoon freshly ground black pepper

1. Cut each mushroom into ½-inch-thick slices. Cut the white part of the scallions into pieces the length of the mushroom strips (about 1½ inches long). Finely chop the scallion greens. Thread the mushroom strips onto skewers so they will lie flat on the grill, alternating with scallion whites and bell pepper strips, threaded on crosswise. Arrange the kebabs in a baking dish.

2. Prepare the marinade. Whisk together the soy sauce, sugar, oil, garlic, half the sesame seeds, and the black pepper in a large bowl. Pour the marinade over the kebabs and marinate at room temperature for 1 to 2 hours, turning once.

3. Preheat the grill to high.

4. When ready to cook, arrange the kebabs on the hot grate and grill, turning with tongs and brushing often with the marinade, until the mushrooms are tender and the scallions and pepper are nicely browned, 3 to 5 minutes per side (6 to 10 minutes in all). Sprinkle with the chopped scallion greens and remaining sesame seeds and serve hot or at room temperature.

Serves 4 to 6

SESAME GRILLED OYSTER MUSHROOMS

KOREA

METHOD:
Direct grilling

Oyster mushrooms are elongated gray mushrooms that have something oysterlike about their slippery, softly chewy consistency. If you can't find them, substitute other exotic mushrooms or even quartered white mushrooms, if desired. This recipe was inspired by the Korea House in Seoul, where it was part of a *hanjongshik*, a dazzling array of more than two dozen different miniature dishes that comprise a traditional Korean *table d'hôte*. For ease in grilling, use a vegetable grate.

**SPECIAL
EQUIPMENT:**
*Vegetable grate
or 12 short
bamboo skewers,
soaked for 1 hour
in cold water to
cover and
drained*

1 pound oyster or medium white mushrooms

½ each medium green and red bell pepper,
    stemmed and seeded

2 cloves garlic, minced

3 scallions, both white and green parts,
    trimmed and minced

3 tablespoons soy sauce

1½ tablespoons Asian (dark) sesame oil

1 tablespoon sugar

1 tablespoon sesame seeds, toasted
    (see box, page 93)

Salt and freshly ground black pepper,
    to taste

1. Trim the ends off the oyster mushrooms. Cut the bell pepper halves on the diagonal into thin slices. Combine the garlic, scallions, soy sauce, oil, sugar, sesame seeds, salt, and plenty of black pepper in a small bowl and stir until the sugar is dissolved. Add the mushrooms and peppers and toss to mix. Let marinate for 15 minutes.

2. Preheat the grill to high. When ready to cook, preheat a vegetable grate (if using) for 5 minutes.

3. Remove the mushrooms and peppers from the marinade. If not using a vegetable grate, thread them onto skewers. Arrange on the hot grate. Grill, turning with tongs, until the vegetables are nicely browned and tender, 3 to 5 minutes per side (6 to 10 minutes in all). Transfer to a platter, plates, or bowls and serve (see Note).

Serves 4 to 6

Note: This dish can be served hot, cold, or at room temperature. Koreans tend to serve side dishes like this at room temperature.

SHIITAKE AND SCALLION KEBABS

JAPAN

METHOD:
Direct grilling

**SPECIAL
EQUIPMENT:**
*8 long bamboo
skewers, soaked
for 1 hour in cold
water to cover
and drained*

These colorful kebabs turn up at yakitori joints around Tokyo and make a wonderful side dish or vegetarian appetizer. I love the way the flavor of the grilled scallions permeates the shiitakes. Fresh shiitakes are widely available, but you could also use dried Chinese black mushrooms (soaked in hot water for 20 minutes) or another type of mushroom.

1 bunch large scallions, both white and
    green parts, trimmed

24 small fresh shiitakes, stemmed,
    caps wiped clean with dampened
    paper towels

3 tablespoons soy sauce

3 tablespoons mirin (sweet rice wine) or
    cream sherry

1 tablespoon sugar

1 clove garlic, minced

1. Preheat the grill to high.

2. Cut the scallions crosswise into pieces the size of the mushroom caps, about 1½ inches. Thread the shiitake caps onto the skewers so they will lie flat on the grill, alternating with pieces of scallion, threaded on crosswise. There should be 3 mushroom caps and 4 scallion pieces on each kebab. Reserve any leftover scallion pieces for another use.

3. Combine the soy sauce, mirin, sugar, and garlic in a small bowl and whisk until the sugar is dissolved.

4. When ready to cook, arrange the kebabs on the hot grate and grill, turning with tongs and brushing with the soy mixture, until the shiitakes are tender and the scallions are nicely browned, 3 to 5 minutes per side (6 to 10 in all). Serve immediately.

Serves 4 as an appetizer or side dish

The Japanese Grill

To most people, Japanese food means sushi, sashimi, sukiyaki, or soba noodles. You may be surprised to learn that Japan has a venerable tradition of grilling. Actually, two traditions of grilling exist here: an haute cuisine style called *robatayaki* and a more populist style called yakitori. This became clear on a recent trip to a country that happens to be especially dear to me: I was born in Nagoya, Japan.

In the course of my grill hopping in Japan, I savored delicate *dengaku* (tofu grilled on "stilts") at a tranquil tea house on the Philosopher's Walk in Kyoto. I munched crisp barbecued rice cakes brushed with mouth-puckeringly tart plum paste from street vendors outside Tokyo's venerated Sensoji Temple. I ate chicken teriyaki and miso-glazed eggplants in the rough and tumble yakitori joints under the train station near the neon-lit Ginza. But my ultimate experience in Japanese grilling was dinner at Tokyo's Inakaya.

Unassuming from the outside, the restaurant occupies the second floor of a small, post-war high-rise in the fashionable Rapongi district. You pass by a bowl of salt (a symbol of hospitality) and a bamboo vase filled with peach blossoms on your way to a dining experience quite unlike anything in North America.

VERY WELCOMED GUESTS

The moment my wife, Barbara, and I entered, a waiter in a blue and white robe shouted out our arrival. His co-workers repeated the announcement in voices that could have roused the dead. We took our seats amid more shouting ("the customer is sitting down," "the customer is ordering") at a U-shaped bar surrounding a dazzling, market-like array of ingredients. There were wicker baskets filled with vegetables (okra, shiitakes, leeks, yams, and baby taro roots to name a few); glistening blocks of ice piled with whole fish, giant prawns, and monstrously large king crab claws; trays of pork, chicken, and marbled kobe beef. I tried to enumerate the individual items displayed here, but lost count after forty.

Kneeling on a platform overlooking all this bounty is a chef wearing a blue and white bandana around his head. We ordered sake. There was another round of shouting and the chef thrust a 10-foot-long wooden paddle at us with a small wooden box in a bowl at the end. A waiter appeared with a flask and filled the bowl with sake, spilling the wine into the shallow box

underneath. Generosity is the name of the game at Inakaya, and for the next two hours we were treated to a largesse that bordered on conspicuous consumption.

Appetizers arrived without our ordering them: a plate of sashimi, a small carrot and *kampyo* (gourd) salad, a cold kebab of Kobe beef, the world's most expensive meat. (The cows are raised on beer and massaged to make the meat tender.) We don't speak Japanese, so we pointed to the various ingredients displayed on the U-shaped counter in front of the chef and the real meal—the *robatayaki*—began.

Robatayaki takes its name from the Japanese words *ro* and *yaki*. The former refers to a square hearth around which peasants would gather for warmth and cooking. *Yaki* means "grilled," and in the old days the grilling would have been done over charcoal. Many yakitori parlors still grill this way, but Inakaya takes a more high tech approach, cooking the food over infrared gas grills that are tiny by American standards. Our entire dinner was cooked on a grill not much longer than my forearm and not much wider than the palm of my hand.

In rapid succession we were served tiny kebabs of grilled asparagus, shiitake mushroom caps, even okra. (The latter are downright amazing grilled.) Nothing is too weird for a *robatayaki* chef: baby yams, quail eggs, even ginko nuts, which taste like waxy potatoes. The shouting goes unabated, the paddle delivers an endless succession of treats. We wanted to continue like this for the rest of the evening, which is exactly what we did.

Perhaps the most remarkable aspect of *robatayaki*—even beyond the noisy theatrics and belt-loosening generosity—is the utter simplicity of the preparation. Sure, there's a brushing of teriyaki sauce here. A dollop of miso sauce there. A drizzle of melted butter. But most of the fare is seasoned solely with salt. The flavors are direct and natural, but from these simple seasonings the chef creates a symphonic range of flavor. The tallest soufflé, the richest French pastry couldn't rival the simple, unadorned slice of exquisitely ripe melon Inakaya serves for dessert.

Given the meticulousness of Japanese cooking, the precise, almost painterly plate presentations, it's easy to lose sight of the joyful aspect of Japanese cuisine. Yet joyful and festive are the operative words at Inakaya, not to mention at virtually every place we dined in Japan. You might expect such refined food to be eaten in sacerdotal silence. But Japanese epicures drink hard and party heartily—especially when partaking of their favorite foods.

HAPPY HOUR, JAPANESE-STYLE

This is especially true at the yakitori joints one finds in or under virtually all of the train stations in Tokyo. The yak-

itori parlor is a uniquely Japanese institution: part pub, part barbecue joint, to which Japanese office workers (aka "salary men") flock after work for a snack, a cigarette, a couple of beers, and some ear-splitting conversation before embarking on the long commute home by train.

The yakitori parlor isn't big (some have only a half dozen seats) and it certainly isn't fancy. For example, one of the most famous yakitori parlors in Tokyo, Tonton, doesn't even have four walls. But to come to Japan without visiting a yakitori parlor would be missing an important cultural experience.

Yakitori takes its name from the Japanese words for "grilled" *(yaki)* and "chicken" *(tori).* Unlike upscale grill restaurants, like Inakaya, yakitori parlors still use charcoal grills—often a trough-like brazier mounted on legs in the front of the restaurant. The traditional charcoal is *bincho,* made from the slow-burning holm oak in the Wakayama Prefecture near Kyoto.

According to some authorities, yakitori (or at least the practice of grilling) originated with Dutch traders who settled in Nagasaki. Indeed, one popular Tokyo yakitori chain goes by the name Nanbantei, literally, "Restaurant of the Southern Barbarians," which is what the Japanese called the early European traders.

As for the *tori* (chicken), most yakitori parlors offer an impressive selection of different cuts. There are *momo yaki* (chicken legs—preferred to breast meat because they have more fat and flavor), *shiitake toriyaki* (chicken and mushroom kebabs), *negi toriyaki*

(chicken and leek kebabs), and *tsukune yaki* (chicken meatballs). Adventurous eaters can move on to *kawa yaki* (grilled chicken skin), *hatsu yaki* (chicken hearts), *bonchiri yaki* ("pope's noses"), and *uzura yaki* (grilled quail eggs). Nor are vegetarians neglected: just order some *nasu yaki* (grilled eggplant brushed with miso glaze), *piiman yaki* (tiny grilled peppers), or *ginnan yaki* (grilled ginkgo nuts).

Not bad for a restaurant that in most incarnations occupies less space than your bedroom! You pay by the skewer, which makes yakitori relatively inexpensive. (This is one of the few dining experiences you will have in Tokyo that leaves you change from a 2,000 yen note—about $16.) The traditional beverage at a *yakitori* parlor is beer.

In the West (particularly in North and South America), the quality of a barbecue is measured in part by how many notches it forces you to loosen your belt. You'd certainly never call it health food. How different is Japanese grilling! Whether at a *robatayaki* restaurant or at a humble yakitori joint, meats are used almost as a condiment. Sauces tend to be based on broths, not oils, eggs, or other fats. The portions are moderate, even modest, with most items being served in bite-size pieces. Small is beautiful in Japan. The food, at least, speaks to you in whispers, not shouts.

For me this sense of moderation is the most important lesson Western grill buffs can learn from Japan. That, and to keep shouting and have fun.

CHORIZO GRILLED MUSHROOMS

SPAIN

METHOD:
Indirect grilling

**SPECIAL
EQUIPMENT:**
*Vegetable grate
(optional)*

Mushroom caps grilled with chorizo, garlic, and olive oil are a popular Spanish tapa—so popular, in fact, that there's a tapas bar in Madrid, the Mesón de Champinone, that serves this and only this dish. The Mesón stands in a row of tapas bars—each with its own specialty—built directly into the retaining wall of the Plaza Mayor. It should be noted that the Mesón cooks its mushroom caps on a *plancha* (griddle), but grilling produces a more interesting flavor. It's also a lot more fun because you get to do it outdoors. This recipe can be served either as an appetizer or as a vegetable side dish.

16 large white mushrooms, stemmed, caps
   wiped clean with dampened paper towels
⅓ **cup olive oil, or more as needed**
4 slices (each ¼ inch thick) cooked chorizo
   sausage (see Note)
4 cloves garlic, minced
¼ **cup chopped Italian (flat-leaf) parsley**
½ **lemon**
Salt and freshly ground black pepper, to taste

1. Set up the grill for indirect cooking (see page 14 or 16) and preheat to high.

2. Generously brush the mushroom caps on both sides with some of the oil and place in a baking dish.

3. Cut each chorizo slice in quarters and place one quarter in each mushroom cap. Divide the garlic and parsley among the mushroom caps. Squeeze a little lemon juice into each mushroom cap and drizzle with any remaining oil. Generously season the mushrooms with salt and pepper.

4. When ready to cook, preheat a vegetable grate (if using) for 5 minutes. Arrange the mushrooms in the center of the hot grate, away from the heat. Cover the grill and cook the mushrooms until tender and nicely browned and the sausage and garlic are sizzling, about 20 minutes. For a smokier flavor, move the mushroom caps directly over the flames for the last 5 minutes of grilling. Transfer the mushrooms to a platter and stick a toothpick in each for serving.

Serves 4 as an appetizer, 8 as a side dish
Note: Chorizo is a spicy Spanish sausage. I've also prepared these mushroom caps with country ham instead of chorizo. You'd need about 2 ounces ham cut into tiny slivers.

GRILLED MUSHROOM CAPS WITH ARUGULA BUTTER

U.S.A.

METHOD:
Indirect grilling

Stuffed mushrooms was one of the first dishes I ever learned to make and I'm still fascinated by the fungus's ability to absorb the flavors of a filling while retaining its own. I like to make this dish with jumbo mushroom caps, behemoths measuring 3 inches across that seem custom grown for stuffing. I fill them with arugula butter and cook them on the grill using the indirect method. Amazing!

1 bunch arugula, stemmed, rinsed, spun dry, and coarsely chopped
1 clove garlic, minced
8 tablespoons (1 stick) unsalted butter, at room temperature
Salt and freshly ground black pepper, to taste
Few drops fresh lemon juice
8 jumbo or 16 large white mushrooms, stemmed, caps wiped clean with dampened paper towels
¼ cup freshly grated Parmesan cheese

1. Set up the grill for indirect cooking (see page 14 or 16) and preheat to high.

2. Prepare the arugula butter. Finely chop the arugula and garlic in a food processor. Add the butter, salt, pepper, and lemon juice. Process until smooth. Spread the butter in the mushroom caps and sprinkle the cheese over the top.

3. When ready to cook, preheat a vegetable grate (if using) for 5 minutes. Arrange the mushrooms in the center of the hot grate (away from the heat). Cover the grill and cook the mushrooms until browned and tender and the butter is melted and sizzling, about 20 minutes. For a smokier flavor, place the mushroom caps directly over the flame for the last 5 minutes. Serve immediately.

Serves 8 as an appetizer, 4 as an entrée

GRILLED OKRA

Okra is the vegetable people love to hate. What they dislike is its tendency to get slimy, especially when boiled or stewed. Others, like me, are drawn to its sweet, earthy flavor. I discovered grilled okra in Tokyo, where it's part of a stunning array of grilled vegetables, meats, and seafood served at a *robatayaki* restaurant (which specializes in Japanese grilling). For a Mediterranean touch, use olive oil instead.

1 pound fresh okra (see Note)
1 tablespoon Asian (dark) sesame oil or extra-virgin olive oil
Salt and freshly ground black pepper, to taste

1. Preheat the grill to high.

2. Trim the tips off the stems of the okra, but do not cut into the pods. This would expose the insides to air, making the okra slimy. Lay 4 or 5 okra side by side in a neat row at the edge of a cutting board. Stick a bamboo skewer through each end of each piece. The idea is to hold them flat for grilling. Transfer the skewered okra to a platter. Lightly brush both sides with sesame oil and season with salt and pepper.

3. When ready to cook, arrange the okra on the hot grate and grill, turning with a flat spatula, until tender and lightly browned, about 4 to 5 minutes per side (8 to 10 minutes in all). Serve the okra at once, letting everyone remove their own skewers.

Serves 4

Note: When buying okra, choose smallish pods of uniform size. They should be about the length and width of your forefinger. Look for crispy, springy, bright green pods, avoiding okra that look brown or shriveled.

GRILLED GREEN ONIONS ROMESCO
Calçots

SPAIN

METHOD:
Direct grilling

ADVANCE PREPARATION:
1 hour to steam onions after grilling

Succulent, tender *calçots* (pronounced "CAL-sots") are Catalan green onions. And what onions! Sweet, fleshy shoots are buried with earth as they grow (much like Belgian endives) to keep them pale and delicately flavored. The *calçots* are charred over burning vine trimmings, then wrapped in newspapers to steam and finish cooking. Every January, when *calçots* are harvested, huge *calçadas* (onion feasts) take place throughout Catalonia. Traditionally the onions are dipped in an almond and roasted tomato sauce called *romesco* and messily devoured by hand. But, you can also enjoy them with olive oil, salt, and pepper.

Note that this recipe can be prepared with green onions or large scallions. I particularly like using green Vidalia onions, which are available from December to April from Bland Farms (see Mail-Order-Sources).

2 bunches green onions or 4 bunches large scallions, both white and green parts, trimmed
Coarse (kosher or sea) salt, to taste
Romesco Sauce, for serving (optional; page 469)
Spanish olive oil, for serving (optional)
Freshly ground black pepper, to taste, for serving (optional)

1. Preheat the grill to high.

2. When ready to cook, arrange the onions on the hot grate and grill, turning with tongs, until charred all over, 8 to 12 minutes (scallions will take less time than green onions). Season the onions with plenty of salt as they cook. Wrap the charred onions in a thick layer of paper towels (or use newspaper as they do in Spain). Let rest for 15 minutes.

3. Unwrap the onions and pick away the charred skin with your fingers. Serve warm with Romesco Sauce for dipping or drizzle with oil and pepper and pop them into your mouth.

Serves 4

MARINATED GRILLED PEPPERS WITH OLIVES AND ANCHOVIES

ITALY

METHOD:
Direct grilling

Like most Italian grilled dishes, this one is simple. Good results depend on the quality of the raw ingredients, rather than on complex marinades or lots of ingredients. You can use any type of bell pepper or even a kaleidoscopic mixture of red, green, yellow, and purple peppers. I first tasted the dish done solely with red bell peppers and that's how I prefer it. For a more rustic dish, leave the pepper skins on as I do here. For a more refined dish, grill the peppers whole and peel them as described in the box on page 372.

3 medium red bell peppers
¼ cup extra-virgin olive oil
Coarse (kosher or sea) salt and
    freshly ground black pepper,
    to taste
2 to 4 oil-packed anchovies,
    drained and cut into
    ¼-inch pieces
2 tablespoons drained capers
4 fresh basil leaves, thinly slivered
¼ cup niçoise or other oil-cured
    black olives
1 tablespoon balsamic vinegar
    (or to taste)

1. Preheat the grill to high.

2. Halve, stem, and seed the bell peppers. Cut each half lengthwise into 2 pieces. Toss the pepper pieces with 1 tablespoon of the oil and salt and pepper.

3. When ready to cook, preheat a vegetable grate (if using) for 5 minutes. Arrange the peppers on the hot grate and grill, turning with tongs, until blistered and nicely browned all over, 3 to 5 minutes per side (6 to 10 minutes in all). Transfer to a cutting board and let cool. Cut each piece into ½-inch-wide strips. Place the strips in a shallow serving bowl.

4. Add the anchovies, capers, basil leaves, olives, balsamic vinegar, and remaining oil to the bowl with the peppers and stir to combine. Marinate for at least 15 minutes or as long as 2 hours before serving.

Serves 4 to 6 as an appetizer or a side dish

GRILLED PLANTAINS

CARIBBEAN

METHOD:
Direct grilling

The plantain is a jumbo cousin of the banana. It's always served cooked, usually as a starch or vegetable. A green plantain tastes bland like a potato. When ripe (the skin will be black), it becomes as sweet as a ripe banana. Both green and ripe plantains can be grilled, but I prefer the latter: The fire caramelizes the sugars in the plantains and makes them candy sweet. The plantain pieces are grilled in their skins, which keeps them moist and tender.

4 very ripe (black) plantains, unpeeled
    (see Note)

1. Preheat the grill to high.
2. Cut 1 inch off each end of the plan-

tains, then cut each plantain crosswise into 2-inch pieces.

3. When ready to cook, place the plantains on the hot grate and grill, turning often with tongs, until the skins are charred, the exposed ends are nicely caramelized, and the flesh in the center is soft. This will take 12 to 15 minutes. To test for softness, press the plaintains with your finger.

4. Serve the grilled plantains in the skins. Cut off the skin before eating.

Serves 4

Note: If you live in an area with a large Hispanic community, you may be able to buy ripe plantains. Otherwise, let green ones ripen at room temperature until the skin is black. (This can take up to a week.)

TWO FOIL-GRILLED POTATOES

The inspirations for the following similarly prepared recipes—both great—couldn't hail from two more disparate sources. When my wife, Barbara, was a young girl, she and her bunkmates at summer camp would prepare a campfire dish called potatoes à la ketchup. Sliced potatoes were tossed with ketchup and butter and grilled in a foil bundle on the fire. Eaten steamy hot, they were camp comfort food at its best. Years later, in quite a different setting, we had another foil-grilled potato dish—this one flavored with sesame seeds and soy sauce—at a Japanese steak house at the Sahid Jaya Hotel in Jakarta.

U.S.A.

METHOD:
Indirect grilling

Potatoes à la Ketchup

Yukon Gold potatoes were not available when Barbara was a kid, but we love their buttery flavor when we make this dish today.

2 tablespoons ketchup
1 tablespoon Worcestershire sauce
1 tablespoon fresh lemon juice
4 tablespoons (½ stick) unsalted butter,
    at room temperature
4 medium potatoes (each about 6 ounces),
    cut into ¼-inch slices
1 small onion, thinly sliced
Salt and freshly ground black pepper, to taste

1. Set up the grill for indirect grilling (see page 14 or 16) and preheat to medium.
2. Mix the ketchup, Worcestershire sauce, and lemon juice in a small bowl and set aside.

3. Cut 4 sheets of heavy-duty aluminum foil, each 14 × 8 inches. Place a sheet of foil, shiny side down, narrow edge toward you, on the work surface. Smear a tablespoon of the butter in the center of the bottom half of the rectangle (the half closest to you). Arrange one-quarter of the potatoes in a mound on top of the butter. Place one-quarter of the onion on top of the potatoes. Spoon 1 tablespoon of the ketchup mixture over the potatoes and season with salt and pepper. Fold the top half of the foil over the potatoes and bring the top and bottom edges together. Fold the edges over several times to make a tight seal. Prepare the remaining packages the same way.
4. When ready to cook, place the foil packages in the center of the hot grate, away from the heat. Cover the grill and cook until the packages are dramatically puffed, 20 to 30 minutes.
5. Serve, warning everyone to open the packages at arm's length, using knives and forks, as the escaping steam will be very hot.
Serves 4

Black Gold

Back in the nineteenth century, when you could buy a black truffle without having to take out a second mortgage, the French would cook truffles in the coals as described in the recipe for onions and potatoes on the facing page. Should you win the lottery, this is a wonderfully extravagant way to enjoy the odoriferous black fungus. You'd need 15 to 20 minutes' cooking time for a 2-inch truffle.

INDONESIA

METHOD:
Indirect grilling

Foil-Grilled Potatoes with Asian Seasonings

Most Westerners don't associate potatoes with Asian seasonings, such as ginger and soy sauce, but the combination is really quite pleasing.

4 tablespoons (½ stick) unsalted butter,
   at room temperature
4 medium potatoes (each about 6 ounces),
   cut into ¼-inch slices
2 tablespoons soy sauce
2 tablespoons sesame seeds, toasted
   (see box, page 93)

1 clove garlic, thinly sliced
2 scallions, both white and green parts,
   trimmed and finely chopped
Salt and freshly ground black pepper,
   to taste

1. Set up the grill for indirect grilling (see page 14 or 16) and preheat to medium.

2. Prepare the packages as described in steps 2 and 3 of the preceding recipe, topping the potatoes with a mixture of soy sauce, sesame seeds, sliced garlic, and chopped scallions. Season with salt and pepper before closing the packages.

3. Grill as described in step 4 above and serve, warning everyone to watch out for the hot steam, which will escape when the packages are opened.
Serves 4

ONIONS AND POTATOES GRILLED IN THE COALS

EUROPE

METHOD:
Direct grilling

This is the most basic, primal way to cook root vegetables—a method as old as mankind itself. The process is simple enough: You bury the vegetables in a mound of glowing coals. The exterior burns, imparting a wonderful smoke flavor, leaving the flesh inside sweet and tender. Sweet onions like Vidalias or Walla Wallas work particularly well for this style of cooking, as do rich-fleshed potatoes, like Yukon Golds.

FOR GRILLING:
4 large baking potatoes, in their skins
4 large sweet onions, in their skins

FOR SERVING:
Balsamic vinegar
Extra-virgin olive oil
Coarse (kosher or sea) salt and
   freshly ground black pepper,
   to taste
Unsalted butter
Sour cream

1. Preheat a charcoal grill to high.

2. When ready to cook, rake half the coals to one side. Place the potatoes and onions on top of the remaining coals, keeping the potatoes together and the onions together (they may cook at different rates, and this allows you to remove each when it's done). Using tongs, place the reserved coals on top of the vegetables.

3. Grill the vegetables, until very soft, 20 to 30 minutes for the onions, 40 to 60 minutes for the potatoes. To test for doneness, poke a skewer into the center of each kind of vegetable. It should slip in very easily. Remove the vegetables from the coals with tongs. Brush away the ashes with a pastry brush and place the vegetables on a platter for serving.

4. To eat, cut open the onions and potatoes and eat the flesh out of the skin (the skin of the potatoes will be too ashy to eat). Sprinkle the onions with a few drops of balsamic vinegar, oil, and salt and pepper (if desired; it's pretty darn good by itself). Eat the potato with butter and/or sour cream, and salt and pepper.

Serves 4

PERUVIAN POTATO MIXED GRILL

PERU

METHOD:
Direct grilling

SPECIAL EQUIPMENT:
Vegetable grate

Where did the universally popular potato originate? There are numerous theories, but the evidence seems to point to Peru. This mountainous country in northern South America is the home of such distinctive potatoes as the purple potato and *camote* (a type of sweet potato, but not as sweet as ours). In fact, Peru probably grows more different types of potatoes than any other country in the world. The following recipe uses a variety of Peruvian potatoes, which are available at gourmet shops and specialty greengrocers. (The Yukon Gold isn't strictly traditional, but it sure tastes good). The purple potato tastes similar to the North American boiling potato. The *camote* has a mild, nutty, semisweet flavor reminiscent of roasted chestnuts.

2 pounds mixed potatoes, including purple potatoes, camotes or sweet potatoes, boniatos (Caribbean sweet potatoes), and/or Yukon Gold potatoes, unpeeled
4 tablespoons (½ stick) unsalted butter, or ¼ cup olive oil
2 cloves garlic, minced
2 tablespoons chopped fresh Italian (flat-leaf) parsley
Salt and freshly ground black pepper, to taste

1. Place the potatoes in a large pot and add cold water to cover. Bring to a boil over medium heat and cook, uncovered, until tender, about 10 minutes for small potatoes, 20 to 30 minutes for large. Drain the potatoes, then rinse under cold running water to stop the cooking. Peel them with a paring knife and cut lengthwise into ½-inch-thick slices.

2. Preheat the grill to high.

3. Melt the butter, with the garlic and parsley, in a saucepan over high heat. Bring to a sizzle and cook, but do not let the garlic brown. Remove the pan from the heat.

4. When ready to cook, preheat a vegetable grate for 5 minutes. Brush the potato slices with the butter mixture and arrange them on the hot grate. Grill, turning with tongs, until golden brown on both sides, 2 to 3 minutes per side. Season the potatoes with salt and pepper as they cook. Serve immediately.

Serves 4 to 6

GREEK GARLIC AND LEMON ROASTED POTATOES

GREECE

METHOD:
Indirect grilling

SPECIAL EQUIPMENT:
1 cup wood chips, soaked for 1 hour in cold water to cover and drained

These potatoes are a traditional accompaniment to Greek spit-roasted lamb (see Index). Lemon is one of the dominating flavors, and although North Americans don't usually associate it with potatoes, I must say it adds a whole new dimension. For extra richness, stir a few tablespoons of butter into the potatoes at the end.

3 pounds small red potatoes, scrubbed and cut in half
¼ cup extra-virgin olive oil
4 cloves garlic, coarsely chopped
2 bay leaves
1 teaspoon dried oregano
Coarse (kosher or sea) salt and freshly ground black pepper, to taste
1 lemon, cut in half
2 tablespoons unsalted butter (optional)
2 tablespoons chopped fresh dill

1. Set up the grill for indirect cooking (see page 14 or 16). *If using a charcoal grill,* preheat to medium.

If using a gas grill, place the wood chips in the smoker box and preheat to high. When smoke appears, turn the heat down to medium.

2. Place the potatoes in a roasting pan and toss with the oil, garlic, bay leaves, oregano, salt, and pepper. Squeeze lemon juice over the potatoes, then place the rind halves on top.

3. When ready to cook, if using a charcoal grill, toss the wood chips on the coals. Set the roasting pan in the center of the grill. Cook the potatoes, with the grill covered, until browned and tender, 1 to 1¼ hours, stirring from time to time to ensure even cooking. Stir in the butter (if using) and dill the last 10 minutes of cooking.

4. To serve, remove and discard the lemon rinds and bay leaves. Taste for seasoning, adding salt and pepper, and serve.

Serves 6 to 8

GRILLED SWEET POTATOES WITH SESAME DIPPING SAUCE

KOREA

METHOD:
Direct grilling

Grilled sweet potatoes are a popular Korean street food. I first partook of this snack at the Tongdaemun Market in Seoul, where it offered a double dose of pleasure. The first was gustatory: the unexpected contrast between the sweetness of the potato and the sesame saltiness of the dipping sauce. The second pleasure was purely tactile: the potato has a wonderful way of warming your hands in Korea's frigid winter air. Sweet potatoes were brought to Korea from Japan in the eighteenth century as a famine-prevention food, and there's nothing quite as satisfying to eat as you're strolling through the market. If you're used to the butter/brown sugar approach to sweet potatoes, this preparation will come as a revelation.

4 medium sweet potatoes (each 4 to
    5 inches long and about
    1½ inches wide)
5 tablespoons soy sauce
5 tablespoons sake or dry sherry
2 tablespoons sugar
2 scallions, both white and green
    parts, trimmed and minced
2 cloves garlic, minced
2 tablespoons sesame seeds, toasted
    (see box, page 93)

1. Preheat the grill to medium-high.

2. Scrub the potato skins and blot dry with paper towels.

3. When ready to cook, oil the grill grate. Place the sweet potatoes on the hot grate and grill, turning often with tongs, until very well browned and squeezably soft, 30 to 50 minutes.

4. Meanwhile, prepare the sauce. Combine the soy sauce, sake, sugar, scallions, garlic, and sesame seeds in a small bowl and whisk until blended and the sugar is dissolved. Spoon the sauce into 4 small bowls or ramekins.

5. Serve the sweet potatoes with bowls of sauce. To eat out of hand, simply dip the potatoes in the sauce and eat away. To serve as a side dish, cut open the potatoes and spoon the sauce over them.

Serves 4

WEST INDIAN PUMPKIN GRATIN

CARIBBEAN

METHOD:
Indirect grilling

This recipe is one of my favorite ways to prepare pumpkin. It is especially good served with Jamaican Jerk Pork, Buccaneer Chicken, or Bahamian Grilled Chicken (see Index), or just about any grilled dish from the Caribbean. It does require using your grill twice, however, first to cook the pumpkin, then to grill the gratin. For this reason, you may wish to prepare the pumpkin on the weekend (when you have plenty of time) and grill the gratin just before serving. This gives an added benefit, too. If bad weather should prevent you from grilling the following day, you can always finish the gratin in the oven. I guarantee the extra grilling is worth the effort—this is one of the tastiest gratins ever!

The traditional pumpkin for this recipe is calabaza, a dense, heavy, dark orange squash with an intense pumpkiny flavor. Calabaza is sold in halves or pieces. The closest squash in North America would be a butternut.

1 piece (about 2 pounds) calabaza or
    2 medium butternut squash
2 cloves garlic
3 tablespoons unsalted butter, chilled, cut
    into ¼-inch pieces, plus additional for
    greasing the gratin dish
1 cup heavy cream
Salt and freshly ground black pepper,
    to taste
Freshly grated nutmeg, to taste
1 cup freshly grated Parmesan cheese
3 tablespoons fresh bread crumbs, toasted
    (see box, page 93)

1. Set up the grill for indirect grilling (see page 14 or 16) and preheat to medium.

2. Scoop the seeds out of the calabaza (or halve and seed the butternut squash) and wrap it loosely in aluminum foil.

3. When ready to cook, place the calabaza on the grill in the center, away from the heat. Cover the grill and cook until the calabaza is very tender, about 1 hour. Remove the calabaza, open the foil (being careful of the escaping steam), and let cool to room temperature.

4. Trim the skin off the calabaza and cut the flesh into 1/4-inch-thick slices. Mince one of the garlic cloves and set aside. Cut the remaining garlic clove in half and rub a 10-inch gratin dish with it; lightly butter the dish. Arrange one-fourth of the calabaza in a layer in the bottom of the dish. Pour one-third of the cream on top, and sprinkle with salt, pepper, nutmeg, one-third of the minced garlic and cheese, and some of the butter pieces. Add another layer of calabaza and top with half the remaining cream, the salt, pepper, nutmeg, half the garlic and cheese, and butter (save a little butter for the top). Continue in this fashion to make another complete layer. Top with the remaining calabaza, sprinkle the bread crumbs over the gratin, and dot with the remaining butter. The recipe can be prepared ahead to this stage. If making ahead, cover loosely with plastic wrap and refrigerate until ready to grill.

5. When ready to cook, place the gratin on the hot grate in the center, away from the heat. Cover and cook until the gratin is crusty and brown, 20 to 30 minutes. Serve immediately. If finishing the dish the next day, you'll have to set up the grill for indirect grilling again and preheat to high.

If making and serving the gratin on the same day, you'll need to add 10 to 12 fresh coals per side to bring the grill heat up to high.

Serves 6 to 8

GRILLED DILLED TOMATOES

CENTRAL ASIA

METHOD:
Direct grilling

SPECIAL EQUIPMENT:
2 long, flat metal skewers

Grilled tomatoes accompany kebabs throughout Central Asia, from Iraq to the Republic of Georgia. Use smallish tomatoes (2½ to 3 inches across) that are firm but ripe. Flat metal skewers work the best for holding the tomatoes, which would slip off a slim metal skewer.

8 fresh, ripe tomatoes or plum
    tomatoes
2 tablespoons olive oil
Salt and freshly ground black pepper,
    to taste
2 tablespoons chopped fresh dill

1. Preheat the grill to high.

2. Thread the tomatoes on the skewers, brush with oil, and season with salt and pepper.

3. When ready to cook, place the skewers on the hot grate and grill the tomatoes, turning as necessary, until the skins are charred and blistered and the flesh inside is hot and soft, about 8 to 12 minutes in all. Ease the tomatoes off the skewers with a fork, then sprinkle the tomatoes with dill and serve immediately.

Serves 4

Vegetarian Grill

Garden-fresh produce makes vegetarian grilling a snap.

Traditionally, the American barbecue was a relentless procession of meat dishes. If you didn't like hamburgers, hot dogs, shish kebab, or steak, you were pretty much out of luck. No wonder many vegetarians found it easier to stay at home rather than to deal with making a meal from coleslaw and potato salad.

Fortunately, times have changed. As more and more Americans switch to at least a partially vegetarian diet, professional chefs and pit masters have turned their talents to meatless grilling. The notion of a vegetarian barbecue has gone from the fringe full force into the culinary mainstream.

This chapter focuses on some of the world's great grilled vegetarian entrées, from Swiss raclette to Indian vegetable kebabs to Japanese *dengaku* (a whimsical dish whose name means "tofu on stilts"). Who says you need to eat meat to have a great time at a barbecue?

THE ORIGINAL GRILLED PIZZA

U.S.A.

METHOD:
*Direct grilling
(two-tiered)*

**ADVANCE
PREPARATION:**
*2 to 3 hours for
making and
raising the dough*

I'll never forget the first time I tasted grilled pizza. The year was 1985; the place was Al Forno restaurant in Providence, Rhode Island. The waitress set before me a rectangle of dough, cracker crisp at the edges, smokily singed on the bottom, moistly chewy in the center, and simply topped with puddles of fresh tomato sauce, a dusting of grated cheese, and a handful of chopped fresh basil. It was everything pizza should be—and more—boasting the primeval smoke flavor of Indian tandoori breads with the puffy moistness of freshly baked pita. It was love at first bite.

Al Forno owners Johanne Killeen and George Germon, created their grilled pizza somewhat by accident. "A vendor told us about a grilled pizza he'd had in Italy," recalls Johanne. "We realized he had probably mistaken a wood-fired oven for a grill, but we were intrigued enough to try to cook the dough on the grill."

Grilled pizza is easy to make, impressive to serve, and about one of the best tasting things you'll ever put in your mouth. Just remember a few simple watchpoints. First, set up the grill so that you have a hotter section (over which to sear the dough) and a cooler section (over which to keep it warm without burning the bottom while you put on the toppings). See the instructions for two-tiered grilling on page 14.

Second, make the pizzas by stretching out the dough in oil instead of rolling it in flour. (The oil helps the dough crisp.) The first stretch will shrink most of the way back. Keep stretching; eventually, you'll achieve the proper shape and thinness.

Finally, keep in mind that the topping goes on a grilled pizza in the opposite sequence of a conventional pizza: first the

oil, then the cheese, finally the tomato sauce or tomatoes. This allows the cheese to melt even though it isn't exposed to direct heat.

Here's the basic dough, plus two grilled pizzas that will change the way you think about pizza forever.

Basic Pizza Dough

Al Forno's dough owes its earthy flavor to the use of three types of flour: white, whole wheat, and stone-ground cornmeal.

1 cup warm water
1 envelope active dry yeast
1 teaspoon sugar
2 teaspoons (kosher or sea) salt
3 tablespoons fine white cornmeal
3 tablespoons whole-wheat flour
**1 tablespoon extra-virgin olive oil,
    plus oil for the bowl**
**3 to 3½ cups unbleached all-purpose
    flour, or as needed**

1. Place the water in a large bowl and add the yeast and sugar. Stir to dissolve and let sit 5 minutes, then stir in the salt, cornmeal, whole-wheat flour, and oil. Gradually stir in enough all-purpose flour to form a dough that comes away from the sides of the bowl. Knead the dough on a floured work surface, or in a food processor or mixer fitted with the dough hook, until smooth and elastic. The dough should be soft and pliable, but not sticky. Kneading should take 6 to 8 minutes.

2. Lightly oil a clean large bowl. Place the

dough in the bowl, brush the top with oil, and cover loosely with plastic wrap. Let the dough rise in a warm, draft-free spot until doubled in bulk, 1 to 2 hours. Punch down the dough.

3. Let the dough rise until doubled in bulk again, 40 to 50 minutes. Punch it down. Divide the dough into 2 equal pieces. Shape each into a ball, then flatten them slightly so they resemble thick disks. You're now ready to make the pizzas.

Makes enough for two 13 X 9-inch rectangular pizzas

Grilled Pizza with Tomato, Basil, and Cheese

Here's a grilled version of the simplest of all pizzas, the *margherita*. To heighten the grilled flavor, I like to char the tomatoes over the fire. Once the slices are charred, you can dice them before topping the crust.

2 large fresh, ripe tomatoes, cored
6 tablespoons extra-virgin olive oil, or
    as needed
Coarse (kosher or sea) salt and freshly
    ground black pepper, to taste
1 recipe Basic Pizza Dough (see above)
2 cloves garlic, minced
²/₃ cup shredded or diced Italian
    Fontina cheese
¹/₃ cup freshly grated pecorino Romano
    cheese
16 basil leaves

1. Preheat your grill so that one side is on high and the other is on medium. If using charcoal, set it up for two-tiered grilling (see page 14), arranging the coals in a double layer on one side and in a single layer on the other.

2. Cut the tomatoes crosswise into ¹/₂-inch-thick slices. Brush each with a small amount of oil and season with salt and pepper. Quickly char the tomato slices on the hot side of the grill, turning with a spatula, about 2 minutes per side. Transfer to a plate and let cool.

3. Generously oil a large baking sheet and place one disk of dough on it. Use the fingers and palms of your hands to stretch out the dough into a 13 × 9 inch rectangle (it needn't be too even). This stretching technique takes a little practice, so don't be discouraged if your first rectangle isn't picture perfect. Stretch out the other disk of dough on another oiled baking sheet.

4. Working with one stretched-out piece at a time, using both hands, gently lift the dough rectangle from the baking sheet. Drape it onto the grill over the hottest part of the fire. Within a minute or so, the underside of the dough will crisp, darken, and harden and the top will puff slightly. Turn the dough over with tongs or two spatulas and move it to the cooler side of the grill.

5. Quickly brush the top of the pizza with 1 tablespoon of the oil. Scatter half the garlic over, then sprinkle with half the cheese and arrange half the tomato slices and basil leaves on top. Drizzle the surface of the pizza with another tablespoon of oil and season with salt and pepper.

6. Slide the pizza back over to the hotter part of the grill, rotating to ensure even cooking. Cook until the underside is slightly charred and the cheese is melted on top, 2 to 4 minutes.

7. Remove the pizza from the grill, cut into serving pieces, and serve while you repeat the procedure with the second stretched-out piece of dough.

Makes 2 pizzas; serves 8 as an appetizer, 2 to 4 as an entrée

Grilled Pizza with Arugula and Italian Cheeses

When making grilled pizza, keep the toppings simple, urge Al Forno owners Johanne and George. You don't want to mask the flavor of the grilled dough.

1 recipe Basic Pizza Dough
    (page 402)
6 tablespoons extra-virgin olive
    oil, or more to taste
2 cloves garlic, minced
1 cup shredded Bel Paese
    cheese
6 tablespoons freshly grated Parmesan
    cheese
2 large fresh, ripe tomatoes, peeled and
    seeded (see page 62), then coarsely
    chopped
24 arugula leaves

1. Prepare as described in the recipe for Grilled Pizza with Tomato, Basil, and Cheese, working with one piece of stretched-out dough at a time. After you turn the dough for each pizza, sprinkle the tops with both of the cheeses, then the chopped tomatoes. Arrange the arugula leaves over all.

2. Slide the pizza back over the high heat and cook, rotating to ensure even cooking, until the underside is slightly charred and the cheese is melted on top, 2 to 4 minutes.

3. Serve as directed above.

Makes 2 pizzas; serves 8 as an appetizer, 2 to 4 as an entrée

RACLETTE

SWITZERLAND

METHOD:
Direct grilling

Raclette is the original grilling cheese. For centuries, this Franco-Swiss favorite has been melted in front of a fire and served over boiled potatoes or bread. The term *raclette* describes both the dish and the cheese used to make it. The latter is a large, disk-shaped semifirm cow's-milk cheese (3 inches thick and 13 to 17 inches in diameter, weighing 13 to 17 pounds), with 45 percent butterfat. The nonedible, dark beige rind encases a robustly flavored cheese.

2 pounds small red potatoes, scrubbed
    and cut in half
Salt, to taste
30 tiny pickled (cocktail) onions,
    drained
30 small sour pickles, such as cornichons,
    drained
6 thick slices rye or country-style bread
1 wedge (2½ to 3 pounds) raclette cheese
    (see Note)

1. If cooking the raclette next to your fireplace or wood stove, build a brisk fire. If using a charcoal or gas grill, preheat to high.

2. Cut the potatoes in half and place in a pot with salted water to cover. Bring to a boil over high heat, then reduce the heat to medium and simmer the potatoes until tender, about 10 minutes. Drain in a colander, rinse with cold water, and drain again. Divide the potatoes, onions, and pickles among 4 serving plates and set aside.

3. When ready to cook, spear the bread on a long-handled fork (or hold with tongs) and toast in front of the fire. Alternatively, grill the bread on the hot grill grate, turning with tongs, 2 to 4 minutes per side. Divide the bread among the plates with the potatoes, onions, and pickles.

4. *Fireplace method:* Using long-handled, spring-loaded tongs, hold the cheese next to the fire until the surface begins to melt, 2 to 4 minutes. Scrape a small amount of the melted cheese onto each plate over the bread, potatoes, onions, and sour pickles. Return the cheese to the fire and continue until you

have melted it all, or as much as you need.

Grill method: Place the cheese directly on the hot grate. Cook until the bottom is melted, about 2 minutes. Scrape a small amount of the melted cheese onto each plate over the bread and vegetables. Return the cheese to the grate and continue until you have melted as much as you need.

Serves 6

Note: You'll need about 2½ pounds of cheese to serve 6 people. But when working in front of a fire, it's easier to work with a larger piece—say 4 to 6 pounds. It will hold up better in front of the flames.

Raclette

Ski lodges in the Alps in the winter are the last places you'd expect to find live-fire cooking. Especially for an ingredient most people don't associate with grilling: cheese. But the French and Swiss Alps are home to one of the world's great live-fire dishes—the après-ski favorite raclette. The word comes from the French verb *racler,* "to scrape."

Raclette (the dish) was traditionally made by placing a half or quarter wheel of cheese on a stone in front of the fireplace. (Today, most restaurants use electric raclette burners instead of the fireplace to do the melting.) As the part of the cheese next to the fire melts, it is scraped onto plates to be enjoyed with such sturdy Alpine fare as crusty bread and boiled potatoes, tangy pickled onion, and cornichons (small sour pickles). *Heidi* fans may remember reading about Grandfather melting the cheese in front of the

fireplace in Johanna Spyri's beloved novel.

Raclette (the cheese) has an aroma that might charitably be described as "pungent"—off-putting to all but the most ardent devotees of Limburger. But melt the cheese next to an open flame and the infamous odor disappears. The cheese becomes as creamy as butter and as mild and sweet as mozzarella. It is widely available at cheese markets and gourmet shops. You won't have trouble locating it: Just use your nose! Raclette is made in both France and Switzerland, and the best ones are made with unpasteurized milk. Steven Jenkins, author of the *Cheese Primer,* recommends raclette from the towns of Bagnes, Conches, Gosmer, and Orsières in Switzerland and Brunnerois and Perrin in France.

Who says you can't enjoy live-fire cooking in the winter? Never did something that smells so bad taste so good!

The Indian Grill

India? Barbecue? Mention Indian cooking and what most comes to mind are curries, chutneys, and rice dishes. What you may not realize is that India is one of the world's great barbecuing capitals, home to a unique style of live-fire cooking called tandoori. Named for a giant clay cooking vessel, tandoori combines the charcoal flavor of Western-style grilling with the fall-off-the-bone tenderness of food cooked in a barbecue pit or oven.

Manjit Gill is the executive chef at Bukhara, a restaurant located in New Delhi's Maurya Sheraton Hotel. The secret to tandoori cooking, he explained the day of my visit, are the ovens. He pointed to the tandoors, the waist-high, urn-shaped clay ovens that are the focal point of the restaurant's exhibition kitchen. These sort of ovens have been in use in India and Central Asia for at least 5,000 years, and they turn up in Iran, where they're called *tanoors,* and in the Caucasus Mountains, where they're called *tones.* They're an indispensable element of northern Indian cooking.

According to Gill, the term *tandoor* may come from the Sanskrit word *kandu* (a bowl-shaped vessel) or perhaps from the Persian words *tata andar,* literally "hot inside." That's putting it mildly. It takes Gill three hours to preheat the tandoors at Bukhara; by the time the food goes in for cooking, the internal temperature exceeds 800°F.

This blast-furnace level heat handsomely chars bull's horn peppers and cauliflower (popular Indian grilled vegetables) in a matter of minutes and produces *raan gosht* (baby leg of goat marinated in yogurt and chickpea flour) so tender you can pull it apart with your fingers. (Which is how Indians eat it.) Kebabs emerge dappled with Rembrandtesque browns, while breads baked directly on the walls of the tandoor come out as smoky and light as wood-oven-baked pizzas.

Lest the lightning-quick activity of the chefs give you the impression that tandoori is fast food, know that each spice-scented mouthful is the result of a lot of advance preparation. Meats and vegetables are patiently marinated—sometimes twice—in tangy pastes of yogurt or yogurt cheese and mouth-puckering mixtures of vinegar, tamarind, or lemon juice. Pungent purées of ginger and garlic build the background flavor, while spice mixes, called *masalas,* weave intricate tapestries of taste. The marinating period can last anywhere from 30 minutes to overnight, and it tenderizes meats so that they quickly cook to perfection.

Once marinated, the foods are threaded onto long metal skewers and lowered into the tandoor. The vertical position of the skewers is another reason why tandoori fare is so succulent: The juices drip on the food below, not on the coals. Additionally, most kebabs are generously basted with *ghee* (clarified butter) before serving.

Vegetarians get short shrift at most North American barbecue joints. Not so in India, where a sizable percentage of the population of one billion doesn't eat meat. Vegetarian kebabs include *paneer tikka* (fresh cheese kebabs coated with chickpea flour) and *tandoori aloo* (spit-roasted potatoes stuffed with a fragrant mixture of cashew nuts, raisins, and coriander). The traditional accompaniments for tandoori include mint chutney, cooling *raita* (a yogurt-based condiment), and an astonishing assortment of breads.

Bread was the first food cooked in a tandoor, and it remains a staple. Every village in northern India has an open-air bakery, where *roti* (whole-wheat flat breads), *paratha* (buttered, layered flat breads), *naan* (sweet, yeasted white breads), and delicate *roomali* (crêpe-like breads whose silken softness lives up to their name, "handkerchief bread") emerge piping hot from the tandoor. If you're lucky enough to dine at Bukhara with a large party, order the "family" *naan,* a huge, bowl-shaped bread that measures a full 2 feet across.

While it's impossible to make authentic tandoori fare at home without a tandoor, you can produce a reasonable approximation using a backyard charcoal or gas grill. The trick is to set up the grill for grateless grilling (see box, page 21), so the meat doesn't touch the grate. After all, the tandoor is only part of what makes Indian barbecue so distinctive. The marinades, spices, and basting play a significant role, too—so much so that when properly done, you can't lose, no matter which way you grill the dish.

WHITE RABBIT

METHOD:
Direct grilling

**ADVANCE
PREPARATION:**
*30 minutes for
draining the
tofu, plus 4 hours
for marinating
the tofu*

This ingenious recipe was inspired by Manu Mehta, executive chef at the Sheraton Rajputana Hotel in Jaipur. Mehta caters to a large vegetarian clientele, so he created a meatless version of the local barbecue, *sula*. He makes the dish with paneer (a white Indian cheese) instead of the traditional game—hence the nickname "white rabbit." Paneer is a soft but solid cheese, not unlike farmer's cheese or Hispanic *queso blanco*. The chef and I agreed you could also make this dish with a thoroughly non-Indian ingredient whose consistency is very similar to paneer: tofu! If you've ever complained that tofu is bland, this is the recipe for you. The bean curd receives a double blast of flavor: first from the cilantro and mint stuffing, then from the garlic, ginger and chile marinade. Add the charcoal flavor imparted by grilling and you have a dish guaranteed to turn skeptics into believers.

FOR THE TOFU AND FILLING:
2 pieces (each 1 pound) extra-firm tofu
3 tablespoons chopped fresh cilantro
**3 tablespoons chopped fresh mint or
 additional cilantro**
**1 scallion, both white and green parts,
 trimmed and roughly sliced**
1 to 2 jalapeños or other hot chiles, seeded
1 tablespoon fresh lemon juice
1 tablespoon vegetable oil
¼ teaspoon salt

FOR THE MARINADE:
3 cloves garlic, sliced
1 piece (1 inch) fresh ginger, sliced
1 jalapeño chile, seeded
2 tablespoons vegetable oil
2 tablespoons water
1 tablespoon paprika
1 teaspoon ground coriander
½ teaspoon cayenne pepper, or more to taste
½ teaspoon salt, or more to taste
¾ cup plain whole-milk yogurt
¼ cup heavy cream or sour cream
3 tablespoons chopped fresh cilantro
**1 tablespoon fresh lemon juice, or more
 to taste**

3 tablespoons unsalted butter, melted

1. Rinse the tofu under cold running water and drain. Place a cutting board on a slight incline in the sink. Place the tofu on the cutting board and put a heavy plate or pot lid on top of it to press out the excess liquid. This will take about 30 minutes. Cut each piece of tofu horizontally in half, then cut each resultant piece in half crosswise. Lay the pieces flat on the edge of the cutting board. Holding the blade of a paring knife parallel to the cutting board, cut a deep pocket in one side of each piece of tofu. Set aside while you prepare the filling.

2. Combine the cilantro, mint, scallion, chile, lemon juice, oil, and salt in a mini chopper or spice mill and process to a coarse paste. Spoon equal amounts of this paste into the pocket in each piece of tofu.

3. Prepare the marinade. Combine the garlic, ginger, chile, oil, and water in a mini chopper or spice mill and process to a smooth paste. Transfer to a small bowl and stir in the paprika, coriander, ½ teaspoon cayenne, ½ teaspoon salt, yogurt, cream, cilantro, and 1 tablespoon lemon juice. Taste for seasoning adding cayenne, salt, and lemon juice as necessary; the marinade should be highly seasoned. Pour one third of the marinade over the bottom of a nonreactive baking dish and place the tofu pieces on top. Pour the remaining marinade over the tofu. Cover and let marinate, in the refrigerator, for 4 hours.

4. Preheat the grill to high.

5. When ready to cook, oil the grill grate.

Remove the tofu from the marinade and arrange the pieces on the hot grate. Grill, turning carefully with a spatula, until nicely browned and thoroughly heated through, about 4 minutes per side. Brush the tofu once or twice with melted butter as it grills. Transfer the tofu to serving plates or a platter and brush once more with melted butter before serving.

Serves 4

TOFU ON STILTS
Dengaku

JAPAN

METHOD:
Direct grilling

ADVANCE PREPARATION:
30 minutes for draining the tofu

SPECIAL EQUIPMENT:
16 long bamboo skewers, soaked for 1 hour in cold water to cover and drained

Dengaku is a popular dish at the tea-houses that line the lovely Philosopher's Walk in Kyoto. The dish takes its curious name from the Japanese word for "stilt." The stilts in question are two bamboo skewers that are used to hold the piece of tofu over the coals for grilling. The traditional grill for cooking *dengaku* does not have a grate. Instead, the skewers are propped up over the flames and the tofu is grilled in midair. Acceptable results can be obtained on a regular grill or hibachi, but you will lose some glaze.

2 pieces (each 1 pound) extra-firm
      tofu
½ cup white miso
2 tablespoons mirin (sweet rice wine) or
      cream sherry
2 tablespoons sake
2 tablespoons sugar
1 tablespoon mayonnaise
1 tablespoon sesame seeds,
      toasted (see box, page 93)

1. Rinse the tofu under cold running water and drain. Place a cutting board on a slight incline in the sink. Place the tofu on the cutting board and put a heavy plate or pot lid on top of it to press out the excess liquid. This will take about 30 minutes.

2. If desired, set up the grill for grateless grilling (see box, page 21). Preheat the grill to high.

3. Combine the miso, mirin, sake, sugar, and mayonnaise in the top of a double boiler and whisk until smooth. Cook the sauce over gently simmering water until thick and creamy, about 3 minutes.

4. Cut each piece of tofu horizontally in half, then cut each of the resultant pieces in half crosswise. Push 2 skewers through each piece of tofu, starting at one narrow end.

5. When ready to cook, arrange the tofu on the grill as described in the grateless method or oil the grill grate and arrange the tofu directly on it. Grill, turning with a spatula, until lightly browned on each side, 3 to 4 minutes per side. Brush with miso glaze as the tofu cooks. Sprinkle with sesame seeds and serve immediately.

Serves 4

MUSHROOM-RICE BURGERS WITH CHEDDAR CHEESE

U.S.A.

METHOD:
Direct grilling

ADVANCE PREPARATION:
4 to 5 hours for chilling the burger mixture and patties

SPECIAL EQUIPMENT:
Vegetable grate

When I was growing up, no one knew from vegetarian burgers. Today, they've become big business, as more and more health-conscious Americans adopt at least partial vegetarian diets. The following recipe combines mushrooms, oats, and brown rice into a patty that looks somewhat like a hamburger and has a rich, earthy flavor that could almost be described as meaty. It's also a great way to use up leftover brown rice. Note that vegetarian burgers are more fragile than beef or lamb burgers. Cook them on a well-oiled vegetable grate and turn as gently as possible with a spatula.

FOR THE BURGERS:
2 tablespoons olive oil
1 medium onion, finely chopped
2 cloves garlic, minced
8 ounces white mushrooms, wiped clean with dampened paper towels and finely chopped
1 cup cooked brown rice
½ cup quick oats
4 ounces coarsely grated sharp Cheddar cheese (about ¾ cup)
1 egg, lightly beaten
Salt and freshly ground black pepper, to taste
2 to 3 tablespoons fine dry bread crumbs, if needed

FOR SERVING:
1 large fresh, ripe, tomato, thinly sliced
1 large onion, thinly sliced (optional)
Pickle slices
½ head iceberg lettuce, thinly sliced
4 whole-wheat hamburger buns
Ketchup and/or mayonnaise and/or mustard

1. Prepare the burger mixture. Heat the oil in a nonstick skillet over medium heat. Add the onion and garlic and sauté until soft but not brown, about 4 minutes. Increase the heat to medium-high, add the mushrooms, and cook, stirring occasionally, until tender and most of the mushroom liquid has evaporated, about 4 minutes.

2. Stir in the brown rice and cook for 1 minute. Remove from the heat and transfer the mixture to a large bowl. Stir in the oats, cheese, and egg. Add salt and pepper. If the mixture seems wet, add the bread crumbs. Cover the mixture and refrigerate until firm, 3 to 4 hours.

3. Line a baking sheet or large plate with plastic wrap. Wet your hands slightly and form the vegetable mixture into 4 patties. Place the patties on the prepared baking sheet, cover loosely with plastic wrap, and refrigerate for 1 hour.

4. Preheat the grill to high.

5. When ready to cook, place a vegetable grate on the hot grill and preheat it for 5 minutes. Arrange the tomato and onion slices, pickles, and lettuce on a platter and set aside. Oil the vegetable grate and place the patties on it. Grill, turning carefully with a spatula, until nicely browned on both sides, 4 to 6 minutes per side. As the burgers cook, toast the buns over the flames as well. Serve as you would any burger, piling the buns high with lettuce, tomato, onion, pickles, and smearing on the ketchup, mayonnaise, or mustard—or all three.

Serves 6

INDIAN SPINACH-CHEESE KEBABS

INDIA

METHOD:
Direct grilling

ADVANCE PREPARATION:
3 hours for chilling the spinach mixture (optional)

SPECIAL EQUIPMENT:
4 long, flat metal skewers

These handsome green kebabs are a specialty of the restaurant Peshawar at the Sheraton Rajputana Hotel in Jaipur. Peshawar is a town on the Indian Pakistan border and a bastion of meat eating if ever there was one. But so deeply ingrained is vegetarianism in India that even grill restaurants like Peshawar offer interesting vegetarian barbecue. The recipe may look complicated because of the number of ingredients, but actually it's quite easy and definitely worth the effort. The interplay of flavors—the sweetness of the nuts and spinach, the saltiness of the cheese, the exotic exuberance of the seasonings—conspires to make this a dish that will delight vegetarians and meat-eaters alike.

FOR THE KEBABS:
Salt, to taste
10 ounces fresh spinach, rinsed and stemmed, or a 10-ounce package frozen spinach
¼ cup coarsely chopped mixed nuts (pistachios, cashews, and/or almonds)
¼ cup chickpea flour (besan) or whole-wheat flour
½ teaspoon Quick Garam Masala (page 499) or ground coriander
¼ teaspoon ground cumin
¼ teaspoon ground fenugreek (optional)
¼ teaspoon cayenne pepper, or more to taste
⅔ cup crumbled farmer's cheese, pot cheese, or dry-curd cottage cheese
1 tablespoon cornstarch
¼ cup grated Gouda or mild Cheddar cheese
3 tablespoons chopped fresh cilantro
1 tablespoon golden raisins, coarsely chopped (optional)
2 teaspoons fresh lemon juice, or more to taste
3 tablespoons unsalted butter, melted

FOR SERVING:
Naan, pita bread, or lavash
Lemon wedges
Sliced onions
Sliced cucumbers
Sliced tomatoes
Sliced chile peppers

1. Pour water to a depth of 1 inch in a large pot, add salt, and bring to a boil over high heat. Add the spinach and cook until wilted and tender, about 3 minutes. (If using frozen spinach, follow package instructions.) Drain the spinach in a colander, rinse with cold water, and drain again. Squeeze fistfuls of spinach in your hands to wring out as much water as possible. Finely chop the spinach in the food processor or by hand. If using a food processor, leave the spinach in the processor bowl; if by hand, transfer to a bowl. You should have about ¾ cup spinach.

2. Heat the nuts in a dry skillet over medium heat until lightly toasted, 2 to 3 minutes, shaking the pan occasionally. Transfer the nuts to a plate to cool. Add the chickpea flour to the skillet and heat until lightly toasted, about 2 minutes, stirring occasionally. Add the chickpea flour to the spinach. Add the *garam masala,* cumin, fenugreek (if using), and ¼ teaspoon cayenne to the skillet and cook until lightly toasted, about 1 minute. Add the spices to the spinach.

3. Add the farmer's cheese to the spinach and process to make a coarse paste or stir to blend. Add the Gouda, cilantro, raisins, 2 teaspoons lemon juice, and nuts and pulse or stir just to mix. Taste for seasoning, adding lemon juice, salt, or cayenne as needed; the mixture should be highly seasoned. You can form the kebabs now, but the mixture will be easier to work with if you refrigerate it, covered, for 3 hours.

4. Oil 4 long, flat metal skewers. Divide the spinach mixture into 4 equal portions. Lightly wet your hands with cold water and mold 1 portion onto a skewer to make a sausage shape 9 to 10 inches long and 1 inch in diameter. Continue making kebabs until the spinach mixture is used up. If making up the kebabs ahead of time, lay them on oiled baking sheets and cover loosely with plastic wrap. Refrigerate until ready to cook.

5. If desired, set up the grill for grateless grilling (see box, page 21). Preheat the grill to high.

6. When ready to cook, lightly brush each kebab with melted butter and arrange them on the grill as described in the grate-less method or oil the grill grate and arrange the skewers directly on it. Grill, turning once or twice, until lightly browned on all sides, about 8 minutes in all. Brush with butter again.

7. Use a piece of *naan,* pita bread, or lavash as a pot holder and unmold the kebabs onto serving plates or a platter. Serve with lemon wedges for squeezing and a platter of sliced onions, cucumbers, tomatoes, and chile peppers.

Serves 4

YAM AND NUT KEBABS

INDIA

METHOD:
Direct grilling

ADVANCE PREPARATION:
3 hours for chilling the yam mixture (optional)

SPECIAL EQUIPMENT:
4 long, flat, metal skewers

How do you cater to a large, affluent vegetarian community in a land of avid meat eaters? Such is the challenge that Nisar Waris faces daily. Waris is the chef of the Peshawar, the signature restaurant in the Sheraton Rajputana Hotel in Jaipur. His staff has created a huge repertoire of vegetarian barbecue items, including the following recipe. Talk about an amazing set of flavors! Here Chef Waris skillfully combines the sweetness of yams and raisins, the nuttiness of cashews and pistachios, and the spicy zing of cardamom and cilantro. It's enough to make you want to give up meat! He molds and grills the mixture on skewers, but you can form the mixture into burgerlike patties. For information on chickpea flour (*besan*), see the Glossary.

FOR THE KEBABS:
1 pound yams or sweet potatoes (enough to make 1 cup purée); see Note

¼ cup chickpea flour (besan) or whole-wheat flour
2 cups coarsely chopped mixed nuts, including cashews, pistachios, and almonds, and/or sunflower seeds
1 tablespoon heavy cream or sour cream
1 teaspoon fresh lemon juice, or more to taste
½ cup golden raisins, finely chopped
⅓ cup chopped fresh cilantro
1 teaspoon freshly ground white pepper
½ teaspoon Quick Garam Masala (page 499) or ground coriander
¼ teaspoon ground cardamom
½ teaspoon salt, or more to taste
3 tablespoons unsalted butter, melted

FOR SERVING:
Naan, pita bread, or lavash
Lemon wedges
Sliced onions
Sliced cucumbers
Sliced tomatoes
Sliced chile peppers

1. If using the grill to cook the yams, set it up for indirect grilling (see page 14 or 16), placing a drip pan in the center, and preheat to medium-high. If using the oven, preheat it to 400°F.

2. Grill (covered) or roast the yams until soft, about 40 minutes. Transfer to a plate and let cool. Peel the yams, then mash in a large bowl with a potato masher, fork, or pestle. (Don't purée in a food processor, or the mixture will become gummy.)

3. Cook the chickpea flour in a dry skillet over medium heat until lightly toasted and fragrant, about 2 minutes. Stir the flour into the yams. Add the mixed nuts to the skillet and cook, stirring, over medium heat until lightly toasted and fragrant, 3 to 5 minutes. Stir the nuts into the yams. Stir in the cream, 1 teaspoon lemon juice, the raisins, cilantro, pepper, *garam marsala,* cardamom, and ½ teaspoon salt. Taste for seasoning, adding more salt or lemon juice as necessary; the mixture should be highly seasoned. You can form the kebabs now, but the mixture will be easier to work with if you refrigerate it, covered, for about 3 hours. You can make the mixture the day before and chill overnight if desired.

4. Oil 4 long, flat metal skewers. Divide the yam mixture into 4 equal portions. Lightly wet your hands with cold water and mold one portion onto a skewer to make a sausage shape 9 to 10 inches long and 1 inch in diameter. Continue making kebabs until the yam mixture is used up. If making up the kebabs ahead of time, lay them on oiled baking sheets and cover loosely with plastic wrap. Refrigerate until ready to cook.

5. If desired, set up the grill for grateless grilling (see box, page 21). Preheat the grill to high.

6. When ready to cook, lightly brush each kebab with melted butter and arrange them on the grill as described in the grateless method or oil the grill grate and arrange them on the hot grate. Grill, turning once or twice, until lightly browned on all sides, about 8 minutes in all. Brush with butter again.

7. Use a piece of *naan,* pita bread, or lavash as a pot holder and unmold the kebabs onto serving plates or a platter. Serve with lemon wedges for squeezing and a platter of sliced onions, cucumbers, tomatoes, and chile peppers.

Serves 4

Note: The preferable yam used here is a true yam, a starchy tuber with minimal sweetness. Look for true yams at Hispanic or Caribbean markets. I've also made the dish with *boniatos* (white-fleshed Caribbean sweet potatoes, which taste like roasted chestnuts) and, of course, American sweet potatoes.

PROVENÇAL DAGWOOD

FRANCE

METHOD:
Direct grilling

If you like grilled vegetables and goat cheese, you'll love this sandwich, which fairly explodes with the evocative flavors of Provence. Rosemary and garlic lend a Mediterranean fragrance to vegetables that are traditionally associated with *ratatouille,* the classic vegetable stew from this region of France. The tangy cheese provides a textural counterpoint to the vegetables. Use a soft, spreadable fresh goat cheese like Montrachet for best results. These sandwiches can be made a few hours ahead of time and are great for picnics, with the vegetable juices soaking into the bread.

FOR THE VEGETABLES:

1 medium eggplant (12 to 14 ounces),
   stem end trimmed off
2 medium zucchini, stem ends trimmed off
2 medium yellow squash, stem ends
   trimmed off
2 medium red bell peppers
1 medium red onion, peeled but root end
   left attached

FOR THE BASTING MIXTURE:

3 tablespoons extra-virgin olive oil
2 tablespoons fresh lemon juice
2 cloves garlic, minced
1 sprig fresh rosemary or 1 teaspoon dried
Salt and freshly ground black pepper, to
   taste

FOR SERVING:

1 long baguette
8 ounces fresh goat cheese, at room
   temperature

1. Preheat the grill to high.

2. Cut the eggplant, zucchini, and squash lengthwise into ¼-inch-thick slices. Stem, seed, and quarter the peppers. Quarter the onion, leaving the root end attached to each piece. (The root will help the onion hold together during grilling.)

3. Prepare the basting mixture. Combine the oil, lemon juice, and garlic in a small bowl. If using dried rosemary, add it directly to the oil.

4. When ready to cook, brush the vegetable slices with the oil mixture, using the rosemary sprig as a basting brush. If you don't have fresh rosemary, use a pastry brush. Arrange each vegetable on the hot grate and grill, turning with tongs, until nicely browned, 3 to 6 minutes per side. Brush the vegetables once or twice with the oil mixture and season with salt and pepper as they cook. Transfer the vegetables to a platter to cool. Cut the root end off the onion wedges and break the layers apart.

5. Cut the bread crosswise into 4 equal pieces. Split each piece lengthwise in half as for a sandwich. Place the bottom halves of the bread on your work surface, brush with any remaining oil mixture, and spread with half the goat cheese. Arrange the eggplant, zucchini, squash, pepper, and onion slices over the goat cheese. Spread the remaining goat cheese over the cut sides of the other pieces of bread and place, cheese side down, on the vegetables. Cut the sandwiches in half and serve warm or at room temperature.

Serves 4

GRILLED PORTOBELLO MUSHROOM SANDWICHES WITH BASIL AIOLI

U.S.A.

METHOD:
Direct grilling

The portobello mushroom has become the *fin de siècle* "steak," a grilled vegetable alternative to beef. The broad fleshy mushroom cap has a rich meaty flavor and luckily, portobellos are available at most supermarkets and gourmet shops. To this, add a fresh basil-flavored *aïoli* (French garlic mayonnaise) and you've got a sandwich that tap dances on your taste buds!

4 large portobello mushrooms, wiped clean with dampened paper towels
3 cloves garlic, cut into thin slivers
Leaves from 1 sprig fresh rosemary (optional)
3 tablespoons extra-virgin olive oil
3 tablespoons balsamic vinegar
1 large fresh, ripe tomato, cut crosswise into ½-inch slices
Salt and freshly ground black pepper, to taste
4 onion rolls, hamburger buns, or 5-inch sections of baguette, split
Basil Aïoli (recipe follows) or mayonnaise
1 bunch arugula, rinsed, dry

1. Preheat the grill to high.

2. Cut the stems off the mushrooms flush with the caps. Using the tip of a paring knife, make tiny holes in the caps, and insert the garlic slivers and rosemary leaves (if using). Combine the oil and vinegar in a small bowl and whisk to mix. Generously brush the portobello caps and tomato slices with this mixture and season with salt and pepper.

3. When almost ready to cook, preheat a vegetable grate for 5 minutes. Arrange the portobello caps, rounded side down, and the tomato slices on the hot grate and grill, turning with a spatula, until nicely browned and soft, 3 to 6 minutes per side. Brush the veg-

etables once or twice as they cook with the oil and vinegar mixture.

4. Spread the insides of the rolls or bread with Basil Aïoli or mayonnaise. Add the grilled vegetables and arugula and serve immediately.

Serves 4

Basil Aïoli

Aïoli is a garlic mayonnaise from the south of France. This version uses commercial mayonnaise as a base to avoid the small but worrisome health risks associated with eating raw egg yolks.

1 cup mayonnaise
3 cloves garlic, put through a garlic press
24 fresh basil leaves, thinly slivered
1 tablespoon fresh lemon juice
Salt and freshly ground black pepper, to taste

Combine the mayonnaise, garlic, basil, lemon juice, salt, and pepper in a small bowl and whisk to mix.

Makes about 1 cup

TANDOORI PEPPERS

Stuffed peppers turn up at tandoori parlors throughout northern India. The pepper in question looks like a miniature green bell pepper, but is hotter. The overall effect is a cross between an American green bell pepper and a Mexican *chile poblano*. I compensate for

the lack of heat in our peppers by adding a good dose of cayenne to the filling. Incidentally, the filling is a meal in itself—a soulful stew of onion, potato, cabbage, and nuts assertively seasoned with spices and cheese. Indians would roast the stuffed peppers on vertical spits in a tandoor. The upright position keeps the filling from falling out. Lacking a tandoor, the best way to cook the peppers is to stand them upright on the grate, using the indirect grilling method. Although not traditional, yellow or red bell peppers are delicious for stuffing too.

FOR THE PEPPERS AND MARINADE:
4 large green, red, or yellow bell
   peppers
2 tablespoons fresh lemon juice
1 tablespoons vegetable oil
1 clove garlic, coarsely chopped
1 piece (½ inch) fresh ginger
¼ teaspoon salt

FOR THE FILLING:
2 tablespoons vegetable oil
½ teaspoon cumin seeds
½ teaspoon ground turmeric
¼ teaspoon cayenne pepper, or more
   to taste
1 medium onion, finely chopped
1 clove garlic, minced
1 large potato (about 10 ounces),
   peeled and cut into ¼-inch dice
⅓ small head green cabbage, cored and
   thinly sliced
1 large fresh, ripe tomato, finely chopped
2 tablespoons cashew nuts, coarsely
   chopped
2 tablespoons golden raisins (optional)
¼ cup finely chopped fresh cilantro
½ cup grated Gouda or mild Cheddar
   cheese
Salt, to taste

1. Carefully cut the caps (the stem ends) off the peppers and set aside. (Each cap section should be about ½ inch deep.) Using a spoon or melon baller, scrape the veins and seeds out of the peppers. Set the peppers aside, with their caps, while you prepare the marinade.

2. Combine the lemon juice, oil, garlic, ginger, and salt in a blender and process until smooth. Paint the insides of the peppers and caps with this mixture, using a pastry brush, then set aside to marinate while you prepare the filling.

3. Heat the oil in a large sauté pan or saucepan over medium heat. Add the cumin seeds, turmeric, ¼ teaspoon cayenne, the onion, and garlic and sauté until the onion is just beginning to brown, about 5 minutes. Stir in the potato, cabbage, tomato, cashews, and raisins (if using) and cook for 2 minutes. Reduce the heat to low, cover the pan, and cook the vegetables until soft, stirring occasionally, 10 to 15 minutes. Check after 10 minutes, and if the vegetables look wet, uncover the pan for the last 5 minutes to evaporate any excess liquid. Stir in the cilantro and cook for 1 minute. Stir in the cheese. Remove from the heat and taste for seasoning, adding salt and additional cayenne as necessary; the mixture should be highly seasoned.

4. Spoon the filling into the peppers. Place the caps on top (see Note).

5. Set the grill up for indirect grilling (see page 14 or 16) and preheat to high.

6. When ready to cook, place the peppers in the center of the hot grate away from the heat. Cover the grill and cook until the peppers are nicely browned and tender, 20 to 30 minutes. I like to move the peppers directly over the flames for a few minutes at the end to lightly char the skins. Serve immediately.

Serves 4

Note: The peppers can be stuffed up to 6 hours ahead to this point and stored, covered loosely with plastic wrap, in the refrigerator.

Rice, Beans,
AND BEYOND

Rice and bean dishes may not be the glamour dishes of a barbecue, but no self-respecting cookout would be complete without them. This chapter focuses on those stalwart dishes that add heft to your plate and round out what could otherwise be a relentlessly carnivorian meal.

Rice is the traditional accompaniment to much of the world's grilled fare, from the sticky short-grain rices popular in Asia to the fluffy long-grain rices featured in the West.

Beans are also universal. North American–style baked beans are familiar, but did you know that Indians serve *dal* (gingery stewed beans) with their tandoori or that Brazilians enjoy *tutu mineira* (cowboy-style black beans) with their grilled meats (*churrasco*)? In this chapter, you'll find recipes for these delectable dishes and more.

This brings me to the less expected accompaniments to barbecue, like polenta and grits, which are delicious grilled, and Yorkshire pudding, which can be cooked on the grill while the rib roast is resting. You'll even find a recipe for toasted manioc flour, which Brazilians like to sprinkle over grilled meats.

Armed with recipes, no one will go hungry. Which is the ultimate goal of any barbecue.

Rice is the classic accompaniment to barbecue in Thailand.

INDIAN-STYLE BASMATI RICE

ON THE SIDE

SPECIAL EQUIPMENT:
Wok ring or Flame Tamer

SAFFRON ROSEWATER BASMATI

Soak ½ teaspoon saffron threads in 2 tablespoons rosewater in a small jar with a lid. Sprinkle a few drops over the rice and toss before serving. Store any extra in the refrigerator.

The traditional Indian method for cooking basmati involves an elaborate but easy sequence of rinsing, soaking, and steaming the rice. This produces the most delicate basmati rice I know.

2 cups basmati rice
2 cups water
1 teaspoon salt

1. Place the rice in a large bowl and add cold water to cover by 3 inches. Swirl the rice around with your fingers until the water becomes cloudy, then pour through a strainer to drain. Repeat the process until the water remains clear. This will take 4 to 6 rinsings. Drain the rice, return it to the bowl, and add the 2 cups water. Let soak for 30 minutes.

2. Drain the rice through a strainer set over a large, heavy pot. Bring the soaking water to a boil over high heat. Add the salt, stir in the rice, and return the water to a boil. Reduce the heat to medium-low and simmer gently, partially covered, until the surface of the rice is riddled with steamy holes, 10 to 12 minutes.

3. Reduce the heat to low, and using a wok ring, raise the pot 1 inch above the burner. (Alternatively, use a flame tamer.) Wrap a clean kitchen towel around the pot lid, piling any excess cloth on top of the lid. (You want to keep the cloth away from the heat.) Place the cloth-covered lid over the rice and steam, over very low heat, for 10 minutes.

4. Gently fluff the rice with a fork and serve immediately.
Serves 4

QUICK-COOK BASMATI RICE

ON THE SIDE

Here's a quick-cook method that produces quite tasty basmati rice for a hurried weeknight. You can also use an American-grown basmati-style rice, like Texmati.

6 cups water
2 tablespoons unsalted butter
1 teaspoon salt
½ teaspoon freshly ground white pepper (optional)
2 cups basmati rice

1. Place the water, butter, salt, and pepper (if using) in a large, heavy pot and bring to a boil. Stir in the rice and return the water to a boil over high heat.

2. Reduce the heat to low, cover the pot tightly, and cook the rice until the grains are tender and all the water is absorbed, about 18 minutes. Remove the pot from the heat and let stand, covered, for 5 minutes.

3. Gently fluff the rice with a fork and serve immediately.
Serves 4

Basmati Rice Five Ways

Basmati is the Rolls-Royce of rices, a long, slender grain with an intensely aromatic taste that is buttery, nutty, milky, and sweet. And that's before you add any flavorings! Grown in the foothills of the Himalayas, basmati owes its extraordinary flavor to several years' aging in silos. Unlike most rices, it doubles in length, not width, when cooked.

Basmati rice is traditionally associated with India, but it's eaten almost on a daily basis as far west as the Caucasus Mountains and as far east as Bangladesh. The traditional method for cooking basmati involves multiple washings, soakings, and steaming. This is the Indian-style recipe you'll find on the facing page. But because basmati rice plays such an important role in the world of barbecue, I offer several recipes, ranging from quick-cook basmati rice, ideal for the weekend cook, to an elaborate Persian rice with cranberries.

Note that basmati rice is sold at most gourmet shops and many supermarkets. If you like it as much as I do, you'll probably want to buy it in bulk at an Indian, Pakistani, or Near or Middle Eastern markets.

PERSIAN-STYLE STEAMED RICE

IRAN

ON THE SIDE

No Persian meal would be complete without rice. Here's a simple steamed rice recipe that's great with any of the Persian or Afghan kebabs in this book. Use this rice or the one below it to prepare Iran's most famous grilled meal: *chelow kebab* (see box on page 420).

3 cups basmati rice
1 tablespoon salt
6 cups water
4 tablespoons (½ stick) unsalted butter, cut into small pieces

1. Place the rice in a large bowl and add cold water to cover by 3 inches. Swirl the rice around with your fingers until the water becomes cloudy, then pour through a strainer to drain. Repeat the process until the water remains clear. This will take 4 to 6 rinsings.

2. Place the rice, salt, and the 6 cups water in a deep, nonstick saucepan. Bring to a boil over high heat. Reduce the heat to medium and simmer the rice gently, uncovered, for about 18 minutes. When the rice has absorbed all the water, reduce the heat to the lowest possible setting and sprinkle the butter pieces over the top.

3. Wrap a clean kitchen towel around the pot lid, piling any excess cloth on top of the lid. (You want to keep the cloth away from the heat.) Place the cloth-covered lid over the rice and steam for 20 minutes. Remove the pot from the heat and let stand, covered, 5 minutes more.

4. Gently fluff the rice with a fork and serve immediately.
Serves 6

A Day with Najmieh Batmanglij:
The Persian Grill

Najmieh Batmanglij is my guru of Persian grilling. I met her on what was probably the least likely day of the year for a barbecue. The charcoal lay neatly piled in her custom-made grill on the terrace of her Georgetown townhouse in Washington, D.C. But by the time I arrived, a freak snowstorm had blanketed the grill, terrace, and gardens with a thick layer of snow.

Never mind—Najmieh Batmanglij is not the sort of cook to let a snowstorm ruin a cookout. A short woman with dark eyes and a cascade of black hair, Najmieh is an author and cooking instructor who comes by her passion for Persian barbecue naturally. One of 11 children, she was born and raised in Tehran in the country now called Iran, but with the ancient and more exotic name Persia. Her books include the stunning *Food of Life, New Food of Life*, and *Persian Cooking for a Healthy Kitchen*. So essential is grilling to Iranian cuisine that she has equipped her kitchen with an indoor grill that would be the envy of many a restaurant. I shook the snow off my overcoat and boots and we set about the task of marinating and skewering meats for

Iranian-style grilling.

On the day I visited, she demonstrated 10 dishes in 3 hours with a dexterity that bordered on legerdemain. A whole beef tenderloin was speedily reduced to neat bite-size strips and doused with onion juice, lime juice, and cracked peppercorns. Lamb and beef shoulder were fed through a noisy meat grinder, then kneaded together by hand over low heat to make Iran's famous *kubideh,* ground meat kebab. Earthenware crocks held chunks of chicken and lamb that had been marinating for 2 days in a colorful mixture of yogurt and saffron. Impressive any time of the year, the display was made more remarkable by the inclement weather outside.

It's unlikely that a cooking technique as universal as roasting meats on a stick over a fire originated at a single time in a single country. But if it had, Iran would make a likely birthplace. Grilling has been inextricably interwoven with Persian culture for hundreds, probably thousands, of years.

Linguistic evidence suggests Iran as the wellspring of Near Eastern–style grilling. After all, kebab is the Persian word for meat. Early Persian literature and art abound with images of grilling. A fourth-century coming-of-age manual, for example, describes a spit-roasted capon that had been raised on a diet of hemp seeds and olive butter. The tenth-century poet Ferdowsi gives a detailed description of a veal marinade made with saffron, rosewater, musk, and old wine.

Persian-style kebabs, with their emphasis on lamb and yogurt-based marinades, turn up as far west as the Balkans and as far east as Bangladesh. They probably inspired Greek *souvlaki* and Indian tandoori. *Souvlaki* may have arrived via the Turks during the Ottoman Empire (if not before, during the Persian Wars in the sixth century B.C.). Tandoori was imported by the Moguls, Persian rulers who brought Islam to northern India in the sixteenth century A.D. (The spicing is more extravagant in the Indian version, but the yogurt- and garlic-based marinade is the same). Even Russia's popular *shashlik* (beef or lamb kebabs) is a likely descendant of Persian *shishlik* (skewered grilled lamb chops).

What accounts for the long-standing popularity of grilled fare in the region we now call Iran? "Ours is an outdoor culture," explains Najmieh. "For eight months a year, most Persians cook, dine, and even sleep outdoors." This love of the outdoors has given rise to a singular style of grilling.

If Iran had a single national dish, it would surely be *chelow kebab*, skewers of lamb, veal, or beef served on a snowy mountain of rice with fire-charred tomatoes, raw egg, raw onions, and a tart purplish powder made from sumac berries. But, almost anything is fair game for the kebabi man: lamb, veal, beef, organ meats, tomatoes, onions, even sumac-dusted fish. Of course, the most popular meat is lamb. "In Iran sheep graze on herbs, which gives them an exceptional flavor," explains Najmieh. Loin and tenderloin are her preferred cuts, but leg and shoulder will do if marinated for at least 48 hours. Tradition calls for interspersing the lamb chunks with moisturizing lumps of tail fat.

Lengthy marinating is one of the cornerstones of Persian grilling. The basic marinade consists of yogurt, lemon or lime juice, onion, garlic, saffron, pepper, and salt. Sometimes candied orange peel is added for a touch of sweetness. Sometimes olive oil is substituted for the yogurt—especially for beef and veal. Iranians marinate their meats much longer than North Americans do—2 to 3 days is not uncommon. A 2- or 3-day soak in an acidic yogurt and lemon juice marinade can work wonders for breaking down tough meat fibers. It also produces an uncommon depth of flavor. "Iranians always have some sort of meat marinating in the refrigerator," explains Najmieh. "That way, we can make kebabs at a moment's notice."

Another hallmark of Persian grilling is the basting mixture, brushed on the meat while it cooks. The basic formula includes lime juice, saffron, and melted butter. The saffron imparts a golden glow to the meat. And the mixture as a whole keeps the meat moist, which is important, since Iranians are fond of grilling over very high heat.

Given the importance of kebabs in Persian cuisine, it's not surprising that Iranians have developed highly distinctive skewers: long, flat ribbons of steel of varying widths with pointed tips for easy penetration. Narrow skewers ($\frac{1}{8}$ inch wide) are used for skewering chunks of meat; medium skewers ($\frac{3}{8}$ inch wide), for holding thin strips of chicken and beef. The widest skewers measure $\frac{1}{2}$ to 1 inch across and are designed for holding ground meats. So effective are these skewers, their popularity has spread throughout the Arab world.

But grilled fare is only part of what makes a Persian barbecue so remarkable, as I learned at my cooking class with Najmieh. The side dishes are also stars of the show. Guests would be welcomed with tiny, gold-rimmed glasses of dulcet tea. The table would be sagging under the weight of a *mokhalafat*, a stunning assortment of dips, salads, chutneys, *torshis* (pickles), and paper-thin lavash bread for wrapping around the meats.

Najmieh accompanied her barbecue with a platter of basil, mint, watercress, and other fresh herbs, not to mention tomatoes, cucumbers, and scallions. She also included chopped onion and delectably tart sumac powder for sprinkling over the meat. To wash it down, she served cool, frothy glasses of *dugh*, a refreshing beverage made from yogurt, mint, and rose petals. Such was Najmieh's hospitality that by the end of the day I felt like I was at a cookout in Tehran, not in a snowstorm in Washington, D.C.

PERSIAN RICE WITH A GOLDEN CRUST
Chelow

This rice dish is one of the glories of Persian (Iranian) gastronomy—tender, sweet, saffroned rice served with an audibly crisp, yogurt-flavored crust. The theory is simple enough (you brown the rice in a single layer on the bottom), but it takes years of practice to achieve a perfect dark-golden crust that comes away from the bottom of the pan in one piece. Here's how my Persian cooking guru, Najmieh Batmanglij, prepares this classic accompaniment to an Iranian barbecue.

3 cups basmati rice
9 cups water
2 tablespoons salt
¼ teaspoon saffron threads
⅔ cup clarified melted unsalted butter
    (see Note) or olive oil
3 tablespoons whole-milk yogurt

1. Place the rice in a large bowl and add cold water to cover by 3 inches. Swirl the rice around with your fingers until the water becomes cloudy, then pour through a strainer to drain. Repeat the process until the water remains clear. This will take 4 to 6 rinsings.

2. Place 8 cups of the water and the salt in a large shallow pot (preferably nonstick; the pot should be 10 to 12 inches across and about 6 inches deep) and bring to a boil over high heat. Reduce the heat to medium-high, add the rice, and cook, uncovered, at a brisk simmer for 6 minutes. Pour the rice into a strainer, rinse under cool running water, and drain well. Wipe out and dry the rice pot with paper towels.

3. Meanwhile, place the saffron threads in a small bowl and grind to a fine powder with a pestle or the end of a wooden spoon.

Add the 1 tablespoon warm water and let soak for 5 minutes.

4. In a separate bowl, combine the clarified butter, yogurt, and another ½ cup water and whisk to mix. Pour this mixture evenly over the bottom of the rice pot. Spoon a ½-inch layer of rice evenly over the yogurt mixture. Without disturbing this layer, add the remaining rice, mounding it toward the center. Sprinkle the top of the mound with the dissolved saffron mixture. Cover the pan and place it over medium heat for 8 minutes.

5. Remove the lid and sprinkle the rice with an additional ½ cup water. Reduce the heat to low. Wrap a clean kitchen towel around the pot lid, piling any excess cloth on top of the lid. (You want to keep the cloth away from the heat.) Place the cloth-covered lid over the rice and cook until the rice on top is tender and the rice on the bottom of the pot has formed a dark golden crust, about 40 minutes. Check after 30 minutes, and if you don't see a crust, increase the heat slightly.

6. To serve, spoon the loose rice on top into a serving bowl, leaving the crusty rice at the bottom. Place a round platter over the pot. Invert the pot and give it a little shake. The crusty rice should slide out in a golden brown disk. Cut the crust into wedges and serve it next to the loose rice.

Serves 6

Note: To clarify butter, melt 1 cup (2 sticks) butter in a small saucepan over medium heat. Remove from the heat and pour off the golden liquid (the clarified butter) into a glass measure or heatproof jar; discard the white milk solids that have settled in the bottom of the pan. Refrigerate any unused clarified butter for up to a month.

PERSIAN RICE WITH CRANBERRIES

IRAN

ON THE SIDE

Rice with sour cherries or bilberries is a popular accompaniment to Persian kebabs. One evening, lacking both, I made the rice with dried cranberries: their sweet-sour flavor was right on the money. Dried cranberries and cherries are sold at gourmet shops, natural foods stores, many supermarkets, and by mail from American Spoon Foods (see Mail-Order Sources).

3 cups basmati rice
9½ cups plus 2
   tablespoons
   water
2 tablespoons salt
1½ cups dried cranberries or dried sour
   cherries
¼ cup sugar
2 tablespoons unsalted butter, plus
   2 tablespoons melted
2 tablespoons plain whole-milk
   yogurt

1. Place the rice in a large bowl and add cold water to cover by 3 inches. Swirl the rice around with your fingers until the water becomes cloudy, then pour through a strainer to drain. Repeat the process until the water remains clear. This will take 4 to 6 rinsings.

2. Place 8 cups of the water and the salt in a large shallow pot (preferably nonstick; the pot should be 10 to 12 inches across and about 6 inches deep) and bring to a boil over high heat. Reduce the heat to medium-high, add the rice, and cook, uncovered, at a brisk simmer for 6 minutes. Pour the rice into a strainer, rinse under cool running water, and drain well. Wipe out and dry the pot with paper towels.

3. Meanwhile, place the cranberries, 1½

cups water, and the sugar in a medium-size saucepan. Bring to a simmer over medium heat and cook until the cranberries are soft and most of the cooking liquid has evaporated, 5 to 8 minutes; the pan juices should be thick and syrupy. Use a slotted spoon to transfer the cranberries to a bowl. Stir the 2 tablespoons butter into the pan juices until melted and bring to a boil. Remove from the heat, cover, and set aside at room temperature.

4. Combine the yogurt, melted butter, and 2 tablespoons water in a bowl and whisk to mix. Pour this mixture evenly over the bottom of the rice pot. Spoon a ½-inch layer of rice evenly over the yogurt mixture. Stir the cranberries into the remaining rice, and without disturbing the rice layer in the pot, add the cranberry rice, mounding it toward the center. Place the pot, uncovered, over medium heat and cook until the rice begins to brown on the bottom, 6 to 8 minutes.

5. Reduce the heat to low. Wrap a clean kitchen towel around the pot lid, piling any excess cloth on top of the lid. (You want to keep the cloth away from the heat.) Place the cloth-covered lid over the rice and cook until the rice on top is tender and the rice on the bottom of the pot has formed a dark golden crust, about 40 minutes. Check after 30 minutes, and if you don't see a crust, increase the heat slightly. Pour the reserved cranberry juices over the rice and remove the pan from the heat. Let stand, covered, for 5 minutes.

6. To serve, spoon the loose rice on top into a bowl, leaving the crusty rice at the bottom. Place a round platter over the pot. Invert the pot and give it a little shake. The crusty rice should slide out in a golden brown disk. Cut the crust into wedges with a spoon and serve it next to the loose rice.

Serves 6

JASMINE RICE

THAILAND

ON THE SIDE

Jasmine rice is a relative newcomer to the North American table, but it's taken the country by storm. With its sweet, delicate, almost floral flavor, it's easy to see why. Jasmine rice can be found at Asian markets and gourmet shops. Serve this rice with any of the Thai grilled dishes in this book.

2 cups jasmine rice
3½ cups water

1. Place the rice in a large bowl and add cold water to cover by 3 inches. Swirl the rice around with your fingers until the water becomes cloudy, then pour through a strainer to drain. Repeat this process until the water remains clear. This will take 4 to 6 rinsings.

2. Place the water in a large, heavy saucepan and bring to a boil over high heat. Stir in the rice and return the water to a boil. Reduce the heat to low and cover the pot tightly. Cook the rice until just tender, 15 to 18 minutes.

3. Remove the pan from the heat. Remove the lid and wrap a clean kitchen towel around the pot lid, piling any excess cloth on top of the lid. Place the cloth-covered lid over the rice and let the rice stand for 5 minutes.

4. Gently fluff the rice with a fork and serve immediately.
Serves 4

BALINESE YELLOW RICE
Nasi Kuning

INDONESIA

ON THE SIDE

This towering cone of rice—gilded with turmeric and perfumed with lemongrass and ginger—symbolizes Bali's sacred Mount Agung. As such, it's a fitting centerpiece for a *megibung*, the Balinese rice table. A *megibung* is a sort of smorgasbord of Balinese delicacies, which would invariably include *babi guling* (Balinese Roast Pork) and a variety of satés.

Note that the traditional rice for this dish is Balinese long-grain rice. The closest approximation available in this country is Thai jasmine rice. Also, coconut water is the liquid inside the coconut.

3 cups jasmine rice
1½ cups coconut water or plain water
1½ cups chicken broth, homemade or
**   canned low-sodium**
¾ cup coconut milk, canned or homemade
**   (page 522)**
1 stalk fresh lemongrass, trimmed and
**   flattened with the side of a cleaver, or**
**   1 teaspoon grated lemon zest**
4 slices fresh galangal or ginger (each ¼
**   inch thick), lightly crushed with the side**
**   of a cleaver**
½ teaspoon ground turmeric
1 tablespoon salt

1. Place the rice in a large bowl and add cold water to cover by 3 inches. Swirl the rice around with your fingers until the water becomes cloudy, then pour through a strainer to drain. Repeat the process until the water remains clear. This will take 4 to 6 rinsings.

2. Place the coconut water, chicken broth, coconut milk, lemongrass, *galangal,* turmeric, and salt in a large, heavy pot and bring to a boil over high heat. Add the rice and return the water to a boil. Reduce the heat to low and cover the pot tightly. Cook the rice until just tender, 15 to 18 minutes. Remove the pot from the heat and let the rice stand, covered, for 5 minutes.

3. Gently fluff the rice with a fork. Remove the lemongrass and *galangal* slices. To serve *nasi kuning* in the traditional Balinese manner, pack it into a lightly oiled large funnel or other cone-shaped mold. Let stand with the wide opening up in a deep bowl or pot covered with aluminum foil for 3 minutes. Place a platter over the base of the mold and invert and unmold the rice onto it.

Serves 6

JAPANESE STEAMED RICE

JAPAN

ON THE SIDE

Rice is more than just a food in Japan. It's the very soul of Japanese culture. Japanese culinary authority Shizuo Tsuji devoted eight pages to the preparation of simple boiled rice in his seminal book *Japanese Cooking: A Simple Art.* It is the inspiration for the following recipe.

You'll need to use a short-grain (aka oval) Asian-style rice for this recipe. Most of the short-grain rice sold in North America is grown in California. Good brands include Calrose and Kokuho Rose. The choicest rice in Japan is *shinmai,* freshly harvested "new rice," which comes to market in the fall. You may be able to find *shinmai* at a Japanese market.

3 cups short-grain rice
4 cups water, approximately
2 teaspoons black sesame seeds (optional)

1. Place the rice in a large bowl and add cold water to cover by 3 inches. Swirl the rice around with your fingers until the water becomes cloudy, then pour through a strainer to drain. Repeat the process until the water remains clear. This will take 4 to 6 rinsings. Once well rinsed, let the rice remain in the strainer for 30 minutes, so it is well drained.

2. Combine the rice and enough water to cover the rice by 1 inch (about 4 cups) in a large heavy pot with a tight-fitting lid. Cook the rice, covered, over medium-high heat until you can hear the water begin to boil. Increase the heat to high and bring the rice to a vigorous boil. (The lid might move from the pressure of the steam.) Boil for 2 minutes. Reduce the heat to low and cook the rice until all the water is absorbed, 15 to 20 minutes. (Do not uncover the rice until it has cooked for a minimum of 15 minutes.)

3. Remove the pot from the heat. Remove the lid and wrap a clean kitchen towel around the pot lid, piling any excess cloth on top of the lid. Place the cloth-covered lid over the rice and let stand for 15 minutes.

4. Gently fluff the rice with a fork before serving. Sprinkle with black sesame seeds (if using) and serve immediately.

Serves 6

GRILLED RICE CAKES

JAPAN

METHOD:
Direct grilling

**ADVANCE
PREPARATION:**
*2 to 8 hours
for chilling the
rice cakes*

Grilled rice cakes are a popular dish in Japan, turning up at street vendors' stalls, at yakitori parlors, and even at highfalutin restaurants. The following recipe was inspired by the vendors outside the Sensoji Temple in Tokyo. You could probably use brown rice, although Japanese barbecue buffs I met in Japan have an almost universal preference for white.

Note that Japanese grill jockeys themselves don't oil the rice cakes. Their grills don't have grates, so the cakes are grilled on chopstick-like skewers held over the fire. The oil enables you to grill the cakes on a Western-style grill.

**Japanese Steamed Rice (page 425), cooled
Classic Teriyaki Sauce or White Miso
　Barbecue Sauce (both page 475),
　or both
1 tablespoon canola oil**

1. Place the rice in a bowl and have a bowl of cold water handy. Lightly oil a large plate. Lightly wet your hands and pinch off 2-inch balls of rice. Mold them into circles, ovals, or heart shapes. Each shape should be about 1 inch thick. Place the shapes as they are made on the prepared plate, rewetting your hands as necessary. When all are made, let stand, loosely covered with plastic wrap, for at least 2 and as long as 8 hours.

2. Preheat the grill to high.

3. When ready to cook, oil the grill grate. Lightly brush the rice cakes on both sides with the canola oil. Brush one side with one or more of the sauces, then arrange the rice cakes, sauce side down, on the hot grate. Cook until nicely browned on both sides, 4 to 5 minutes per side, brushing the cakes with the sauces again before turning. Serve immediately.

Makes 16 to 18 cakes; serves 6 to 8 as a side dish

BAHAMIAN PEAS AND RICE

BAHAMAS

ON THE SIDE

Peas and rice are a staple on every island in the Caribbean. The "peas" in this case are pigeon peas, a greenish-brown, earthy-flavored bean native to Africa. The African origins are evident in some of the bean's local names. Jamaicans call it "Gunga pea" (Congo pea). In the French West Indies, it's known as *pois d'angole* (pea from Angola), a name echoed in the Spanish term *gandule.* If you live in the American South, you probably know it as "crowder."

Whatever you call it, pigeon peas come in ridged pods and are widely available canned and frozen at Hispanic markets and most supermarkets. If you can't find them, you can certainly substitute black-eyed peas or small red kidney beans.

1 tablespoon vegetable oil
4 strips bacon, cut into ¼-inch slivers
1 medium onion, finely chopped
1 medium green bell pepper, stemmed, seeded, and finely chopped
3 cloves garlic, minced
6 fresh basil leaves, thinly slivered, or 1 teaspoon dried basil
1 teaspoon fresh thyme or ½ teaspoon dried
2½ teaspoons salt, or more to taste
½ teaspoon freshly ground black pepper, or more to taste
2 tablespoons tomato paste
½ teaspoon sugar
5½ cups water, or more as needed
3 cups long-grain white rice
1 tablespoon fresh lime juice
2 cups cooked pigeon peas, black-eyed peas, or kidney beans

1. Heat the oil in a large, heavy pot over medium heat. Add the bacon and cook until lightly browned, about 4 minutes. Pour off all but 2 tablespoons fat. Add the onion, bell pepper, garlic, basil, thyme, 2½ teaspoons salt, and ½ teaspoon black pepper and cook until the onion is golden brown, about 5 minutes. Stir in the tomato paste and sugar and cook about 2 minutes more.

2. Add 5½ cups water and bring to a boil. Stir in the rice and lime juice and return to a boil. Reduce the heat to low and cover the pot tightly. Cook until the rice is tender, about 18 minutes, but check after 15 minutes: If the rice is too wet, set the cover ajar to allow some of the liquid to evaporate; if too dry, add 2 to 3 tablespoons water. Stir in the pigeon peas during the last 3 minutes of cooking. Remove the pot from the heat and let stand for 5 minutes. Just before serving, fluff the peas and rice with fork and correct the seasoning, adding more salt or black pepper as needed.

Serves 8

CRAZY RICE
Arroz Loco

BRAZIL

ON THE SIDE

A VEGETARIAN VARIATION
To make a vegetarian version of this dish, simply leave out the bacon and increase the oil to 2 tablespoons.

This colorful side dish is the Brazilian version of fried rice. It turns up at *churrascarias* and restaurants in Rio de Janeiro and São Paolo, with each chef trying to outdo his peers with the elaborateness of the flavorings. This version comes from a wonderful restaurant called Candidos, located in the port town of Pedra de Guaratiba, an hour south of Rio.

FOR THE RICE:
1½ cups long-grain rice
2½ cups water, or more as needed
½ teaspoon salt
1 tablespoon unsalted butter

FOR THE FLAVORINGS:
1 tablespoon olive oil
3 strips bacon, cut into ¼-inch slivers
½ medium red onion, diced
1 clove garlic, minced
½ medium green bell pepper, stemmed, seeded, and cut into ¼-inch dice
½ medium red bell pepper, stemmed, seeded, and cut into ¼-inch dice
½ cup cooked corn kernels
¼ cup dark raisins
¼ cup golden raisins
3 tablespoons chopped fresh Italian (flat-leaf) parsley
Salt and freshly ground black pepper, to taste

1. Place the rice in a large bowl and add cold water to cover by 3 inches. Swirl the rice around with your fingers until the water becomes cloudy, then pour through a strainer to drain. Repeat the process until the water remains clear. This will take 4 to 6 rinsings.

2. Place the rice in a large, heavy pot. Add enough water to cover the rice by ¾ inch (about 2½ cups). Stir in the salt and butter and bring the rice to a boil over high heat. Tightly cover the pan, reduce the heat to low, and cook the rice until tender, about 18 minutes, but check after 15 minutes: If the rice is too wet, set the cover ajar to allow some of the liquid to evaporate; if too dry, add 2 to 3 tablespoons water. Remove the pot from the heat and let the rice stand, covered, for 5 minutes. Fluff it with a fork and set aside.

3. Meanwhile, prepare the flavorings. Heat the oil in a large sauté pan over medium heat. Add the bacon and cook until lightly browned, about 4 minutes. Pour off all but 2 tablespoons fat. Add the onion, garlic, bell peppers, corn, both raisins, and the parsley. Cook until the onion begins to brown, about 5 minutes. Stir the rice into the vegetable mixture and cook until thoroughly heated, about 2 minutes. Correct the seasoning, adding salt and black pepper as needed.

Serves 4

GRILLED POLENTA

ITALY

METHOD:
Direct grilling

ADVANCE PREPARATION:
4 hours to 2 days for chilling the polenta

Polenta is Italian cornmeal mush. But, oh, what mush! Cornmeal simmered to a savory paste and, here, enriched with butter and cream, then smokily browned on the grill. You can serve grilled polenta by itself as a side dish or you can top it with your favorite tomato sauce. For a whimsical touch, use a cookie cutter to cut out stars, triangles, circles, or other fanciful shapes.

To further enrich the polenta, I add 2 tablespoons melted butter to the cornmeal in step 2 and you may also wish to do the same.

2 cups coarse yellow cornmeal
6 cups water
1 teaspoon salt, or more to taste
½ teaspoon freshly ground black
**   pepper, or more to taste**
½ cup heavy cream
2 to 4 tablespoons unsalted butter,
**   melted, or olive oil**

1. Combine the cornmeal, water, 1 teaspoon salt, and ½ teaspoon pepper in a large, heavy saucepan and whisk until smooth. Bring the mixture to a boil over high heat and boil for 2 minutes, whisking steadily.

2. Reduce the heat to a gentle simmer and stir in the cream and, if desired, 2 tablespoons melted butter or oil. Simmer the polenta gently, uncovered, until the mixture thickens enough to pull away from the sides of the pan, 30 to 40 minutes. It should be the consistency of soft ice cream. You don't need to whisk the polenta continuously, but you should keep a careful eye on it, giving it a stir every 5 minutes. As it thickens, you'll need to switch from a whisk to a wooden spoon. Correct the seasoning, adding salt and pepper to taste; the polenta should be highly seasoned.

3. Pour the polenta into a nonstick jellyroll pan or cake pan and even out the top with a spatula. The polenta should be about ½ inch thick. Let cool to room temperature, then cover loosely with plastic wrap and refrigerate until firm, at least 4 hours or as long as 2 days.

4. Preheat the grill to high.

5. While the grill is heating, cut the cold polenta with a knife or cookie cutter into squares, rectangles, or fanciful shapes. (The pieces should be no more than 3 to 4 inches across.) Use a spatula to remove them from the pan to a large plate.

6. When ready to cook, oil the grill grate. Brush both sides of the polenta pieces with 2 tablespoons melted butter or oil. Arrange the polenta on the hot grate and cook, turning with a spatula, until sizzling hot and nicely browned on both sides, 3 to 4 minutes per side. Serve immediately.

Serves 4

GRILLED GRITS

U.S.A.

METHOD:
Direct grilling

ADVANCE PREPARATION:
4 hours to 2 days for chilling the grits

GRILLED GRITS PLUS

Add any of the following in step 1, when you add the grits.

Cheese grits: Add ½ cup finely grated sharp Cheddar, Gouda, or manchego cheese.

Corn grits: Add 1 cup grilled corn kernels (see box, page 372).

Chile grits: Add 2 to 6 chopped pickled jalapeño chiles and ½ cup grated jack or Cheddar cheese.

Grilling polenta is a long-standing Italian tradition. This gave me the idea to grill the American equivalent, grits. Grilled grits go really well with southern- or Texas-style barbecue.

3 cups water or chicken broth,
   homemade or canned low sodium
1 clove garlic, minced
1 teaspoon of your favorite hot sauce
1 teaspoon salt, or more to taste
½ teaspoon freshly ground black pepper,
   or more to taste
3 cups quick-cook grits
4 tablespoons (½ stick) unsalted butter,
   melted, or olive oil

1. Combine the water, garlic, hot sauce, 1 teaspoon salt, and ½ teaspoon pepper in a large, deep pot and bring to a boil over high heat. Stir in the grits and 2 tablespoons melted butter and return to a boil. Reduce the heat to a gentle simmer and cook the grits, uncovered, until thick, 5 to 8 minutes, stirring often. The heat should be high enough to cause bubbles to break the surface, but low enough so that the grits don't spatter. Correct the seasoning, adding salt and pepper to taste.

2. Pour the cooked grits onto a nonstick baking sheet or pie pan and even out the top with a spatula. The grits should be about ½ inch thick. Let cool to room temperature, then cover loosely with plastic wrap and refrigerate until firm, at least 4 hours or as long as 2 days.

3. Preheat the grill to high.

4. While the grill is heating, cut the grits into rectangles or wedges and use a spatula to remove them from the pan to a large plate.

5. When ready to cook, brush both sides of the grits pieces with some of the remaining melted butter or oil. Oil the grate, then arrange the grits pieces on it and cook, turning with a spatula, until sizzling hot and nicely browned on both sides, 3 to 4 minutes per side. Brush the grits with any remaining butter or oil as they cook.

Serves 6

RAINBOW MANIOC
Farofa

ON THE SIDE

TOASTED MANIOC

A simpler farofa is served as a condiment at Brazilian grill joints, where it is sprinkled over steaks and chops to soak up the meat juices. It may strike you as odd but it quickly becomes addictive. You even find it at steak houses in Uruguay and Argentina.

*F*arofa is one of the world's most unusual accompaniments to barbecue, although little known outside its native Brazil. In its simplest form, it looks somewhat like sautéed bread crumbs, but the flavor is nutty, earthy, and buttery—much more complex. The texture is delectably gritty.

Farofa (accent on the second syllable) is made from ground dried manioc (also known as cassava), the starchy tuber that gives us tapioca. A simple *farofa* is made by sautéing manioc flour in butter or oil with a little onion or garlic for flavor. A more elaborate *farofa,* like this one, is garnished with a rainbow-colored array of dried fruits, vegetables, and scrambled eggs.

Manioc flour can be found at Brazilian and Portuguese grocery stores and gourmet shops. Matzo meal could be used as a substitute, but the flavor wouldn't be quite the same.

2 tablespoons unsalted butter
4 tablespoons olive oil
1 large onion, finely chopped
2 cloves garlic, minced
1 medium red bell pepper, stemmed, seeded, and cut into ½-inch diamonds
1 medium green bell pepper, stemmed, seeded, and cut into ½-inch diamonds
1 medium yellow bell pepper, stemmed, seeded, and cut into ½-inch diamonds
⅓ cup raisins or dried currants
⅓ cup diced pitted prunes
2 cups manioc flour
2 large eggs, beaten
Salt and freshly ground black pepper, to taste

1. Heat the butter and 2 tablespoons of the oil in a large nonstick skillet over medium heat. Add the onion and garlic and sauté until soft but not brown, about 4 minutes. Add the bell peppers, raisins, and prunes and sauté until the peppers have softened slightly, about 4 minutes.

2. Add the manioc flour and sauté, stirring frequently, until golden brown, 6 minutes. Push the mixture to the sides of the pan.

3. Add the remaining 2 tablespoons oil to the center of the skillet and heat well. Pour the eggs into the skillet and cook, stirring vigorously with a wooden spoon, until scrambled. Stir the scrambled eggs into the manioc mixture and cook until thoroughly heated, 2 to 4 minutes more. Season with salt and pepper, transfer to a platter, and serve.

Serves 6 to 8

QUICK AND SMOKY BAKED BEANS

METHOD: *Indirect grilling*

*N*ot everyone has the time to make baked beans from scratch. This recipe starts with canned beans, but a quick smoke on the grill produces such rich flavor, you'd swear they had been cooked for hours. For the best results, add

SPECIAL EQUIPMENT:
2 cups wood chips or chunks, soaked for 1 hour in cold water to cover and drained

a couple of cups of diced barbecued pork, ham, or brisket left over from a previous cookout. These beans can also be prepared in the oven. Cook for 30 minutes at 350°F.

4 ounces bacon, cut into ¼-inch slivers
2 cups finely chopped onion
3 cloves garlic, minced
1 tablespoon grated fresh ginger
2 cans (each 15 ounces) Great Northern or kidney beans, drained and rinsed in a colander
¼ cup firmly packed dark brown sugar
¼ cup molasses
¼ cup barbecue sauce
¼ cup ketchup
2 tablespoons Worcestershire sauce
1 tablespoon dry mustard
1 tablespoon prepared mustard
1 tablespoon cider vinegar
1 to 2 cups diced smoked or barbecued pork, ham, or brisket (optional)
1 tablespoon barbecued meat drippings (optional)
Salt and freshly ground black pepper, to taste

1. Set up the grill for indirect grilling (see page 14 or 16). *If using a charcoal grill,* preheat to medium.

If using a gas grill, place all the wood chips in the smoker box and preheat to high. When smoke appears, reduce the heat to medium.

2. Place the bacon in a large, heavy pot and cook over medium heat until lightly browned, about 5 minutes. Discard all but 2 tablespoons fat.

3. Add the onion, garlic, and ginger and sauté until the vegetables are soft, about 5 minutes. Remove the pot from the heat and stir in the beans, sugar, molasses, barbecue sauce, ketchup, Worcestershire sauce, mustard powder, prepared mustard, vinegar, meat (if using), and drippings (if using). Transfer the beans to a baking dish.

4. When ready to cook, if using a charcoal grill, toss the wood chips on the coals. Place the dish in the center of the grill, away from the flames. Cover the grill and bake the beans until thick, about 30 minutes. Season with salt and pepper and serve.

Serves 6 to 8

INDIAN "BAKED BEANS"
Dal Bukhara

INDIA

ON THE SIDE

It's hard to conceive of a North American barbecue without baked beans. Halfway around the world, New Delhi's famous tandoori palace, Bukhara, attracts a cult-like following for an exquisitely rich, creamy bean dish called *dal bukhara*. In other words, baked beans. Like traditional Yankee beans, *dal bukhara* is cooked overnight in a giant pot over charcoal.

The bean of choice for *dal bukhara* is the *urad dal* (also called *kali dal*), a small black bean that looks like a mung bean. (The English name is "whole black gram bean.") The cream and butter give the beans a silky consistency and concentrated richness unequaled in Indian bean dishes. *Urad dal* is available at Indian markets and natural food stores. In a pinch, you can use mung beans.

Traditional *dal bukara* takes 12 hours to make. I've streamlined the recipe by making it in a pressure cooker.

1 cup (8 ounces) dried whole black gram
    beans or mung beans
4 cups water
1 large fresh, ripe tomato
1 tablespoon grated fresh ginger
3 cloves garlic, minced
½ medium onion, minced
1 tablespoon tomato paste
2 teaspoons ground coriander
1 teaspoon salt, or more to taste
½ teaspoon ground black pepper, or
    more to taste
¼ to teaspoon cayenne pepper, or
    more to taste
6 tablespoons unsalted butter
½ cup heavy cream

1. Spread out the beans on a baking sheet and pick out and discard any twigs or stones. Place the beans in a large bowl and add cold water to cover by 3 inches. Swirl the beans with your fingers, then pour through a strainer to drain. Repeat the process another 3 or so times.

2. Place the beans in a pressure cooker and add the 4 cups water. Pressure-cook over medium heat until you hear an even hiss and the valve in the lid dances in a lively fashion, about 10 minutes.

3. Meanwhile, core and cut the tomato into chunks. Place the tomato in a food processor and process until puréed.

4. Cool the cooker completely (top and sides) under cold running water for 5 minutes, then remove the lid.

5. Stir the ginger, garlic, onion, puréed tomato, tomato paste, coriander, 1 teaspoon salt, ½ teaspoon pepper, ¼ teaspoon cayenne, and 4 tablespoons of the butter into the beans. Pressure-cook again until the beans are reduced to a thick, creamy purée, about 5 minutes (see Note). Once again, cool the cooker completely under cold running water.

6. Shortly before serving, stir in the cream. Gently simmer the *dal* until rich and creamy, 2 minutes in the pressure cooker (with its lid off) or in a saucepan. Correct the seasoning, adding salt and black and cayenne pepper as needed. Transfer the *dal* to a serving bowl and dot the top with the remaining butter. Serve immediately.

Serves 8

Note: The beans can be prepared several hours or even a day ahead to this point and stored, covered, in the refrigerator.

BRAZILIAN BLACK BEANS WITH BACON
Tutu Mineira

BRAZIL

ON THE SIDE

Here's the Brazilian version of baked beans. Actually, it's only one of the versions. Brazilians love beans so much they have dozens of dishes to choose from. *Tutu* comes from Minas Gerais (a mining province in northwest Brazil), where it's made with black beans and bacon. I've lightened up the recipe a little—the original is the sort of fare you want to eat before engaging in strenuous physical labor. Serve *tutu mineira* with any of the Brazilian barbecue entrées in this book.

If you can't find manioc flour (see page 430), substitute toasted bread crumbs (see box, page 93).

VEGETARIAN BEANS

To make a vegetarian version of tutu, substitute chopped pine nuts for the bacon and 2 tablespoons olive oil for the bacon fat. In step 1, heat the oil over medium heat, add the pine nuts, and sauté until lightly golden, 2 to 3 minutes. Continue with the recipe as written.

4 strips bacon
1 medium onion, finely chopped
4 cloves garlic, minced
¼ cup chopped fresh Italian (flat-leaf) parsley
1 bay leaf
4 cups cooked black beans (if using canned beans, you'll need two 15-ounce cans)
½ to 1 cup reserved bean cooking liquid or chicken broth, homemade or canned low-sodium
¼ teaspoon Portuguese Hot Sauce (page 478) or your favorite hot sauce
3 to 4 tablespoons manioc flour
Salt and freshly ground black pepper, to taste
2 hard-cooked eggs, coarsely chopped

1. Place the bacon in a large skillet and cook over medium heat until lightly browned, about 5 minutes. Pour off all but 2 tablespoons bacon fat. Add the onion, garlic, half the parsley, and the bay leaf and cook until the onion is soft but not brown, about 4 minutes.

2. Add the beans, ½ cup bean cooking liquid, and the hot sauce to the pan and simmer for 5 minutes. Discard the bay leaf. Using a pestle, potato masher, or the back of a wooden spoon, mash half the beans. Stir in 3 tablespoons manioc flour. Simmer the beans, uncovered, until nice and thick, about 3 minutes. If it's too thick, add a little more bean cooking liquid; if it's too thin, add the remaining manioc flour.

3. Correct the seasoning, adding salt, pepper, and additional hot sauce, as needed. Sprinkle the *tutu* with the chopped eggs and remaining parsley and serve immediately.

Serves 8

GRILLED YORKSHIRE PUDDING

ENGLAND

METHOD:
Indirect grilling

ADVANCE PREPARATION:
30 minutes for chilling the batter

Grilled Prime Ribs (see Index) just isn't complete without Yorkshire pudding. And you can cook the pudding on the grill while resting the meat before carving. The trick to achieving a dramatic puff is to start with ice-cold batter and add it to a smoking hot pan. For the most authentic flavor, use melted meat drippings—however nutritionally incorrect they may be.

You can collect drippings from a roast while it cooks, using a turkey baster to extract them from the drip pan, or save drippings from a previous bout of cooking.

6 large eggs
2¼ cups milk
1 teaspoon salt
½ teaspoon freshly ground black pepper
2 cups all-purpose unbleached flour
¼ cup prime rib drippings, melted unsalted butter, or olive oil

1. Place the eggs, milk, salt, and pepper in a large bowl and whisk to mix. Whisk in the flour and 2 tablespoons of the drippings. Cover and chill the mixture in the freezer for 30 minutes.

2. Set up the grill for indirect grilling (see page 14 or 16) and preheat to high (see Note).

3. Add the remaining 2 tablespoons drippings to a clean 14 × 9-inch roasting pan, place in the center of the hot grill grate, and heat to smoking, about 3 minutes. Pour the batter into the pan and cover the grill tightly. Cook until the pudding is puffed and nicely browned, about 20 minutes (don't peek). Cut into squares for serving.

Serves 8

Note: If you have just prepared a roast, your grill will already be set up for the indirect method. Just add 10 to 12 fresh coals to each side in a charcoal grill.

Sidekicks:
PICKLES, RELISHES, SALSAS & SLAWS

"Hunger is the best pickle."

—*BENJAMIN FRANKLIN*

Every great performance has its divas and chorus lines. So it is with barbecue. The meats or seafood may fetch the lion's share of the bravos. But it's the condiments—the pickles, relishes, salsas, and slaws—that expand what would be a simple solo into a performance of operatic virtuosity.

Pickles and relishes play an important role in the world of barbecue, where their texture and bite offer an exquisite contrast to grilled meats. Following are recipes for the *encurtidos* (pickled onion mixtures) of Central America, the *torshis* (pickled vegetables) of Central Asia,

This North African grocer sells all the fixings for barbecue side dishes.

the fiery *sambals* of Indonesia and Malaysia, and the chutneys of the Indian subcontinent.

A large and distinguished family of salsas comes from closer to home, ranging from Argentina's mild *salsa criolla* (Argentinian Tomato Relish) to the excruciatingly fiery *xni pec* ("Dog's Nose" Salsa) of the Yucatán to the Smoky Apple-Banana Salsa and Grilled Pineapple Salsa of Florida.

Finally, no barbecue would be complete without slaw. In this chapter you'll find recipes for several slaws, including one with fiery scotch bonnet chiles.

I can hear the bravos already.

CENTRAL ASIAN PICKLES
Torshi

AFGHANISTAN

ON THE SIDE

**ADVANCE
PREPARATION:**
3 days

**SPECIAL
EQUIPMENT:**
*1 large jar
(3 quarts or
larger), well
washed*

Torshi refers to a family of pickled vegetables found throughout Central Asia, especially in Afghanistan, Iraq, and Iran. Obviously, the formula varies from country to country, but the basic recipe includes carrots, celery, cauliflower, and cucumbers cured in vinegar, salt, and *sev gundig* (black onion seeds found in Middle and Near Eastern groceries). No Central Asian barbecue would be complete without one or more bowls of *torshi*. This recipe makes a mild pickle. If you'd prefer yours hot, add 2 to 12 dried red chile peppers.

FOR THE PICKLING SOLUTION:
4½ cups distilled white vinegar
3 cups water
⅓ cup salt
¼ cup sugar, or more
    to taste
1 teaspoon black onion seeds
    (sev gundig; optional)
1 teaspoon dried oregano
1 teaspoon black
    peppercorns
½ teaspoon ground
    turmeric

FOR THE VEGETABLES:
1 head cauliflower, cut into bite-size florets
8 ounces carrots, peeled and cut into 1-inch
    pieces
4 medium ribs celery, cut into 1-inch pieces
1 turnip, cut lengthwise in half, then
    crosswise into ¼-inch slices
1 onion, cut into ¼-inch slices
3 cloves garlic, peeled

1. Combine the vinegar, water, salt, sugar, black onion seeds (if using), oregano, peppercorns, and turmeric in a large jar. Cover the jar tightly and shake until the sugar is dissolved.

2. Add the cauliflower, carrots, celery, turnip, onion, and garlic to the jar and stir. Correct the seasoning, adding sugar to taste. Press a piece of plastic wrap directly on top of the mixture to keep the vegetables submerged. Cover the jar, placing another piece of plastic wrap between the mouth of the jar and the lid (to prevent the vinegar from corroding the metal lid). Let cure, at room temperature or in the refrigerator, for at least 3 days; the *torshi* will keep, tightly covered in the refrigerator, for several weeks.

Makes about 3 quarts; enough to serve 12

GEORGIAN PICKLES

REPUBLIC OF
GEORGIA

ON THE SIDE

Whenever Georgians eat barbecue (indeed, whenever they feast in general), you'll find a lavish assortment of pickles—vegetables you expect to find pickled, like cucumbers and cabbage, and vegetables you wouldn't think of pickling, like lettuce and watermelon (the fruit, not just the rind). Georgian pickles can be made in a matter of minutes, but leave yourself 3 days for the vegetables to cure.

FOR THE PICKLING SOLUTION:
5 cups distilled white vinegar
3 cups water
5 tablespoons salt
5 tablespoons sugar, or more to taste
8 cloves garlic, peeled
8 sprigs fresh cilantro
8 sprigs fresh dill
8 dried hot peppers

FOR THE VEGETABLES:
1 head iceberg lettuce
1 pound fresh, ripe plum tomatoes
1 pound pickling cucumbers, such
   as Kirby
1 piece (1 pound) watermelon with rind

1. Combine the vinegar, water, salt, and sugar in a nonreactive saucepan and bring to a boil over high heat. Remove from the heat and stir in the garlic, cilantro, dill, and hot peppers. Let the mixture cool to room temperature, about 1 hour. Correct the seasoning, adding sugar to taste.

2. Meanwhile, trim the lettuce and cut into 1-inch wedges. Rinse the tomatoes and cucumbers under cold running water, blot dry with paper towels, and prick 5 to 6 times with a fork. Cut the watermelon, both rind and flesh, into 1-inch wedges. Divide the vegetables and melon among three clean 1-quart jars. Add enough cooled pickling mixture to cover. Press a piece of plastic wrap directly on top of the mixture in each jar to keep the vegetables submerged.

3. Cover the jars, placing another piece of plastic wrap between the mouth of the jar and the lid. (The second piece of plastic wrap will prevent the vinegar from corroding the metal lid.) Let the vegetables pickle, in the refrigerator, for at least 3 days. The pickles will keep, tightly covered in the refrigerator, for several weeks.

Makes about 3 quarts; enough to serve 10 to 12

CARROT AND PINEAPPLE ESCABECHE

Escabeche is the Spanish term for a food preserved in vinegar. Part relish, part pickle, part salsa, this one is 100 percent delicious. Serve it as an accompaniment to turkey, for example, the way you would cranberry sauce. One chile will give you a warm *escabeche*, 6 chiles an infernally hot one.

2 cups rice vinegar
⅔ cup sugar
5 cups julienned carrots (6 to 8 medium
   carrots; about 10 ounces)
1 to 6 serrano or jalapeño chiles, sliced
   crosswise as thinly as possible
3 cups diced fresh pineapple
Salt and freshly ground black pepper, to taste
3 tablespoons chopped fresh cilantro

1. Bring the vinegar and sugar to a boil in a large, shallow nonreactive saucepan over high heat. Add the carrots, reduce the heat to medium, and simmer until just tender, 1 to 2 minutes. Add the chiles and simmer for 20 seconds. Transfer the carrots and chiles with a slotted spoon to a heatproof serving bowl.

2. Add the pineapple to the simmering vinegar mixture and cook until just tender, 2 to 4 minutes. Transfer the pineapple with a

slotted spoon to the serving bowl. Add enough of the poaching liquid to nicely coat the vegetables and stir in salt and pepper.

3. Let the *escabeche* cool to room temperature, then refrigerate, covered, until serving time, at least 2 hours (see Note).

4. Just before serving, correct the seasoning and stir in the cilantro.

Makes about 2 quarts; enough to serve 8 to 10

Note: The *escabeche* can be prepared to this point up to 48 hours ahead.

PICKLED ONIONS
Cebollita

NICARAGUA

ON THE SIDE

ADVANCE PREPARATION:
6 to 8 hours for pickling the onions

SPECIAL EQUIPMENT:
One 1-pint jar, well washed

In Nicaragua, grilled beef is always served with pickled onions. This is one of the quickest and easiest pickle recipes there is—perfect for any grilled meat.

1 cup distilled white vinegar
1½ teaspoons salt
½ teaspoon sugar
1 large white onion, cut into thin wedges
1 to 2 fresh jalapeño chiles, thinly sliced

1. Whisk the vinegar, salt, and sugar in a nonreactive bowl until the sugar is dis-

solved. Stir in the onion and chile. Press a piece of plastic wrap directly on top of the mixture to keep the onions submerged.

2. Let the onions and chiles pickle at room temperature for 6 to 8 hours. Transfer to a clean 1-pint jar and cover, placing a piece of plastic wrap between the mouth of the jar and the lid (to prevent the vinegar from corroding the metal lid). The *cebollita* will keep, tightly covered in the refrigerator, for several weeks.

Makes about 2 cups; enough to serve 6

PICKLED VEGETABLES
Encurtido

CENTRAL AMERICA

ON THE SIDE

This tangy condiment turns up throughout Central America, where it's used as an all-purpose condiment for grilled steaks and sausages, rice and bean dishes—and just about everything

else. The chile of choice is the habanero, a Mexican/Central American cousin of the Caribbean scotch bonnet chile. The two are interchangeable.

2 cups distilled white vinegar
1 tablespoon salt
2 large white onions, finely diced
1 cup finely diced carrots
½ medium green bell pepper, stemmed,
   seeded, and finely diced
½ medium red bell pepper, stemmed,
   seeded, and finely diced
1 to 3 fresh habanero chiles, thinly
   sliced
3 tablespoons chopped fresh cilantro
1 tablespoon chopped fresh oregano
   or 2 teaspoons dried
8 black peppercorns
2 allspice berries

1. Combine the vinegar and salt in a non-reactive bowl and whisk until the salt is dissolved. Stir in the onions, carrots, bell peppers, chile, cilantro, oregano, peppercorns, and allspice berries. Transfer the mixture to two 1-pint jars.

2. Cover the jars, placing a piece of plastic wrap between the mouth of each jar and the lid. (The plastic wrap will prevent the vinegar from corroding the metal lid.) Let the vegetables pickle, at room temperature, for at least 1 day (see Note).

***Makes about 2 pints; enough to serve
8 to 10***

Note: *Encurtido* will keep for several weeks in the refrigerator (the flavor improves as the mixture sits).

PENANG SHALLOT RELISH
Chung Gao Jai

MALAYSIA

ON THE SIDE

Shallot relishes turn up widely on the world's barbecue trail. I've enjoyed them in countries as diverse as Morocco, Malaysia, and Turkey. One reason for their popularity is that shallots have a milder, more refined flavor than onions. This relish comes from the island of Penang in northwestern Malaysia, where it is served with Grilled Skate Wings (see Index). In fact, it's delicious with just about any type of fish and even over steak. Warning, though: This baby is hot!

Sambal ulek is a fiery red chile paste from Indonesia and Malaysia, widely available at Asian markets and in some gourmet shops. Substitutes include Thai and Vietnamese red chile sauces (unsweetened) and Chinese chile pastes.

1 cup thinly sliced shallots
½ cup fresh lime juice, or more to taste
1½ teaspoons salt, or more to taste
1½ teaspoons sugar
1 tablespoon sambal ulek or other
   chile paste, or more to taste
¼ cup water

Place the shallots in a large bowl and add ½ cup lime juice, 1½ teaspoons salt, the sugar, 1 tablespoon *sambal ulek,* and the water, stirring until the sugar is dissolved. Correct the seasoning, adding salt, lime juice, or *sambal ulek* to taste. The sambal will taste good right away and even better after 30 minutes, as the flavors blend and merge.

***Makes about 1¼ cups; enough to serve
4 to 6***

ONION-CILANTRO RELISH

MEXICO

ON THE SIDE

This simple relish turns up in Mexico wherever you find *barbacoa* (see Index), grilled fish, or grilled meats. I love the way the relish launches a triple assault on your tongue: the pungency of the onion, the peppery bite of the radishes, and the aromatic punch of the fresh cilantro. By the way, the latter has a neutralizing effect on the onion; you're less likely to get "onion breath" when you eat the two ingredients together.

1 bunch fresh cilantro
1 bunch radishes
1 large white onion, peeled

Rinse the cilantro under cold running water, blot it dry with paper towels, and pluck the leaves from the stems. Trim and rinse the radishes, then cut them into $\frac{1}{4}$-inch dice (see Note). Cut the onion into $\frac{1}{4}$-inch dice. Combine the cilantro, radishes, and onion in a serving bowl and toss to mix. The relish is best served within 2 hours of preparing.

Serves 6 to 8

Note: If desired, save the radish leaves for Swordfish with Pipián Sauce (see Index).

FIERY CHILE AND SHALLOT RELISH

Sambal Chobek

INDONESIA

ON THE SIDE

This relish (or *sambal,* as it is called in Indonesia) features an incendiary blend of shallots and red chiles. *Chobek* is a black lava-stone mortar and pestle traditionally used to grind the ingredients for *sambals* in Java. There are lots of options for chiles: red jalapeños or serranos, bird peppers or tabasco peppers. I've given a range to suit every degree of heat tolerance. (An Indonesian would use the full 15). You'll need to know about one offbeat ingredient: shrimp paste. Called *trasi* in Indonesia and *belacan* in Malaysia, it's a malodorous purple-brown paste of ground, salted, fermented shrimp. It tastes a lot better than it smells. If unavailable, you could use a few drops of Asian fish sauce or omit it entirely.

$\frac{1}{2}$ teaspoon shrimp paste (optional)
5 to 15 fresh red chiles, stemmed and thinly sliced
4 shallots, coarsely chopped
$\frac{2}{3}$ cup fresh lime juice, or more to taste
1 tablespoon salt, or more to taste

1. Roll the shrimp paste (if using) into a ball and place it on the end of a fork or skewer. Hold it over a live flame (either a barbecue grill or gas burner) until lightly toasted and very aromatic, 2 to 4 minutes.

Alternatively, place the shrimp paste on a square of aluminum foil and roast it under the broiler.

2. Combine the shrimp paste, chiles, shallots, ⅔ cup lime juice, and 1 tablespoon salt in a mini chopper, food processor, or blender, and blend to a coarse paste. Correct the seasoning, adding lime juice or salt; the *sambal* should be very spicy. *Sambal chobek* will keep, tightly covered in the refrigerator, for up to 3 days.

Makes about 1 cup; enough to serve 4 to 6

MOROCCAN SHALLOT RELISH

MOROCCO

ON THE SIDE

This simple relish is a traditional accompaniment to Moroccan barbecue. Serve it with any of the Moroccan lamb dishes in the lamb chapter or the Bani Marine Street Beef Kebabs (see Index).

½ cup finely chopped shallots
½ cup finely chopped Italian (flat-leaf) parsley
2 tablespoons extra-virgin olive oil
2 tablespoons fresh lemon juice, or more to taste

½ teaspoon salt, or more to taste
½ teaspoon freshly ground black pepper, or more to taste

Combine the shallots, parsley, oil, and lemon juice in a mixing bowl and toss to mix. Add ½ teaspoon salt and ½ teaspoon pepper and toss again. Correct the seasoning, adding more salt, pepper, and lemon juice, if desired. The relish is best served within 2 hours of preparing.

Makes about 1 cup; enough to serve 4

ONION RELISH WITH POMEGRANATE MOLASSES

TURKEY

ON THE SIDE

This tangy relish turns up in one form or another at kebab houses and private homes throughout Turkey. A simple version might consist solely of parsley and sliced onions. Here's a more elaborate relish—flavored with sumac, Aleppo peppers, and pomegranate molasses. I first sampled it at the home of Turkish cooking authority Ayfer Unsal. The unfamiliar ingredients are described in the Glossary and can be purchased at Middle and Near Eastern markets (not to mention at many gourmet shops) or ordered from one of the mail-order sources listed at the end of this book.

1 medium white onion, thinly sliced lengthwise
½ medium red bell pepper, stemmed,
    seeded and thinly sliced
¼ cup coarsely chopped Italian (flat-leaf)
    parsley
1 tablespoon Aleppo pepper flakes or sweet
    or hot paprika
1 tablespoon ground sumac or
    2 teaspoons fresh lemon juice
1 tablespoon Pomegranate Molasses
    (page 227)
Salt, to taste

Combine the onion, bell pepper, parsley, pepper flakes, sumac powder, and Pomegranate Molasses in an attractive bowl. Mix well with your hands or a wooden spoon. (Mixing with your hands helps soften the onions.) Let stand 5 to 10 minutes, then taste, adding salt as needed. Serve immediately.

Makes about 2 cups; enough to serve 4 to 6

GUYANESE MANGO FIRE RELISH

GUYANA

ON THE SIDE

Alarmingly hot and delectably fruity is this popular condiment from Guyana. Tradition calls for the relish to be made with green mangoes, but I like the peachy-apricoty tones that come with using ripe ones. Use the relish sparingly—it's *really* hot! To make a slightly less fiery version, seed the chiles before puréeing.

Serve this relish with any simply grilled seafood, poultry, or meat dish.

1 pound ripe mangoes, peeled, pitted,
    and cut into ½-inch dice
    (about 2 cups)
1 to 4 scotch bonnet chiles, or more,
    if you can bear it, stemmed

4 cloves garlic, crushed
2 teaspoons salt, or more to taste
2 teaspoons sugar
⅓ cup fresh lime juice, or more to taste
2 to 4 tablespoons water

Combine the mangoes, chile, garlic, 2 teaspoons salt, the sugar, ⅓ cup lime juice, and 2 tablespoons water in a blender and purée until smooth. Add more water as needed to obtain a thick but pourable sauce. Correct the seasoning, adding more salt or lime juice as necessary. The relish will keep, tightly covered in the refrigerator, for up to 1 week.

Makes about 2 cups; enough to serve 8

PINEAPPLE ACHAR

SINGAPORE

ON THE SIDE

Achar is an Indian and Southeast Asian relish-like dish often made with fruit. This one contrasts the cooling succu-

lence of fresh pineapple with the fiery bite of chiles. There is one ingredient that may take you by surprise here: fish sauce. Yet, throughout Southeast Asia this briny condiment is paired with fruit. You'll be amazed how the salt in the fish sauce brings out the sweetness of the pineapple. And how the acidity in the fruit eliminates the fishy flavor in the fish sauce. So try it even if you have misgivings. I promise you'll be delighted. This recipe was inspired by an *achar* I tasted at a food stall in the Arab market in Singapore.

1 tablespoon Asian fish sauce, or more to taste
1 tablespoon fresh lime juice, or more to taste

1 tablespoon sugar, or more to taste
3 cups diced fresh pineapple
1 to 3 hot Asian red or green chiles or jalapeños, thinly sliced (for a milder achar, seed the chiles)

Combine 1 tablespoon each fish sauce, lime juice, and sugar in an attractive bowl and whisk until the sugar dissolves. Stir in the pineapple and chile. Taste for seasoning, adding more fish sauce, lime juice, or sugar as necessary; the mixture should be sweet, fruity, tart, and a little salty. Serve immediately.

Makes about 3 cups; enough to serve 6

MIXED VEGETABLE ACHAR

INDONESIA

ON THE SIDE

ADVANCE PREPARATION:
8 to 10 hours for marinating the relish

Here's another *achar*—this one from the Amandari Resort in Bali. It's one of the most refreshing relishes ever to grace a table. I love the way the sweetness of the cinnamon and star anise balance the bite of the shallots and vinegar.

FOR THE VEGETABLES:
1 cucumber, peeled and seeded (see box, page 89)
3 carrots, peeled
1 medium red bell pepper, stemmed and seeded
1 medium green bell pepper, stemmed and seeded
4 shallots, peeled

FOR THE MARINADE:
1⅓ cups distilled white vinegar
½ cup sugar
5 whole cloves
4 cinnamon sticks (3 inches each)
2 star anise
2 slices (each ¼ inch thick) fresh ginger, smashed with the side of a cleaver
Salt, to taste (optional)

1. Cut the cucumber, carrots, and bell peppers into 4 × ¼-inch strips. Thinly slice the shallots. Place the vegetables in a large nonreactive bowl, toss to mix, and set aside.

2. Combine the vinegar, sugar, cloves, cinnamon, star anise, and ginger in a small nonreactive saucepan. Bring to a boil over high heat. Reduce the heat to medium and simmer until richly flavored, about 10 minutes. Taste, adding salt if desired. Cool slightly, then strain over the vegetables. Marinate the vegetables, covered, in the refrigerator for 8 to 10 hours, stirring from time to time. The *achar* will keep for 1 week in the refrigerator.

Serves 6

Stuck on Saté:
The Indonesian Grill

Indonesia is a country of mind-boggling ethnic diversity, with 300 different races and religions. I visited two of the best known of the 12,000 islands in the Indonesian archipelago—Java and Bali—and no matter where I went I found saté (pronounced "sah-tay"). Indonesia's culinary common denominator, these tiny kebabs are served everywhere, from roadside pushcarts to swank hotel restaurants, as a snack or full meal, at religious festivals, sporting events, and at the beach, pretty much any time of the day or night.

Simple to make, easy to eat, economical, nutritious, infinitely varied in shape and flavor, satés are one of the most perfect foods devised by man. Not surprisingly, their popularity extends far beyond Indonesia's borders. Satés have become an integral part of the Thai, Malaysian, and Singaporean diet ("satay" is the Malaysian spelling). In the last decade, they've been embraced with equal enthusiasm by contemporary American chefs.

A great many misconceptions surround saté, not the least of which is its main ingredient. To most Americans, saté means a small (although rather large by Indonesian standards) chicken or beef kebab served with peanut sauce. In Indonesia, however, there are hundreds of different types of satés to choose from, ranging from the tiny *saté lalat* (a beef and coconut saté made in such diminutive proportions, its name literally means "fly") to the *saté buntel* (a ground lamb saté so large it takes four skewers to hold it).

The saté—or at least the idea of grilling meat on a stick—seems to have originated with Arab spice traders, who arrived on the island of Sumatra in the eleventh century A.D. The Arabs introduced the Islamic religion to the region, and it's possible they also introduced the Middle Eastern–style kebab. To support this theory, scholars point to Padang, which was one of the first cities in Sumatra to adopt Islam. *Saté padang* became one of Indonesia's most beloved satés and remains so to this day. (Of course, the idea of meat on a stick is so universal, it may have originated long before the arrival of the Arabs.)

If saté was inspired by the Arab kebab, it quickly acquired its own personality. First, it shrank. The average *saté ayam* (chicken saté) or *saté kambing* (lamb or goat saté) is about the size

of your baby finger. This makes for great snacking: It's not uncommon for an Indonesian to down 20 or 30 satés at a single sitting. And still not leave the table stuffed.

According to Jakarta tourism representative Yuni Syafril, the saté takes its name from a Sumatran word meaning "to stick, stab, or skewer." When you're really angry with someone, explained Syafril you threaten to "saté" them. This sort of etymology is certainly not without precedent in the world of barbecue: Jamaican jerk, for example, is named for *juk,* the local dialect word for "to stab."

SEARCHING OUT THE BEST

Syafril was my host in Jakarta, the capital of Indonesia, and the largest city on Java, and he acquitted his duties with the hospitality for which Indonesians are famous. My first night there, he took me on the Indonesian equivalent of a bar crawl. Our first stop was the Jalan Sabang, a noisy street lined with restaurants (including the famous Padang restaurant Natrabu, not to mention a Kentucky Fried Chicken and a Sizzler Steak House). Our destination wasn't a dining establishment, however, but a tiny pushcart on bicycle wheels run by Nurul Phamid, a willowy young man with a faint moustache.

Like his father, who set up shop here in 1960, Phamid begins work at 5 P.M. and continues until 3 A.M. His stock in trade is *saté ayam,* which he prepares and grills by the light of a kerosene lamp. Phamid spends his afternoons threading tiny pieces of chicken thigh, liver, skin, and embryonic chicken eggs onto bamboo skewers not much bigger than broom straws.

When you place your order, Phamid prepares the marinade on the spot, mixing *ketjap manis* (sweet soy sauce), peanut sauce, a squeeze of lime juice, and chopped onion on a dinner plate. He dabs a handful of satés into the mixture, as you would a paint brush, then places them on a tiny charcoal brazier. A few waves of a bamboo fan—the most important piece of equipment in a saté man's kitchen after the grill—and the coconut husk charcoal blazes to life. Phamid bastes the sizzling satés with his secret ingredient—rendered chicken fat. A moment later, they're ready to eat.

The accompaniments to this splendid saté include a dollop of peanut sauce, a splash of *ketjap manis,* and a spoonful of *sambal* (fiery chili sauce), which are mixed together in a bowl. We were also served a steamed cake of sticky rice, called *lontong,* which is cooked in a banana leaf. We sprinkled everything with fried shallots. The cost for this princely feast—and it is princely—is 3,000 rupiahs, about 35 cents.

NOW FOR SATE PEDANG

Our next stop was a brightly lit sidewalk eatery called Gunung Sari, near Jakarta's lively Kota district. Jakarta operates on a diurnal economy: daytime businesses close their shutters at nightfall and a veritable city of portable restaurants spring up on the sidewalks in front of them. Some, like Gunung Sari, are quite elaborate, complete with generators, fluorescent lighting systems, and white Formica tables. I peered into an enormous cauldron bubbling away over a charcoal fire to see the next dish I was to sample: *saté pedang.*

To make it, beef hearts, tongues, and tripe are simmered for several hours in a fiery broth flavored with ginger, galangal, turmeric, garlic, and palate-blasting doses of black pepper. The cooked meats are cut into tiny dice, threaded on skewers, and grilled over coconut husk charcoal. Meanwhile, the broth has been heavily thickened with rice flour into a starchy gravy. The kebabs and gravy are served on a banana leaf. To wash them down there's iced tea chilled with a chips off a huge block of ice that sits on the sidewalk.

I must confess, I'm not a big fan of heart or tongue, and years of restaurant reviewing have conditioned me to disdain starchy gravies. But Gunung Sari's *saté padang* was one of the most delicious things I've ever tasted. I understood why this rough-and-tumble eatery does such a lively business.

During the weeks I spent on the islands of Bali and Java, I sampled an astonishing array of satés. Sausage-size *saté buntel* (ground lamb and coriander satés) served with sweet-sour tamarind sauce. Tiny *saté kalong* ("flying fox" satés), a sweet, garlicky ground beef saté named for a nocturnal squirrel that comes out about the same time of day the saté vendors do in the city of Cirebon on the north coast of Java. One night, I feasted on what was the last kind of saté I expected to find on this staunchly Muslim island: *saté babi manis* (sweet pork saté). I ate it, logically enough, in Jakarta's Chinatown. In Bali I enjoyed one of my all-time favorites, *saté lilit,* a spicy fish mousse flavored with exquisitely aromatic kaffir lime leaves and grilled on fresh lemongrass stalks.

Recipes for these satés and others appear throughout this book—some are better as appetizers, some are better as entrées, and most work well as either. Satés are the perfect grilled food for the new millennium: high in flavor, low in fat, great for casual eating and entertaining, and quick and easy to make. One traditionally eats a relatively small amount of meat in proportion to the vegetable-based accompaniments.

MANGO ACHAR

Here's the third of our trio of *achars,* this one from Malaysia. I like to think of it as Southeast Asian coleslaw. The sweetness of the mango and coconut milk makes a particularly welcome addition to a barbecue, as does the contrast of sweet and savory, of hot and cold. As elsewhere in the book, I've given a range of chiles. One will make a mild *achar*; 6 will be Malaysian in its firepower.

FOR THE DRESSING:

½ cup coconut milk, canned or homemade (page 522)
¼ cup distilled white vinegar
1 tablespoon sugar, or more to taste
1 tablespoon Asian fish sauce or soy sauce (see Note)
2 teaspoons minced fresh ginger
1 clove garlic, minced
½ teaspoon salt, or more to taste
½ teaspoon freshly ground black pepper, or more to taste

FOR THE RELISH:

1 ripe mango, peeled, pitted, and cut into ½-inch dice (about 2 cups)
¼ head green cabbage (8 ounces), cut into ½-inch dice (about 2 cups)
2 shallots, thinly sliced
1 to 6 hot chiles, such as Thai or serrano, thinly sliced (for a milder achar, seed the chiles)

1. Prepare the dressing. Combine the coconut milk, vinegar, 1 tablespoon sugar, the fish sauce, ginger, garlic, ½ teaspoon salt, and the pepper in a small nonreactive saucepan and bring to a boil over medium heat, whisking until the sugar dissolves. Transfer the dressing to a serving bowl and let cool to room temperature.

2. Stir in the mango, cabbage, shallots, and chile. Correct the seasoning, adding sugar or salt as needed; the *achar* should be a little sweet, a little salty, and electrifyingly spicy. You can serve the *achar* right away, but it will taste even richer if you let it stand for an hour or so (no longer) before serving.

Makes about 4 cups; enough to serve 6 to 8

Note: Traditionally, the *achar* would be flavored with a malodorous condiment called shrimp paste (see the Glossary). I call for fish sauce, which has a similar flavor and is easier to find and use.

LEMONGRASS SAMBAL

Sambals are spicy pastes made of hot chiles and aromatic vegetables (sometimes with seafood added), served as condiments in Indonesia and Malaysia. A tiny bowl or spoonful of *sambal* (or several different *sambals*) is placed on the plate and served as an accompaniment to saté or grilled chicken or fish. This one features the haunting flavor of fresh lemongrass. To be strictly authentic, you'd use fresh turmeric, palm sugar, and tamarind water—all available at Asian markets. But a highly tasty *sambal* can be made using ginger and ground turmeric instead of the fresh; brown sugar in place of the palm sugar; and lemon juice in place of the tamarind.

6 stalks fresh lemongrass, trimmed and thinly sliced

2 to 3 large shallots, coarsely chopped

6 cloves garlic, peeled

1 to 3 Thai or serrano chiles, coarsely chopped (for a milder sambal, seed the chiles)

1 fresh, ripe plum tomato, cut into ½-inch dice (with juices)

1 tablespoon chopped fresh ginger

1 tablespoon chopped fresh turmeric or an additional 1 tablespoon chopped fresh ginger mixed with ½ teaspoon ground turmeric

1 tablespoon palm sugar or firmly packed light brown sugar

2 tablespoons Tamarind Water (page 219) or fresh lemon juice

1 tablespoon sweet soy sauce (ketjap manis) or 1½ teaspoons each regular soy sauce and molasses

½ teaspoon salt, or more to taste

½ teaspoon freshly ground black pepper, or more to taste

½ cup peanut oil

1. Place the lemongrass, shallots, garlic, chile, tomato with its juices, the ginger, turmeric, and palm sugar in a food processor. Process to a coarse paste. Add the Tamarind Water, sweet soy sauce, ½ teaspoon salt, and ½ teaspoon pepper. Process to blend.

2. Heat the oil in a wok or frying pan over medium heat. Add the lemongrass mixture. Cook, stirring with a wooden spoon, until lightly browned and very fragrant, about 10 minutes. Season to taste with additional salt and pepper. Cool to room temperature before serving. This delicious *sambal* will keep, tightly covered in the refrigerator, for up to 1 week.

Makes about 1¼ cups; enough to serve 4 to 6

TOMATO PEANUT SAMBAL
Sambal Achan

INDONESIA

ON THE SIDE

This is one of the milder *sambals* in the Indonesia repertory—a delectably creamy condiment made nutty with peanut butter, aromatic with cilantro and coriander, and piquant with lime juice.

Serve this *sambal* with any of the Indonesian satés in this book or with Vietnamese, Thai, or Malaysian-style grilled meats.

¼ **cup chunky peanut butter**

¼ **cup fresh lime juice or distilled white vinegar, or more to taste**

¼ **cup sweet soy sauce (ketjap manis) or 2 tablespoons each regular soy sauce and molasses, or more to taste**

2 to 3 teaspoons sambal ulek (see Glossary) or other chile paste, or more to taste

1 large fresh, ripe tomato, peeled and seeded (see box, page 62), then diced

2 scallions, both white and green parts, trimmed and minced

1 clove garlic, minced

3 tablespoons minced fresh cilantro leaves

1 teaspoon ground coriander

½ **teaspoon salt**

½ **teaspoon freshly ground black pepper**

1. Combine the peanut butter, ¼ cup lime juice, ¼ cup sweet soy sauce, and 2 teaspoons *sambal ulek* in a small bowl and whisk to mix.

2. Stir in the tomato, scallions, garlic, cilantro, coriander, salt, and pepper. Correct the seasoning, adding *sambal ulek,* lime juice, or sweet soy sauce as necessary. The *sambal* will keep, tightly covered in the refrigerator, for up to 1 week.

Makes about 1¼ cups; enough to serve 4 to 6

MOROCCAN TOMATO JAM

MOROCCO

ON THE SIDE

This thick, spicy "jam" is unlike any tomato dish you've ever tasted. Sweet, fruity, and perfumed, it is traditionally part of the lavish assortment of salads served at the beginning of a Moroccan meal. I like to serve it in a more unconventional fashion—as a relish for grilled meats.

8 fresh, ripe tomatoes (3 to 3½ pounds)

½ **cup sugar, or more to taste**

3 tablespoons vegetable oil

2 tablespoons red wine vinegar, or more to taste

2 teaspoons ground cinnamon, or more to taste

1. Cut the tomatoes in half crosswise and gently squeeze the halves, cut side down, over a bowl to wring out the seeds. (You can save the seeds and liquid for stock or soups.) Grate the tomatoes, on the coarse side of a grater, into a large nonstick skillet.

2. Stir in ½ cup sugar, the oil, 2 tablespoons vinegar, and 2 teaspoons cinnamon and bring the mixture to a boil over high heat. Reduce the heat to medium and gently cook the mixture, stirring occasionally with a wooden spoon, until thick and jam-like, 5 to 10 minutes. Correct the seasoning, adding more sugar, vinegar, or cinnamon as necessary. The mixture should be sweet and spicy. Transfer the jam to a dish or bowl and cool to room temperature. It will keep, covered in the refrigerator, for up to 1 week.

Makes about 1 cup; enough to serve 4 to 6

PINEAPPLE CHUTNEY

SRI LANKA

ON THE SIDE

Here's a quick, easy pineapple chutney that is often served with chicken satés in Sri Lanka. The tamarind gives the chutney a complex, smoky, sweet-sour flavor. For best results, use one of the new golden pineapples, which are richer and sweeter than the conventional hard, green supermarket variety.

2 cups diced fresh, ripe pineapple (with juices)

½ medium red bell pepper, stemmed, seeded, and cut into ¼-inch dice

¼ cup dark or golden raisins

1 to 4 serrano or other hot chiles, seeded and finely chopped

3 tablespoons chopped fresh cilantro

½ cup Tamarind Water (page 219) or ¼ cup balsamic vinegar mixed with 1 tablespoon firmly packed light brown sugar

½ cup pineapple juice

¼ cup cider vinegar

2 tablespoons firmly packed light brown sugar, or more to taste

1 cinnamon stick (3 inches)

3 white cardamom pods or 1 teaspoon ground cardamom

½ teaspoon sambal ulek or other hot sauce

1. Combine the pineapple with its juices, the bell pepper, raisins, chile, cilantro, Tamarind Water, pineapple juice, vinegar, 2 tablespoons sugar, the cinnamon stick, cardamom, and *sambal ulek* in a heavy nonreactive saucepan and bring to a boil over high heat. Cook, uncovered, until the pineapple is soft and the chutney is thick and richly flavored, about 5 minutes. Remove from the heat and correct the seasoning, adding sugar as necessary.

2. Transfer the chutney to a bowl and cool to room temperature. Discard the cinnamon stick before serving. The chutney will keep, tightly covered in the refrigerator, for several weeks.

Makes about 2 cups; enough to serve 4 to 6

OAXACAN-STYLE GUACAMOLE

MEXICO

ON THE SIDE

Just about everybody is familiar with the puréed avocado preparation known as guacamole. What you may not realize is that it serves more as a sauce than a dip in Mexico and that it changes from region to region. Guacamole is easy to prepare, but if you don't use ripe avocados (the sort that go splat when you drop them), it will never taste right. Here's the Oaxacan version—perfect for spooning over grilled meats.

2 ripe avocados

¼ cup chopped onion

1 clove garlic, minced

1 to 3 serrano or jalapeño chiles, coarsely chopped

¼ cup fresh lime juice, or more to taste

¼ cup chopped fresh cilantro

½ teaspoon salt, or more to taste

1. Peel, pit, and coarsely chop the avocados. Combine the onion, garlic, and chile in a food processor and process until finely chopped. Add the avocados and process to a purée. Add ¼ cup lime juice, the cilantro, and ½ teaspoon salt and process just to blend. Taste for seasoning, adding lime juice and salt as needed.

2. Transfer the guacamole to an attractive bowl and serve immediately.

Serves 4 to 6

ARGENTINIAN TOMATO SALSA
Salsa Criolla

ARGENTINA

ON THE SIDE

This colorful salsa turns up wherever grilled meats are served in Argentina. The recipe varies from restaurant to restaurant and from family to family. Sometimes it's nothing more than chopped tomatoes and onions. Here's a slightly more elaborate version that tastes great with just about any type of grilled fare.

2 large fresh, ripe tomatoes (about
   1 pound), cored and seeded
   (see box, page 62), then cut into
   ¼-inch dice
1 sweet onion, such as Vidalia or Walla Walla,
   cut into ¼-inch dice
1 medium green bell pepper, stemmed,
   seeded, and cut into ¼-inch dice

2 tablespoons extra-virgin olive oil
2 tablespoons red wine vinegar, or
   more to taste
3 tablespoons fresh Italian (flat-leaf) parsley
1 teaspoon dried oregano
Salt and freshly ground black pepper,
   to taste

Combine the tomatoes, onion, bell pepper, oil, 2 tablespoons vinegar, the parsley, and oregano in a medium-size bowl and toss to mix. Correct the seasoning, adding more vinegar and salt and pepper; the mixture should be highly seasoned. The salsa can be prepared up to 4 hours ahead of time. Reseason just before serving.

Makes 3 to 4 cups; enough to serve 6 to 8

GRILLED HABANERO SALSA

MEXICO

METHOD:
Direct grilling

The habanero is one of the world's two or three hottest chiles. Grilling blunts its fiery bite and enhances the chile's smoky, fruity flavor. Still, this is one of the most scorching salsas you'll ever taste. If you like them hellish, also try the "Dog's Nose" Salsa on page 453.

12 to 15 habanero or scotch bonnet
   chiles
1 small onion, cut lengthwise in half
1 clove garlic, minced
¼ cup fresh sour orange juice or fresh
   lime juice
¼ cup fresh regular orange juice
½ teaspoon salt
¼ teaspoon sugar (optional)

1. Preheat the grill to high.

2. When ready to cook, place a vegetable grate on the hot grill and preheat it for 5 minutes.

3. Arrange the chiles and onion halves (cut side down) on the hot grate and grill, turning often, until browned all over, 3 to 6 minutes. (The skins should be charred but the chiles and onion should not be cooked through.) Transfer the chiles and onions to a cutting board and let cool.

4. Scrape off any particularly burnt pieces of skin and finely chop the chiles and onion halves. Place in a serving bowl and stir in the garlic, sour orange juice, regular orange juice and ½ teaspoon salt. Stir in the sugar (if using). Use this salsa sparingly; it's ornery! It is best served within 3 hours of preparing.

Makes about 1 cup; enough to serve 8

THREE FRUIT SALSAS

Fruit salsas are a uniquely North American invention and are of relatively recent date. They've become an indispensable part of the American table and are a perfect companion for grilled meats, poultry, and seafood. They're also healthy, containing little if any fat. Here are three of my favorites. Once you have the basic idea, you can make salsa with just about any type of fruit.

Grilled Pineapple Salsa

Grilling imparts a distinctive smoky flavor to this salsa, but if you're in a hurry, a perfectly delectable salsa can be made without grilling. Serve this alongside grilled pork.

1 ripe pineapple
1 medium red bell pepper
1 medium yellow bell pepper
1 poblano chile or medium green bell pepper
½ to 1 scotch bonnet chile or other hot
   chile, seeded and minced (for a hotter
   salsa, leave the seeds in)
1 tablespoon minced candied ginger
½ medium red onion, finely chopped
½ cup chopped fresh cilantro leaves
3 tablespoons fresh lime juice, or more
   to taste
1 tablespoon firmly packed light brown sugar,
   or more as needed

1. Preheat the grill to high.

2. Peel the pineapple, cut it in half lengthwise, and remove the core. Cut each half lengthwise into quarters. You should have 8 pieces.

3. When ready to cook, arrange the pineapple pieces, bell peppers, and poblano chile on the hot grate and grill, turning with tongs, until nicely charred on all sides, 8 to 12 minutes. Transfer to a bowl and let cool.

4. Cut the cooled pineapple into 1-inch dice. Stem and seed the peppers and cut into 1-inch dice. Combine the pineapple, bell pepper, poblano, scotch bonnet, ginger, onion, cilantro, 3 tablespoons lime juice, and 1 tablespoon sugar in a serving bowl and toss gently to mix. Correct the seasoning, adding more lime juice or sugar as necessary; the salsa should be highly seasoned. Serve within 3 hours of making.

Makes 4 to 6 cups; enough to serve 6 to 8

Smoky Apple-Banana Salsa

The apple banana (*platano manzano* in Spanish) is one of the tastiest exotic fruits ever to cross the North American table. Short and stubby, it has a tart, apply-banana flavor that makes you want to throw stones at regular bananas. Look for it in Hispanic markets and in some large supermarkets. This is the salsa to serve with grilled duck or chicken; the smoke flavor comes from the chipotle chiles.

1 to 2 chipotle chiles (see Note)
4 apple-bananas, peeled and diced (about 2 cups), or 2 large bananas
½ medium red bell pepper, stemmed, seeded, and finely diced
½ poblano chile or medium green bell pepper, stemmed, seeded, and finely diced
¼ cup finely diced red onion
3 tablespoons chopped fresh mint
3 tablespoons fresh orange juice
2 tablespoons fresh lime juice, or more to taste
1 tablespoon honey, or more to taste

1. If using dried chipotle chiles, soak in warm water to cover for 30 minutes. Remove the chiles from the water and blot dry with paper towels. Stem, seed, and mince the chiles. (If using canned chipotles, mince them.)

2. Combine the chipotles, apple-bananas, bell pepper, poblano, onion, mint, orange juice, 2 tablespoons lime juice, and 1 tablespoon honey in a serving bowl and toss gently to mix. Correct the seasoning, adding more lime juice or honey to taste. This salsa tastes best served within 3 hours of making.

Makes about 3 cups; enough to serve 4 to 6

Note: Chipotles (smoked jalapeño chiles) come dried and canned. (The latter are packed in a spicy tomato sauce called *adobo.*) If using dried chipotles, you'll need to soak them in warm water for 30 minutes. If using canned, no soaking is required. Simply fish them out of the can and mince.

Mango-Mint Salsa

When buying mangoes, look for heavy, unblemished fruits. Let them ripen at room temperature until squeezably soft and very fragrant. Many (but not all) varieties turn red when ripe, so you really need to judge ripeness by smell and touch. If you have sensitive skin, wear rubber gloves when handling mangoes: The sap can cause a poison ivy–like reaction. This salsa is delicious made with other fruits, such as peaches, nectarines, or melons, and is a perfect companion to poultry or seafood. Note that the ingredients can be chopped ahead of time, but do the mixing within 20 minutes of serving.

2 ripe mangoes

1 medium cucumber, peeled, seeded, and cut into ¼-inch dice

½ cup finely chopped scallions, both white and green parts

½ medium red bell pepper, stemmed, seeded and cut into ¼-inch dice

1 tablespoon minced candied ginger or fresh ginger

1 to 3 jalapeño chiles, seeded and minced (for a hotter salsa, leave the seeds in)

¼ cup chopped fresh mint

3 tablespoons fresh lime juice, or more to taste

2 tablespoons firmly packed light brown sugar, or more to taste

1. Peel and pit the mangoes. Cut the mango flesh into ¼-inch dice. You should have about 2 cups.

2. Combine the mangoes, cucumber, scallions, bell pepper, ginger, chile, mint, 3 tablespoons lime juice, and 2 tablespoons brown sugar in a large serving bowl and toss gently to mix. Correct the seasoning, adding more lime juice or sugar as necessary; the salsa should be highly seasoned. The salsa tastes best served within 3 hours of making.

Makes 3 to 4 cups; enough to serve 4 to 6

"DOG'S NOSE" SALSA
Xni Pec

MEXICO

ON THE SIDE

The world's most colorfully named salsa—*xni pec* (pronounced "shnee pek")—is also one of the world's hottest. *Xni* is the Mayan word for "dog," *pec* for "nose." Just why it's thus named is a matter of debate. The likely explanation is that the chiles make your nose run, an effect I can readily attest to. And a dog's nose is always wet. I've given a range of chiles—a person from the Yucatán would use the full 8. There is more to this fighter than heat alone. The onion, tomato, cilantro, and sour orange create a complex play of flavors.

2 to 8 habanero or scotch bonnet chiles, finely chopped (see Note)

1 large fresh, ripe tomato, cut into ¼-inch dice (with juices)

½ cup finely chopped white onion

3 tablespoons chopped fresh cilantro

3 tablespoons fresh sour orange juice or 2 tablespoons fresh lime juice plus 1 tablespoon fresh orange juice, or more to taste

½ teaspoon salt

Combine the chiles, tomato, onion, cilantro, 3 tablespoons sour orange juice, and salt in a serving bowl. Toss to mix. Correct the seasoning, adding more sour orange juice as necessary. The salsa tastes best served within 3 hours of making.

Makes about 1 cup; enough to serve 4 to 6

Note: You can blunt the salsa bite a little by seeding the chiles. Of course, you'll lose a great measure of authenticity.

TWO RAITAS

INDIA

ON THE SIDE

ADVANCE
PREPARATION:
2 hours for
draining the
yogurt (optional)

*R*aita is a cooling condiment made with yogurt, vegetables or fruits, and aromatic spices. It's the perfect accompaniment to the Indian grilled fare in this book, not to mention an effective soother of any chile-inflamed palate. Below are two traditional Indian raitas.

Both recipes call for the yogurt to be drained to concentrate its richness. If you're in a hurry, you can omit this step, but reduce the amount of yogurt by ½ cup. You can make the *raita* with fat-free yogurt, but it won't be quite as rich.

Pineapple Raita

*P*ineapple lends this *raita* an unexpected touch of sweetness.

1½ to 2 cups plain whole-milk yogurt
½ teaspoon cumin seeds
1 cup finely diced ripe pineapple
1½ tablespoons fresh mint or 2 teaspoons
    dried
1 teaspoon Quick Garam Masala (page 499)
Salt and freshly ground black pepper,
    to taste

1. If you are draining the yogurt, place 2 cups in a yogurt strainer, or regular strainer lined with a double layer of dampened cheesecloth, and set the strainer over a bowl. Let the yogurt drain, in the refrigerator, for 2 hours.

2. Toast the cumin seeds in a dry skillet over medium heat until toasted and fragrant, about 2 minutes.

3. Transfer the yogurt to a serving bowl and stir in the cumin seeds, pineapple, mint, half the *garam masala*, and salt and pepper. Sprinkle the remaining *garam masala* on top and serve immediately, or at least within 4 hours of making; the *raita* may be served at room temperature or cold.

Makes about 3 cups; enough to serve 4 to 6

Tomato-Cucumber Raita

1½ to 2 cups plain whole-milk yogurt
½ teaspoon cumin seeds
1 small or ½ large cucumber, peeled, seeded,
    and finely diced
1 medium fresh, ripe tomato, peeled, seeded,
    and finely diced
Salt and freshly ground black pepper, to taste

1. If you are draining the yogurt, place 2 cups in a yogurt strainer, or regular strainer lined with a double layer of dampened cheesecloth, and set the strainer over a bowl. Let the yogurt drain, in the refrigerator, for 2 hours.

2. Toast the cumin seeds in a dry skillet over medium heat until toasted and fragrant, about 2 minutes.

3. Transfer the yogurt to a serving bowl and stir in the cumin seeds, cucumber, tomato, and salt and pepper. Serve immediately or at least within 4 hours of making; serve at room temperature.

Makes about 3 cups; enough to serve 4 to 6

THREE SLAWS

U.S.A.

ON THE SIDE

Coleslaw has been part of America's barbecue landscape since the founding of our nation—if not before. The name comes from the Dutch words *cole* (cabbage) and *slaw* (salad)—a reminder of the days when Manhattan was a Dutch colony. Amelia Simmons mentions slaw in *American Cookery,* the first American cookbook, which was published in 1796. Here's a sampling of slaws ranging from mild to fiery that would do any barbecue justice.

Your Basic Slaw

This is the basic mild and creamy, mayonnaise-based coleslaw that is served at barbecue joints throughout the country. To make a low-fat version, substitute low or no-fat sour cream for the mayonnaise.

FOR THE DRESSING:
5 tablespoons mayonnaise
3 tablespoons cider vinegar
1 tablespoon Dijon mustard
1 tablespoon fresh lemon juice
2 teaspoons sugar, or more to taste
1 clove garlic, minced (optional)
2 teaspoons celery seeds
Salt and freshly ground black pepper, to taste

FOR THE SLAW:
5 cups packed shredded green cabbage (about ½ medium head cabbage; see Note)
2 medium carrots, peeled and shredded or julienned (see Note)
½ medium green bell pepper, stemmed, seeded, and shredded (optional; see Note)
1 medium rib celery, finely chopped (optional)

1. Prepare the dressing. Combine the mayonnaise, vinegar, mustard, lemon juice, 2 teaspoons sugar, the garlic (if using), and celery seeds in a small bowl and whisk to mix. Add salt and pepper and taste. Correct the seasoning, adding more salt, pepper, or sugar as needed; the dressing should be highly seasoned.

2. Combine the cabbage, carrots, and bell pepper and celery (if using) in a large bowl. Add the dressing and toss to mix. The slaw is best served within 4 hours of making. Season with more salt and pepper just before serving.

Serves 6

Note: The quickest, easiest way to shred cabbage for coleslaw is to use the slicing disk of a food processor. Shred the carrot and the bell pepper (if using) on the shredding or julienne disk.

Shogun Slaw

Ginger, rice vinegar, and sesame oil give this slaw a Japanese accent that would do any Asian barbecue proud. Wasabi is Japanese horseradish—the green toothpaste-looking stuff served with sushi. I've made it optional, but it does give the slaw a nice bite. Napa is an elongated Asian cabbage. You could also use green or savoy cabbage. Wasabi, rice vinegar, and black sesame seeds can be found in Japanese markets and in some large supermarkets.

FOR THE DRESSING:

2 teaspoons wasabi powder
(optional)
2 teaspoons water (optional)
1 clove garlic, minced
1 tablespoon minced fresh ginger, or
more to taste
5 tablespoons rice vinegar, or more
to taste
2 tablespoons sugar, or more to taste
½ teaspoon salt, or more to taste
1 tablespoon dark sesame oil
2 tablespoons black sesame seeds or
toasted white sesame seeds
(see box, page 93)

FOR THE SLAW:

3 cups thinly shredded napa cabbage,
(about ½ small head cabbage)
2 medium carrots, peeled and
shredded or julienned
½ medium red bell pepper, stemmed,
seeded, and very thinly sliced
4 scallions, trimmed, white part
minced, green part thinly sliced
lengthwise
½ cup snow peas, ends trimmed,
strings removed, and pods cut
into thin slivers

1. Prepare the dressing. Mix the wasabi and water (if using) in a small bowl and let stand for 5 minutes to form a thick paste. Add the garlic, ginger, 5 tablespoons vinegar, 2 tablespoons sugar, and ½ teaspoon salt. Whisk until the sugar dissolves. Whisk in the sesame oil and sesame seeds.

2. Stir in the cabbage, carrots, bell pepper, scallions, and snow peas. Toss to mix. The slaw tastes best served within 4 hours of preparing. Correct the seasoning, adding vinegar, sugar, or salt as necessary just before serving.

Serves 4 to 6

Haitian Slaw
Pikliz

This is about the hottest slaw I've found on the barbecue trail, and it owes its firepower to the Dame Jeanne, a Haitian cousin of the scotch bonnet pepper. As the name suggests, *pikliz* is a sort of pickled cabbage or sauerkraut. I call for a range of chiles here: 2 will give you a nice fiery slaw; the full 10 would satisfy even the most pyromaniacal Haitian. Sour orange looks like an orange but tastes like a lime; look for it at West Indian markets.

FOR THE DRESSING:

1½ cups distilled white vinegar
1½ cups fresh sour orange juice or
1 cup fresh lime juice plus
½ cup fresh regular orange juice
2 tablespoons salt
½ teaspoon freshly ground pepper
3 whole cloves

FOR THE SLAW:

6 cups shredded green or savoy cabbage
(about 1 small head)
2 medium carrots, peeled and
shredded
2 medium ribs celery, finely chopped
1 large onion, thinly sliced
1 bunch scallions, both white and green
parts, trimmed and finely chopped
5 cloves garlic, finely chopped
2 to 10 scotch bonnet or habanero
chiles, seeded and thinly sliced
(for an even hotter slaw,
leave the seeds in)

1. Prepare the dressing. Combine the vinegar, sour orange juice, salt, pepper, and cloves in a 2-quart crock, jar, or large nonreactive bowl. Whisk until the salt dissolves.

2. Stir in the cabbage, carrots, celery, onion, scallions, garlic, and chiles. Cover the crock with plastic wrap and let the slaw pickle in the refrigerator for at least 24 hours before serving. Stir several times to ensure even curing. The slaw can be made up to a week in advance; store, tightly covered, in the refrigerator.

Serves 8 to 10

Sauces

A splash of fish sauce adds zing to Southeast Asia barbecue.

Not so long ago, I served as a judge at the Memphis in May International World Championship Barbecue Cooking Contest. I was dazzled by the virtuosity of the pork shoulders, astonished by the penetrating smoke flavor of the ribs. But what really took my breath away was the sheer diversity of the sauces.

Sauces have always been a touchstone of a pit master's art. In North America they range from the sweet, tomatoey sauces of Kansas City to the vinegar-based sauces of northern North Carolina, from the mustard-based sauces of southern North Carolina to the fiery salsas of the American Southwest.

Grill jockeys are equally ingenious elsewhere. No South American barbecue would be complete without a garlic-parsley sauce called *chimichurri*, while it's hot peppers that give the North African *harissa* its kick. Spaniards dote on the roasted sweet red peppers and nuts that flavor their *romesco*, while fruit dominates many other of the world's barbecue sauces. Note that this chockablock chapter includes sauces that accompany other recipes in this book and also ones that are terrific served with any of your favorite grilled entrées. Your notion of barbecue sauce will never be the same.

BASIC BARBECUE SAUCE

A good barbecue sauce is a study in contrasts: sweet versus sour, fruity versus smoky, spicy versus mellow. Here's a great all-purpose sauce that's loaded with flavor, but not too sweet. It goes well with all manner of poultry, pork, or beef.

The minced vegetables give you a coarse-textured sauce, which I happen to like. If you prefer a smooth sauce, purée it in a blender.

3 tablespoons vegetable oil
1 medium onion, minced
1 clove garlic, minced
¼ green bell pepper, stemmed, seeded, and minced
½ cup ketchup
½ cup tomato sauce
1 cup water, or more if needed
3 tablespoons cider vinegar, or more to taste
3 tablespoons Worcestershire sauce
2 tablespoons fresh lemon juice
2 tablespoons pineapple juice (optional)
1 teaspoon of your favorite hot sauce, or more to taste
½ teaspoon liquid smoke or 2 tablespoons meat drippings
2 tablespoons molasses

3 tablespoons firmly packed dark brown sugar, or more to taste
2 tablespoons prepared mustard of choice
1 teaspoon dry mustard
½ teaspoon freshly ground black pepper
Salt, to taste

1. Heat the oil in a large nonreactive saucepan over medium heat. Add the onion, garlic, and bell pepper and sauté until softened but not brown, about 4 minutes.

2. Stir in the ketchup, tomato sauce, 1 cup water, 3 tablespoon vinegar, Worcestershire sauce, lemon juice, pineapple juice (if using), hot sauce, liquid smoke, molasses, sugar, both mustards, and black pepper and bring to a boil. Reduce the heat to low and simmer, uncovered, until thickened, about 15 minutes, stirring often to prevent scorching. If the sauce becomes too thick, add a little water. Remove from the heat and taste for seasoning, adding salt and vinegar, hot sauce, and sugar as necessary; the sauce should be highly seasoned.

3. Transfer to a serving bowl and serve warm or at room temperature. The sauce will keep, tightly covered in the refrigerator, for several weeks.
Makes 2½ to 3 cups

NORTH CAROLINA VINEGAR SAUCE

North Carolina (particularly north-western North Carolina) occupies a unique position in the realm of American barbecue. Unlike the rest of the country (which enjoys tomato-based sauces), the preferred condiment here is a piquant mixture of vinegar and pepper flakes, with just a little sugar to take off the sharp edge. The meat served is always pork, and it's shredded or finely chopped, not sliced. Put the pork and vinegar sauce together and you have one of the most delectable barbecues ever to grace a bun. The jalapeño chiles aren't strictly traditional, but I like their added bite.

1½ cups cider vinegar
1 cup water
1 tablespoon sugar, or more
   to taste
1 tablespoon hot red pepper flakes

1 small onion, thinly sliced
1 jalapeño chile, thinly sliced
   (for a milder sauce, seed the chile)
2 teaspoons salt, or more to taste
½ teaspoon freshly ground black pepper

1. Combine all the ingredients in a medium-size nonreactive bowl and stir until the sugar and salt are dissolved. Taste for seasoning, adding salt and sugar as necessary.
2. Use the sauce immediately, or at least the same day; it does not store well.
Makes about 2½ cups

MARK MILITELLO'S MANGO BARBECUE SAUCE

U . S . A .

METHOD:
Direct grilling

SPECIAL EQUIPMENT:
1 cup wood chips, soaked for 1 hour in cold water to cover and drained

Here's a mango-based barbecue sauce that fairly explodes with tropical flavor. Grilled peppers and tomatoes pump up the smoke, while scotch bonnets stoke the fire. (Tender of tongue take comfort: The sauce is piquant but not incendiary.) This sauce was inspired by Florida superchef Mark Militello, who serves it with grilled swordfish. I can't think of a single grilled food that doesn't shine in its presence, but it goes especially well with seafood and chicken.

1 medium green bell pepper
1 medium red bell pepper
2 large fresh, ripe tomatoes
1 large or 2 small ripe mangoes, peeled,
   seeded, and diced (about 2 cups)
⅔ cup finely chopped red onion
1 tablespoon minced garlic
1 scotch bonnet chile, cut in half
   (for a milder sauce, seed the chile)
⅓ cup cider vinegar

½ cup firmly packed dark brown sugar
2 tablespoons molasses
2 tablespoons Dijon mustard
2 tablespoons Tamarind Water
   (page 219), frozen tamarind purée,
   thawed, or fresh lime juice
1 tablespoon soy sauce
1 cinnamon stick (3 inches)
1½ teaspoons fresh thyme or
   ¾ teaspoon dried
1½ teaspoons fresh marjoram or
   ¾ teaspoon dried
1½ teaspoons ground cumin
½ cup water, or more as needed
Salt and freshly ground black pepper,
   to taste

1. Preheat the grill to high. If using a gas grill, heat the chips in the smoker box until they begin to smoke.
2. When ready to grill, if using a charcoal gril, toss the wood chips on the coals. Oil the grill grate and arrange the bell peppers and

tomatoes on the hot grate. Grill covered, uncovering to turn with tongs, until charred on all sides, 12 to 20 minutes in all. Transfer to a cutting board and cool.

3. Scrape most of the charred skin off the peppers and tomatoes. Cut the peppers and tomatoes in half, then core, seed, and coarsely chop them. Transfer to a large nonreactive saucepan and add the mango, onion, garlic, chile, vinegar, sugar, molasses, mustard, Tamarind Water, soy sauce, cinnamon stick, thyme, marjoram, cumin, ½ cup water, and a little salt and pepper. Bring to a simmer over low heat and cook gently,

uncovered, until richly flavored, about 20 minutes, stirring occasionally. Add water as needed to keep the sauce soupy. Discard the cinnamon stick.

4. Transfer the sauce to a blender and process to a smooth purée. For extra smoothness, press it through a fine-meshed strainer. Taste for seasoning, adding salt and black pepper as necessary.

5. Transfer to a serving bowl and serve warm or at room temperature. The sauce will keep, tightly covered in the refrigerator, for several weeks.

Makes about 3 cups

ELIDA'S HONEY-GUAVA BARBECUE SAUCE

CUBA

ON THE SIDE

Readers of my previous books will recognize the name Elida Proenza, a good friend and Cuban cook extraordinaire. Elida is forever proving this central gastronomic truth: While anyone can make a great-tasting dish with a lot of ingredients, it takes a true genius to make unforgettable food with only two or three. Elida watched with what I imagine was secret amusement as I lined up several dozen bottles of spices and condiments to experiment with barbecue sauces. When I wasn't looking, she blended honey, guava paste, and commercial barbecue sauce to make this exotically fruity sauce, which instantly became a Raichlen family favorite. It is particularly good with chicken and pork.

Guava paste is a thick, fragrant red tropical fruit jelly sold in flat tins at Hispanic markets and most supermarkets. Once opened, it keeps for months wrapped in plastic in the refrigerator. Don't be disconcerted if the paste becomes crystallized or grainy—the sugar will melt back in when you cook the sauce.

¼ cup honey
3 tablespoons guava paste
⅔ cup commercial barbecue sauce (see Note)
Squeeze of fresh lemon juice (optional)

1. Combine the honey, guava paste, and barbecue sauce in a small, heavy saucepan and bring to a boil over medium heat. Reduce the heat to low and simmer for 5 minutes, whisking to mix. The sauce is ready when all the guava paste is dissolved. If it tastes too sweet, add a squeeze of lemon juice.

2. Transfer to a serving bowl and serve warm or at room temperature. The sauce will keep, tightly covered in the refrigerator, for several weeks.

Makes about 1 cup

Note: What's amazing about this recipe is that you can use almost any commercial barbecue sauce to make it. Elida favors Kraft or KC Masterpiece, but she has also made it with vinegar-based sauces in the style of Arthur Bryant's with equal success.

CAROLINA MUSTARD BARBECUE SAUCE

U.S.A.

ON THE SIDE

Tomato- or ketchup-based barbecue sauces rule most parts of the country. But in the southern part of North Carolina (and in a few parts of South Carolina and Florida), barbecue simply isn't barbecue unless it's served with a bright yellow sauce made from mustard, honey, and vinegar. If you haven't grown up with such a sauce, the very notion might seem revolting. But even if you come from tomato sauce country, mustard barbecue sauce quickly becomes addictive.

Tradition calls for using inexpensive ballpark-style mustard and you'll certainly be in good company if you use this kind of mustard. But I like the sharper, more refined flavor of Dijon mustard—particularly an "old-fashioned style" mustard imported from France. Look for the words *à l'ancienne* on the label.

½ cup prepared mustard of choice
½ cup honey
¼ cup light brown sugar
¼ cup distilled white vinegar
Salt and freshly ground black pepper, to taste

1. Combine the mustard, honey, sugar, and vinegar in a nonreactive saucepan and whisk to mix. Bring to a simmer over low heat and cook gently, uncovered, until richly flavored, about 5 minutes, whisking from time to time. Remove from the heat and season with salt and pepper.

2. Transfer to a serving bowl and serve warm or at room temperature. The sauce will keep, tightly covered in the refrigerator, for several weeks.

Makes about 1½ cups

GEORGIAN PICKLED PLUM SAUCE
Tkemali

REPUBLIC OF GEORGIA

ON THE SIDE

Tkemali, a deliciously tart table sauce made with sour plums and cilantro, is the Republic of Georgia's answer to ketchup. Pronounced "tek-MA-lee," it accompanies everything from grilled sausages to fish. Since dark red *tkemali* plums are very sour, I suggest using large underripe red plums found at most American supermarkets. They work well for this recipe. You can also use other tart fruits, like rhubarb (see Note).

1 pound underripe red plums
¾ cup water
3 tablespoons fresh lemon juice or red wine vinegar, or more to taste
1 tablespoon olive oil
3 cloves garlic, minced
1½ teaspoons ground coriander
½ teaspoon salt, or more to taste
½ teaspoon hot red pepper flakes, or more to taste
¼ cup minced fresh cilantro or dill

1. Fill a large saucepan half full of water and bring to a boil over medium-high heat. Immerse the plums in the water for 1 minute, then drain and rinse under cold running water. Slip off the skins, using a sharp paring knife. Cut each plum around its circumference all the way to the stone, then twist the halves in opposite directions to separate them. Use a spoon to pop out the stone. Cut each plum half in half again.

2. Combine the plums, water, 3 tablespoons lemon juice, the oil, garlic, coriander, ½ teaspoon salt, and ½ teaspoon hot pepper flakes in a small nonreactive saucepan and bring to a boil over medium heat. Reduce the heat to low and simmer, covered, until the plums are very soft, about 5 minutes. Transfer the mixture to a food processor or blender and process to a smooth purée. Return the purée to the saucepan and stir in the cilantro. Bring to a boil over medium heat, then reduce the heat to medium-low and simmer until the sauce is reduced to about 2 cups, about 5 minutes. Remove from the heat and taste for seasoning, adding salt, pepper flakes, or lemon juice as necessary; the sauce should be highly seasoned. Cool to room temperature and serve at once, or store, tightly covered in the refrigerator, for up to 2 weeks.

Makes about 2 cups

Note: Prepare rhubarb as described above in step 2, substituting 1 pound fresh rhubarb, trimmed and diced, for the plums. You may need a tablespoon or so more sugar to balance the rhubarb's acidity.

BENGALI MANGO-TAMARIND BARBECUE SAUCE

BANGLADESH

ON THE SIDE

This recipe is based on a sauce I never actually tasted prior to making it. But the Bengali cab driver who told me about it described it with such passion I could easily imagine its flavor. The sauce belongs to a family of tamarind chutneys popular throughout the Indian subcontinent. Spoon it over grilled meats, poultry, and seafood.

1½ cups Tamarind Water (page 219) or
   frozen tamarind purée, thawed
1 cup diced ripe mango
1 medium onion, finely chopped
1 piece (3 x 2 inches) green bell pepper,
   finely chopped
2 serrano or jalapeño chiles,
   seeded and finely chopped
1 tablespoon minced fresh ginger
3 tablespoons firmly packed
   dark brown sugar, or more
   to taste
¼ teaspoon salt, or more
   to taste
¼ cup chopped fresh cilantro
1 tablespoon fresh lime juice

1. Place the Tamarind Water, mango, onion, bell pepper, chiles, ginger, 3 tablespoons sugar, and ¼ teaspoon salt in a heavy saucepan. Bring to a boil over medium heat, then reduce the heat to medium-low and simmer, uncovered, until the mango and onion are very soft, about 20 minutes, stirring often. Stir in the cilantro and lime juice and remove from the heat.

2. Transfer the mixture to a blender or food processor and process to a purée. Taste for seasoning, adding sugar or salt as neces-

sary; the sauce should be both sweet and sour.

3. Transfer to small individual serving bowls and serve at room temperature. The sauce will keep, tightly covered in the refrigerator, for several days.

Makes about 1¾ cups

JAKE'S TURKISH COFFEE BARBECUE SAUCE

U.S.A.

ON THE SIDE

This isn't like any barbecue sauce Bubba used to make. Not with ingredients like cardamom, coffee, and hoisin sauce. The recipe comes from chef Jake, my stepson, who likes to serve it with grilled grouper and rich meats like pork and lamb at his smashing new restaurant, JADA, located in South Miami.

2 tablespoons olive oil
1 medium onion, finely chopped
1 medium red bell pepper, stemmed,
    seeded, and finely
    chopped
3 cloves garlic, minced
1 tablespoon minced fresh ginger
1½ cups brewed Turkish coffee or
    espresso
¼ cup hoisin sauce
2 tablespoons balsamic vinegar
1½ teaspoons unsweetened cocoa
    powder
2 teaspoons ground cardamom
2 tablespoons honey, or more
    to taste
Salt and freshly ground black pepper,
    to taste

1. Heat the oil in a large nonreactive saucepan over medium heat. Add the onion, bell pepper, garlic, and ginger and sauté until the vegetables are softened but not brown, about 5 minutes. Add the coffee, hoisin sauce, vinegar, cocoa powder, and cardamom. Increase the heat and bring to a boil.

2. Reduce the heat to low and simmer gently, uncovered, until thick and richly flavored, about 10 minutes, stirring occasionally. If the sauce seems too thick, add a little water. Purée the sauce in a blender, adding 2 tablespoons honey to give the sauce sheen. Taste for seasoning, adding salt, black pepper and honey as necessary.

3. Transfer to a serving bowl and serve warm or at room temperature. The sauce will keep, tightly covered in the refrigerator, for several weeks.

*Makes about
2 cups*

The Four Styles of American Barbecue

Everyone agrees that barbecue is a distinctly North American delicacy. But what you get will be very different, depending on where you order it. East of the Mississippi, barbecue means pork, while west of the mighty river—especially in Texas—barbecue means beef. Ribs are the stock and trade of Kansas City pit masters, while pork shoulder remains the cut of choice in the Carolinas. To confuse matters further, more and more barbecue joints are serving chicken, a reflection of the general lightening-up of the American diet.

As you feast your way along America's barbecue trail, you'll find considerable overlap in meat cuts, sauces, and cooking techniques. Here's a guide to the basic regional styles.

NORTH CAROLINA

In the Carolinas barbecue means pork, specifically pork shoulder (also known as Boston butt). Sometimes the meat is rubbed with a mixture of paprika, salt, sugar, and other seasonings. But just as often, pit masters forgo the seasonings. The pork shoulders are smoke-cooked over oak or hickory for 6 to 8 hours, or until tender enough to be pulled into shreds with your fingers.

Which is precisely what local pit masters do, for the ultimate Carolina barbecue is "pulled pork," a well-smoked and exceedingly tender pork shoulder, teased by hand into soft meaty shreds. Other pit maestros (particularly at restaurants) prefer to chop the shoulders into tiny pieces with a meat cleaver. The

pulling or chopping is important, because it allows the tiny pieces of meat to soak up the sauce like a sponge. Unlike other parts of the country, Carolina-style barbecue is rarely served sliced.

Some cooks use vinegar-based mop sauces to keep meat moist during cooking. Other cooks simply let time and wood smoke do the job, without other culinary artifice. Sometimes, Carolinians go hog wild, barbecuing a whole pig in this fashion. The occasion is called a "pig picking," and it becomes a community event.

Another factor that distinguishes Carolina barbecue from that of the rest of the country is the use of sauces. There are three main styles, each different from the sweet, thick, red condiment most Americans think of as classic barbecue sauce. In northeastern North Carolina (the capital of Carolina barbecue), folks favor a thin, clear sauce made of distilled white or cider vinegar flavored with salt, hot red pepper flakes, and a little sugar. In the western part of the state, they often add ketchup or tomato sauce to this mixture. The result

is a peppery, tart, red sauce unlike any elsewhere in the U.S. In southern North Carolina and South Carolina, the preferred condiment is a lurid yellow sauce made with vinegar, a sweetener (sugar, molasses, and honey are all used), and ballpark mustard. This is the sweetest of the Carolina-style barbecue sauces, but even it isn't particularly sweet.

The traditional way to eat Carolina-style barbecue is on a bun with coleslaw and vinegar sauce.

MEMPHIS

Memphis knows its stuff when it comes to barbecue. This Tennessee city on the banks of the Mississippi hosts one of the world's largest barbecue contests, The Memphis in May World Championship Barbecue Cooking Contest, a three-day orgy of beer and barbecue, drawing three hundred teams from thirty states and half a dozen countries to compete for tens of thousands of dollars in prize money.

Although you find all sorts of barbecued meats and even seafood in Memphis (locals like to say that the Mississippi Delta begins here), two cuts reign supreme: pork shoulder and ribs. The former is slow-smoked to fork-tender perfection, then served thinly sliced with barbecue sauce. But the ribs are what set Memphis apart from the rest of American barbecue.

Memphis is the home of the dry rib, a rack of baby back ribs or spareribs thickly crusted with a dry rub, then smoke-cooked and sprinkled with more rub before serving. My favorite are the ribs served at Charlie Vergos's Rendezvous, a subterranean restaurant in downtown Memphis. Vergos uses a hybrid method for cooking his ribs: The meat is grilled directly over charcoal, but the grate is positioned high above the coals so the heat is somewhat indirect.

Dry-rub ribs are my personal favorite way of making ribs. The rub reinforces the flavor and texture of the meat without overpowering it, the way wet barbecue sauce sometimes does.

KANSAS CITY

Kansas City rivals Memphis as the epicenter of American barbecue. Also located on the Mississippi River, it boasts more than 90 barbecue joints, ranging from Arthur Bryant-esque "grease houses" to proper restaurants with Tiffany-style lamps. Kansans are ecumenical when it comes to barbecue itself. Like their brethren in Tennessee and the Carolinas, Kansans love pork—especially ribs. Indeed, they've developed a whole vocabulary to describe the fine points of rib cookery.

"Rib tips" are the burnt edges of spareribs—greasy, gristly, and delicious. "Long ends" are the lean fore-sections of a rack of spareribs, and "short ends" are the shorter, fatter, meatier hind sections. Most succulent of all are "baby back ribs," which are cut from the sections closest to the backbone.

But Kansans are also broad-minded enough to share the Texas enthusiasm for beef. Since Kansas City was an important meat-packing center until the 1960s, the stockyards have traditionally supplied pit masters with brisket and less expensive cuts of beef. And like Memphans, many Kansan barbecue buffs rub their meats with a dry rub (a mixture of salt, paprika, and other spices) before cooking, but they don't tend to use mop sauces. Perhaps the most defining characteristic of Kansas City barbecue is the prominent role played by the sauce.

A typical Kansas City barbecue sauce is thick and sweet, a complex blend of ketchup or tomato sauce, brown sugar, corn syrup, molasses, vinegar, onion, garlic, hot red pepper flakes, liquid smoke, and sometimes even apple juice. The most typical Kansas City sauce (certainly the best selling) is KC Masterpiece, a brand created by child psychologist turned barbecue mogul Rich Davis. But no survey of Kansas City sauces would be complete without a shot of Arthur Bryant's sauce, a sharp, chalky, no-nonsense (and not the least bit sugary) blend of vinegar and paprika.

Kansas City is home to one delicacy seldom seen elsewhere. Called "burnt edges" (aka, "brownies"), they are the crisp, charred ends of smoked briskets. (Beware of "burnt edges" that are cut from the center of the brisket—they don't have the fat content that makes the real edges so damnably delectable). The world's best burnt edges come from Arthur Bryant's, the bare-bones grease house immortalized by Calvin Trillin.

TEXAS

I'll never forget my first taste of Texas barbecue—although it has been more than 20 years now. The place was Bodacious Barbecue in Longview, Texas. The meat was beef brisket and it was as smoky as a fireplace, as succulent as stew, and tender enough to pull apart with my fingers.

In Texas, beef reigns supreme. (Where else would you find a monumental bronze sculpture of a herd of steer?) The preferred cut of meat for barbecue is brisket and the preparation is almost Zen in its simplicity, consisting chiefly of time and wood smoke. The wood can be oak, hickory, or even mesquite. As for the time, well, a properly prepared brisket can spend up to 18 hours in the pit, resulting in a pinkish-red tinge around the edge of the meat. This is the smoke ring, a naturally occurring band of color found in meats that are lengthily smoked. Most Texan pit masters don't even bother to use rubs or mop sauce.

The beef generally comes sliced (not chopped), and it's more at home on a slice of cheap, soft, white bread than a bun. Texan barbecue sauces tend to be based on tomatoes and chile powder and are rather thin, tart, and vinegary. "We don't go in for a lot of sugar," says Mike DeMaster, pit master of the original Sonny Bryan's in Dallas, who gives his sauce its deep, rich flavor by smoking it in the pit.

Just how barbecue came to Texas is a matter of debate. The lengthy smoke-cooking in a pit recalls the barbecue of the Carolinas and Kansas City. The use of beef and mesquite suggest parentage with the *carnes asados* of northern Mexico. Perhaps both influences are at play.

Today, there are more than 3,800 barbecue joints in Texas (according to the Texas Restaurant Association), and most of them serve ribs, pork shoulder, sausage (jalapeño sausage is a popular item these days), turkey, and other meats.

But to taste Texas barbecue at its best, you've got to order brisket.

GINGER-PLUM BARBECUE SAUCE

ON THE SIDE

Here's a contemporary Asian barbecue sauce, made with tangy sweet plums, that is delicious on duck, pork, and ribs. The recipe was inspired by Romy Dorotan, chef-owner of the restaurant Cendrillon in New York, and it far surpasses the sugary bottled plum sauces from China. To pit a plum, cut it around its circumference all the way to the stone, then twist the halves in opposite directions to separate them. Use a spoon to pop out the stone left in one of the halves.

12 ounces ripe plums (4 to 5 plums), pitted
1 tablespoon minced fresh ginger
1 stalk fresh lemongrass, trimmed and finely chopped, or 1 strip lemon zest (2 x ½ inches; removed with a vegetable peeler)
1 hot chile, seeded (for a hotter sauce, leave the seeds in)
2 scallions, both white and green parts, trimmed and finely chopped
1 large clove garlic, minced
2 tablespoons soy sauce, or more to taste
2 tablespoons sweet soy sauce (ketjap manis) or 1 tablespoon each regular soy sauce and molasses
2 tablespoons honey, or more to taste
1 tablespoon rice vinegar
2 teaspoons fresh lemon juice, or more to taste
½ cup water, or more if needed

1. Combine all the ingredients, including 2 tablespoons each soy sauce and honey, 2 teaspoons lemon juice, and ½ cup water, in a heavy nonreactive saucepan and bring to a boil over medium heat. Reduce the heat to medium-low and simmer, uncovered, until the plums are very soft, about 5 minutes. Transfer the mixture to a blender to process to a purée, then return to the pan. Taste for seasoning, adding soy sauce, honey, or lemon juice as necessary; the sauce should be sweet, sour, and spicy. If too thick, thin with a little more water.

2. Transfer to a serving bowl and serve warm or at room temperature. The sauce will keep, tightly covered in the refrigerator, for up to 1 week.

Makes about 1 cup

NICARAGUAN TOMATO SAUCE
Salsa Marinara

ON THE SIDE

Nicaraguans call this tangy tomato sauce *marinara,* but it sure doesn't taste like any pasta sauce I've ever sampled. It is one of the three traditional accompaniments to Nicaraguan grilled meats. (The other two are *chimichurri* and *cebollita* (see the Index). Serve with Nicaraguan-Style Steak (see Index).

½ cup water

3 tablespoons distilled white vinegar, or more to taste

3 tablespoons ketchup

3 fresh, ripe tomatoes, peeled and seeded (see page 62), then finely chopped

2 medium onions, thinly sliced

½ medium green bell pepper, stemmed, seeded, and thinly sliced

2 cloves garlic, minced

3 tablespoons finely chopped fresh Italian (flat-leaf) parsley

1 to 2 jalapeño chiles, seeded and diced

Salt and freshly ground black pepper, to taste

Combine the water, 3 tablespoons vinegar, and the ketchup in a small nonreactive saucepan. Bring to a boil over medium heat. Add the tomatoes, onions, bell pepper, garlic, parsley, and chiles. Reduce the heat to low and simmer gently until the sauce is thick and flavorful, 5 to 10 minutes. Remove from the heat and taste for seasoning, adding salt and black pepper and more vinegar as necessary; the sauce should be highly seasoned. Serve at once, or store, tightly covered in the refrigerator, for up to 3 days.

Makes about 2 cups

ROMESCO SAUCE

SPAIN

METHOD:
Direct grilling

SPECIAL EQUIPMENT:
Vegetable grate

Romesco is the most famous sauce in Catalonia, a gutsy purée of tomatoes, garlic, and fresh and dried chiles bound together with two characteristic Catalan thickeners: toasted bread and ground almonds. Traditionally, these ingredients would be roasted in the oven to intensify their flavor before puréeing. That set me thinking about an even better way to heighten the flavor: charring the vegetables and bread on the grill. Catalans would use a dried chile called *anorra*. These are difficult to find in the U.S., but a Mexican ancho or pasilla chile makes a good substitute. (In a worst-case scenario, you could use 1 to 2 tablespoons chile powder.) *Romesco* is traditionally served with grilled seafoods, chicken, and meats. I like to eat it straight off the spoon!

3 dried anorra chiles or 1 ancho or pasilla chile

1 small red bell pepper

2 large or 3 medium fresh, ripe tomatoes

5 cloves garlic, peeled

3 tablespoons whole almonds, blanched or unblanched

1 small onion, quartered

⅓ cup olive oil

1 slice country-style white bread

1 bay leaf

3 tablespoons finely chopped fresh Italian (flat-leaf) parsley

2 tablespoons red wine vinegar, or more to taste

Salt and freshly ground black pepper, to taste

1. Place the chiles in a bowl and add warm water to cover. Soak until soft and pliable, about 30 minutes.

2. Drain the chiles, reserving the soaking liquid; blot dry with paper towels. If a milder sauce is desired, remove the seeds.

3. Preheat the grill to high.

4. When ready to cook, preheat a vegetable grate for 5 minutes. Brush the bell pepper and tomatoes with oil and grill until the skins are nicely charred, 10 to 15 minutes in all. Toss the garlic, almonds, and onion pieces with 2 tablespoons of the oil in a small bowl, then arrange these ingredients on the hot grate and cook, turning with a spatula, until each is nicely browned and aromatic, 1 to 2 minutes for the almonds, 4 to 8 minutes for the vegetables. Brush the bread on both sides with oil and grill until nicely browned, 1 to 2 minutes per side. Grill the soaked and drained chiles until crisp and fragrant, about 20 seconds per side. As they are done, transfer the grilled almonds, vegetables, bread, and chiles to a platter and let cool.

5. Remove any very charred skin from the tomatoes and peppers; core and seed the peppers. Transfer the tomatoes to a blender or food processor and purée to a smooth paste. Add the garlic, onion, bell pepper, almonds, bread, chiles, bay leaf, parsley, vinegar, remaining olive oil, and salt and black pepper. Process until smooth, adding enough of the reserved chile soaking liquid to make a pourable sauce. Correct the seasoning, adding salt or vinegar as necessary.

6. Serve the sauce at room temperature; it will keep, tightly covered in the refrigerator, for up to 3 days.

Makes about 2 cups

CHARRED TOMATO SAUCE WITH POMEGRANATE MOLASSES
Khashkesh

LEBANON

METHOD:
Direct grilling

Khashkesh isn't your typical tomato sauce. Not by a long shot. Charring the tomatoes lends a distinctive smoke flavor, while the pomegranate molasses adds an unexpected sweetness and tartness. (The latter is available at Middle and Near Eastern markets, but I have also included a recipe for it.)

1 large fresh, ripe tomato
1 clove garlic, minced
2 tablespoons Pomegranate Molasses
    (page 227) or 1 tablespoon balsamic
    vinegar
¼ teaspoon cayenne pepper, or more to taste
Salt and freshly ground black pepper, to taste

1. Preheat the grill to high.

2. Place the tomato on the hot grate and grill, turning with tongs, until charred on all sides, 8 to 12 minutes. Transfer to a platter to cool.

3. Scrape most of the burnt skin off the tomato, then combine with the garlic, Pomegranate Molasses, ¼ teaspoon cayenne, and salt and black pepper in a food processor. Process to a coarse paste. Taste for seasoning, adding salt or cayenne as necessary; the sauce should be highly seasoned.

4. Serve, at room temperature, within 4 hours of making.

Makes about 1 cup

HOISIN-CHILE SAUCE

CHINA

ON THE SIDE

Enjoyed over a huge area, including China and Southeast Asia, this sauce is simplicity itself. It contains only two ingredients: hoisin sauce (a dark sweet sauce made from soybeans) and chile sauce. There are lots of options for the latter: I like a Thai chile sauce, like Sriracha, but almost any good-quality bottled chile sauce will do. Increase or decrease the proportion of chile sauce according to the intensity of the sauce and your tolerance to heat. Serve this sauce with satés and other Asian-style grilled meats.

⅔ cup hoisin sauce
⅓ cup chile sauce

Combine the ingredients in a bowl and whisk to mix (see Note). Transfer to tiny bowls to serve.
Makes about 1 cup
Note: For a more striking presentation, spoon the hoisin sauce into tiny bowls and squirt or spoon a puddle of the chile sauce in the center of each. Mix the sauces in the bowl with the tip of chopsticks and use the sauce for dipping.

A SIMPLE TAMARIND BARBECUE SAUCE

THAILAND

ON THE SIDE

Most North American barbecue sauces play the sweetness of sugar or molasses against the sharpness of vinegar and hot sauce. A similar contrast of sweet and sour characterizes the barbecue sauces of Thailand. The following sauce, inspired by one served at the restaurant Bahn Thai in Bangkok, derives its piquant flavor from tamarind. It is particularly good with grilled chicken or fish.

I leave the number of chiles you use up to you.

¼ cup Tamarind Water (page 219)
    or frozen tamarind purée, thawed
¼ cup Asian fish sauce
¼ cup sugar
2 tablespoons water
2 large shallots, finely chopped
1 to 6 Thai, serrano, or jalapeño chiles,
    thinly sliced (for a milder sauce,
    seed the chiles)

Combine the Tamarind Water, fish sauce, sugar, and water in a small bowl and whisk until the sugar is dissolved. Whisk in the shallots and chiles and serve immediately, or at least the same day you make it; serve at room temperature.
Makes about 1 cup

INDONESIAN KETCHUP
Ketjap Manis

ON THE SIDE

Ask for ketchup in the world's fourth most populous nation, and you're likely to be served *ketjap manis*, a thick, syrupy, sweet, spiced soy sauce. At first glance, nothing could be more different than the blood-red sauce most of Americans think of as ketchup. But the two condiments are closely related, kissing cousins as it were, descended from a common historical ancestor.

Here's a homemade *ketjap manis* that makes an intriguing condiment for simple grilled meats and seafood. Note: Mix equal parts *ketjap* and melted butter to make a fabulous basting mixture for grilled fish. For the sake of convenience, I've westernized the recipe slightly, substituting the more readily available ginger and bay leaves for the traditional galangal and salam leaf. If you have the patience to search out these ingredients at an Asian market, your *ketjap* will taste even more authentic.

Throughout the book, I have suggested an even easier substitute for the *ketjap*—equal parts soy sauce and molasses—but if you like Indonesian grilling as much as I do, it's worth buying real *ketjap manis* or making your own.

2 cups soy sauce
1½ cups firmly packed light brown sugar, or more to taste
¾ cup molasses, or more to taste
2 cloves garlic, flattened with the side of a cleaver and peeled
2 slices ginger (each ¼ inch thick), flattened with the side of a cleaver
2 whole star anise or 1 teaspoon anisette liqueur plus ¼ teaspoon liquid smoke
1 bay leaf
1 teaspoon coriander seeds

1. Combine the soy sauce, 1½ cups sugar, ¾ cup molasses, the garlic, ginger, star anise, bay leaf, and coriander seeds in a medium-size, heavy saucepan. Bring to a boil over medium heat, stirring until the sugar is dissolved. Reduce the heat to medium-low and simmer, uncovered, until the mixture is richly flavored and slightly syrupy, about 8 minutes. Stir the mixture as it cooks. Taste for seasoning, adding sugar or molasses as necessary; the sauce should be quite sweet.

2. Strain the *ketjap* into a clean jar and let cool; it will keep, tightly covered in the refrigerator, for several months.

Makes about 3 cups

THAI PEANUT SAUCE

ON THE SIDE

Peanut sauce is the traditional accompaniment to Southeast Asian satés. There are probably as many individual recipes as there are street vendors. You might find this version—enriched with coconut milk—at a Thai saté stall.

2 teaspoons minced fresh ginger

1 to 2 Thai, serrano, or jalapeño chiles, seeded and minced (for a spicier sauce, leave the seeds in)

1 clove garlic, minced

2 scallions, both white and green parts, trimmed and minced

⅓ cup chunky peanut butter

⅓ cup coconut milk, canned or homemade (page 522), or more as needed

2 tablespoons Asian fish sauce or soy sauce, or more to taste

1 tablespoon fresh lime juice, or more to taste

2 teaspoons sugar, or more to taste

¼ cup chopped fresh cilantro (optional)

1. Combine the ginger, chile, garlic, scallions, peanut butter, ⅓ cup coconut milk, 2 tablespoons fish sauce, 1 tablespoon lime juice, 2 teaspoons sugar, and the cilantro (if using) in a small, heavy saucepan. Bring to a boil over medium heat, stirring well to mix, then reduce the heat to low and simmer, uncovered, until richly flavored, about 10 minutes. The sauce should be thick but pourable; thin with coconut milk, if needed.

2. Remove from the heat and taste for seasoning, adding fish sauce, lime juice, or sugar as necessary; the sauce should be highly seasoned. Serve warm or at room temperature. The sauce will keep, tightly covered in the refrigerator, for up to 3 days.

Makes about 1 cup

DUTCH WEST INDIAN PEANUT SAUCE

DUTCH WEST INDIES

ON THE SIDE

Tamarind lends a fruity tartness to this peanut sauce, a West Indian version of an Indonesian classic. The sauce is designed to be served with Dutch West Indian Chicken Kebabs, (see Index), but it's great with any type of saté, as well as grilled chicken or seafood.

¼ cup finely chopped onion

1 clove garlic, minced

1 teaspoon sambal ulek or other chile paste or sauce

¾ cup creamy peanut butter

¼ cup Tamarind Water (page 219)

2 tablespoons sweet soy sauce (ketjap manis), or 1 tablespoon each regular soy sauce and molasses, or more to taste

2 tablespoons distilled white vinegar, or more to taste

¾ to 1 cup water

1. Combine the onion, garlic, and *sambal ulek* in a mortar and pound to a smooth paste with the pestle; or process in a blender or mini chopper. Transfer the mixture to a nonreactive heavy saucepan and stir in the peanut butter, Tamarind Water, 2 tablespoons sweet soy sauce, 2 tablespoons vinegar, and ¾ cup water.

2. Bring the mixture to a boil over medium heat, then reduce the heat to low and simmer, uncovered, until dark and well flavored, about 5 minutes, adding water as necessary to obtain a thick but pourable sauce. Remove from the heat and taste for seasoning, adding sweet soy sauce or vinegar as necessary; the sauce should be highly seasoned.

3. Serve warm or at room temperature. The sauce will keep, tightly covered in the refrigerator, for up to 3 days.

Makes about 2 cups

VIETNAMESE APPLE AND SHRIMP SAUCE
Mam Nem

VIETNAM

ON THE SIDE

Mam nem is certainly one of the more exotic dipping sauces in the Vietnamese culinary repertoire. Despite the odd-sounding combination of flavors, it's extremely tasty and easy to make. I first sampled this sauce in Saigon, where it was made with puréed pineapple. I like the no-fuss sweetness of applesauce. Serve with any sort of grilled fish or pork.

1 tablespoon vegetable oil
1 clove garlic, minced
4 ounces shrimp, peeled and deveined (see box, page 349), then very finely chopped
2 tablespoons Asian fish sauce, or more to taste
1 teaspoon sambal ulek or other chile paste or sauce
½ cup unsweetened applesauce

1. Heat the oil in a small, heavy saucepan over medium-high heat. Add the garlic and cook until fragrant but not brown, about 15 seconds. Add the shrimp and cook, stirring, until opaque, 1 to 2 minutes. Stir in 2 tablespoons fish sauce, 1 teaspoon hot sauce, and the applesauce and bring to a boil, then remove from the heat. Taste for seasoning, adding fish sauce or hot sauce as necessary; the sauce should be highly seasoned.

2. Transfer the sauce to a bowl and let cool to room temperature. Serve immediately, or store, tightly covered in the refrigerator, for up to 3 days. Serve at room temperature.

Makes about ¾ cup

TWO MISO BARBECUE SAUCES

JAPAN

ON THE SIDE

These creamy, sweet-salty sauces are two of the glories of Japanese grilling. You find them at humble yakitori parlors and at grand restaurants. They owe their rich tangy flavor to miso, a nutritious paste made from cultured (fermented) soy beans and grains. It's impossible to describe the exact flavor of miso, but if you imagine the salty tang of a bouillon cube crossed with the richness of cream cheese, you'll start to get the idea. Miso is readily available in natural foods stores and Japanese markets, and in the produce section of many supermarkets. Stored in the refrigerator, it keeps almost indefinitely. Below are two miso barbecue sauces used widely in Japanese grilling.

White Miso Barbecue Sauce

White miso (actually it's beige in color) is the most readily available miso, and is best known as an ingredient in miso soup and miso salad dressing. Called *shiro-miso* in Japanese, it's made with soybeans and rice, which give it a sweet flavor. This recipe breaks with tradition in two ways. First, I've substituted commercial mayonnaise for the customary egg yolks. Sometimes the sauce is served warmed but not cooked, so I prefer not to use raw yolks. Second, I use vegetable stock instead of *dashi* (a light fish broth made with dried bonito flakes and kelp). The purist could certainly use 2 egg yolks and 2 tablespoons *dashi* instead. White miso is delicious on grilled tofu and vegetables.

1 cup white miso
2 tablespoons sake or dry sherry
2 tablespoons mirin (sweet rice wine),
  or cream sherry
2 tablespoons sugar
2 tablespoons mayonnaise
2 tablespoons vegetable stock,
  dashi, or water

1. Combine the miso, sake, mirin, sugar, and mayonnaise in the top of a double boiler and whisk until smooth. Gradually whisk in the stock. Cook the sauce over simmering water, stirring occasionally, until thick and creamy, about 5 minutes. Remove the pan from over the water and let the sauce cool to room temperature.

2. Transfer to a serving bowl, cover, and refrigerate until ready to use, up to 3 days. Serve at room temperature.

Makes about 1½ cups

Red Miso Barbecue Sauce

Red miso (actually a reddish brown in color) has a deep, rich, salty flavor and isn't quite as sweet as white miso. Known as *aka-miso* in Japanese, it contains barley as well as soybeans and rice. Red miso barbecue sauce is particularly good on grilled vegetables and salmon.

Prepare and store as above, substituting red miso for the white. You may need a little more sugar; taste for seasoning after cooling, and be sure to stir any added sugar in thoroughly.

Makes about 1½ cups

CLASSIC TERIYAKI SAUCE

JAPAN

ON THE SIDE

Many Americans think of teriyaki as a marinade, but in traditional Japanese cuisine it's actually a glaze or barbecue sauce brushed on simply grilled meats and seafood. (*Teri* is the Japanese word for "gloss" or "luster"; *yaki* means "grilled.") Zen-like in its simplicity, this recipe was inspired by the late Shizuo Tsuji, founder of the Ecole Technique Hôtelière Tsuji in Osaka and author of the authoritative book *Japanese Cooking: A Simple Art.*

½ cup dark soy sauce
½ cup sake or dry sherry
½ cup mirin (sweet rice wine) or
    cream sherry
2 tablespoons sugar

1. Combine the soy sauce, sake, mirin, and sugar in a small, heavy saucepan and bring to a boil over high heat. Reduce the heat to medium and simmer until the sugar is dissolved and the sauce is thick and syrupy, about 5 minutes.

2. Remove from the heat and let cool before using as a glaze or as a sauce for serving. The sauce will keep, tightly covered in the refrigerator, for up to 2 weeks.

Makes about 1½ cups

BASIC CHIMICHURRI

ON THE SIDE

CHIMICHURRI VARIATIONS
Some cooks add grated onion to their chimichurris (1 small onion for the quantities at right), while others add ¼ cup diced red bell pepper or fresh hot chiles.

Chimichurri is the traditional accompaniment to South American grilled meats. It turns up everywhere, from roadside barbecue stalls to pricey steak palaces, as far north as Nicaragua, as far south as Chile, and in just about every Spanish-speaking country in between. No two *chimichurri* recipes are exactly alike, although the basic recipe contains just four ingredients: parsley, garlic, olive oil, and salt. This recipe comes from Marono Fraga, owner of the Estancia del Puerto in Montevideo's colorful Mercado del Puerto (Port Market). Don't be alarmed by the seemingly enormous quantity of garlic. The parsley acts as a breath sweetener.

1 bunch fresh Italian (flat-leaf) parsley,
    stemmed
1 small head garlic, broken into cloves
    and peeled (8 to 10 cloves in all)
1 medium carrot, peeled and grated on
    the coarse side of a grater
1 cup extra-virgin olive oil
⅓ cup white wine vinegar or distilled
    vinegar, or more to taste
¼ cup water
1 teaspoon salt, or more to taste
1 teaspoon dried oregano
½ teaspoon hot red pepper flakes, or
    more to taste
½ teaspoon freshly ground black pepper

1. Combine the parsley and garlic in a food processor and pulse to chop as fine as possible.

2. Add the carrot, oil, ⅓ cup vinegar, the water, 1 teaspoon salt, the oregano, ½ teaspoon hot pepper flakes, and the black pepper. Process to mix. Taste for seasoning, adding vinegar, salt, or pepper flakes as necessary; the sauce should be highly seasoned. The *chimichurri* will keep for several days in the refrigerator (you may need to reseason it just before serving), but it tastes best served within a few hours of making.

Makes about 2 cups

RED CHIMICHURRI

ARGENTINA

ON THE SIDE

Traditional *chimichurri* is a garlicky green sauce made with olive oil and fresh parsley. But many variations exist in Argentina and Uruguay, including red *chimichurri*—a specialty of the venerable Buenos Aires steak house La Cabaña. This *chimichurri* differs from most in two significant ways: It's cooked (most are raw) and it's flavored with anchovies and tuna. The former suggests parentage with two other of the world's great steak sauces, A-1 and Worcestershire, while the latter recalls Italy's *tonnato* sauce, which is so delightful with cold roast veal or grilled beef and seafood. Here's how I imagine La Cabaña prepares the sauce.

½ cup olive oil
½ medium red bell pepper, stemmed,
　　seeded, and diced
½ medium carrot, peeled and diced
2 scallions, both white and green parts,
　　trimmed and diced
¼ medium onion, diced
1 medium rib celery, diced
1 clove garlic, finely chopped
3 tablespoons drained canned water-
　　pack tuna
1 canned anchovy fillet, drained and chopped
2 tablespoons chopped fresh Italian
　　(flat-leaf) parsley
2 teaspoons drained capers
1 cup tomato sauce
½ cup chicken broth or water
¼ cup tomato paste
1 tablespoon red wine vinegar, or
　　more to taste
1 teaspoon dried oregano
Salt and lots of freshly ground black
　　pepper

1. Heat the oil in a medium-size nonreactive saucepan over medium heat. Add the bell pepper, carrot, scallions, onion, celery, and garlic and sauté until softened but not brown, about 5 minutes.

2. Stir in the tuna, anchovy, parsley, capers, tomato sauce, broth, tomato paste, 1 tablespoon vinegar, oregano, and salt and black pepper and cook, uncovered, until thick and fragrant, about 10 minutes.

3. Transfer the sauce to a blender or food processor and process to a purée, then return to the pan and cook over medium-low heat for 5 minutes. Remove from the heat and taste for seasoning, adding salt or vinegar as necessary; the sauce should be highly seasoned. Transfer to a serving bowl and serve hot or at room temperature. The sauce can be stored, tightly covered in the refrigerator, for up to 3 days.

Makes about 2½ cups

"DRY" CHIMICHURRI

ARGENTINA

ON THE SIDE

This is the simplest of *chimichurris:* olive oil flavored with dried herbs and hot red pepper flakes. I first tasted it at the Estancia Cinacina, a horse ranch in Argentina that also stages barbecues and equestrian events for tourists. Argentinian food markets sell packages of premixed *chimichurri* herbs for people who don't

have time to buy and chop fresh herbs.
Spoon the *chimichurri* over grilled beef.

- ¾ cup extra-virgin olive oil
- 3 tablespoons red wine vinegar
- 1 tablespoon dried oregano
- 1 tablespoon dried basil
- 2 teaspoons sweet paprika
- 1 teaspoon dried thyme
- 1 teaspoon hot red pepper flakes
- ½ teaspoon coarse (kosher or sea) salt, or more to taste
- ½ teaspoon freshly ground black pepper, or more to taste

Place all the ingredients, including ½ teaspoon each salt and pepper, in a mixing bowl and whisk to mix. Taste for seasoning, adding salt and pepper as necessary. The sauce will keep, tightly covered in the refrigerator, for up to 3 days.

Makes about ¾ cup

PORTUGUESE HOT SAUCE
Piri-Piri

PORTUGAL

ON THE SIDE

ADVANCE PREPARATION:
3 to 48 hours

SPECIAL EQUIPMENT:
One 1-pint jar, well washed

The Portuguese learned to love chiles in their former colony, Brazil. The chile in question here is one of the smallest members of the capsicum family, a bullet-shaped brute ¼ to ½ inch in length, whose diminutive size belies its ferocious bite. Piri-piri peppers go by the name of *pimenta malagueta* in Brazil and *gindungo* in Angola. Piri-piri sauce has become an indispensable part of barbecue all over the Portuguese-speaking world. If you live near a Portuguese or Brazilian market, you may be able to find fresh or bottled piri-piri or malagueta peppers. Acceptable substitutes include fresh or pickled cayenne peppers; péquin chiles from Mexico; serrano; Thai or Indian peppers; or in a pinch jalapeño chiles.

The sauce goes especially well with grilled fish or chicken; serve it with any dish you feel could use an Iberian blast of heat.

- 6 to 12 pimenta malagueta or other hot red chiles
- 1 teaspoon coarse (kosher or sea) salt, or more to taste
- ⅓ cup red wine vinegar
- ¾ cup olive oil
- ¼ cup hot water

Thinly slice the chiles, then combine with the salt and vinegar in a clean 1-pint jar with a lid. Cover and shake until blended and the salt is dissolved. Add the oil and water and shake again. Let sit, in a cool place, for a few hours or even days, so the flavors ripen. Taste for seasoning, adding more salt if desired. The sauce will keep, tightly covered in the refrigerator, for several weeks. For prolonged storage, place a piece of plastic wrap over the mouth of the jar before screwing on the lid, to keep the lid from corroding.

Makes about 1½ cups

TWO HARISSAS

NORTH AFRICA

ON THE SIDE

Harissa is North Africa hot sauce. The concept is sufficiently broad to include simple fresh tomato purées warmed with onion and hot paprika and complex sauces flavored with preserved lemons and cayenne. Homemade *harissa* is quite different and vastly more tasty than the salty canned *harissas* one finds in gourmet shops and ethnic markets.

A Simple Harissa

Here's a quick, simple version of *harissa*. Serve it alongside grilled lamb, kebabs, and other North African–style meats.

2 large fresh, ripe tomatoes
1 small onion or 2 shallots, peeled
3 tablespoons minced fresh Italian
    (flat-leaf) parsley
1 tablespoon hot paprika or 1½ teaspoons
    cayenne pepper (see Note), or
    more to taste
2 tablespoons extra-virgin olive oil
1 tablespoon fresh lemon juice
Salt and freshly ground black pepper, to taste

Cut the tomatoes in half and gently wring out the seeds and liquid over the sink. Grate each tomato half on the coarse side of a grater into a bowl by holding the cut side of the tomato half against the grater and grating the flesh just to the skin. Discard the skin. Grate the onion into the bowl. Stir in the parsley, paprika, oil, and lemon juice, salt and black pepper to taste; the mixture should be highly seasoned. Serve immediately, or no longer than 4 hours after making, at room temperature.

Makes about 1½ cups

Note: For a milder *harissa*, omit the hot paprika or cayenne pepper.

Preserved Lemon Harissa

Here's a more sophisticated *harissa* flavored with fresh chiles and preserved lemons. The latter—one of the most distinctive flavors in Moroccan cuisine—are a sort of pickle made with fresh lemons and salt. You can buy them in North African and Middle Eastern markets and gourmet shops. A little of this intensely flavored pickle goes a long way.

4 to 10 hot chiles, such as
    jalapeños or serranos
    (for a milder sauce, seed the chiles)
3 shallots, thinly sliced
2 cloves garlic, peeled
1 tablespoon chopped preserved lemon
2 large fresh, ripe tomatoes, peeled and
    seeded (see page 62)
1 tablespoon hot paprika or 1½ teaspoons
    cayenne pepper
½ teaspoon ground cumin
3 tablespoons vegetable oil
2 tablespoons fresh lemon juice
Salt and freshly ground black pepper, to taste

1. Place the chiles, shallots, garlic, preserved lemon, and tomatoes in a mortar and grind to a purée with the pestle, then work in the remaining ingredients, adding salt and pepper to taste. Or process all the ingredients at once in a blender. Go easy on the salt; the preserved lemon is already quite salty.

2. The *harissa* should be tart and spicy, but there should be more to it than just heat. Transfer to a bowl and serve immediately, or at least within 4 hours of making; serve at room temperature.

Makes about 2 cups

CORIANDER SAUCE

AFGHANISTAN

ON THE SIDE

Coriander sauce is a tart, tangy condiment that is spooned over grilled kebabs, chops, and chicken. This version is a permanent fixture on the Afghan table. Similar sauces are found as far east as India and as far west as the Republic of Georgia. Walnuts help thicken and bind the sauce.

1 bunch fresh cilantro, stemmed
(about 1 cup loosely packed leaves)
3 cloves garlic, peeled
1 jalapeño or other hot chile, seeded
(for a spicier chutney, leave the seeds in)
½ cup walnut pieces
⅓ cup fresh lemon juice or distilled white
vinegar, or more to taste

1 teaspoon salt, or more to taste
½ teaspoon freshly ground black pepper
¼ teaspoon ground cumin (optional)
2 to 4 tablespoons water, or as needed

1. Combine the cilantro, garlic, chile, and walnuts in a blender or food processor. Add ⅓ cup lemon juice, 1 teaspoon salt, the pepper, and cumin (if using) and process to a smooth paste. Add enough water to obtain a pourable sauce.

2. Taste for seasoning, adding salt and lemon juice as necessary; the sauce should be very highly seasoned. Serve immediately, or at least within 4 hours of making; serve at room temperature.

Makes about 1 cup

COUNTRY HOT SAUCE
Molho da Companha

VIETNAM

ON THE SIDE

This salsa-like hot sauce turns up wherever Brazilians grill meats. The chile of choice is a pepper called *pimenta*

malagueta, the strength of whose fiery bite is inversely proportional to its tiny dimensions. *Pimenta malagueta* come packed in vinegar in bottles at Brazilian markets. Other possibilities for chiles include Thai or bird peppers, serrano or jalapeño chiles, or even hot red pepper flakes; the number of chiles to use is up to you. The traditional way to eat grilled meats in Brazil is to spoon this sauce on top, then sprinkle the meat with *farofa* (toasted manioc flour—see the Index for Rainbow Manioc, a more exotic version).

1 medium onion, finely chopped
1 large fresh, ripe, tomato, finely chopped
½ green bell pepper, stemmed, seeded, and finely chopped
1 to 6 pimenta malaqueta or other hot red chiles, minced

¼ cup water
3 tablespoons extra-virgin olive oil
2 tablespoons fresh lime juice
1 tablespoon red wine vinegar, or more to taste
Salt and freshly ground black pepper, to taste

Combine the onion, tomato, bell pepper, chile, water, oil, lime juice, and 1 tablespoon vinegar in a small nonreactive bowl and stir to mix. Taste for seasoning, adding salt and black pepper and more vinegar, if necessary; the sauce should be highly seasoned. Serve immediately or at least the same day you make it; serve at room temperature.
Makes about 2 cups

FRENCH WEST INDIAN "DOG" SAUCE
Sauce Chien

FRENCH WEST INDIES

ON THE SIDE

Sauce chien (literally, "dog sauce") is a sort of high-voltage vinaigrette served throughout the French West Indies. How did it get its odd name? One theory holds that the "dog" refers to the fierce bite of the chiles. Another refers to the fact that this is a humble sauce, made without the egg yolks, butter, or cream found in more "noble" French sauces. Whatever its origins, *sauce chien* is an indispensable accompaniment to grilled seafood, chicken, and vegetables throughout the French West Indies.

2 cloves garlic, minced
½ teaspoon salt, or more to taste
½ to 2 scotch bonnet chiles, seeded and minced (for a hotter sauce, leave the seeds in)
1 shallot, minced
2 tablespoons finely chopped fresh chives or scallion greens
2 tablespoons finely chopped fresh cilantro
2 tablespoons finely chopped fresh Italian (flat-leaf) parsley
½ teaspoon chopped fresh thyme
Freshly ground black pepper, to taste
3 tablespoons fresh lime juice, or more to taste
¼ cup extra-virgin olive oil
¼ cup boiling water, or more as needed

1. Combine the garlic and ½ teaspoon salt in a mortar and grind to a paste with the pestle. Then pound in the chiles, shallot, chives, cilantro, parsley, thyme, pepper, and 3 tablespoons lime juice. Work in the oil, then add enough boiling water to obtain a mellow, pourable sauce. Or combine all the ingredients at once in a blender or mini chopper and run the machine in short bursts until just coarsely puréed. Taste for seasoning, adding salt or lime juice as necessary; the sauce should be highly seasoned.

2. Serve immediately, or at least no longer than 4 hours after making; serve at room temperature.

Makes about 1 cup

HOT AND SWEET MINT SAUCE

GREAT BRITAIN

ON THE SIDE

Mint sauce is such a popular accompaniment to lamb in Britain and other Commonwealth countries that it would seem a grievous omission to leave it out here—even though said sauce is usually served with roasted or boiled lamb, not grilled. To jazz up the traditional recipe, I've added fresh mint and scotch bonnet chiles. Serve hot or cold with any sort of grilled lamb.

¾ **cup mint jelly**
¼ **cup distilled white vinegar, or more to taste**
1 **scotch bonnet, habanero, or jalapeño chile, seeded and minced (for a spicier sauce, leave the seeds in)**
3 **tablespoons thinly slivered fresh mint leaves or 2 teaspoons dried**

Combine the mint jelly, ¼ cup vinegar, and the chile in a small nonreactive saucepan and bring to a boil over medium heat. Reduce the heat to medium-low and simmer gently, uncovered, until thick and richly flavored, about 5 minutes. Stir in the mint leaves and cook for 1 to 2 minutes more. Remove from the heat, and if the sauce tastes too sweet, add a little more vinegar, and if it's too thick, add a little water. Serve immediately or allow to cool, then refrigerate, tightly covered, for up to 3 days.

Makes about 1 cup

GARLIC SAUCE

TRINIDAD AND TOBAGO

ON THE SIDE

You might think that the staggering amount of garlic in this recipe would render the sauce inedible, but the lime juice and salt have a mellowing effect that makes it mild and palatable. This sauce was originally designed to be served with

Shark and Bake (see Index), although it's hard to imagine a grilled dish that wouldn't benefit from a spoonful of this elixir.

8 cloves garlic, peeled
½ cup fresh lime juice, or more to taste
½ cup distilled white vinegar
¼ cup water
1 tablespoon salt, or more to taste

Combine the garlic, ½ cup lime juice, the vinegar, water, and 1 tablespoon salt in a blender and process until creamy and smooth. Taste for seasoning, adding lime juice or salt as necessary; the sauce should be highly seasoned. Serve immediately, or store, tightly covered in the refrigerator, for up to 3 days. Serve at room temperature.

Makes about 1¼ cups

LEMON-HONEY SAUCE WITH GARLIC

THAILAND

ON THE SIDE

Sweet, sour, slightly hot, and decidedly pungent, this sauce is the quintessence of Thai cooking. To be strictly authentic, you'd use cilantro root, which tastes like a cross between fresh cilantro and parsnip. If you live near an Indian, Hispanic, or Southeast Asian market, you can probably buy cilantro with the roots still attached. If not, use cilantro leaves—the sauce will be almost as good. Don't be put off by the seemingly large quantity of garlic and chiles: The lemon juice and honey seem to neutralize these ingredients. This sauce can be served with grilled chicken, beef, or pork, but it's particularly good with seafood.

12 cloves garlic, minced
3 to 6 Thai, serrano, or other hot chiles, seeded and finely chopped
3 tablespoons minced fresh coriander roots or leaves
½ cup fresh lemon juice
½ cup Asian fish sauce
3 tablespoons honey

Combine the garlic, chiles, coriander root, lemon juice, fish sauce, and honey in a bowl and whisk to mix. Taste for seasoning, adding more of any of the ingredients as desired. Serve immediately or cover and refrigerate for up to 8 hours.

Makes about 1½ cups

CATALAN VINAIGRETTE

SPAIN

ON THE SIDE

This is one of the three sauces that invariably accompany grilled meats and seafood in Barcelona (the others are *romesco*—also in this chapter—and *alioli,* cousin of the Provençal *aïoli,* a simple garlic-spiked mayonnaise). If you think of vinaigrette as too delicate a sauce to stand up to a steak, try this caper-, shallot-, and pickle-flavored version. You'll be pleasantly surprised.

2 tablespoons red wine vinegar

2 tablespoons hot water

½ teaspoon salt, or more to taste

½ teaspoon freshly ground black pepper, or more to taste

½ cup extra-virgin olive oil

1 large shallot, finely chopped

1 small sour pickle, such as cornichon, finely chopped

1 fresh, ripe plum tomato, finely chopped

1 tablespoon capers, drained and coarsely chopped, if large

1. Combine the vinegar, water, ½ tea-spoon salt, and ½ teaspoon pepper in a small nonreactive bowl and whisk until the salt is dissolved. Add the oil in a thin, steady stream, whisking constantly to make an emulsified sauce. Whisk in the shallot, pickle, tomato, and capers.

2. Taste for seasoning, adding salt and pepper if necessary. Let stand for at least 10 minutes and up to 4 hours before serving. If you refrigerate the sauce while it stands, bring it to room temperature before serving, making sure you restir it and check it for seasoning as well.

Makes about 1 cup

TAMARIND DIPPING SAUCE

THAILAND

ON THE SIDE

Tamarind is the sweet-sour pulp of a tropical seed pod, and its mouth-puckering tartness makes a nice counterpoint to the grilled fare of Southeast Asia. Serve this lively sauce with saté, but don't stop there. Grilled shrimp, chicken, pork, and even hamburgers shine in its presence.

2 tablespoons peanut oil

2 cloves garlic, minced

2 shallots or 1 small onion, minced

1 tablespoon minced fresh ginger

1 to 2 hot chiles, seeded and minced (for a hotter sauce, leave the seeds in)

¾ cup Tamarind Water (page 219)

¼ cup Asian fish sauce, or more to taste

2 tablespoons sugar, or more to taste

2 tablespoons chopped fresh cilantro (optional)

1. Heat the oil in a wok or large, heavy skillet over high heat. Add the garlic, shallots, ginger, and chiles and sauté until fragrant but not brown, about 30 seconds, stirring constantly.

2. Stir in the Tamarind Water, ¼ cup fish sauce, and 2 tablespoons sugar and bring to a boil over medium heat. Reduce the heat to medium-low and simmer gently, uncovered, until thickened and the flavors are well blended, about 5 minutes. Remove from the heat and taste for seasoning, adding fish sauce or sugar as necessary; the sauce should be highly seasoned. Stir in the cilantro (if using), then transfer the sauce to bowls and let cool to room temperature. Serve immediately.

Makes about 1 cup

BASIC VIETNAMESE DIPPING SAUCE
Nuoc Cham

VIETNAM

ON THE SIDE

Nuoc cham is Vietnam's national table sauce—a delicate, topaz-colored, slightly sweet, salty, and sour condiment that is obligatory for any Vietnamese grilled fare. Traditionally, finely slivered carrots are added for color and texture. And when I say finely slivered, I mean like dental floss!

1 piece of carrot (2 inches), peeled
½ cup warm water
2 tablespoons sugar, or more to taste
⅓ cup Asian fish sauce, or more
    to taste
¼ cup fresh lime juice
2 tablespoons rice vinegar or distilled
    white vinegar
1 small hot red chile, thinly sliced, or
    ¼ teaspoon hot red pepper flakes
2 cloves garlic, minced

1. Slice the carrot lengthwise with a vegetable peeler and pile the slices on top of one another, then slice lengthwise with a sharp slender knife into the thinnest imaginable strips.

2. Combine the water and 2 tablespoons sugar in a small bowl and whisk until the sugar is dissolved; stir in ⅓ cup fish sauce, ¼ cup lime juice, 2 tablespoons vinegar, the chile, garlic, and carrot strips (see Note). Taste for seasoning, adding fish sauce or sugar as necessary; the *nuoc cham* should strike a delicate balance between salty, tart, and sweet.

3. Serve the sauce immediately, or at least the same day you make it; serve at room temperature.
Makes about 1 cup
Note: You can also blend the ingredients for the sauce by shaking them in a sealed jar

PEANUT CHILE DIPPING SAUCE

VIETNAM

ON THE SIDE

Here's a simple tasty dipping sauce modeled on Vietnamese *nuoc cham*. The peanuts add a characteristic Southeast Asian sweetness.

1 piece of carrot (2 inches), peeled
2 cloves garlic, coarsely chopped
2 tablespoons sugar, or more to taste
¼ cup Asian fish sauce, or more to taste
¼ cup fresh lemon or lime juice, or
    more to taste
2 tablespoons rice vinegar or distilled
    white vinegar

1 or 2 jalapeño or serrano chiles,
    thinly sliced (for a milder sauce,
    seed the chiles)
3 tablespoons chopped dry-roasted peanuts
5 to 6 tablespoons water

1. Slice the carrot lengthwise with a vegetable peeler and pile the slices on top of one another, then slice lengthwise with a sharp slender knife into the thinnest imaginable strips.

2. Combine the garlic and 2 tablespoons sugar in a mortar and grind to a fine paste with the pestle. Or mash them in the bottom of a bowl with the back of a wooden spoon. Stir in ¼ cup fish sauce, ¼ cup lemon juice, the vinegar, carrot strips, chiles, peanuts, and enough water to obtain a mild, mellow sauce. Taste for seasoning, adding fish sauce, lemon juice, or sugar to taste; the sauce should be a little sweet, a little salty, and a little sour.

3. Serve within 4 hours of making, at room temperature.

Makes about 1¼ cups

ASIAN PEAR DIPPING SAUCE

KOREA

ON THE SIDE

Readers of this book will know of my unbridled enthusiasm for Korean cooking, a cuisine, I might add, that is grossly underappreciated in the West. This sauce reflects the Korean penchant for combining sweet, salty, and nutty flavors in a single dish. Serve it with any Korean meat dish.

½ cup soy sauce
½ cup sake or dry sherry
¼ cup sugar
1 small Asian pear, peeled, cored, and
    finely chopped

4 scallions, both white and
    green parts, trimmed and
    finely chopped
¼ cup finely chopped onion
2 tablespoons sesame seeds,
    toasted (see page 93)

Combine all the ingredients in a medium-size bowl and stir until thoroughly mixed and the sugar is dissolved. Divide the sauce among as many small bowls as there are people, so each person has his own for dipping, and serve immediately.

Makes about 2½ cups

A SIMPLE JAVANESE DIPPING SAUCE

JAVA

ON THE SIDE

Mention Indonesian saté and most Westerners will think of peanut sauce. Equally beloved in Indonesia is this simple dipping sauce made at the table by the eater, who customizes it by adding his preferred proportions of lime juice, fried shallots, and chiles. Sweet and salty, tart and hot, smooth yet crispy with bites of fried shallot, the sauce launches a bold assault on the taste buds. And it goes without saying that any food you make and mix at the table is fun food.

Serve as a dip with any type of saté or grilled meats.

1 cup peanut oil

1 large shallot, cut into thin
   wedges

¾ cup sweet soy sauce (ketjap manis)
   or 6 tablespoons each regular soy
   sauce and molasses

2 to 4 Thai, serrano, or other hot
   chiles, thinly sliced (for a
   spicier sauce, leave the
   seeds in)

4 juicy lime wedges, for serving

1. Heat the peanut oil in a small, heavy skillet, over medium-high heat until rippling (350° F). Add the shallot wedges and fry until crisp, about 30 seconds. Remove with a slotted spoon to paper towels to drain.

2. Divide the sweet soy sauce among 4 small bowls. Sprinkle each with sliced chiles and fried shallots, then with a generous squeeze of fresh lime juice. Use as a dip; the dipping action will mix the ingredients.

Serves 4

Rub It In

"He who has spice enough may season his meat as he pleases."
—ENGLISH PROVERB

Spices from this market in the south of France make memorable rubs and marinades.

One of the secrets shared by the world's great grill jockeys is a savvy use of rubs, marinades, butters, and bastes.

Rubs are spice mixes applied to meats to flavor and cure them before grilling. In this chapter you'll find recipes for a wide world of rubs, from Israeli *hawaij* to Indian *garam masala,* from Puerto Rican *sazón* to Sichuan-seasoned salt.

Marinades are the lifeblood of barbecue, lending distinct ethnic or regional character to commonplace meats, poultry, and fish. Here you'll find recipes for some of the world's best, from the vibrant flavors of Mexican *adobo* to a fiery Berber marinade from the Atlas Mountains.

The butters and bastes in this chapter are designed to combat the one drawback to grilling—its tendency to dry foods out. A diligent program of basting will keep even the leanest meats moist and juicy. As for flavor, well, the Japanese Garlic Butter, Bourbon Basting Sauce, and North Carolina Mop Sauce will keep any meat moist and sizzling with taste.

Use these recipes to customize your grilling and add excitement to even the simplest fare.

MEMPHIS RUB

I'm not sure where the American version of a spice rub was born, but if I had to guess a birthplace, I'd name Memphis. Memphans make extensive use of rubs—often to the exclusion of mop sauces or barbecue sauces. This rub is especially delicious on smoke-cooked ribs and pork shoulders.

¼ cup paprika
1 tablespoon firmly packed dark
    brown sugar
1 tablespoon granulated sugar
2 teaspoons salt

2 teaspoons Accent (MSG; optional)
1 teaspoon celery salt
1 teaspoon freshly ground black pepper
1 to 3 teaspoons cayenne pepper, or to taste
1 teaspoon dry mustard
1 teaspoon garlic powder
1 teaspoon onion powder

Combine all the ingredients in a jar, twist the lid on airtight, and shake to mix. Store away from heat and light for up to 6 months.
Makes about ½ cup; enough for 4 to 6 racks of ribs

MIAMI SPICE

I created this rub to celebrate the launch of my book *Miami Spice*. Use it to give a South Floridian accent to grilled meats and seafood. Habanero chile powder is available at gourmet shops and from the hot sauce mail-order companies (see Mail-Order Sources).

5 tablespoons coarse (kosher or sea) salt
3 tablespoons paprika
3 tablespoons freshly ground black pepper

2 tablespoons ground cumin
2 tablespoons dried oregano
1 tablespoon habanero chile
    powder

Combine all the ingredients in a jar, twist the cap on airtight, and shake to mix. Store away from heat and light for up to 6 months.
Makes about 1 cup; enough for 6 to 8 pounds meat, poultry, or seafood

CREOLE RUB SEASONING

This seasoning, suffused with the warm glow of paprika and cayenne, lies at the very soul of Creole cooking. Use it to spice up seafood (especially shrimp and crawfish) as well as chicken.

3 tablespoons paprika
2 tablespoons salt
1 tablespoon garlic powder
1 tablespoon freshly ground black pepper
1 tablespoon onion powder
1 tablespoon cayenne pepper
1 tablespoon dried oregano
1 tablespoon dried thyme

Combine all the ingredients in a jar, twist the cap on airtight, and shake to mix. Store away from heat and light for up to 6 months.

Makes about ¾ cup; enough for 4 pounds seafood or poultry

CAJUN RUB

U.S.A.

ON THE SIDE

This pungent blend originated as a spice mix for pan-blackening (a method popular in Cajun cooking that involves charring highly seasoned foods in a super-hot skillet). This rub is delectable when applied to almost any seafood or meat at least 30 minutes before grilling.

¼ cup coarse (kosher or sea) salt
2 tablespoons garlic powder
2 tablespoons onion powder
2 tablespoons dried thyme

2 tablespoons dried oregano
2 tablespoons paprika
1 tablespoon freshly ground black pepper
1 tablespoon freshly ground white pepper
1 to 3 teaspoons cayenne pepper, or to taste

Combine all the ingredients in a jar, twist the lid on airtight, and shake to mix. Store away from heat and light for up to 6 months.

Makes about 1 cup; enough for 6 to 8 pounds of meat or seafood

PUERTO RICAN SEASONING SALT
Sazón

PUERTO RICO

ON THE SIDE

Sazón, a seasoned salt fragrant with cumin, garlic, and oregano, is the ubiquitous seasoning of Puerto Rico. Commercial blends are widely available, but most are loaded with MSG. Here's a homemade version chock-full of flavor. It calls for whole spices (peppercorns and cumin seeds) that are freshly toasted before grinding. For a quicker version, skip the roasting and grinding. Use preground pepper and cumin—the mixture will still be quite tasty.

2 tablespoons black peppercorns
2 tablespoons cumin seeds
2 tablespoons drled oregano
½ cup coarse (kosher or sea) salt
2 tablespoons garlic powder

1. Combine the peppercorns and cumin seeds in a dry skillet and cook over medium heat, shaking the pan to ensure even cooking, until toasted and fragrant, about 3 minutes. Transfer to a bowl and let cool.

2. Place the mixture in a mortar, add the oregano and grind to a fine powder with the pestle. Or use a spice mill. Add the salt and garlic powder. Store in an airtight jar away from heat and light for up to 6 months.

Makes about 1 cup; enough for 6 to 8 pounds meat, poultry, or seafood

NIÇOISE RUB FOR LAMB AND STEAKS

FRANCE

ON THE SIDE

The Rue Pairolière, located in the Old Quarter of Nice, is a narrow, winding street lined with bakeries, olive shops, and spice vendors. This rub, a specialty of the store called Maison d'Olive, caught my eye—and nose—as a colorful and fragrant embellishment for grilled meats.

½ cup dried parsley
3 tablespoons dried garlic flakes
3 tablespoons cracked coriander seeds or ground coriander

2 tablespoons coarse (kosher or sea) salt
2 tablespoons cracked black peppercorns
2 tablespoons hot red pepper flakes

Combine all the ingredients in a jar, twist the lid on airtight, and shake to mix. Store away from heat and light for up to 6 months.

Makes about 1 cup; enough for 6 to 8 pounds lamb or steak

HERBES DE PROVENCE

FRANCE

ON THE SIDE

Herbs and spices are the very soul of Provençal cooking. As you drive through this sunny corner of southwestern France, you see them growing everywhere: purple fields of fresh lavender, shrub-size bushes of rosemary; fennel so abundant it grows wild by the side of the road. Sometimes these herbs are used fresh, by themselves, but more often they're dried and mixed to make a perfumed blend called *herbes de Provence*.

The formula varies from region to region and cook to cook, but the basic ingredients are rosemary, thyme, marjoram, savory, basil, bay leaf, and, for a touch of sweetness, fennel and lavender. *Herbes de Provence* is sold in most gourmet shops, often in decorative jars at inflated prices. But it's easy to make your own for a lot less money. (Pots of home-made *herbes de Provence* make great holiday presents.) There's nothing like this fragrant blend for enhancing the flavor of grilled lamb, steaks, and even seafood or poultry.

3 tablespoons dried rosemary
3 bay leaves
3 tablespoons dried basil
3 tablespoons dried marjoram

3 tablespoons dried summer savory
3 tablespoons dried oregano
2 tablespoons dried thyme
1 teaspoon fennel seeds
1 teaspoon dried lavender
1 teaspoon freshly ground white pepper
1 teaspoon ground coriander

In a small bowl crumble the rosemary and bay leaves between your fingers to break them into small pieces. Whisk in the remaining ingredients. Store the *herbes de Provence* in an airtight jar away from heat and light for up to 6 months.

Makes about 1¼ cups; enough for 8 pounds meat, poultry, or seafood

COLOMBO POWDER

FRENCH WEST INDIES

ON THE SIDE

Colombo is the French West Indian version of curry powder. What sets it apart is the addition of an unexpected ingredient: toasted rice. The rice acts as both a flavoring and natural thickener. Toasting gives the rice a pleasing nutty flavor and makes it easier to grind.

¼ cup white rice
¼ cup cumin seeds
¼ cup coriander seeds
1 tablespoon mustard seeds, preferably black (see Note)
1 tablespoon black peppercorns
1 tablespoon fenugreek seeds (optional; see Note)
1 teaspoon whole cloves
¼ cup ground turmeric

1. Place the rice in a dry skillet and cook over medium heat, shaking the pan to ensure even cooking, until lightly browned, 2 to 3 minutes. Transfer the rice to a bowl and let cool.

2. Add the cumin seeds, coriander seeds, mustard seeds, peppercorns, fenugreek seeds, and cloves to the skillet and cook over medium heat, shaking the pan, until lightly toasted and fragrant, about 3 minutes. Transfer the spices to a bowl and let cool.

3. Combine the rice and toasted spices in a spice mill or blender and grind to a fine powder. Grind in the turmeric. Store the powder in an airtight jar away from heat and light for up to 6 months.

Makes about 1 cup; enough for 6 to 8 pounds meat, poultry, or seafood

Note: Black mustard seeds are hotter than white, but the latter will work in a pinch. Fenugreek is a spice made up of tiny, rectangular tan pieces with a slight but agreeable bitterness. Both are available at Indian markets, gourmet shops, and natural foods stores.

PROVENÇAL GRILLING MIXTURE FOR FISH

The town of Isle Sur la Sorge lives up to its nickname, the Venice of Provence. The Sorge River flows through and around the center of this picturesque town, creating broad quays and waterfront terraces. On Sunday (market day), the quays fill with vendors selling Provençal provender and handicrafts. The following recipe was inspired by the spice vendors at the market.

1 tablespoon fennel seeds
¼ cup cracked coriander seeds or ground coriander
2 tablespoons cracked black peppercorns
2 tablespoons hot red pepper flakes
2 tablespoons coarse (kosher or sea) salt
3 bay leaves, crumbled

Combine all the ingredients in a jar, twist the lid on airtight, and shake to mix. Store away from heat and light for up to 6 months.

Makes about ½ cup; enough for 3 to 4 pounds seafood

ISRAELI RUB
Hawaij

Hawaij (pronounced "ha-WHY-idge") is the national spice mix of Yemen. Yemenite Jews brought it to Israel, where Israelis of all ethnic backgrounds adopted it with gusto. This recipe comes from *New York Daily News* food editor Lenore Skenazy, whose husband is a Yemenite Jew. Like Chinese five-spice powder or French *herbes de Provence, hawaij* is rubbed on meats and seafood prior to grilling. It's also added to soups and stews. There's even a version for sprinkling in coffee.

6 tablespoons black peppercorns
5 tablespoons cumin seeds
1 teaspoon whole cloves
1 teaspoon cardamom seeds or
    1 tablespoon cardamom pods
3 tablespoons ground turmeric
3 tablespoons coarse (kosher or sea) salt (optional; see Note)

1. Combine the peppercorns, cumin, cloves, and cardamom in a dry skillet and cook over medium heat, shaking the pan to ensure even cooking, until toasted and fragrant, about 3 minutes. Transfer to a bowl and let cool.

2. Place the toasted spices, turmeric, and salt (if using) in a spice mill or blender and grind to a fine powder. Store in an airtight jar away from heat and light for up to 6 months.

Makes about 1 cup; enough for 6 to 8 pounds meat, poultry, or seafood

Note: North Americans tend to put salt in their rubs; Israelis do not. I like the way the salt rounds out the flavor.

QUICK HAWAIJ

ISRAEL

ON THE SIDE

Here's a quick *hawaij* that requires no toasting. The salt makes it a North American–style rub.

- 3 tablespoons freshly ground black pepper
- 3 tablespoons ground cumin
- 3 tablespoons ground turmeric
- 3 tablespoons coarse (kosher or sea) salt
- 1 teaspoon ground cardamom

Combine all the ingredients in a jar, twist the lid on airtight, and shake to mix. Store away from heat and light for up to 6 months.

Makes about ¾ cup; enough for 4 to 6 pounds of meat, poultry, or seafood

MARRAKESH RUB

MOROCCO

ON THE SIDE

The Herboriste de Paradis is a spice shop in the Souk (old market) of Marrakesh. This tiny stall, run by Majid Ouadouane, conveys all the mystery and mystique of the spice trade in North Africa. The hundreds of spices and seasonings on sale here blur the traditional distinctions between cooking, cosmetics, and medicine. The spices used range from commonplace coriander and cardamom to antimony for making kohl (eye shadow) and Spanish fly (an aphrodisiac made from dried beetles). Monsieur Ouadouane cre-

ated the following blend as a seasoning for grilled lamb. For a quicker version, make a tasty rub using commercially ground spices and omit the toasting.

- 2½ tablespoons coriander seeds
- 2 tablespoons cumin seeds
- 1 tablespoon black peppercorns
- ½ teaspoon cardamom seeds or 1 teaspoon cardamom pods
- 2 tablespoons ground ginger
- 2 tablespoons coarse (kosher or sea) salt (optional)

1. Combine the coriander seeds, cumin seeds, peppercorns, and cardamom seeds in a dry skillet and cook over medium heat, shaking the pan to ensure even cooking, until the spices are fragrant and just beginning to brown, about 3 minutes. Transfer to a bowl and let cool.

2. Place the toasted spices in a mortar and grind to a fine powder with the pestle. Or use a spice mill. Transfer to a bowl and mix in the dried ginger and salt (if using). Store in an airtight jar away from heat and light for up to 6 months.

Makes ½ cup; enough for 4 pounds lamb

GREEK RUB

GREECE

ON THE SIDE

Here's a simple rub that will give any grilled meat (but especially lamb) or fish a Greek accent. For best results, use Greek oregano—it has a sharper, mintier flavor than Italian or Mexican. Look for it at Greek markets or see Mail-Order Sources. Olive oil gives the rub a flavorful luster, without making it sticky.

⅓ cup coarse (kosher or sea) salt
⅓ cup cracked black peppercorns
⅓ cup coarsely crumbled oregano, preferably Greek
2 tablespoons dried dill
2 tablespoons extra-virgin olive oil

Combine the salt, peppercorns, oregano, dill, and oil in a bowl and stir to mix. The spices should be coated with oil but not stick together. Store in an airtight jar away from heat or light for up to 6 months.

Makes about 1 cup; enough for 6 to 8 pounds lamb or fish

TUNISIAN RUB
Tabil

TUNISIA

ON THE SIDE

Pungent, spicy, and aromatic is this simple mix from Tunisia, known locally as *tabil*. Caraway seeds aren't normally associated with barbecue, but they add a complex, earthy flavor to almost any grilled fish, chicken, or meat.

2 tablespoons coriander seeds
2 tablespoons cumin seeds
2 tablespoons caraway seeds
2 tablespoons hot red pepper flakes
2 tablespoons coarse (kosher or sea) salt

1. Combine the coriander, cumin, and caraway seeds in a dry skillet and cook over medium heat, shaking the pan to ensure even cooking, until toasted and fragrant, about 3 minutes. Transfer to a bowl and let cool.

2. Place the mixture in a mortar and grind to a fine powder with the pestle. Or use a spice mill. Store in an airtight jar away from heat and light for up to 6 months.

Makes about ½ cup; enough for 3 to 4 pounds meat, poultry, or seafood

KOREAN SESAME SALT

KOREA

ON THE SIDE

Sesame is one of the defining flavors of Korean cuisine. In this recipe toasted sesame seeds are combined with salt, pepper, and hot red pepper flakes to make an uncommon seasoning for grilled meats and seafood.

3 tablespoons white sesame seeds
1 tablespoon black sesame seeds
   (see Note)
2 tablespoons coarse (kosher or sea) salt
2 teaspoons cracked black peppercorns
1 teaspoon hot red pepper flakes
   (optional)

1. Place the white sesame seeds in a dry skillet and cook over medium heat, shaking the pan to ensure even cooking, until toasted and lightly browned, about 3 minutes. Transfer to a bowl and let cool.

2. Stir in the black sesame seeds, salt, pepper, and pepper flakes (if using). Store in an airtight jar away from heat and light for up to 6 months.

Makes about ⅓ cup; enough for 3 pounds of meat or seafood

Note: If you can't find black sesame seeds, increase the white ones to 4 tablespoons.

SICHUAN SEASONED SALT

CHINA

ON THE SIDE

Seasoned salt isn't unique to North America. The Chinese version features the tongue-popping aromatics of black and Sichuan peppercorns. The latter aren't really peppers at all, but a reddish-brown, peppercorn-size berry native to China's Sichuan province. Sichuan peppercorns have a clean, piney, woodsy flavor that's unique in the world of seasonings.

(The name notwithstanding, they aren't especially hot.) They can be found in Asian markets and gourmet shops. Toasting the spices intensifies their flavor and makes this an especially good seasoning for grilled chicken, squab, and shrimp.

½ cup coarse (kosher or sea) salt
⅓ cup Sichuan peppercorns
3 tablespoons black peppercorns

1. Combine the salt and both peppercorns in a dry skillet and cook over medium heat, shaking the pan to ensure even cooking, until the mixture begins to darken and smoke, 3 to 6 minutes. Transfer to a bowl and let cool.

2. Place the mixture in a mortar and grind to a fine powder with the pestle. Or use a spice mill. Store in an airtight jar away from heat and light for up to 6 months.

Makes about 1 cup; enough for 6 to 8 pounds poultry or seafood

INDIN ROASTED SPICE POWDER
Garam Masala

INDIA

ON THE SIDE

aram masala is the most ubiquitous of India's spice blends. There are almost as many recipes as there are Indian cooks. You can buy a commercial mix at an Indian market, but most households and restaurants there make their own. The dominant flavors of *garam masala* are cumin, coriander, black pepper, and green and black cardamom. The latter is a large, almond-shaped black pod with a richly aromatic smoky flavor. (I've made it optional, as you have to go to an Indian market or mail-order source to find it. It's well worth tracking down.) *Garam masala* is a key flavoring in Indian tandoori marinades. Make a batch every few months and keep some on hand.

3 tablespoons cumin seeds
3 tablespoons coriander seeds
1 tablespoon black peppercorns
2 teaspoons green cardamom pods
1 teaspoon black cardamom pods (optional)
1 piece (2 inches) cinnamon stick
½ whole nutmeg
2 bay leaves
½ teaspoon mace blades
¼ teaspoon whole cloves
1 teaspoon ground ginger

1. Combine the cumin seeds, coriander seeds, peppercorns, green and black cardamom, cinnamon stick, nutmeg, bay leaves, mace, and cloves in a dry skillet. Cook over medium heat, shaking the pan, until lightly toasted and fragrant, about 3 minutes. Transfer to a bowl and cool.

2. Place the mixture in a mortar and grind to a fine powder with the pestle. Or use a spice mill. Place the mixture in a jar, add the ginger, and twist the lid on airtight; shake to mix. Store away from heat and light for up to 6 months.

Makes about ½ cup; enough for 3 to 4 pounds meat, poultry, or seafood

QUICK GARAM MASALA

INDIA

ON THE SIDE

If you don't have time to toast and grind whole spices, here's a *garam masala* you can make in a couple of minutes.

2 tablespoons ground cumin
2 tablespoons ground coriander
2 teaspoons freshly ground black pepper
1 teaspoon ground cardamom
1 teaspoon ground ginger
⅛ teaspoon ground cinnamon
⅛ teaspoon ground cloves
⅛ teaspoon ground nutmeg

Combine all the ingredients in a jar, twist the lid on airtight, and shake to mix. Store away from heat and light for up to 6 months.

Makes about ⅓ cup; enough for 3 pounds meat, poultry, or seafood

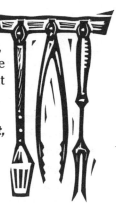

JAMAICAN JERK MARINADE

JAMAICA

ON THE SIDE

Jerk is a traditional ethnic food that has entered America's culinary mainstream. In the process, it's lost a lot of its fire, spice, and salt. Here's how they make it in the birthplace of jerk—a town called Boston Beach on the north coast of Jamaica. Count yourself lucky to have a blender. In Boston Beach they grind the seasonings in a hand-cranked spice mill. Use the jerk marinade to marinate pork for 6 hours, chicken breasts for 3 hours, and fish fillets or shrimp for 1 hour.

4 to 15 scotch bonnet chiles, seeded
    (for a hotter marinade, leave
    the seeds in)
1 bunch scallions, both white and
    green parts, trimmed and
    coarsely chopped
2 shallots, halved
1 small onion, quartered
2 cloves garlic, peeled
1 tablespoon grated fresh ginger

2 teaspoons chopped fresh thyme or
    1 teaspoon dried
2 teaspoons ground allspice
3 tablespoons canola oil
3 tablespoons soy sauce
3 tablespoons fresh lime juice, or more
    to taste
2 tablespoons firmly packed dark
    brown sugar
2 tablespoons salt, or more to taste
1 teaspoon freshly ground black pepper
1 cup water

Combine the chiles, scallions, shallots, onion, garlic, ginger, thyme, allspice, oil, soy sauce, 3 tablespoons lime juice, sugar, 1 tablespoon salt, pepper, and water in a blender. Blend until smooth. Correct the seasoning, adding salt and lime juice as necessary. Store, tightly covered in the refrigerator, for up to 2 weeks.

Makes about 2 cups; enough to marinate 4 pounds meat, chicken, or seafood

Barbecue Alley: The Mexican Grill

To many North Americans, Mexican cooking means tacos, burritos, and enchiladas. Grill buffs, though, will be pleased to learn that Mexico has a venerable, varied, and lively tradition of live-fire cooking, from the mesquite-grilled steaks of the north to the spicy grilled fish of the Yucatán.

There's even a version of pit-cooked barbecue known as *barbacoa*, a term that has different meanings in various parts of the country. In the north, *barbacoa* is made with beef, in the south with pyrotechnically spiced goat, and in Mexico City with lamb wrapped in the leaves of *maguay* cactus and roasted in a wood-heated brick pit: There is no marinade, no spice rub, nor are there fancy condiments—just lamb cooked to fall-off-the-bone tenderness in a pit.

Mexico offers plenty of interesting barbecue cooked over direct heat, too. Consider the gracious colonial city of Oaxaca in the south-central part of the country. Famous for its *moles* (complex, slow-simmered sauces made from nuts, fruits, and a dazzling array of chiles), Oaxaca is also a hotbed of thrilling grilling. "Barbecue alley," as it is known, in the Mercado 20 de Noviembre (November 20 Market) is a great place to sample the best of Mexican live-fire fare.

To find the "alley," you just follow your nose to a smoky arcade on the east side of the market. Lining the arcade are rows of barbecue stalls—each sending thick billows of smoke toward the skylight. The ordering procedure is a little confusing to newcomers, but it ensures that everything you eat will be hot off the grill.

As you enter the arcade, pause at the vegetable stalls on the right or left. (I liked the first stall on the right, where two of the servers, Yolanda and Gloria, delight in pulling your leg as they take your order.) Ask for a bunch of scallions and a couple of *chiles de agua*. (The latter are rather innocent-looking peppers that resemble American cubanelles. There all innocence ends.) The vegetables will be handed to you in a paper-lined wicker basket.

Continue down the arcade. To the right and left you'll see a series of meat stalls. There are four or five basic meats to choose from: *carne de res* (beef), *tazajo* (dried beef), *cecino* (cured pork), *chorizo* (strings of egg-shaped, blood-colored sausages), and rope-like hanks of tripe. The meats are cut into broad, thin strips and are displayed on tables. No, they're not refrigerated, but the high heat of the charcoal acts as a powerful disinfectant.

Pick a stall (I liked no. 189) and point to the type of meat you want. The owner will cut off a few pieces of beef, pork, or tripe and weigh them on a scale. Enter a woman who relieves you of your scallions and chiles, nestling them amid the coals of an enormous brazier fashioned from a washtub filled with concrete.

She's the *asador* (grill jockey), and while you watch, she'll fire-char your vegetables and grill your meats on a wire grate resting directly on the coals. While she does, the tortilla lady arrives and counts out the desired number of tortillas and warms them for you on the grill. Meanwhile, a fifth lady stops to sell you a *nopalito* (cactus paddle) salad, neatly packaged in a tiny plastic bag. Give her a large bill to pay for the salad and she'll place the tray on her head while she makes change.

When the meats and vegetables are cooked, the *asador* returns them to your basket. Go back to the first stall where Yolanda will peel and seed your chiles, scrape the burnt parts off your scallions, and douse both with lime juice and salt. Then Gloria will give you dishes of guacamole and *salsa mexicana*, whose colors, appropriately, mirror the Mexican flag: green serrano chiles, white onions, and shockingly red tomatoes. (Texans will recognize the preparation as *pico de gallo*.)

Take your seat at one of the low stone communal tables, and let the feast begin. To eat *carne asado*, place a sliver of meat on a tortilla and top it with charred onions, some chiles, a bit of salsa, and a little guacamole. Roll it up and pop it into your mouth. If you're feeling particularly macho you can eat the chile straight, otherwise wrap it in the tortilla with the other ingredients.

A meal of *carne asado* is fun—you interact with vendors and fellow diners at the communal tables and enjoy a spicy treat you won't soon forget. A trip to "barbecue alley" is worth a detour!

MEXICAN SMOKED CHILE MARINADE

Adobo

MEXICO

ON THE SIDE

Adobo refers to a large family of marinated pork dishes found throughout the Spanish-speaking world. In central Mexico, the term describes a fiery marinade made with chipotle chiles (smoked jalapeño chiles). Chipotles are sold both dried and canned (in tomato sauce). I prefer the latter for this recipe. Look for them in Mexican markets and gourmet shops or see the Mail-Order Sources.

Use *adobo* to marinate seafood for 30 minutes, chicken breasts for 1 hour, and whole chickens and meat for 4 to 6 hours. *Adobo* goes particularly well with pork.

6 canned chipotle chiles with 2 tablespoons
    canning juices
5 cloves garlic, peeled
1 strip orange zest (2 x ½ inches; removed
    with a vegetable peeler)

1 cup fresh sour orange juice or
    ¾ cup fresh orange juice and
    ¼ cup fresh lime juice
1 tablespoon tomato paste
2 teaspoons dried oregano
1 teaspoon ground cumin
2 tablespoons red wine vinegar
1 teaspoon salt
½ teaspoon freshly ground black pepper

1. Combine all the ingredients in a medium-size saucepan. Bring to a boil over high heat and boil until reduced by half, 5 to 8 minutes.

2. Place the mixture in a blender or food processor and process to a smooth paste. Store, tightly covered in the refrigerator, for up to 3 days.

Makes about 1 cup; enough to marinate 3 pounds meat or chicken

BASIL MARINADE

U.S.A.

ON THE SIDE

Here's a colorful, fragrant, and intensely flavorful basil marinade that's great for chicken and seafood. Set about a third of the marinade aside to use as a basting sauce. If using chicken, marinate for 2 hours; seafood, 1 hour.

⅓ cup extra-virgin olive oil
⅓ cup fresh lemon juice
⅓ cup boiling water
3 cloves garlic, peeled

1 large bunch fresh basil, stemmed
1 teaspoon salt
1 teaspoon freshly ground black pepper

Combine the oil, lemon juice, water, garlic, basil, salt, and pepper in a blender and process to a smooth paste. Store, tightly covered in the refrigerator, for up to 3 days.

Makes about 1 cup; enough to marinate 3 pounds poultry or fish

A Griller's Guide to the World's Chiles

Where there's smoke, there's fire, goes the saying. And where there's fire, there's heat. Chiles are absolutely essential to barbecue: grilled on their own; added to a myriad of marinades, rubs, and spice mixes; served pickled or straight up as an accompaniment to grilled fare. If you have sensitive skin, don't handle chiles directly. Instead, wear rubber or plastic gloves. Remember that the hottest parts of a chile are the seeds and veins. If you have a low tolerance for heat, remove them by cutting the chile in half and scraping out the seeds with a small spoon or a blunt knife. When working with chiles, never rub your eyes, nose, or mouth—the oils will cause a burning sensation in these sensitive areas. And always wash your hands (or gloves) thoroughly with soap and water when done.

Here's a field guide to some of the many chiles you will encounter on the barbecue trail.

AJI AMARILLO: Literally, "yellow chile." A fiery, fleshy, yellow-orangish Peruvian chile used as a flavoring for kebabs. *Aji amarillo* comes in three forms: powdered, paste, and pickled. Look for it in Hispanic markets or see Mail-Order Sources.

BIRD PEPPER: A small (about 1 inch long), cone-shaped red or reddish-orange chile related to the cayenne and found in the Bahamas and elsewhere in the Caribbean. If unable to find, substitute red serrano or jalapeño chiles.

BULL'S HORN PEPPERS: These chiles are popular all along the barbecue trail. The bull's horn pepper has a pleasant bell pepper flavor. The bite can range from a bit hot to moderately hot. The long, slender shape of the bull's horn pepper makes it popular for grilling. Simply thread the peppers crosswise on skewers and char on all sides.

CAYENNE: A small (2 inches long), fiery red chile native to the Gulf of Mexico and Guyana and used mostly in powdered form. Today, cayenne is widely used throughout Africa, India, and Asia. Cayenne is very hot, but its flavor is fairly one-dimensional.

CHIPOTLE: The jalapeño chile smoked, the chipotle is an essential ingredient in Mexican *adobo* (a smoked chile marinade) and many salsas. Chipotles comes in two varieties—the small red *morena* and large tan *grande*—the latter with a more complex flavor. Chipotles also come in two forms: dried and canned (the latter in a sour orange and tomato sauce). The canned has a

TERIYAKI MARINADE

JAPAN

ON THE SIDE

Here's a sweet-salty marinade modeled on classic Japanese teriyaki sauce. To make a safe glaze for brushing on the food while it cooks, I boil the marinade after the food—meat or seafood—has been removed.

2 cloves garlic, minced
1 tablespoon minced fresh ginger

2 scallions, both white and
    green parts, trimmed and
    thinly sliced
½ cup tamari or soy sauce
½ cup mirin (sweet rice wine) or
    cream sherry
¼ cup sake or dry sherry
¼ cup firmly packed light
    brown sugar

richer flavor. Chipotles are available at Mexican markets and gourmet shops, or try one of the Mail-Order Sources.

DE ARBOL: A long (3 to 4 inches), skinny dried red Mexican chile that's moderately fiery. It is used in the charred tomato salsas that accompany grilled beef in northern Mexico.

GOAT PEPPER: A crinkly, round green chile about $1\frac{1}{2}$ inches long, similar in flavor and heat to the scotch bonnet. It is popular in the Bahamas.

GUAJILLO: A long, smooth-skinned, reddish-brown dried chile, flavorful but relatively mild, from Mexico. It is often ground into chile powder and used to marinate pork in central Mexico.

HABANERO: A smooth, acorn-shaped red, green, or yellow chile similar in flavor and tongue-torturing heat to the scotch bonnet.

JALAPENO: A bullet-shaped green or red pepper available just about everywhere. Despite its reputation, the jalapeño is relatively mild as chiles go. The heat of a chile is measured in units called scovilles, and jalapeños ring in at about 5,000 scovilles. Compare that to the 200,000 scovilles of the habanero or scotch bonnet chile.

KOREAN CHILE: A hot dried red chile that's indispensable in Korean cooking. Hungarian hot paprika makes a good substitute.

PIMENTA MALAGUETA: A tiny, ridged red or green chile (usually pickled or dried). Adds zip to Brazilian table sauces.

POBLANO: A large (up to 3 inches), dark green, tapered fresh chile from Mexico. Similar in flavor to a green bell pepper, but hotter and more aromatic. Great for stuffing and grilling. The dried version is called *ancho.*

SCOTCH BONNET: To call this Chinese lantern–shaped chile hot would be an understatement: The scotch bonnet is about 50 times more fiery than a jalapeño! But behind the heat, there's a floral, almost fruity flavor that makes me think of apricots. Mexico's habanero chile, Jamaica's country pepper, Haiti's Dame Jeanne, and Florida's datil pepper are closely related and make satisfactory substitutes. Scotch bonnets are available at West Indian and Mexican markets, gourmet shops, and at most major supermarkets.

SERRANO: A thin, tapered bright green chile smaller and slightly hotter than a jalapeño. The two are interchangeable.

THAI CHILE PEPPERS: You need to know about two: The *prik kee noo,* a tiny ridged, mercilessly hot chile whose Thai name literally means "mouse dropping"; and the *prik kee far,* a slender, horn-shaped green chile that is very hot, but milder than its little brother. Look for Thai chiles at Asian and Indian markets.

1. Combine the garlic, ginger, scallions, tamari, mirin, sake, and sugar in a small bowl and whisk until the sugar is dissolved. Marinate meat or seafood in this mixture for 1 hour. Remove the food from the marinade and drain.

2. If you wish to use the marinade as a glaze, strain it into a saucepan and boil until thick and syrupy, about 5 minutes. Brush it on the food during the last 5 minutes of cooking. After boiling, store, tightly covered in the refrigerator, for up to 1 week.

Makes about $1\frac{1}{2}$ cups before boiling; enough to marinate 2 pounds seafood, chicken, or beef

BERBER MARINADE

MOROCCO

ON THE SIDE

The Berbers are a rugged, rug-weaving people who live in Morocco's Atlas Mountains. They season lamb and other meats with this vibrant paste of typical North African seasonings. Fenugreek is a rectangular seed with a pleasantly bitter flavor—look for it in Indian and Middle Eastern grocery stores. I have used this marinade with great success on tuna, pork tenderloin, and sirloin steak. Spread the Berber marinade on the meat, poultry, or seafood and marinate, covered, for 8 hours in the refrigerator. A little of this fiery mixture goes a long way!

1 medium onion, finely chopped
4 cloves garlic, finely chopped
2 tablespoons chopped fresh ginger
3 tablespoons mild paprika
3 tablespoons hot paprika
1 tablespoon ground coriander
2 teaspoons freshly ground black pepper
½ teaspoon ground cardamom
1 teaspoon hot red pepper flakes, or to taste

½ teaspoon ground fenugreek (optional)
½ teaspoon ground cinnamon
¼ teaspoon ground allspice
⅛ teaspoon ground cloves
4 teaspoons salt, or to taste
1 teaspoon honey or sugar
¾ cup olive oil
¼ cup fresh lemon juice

Place the onion, garlic, ginger, both paprikas, coriander, pepper, cardamom, 1 teaspoon hot pepper flakes, fenugreek (if using), cinnamon, allspice, cloves, and 4 teaspoons salt in a food processor and process to a coarse paste. Work in the honey, oil, and lemon juice. Alternatively, combine all the ingredients at once in a blender and purée to a smooth paste. Taste for seasoning, adding pepper flakes and salt as necessary. This marinade will keep, covered in the refrigerator, for 1 week.

Makes about 1½ cups; enough to marinate 2 to 3 pounds seafood, poultry, or meat

BRAZILIAN LAMB MARINADE

BRAZIL

ON THE SIDE

Beef is what generally comes to mind when you think of Brazilian barbecue, but the legendary barbecue restaurant chain, Porcão, with branches in Rio, São Paulo, and Miami, also does a lively business in lamb. This is a great marinade for either whole (bone-in) or butterflied legs of lamb. Allow the meat to marinate, covered in the refrigerator, for 1 day before grilling.

1 medium onion, quartered
6 cloves garlic, peeled
1 bunch scallions, both white and green parts, trimmed
½ cup fresh cilantro leaves
2 bay leaves
1 teaspoon salt
1 teaspoon freshly ground black pepper
½ cup dry white wine
½ cup olive oil

Combine all the ingredients in a blender or food processor and process to a coarse paste. Transfer to a bowl or jar and store, tightly covered in the refrigera- tor, for up to 2 days.

Makes about 2 cups; enough to marinate 3 pounds lamb

WHITE WINE MARINADE FOR SEAFOOD

FRANCE

ON THE SIDE

Here's a simple white wine marinade that's good for any seafood. To give it an Asian accent, substitute sesame oil for the olive oil and sake or mirin for the wine. Marinate the seafood, covered in the refrigerator, 1 to 2 hours.

½ cup dry white wine or white vermouth
¼ cup extra-virgin olive oil
3 tablespoons fresh lemon juice
3 tablespoons chopped fresh Italian (flat-leaf) parsley
2 sprigs fresh rosemary or 1 tablespoon dried
2 bay leaves
½ medium onion, thinly sliced
2 cloves garlic, thinly sliced
1 teaspoon salt
½ teaspoon freshly ground black pepper

Combine all the ingredients in a small bowl and whisk to mix. Use this marinade within an hour of preparing.

Makes about ¾ cup; enough to marinate 2 pounds seafood

SIX COMPOUND BUTTERS

FRANCE

ON THE SIDE

Back in the B.C.C. (Before Cholesterol Consciousness) era, butter was an indispensable ingredient, not only to the chef, but also the grill jockey. The French have a venerable tradition of crowning meats with a disk of flavored butter. The butter melts on contact with the hot meat or seafood—anointing, basting, and moisturizing it. This compensates for the tendency of many foods to dry out when cooked on the grill.

Compound butters are easy to make, and a small portion certainly won't kill you. The butter is creamed (beaten until light and fluffy—a stage the French call *en pommade*), then seasoned with intense flavorings. The resulting mixture is rolled in a sheet of plastic wrap or parchment paper to form a thick cylinder. Thus prepared, the compound butter can be stored in the refrigerator or freezer. When you need it, simply cut off a slice and place it atop a piece of grilled meat or seafood.

I keep several compound butters on hand in my freezer, knowing that a moist, memorable, flavorful dish is only a moment away. Below are six traditional compound butters. All keep for 1 week refrigerated or up to 2 months frozen.

Maître d'Hôtel Butter

Here's an updated version of the most classic of all compound butters—a perfect adornment to a piece of grilled salmon, cod, halibut, or sole.

8 tablespoons (1 stick) salted butter,
    at room temperature
3 tablespoons chopped fresh Italian
    (flat-leaf) parsley
1 clove garlic, minced
½ teaspoon grated lemon zest
2 teaspoons fresh lemon juice
¼ teaspoon freshly ground white pepper

1. Cream the butter in a bowl, mixer, or food processor. Beat in the parsley, garlic, lemon zest, lemon juice, and pepper.

2. Spread the butter on a piece of parchment paper or plastic wrap and roll into a compact cylinder. Store the butter in the refrigerator or freezer. Cut off 1-inch slices as needed.

Serves 6 to 8

Escargot Butter

This garlic-parsley butter is the classic topping for *escargots* (snails), but it goes great with any seafood. I also like to spread it on bread and grill the bread to make garlic toast.

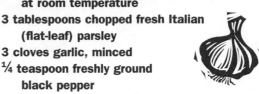

8 tablespoons (1 stick) salted butter,
    at room temperature
3 tablespoons chopped fresh Italian
    (flat-leaf) parsley
3 cloves garlic, minced
¼ teaspoon freshly ground
    black pepper

1. Cream the butter in a bowl, mixer, or food processor. Beat in the parsley, garlic, and pepper.

2. Spread the butter on a piece of parchment paper or plastic wrap and roll into a compact cylinder. Store the butter in the refrigerator or freezer. Cut off 1-inch slices as needed.

Serves 6 to 8

Roquefort Butter

The salty tang of Roquefort cheese goes especially well with grilled lamb and beef. Stilton or Gorgonzola butter is made the same way.

8 tablespoons (1 stick) unsalted butter,
    at room temperature
2 ounces Roquefort cheese, at room
    temperature

1. Cream the butter in a bowl, mixer, or food processor. Push the Roquefort through a sieve into the butter and whisk to mix.

2. Spread the butter on a piece of parchment paper or plastic wrap and roll into a compact cylinder. Store the butter in the refrigerator or freezer. Cut off 1-inch slices as needed.

Serves 6 to 8

Anchovy Butter

Anchovies make great appetizers, as the seventeenth-century English writer Thomas Flatman observed:

To quicken appetite it will behoove ye
To feed courageously on good Anchovie.

Anchovy butter is particularly good on grilled swordfish, tuna, and steak.

6 to 8 canned anchovy fillets, drained and rinsed
8 tablespoons (1 stick) unsalted butter, at room temperature
¼ teaspoon freshly ground black pepper

1. Place the anchovies in a mortar and mash to a paste with the pestle. Or place in a small bowl and mash using the back of a wooden spoon. Add the butter and pepper and beat until smooth.

2. Spread the butter on a piece of parchment paper or plastic wrap and roll into a compact cylinder. Store the butter in the refrigerator or freezer. Cut off 1-inch slices as needed.

Serves 6 to 8

Curry Butter

Curry butter is particularly well suited to seafood.

8 tablespoons (1 stick) salted butter, at room temperature
3 tablespoons minced shallots
1 clove garlic, minced
2 teaspoons curry powder

1. Melt 2 tablespoons of the butter in a small saucepan over medium heat. Add the shallots, garlic, and curry powder and cook, stirring often, until the shallots are soft but not brown, about 3 minutes. Let the mixture cool completely.

2. Cream the remaining butter in a bowl, mixer, or food processor. Add the curry mixture.

3. Spread the butter on a piece of parchment paper or plastic wrap and roll into a compact cylinder. Store the butter in the refrigerator or freezer. Cut off 1-inch slices as needed.

Serves 6 to 8

Marchand de Vin Butter

Reduced red wine and shallots account for the name of this butter, which means "wine merchant." Serve on steak.

1 cup dry red wine
2 shallots, finely chopped
8 tablespoons (1 stick) salted butter
3 tablespoons finely chopped fresh Italian (flat-leaf) parsley
¼ teaspoon freshly ground black pepper

1. Combine the wine and shallots in a heavy saucepan and bring to a boil over high heat. Boil until thick, syrupy, and reduced to 3 to 4 tablespoons, about 7 minutes. Let the mixture cool completely.

2. Cream the butter in a bowl, mixer, or food processor. Add the wine mixture, parsley, and pepper.

3. Spread the butter on a piece of parchment paper or plastic wrap and roll into a compact cylinder. Store the butter in the refrigerator or freezer. Cut off 1-inch slices as needed.

Serves 6 to 8

JAPANESE GARLIC BUTTER

East meets West in this recipe—a Japanese butter sauce used as a baste and serving sauce for grilled vegetables, seafood, and meat.

5 tablespoons unsalted butter
3 tablespoons soy sauce
2 tablespoons fresh lemon juice
1 clove garlic, minced

Melt the butter in a small saucepan over medium heat. Stir in the remaining ingredients and simmer briskly until the garlic has lost its rawness and the sauce is rich-tasting and mellow, about 3 minutes. The butter keeps, covered in the refrigerator, for up to 3 days. Reheat over low heat before using.

Makes about ½ cup

KETJAP BUTTER

Ketjap manis (spiced, sweet soy sauce) is Indonesia's national table sauce. It is an essential ingredient in marinades and the traditional accompaniment to Indonesian satés. Cooks at the famous Sunda Kelapa fish house in Jakarta use this *ketjap* butter as a baste for grilled fish and seafood. If *ketjap manis* is unavailable, or you don't have the time to make it, combine equal parts soy sauce and molasses and add ½ teaspoon ground coriander.

4 tablespoons (½ stick) unsalted butter
¼ cup ketjap manis, store-bought or homemade (page 472)

Melt the butter in a small saucepan over medium heat. Stir in the *ketjap manis* and simmer briskly to blend, about 2 minutes. The butter keeps, covered in the refrigerator, for up to 3 days. Reheat over low heat before using.

Makes about ½ cup

VINEGAR-BASED MOP SAUCE

Mop sauces are an integral part of the long, slow, smoky, indirect grilling method known as barbecue. You find them in North Carolina, where they're brushed on slow-roasting pork shoulders. You find them in Memphis, where they're applied to ribs. The traditional instrument for basting is a cotton floor mop (a clean, brand new-one, of course), hence the name mop sauce.

1 quart cider vinegar
1 medium onion, thinly sliced
3 jalapeño chiles, thinly sliced
4 teaspoons coarse (kosher or sea) salt
2 teaspoons hot red pepper flakes
2 teaspoons freshly ground black pepper

Combine the vinegar, onion, jalapeños, salt, pepper flakes, and black pepper in a large plastic container. Stir until the salt is dissolved. This mixture keeps, covered in the refrigerator, for up to 3 days.

Makes about 1 quart

BOURBON BUTTER BASTING SAUCE

U.S.A.

ON THE SIDE

Here's a sweet, boozy baste from Tennessee that's great on grilled or barbecued pork. To make a Caribbean version, substitute dark rum for the bourbon and pineapple juice for the apple cider. Use this sauce to baste grilled or smoked pork.

8 tablespoons (1 stick) salted butter
1 cup apple cider
¼ cup firmly packed dark brown sugar
1 tablespoon fresh lemon juice
½ teaspoon salt, or more as needed
½ teaspoon freshly ground black pepper
1 cup bourbon

1. Melt the butter in a medium-size saucepan over medium heat. Add the cider, sugar, lemon juice, ½ teaspoon salt, and pepper. Increase the heat to high and bring to a boil. Boil until slightly thickened, about 5 minutes.

2. Remove from the heat and stir in the bourbon. Taste for seasoning, adding salt as necessary. The basting sauce keeps, covered in the refrigerator, for up to 1 week. Reheat over low heat before using.

Makes about 2½ cups

MEXICAN FISH BASTE

MEXICO

ON THE SIDE

Tart and salty, this is a baste used by cooks in the Yucatán to heighten the flavor of almost any grilled seafood. Hotheads could add a sliced habanero chile or two. Sour orange juice (see Glossary) is used in the Yucatán; if unavailable, use lime juice.

½ cup fresh sour orange juice or lime juice
2 teaspoons salt
2 cloves garlic, minced

Combine the sour orange juice, salt, and garlic in a bowl and stir until the salt is dissolved. This baste keeps, covered in the refrigerator, for up to 3 days.

Makes about ½ cup

FIRE AND ICE:
DESSERTS

> *"The gods give everything to the eater of sugar."*
> —INDIAN PROVERB

Bananas await grilling in Manaus, Brazil.

"**S**ome say the world will end in fire, some say in ice," wrote the poet Robert Frost. I hold that a barbecue should end with both.

Just because you've finished the main course doesn't mean you should turn off your grill. This truth is not lost on the Bangkok banana vendor, who bastes his fruit with coconut milk and chars it over coconut charcoal. Nor is it lost on the French *pâtissier,* who uses a blowtorch to caramelize the top of his crème brûlée. The high heat of a fire does wonders for caramelizing sugar, helping it acquire an extraordinary depth of flavor.

Here you'll find recipes for *crema catalana,* grilled pineapples, grilled bananas, an updated version of s'mores, and other fire-charred desserts.

As for ice, well, many people (myself included) would argue that no barbecue is complete without ice cream. Next to beer, there's nothing like it for refreshing a grill jockey who has been tending a blazing fire. The iced desserts in this chapter range from *kulfi* (Indian ice milk) to *faluda* (a Persian rosewater and noodle sherbet) to a freshly made coconut ice cream from Guadeloupe.

UPTOWN S'MORES

U.S.A.

METHOD:
Direct grilling

**SPECIAL
EQUIPMENT:**
4 long metal
skewers or 8
short bamboo
skewers, soaked
for 1 hour in cold
water to cover
and drained

Anyone who ever attended camp or a Boy or Girl Scout cookout will remember s'mores. To make them you sandwiched freshly roasted marshmallows between graham crackers and chocolate candy bars. The marshmallows melted the chocolate, which got all over your face and fingers. The overall effect was so tasty, you cried out for "s'more" (some more). Here's a s'more for grown-ups, made with chocolate chip cookies and super-premium chocolate.

8 large marshmallows
8 thin squares (each 2 inches) superior
    dark chocolate, such as Lindt
16 chocolate chip cookies, preferably
    homemade

1. Skewer the marshmallows and set aside.

2. *If using a charcoal grill,* prepare this dessert once the coals have died down after the main course. Carefully remove the grill grate and rake the coals into a hot, glowing pile. Roast the marshmallows over the fire until sizzling, melted, and darkly browned all over, turning to ensure even cooking. This will take 3 to 6 minutes.

If using a gas grill, preheat to high and oil the grate. Place the skewer directly on the hot grate and, watching carefully, grill until the marshmallows are lightly browned, about 1 minute. Lift the skewer and brown the other side, 1 minute more.

3. Place a piece of chocolate on the bottom (the flat side) of a cookie. Ease a hot marshmallow off the skewer onto the chocolate. Place a second cookie (flat side down) on top of the marshmallow to make a sandwich. Wait a few seconds for the hot marshmallow to melt the chocolate, then eat the s'more like a sandwich. Nostalgia never tasted so good!

Makes 8; serves 4 to 8

FIRE-ROASTED APPLES

U.S.A.

METHOD:
Indirect grilling

**SPECIAL
EQUIPMENT:**
1 cup wood
chips, preferably
apple or maple,
soaked for 1 hour
in apple cider or
cold water to
cover and
drained

Once you master the concept of indirect grilling, you can cook pretty much anything you once baked in the oven on the grill. Even baked apples. But why would you bother? Well, smoke has a natural tie to sugar, a fact that is apparent in such classic sugar-cured foods as smoked salmon, turkey, and ham. It also seems to bring out the autumnal sweetness of apples, which here are stuffed with a tasty filling of brown sugar and graham-cracker crumbs before hitting the grill.

8 firm, sweet apples, like Cortlands or Galas
4 tablespoons (½ stick) unsalted butter,
    at room temperature
¼ cup firmly packed dark brown sugar
¼ cup dried currants
¼ cup graham-cracker crumbs,
    toasted bread crumbs, or
    ground almonds
½ teaspoon ground cinnamon
¼ teaspoon freshly grated nutmeg
1 teaspoon vanilla extract
4 marshmallows, cut in half (optional)

1. Set up the grill for indirect grilling (see page 14 or 16). *If using a charcoal grill,* preheat to medium.

If using a gas grill, add the wood chips to the smoker box and preheat to high; when smoke appears, lower the heat to medium. Lightly grease an aluminum-foil roasting pan.

2. Core the apples, using an apple corer or melon baller, but don't cut all the way through the bottom. The idea is to create a cavity for stuffing.

3. Cream the butter and sugar in a medium-size bowl until light and fluffy. Beat in the currants, graham-cracker crumbs, cinnamon, nutmeg, and vanilla. Spoon this mixture into the apples. Place a half marshmallow (if using) on top of each. Set the apples in the prepared foil pan.

4. When ready to cook, if using a charcoal grill, toss the wood chips on the embers. Place the pan of apples on the grill grate away from the heat. Cover the grill and cook the apples until soft, 40 to 60 minutes. Check after 40 minutes, and if the marshmallows start to brown too much, cover the apples with a piece of foil. Serve immediately.
Serves 8

BALINESE GRILLED BANANAS IN COCONUT MILK CARAMEL

INDONESIA

METHOD:
Direct grilling

I like to think of this recipe as a Balinese banana split. Imagine a sugar-crusted, smokily grilled banana served with a silken caramel sauce flavored with coconut milk, lemongrass, and palm sugar. (The latter is a malty sweetener made from palm sap that is similar in flavor to light brown sugar.) You can simply serve the grilled bananas in a bowl topped with this luscious, offbeat sauce and, if you prefer, with ice cream, which I've made optional in this recipe.

The Balinese prepare this dish with finger bananas, sweet fruit about the size of your forefinger. I've called for regular bananas, but if you can find finger bananas or apple bananas (which have a tart, appley flavor), by all means use them instead. Choose bananas that are ripe, but not too soft.

FOR THE CARAMEL SAUCE:
⅔ cup palm sugar or firmly packed light
   brown sugar
2 cups coconut milk, canned or homemade
   (page 522)
1 cinnamon stick (3 inches)
1 stalk lemongrass, trimmed and lightly
   flattened with the side of a cleaver
2 teaspoons cornstarch
1 tablespoon water

FOR THE BANANAS:
6 firm, ripe bananas
   (each about 6 inches long)
1 cup coconut milk, canned or
   homemade (page 522)
1 cup granulated sugar
1 quart vanilla ice cream (optional),
   for serving

1. Prepare the sauce. Place the sugar in a large, deep, heavy saucepan (preferably nonstick) and melt it over medium heat, stirring constantly with a wooden spoon. (It will take the sugar 2 to 3 minutes to melt.) Continue cooking the sugar until it begins to caramelize (turn brown), 3 to 5 minutes. You're looking for a rich brown color, but not the dark brown of chocolate. Do not overcook, or the sugar will burn and the sauce will be bitter.

2. Immediately remove the pan from the heat and stir in the coconut milk. (Be careful, it will sputter and hiss.) Return the pan to the heat and bring the coconut milk to a boil, stirring to dissolve the sugar. Stir in the cinnamon stick and lemongrass. Reduce the heat and simmer the mixture, uncovered, until thick and richly flavored, about 10 minutes, stirring from time to time to prevent scorching.

3. Dissolve the cornstarch in the water and stir it into the sauce. Simmer for 1 minute; the sauce will thicken even more. Remove the pan from the heat, transfer the sauce to a bowl, and let cool to room tem-

perature. Remove the cinnamon stick and lemongrass with tongs and discard. Cover and refrigerate the sauce until cold.

4. Preheat the grill to high.

5. Peel the bananas. Cut the bananas into quarters on the diagonal. Place the coconut milk and sugar in separate shallow bowls at grillside.

6. When ready to cook, oil the grate. Dip each banana piece first in coconut milk, then in sugar, and place on the hot grate. Grill, turning with tongs, until nicely browned all over, 6 to 8 minutes in all.

7. To serve, arrange the bananas on plates or in bowls and spoon the sauce on top. If serving with ice cream, place scoops of it in the bowls and arrange the bananas on top. Spoon the caramel sauce on top and serve immediately.

Serves 6

THE POMPANO GRILLE'S FIRE-GRILLED BANANA SPLIT

U. S . A .

METHOD:
Direct grilling

ADVANCE PREPARATION:
3 hours for marinating the bananas

Philadelphia's Book and The Cook is one of the nation's foremost food festivals, a 10-day orgy of wining and dining that pairs cookbook authors with the city's top restaurants.

A few years ago, I worked with the Pompano Bar & Grille, where I found a kindred spirit in the restaurant's owner, Bill Beck. The Pompano's Caribbean menu has a lot in common with my book *Miami Spice,* which Bill says was an inspiration for his restaurant. It looks like we're also kindred spirits when it comes to the subject of grilling. Consider the following grilled banana split.

FOR THE BANANAS AND MARINADE/SAUCE:
1 cup maple syrup
½ cup dark rum
¼ cup sugar
½ teaspoon ground cinnamon
¼ teaspoon freshly grated nutmeg
4 slightly green bananas, peeled

FOR THE BANANA SPLITS:
1 quart Coconut Ice Cream (page 522; or use a good store-bought brand)
2 cups Whipped Cream (recipe follows)
¼ cup shredded coconut, toasted (see facing page)
2 tablespoons chopped macadamia nuts, toasted (see box, page 93)

TOASTING COCONUT

Spread shredded coconut on a baking sheet and toast in a preheated 400°F oven, stirring once, until lightly browned, 4 to 6 minutes.

1. Preheat the grill to high.

2. Combine the syrup, rum, sugar, cinnamon, and nutmeg in a large bowl and whisk until the sugar is dissolved. Set aside to cool.

3. When ready to cook, oil the grill grate. Arrange the bananas on the hot grate and grill, turning with tongs, until nicely browned all over, 6 to 8 minutes in all. Transfer the bananas to a cutting board and slice on the diagonal into bite-size pieces. Stir the hot bananas into the syrup mixture and allow to cool to room temperature. Cover and let marinate, in the refrigerator, for 3 hours.

4. Prepare the banana splits. Mound one-quarter of the ice cream in the center of each of 4 shallow dessert bowls. Spoon the bananas with a little syrup mixture over the ice cream. Spoon or pipe rosettes of whipped cream on top and sprinkle with toasted coconut and macadamia nuts. Serve immediately.

Serves 4

Whipped Cream

For best results, chill bowl and beaters for 30 minutes before whipping the cream.

1 cup heavy cream
3 tablespoons confectioners' sugar
½ teaspoon vanilla extract

1. Place the cream in a chilled large bowl and beat it with an electric mixer, first on slow speed, then medium speed, then high, until soft peaks form, about 5 minutes.

2. Add the sugar and vanilla and continue beating until the cream is thick a. d stiff, about 2 minutes more. Do not overbeat or the cream will separate.

Makes about 1½ cups

GRILLED SUGAR-DIPPED PINEAPPLE

U.S.A.

METHOD:
Direct grilling

Americans don't customarily grill fruit, but elsewhere in the world—especially in Southeast Asia—bananas and other fruits are often charred over glowing coals for dessert. Pineapples taste particularly good grilled, the charred flavor meshing nicely with the caramelized sweetness of the fruit. When buying pineapple, go for the gold: Look for fruit with a golden rind. It will be juicier and sweeter than the usual green-rind pineapples.

1 ripe pineapple
8 tablespoons (1 stick) unsalted butter, melted
¾ cup sugar
1 teaspoon grated lime zest
1 teaspoon ground cinnamon
⅛ teaspoon ground cloves
½ cup dark rum, for flambéing (optional)

1. Preheat the grill to high.

2. Cut the leafy top off the pineapple, then cut off the rind. Slice the fruit into 8 or 10 even rounds. Using a pineapple corer or paring knife, remove the core from each round.

3. When ready to cook, place the melted

butter in a shallow bowl; combine the sugar, lime zest, and cinnamon in a separate bowl. Bring both bowls to grillside. Oil the grill grate. Dip each slice of pineapple first in melted butter, then in the sugar mixture, shaking off the excess. Arrange the pineapple slices on the hot grate and grill, turning with tongs, until browned and sizzling, 5 to 8 minutes per side. Transfer the pineapple slices to plates or a platter, arranging the slices in an overlapping fashion.

4. If using the rum, warm it in a small flameproof saucepan on one side of the grill; do not let it boil or even become hot. Remove from the heat and then, making sure your sleeves are rolled up and hair is tied back, light a long match and use it to ignite the rum, averting your face as you do so. Very carefully pour the flaming rum over the pineapple and serve immediately.

Serves 8 to 10

LEMON-GINGER CREME BRULEES

U . S . A .

METHOD:
Direct fire

ADVANCE PREPARATION:
6 to 8 hours for chilling the custard

SPECIAL EQUIPMENT:
Kitchen blowtorch (optional)

This is a book about live-fire cooking, so I thought it only natural to include a few variations on crème brûlée (literally "burnt cream"). Despite their current trendiness, these burnt sugar desserts have been around a long time. Originally, the sugar was caramelized with a fire-heated poker. Although you could caramelize the sugar by running the brûlées under the broiler, these days there's a better method available—the kitchen blowtorch. This is my favorite method—first, because it's in keeping with the live-fire theme of this book, then, because it gives you a very hot, concentrated, and controlled flame that burns the sugar without warming the custard beneath it. On page 521 you'll find a discussion of kitchen blowtorches.

As for the following crème brûlée, fresh ginger and lemon zest give it a haunting Asian accent that makes for a particularly refreshing summer dessert.

3 cups heavy cream
6 slices (each ¼ inch thick) fresh ginger, flattened with the side of a cleaver
6 strips lemon zest (each 2 x ½ inches; removed with a vegetable peeler)
10 large egg yolks
⅓ cup granulated sugar
¼ cup turbinado sugar (Sugar in the Raw) or additional granulated sugar

1. Combine the cream, ginger, and lemon zest in a heavy saucepan. Bring just to a boil over medium heat. Remove from the heat and let the cream cool to room temperature.

2. Preheat the oven to 300°F. Bring a large saucepan or kettle of water to a boil.

3. Combine the egg yolks and granulated sugar in a large bowl and whisk just to mix. Whisk the cooled cream into the yolk mixture. Strain this custard mixture into 6 crème brûlée dishes or ramekins. Pour boiling water to a depth of ½ inch into a roasting pan. Place the dishes or ramekins in the roasting pan.

4. Bake the custards until just set, 45 minutes to 1 hour. To test for doneness, gently shake a dish; the top should jiggle just a little. Remove the dishes from the roasting pan and let cool to room temperature. Cover loosely with plastic wrap and refrigerate for at least 6 hours or overnight.

5. When ready to serve, sprinkle each custard with 2 teaspoons of the turbinado sugar in a thin layer. Light a kitchen blowtorch following the manufacturer's directions. Or preheat the broiler and set the broiling rack 2 to 4 inches from the source of heat.

6. Use the kitchen blowtorch to caramelize the tops of the custards, following the instructions on page 521. Or set the dishes on the broiling rack and broil until the tops have crusted to a rich, golden brown, about 3 minutes; watch carefully to prevent burning and shift the brulées as needed to ensure even browning. Serve immediately.
Serves 6

COCO LOCO BRULEE

U.S.A.

METHOD:
Direct fire

ADVANCE PREPARATION:
4 to 8 hours for chilling the custard

Here's a twist on classic crème brûlée —not to mention a wow dessert of the highest order. Talk about drama! The custard is made with coconut milk and coconut cream and is served in a hollowed coconut shell—an idea I got from chef Douglas Rodriguez of the restaurant Patria in New York.

Coco Loco Brûlée isn't really grilled, but it does involve the application of that live fire in order to caramelize the sugar. I like to do it with a blowtorch, but you can use the broiler. Save the coconut water for making drinks, like Sky Juice (see Index).

3 ripe (hard) coconuts
2 cups heavy cream
¾ cup coconut milk, canned or homemade (page 522)
¾ cup canned coconut cream, such as Coco Lopez
1 vanilla bean, split
2 strips lemon zest (each 2 x ½ inches; removed with a vegetable peeler)
¾ cup sugar
8 large egg yolks
2½ tablespoons cornstarch
8 cups crushed ice

1. Cut the coconuts in half. The easiest way to do this is to tap the shell repeatedly with the back of a cleaver along an imaginary line going around the middle. After 10 to 20 taps, the shell will break neatly in two. Work over a bowl with a strainer to collect the coconut water, if desired, for making drinks. Blot the insides of the coconut dry with paper towels. Place the coconuts in plastic bags and refrigerate until ready to fill.

2. Combine the cream, coconut milk, coconut cream, vanilla bean, and lemon zest in a heavy saucepan and gradually bring to a boil over medium heat, 6 to 8 minutes. Remove the pan from the heat and let cool for 3 minutes.

3. Meanwhile, combine ½ cup of the sugar and the egg yolks in a medium-size heatproof bowl and whisk just to mix. Whisk in the cornstarch. Pour the cream mixture into the yolk mixture in a thin stream and whisk to mix. Return this mixture to the saucepan and gradually bring to a gentle simmer over medium heat, whisking steadily. Once the mixture thickens, simmer for 1 to 2 minutes. Do not boil rapidly or overcook, or the mixture will curdle. Remove the pan from the heat and let the custard cool to room temperature. Discard the vanilla bean and lemon zest. Spoon the custard mixture into the coconut shells and smooth the tops with the back of a spoon. Refrigerate the custards for at least 4 hours or even overnight.

4. When ready to serve, sprinkle each custard with 2 teaspoons of the remaining sugar in a thin layer. Light a kitchen blowtorch following the manufacturer's directions. Or preheat the broiler and set the broiling rack 4 to 6 inches from the source of heat.

5. Place a layer of crinkled aluminum foil in the bottom of a roasting pan and arrange the custard-filled coconut shells in the prepared pan, using the foil to steady them. Use the kitchen blowtorch to caramelize the tops of the custards, following the instructions on page 521. Or, broil until the tops have crusted to a golden brown, about 3 minutes; watch carefully to prevent burning, shifting the pan as needed to ensure even browning.

6. Divide the crushed ice among 6 shallow bowls. Place a coconut shell in each bowl and serve.
Serves 6

CATALAN CREAM
Crema Catalana

SPAIN

METHOD:
Direct fire

**ADVANCE
PREPARATION:**
*6 hours for
chilling the
custards*

**SPECIAL
EQUIPMENT:**
*Kitchen
blowtorch
(optional)*

Crema catalana is Spain's answer to crème brûlée, and a splendid answer it is. This recipe comes from the Set Portes restaurant in Barcelona, which opened its doors in 1836.

2 cups milk
1 cup heavy cream
6 strips fresh lemon zest (each 2 x ½ inches; removed with a vegetable peeler)
6 strips fresh orange zest (each 2 x ½ inches; removed with a vegetable peeler)
1 cinnamon stick (3 inches)
1 cup sugar
7 large egg yolks
2½ tablespoons unbleached all-purpose flour

1. Combine the milk, cream, orange and lemon zests, and cinnamon stick in a medium-size heavy saucepan and bring almost to a simmer over low heat. Let the mixture cook for about 10 minutes, but do not allow to boil. Remove from the heat and let cool to room temperature.

2. Whisk together ¾ cup of the sugar and the egg yolks in a medium-size bowl. Whisk in the flour, then strain the milk into the yolk mixture in a thin stream and whisk to mix. Return this mixture to the saucepan and bring gradually to a gentle simmer over medium heat, whisking steadily. Once the mixture thickens, gently simmer for 1 to 2 minutes. Do not boil rapidly or overcook, or the custard will curdle.

3. Immediately divide the custard among 6 individual gratin dishes or ramekins. Cool to room temperature, then cover loosely with plastic wrap and refrigerate 6 hours.

4. When ready to serve, sprinkle each custard with 2 teaspoons of the remaining sugar in a thin layer. Light a kitchen blowtorch following the manufacturer's directions. Or preheat the broiler and set the rack 6 to 8 inches from the heat source.

5. Use the kitchen blowtorch to caramelize the tops of the custards, following the instructions on page 521. Or arrange the dishes on the broiling rack and broil until the tops have crusted to a rich, golden brown, about 3 minutes; watch carefully to prevent burning, shifting the creams as needed to ensure even browing. Serve immediately.
Serves 6

Cooking with a Blowtorch

Okay, it may not be grilling. But it is live-fire cooking. Many chefs and pit masters use a tool once relegated to the workshop to lend a flame-charred taste to their food: a blowtorch.

The blowtorch made its appearance in the kitchen in the 1970s, when French pastry chefs began using it to brown meringues and caramelize sugar on custard desserts, like crème brûlée.

Using a blowtorch may seem a little intimidating at first, but there's nothing like it for creating a high, focused flame and sharp blast of heat. Nowadays there are torches specially created for use in the kitchen. Cookware shops, such as Williams-Sonoma, sell them. If you decide to use one, keep these watchpoints in mind:

■ Make sure your sleeves are rolled up, your hair is tied back, and there are no children underfoot.

■ Have the food on a heatproof plate or baking dish. Never torch a pastry on a glass plate or platter.

■ Place the plate or baking dish on a heatproof surface.

■ Light the flame and adjust it to obtain a pointed, glowing, red-yellow cone of heat in the center of the lavender blue flame. This cone is where the heat is concentrated. Hold it 2 to 3 inches above the surface of the food, moving it back and forth to ensure even browning.

■ Remember that sugar and meringue will continue to cook for a few seconds even after the flame has been removed. Stop torching just before you get the desired degree of doneness.

PERSIAN LEMON AND ROSEWATER "SUNDAE" WITH SOUR CHERRY SYRUP

Faluda

IRAN

ON THE SIDE

One of the most refreshing desserts ever to grace a barbecue is *faluda* (aka *faludeh*). I first sampled it at a Persian restaurant in New York called Persepolis. *Faluda* also turns up in Afghanistan, where it is made with fresh mountain snow. It belongs to a large family of Asian frozen desserts that include Indian *kulfi* and Turkish *sorpa* (sorbet). The Persian version offers the haunting flavors of sour cherry syrup and rosewater. But what really sets *faluda* apart is the addition of rice noodles, which creates a wonderfully exotic and unexpected texture.

Rosewater and sour cherry syrup are available at Middle and Near Eastern markets. Use a thin rice noodle, like Thai rice sticks or Vietnamese rice vermicelli, for the noodles.

⅔ cup fresh lemon juice
⅔ cup rosewater
1½ cups sugar
1 skein (1 ounce) rice noodles
8 cups crushed ice
½ cup sour cherry syrup or grenadine

1. Combine the lemon juice, rosewater, and sugar in a heavy saucepan and bring to a boil over medium-high heat. Boil, stirring constantly, until the sugar is dissolved and the mixture is syrupy, about 5 minutes. Remove the pan from the heat and let the syrup cool to room temperature, then cover and refrigerate until cold, about 2 hours.

2. Meanwhile, soak the rice noodles in cold water to cover for 20 minutes.

3. Bring 4 cups of water to a boil in a large saucepan. Drain the noodles in a colander and cook in the boiling water until soft, 3 to 5 minutes. Drain in the colander and rinse under cold running water until cool. Drain again. Cut the noodles into 1-inch pieces, using scissors.

4. Working in batches, combine the crushed ice and chilled rosewater syrup in a blender and process to an icy purée. Transfer the mixture to a bowl and stir in the rice noodles. Transfer the mixture to 8 wine glasses. Drizzle a spoonful of sour cherry syrup over each *faluda* and serve immediately (see Note).

Serves 8

Note: You can make the *faluda* ahead and freeze it in paper cups. To serve, let warm for 5 to 10 minutes, then crush the *faluda* by gently squeezing the sides of the cups with your fingers to loosen up the ice crystals. Transfer it to wine glasses and drizzle with the cherry syrup.

ARGENTINIAN CARAMEL CREAM
Dulce de Leche

ARGENTINA

ON THE SIDE

This thick, sweet, sauce-like caramel is Argentina's national dessert. It turns up at highfalutin restaurants and homey eateries, spooned over everything from fruit to cake to ice cream. It's also good eaten right off the spoon. *Dulce de leche* (literally "milk sweet") isn't particularly difficult to make, but it does require conscientious stirring to keep the caramel from boiling over. Be comforted by the fact that it keeps for months and a little goes a long way.

1 quart whole milk (see Note)
1⅓ cups sugar
1 vanilla bean
½ teaspoon baking soda

1. Combine all the ingredients in a large, heavy saucepan and bring to a boil over high heat, stirring to dissolve the sugar. Reduce the heat to medium and simmer the mixture briskly, stirring often with a wooden spoon, until thick, caramel colored, and reduced by half, 30 to 40 minutes. You'll need to adjust the heat, now up, now down, to keep the mixture at a brisk simmer, but without it boiling over. The traditional test for doneness is to pour a spoonful of caramel cream on a plate. When it gathers in a thick puddle and no longer runs to the edges, the mixture is ready. Remove the vanilla bean with tongs and discard.

2. Transfer the caramel cream to a serving bowl and cool to room temperature. You can eat it now or cover and refrigerate if you prefer to serve it chilled.

Serves 4 to 6

Note: You must use whole milk for *dulce de leche*. Skim milk will burn during the reduction process.

INDIAN CARDAMON-PISTACHIO RICE PUDDING

Kheer

INDIA

ON THE SIDE

It's hard to imagine a meal of tandoori or kebabs without *kheer,* an exquisitely creamy rice pudding dessert, popular in Central Asia and the Indian subcontinent. *Kheer* owes its exotic, perfumed fragrance to cardamom and rosewater and its richness to the milk, which is boiled until reduced by almost half to concentrate its flavor.

2 quarts whole milk (see Note)
12 green cardamom pods, crushed and tied in a piece of cheesecloth
¼ cup basmati rice
½ cup sugar
¼ cup finely chopped unsalted pistachio nuts, plus 2 tablespoons for garnish
¼ cup slivered almonds
¼ cup golden raisins
Pinch of salt
1 tablespoon rosewater

1. Combine the milk, cardamom, and rice in a large, heavy saucepan and bring gradually to a boil over medium high heat. Reduce the heat to medium and simmer the mixture, stirring often with a wooden spoon, until the milk is reduced to 6 cups, about 30 minutes. Remove and discard the cardamom.

2. Stir the sugar, ¼ cup pistachio nuts, the almonds, raisins, and salt into the reduced milk. Gently simmer the mixture, stirring often, until the rice is very soft and the pudding has thickened, about 20 minutes more. You should have about 5½ cups in all. Stir in the rosewater and cook for 1 minute.

3. Remove the pan from the heat and let the mixture cool to room temperature, then spoon it into 6 bowls or wine glasses. The pudding tastes best served at room temperature or just slightly chilled. Just before serving, sprinkle the desserts with the remaining chopped pistachio nuts.

Serves 6

Note: Use whole milk for *kheer*. Skim milk will burn during the reduction process.

COCONUT ICE CREAM

GUADELOUPE

ON THE SIDE

SPECIAL EQUIPEMNT:
Ice cream machine

This lovely ice cream comes from Guadeloupe's Point Château Beach, where it's churned by hand by women working under beach umbrellas or from the backs of their station wagons. For the best results, use made-from-scratch coconut milk. In a pinch you can use canned (try Goya or A Taste of Thai); do not use coconut cream.

2 cups coconut milk, homemade (recipe follows) or canned.
⅔ cup sugar, or more to taste
1 teaspoon vanilla extract
½ teaspoon almond extract
1 teaspoon grated lemon zest
½ teaspoon ground cinnamon
¼ teaspoon freshly grated nutmeg

1. Combine all the ingredients in a medium-size bowl, including ⅔ cup sugar, and whisk until the sugar is dissolved. Correct the seasoning, adding sugar if necessary.

2. Transfer the mixture to an ice cream machine and freeze, following the manufacturer's instructions.

Serves 4

Coconut Milk

Here's a quick, easy way to make coconut milk from scratch.

1 ripe (hard) coconut
2 cups boiling water

1. Prepare the coconut, through removing the brown skin, as directed in the box on page 89. Break the large pieces into 1- to 2-inch pieces.

2. Place the coconut, reserved coconut water, and boiling water in a blender and blend for 3 minutes. You may need to work in two or three batches to reduce the risk of overflow. Let the mixture stand for 5 minutes, then pour it through a fine-meshed strainer or a strainer lined with several layers of dampened cheesecloth. Twist the cheesecloth tightly to extract as much milk as possible. Store coconut milk, covered, in the refrigerator for up to 3 days. It can also be frozen for up to 1 month.

Makes 2 to 3 cups

CARDAMOM CARAMEL ICE CREAM
Kulfi

CENTRAL ASIA

ON THE SIDE

ADVANCE PREPARATION:
2 hours for chilling the ice cream

SPECIAL EQUIPMENT:
Ice cream machine

Grilled fare and ice cream are one of the constants of the world of barbecue. This one, *kulfi*, has a haunting flavor that lies midway between malt and caramel—the result of the long, slow simmering of the milk to reduce it by two thirds. To this add the exotic flavors of cardamom and pistachio nuts and you've got an ice cream quite unlike anything in the North American repertoire.

2 quarts whole milk (see Note)
6 green cardamom pods, crushed and tied in a piece of cheesecloth
½ cup sugar, or more to taste
3 tablespoons chopped pistachio nuts
3 tablespoons chopped blanched almonds

1. Combine the milk and cardamom in a large, heavy saucepan and gradually bring to a boil over medium-high heat. Reduce the heat to medium and simmer the milk briskly, stirring often with a wooden spoon, until reduced to 3 cups, about 1 hour. Remove and discard the cardamom.

2. Stir in ½ cup sugar, the pistachio nuts, and almonds and simmer for 3 minutes. Remove from the heat and correct the seasoning, adding sugar if necessary. Let the mixture cool to room temperature, then transfer to a bowl. Cover and refrigerate until cold, about 2 hours.

3. Transfer the *kulfi* mixture to an ice cream machine and freeze, following the manufacturer's instructions.

Serves 4 to 6

Note: Use whole milk for *kulfi*. Skim milk will burn during the reduction process.

FRUIT COOLER

SOUTHEAST ASIA

ON THE SIDE

A cross between a milk shake and a dessert, this refreshing cooler is sold at street stalls and markets throughout Southeast Asia. Sweetened condensed milk is the dairy product of choice here because it won't spoil in the tropical heat. Feel free to vary the fruits.

3 cups seeded, diced watermelon
3 cups diced fresh strawberries, plus 6 small whole ones, for garnish
2 ripe bananas, peeled and diced
⅓ cup fresh lime juice, or more to taste
⅓ cup sugar, or more to taste
⅓ cup sweetened condensed milk
6 cups crushed ice

Working in batches, combine the fruits, ⅓ cup lime juice, ⅓ cup sugar, the condensed milk, and ice in a blender and blend until smooth. Correct the flavoring, adding the lime juice or sugar as necessary. Serve immediately in tall glasses garnished with whole strawberries and straws.

Serves 6

Barbecue from the Land of Morning Calm: The Korean Grill

When I was a bachelor in Boston, my favorite neighborhood restaurant was a small, unassuming storefront called Korea Garden. At least once a week, I would retreat to this oasis of calm and warmth for a sorely needed dose of *mandoo* (garlicky beef ravioli), *kimchi* (fiery pickled napa cabbage), and *bool kogi* (sweet-salty sesame grilled beef).

In matters culinary, Korea tends to be eclipsed by its two giant neighbors, China and Japan. Most Americans have had a lifelong experience with some sort of Chinese cooking, while sushi, teriyaki, and other Japanese dishes are now so popular, they've become part of the North American repertoire. But most of us would be hard pressed to name a single dish from Korea.

This is a shame, for Korea offers some of the most refined, sophisticated, and intrinsically healthy food I have eaten on five continents. Dishes designed with a dazzling array of colors, textures, and flavors. Menus remarkable for their sparing use of meats and seafoods and high proportion of grains and vegetables. Korean cooking lacks the oiliness associated with many Chinese dishes, while its flavors are more vibrant than the restrained, disciplined tastes of Japan.

Actually, barbecue was about the last thing on my mind when I visited Korea. The month was February, and the bone-numbing cold had frozen the water in the moats around Seoul's Kyongbuk-kung Palace. This was the time of year for hearty soups and stews.

Curiously, though, wherever I went, I found barbecue—in showy restaurants, homey neighborhood eateries, and back-alley cookshops. In the process, I dis-

covered that in Korea grilling is done, as often as not, indoors and is popular all year round. Koreans gather around their tabletop charcoal braziers with the same fervor, the same hunger for warmth that bring skiers to crowd around fireplaces at ski lodges in the Alps.

This truth was brought home to me by a restaurant called Dae Won Gak. Actually, the term "restaurant" is a bit of an understatement. Dae Won Gak is a veritable village of 60 traditional Korean houses on several acres of hillside overlooking Seoul. Some of the structures are large enough to accommodate 300 people, others cozy and intimate enough to seat only two. Each boasts the gracefully curved eaves, ceramic tile roofs, rope mats, and intricate woodwork of a traditional Korean home.

I took my seat on the floor at a

KOREAN FRUIT "PUNCH"

KOREA

ON THE SIDE

Part beverage and part fruit salad, this cool, syrupy dish is served as a refresher at the end of a Korean meal. I've had it made with everything from dried persimmons to jujubes (a type of date); the ingredients are really limited only by your imagination. I like a mixture of hard fruits, like Asian pears or apples; soft fruit, like bananas or melon; and berries, like strawberries or blueberries.

3 cups mixed diced or sliced fresh fruit
¾ cup sugar
4 cups water
4 slices fresh ginger (each ¼ inch thick), flattened with a cleaver
3 strips lemon zest (each 2 x ½ inches; removed with a vegetable peeler)
2 cinnamon sticks (each 3 inches)
2 tablespoons pine nuts, lightly toasted (see box, page 93)

knee-high table with a ceramic brazier in the center. Our waitress filled it with blazing coals, then, leaning over with her chopsticks, arranged thin sheets of marinated beef and tiny skewers of garlic cloves on the concave grill over the brazier. Smoke filled our nostrils, the sounds of sizzling meat sang in our ears, as the *bool kogi* was grilled before our eyes.

The traditional way to eat *bool kogi* is wrapped, much like moo shu pork or fajitas (although this is not how it's usually served at Korean restaurants in the U.S.). I placed a snippet of meat and a grilled garlic clove on a romaine lettuce leaf, rolled it up, dipped it in a delicately flavored Asian pear sauce, then popped it into my mouth. The contrast of sweet and salty, of pungent and fruity, of crisp vegetable and chewy but tender meat was as haunting and complex as the twangy *kal ya kum* music that played in the background.

To round out the meal, there was an impressive array of refreshing side dishes: spicy daikon radish salad, onion and lettuce salad, nutty bean sprout salad, three types of *kimchi,* plates of lettuce leaves, sliced cucumbers, and rice.

KOREAN BARBECUED RIBS

Koreans have raised the beef short rib to the level of art in a dish called *kalbi kui* (literally, "grilled ribs"). I enjoyed my rib experience in one of Seoul's most famous grill restaurants, Samwon Garden. I didn't enjoy it alone: This behemoth eatery seats 700 and serves 2,000 people on a busy day. Samwon means "three utmosts" in Korean, explained the restaurant's manager, Mr. Park. The three utmosts in question here are cleanliness, kindness, and deliciousness. I might add a fourth utmost, entertainment, as Samwon is a veritable theme park, complete with its own pond, mountain, and waterfalls.

Mr. Park led me down to an immaculate kitchen, where 70 chefs toil round the clock to feed the appreciative multitudes upstairs. One whole room has been consecrated to the preparation of the *kalbi.* The restaurant starts with whole rib sections of beef, which are cut into 2-inch cross sections on a band saw, then butterflied into thin strips. According to Mr. Park, *kalbi kui* is a relatively new addition to the Korean repertoire, originating in restaurants, not in the home, in the 1950s. As with *bool kogi, kalbi kui* is cooked on a brazier in the center of the table and is eaten wrapped in lettuce leaves.

Like most Korean dishes, Korean barbecue is built from a simple palate of flavors: the salty succulence of soy sauce, the sweetness of sugar or honey, the nutty tang of sesame oil and sesame seeds. Accents are provided by the pungency of garlic and scallion, the tingle of ginger, the bite of chile powder and chile paste.

What this means in practical terms is that Korean food is much easier to prepare in an American kitchen than, say, Chinese or Japanese. It requires few esoteric ingredients or tricky cooking techniques. Using a relatively limited number of ingredients, Koreans create an astonishing range of flavors.

1. Toss the fruit with ¼ cup of the sugar in a serving bowl and let stand for 15 minutes.

2. Meanwhile, combine the remaining ½ cup sugar, the water, ginger slices, lemon zest, and cinnamon sticks in a saucepan and bring to a boil over high heat. Reduce the heat and simmer until well flavored and lightly syrupy, about 5 minutes. Remove the pan from the heat and let cool completely.

3. Strain the syrup over the fruit and stir gently to mix. Sprinkle the pine nuts on top and serve immediately. I like to serve the punch in glass bowls or brandy snifters. It's perfectly acceptable to raise the bowl to your lips to sip the syrup.

Serves 6

RAICHLEN'S TOP TWENTY-FIVE:
The World's Best Grilling Emporiums and Barbecue Joints

What are the world's best places for barbecuing and grilling? My three years on the barbecue trail have taken me to some pretty remarkable dining establishments, not all of them fancy—for that matter, not all of them even restaurants. In fact, many are greasy dives and even sidewalk pushcarts, but all serve superlative grilled fare.

Picking the best is a little like asking a parent to name his favorite child. Here, in alphabetical order, are my top twenty-five:

ARROYO
Av. Insurgentes Sur 4003, Coyoacán
Mexico City, Mexico
5-573-4344
A gigantic, Disneyesque food emporium complete with its own bullfighting ring. Order *barbacoa* (pit-roasted lamb cooked in maguey cactus leaves).

ARTHUR BRYANT'S
1727 Brooklyn Avenue
Kansas City, Missouri
(816) 231-1123
Immortalized by Calvin Trillin and as grungy as a bus station. But nobody in Kansas City serves better barbecued brisket or burnt edges (the singed, chopped trimmings removed from the barbecued brisket).

BUKHARA
At the Maurya Sheraton Hotel & Towers
Diplomatic Enclave
New Delhi, India
011-3010101
The ultimate tandoori palace, decorated like an Indian frontier-style hunting lodge. Order any dish marked tandoori, and save room for the *dal bukhara* (buttery stewed gram beans).

DA DELFINA
Artimino, near Carmignano
Tuscany, Italy
055-8718074
Rosemary-scented, spit-roasted pheasant and superlative *bistecca alla fiorentina*.

DEVELI
Samatya Balikazari
Gumusyuzuk Sok. No. 7
Samatya, Istanbul, Turkey
212-5290833
Not much better than dozens of other restaurants serving upscale kebabs and traditional Turkish dishes in Istanbul. Which is to say superb. Try the pistachio lamb kebabs and *ali-nasik kebab* (grilled ground lamb served on grilled eggplant purée).

EAST COAST GRILL
1271 Cambridge Street
Cambridge, Massachusetts
(617) 491-6568
Cutting-edge American grilling served up by barbecue guru Chris Schlesinger.

IMAM CAGDAS
Hamdi Kutlar Cad.
Uzun Carsi 14
Gaziantep, Turkey
90-342-231-2678 or
90-342-234-4000
Over 100 years old and still going strong! Enjoy the most exotic kebabs in Turkey (not to mention the best baklava) in a city that owes its extraordinary cuisine to its strategic location on the Silk Route.

INAKAYA
7-8-4 Roppongi
Minato-ku, Tokyo, Japan
3405-9866
Japan's most famous *robatayaki* restaurant, offering an astonishing array of meats, seafood, and vegetables grilled to order and served on 10-foot-long paddles, amid much shouting. One of the most extraordinary grilling experiences in the world and one of the most expensive. Bring lots of yen. Better still, come on someone else's expense account.

LA CABANA
Av. Entre Rios 435. Congreso
Buenos Aires, Argentina
381-2373
The granddaddy of Buenos Aires steak houses, stately, dignified, and the place to come for *costilla* (bone-in rib steak)—La Cabaña's tips the scale

at 3½ pounds! Highly unusual is the house steak sauce, a red *chimichurri*.

LAS NAZARENAS
1132 Reconquista Street
Buenos Aires, Argentina
011-54-1-312-5559
One of the most respected steak houses in Buenos Aires, boasting both *asado* (whole sides of beef and kid roasted in front of a campfire) and *parillada* (steaks, sausages, and other meats cooked on a grill). Don't miss the *parrillada Las Nazarenas*, a belt-loosening mixed grill featuring just about every imaginable sort of grilled sausage and organ meat.

LA TOMAQUERA
Margarit 58
Barcelona, Spain
This smoky, one-room chop house serves huge portions of grilled meats, seasoned with romesco sauce and *alioli* so tasty you'll want to lick the spoon. But the real star of the show are the grilled artichokes, which are smoky, buttery, garlicky, and crisp—and simply the best artichokes I've ever tasted. Anywhere.

LEXINGTON BARBECUE NO. 1
10 Highway 29-70 S.
Lexington, North Carolina
(704) 249-9814
The town of Lexington, located 20 miles north of Winston Salem, is the capital of Carolina barbecue, with dozens of barbecue joints to choose from. The best of the bunch is "Honey Monk's," as Lexington Barbecue is referred to by the locals. The finest pork shoulder ever to grace a hamburger bun.

LIL' JAKE'S EAT IT & BEAT IT
1227 Grand Avenue
Kansas City, Missouri
(816) 283-0880
The quintessential Kansas City grease house. (With only 18 seats, the owner really does want you to "eat it and beat it"). Fantastic ribs and brisket.

MARIUS
Rua Francisco Otaviano, 96
Ipanema, Rio de Janeiro, Brazil
021-521-0500
(and other locations)
The most fashionable *churrascaria* in Rio. (Unlike most Brazilian grill houses, the service here is à la carte.)

MERCADO DEL PUERTO
Located at the corner of the Calle Piedras and Calle Perez Castellano, across the street from the old port, in downtown Montevideo, Uruguay
Any of the two dozen stalls and restaurants in this restored 1868 food market will serve you superlative Uruguayan-style grilled meats, which include *choto* (coiled, grilled lamb's intestines—better than it sounds) and *tira de asado* (an unusual but highly flavorful steak cut from a cross section of beef ribs). My favorite restaurant here is El Palenque.

MITLA
Hermanos Escobar 2325
Juarez, Mexico
A one-room steak house whose walls are blackened with four decades of wood smoke. Steaks grilled over blazing mesquite are the house specialty: Enjoy them with fresh tortillas and *chile de arbol* salsa.

PORCAO
Ilha do Governador
Praia Belo Jardin, 285 (Estrada do Galeão)
Rio de Janeiro, Brazil
55 (21) 462-3209
The name means "big pig," which is what patrons make of themselves when they dine here. Porcão is the quintessential *churrascaria*, with squadrons of waiters marching through the dining room bearing sword-like spits of meats, which they carve directly onto your plate. There's a Porcão in Miami, as well as in other locations in Brazil.

RENDEZVOUS RESTAURANT
52 S. Second Street
Memphis, Tennessee
(901) 523-2746
My favorite barbecue joint in Memphis. The dry-cooked ribs are the very exemplar of the species.

SAMWON GARDEN
135-120 623-1, Sinsa-dong
Kangnam-gu, Seoul, Korea
544-5351
A mammoth (700-seat) restaurant specializing in *bool kogi*, *kalbi kui*, and other Korean meats grilled on a brazier in the center of your table.

SATAY GELUGOR
Gurney Drive
Georgetown
Penang Island, Malaysia
04-83-4761
Asmavy Mustadi serves some of the most exotic saté in Malaysia. Exotic? How about rabbit or venison saté? His basting brush is a stalk of lemongrass. Of course you can get superb saté from just about any of the grill stalls on Gurney Drive, a bayfront hawkers' center on the island of Penang in northern Malaysia that offers some of the best street food in Asia.

SONNY BRYAN'S
2202 Inwood Road
Dallas, Texas
(972) 357-7120
Home of the barbecued brisket that made Dallas famous. (Also try the

jalapeño sausage and hand-cut onion rings.) Note: To have the full experience of Sonny Bryan's, you must visit this, the original location, and be there by noon or no later than 1 P.M. (The restaurant closes when the brisket is sold out.)

SUFFERER'S JERK PORK FRONT LINE NO. 1
Boston Beach, Jamaica

Simply the best jerk in Jamaica. Round out your meal with breadfruit roasted in the embers.

SUNDA KELAPA
J1 Ancol Barat IV 28-29
Old Port
Jakarta, Indonesia
692-4954, 690-8765

The most famous seafood restaurant in Jakarta. Order the grilled prawns and any of the grilled fish.

THE RIVERSIDE TERRACE AT THE ORIENTAL HOTEL
Oriental Avenue
Bangkok, Thailand
437-6211

Okay, so it's a little touristy. Okay, so it's a lot touristy. (The only Thais you'll see here work here.) But you get to enjoy the explosive flavors of Thai barbecue in a gorgeous riverside setting—without enduring the city's hellish traffic or risk of gastrointestinal distress.

TON TON
Under the tracks, 1,
Yurakucho 2-chome
Chiyoda-ku, Tokyo, Japan

Smoky, noisy, crowded, and cramped. Everything a rough-and-tumble yakitori joint should be.

GLOSSARY OF SPECIAL INGREDIENTS

Grilling is the world's most straight-forward cooking technique, but as you grill your way along the barbecue trail, you'll need to know about some special ingredients. Here's what they are. For specific mail-order sources, see page 533.

ALEPPO PEPPER: A round, reddish-brown chile from Syria and eastern Turkey, usually sold powdered or in flakes. Used in a number of preparations—notably in this book in the Onion Relish with Pomegranate Molasses. The Aleppo pepper has a complex flavor that's simultaneously earthy, salty, piquant, fruity, and hot. Look for it in Middle Eastern grocery stores. The closest approximation would be equal parts ancho chile powder and hot red pepper flakes with a sprinkle of salt and lime juice.

ALLSPICE: The perfumed berries of this Caribbean tree are one of the most defining flavors of Jamaican jerk. The best allspice comes from Jamaica: Look for it in West Indian markets and buy the berries whole.

AMBA: A hot, sour pickling paste from India and the Middle and Near East. *Amba* is the Hindu word for mango (think mango pickle here). *Amba* paste, whose main ingredients are vinegar, turmeric, and fenugreek, is the flavoring for the hot pickles that invariable accompany Afghan, Iraqi, and Israeli barbecue.

ANNATTO SEED: A hard, squarish, rust-colored seed with a tangy, earthy, iodine flavor. The spice, also known by its Spanish name *achiote,* is native to the Caribbean and Central America. Annatto is an essential ingredient in *recado* (Yucatecan spice paste) and *tikin xik* (Yucatán-style marinated fish). There are two ways to use this hard seed: Grind it to a powder in a spice mill or soak it in sour orange juice (or water) until soft, then crumble or pureé.

BLACK SESAME SEEDS: A jet-black variety of sesame seed known as *gomen* in Japanese. Use toasted white sesame seeds as a substitute.

CANDLENUT: An essential ingredient in Balinese spice pastes, the candlenut tastes like a somewhat bitter cashew. Look for it in Asian markets that carry Indonesian ingredients. There's no taste equivalent in the West, but macadamia nuts and cashews have the right texture and mouth feel.

CARDAMOM: A spice with a sweet, perfumed flavor used throughout North Africa, the Middle East, and India. Actually there are two types: Green cardamom is a greenish-tan, coffee bean–size pod with small, fragrant black seeds inside; black cardamom is the size of a plum pit and has a smoky flavor. Green cardamom is available in the spice rack of almost any supermarket; black cardamom can be found in Indian markets.

CHAAT MASALA: A traditional Indian spice mix sprinkled on salads and cold grilled dishes. *Chaat masala* owes its distinctive sourish, sulphurous flavor to the addition of a sulphur-rich mineral called black salt.

CHICKPEA FLOUR (also known as besan): A fine, aromatic flour made from roasted chickpeas. It has a tart, nutty, earthy flavor that's unique in the world of cooking. *Besan* is used extensively in Indian barbecue to thicken and flavor marinades. It is also used in the south of France to make pancakes (*socca,* traditionally baked in a wood-fired oven) and in North Africa to make a sort of french fry.

CHILES: Individual chiles are described on page 502.

CILANTRO (also known as coriander leaf and Chinese parsley): This pungent plant is probably the most widely used herb in the world of barbecue. The leaves turn up in salsas and marinades and are sprinkled whole over grilled fare from Malaysia to Mexico City. Cilantro roots are a key ingredient in Thai and Malaysian spice pastes. The seed of the plant (coriander) is an essential flavoring in North African and Indian barbecue.

Cilantro can also be found at Asian, Indian, and Hispanic markets, gourmet shops, and in most supermarkets. There is no substitute for the fresh herb, and it doesn't dry particularly well. Nonetheless, fresh mint can be used as a substitute in many recipes. Cilantro is one of those flavorings people either love or hate. If the herb tastes like soap to you, you may be mildly allergic to it.

COCONUT MILK: A creamy white liquid extracted from freshly grated coconut. (Contrary to popular belief, it's not the clearish liquid inside a coconut—that's coconut water.) Coconut milk is used widely throughout Southeast Asia and the Caribbean, and in Brazil. On page 522, you'll find instructions on how to make it from scratch. Canned coconut milk will work fine for the recipes in this book and is available at Asian and Hispanic supermarkets. Be sure to buy unsweetened coconut milk, and avoid coconut cream. One good brand is A Taste of Thai.

EPAZOTE: A refreshing, astringent, and strongly aromatic Mexican herb whose peculiar aroma lives up to its English name, pigweed. Sold in Mexican and Hispanic markets.

FENUGREEK: A rectangular tan seed with pleasantly bitter flavor. Fenugreek is used widely in India (where it's known as *methi*) and in the Middle East (where it's known as *hilbeh*).

FISH SAUCE (called *nam pla* in Thai and *nuoc mam* in Vietnamese): A salty condiment made from pickled anchovies. Fish sauce is used in Southeast Asia the way soy sauce is used in Japan and China. Its aroma can be off-putting, but its distinctive flavor enriches all that it touches. Look for fish sauce in Asian markets, gourmet shops, and in many large supermarkets. The best-quality brands come in glass, not plastic, bottles. Good brands include Flying Lion, Three Crabs, and Squid. A smaller amount of soy sauce can be substituted, but the flavor won't be quite the same.

GALANGAL: A root in the ginger family with a peppery, aromatic flavor (imagine the heat of ginger without the sweetness). It usually comes fresh or frozen in Asian markets. There's also a powdered form from Indonesia that is sometimes sold by the name of *laos*. Fresh ginger mixed with freshly ground black pepper makes an acceptable substitute.

GARAM MASALA: An Indian spice mix with as many as 20 different herbs and spices, including cumin, coriander, green and black cardamom seeds, black pepper, and bay leaves. On page 498 you'll find a recipe for making *garam masala* from scratch. Or use a commercial brand, available at Indian markets and in some gourmet shops.

GINGER: Widely available and best used fresh. Choose "races" (clusters) of ginger that feel heavy in your hand. The thinner the skin, the better. Avoid old, fibrous ginger (break off a small piece to check the state of the fibers). One good way to prepare ginger is to grate it.

GRAPE LEAVES: Sold pickled in jars at Middle Eastern markets and in many supermarkets. It is often used to make the wrapped grilled fish dishes of Turkey and the Republic of Georgia.

GRAPE SYRUP (also known as *grape molasses*): A tart, molasseslike sweetener used in Middle Eastern and Iranian cooking. (Try a little drizzled over grilled kebabs or pork chops). Grape syrup is sold in Middle and Near Eastern markets.

HUNG YOGURT (also known as *yogurt cheese*): This is the soul of barbecue marinades from Turkey to Bangladesh. Indians make it by tying and hanging fresh whole-milk yogurt in cheesecloth and allowing the whey to drain off (hence the name "hung yogurt"). In the West, we would use a yogurt strainer or strainer lined with dampened cheesecloth or a coffee filter. Save the whey for one of the yogurt drinks in the Thirst Quenchers chapter.

KACHIRI POWDER: A souring agent made from a small, round dried fruit from Rajasthan, used for marinades in North Indian grilling.

KETJAP MANIS: This thick, sweet soy sauce is Indonesia's national flavoring for satés and table sauces. It is available in Asian markets and in some gourmet shops. You can make the real thing by following the recipe on page 472, but a quick substitute can be made by combining equal parts regular soy sauce and molasses.

LAVASH: These large sheets of paper-thin flat bread are served with grilled fare in Iraq, Iran, and the Caucasus Mountain republics of the former Soviet Union (Azerbaijan, Uzbekistan, Turkmenistan, etc.) Central Asians wrap grilled lamb in lavash the way Mexicans serve beef and pork in tortillas. Look for lavash at Middle Eastern markets and in many supermarkets. Dried lavash needs to be softened in water. Pita bread can be used as a substitute.

LEMONGRASS: The quintessential flavoring of Southeast Asia, where it's used in innumerable marinades and spice pastes. The Balinese grill shrimp mousse on whole lemongrass stalks. Malaysian grill jockeys use the leafy shoots as a basting brush.

Lemongrass looks somewhat like a large scallion, with a bulbous base that tapers to slender, pointed leaves. The top two-thirds of the fibrous stalks are generally trimmed off, as are the outside leaves covering the base and the root. (I like to put them in the cavity of fish or chicken before grilling.) The core that remains has a haunting lemon flavor—without the tartness—that goes exceedingly well with seafood, chicken, and beef.

Fresh lemongrass can be found at Asian markets and in an increasing number of supermarkets. Dried lemongrass can be found at most natural foods stores. There's no real substitute for lemongrass, but fresh lemon zest (the lemon's oil-rich outer rind) works better than nothing.

When buying lemongrass, look for stalks that feel firm and heavy. (Press your thumbnail into the base of the stalk: it should feel moist.) To trim lemongrass, cut off the root end and the slender greenish leaves. What remains will be a cream-colored core 4 to 6 inches long and ¼ to ½ inch thick.

MIRIN: Sweet Japanese cooking wine. If unavailable, use cream sherry or sake or white wine sweetened with a little sugar or honey.

MISO: A richly flavored and highly nutritious paste made from cultured soy beans and grains. The Japanese make a barbecue sauce for grilled tofu and eggplant by mixing miso, mirin, sugar, and egg yolks. Miso comes in many colors and flavors, but the white is the most often used for grilling. Look for it at Japanese markets and natural foods stores.

OLIVE OIL: Use the best extra-virgin olive oil you can buy for marinating and basting. (Extra-virgin has the lowest acidity and the most intense flavor.) Every country on the Mediterranean makes olive oil and the flavors vary widely. I like to use Spanish oil for Spanish grilled dishes, Italian oil for Italian dishes, etc. The best oils for the money come from Turkey, Greece, and Lebanon.

PALM SUGAR: A creamy, light brown sugar made from the sap of the date palm. Used throughout Southeast Asia, it has overtones of toffee and maple syrup. Look for it at Asian markets or use light brown sugar or maple sugar.

PEPPER: One of the indispensable barbecue seasonings. Black is the preferred pepper in North America. Asian and Europeans often use white pepper. Nothing can beat the flavor of freshly ground peppercorns, of course, but I find it inconvenient to reach for a peppercorn grinder when I'm in the middle of cooking (hard to grip with wet hands). My compromise is to pregrind black and white peppercorns in a spice mill every few weeks and store them in jars. That way, you always have a pinch on hand.

POMEGRANATE MOLASSES: A thick, sweet-sour syrup made from boiled-down pomegranate juice. Called *narshrab* in Central Asia, it's commonly drizzled on grilled meats in Turkey, Iran, and the Central Asian Republics of the former Soviet Union. Pomegranate syrup is sold at Middle and Near Eastern markets.

SAFFRON: The fragrant, rust-colored stigmas of a crocus grown in Spain and India. Saffron is a key flavoring in Iranian barbecue, where it's used in both marinades and basting mixtures. Seventy thousand flowers are needed to make a single pound of saffron (each must be processed by hand), which accounts for saffron's high price. Always buy saffron threads, not powder (the latter is easier to adulterate). For best results, buy small quantities in tiny glass tubes. Store tightly sealed and away from light. (I keep mine in the refrigerator.) It will keep for several months. If the saffron lacks an intense aroma when you open the bottle, it's probably past its prime. To grind saffron, place the threads in a small bowl and pulverize with the end of a wooden spoon.

SAKE: Japanese rice wine. An ingredient in teriyaki sauce, as well as the traditional beverage for Japanese barbecue. (If you really want to be traditional, serve the sake in a wooden box with a pinch of salt.)

SALT: The primal seasoning for barbecue; indeed it is the only seasoning for grilled beef in many countries, including Argentina and Brazil. Not all salts are created equal, however. My favorite seasoning is coarse sea salt. (The coarse texture keeps it from dissolving completely, so you get little bursts of salty flavor. Also, the minerals in sea salt add flavor. Besides, I like the way it feels between my fingers). I also like kosher salt—again for its coarse texture.

SAMBAL ULEK: A fiery red chile paste from Indonesia. Available at Asian markets, gourmet shops, and at an increasing number of supermarkets. Substitute Thai or Vietnamese chile paste or a spoonful of your favorite hot sauce.

SESAME OIL: A dark, nutty oil extracted from roasted sesame seeds, used extensively in Japanese and Korean grilling. One good brand is Kadoya from Japan. Look for it at Asian markets and in natural foods stores. (Steer clear of domestic sesame oils, most of which lack the roasted flavor of the Asian).

SHRIMP PASTE: A malodorous paste made from fermented shrimp and used in Southeast Asian cooking, especially in Indonesia, where it goes by the name of *trasi,* and in Malaysia, where it goes by the name of *belacan.* A small, pea-size piece goes a long way. It's customary to toast the shrimp paste on the end of a skewer over the fire for a few minutes before using. If your fire isn't in operation when you're preparing to use the shrimp paste, sauté it in a skillet or broil on a piece of aluminum foil under the broiler.

SOUR ORANGE: A citrus fruit that looks like an orange (although much less uniform in appearance), but tastes like a lime. Known as *naranja agria* in Spanish, sour orange is widely used in Caribbean and Central American marinades. If unavailable, substitute 3 parts fresh lime juice to 1 part regular orange juice.

SOY SAUCE: The lifeblood of Chinese and Japanese cuisine. *Shoyu* is Japanese soy sauce made with wheat and soybean starter. Tamari is a naturally brewed Japanese soy sauce made with soybean starter. Its clean, elegant flavor makes it my hands-down favorite. Chinese soy sauce is thicker and sweeter than Japanese. Mushroom soy sauce is a thick, sweet Chinese soy sauce flavored with straw mushrooms.

STAR ANISE: The dried, star-shaped fruit of a small evergreen tree that grows in southwestern China and Vietnam. Its smoky licorice flavor is as unique as its eight-pointed pod. A member of the magnolia family, star anise is one of the ingredients in Chinese five-spice powder. Look for it in Asian and Hispanic markets and gourmet shops.

SUMAC: A sour, purplish powder made from the berries of the Middle Eastern sumac tree. Tart and lemony, sumac is used as a seasoning for grilled meats and seafood throughout the Middle East, the Caucasus Mountain republics, and Central Asia.

TAHINI: Refers both to a chalky paste made from sesame seeds and a sauce made from this paste mixed with lemon juice and water. The latter is a popular accompaniment to Lebanese and Middle Eastern–style grilled seafood. Tahini can be purchased at Middle Eastern markets, natural foods stores, and in the ethnic food section of most supermarkets. Store tahini at room temperature, but know that when it sits for any length of time, the oil tends to separate. Stir with a fork until smooth before using.

TAMARIND/TAMARIND WATER: Tamarind is a long brown tropical seed pod whose sweet-sour pulp tastes like puréed prunes mixed with lime juice. You've probably had it, even if you've never heard of it, as tamarind is a flavoring in Worcestershire sauce and in A-1 steak sauce. Tamarind is a staple in the Caribbean, India, and Southeast Asia, and it's finally becoming known in this country. If you live in a city with a large Hispanic or Asian

population, you may be able to find fresh tamarind pods. Asian and Indian markets often sell sticky balls of peeled tamarind pulp. Tamarind purée (also known as tamarind water) can be found frozen at Hispanic markets and in many supermarkets.

TURMERIC: A pungent, orange-fleshed cousin of ginger. Sometimes you can find it fresh or frozen at Asian markets. More often, it's used in powdered form and is available in supermarkets. Fresh turmeric is an essential ingredient in the spice pastes of Indonesia. To approximate its flavor, combine ½ teaspoon ground turmeric with 1 tablespoon fresh ginger.

UMEBOSHI PLUMS/PLUM PASTE: Japanese pickled plums flavored with a basil-like herb called *shiso* (beefsteak leaf). Japanese grill jockeys make a piquant *umeboshi* plum sauce for brushing on grilled rice and other grilled vegetables.

ZA'ATAR: A Middle Eastern spice mix made of sumac, wild marjoram, toasted sesame, and sometimes thyme. (*Za'atar* is the Arabic name for wild marjoram). In Israel and Jordan, marjoram predominates, resulting in a green blend. Armenians and Syrians add proportionally more sumac to make a reddish *za'atar*. Elsewhere in the Near East, chickpeas or grains are added to make brownish *za'atar*.

MAIL-ORDER SOURCES

Grills & Accessories

CHAR-BROIL
P.O. Box 1240
Columbus, GA 31902
(800) 241-7548
All manner of grills, accessories, vegetable grates, smoker boxes, grill lights, etc.

CHEF'S CATALOGUE
3215 Commercial Avenue
Northbrook, IL 60062-1900
(800) 338-3232
Grills, vegetable grates, accessories, general cookware.

WILLIAMS-SONOMA
3250 Van Ness Avenue
San Francisco, CA 94109
(800) 541-2233
High-end grills and accessories, exotic woods and chips, condiments, etc.

YEKTA MIDDLE EASTERN GROCERIES
1488 Rockville Pike
Rockville, MD 20852
(301) 984-1190
Flat skewers for Central Asian–style grilling.

Woods, Chips, & Charcoals

NATURE'S OWN/PEOPLES WOODS
55 Mill Street
Cumberland, RI 02864
(800) 729-5800
Grapevine trimmings, dried herbs, and exotic woods, as well as premium charwood.

BARBECUE WOOD FLAVORS CO.
Route 1, Box 51 A
Ennis, TX 75119
(972) 875-8391

W W WOOD, INC.
P.O. Box 244
Pleasanton, TX 78064
(830) 569-2501

Ingredients

GENERAL

DEAN & DELUCA
Catalog Department
560 Broadway
New York, NY 10012
(800) 221-7714
All manner of oils, vinegars, spices, condiments, hot sauces, exotic grains, etc., from all over the world.

FOODALICIOUS
2055 N.E. 151st Street
North Miami, FL 33162
(305) 945-0502
Chiles, spices, Asian ingredients, exotic rices, peanut flour.

FRIEDA'S, INC.
4465 Corporate Center Drive
Los Alamitos, CA 90720
(800) 241-1771; (714) 826-6100
Exotic produce, including habaneros and other chiles, fresh sugarcane, tamarind, tomatillos, etc. In addition to mail order, they'll also tell you which store in your area sells their products.

MELISSA'S SPECIALTY FOODS
P.O. Box 21127
Los Angeles, CA 90021
(800) 588-0151
Fresh and dried Latin American produce, chiles, and grains.

ASIAN

Ketjap manis, dried lemongrass, dried galangal, rice wine, sesame oil, Asian rices, etc.

ANZEN JAPANESE FOODS AND IMPORTS
736 N.E. Martin Luther King Boulevard
Portland, OR 97232
(503) 233-5111

THE ORIENTAL PANTRY
at Joyce Chen Unlimited
423 Great Road
Acton, MA 01720
(800) 828-0368

CARIBBEAN

Colombo powder and West Indian curry powder, Caribbean spices and seasonings, etc.

ISLA
P.O. Box 9112
San Juan, Puerto Rico
(800) 575-4752
Traditional Puerto Rican seasonings and hot sauces.

JAMAICA GROCERIES & SPICES
Colonial Shopping Centre
9587 S.W. 160th Street
Miami, FL 33157
(305) 252-1197

INDIAN

Spices (*garam masala, chat masala, ajwain, etc.*), *besan* (chickpea flour), rosewater, basmati rice, etc.

FOODS OF INDIA
121 Lexington Avenue
New York, NY 10016
(212) 683-4419
$50 minimum for mail orders.

PATEL BROTHERS
18636 South Pioneer
Artesia, CA 979701
(562) 402-2953
$50 minimum for mail orders.

INDIA SPICE AND GIFT SHOP
3295 Fairfield Avenue
Bridgeport, CT 06605
(203) 384-0666

INDIAN EMPORIUM
68-48 New Hampshire Avenue
Tacoma Park, MD 20012
(301) 270-3322

INDIAN GROCERY STORE
2342 Douglas Road
Coral Gables, FL 33134
(305) 448-5869

SEEMA ENTERPRISES
10635 Page Avenue
St. Louis, MO 63132
$15 minimum for mail orders.

MIDDLE & NEAR EASTERN, CENTRAL ASIAN & AFRICAN

Aleppo peppers, sumac, *sev gundig* (black onion seeds), pomegranate molasses, rosewater, basmati rice, etc.

APHRODISIA PRODUCTS, INC.
264 Bleecker Street
New York, NY 10014
(212) 989-6440
Greek oregano and other Middle Eastern spices and condiments.

GREATER GALILEE GOURMET, INC.
2118 Wilshire Boulevard, Suite 829
Santa Monica, CA 90403
(800) 290-1391; (310) 459-9120
Fax: (310) 459-1276
Israeli seasonings.
$50 minimum for mail orders.

HAJI BABA MIDDLE EASTERN FOOD & RESTAURANT
1513 E. Apache
Tempe, AZ 85281
(602) 894-1905

NEAMS MARKET
3217 P Street N.W.
Washington, DC 20007
(202) 338-4694

ORIENTAL PASTRY AND GROCERY
170-172 Atlantic Avenue
Brooklyn, NY 11201
(718) 875-7687

PARS MARKET
9016 West Pico
Los Angeles, CA 90035
(310) 859-8125

SHALLAH'S MIDDLE EASTERN IMPORTING COMPANY
290 White Street
Danbury, CT 06810
(203) 743-4181

WEST AFRICAN GROCERY
535 9th Avenue
New York, NY 10018
(212) 695-6215
Mail order available.

YEKTA MIDDLE EASTERN GROCERY
1488 Rockville Pike
Rockville, MD 20852
(301) 984-1190
$50 minimum for mail orders.

MEXICAN & SOUTHWESTERN

Chiles, Mexican oregano, and other herbs and spices, etc.

CASA LUCAS MARKET
2934 24th Street
San Francisco, CA 94110
(415) 826-4334
They also carry Peruvian *aji amarillo*.

THE CHILE SHOP
109 E. Water Street
Santa Fe, NM 87501
(505) 983-6080
Fax: (505) 984-0737

COYOTE CAFE GENERAL STORE
132 W. Water Street
Santa Fe, NM 87501
(505) 982-2454
Dried chiles and Southwestern seasonings.

THE EL PASO CHILE COMPANY
909 Texas Avenue
El Paso, TX 79901
(800) 274-7468; (915) 544-3434

MONTERREY FOODS PRODUCTS
3939 Cesar Chavez
Los Angeles, CA 90063
(213) 263-2143
$50 minimum on most mail orders.

RUSSIAN & CAUCASUS REPUBLICS

THE SPICE HOUSE
1031 N. Third Street
Milwaukee, WI 53203
(414) 272-9077
Pomegranate molasses.

SOUTH & CENTRAL AMERICA

Peruvian *aji amarillo*, malagueta peppers, *farinha de manioca (cassava flour)*, etc.

CATALINA'S MARKET
1070 Northwestern Avenue
Santa Monica, CA 90029
(213) 461-2535
Peruvian *aji amarillo*.

TRANSAMERICA
2759 S.W. 27th Avenue
Miami, FL 33133
(305) 858-8756
Fax: (305) 858-7669

BARBECUE & HOT SAUCES

MO HOTTA MO BETTA
P.O. Box 4136
San Luis Obispo, CA 93403
(800) 462-3220

PEPPERS
2009 Highway One at Salisbury Street
Dewey Beach, DE 19971
(800) 998-3473; (302) 227-4608

SPECIALTY POULTRY, GAME & MEATS

D'ARTAGNAN, INC.
280 Wilson Avenue
Newark, NJ 07105
(800) 327-8246
Foie gras, artisanally raised ducks, chickens, and game hens.

HARRINGTON'S HAMS
P.O. Box 288
Richmond, VT 05477
(802) 434-3188

NUESKE'S HILLCREST FARM
Rural Route 2, P.O. Box D
Wittenberg, WI 54499
(800) 392-2266

MUSHROOMS, VIDALIA ONIONS, TRUFFLES, & DRIED FRUITS

AMERICAN SPOON FOODS
P.O. Box 566
Petoskey, MI 49770
(800) 222-5886
Specializing in preserves and dried fruits; $50 minimum for mail orders.

BLAND FARMS
P.O. Box 506
Glennville, GA 30427
(800) 671-7901
Vidalia onions; $50 minimum for mail orders.

COMPTOIR EXOTIQUE
120 Imlay Street
Brooklyn, NY 11231
(888) 547-5471; (718) 858-5277
Truffles and exotic mushrooms.

SEAFOOD & LOBSTER

LEGAL SEA FOODS
33 Everett Street
Boston, MA 02134
(800) 477-5342

Conversion Table

LIQUID CONVERSIONS

US	IMPERIAL	METRIC
2 tbs	1 fl oz	30 ml
3 tbs	1½ fl oz	45 ml
¼ cup	2 fl oz	60 ml
⅓ cup	2½ fl oz	75 ml
⅓ cup + 1 tbs	3 fl oz	90 ml
⅓ cup + 2 tbs	3½ fl oz	100 ml
½ cup	4 fl oz	125 ml
⅔ cup	5 fl oz	150 ml
¾ cup	6 fl oz	175 ml
¾ cup + 2 tbs	7 fl oz	200 ml
1 cup	8 fl oz	250 ml
1 cup + 2 tbs	9 fl oz	275 ml
1¼ cups	10 fl oz	300 ml
1⅓ cups	11 fl oz	325 ml
1½ cups	12 fl oz	350 ml
1⅔ cups	13 fl oz	375 ml
1¾ cups	14 fl oz	400 ml
1¾ cups + 2 tbs	15 fl oz	450 ml
1 pint (2 cups)	16 fl oz	500 ml
2½ cups	1 pint	600 ml
3¾ cups	1½ pints	900 ml
4 cups	1¾ pints	1 liter

WEIGHT CONVERSIONS

US/UK	METRIC	US/UK	METRIC
½ oz	15 g	7 oz	200 g
1 oz	30 g	8 oz	250 g
1½ oz	45 g	9 oz	275 g
2 oz	60 g	10 oz	300 g
2½ oz	75 g	11 oz	325 g
3 oz	90 g	12 oz	350 g
3½ oz	100 g	13 oz	375 g
4 oz	125 g	14 oz	400 g
5 oz	150 g	15 oz	450 g
6 oz	175 g	1 lb	500 g

APPROXIMATE EQUIVALENTS

1 stick butter = 8 tbs = 4 oz = ½ cup
1 cup all-purpose presifted flour/dried bread crumbs = 5 oz
1 cup granulated sugar = 8 oz
1 cup (packed) brown sugar = 6 oz
1 cup confectioners' sugar = 4½ oz
1 cup honey/syrup = 11 oz
1 cup grated cheese = 4 oz
1 cup dried beans = 6 oz
1 large egg = 2 oz = about ¼ cup
1 egg yolk = about 1 tbs
1 egg white = about 2 tbs

OVEN TEMPERATURES

FAHRENHEIT	GAS MARK	CELSIUS
250	½	120
275	1	140
300	2	150
325	3	160
350	4	180
375	5	190
400	6	200
425	7	220
450	8	230
475	9	240
500	10	260

Note: Reduce the temperature by 20 °C (68 °F) for fan-assisted ovens

Please note that all the above conversions are approximate, but close enough to be useful when converting from one system to another.

INDEX

D

E

F

U, V